ANGLO-NORMAN STUDIES XIX

PROCEEDINGS OF THE BATTLE CONFERENCE
1996

The Proceedings of the 1996 Battle Conference contain the usual wide range of topics, from the late tenth century to 1200 and from Durham to Southern Italy, demonstrating once again its importance as the leading forum for Anglo-Norman studies. Many different aspects of the Anglo-Norman world are examined, ranging from military technology to the architecture of Durham Cathedral; there are also in-depth investigations of individual families and characters, including William Malet and Abbot Suger.

ANGLO-NORMAN STUDIES

XIX

PROCEEDINGS OF THE BATTLE CONFERENCE

1996

Edited by Christopher Harper-Bill

THE BOYDELL PRESS

First published 1997
The Boydell Press, Woodbridge

ISBN 0 85115 707 6

ISSN 0954–9927
Anglo-Norman Studies

(Formerly ISSN 0261–9857: Proceedings of the Battle Conference
on Anglo-Norman Studies)

The Boydell Press is an imprint of Boydell & Brewer Ltd
PO Box 9, Woodbridge, Suffolk IP12 3DF, UK
and of Boydell & Brewer Inc.
PO Box 41026, Rochester, NY 14604–4126, USA

A catalogue record for this series is available
from the British Library

Library of Congress Catalog Card Number: 89–646512

This publication is printed on acid-free paper

Printed in Great Britain by
St Edmundsbury Press Ltd, Bury St Edmunds, Suffolk

754425
4

CONTENTS

ILLUSTRATIONS

The editor and publishers gratefully acknowledge
the generosity of the
Trustees of the R. Allen Brown Memorial Fund
in providing a grant towards publication of this volume.

EDITOR'S PREFACE

The nineteenth Battle Conference was held, as usual, at Pyke House, 26–31 July 1996, and the present volume contains all the papers there delivered. The opening reception was again held in the Abbot's Hall, by courtesy of the Headmaster of Battle Abbey School. The outing was to Bodiam Castle and Bayham Abbey, for expert guidance at which we were indebted to, respectively, Dr Charles Coulson and Jonathan Coad. For the smooth running of the conference, for much administrative work beforehand, for comfortable accommodation and for excellent cuisine, we are grateful to Wendy Hughes and all her staff at Pyke House, where, miraculously these days, the warmth of the welcome has in no way been diminished by new management. As always, Ian Peirce provided help and encouragement in many ways, and the staff of Boydell & Brewer both facilitated the production of the volume and made working with them a pleasure.

Strawberry Hill   *Christopher Harper-Bill*
Twickenham

ABBREVIATIONS

AD	Archives Départmentales
ANS	*Anglo-Norman Studies*
Antiqs Journ.	*The Antiquaries Journal (Society of Antiquaries of London)*
ANTS (OPS; PT)	Anglo-Norman Text Society (Occasional Publications Series; Plain Texts)
Arch. Journ.	*Archaeological Journal* (Royal Archaeological Institute)
ASC	*Anglo-Saxon Chronicle*, ed. D. Whitelock *et al.*, London 1969
Battle Chronicle	*The Chronicle of Battle Abbey*, ed. Eleanor Searle, OMT, 1980
BIHR	*Bulletin of the Institute of Historical Research*
BL	British Library
BN	Bibliothèque Nationale
Cal. Docs France	*Calendar of Documents preserved in France . . .* i, 918–1216, ed. J.H. Round, HMSO, 1899
Carmen	*The Carmen de Hastingae Proelio of Guy Bishop of Amiens*, ed. Catherine Morton and Hope Munz, OMT, 1972
De gestis pontificum	William of Malmesbury, *De gestis pontificum Anglorum*, ed. N.E.S.A. Hamilton, RS 1870
De gestis regum	William of Malmesbury, *De gestis regum Anglorum*, ed. W. Stubbs, RS 1887
Domesday Book	*Domesday Book, seu liber censualis . . .* , i, ii, ed. A. Farley, 2 vols, 'Record Commission', 1783; iii, iv, ed. H. Ellis, 1816
Dudo	*De moribus et actis primorum Normanniae Ducum auctore Dudone Sancti Quintini Decano*, ed. J. Lair, Société des Antiquaires de Normandie, 1865
Eadmer	*Historia novorum in Anglia*, ed. M. Rule, RS 1884
EHD	*English Historical Documents*, 2nd edn, i, ed. D. Whitelock, London 1979; ii, ed. D.C. Douglas, London 1981
EHR	*English Historical Review*
Fauroux	*Recueil des actes des ducs de Normandie (911–1066)*, ed. M. Fauroux, Mémoires de la Société des Antiquaires de Normandie xxxvi, 1961
GEC	*Complete Peerage of England, Scotland, Ireland, Great Britain and the United Kingdom*, 13 vols in 14, London 1910–59
Gesta Guillelmi	William of Poitiers, *Gesta Guillelmi . . .* , ed. R. Foreville, Paris 1952
Historia Novella	*William of Malmesbury, Historia Novella*, ed. K.R. Potter, NMT, London 1955
HMSO	Her Majesty's Stationery Office, London

Huntingdon	Henry of Huntingdon, *Historia Anglorum*, ed. T. Arnold, RS 1879
John of Worcester ii	*The Chronicle of John of Worcester* ii, ed. R.R. Darlington and P. McGurk, OMT 1995
JMH	*Journal of Medieval History*
Journ. BAA	*Journal of the British Archaeological Association*
Jumièges	Gesta Normannorum Ducum *of William of Jumièges, Orderic Vitalis and Robert of Torigni*, ed. E.M.C. van Houts, 2 vols, OMT 1992–95.
Lanfranc's Letters	*The Letters of Lanfranc Archbishop of Canterbury*, ed. H. Clover and M. Gibson, OMT, 1979
Med. Arch.	*Medieval Archaeology*
MGH SS	*Monumenta Germaniae Historica, Scriptores*
Monasticon	William Dugdale, *Monasticon Anglicanum*, ed. J. Caley, H. Ellis and B. Bandinel, 6 vols in 8, London 1817–30
NMT	Nelsons Medieval Texts
ns	new series
OMT	Oxford Medieval Texts
Orderic	Ordericus Vitalis, *Historia Ecclesiastica*, ed. M. Chibnall, OMT, 1969–80
os	old series
PL	*Patrologiae cursus completus, series Latina*, ed. J.P. Migne, Paris 1841–64
PR	Pipe Roll (as published by Pipe Roll Society)
PRO	Public Record Office
Procs BA	*Proceedings of the British Academy*
PRS	Pipe Roll Society
Regesta	*Regesta Regum Anglo-Normannorum*, i, ed. H.W.C. Davis, Oxford 1913; ii, ed. C. Johnson, H.A. Cronne, Oxford 1956; iii, ed. H.A. Cronne, R.H.C. Davis, Oxford 1968
RHF	*Recueil des historiens des Gaules et de la France*, Paris 1738–1904
RS	Rolls Series, London
SATF	Société des Anciens Textes Français
ser.	series
Trans.	Transactions
TRHS	*Transactions of the Royal Historical Society*
VCH	*Victoria County History*
Vita Eadwardi	*The Life of Edward the Confessor*, ed. F. Barlow, OMT, Oxford 1992
Wace	Wace, *Le Roman de Rou*, ed. A.J. Holden, 3 vols, Société des anciens textes français, Paris 1970–3
Worcester	Florence of Worcester, *Chronicon ex Chronicis*, ed. B. Thorpe, English Historical Society, London 1848–9

R. Allen Brown Memorial Lecture

PEACEMAKING IN THE TWELFTH CENTURY

Christopher Holdsworth

I am only too sensible of the honour and privilege of giving this lecture dedicated to the memory of Allen Brown.[1] None of us would be gathered together were it not for his tireless work and deep commitment to Anglo-Norman studies. What, however, made his life so special was that he created around his scholarship a community of friends, amongst whom he presided here so genially year after year. I knew him many years before Battle began, so to say, and owe to him, as some already know, one of the crucial introductions of my life. It happened when he took me into one of the behind-the-scenes rooms in the old Public Record Office and opened a large tin box full of brown paper envelopes from which he then drew out a number of twelfth-century charters concerned with an English Cistercian abbey about which I then knew almost nothing. Next he invited me, his junior in years and a novice historian, whether I would like to collaborate with him in editing those Rufford charters, and so began what turned out to be well over ten years' work. Gradually he withdrew from the project, but to the end he was a wise and helpful guide to someone who had scarcely ever looked at a charter, let alone transcribed one, before. So for me Christopher Harper-Bill's invitation to give this lecture came as something which I could not possibly refuse because it gave me a new opportunity to express my gratitude to Allen.

I hope that he would have approved of my choice of subject, even though I suspect that he would himself have been easier mounted upon a destrier on a twelfth-century battle-field than sitting under a tree on the borders of France and England trying to thrash out the conditions of a truce or the broad lines of a peace settlement of longer duration. My recollection is that he never much enjoyed attending committee meetings, especially those of the Board of Studies in History in the University of London, and that he found it more congenial to argue at meetings of Boards of Examiners where the fate of a student might be at stake. Not that meetings of either kind were regularly peaceful when we were both lowly lecturers in different colleges: the feats of arms between Reginald FitzDarlington, Joan, domina de Hussey and other defenders of the status quo with those who even dared to suggest that all was not altogether for the best in the London History School were fairly bloody.[2] I well recall a particular episode when after another defender of old ways, S.T. Bindoff, had reacted cooly to a minor proposal for change, Michael Howard, then Reader in War Studies at King's College, was

---

[1] I am grateful for comments made by those who heard this lecture, which have considerably enriched its argument.

[2] This light-hearted way of referring to two eminent scholars may surprise some; it is not intended to belittle their great achievements but rather to underline one side of their public manner.

moved to respond 'That's exactly the kind of argument which has been used against any reform since the era of the Great Reform Bill.' Then, to adopt Macaulay's words, 'Even the ranks of Tuscany', those lesser participants on the Board, 'Could scarce forbear to cheer.' I think that in some of those battles Allen and I stood on different ground, but I hope that he would have agreed that there was a place for a paper on peacemaking here, and that you will do so too.

Peace, in one sense or another, has not been a theme to attract much attention either here at Battle itself, or in the wider scholarly world, whilst war has.[3] Searching the literature, something I never do too well, I was astonished to find that little germane to the theme has been written recently. As far as I know Ganshof's manual on International Relations in the Middle Ages, published in 1953, seems not to have been superseded.[4] I cannot help sharing my amusement in discovering that my own copy, bought new in 1956 from Parkers, cost the splendid sum of eighteen shillings and sixpence: say 85 new pence. For that I got a paperback of over three hundred pages, and the opportunity to exercise a knife to separate each of those pages from their neighbours. Since I decided on my topic it has occurred to me, more than once, that the explanation for so little writing on it could be because there is nothing meaningful to say: the evidence might be too sparse. You are about to find out whether or not that be the case. In fact, to me now the evidence seems so extensive that if I am to say anything meaningful I must limit my view. Plunging a large needle into a big canvas, to adapt a metaphor from needlework, is all very well, but if one wants to provide more detailed colouring, then smaller needle and canvas are necessary. Although my title promises more (how often are we not tripped up by words which we adopted long before we had really started work), this lecture is restricted to peacemaking involving England, and to the two reigns of Henry I and Henry II. For these two reigns I have tried to read the main sources for information about peacemaking with other rulers. Such people will from time to time include some who were not kings, but who behaved often independently. My hope is that by taking two discrete periods it may be possible to highlight some significant changes in practice. I am only too well aware that much that was relevant to the making of peace cannot be mentioned on one occasion: the ideas which had grown up about the place of peace in the universe, the way that the church tried to encourage peace through its liturgy and the encouragement of specific ways of protecting peace, even the very contribution of arms and fortifications to peace-keeping, all these have had to be left on one side. But I hope that what has become fresh and unexpected to me may prove so for you.

Henry I, thanks largely to the work of Orderic Vitalis, has come down to us as one deeply concerned about peace. Most of Orderic's references make clear that he had principally in mind Henry as a peace-keeper within Normandy, but once, at least, he called the king 'the lover of peace' in an 'international' setting, namely

---

[3] The great exception, of course, is the huge interest in the Peace of God and associated movements: see *The Peace of God: Social Violence and Religious Response in France around the Year 1000*, ed. T. Head and R. Landes, Ithaca and London 1992, and J. Martindale, 'Peace and War in Early Eleventh-Century Aquitaine', *Medieval Knighthood, IV: Papers from the Fifth Strawberry Hill Conference, 1990*, ed. C. Harper-Bill and R. Harvey, Woodbridge 1992, 147–76.

[4] Francois-L. Ganshof, *Le Moyen Age* (*Histoire des Relations Internationales*, ed. Pierre Renouvin, i), Paris 1953, chapters VI–VII, 91–155 provide a wide setting for my paper.

Louis VI's failure to capture Breteuil.[5] It is, therefore, not quite clear which part of Henry's work he had in mind when in his panegyric on the dead king he lamented that the Normans on the whole, 'find peace abhorrent': 'Luce patet clara quod eis pax extat amara . . .'.[6] In any case Professor Hollister has recently made a convincing case for holding that in fact both England and Normandy enjoyed internal peace for by far the greatest part of his reign, and that his overall aim was not to expand the area over which he ruled 'beyond the limits of his patrimony'.[7] My intention now is not to explore directly how that peace was maintained, but rather, how agreements intended to ensure peaceful relations with neighbouring powers were made.

Four major treaties have to be examined: those made in 1101, 1109, 1113 and 1120. At the outset we are faced with a real difficulty: no texts of what was agreed have come down to us, indeed, we seem to be in an era when such agreements were not written down. We are, therefore, dependent upon what chroniclers tell us, and some of them may have been much better informed than others. Having admitted that, let us turn to the first significant 'treaty' of Henry's reign, that made between him and Robert Curthose his brother, usually known as the treaty of Alton.

Robert, you will recall, had come to England to try to force his brother to submit to him and hand over the kingdom, but in fact Henry held his own and a stalemate was reached. At this point people merely described in the sources as 'the chief men' or the 'wiser men of both sides' acted as intermediaries and were able to reconcile the two brothers.[8] It seems clear that Robert had to concede most, since he renounced his claim to the English throne, but Henry, too, had to make some concessions. He promised to give up what he had gained in Normandy, to restore what he had taken from Robert's supporters in England, and to allow Count Eustace of Boulogne to have his father's lands in England. He also committed himself to pay Robert no less than three thousand marks a year. The only other component known, that if one of the brothers died the survivor would inherit everything, could be so far in the future that it involved no very significant concession for either. A third element in the agreement was that it was guaranteed by the oaths of twelve notable men on either side, a provision mirroring the guarantee in the agreement of 1091 made between William Rufus and Robert.[9]

This agreement, we may note here, did not, in fact last very long. Within two years, Robert on a visit to England released Henry from payment of the subsidy, perhaps as some sources have it, moved by the intercession of Henry's queen, to

---

[5] Orderic, XII.19 (vi, 247). For Henry and internal peace see, for example, XI.23 (vi, 99), XII.6 and 22 (vi, 203, 279). For his view on relations between England and France see M. Chibnall, 'Anglo-French Relations in the Work of Orderic Vitalis', *Documenting the Past: Essays in Medieval History presented to George Peddy Cuttino*, ed. J.S. Hamilton and P.J. Bradley, Woodbridge 1989, 5–19.

[6] Orderic, XIII.19 (vi, 453).

[7] C.W. Hollister, with T.K. Keefe, 'The Making of the Angevin Empire', *Journal of British Studies* xii, 1973, 1–25, as reprinted in *Monarchy, Magnates and Institutions in the Anglo-Norman World*, London and Ronceverte 1986, 250: cf. also his 'War and Diplomacy in the Anglo-Norman World: the Reign of Henry I', *ANS* vi, 1984, 72–88, reprinted same volume, 274–89. esp. 279.

[8] *ASC*, AD 1101, 177; *Historia Regum Symeonis Monachi*, ed. T. Arnold, 2 vols, RS LXXV, 1882–85, ii, 233. My discussion is greatly indebted to Hollister, 'The Anglo-Norman Civil War: 1101', *EHR* lxxxviii, 1973, 315–34, reprinted in *Monarchy, Magnates*, 77–95, esp. 90–1, 92–4.

[9] *ASC*, AD 1091, 169.

whom Robert may have listened with sympathy since she was his god-daughter,[10] though Wace suggests that Henry threatened to imprison his brother.[11] Only a year later, in 1104, the underlying tensions between the brothers led to renewed hostilities, when Henry accused Robert of having broken the treaty, at which, according to Orderic, Robert was unable to clear himself 'by purgation on the oath of his culpable companions'.[12] The crucial issue here seems to have been that Robert had made peace with Robert of Bellême whom Henry had exiled two years earlier.[13]

What we need to emphasise now is that in the agreement of 1101 a number of elements can be distinguished, all or some of which will be present in all the agreements which will pass before us: negotiators or intermediaries, the actual terms of the agreement, and methods intended to ensure that it was kept.

The next negotiation which deserves some consideration is one which, according to the record, did not result in any longer-term peace, but which, events suggest, did secure a truce, that is to say peace for a limited time. I refer to the negotiations which took place early in 1109 at Néaufles on the river Epte, not very far to the south-west of Gisors in the Vexin.[14] They came about soon after Louis VI had succeeded to the throne, following the death of his father. The only coherent account to survive – there are less coherent echoes of events in the Chronicle of Hyde, and the chronicle of Clarius of Sens – is in Suger's Life of the King, itself, of course, a source slanted in his favour.[15] Yet it should also be remembered that by the time he wrote Suger had become extremely close to the English ruler, as a result of frequent missions to him to try to ensure peace. One may deduce that his own motive on those occasions was to ensure that the lands of Saint-Denis in Normandy should survive undisturbed, since our only knowledge of them comes from a letter he later wrote to Geoffrey of Anjou asking him to protect those lands just as Henry had done in the past.[16] Suger's account in the Life, which Dr Grant will argue reads as though written by a witness, is sufficiently extraordinary, yet almost without comment in the secondary literature, that it deserves summary.

The negotiations came about after the lands of Robert, count of Meulan had been ravaged by a force composed of Robert of Flanders, Theobald of Blois, the

[10] Orderic, XI.2 (vi, 15); William of Malmesbury, *De Gestis Regum Anglorum*, ed. W. Stubbs, 2 vols, RS XC, 1887–89, ii, 462.

[11] Wace, *Le Roman de Rou et des ducs de Normandie*, ed. H. Andresen, 2 vols, Heilbronn 1877–79, ii, 448–55; Hollister, 'Anglo-Norman Civil War', *Monarchy, Magnates*, 94, puts weight on the threat.

[12] Orderic, XI.10 (vi, 57).

[13] Hollister, 'Anglo-Norman Civil War', *Monarchy, Magnates*, 94, n. 4.

[14] There are brief discussions in Hollister, 'Normandy, France and the Anglo-Norman Regnum', originally *Speculum* li, 1976, 202–42, reprinted *Monarchy, Magnates*, 17–57, at 39, and 'War and Diplomacy', *Monarchy, Magnates*, 281.

[15] *Chronica monasterii de Hida juxta Wintoniam*, in *Liber Monasterii de Hyda*, ed. E. Edwards, RS XLV, 1866, 309; Clarius of Sens, *Chronicon S. Petri Vivi Senonensis*, in M. Bouquet, *Recueil des historiens des Gaules et de la France*, 24 vols, Paris 1738–1904, xii, 281; Suger, *Vie de Louis VI le Gros*, ed. H. Waquet, Paris 1929, cap. 16, 104–110 (Eng. trans. *Suger, The Deeds of Louis the Fat*, R.C. Cusimano and J. Moorhead, Washington, DC, 1992, 69–75).

[16] Suger, ep. 153 (*PL*, 186, cols 1419–21). Cf. Lindy Grant's discussion of this same episode and the Norman estates, 51–64 below. I am grateful to her for drawing this letter to my attention. Evidence of Suger's continuing role as intermediary is in a letter from Henry of Blois to Suger, c.1144–51: P. Chaplais, *English Medieval Diplomatic Practice, Part I: Documents and Interpretation*, 2 vols, London 1982, i, 46.

count of Nevers and others. The cause of these attacks was probably Count Robert's attachment to Henry and his increasing influence in the Seine valley.[17] Henry himself, however, seems to have been the real objective, since when the negotiations began Louis demanded that Henry give up or destroy the castle at Gisors, which seems to have come into his hands around the time of Tinchebrai.[18] The French negotiators, drawn from 'the noblest and most wise among the French', asserted that when it had been agreed that Henry should hold Normandy, by which I presume an agreement (of which we otherwise know nothing) made after the battle of Tinchebrai is meant, it had been determined that if either of them obtained Gisors or Braye they would not keep it, but destroy it within forty days. The French offered to prove the truth of their assertions by combat by two or three barons. To this the Normans made no effective reply, and when the French team returned, afforced by Count Robert of Flanders, they repeated their willingness to prove their case by fighting. Again the Normans stayed dumb, at which Louis himself upped the stakes by offering single combat with Henry. He suggested that the two armies should withdraw, the English sufficiently far north of the river for there to be space for the combat to take place, and that noble hostages should be exchanged to ensure that the combat remained restricted to the two monarchs. Henry refused to agree to this, and the negotiations came to a sudden end. According to Suger, the French king attacked Gisors the very next day, setting off hostilities for two years. How much credence can we give this account?

Clearly it contains some errors; we know that war probably did not break out at once because Henry and Louis were well away from Normandy for much of the next two years.[19] Yet Suger's account overall makes some kind of sense, despite the echoes it contains of heroic literature. Louis at this stage of his life, a young, tall and vigorous person, albeit already fat (though not as gross as he later became), could well have felt that his chance of defeating the older Henry – cheek by jowl, so to say – was good, whilst Henry may well have put more of his trust in money.[20] A letter which he sent to Anselm soon after the events certainly shows that some kind of an agreement involving a truce must have been patched up, since he claimed that the French hostages whom he held, once they had heard his side of the quarrel, had come to accept it.[21] Here we may notice another element in peacemaking: the exchange of hostages. They are not mentioned at Alton, but they are so common that I can not help wondering whether chroniclers took them for granted, just as whilst there must have been recognised means by which intermediaries made their peaceful intentions known to the other side as they approached them, these too are not mentioned.[22]

[17] D. Crouch, *The Beaumont Twins: the Roots and Branches of Power in the Twelfth Century*, Cambridge 1986, 60, 74.

[18] Hollister, 'War and Diplomacy', *Monarchy, Magnates*, 281, n. 52.

[19] Hollister, 'Normandy, France', *Monarchy, Magnates*, 39, n. 125.

[20] Cf. Orderic's description of Louis at the Council of Rheims, Oct. 1118, XII.21 (vi, 253). In 1109 Henry was forty-one and Louis about twenty-eight years old.

[21] Anselm, ep. 461, *S. Anselmi Cantuariensis Archiepisopi Opera Omnia*, ed. F.S. Schmitt, 6 vols, Edinburgh and London 1938, v, 410–11.

[22] Dr Chibnall suggested in the discussion that hostages were only mentioned when something untoward occurred to them. This needs further exploration. Geoffrey of Monmouth twice has intermediaries who seek peace approach bearing olive branches: *Geoffrey of Monmouth: The History of the Kings of Britain*, V.11, IX.15, trans. L. Thorpe, Harmondsworth 1966, 136–7, 230.

The next treaty to be considered is that made by the two kings near Gisors at the end of March 1113.[23] This had been preceded by negotiations between Henry and Count Fulk of Anjou, then allied to Louis, near Alençon in the last week of February. Then Fulk swore fealty to Henry, received the county of Maine and agreed that his daughter should marry William Adelin, Henry's son and heir. Although all this might suggest that Fulk had given a lot up, the agreement included concessions by the king. He would give the county of Evreux to William, its count, who had been living in exile in Anjou, pardon Amaury de Montfort and William Crispin, allies of Fulk, and recall to Normandy those exiled by Robert Curthose (though this last could have been something Henry would have been content to promise). At Gisors, on the other hand, the concessions were very much heavier on Louis' part, for after the two had sworn to keep the peace, and bound themselves in a chain of love to the great joy of all those present, as Orderic put it (*iurata pace cum magno multorum gaudio amoris vinculo complexati sunt*), the French king gave Bellême, the county of Maine, and the whole of Brittany to Henry. Only Orderic provides us with these details, perhaps because it resulted in gifts to his own monastery, thus confirming what Suger says, namely that the magnates and monks worked hard for this particular peace.[24] Others writing further away may not have given these negotiations much thought since they knew that within about two years war had begun again in the Vexin.[25]

The last treaty made between Henry and Louis followed in 1120, and was called by Orderic a confirmation of the treaty with France, that is to say a renewal of Gisors.[26] He also called it the treaty made by the pope, alerting us at once to the fact that it came about partly as a result of the complaint laid by Louis about Henry to Calixtus II at his Council held at Rheims in October the year before.[27] The pope had been sufficiently impressed to visit Henry when the Council ended to hear his side of the dispute, and where should they meet but, again, near Gisors. Hugh the Chanter provides the significant detail that they met at a church halfway between the two castles where they were staying, Gisors in Henry's case, Chaumont-en-Vexin in the pope's.[28] Gisors, it is worth emphasising, was on the north side of the Epte, and therefore in the 'Norman' Vexin, Chaumont, on the south, within the French dominated area.[29] All this is but to underline that the choice of a church as a meeting place, and one midway between castles held by the two warring sides, was surely made to try and find as neutral a site as possible. We should be wrong,

[23] Orderic, XI.45 (vi, 180–1), discussed Hollister, 'Normandy, France', *Monarchy, Magnates*, 39, 53–4, and 'War and Diplomacy', *Monarchy, Magnates*, 281–4.

[24] *Louis le Gros*, cap. 23, 170–3 (trans. 105, 194).

[25] *ASC*, 182, for example, has nothing on the negotiations, although it mentions Henry's deprivation of William Crispin under 1112.

[26] Orderic, XII.24 (vi, 290–1): 'Confirmata itaque concordia principuum', which harks back to Henry's reported words 'Pactum amiciciae quod est inter nos erat ipse [sc. Ludovicus] prior uiolauit . . .' (288–9), so Dr Chibnall's translation 'When the treaty between the princes had been ratified' may be too precise.

[27] Orderic, XII.37 (vi, 346–7). For the Council and subsequent events, Orderic, XII.21 (vi, 257–65) and XII.24 (vi, 282–91). Hollister discusses them, 'War and Diplomacy', *Monarchy, Magnates*, 276–7.

[28] *Hugh the Chantor: the History of the Church of York, 1066–1127*, ed. C. Johnson, London 1961, 75–7.

[29] There is a useful map in J.A. Green, 'Lords of the Norman Vexin', *War and Government in the Middle Ages*, ed. J. Gillingham and J.C. Holt, Woodbridge 1984, 46.

however, if we assumed that pope and king went there unaccompanied: the pope had cardinals, bishops and abbots and other Frenchmen with him, whilst Henry had Prince William, bishops and abbots, as well as many nobles and knights. After a cordial greeting pope and king spoke alone, one may suppose in the chancel of the church, when Henry was able to put his case with some success, perhaps because the two men were, after all, second cousins once removed.[30] After such a boost to the peace process (to adopt a current term), it was not long before Louis and Henry themselves met, though there seems to have been a good deal of coming and going by intermediaries, including at least one cardinal, Cuno of Praeneste, and Thurstan of York, recently consecrated at Rheims by Calixtus. Thurstan had become a friend, too, of the French king during his exclusion from England and must have seemed a very suitable intermediary for both sides. The result of the agreement, finally thrashed out in the summer of 1120, was that William Adelin did homage to the king of France and received Normandy to hold of him.[31] In this way both parties gained something: Henry himself did not have to do homage, whilst Louis got his overlordship recognised, but implicitly would not in future be able to support the claim of William Clito to the duchy. Professor Hollister has called this agreement 'a dazzling diplomatic triumph', which secured what Henry had offered five years before. Then, just after the Normans had sworn fealty to William Adelin, he had tried to get Louis to accept such an arrangement, proffering a substantial bribe.[32] Finally, we must notice that here again we have a treaty which does not seem to have been written down, and again one which only held for a fairly short period, say two years.

If we now turn, briefly, to consider two agreements reached with very different opponents, namely the Welsh princes, a different and less detailed picture emerges. We have extremely brief accounts in the 'English' sources about agreements made in 1114 and 1121. In the first case the princes of Powys and Gwynedd, pressed hard by a three-pronged attack mounted by Henry, came to him and, as the Chronicle puts it, 'became his men and swore him oaths of allegiance'. Gruffyd ap Cynan later attended Henry's court.[33] Seven years later only the prince of Powys was involved. He had risen against the Normans when the news of the loss of the White Ship reached him, removing as it did one of those Normans with a particular concern for Wales, Richard earl of Chester.[34] In response to his burning of two castles, pillaging and murder, Henry led an army right into the northern mountains, where Maredudd ap Bledlyn submitted and was reconciled to Henry, 'having pacified him (Henry) with the gifts and hostages which he demanded' as Symeon

---

[30] Orderic, XII.24 (vi, 282–3) notes Henry recognised the pope both as 'shepherd of the whole Church and his own close kinsman'. Dr Chibnall (vi, 283, n. 4) explains.

[31] Chronicle, AD 1120, 187: Symeon ii, 258 is the only one to mention the homage, whilst Orderic is extremely vague: XII.24 (vi, 290–1). The significance of homage deserves separate treatment in view of the wide-ranging discussion by S. Reynolds, *Fiefs and Vassals: the Medieval Evidence Reinterpreted*, Oxford 1994. My impression is that J.F. Lemarignier, *Recherches sur l'hommage en marche et les frontières féodales*, Lille 1945, now looks far too tightly structured.

[32] 'War and Diplomacy', *Monarchy, Magnates*, 277, and 275–7.

[33] *ASC*, versions E and H, AD 1114, 183. This episode and the subsequent one are well discussed by R.R. Davies, *Conquest, Coexistence, and Change: Wales 1063–1415*, Oxford 1987, 42, and more fully in his 'Henry I and Wales', *Studies in Medieval History presented to R.H.C. Davis*, ed. H. Mayr-Harting and R.I. Moore, London and Ronceverte 1985, 133–47.

[34] *ASC*, AD 1121, 187; Symeon ii, 263–4 mentions the significance of the death of the earl.

puts it. In both these cases (and in lesser agreements mentioned in the *Brut* under 1102, 1110 and 1111) one thing stands out: the Welsh generally adopted a subordinate posture to Henry, entirely proper to people who had been defeated.[35] This distinguishes these agreements from the other four which we have just considered where, even though the military background had shifted, no one had been forced so low. On the other hand these Welsh agreements share with the French-Norman agreements oaths and hostages, and the fact that no texts have come down to us.

One other feature of these agreements made under Henry I is worth a brief mention now, namely that some peacemaking is described in a language of affection and concord, and so brings international treaties, if this is not an overmighty description, alongside those agreements made in many parts of Europe where recourse to love was preferred to recourse to justice.[36] Such agreements have recently been discussed by many scholars, running from Frederick Cheyette at one end of the alphabet to Stephen White at the other.[37] There was, after all, in the twelfth century, no clearly established law between states; it may not, therefore, be surprising that chroniclers seem, on occasion, to have used language reminiscent of conventions made between great men within one kingdom, or part of a kingdom. And what chroniclers did probably reflects what men who made peace said about the process. This language was that often found in the arrangements made by the nobility of England during the disturbed reign of Stephen. Such English *conventiones* often survive in actual documents, well-known to us now thanks to the work of many scholars. One can recall, for example, Edmund King's paper read here five years ago.[38] As we move towards the reign of the second Henry, one of the questions to bear in mind is whether this language of love and friendship is still found there, and another whether any other aspects of the agreements made in the disturbed reign of Stephen are echoed in treaties made by his successor.

Once we find ourselves under Henry Plantagenet the sheer mass of evidence about peacemaking is the first thing to strike us, even though the reigns are of roughly the same length (August 1100 – Dec. 1135; Dec. 1154 – July 1189). The change, I need scarcely remind you, reflects that fundamental shift going on which Michael Clanchy so memorably characterised in the title of his great book, *From Memory to Written Record*. We are in a time when people increasingly feel the need to write things down, as they become more and more used to read every kind of writing, sometimes just for pleasure, more often with a practical end in view. For this present purpose this change means that it is quite impossible to discuss all the

---

[35] *Brut y Tywysogyon*, trans. T. Jones, Board of Celtic Studies, University of Wales, History and Law, ser. XI, Cardiff 1952, 24, 32, and 36; and for 1114 and 1121, 38, 48.

[36] This seems particularly true of Orderic: see his words on the agreements of 1113 and 1120, cited at n. 23, n. 26 above; Symeon also calls 1120 a concord, ii, 258.

[37] F. Cheyette, 'Suum Cuique Tribuere', *French Historical Studies* vi, 1970, 287–99; S. White, '*Pactum legem vincit et amor judicium*: the Settlement of Disputes by Compromise in Eleventh-Century France', *American Journal of Legal History* xxii, 1978, 281–304. See also P.J. Geary, 'Vivre en conflit dans une France sans état: typologie des mécanismes de règlement des conflits', *Annales Économies Sociétés Civilisations* xli, 1986, 1107–33, and for a wide discussion of English evidence, M. Clanchy, 'Law and Love in the Middle Ages', *Disputes and Settlements: Law and Human Relations in the West*, ed. J. Bossy, Cambridge 1983, 47–67.

[38] 'Dispute Settlement in Anglo-Norman England', *ANS* xiv, 1992, 115–30. See also D. Crouch, 'A Norman "conventio" and Bonds of Lordship in the Middle Ages', *Law and Government in Medieval England and Normandy: Essays in honour of Sir James Holt*, ed. G. Garnett and J. Hudson, Cambridge 1994, 299–324.

negotiations concerning peace which took place, and instead a different strategy must be adopted. That will be to highlight a number of areas, where, it may be, both change and continuity with the reign of Henry's grandfather may strike us. I shall look in turn at the three aspects which we first met in the treaty of Alton, namely, intermediaries, the content of treaties, and provision for compliance. But first a brief further word upon the evidence.

It will not, I am sure, be unknown to many here that the narrative sources, and it is they which preserve most of the evidence, are very much richer for the years from 1170 onwards. Some of them actually embody the complete texts of peace treaties, just as they incorporate new assizes, or decisions of church councils. One of these sources, the *Gesta Henrici*, since Stubbs usually attributed to Benedict of Peterborough, but now often attributed to Roger of Howden, tells us far more about peacemaking than any other single source, though Roger himself, Ralph of Diceto, Gerald of Wales and others are significant.[39] In comparison, Robert of Torigni, who provides us with the main narrative for the first part of the reign, is far less informative, and, as we shall see, in one sense he echoes the language of the previous period. One explanation of his distinction from the other historians of the second Henry's reign is that he was a monk, whilst they, with the one exception of Gerald, were involved with the royal court.

For the period up to 1170 the sources make very few references to the role played by intermediaries, although one must suppose that there must have been people who went between the main parties and helped them believe that each side was serious about finding peace. The first-named intermediaries whom I have noticed were involved in the cessation of hostilities which had arisen about castles in the Vexin, and further to the south-west, in 1159. The fact that a truce was made that winter, and that Louis and Henry made a treaty the following year, is well-known, thanks to Robert of Torigni, but the involvement of two Cistercian abbots in the process has rarely been noticed.[40] The two were Peter, bishop of Pavia, who had been abbot of Locedio, in Piedmont, and Philip, abbot of L'Aumône in the diocese of Chartres, whose role has recently been highlighted by Martha Newman.[41]

The intervention of a papal legate was asked for by the French king, and following Peter's despatch in September 1159, very soon after his own consecration, Alexander III sent Philip to Henry the following month, armed with letters addressed both to him and the French king asking for their acknowledgement of his own position.[42] Henry already knew Philip since he had been present in Tours earlier in 1159 when an agreement was made before the king between the abbeys

---

[39] On 'Benedict' and Roger see the balanced discussion in A. Gransden, *Historical Writing in England c.550–c.1307*, London 1974, 220–30.

[40] *The Chronicle of Robert of Torigni* in *Chronicles of the Reigns of Stephen, Henry II and Richard I*, ed. R. Howlett, 4 vols, RS LXXXII, 1884–89, iv, 206–7. R.W. Eyton, *Court, Household, and Itinerary of King Henry II*, Dorchester 1878, 48, places the truce negotiations in November 1159 and the peace in May 1160. Neither Eyton, nor J. Boussard, *Le Gouvernement d'Henri II Plantagenêt*, Paris 1956, nor W. L. Warren, *Henry II*, London 1973, mention the abbots.

[41] M.G. Newman, *The Boundaries of Charity: Cistercian Culture and Ecclesiastical Reform 1098–1180*, Stanford, Cal., 1995, 204–5.

[42] This is clear from Philip's own letter to Alexander reporting on his delivery of both letters and expressing the hope that peace between the kings would soon be made: Bouquet, *Recueil* xv, 762.

of St Julien there, and La Trinité, Vendôme.[43] Indeed, as the father abbot of a cluster of English houses sprung from Waverley (itself a daughter of L'Aumône), he may very well have met Henry in England.[44] Be that as it may, he does not appear in the text of the treaty which the two kings concluded next year, but Peter does, though earlier scholars may have missed him because he witnesses merely as Peter the bishop, placed after the Master of the Temple and three other Templars, people probably given prominence because of the part the treaty gave them to guard the Vexin castles.[45] The role of two Cistercians, one whom, Philip of L'Aumône, had been attracted to Clairvaux under St Bernard, and gone on to serve as his prior, may well point to a significant continuity of tradition of concern with the wider church within the order.[46]

Papal legates appear again in negotiations of 1167, 1172, 1174, 1177, 1180, 1182, 1187, 1188 and 1189.[47] I have excluded from this list negotiations mainly concerned with Thomas Becket, although for a full study of papal-royal relations they would be extremely significant. Here we may merely note that just as many of the same people were involved, many of the same techniques, for example, truces, were used. Most of the legates only acted once, only two twice, one of whom was

---

[43] L. Delisle and M.E. Berger, *Recueil des Actes de Henri II roi d'Angleterre et duc de Normandie, concernant les provinces françaises et les affaires de France*, 3 vols, Paris 1916–27, i, 234–6. Delisle dates this document 1159, and notes that Adrian IV named at its end died on 1 September. Eyton, *Itinerary*, 45, was unaware of it and does not have Henry in Tours that year, but it could be fitted into his movements between April and June. It is significant that Arnulf of Lisieux witnessed the same agreement, for he proved to be one of the protagonists for Alexander. F. Barlow, *The Letters of Arnulf of Lisieux*, Camden 3rd ser. LXI, 1939, xiv, xvi, 15, noted the connection between Arnulf and Philip. For Arnulf's role see C.P. Schriber, *The Dilemma of Arnulf of Lisieux: New Ideas versus Old Ideals*, Bloomington and Indianapolis 1990, 40–5.

[44] For the abbeys see J. Burton and R. Stalley, 'Tables of Cistercian Affiliations', *Cistercian Art and Architecture in the British Isles*, ed. C. Norton and D. Park, Cambridge 1986, 395. Philip played an obscure role in a schism involving Kingswood, Tintern and Waverley: see *The Letters and Charters of Gilbert Foliot*, ed. A. Morey and C.N.L. Brooke, Cambridge 1967, 510–13.

[45] Delisle and Berger, i, 251–3.

[46] There is an important note on Philip's career by F. Gastaldelli in *Opere di San Bernardo*, Milan 1984–, VI/1, 670–71, making clear that he was not archdeacon of Liège before he entered Clairvaux as usually stated, but a secular priest elected to the see of Tours in 1133, promoted by Anacletus to the archbisopric of Taranto, from which post he was deposed by the Lateran Council of 1139.

[47] I give here merely the most significant source for each negotiation with the cardinals, or other legates, in brackets. 1167, *The Historical Works of Gervase of Canterbury*, ed. W. Stubbs, 2 vols, RS LXXIII, 1879–80, i, 203 (William cardinal priest of St Peter ad Vincula, Otto, cardinal deacon of St Nicholas in Carcere Tulliano); 1172, *Gesta regis Henrici secundi Benedicti abbatis*, ed. W. Stubbs, 2 vols, RS XLIX, 1867, i, 31 (who does not name the legates, Theodwin cardinal priest of St Vitale and Albert cardinal deacon of St Lorenzo in Lucina: on this mission see F. Barlow, *Thomas Becket*, London 1985, 260); 1174, Robert of Torigni, 263 (Peter archbishop of Tarentaise and Alexander abbot of Cîteaux); 1177, Benedict i, 191–4 (Peter, cardinal deacon of St Chrysogonus); 1180, *Radulfi de Diceto decani Lundoniensis opera historica*, ed. W. Stubbs, RS LXVIII, 2 vols, 1876, ii, 6 (Peter again); 1182, Diceto ii, 10–11, who places this in 1181, but see Eyton, *Itinerary*, 247 (Henry, cardinal bishop of Albano); 1187, Benedict ii, 3–7 (Octavian, cardinal deacon of SS Sergius and Bacchus, Hugh de Nonant, bishop of Coventry); 1188, Benedict ii, 50–1 (Henry of Albano); 1189, Benedict ii, 61–2 (John of Anagni, cardinal deacon of St Maria in Porticu). I.S. Robinson, *The Papacy 1073–1198: Continuity and Innovation*, Cambridge 1990, 169, also mentions Bobo of S. Angelo and Soffred of S. Maria in Via Lata as being sent to reconcile the English and French kings in 1187, but I have not been able to consult his authority, W. Janssen, *Die päpstlichen Legaten in Frankreich vom Schisma Anaklets II, bis zum Tode Coelestins III. (1130–1198)*, Kölner Historische Abhandlungen 6, Cologne-Graz 1961, 128–30.

Henry de Marcy, cardinal bishop of Albano, acting in 1182 and 1188. He again turns out to have been a Cistercian, having been abbot of Hautecombe and then Clairvaux, still in the 1170s one of the most important positions in the whole monastic world. He was one of the cardinals created by Alexander III, widely used on papal business as legate and preacher against heretics so that it was not surprising that he was considered seriously as a possible pope when Urban II died in 1187.[48] A formidable trio of white monks acted in 1174 to attempt to reconcile Henry with Louis VII.[49] They were Peter, the second of that name to be archbishop of Tarentaise, a former monk of Bonnevaux, and abbot of Tamié, Alexander, abbot of Cîteaux, and Pons bishop of Clermont, Henry de Marcy's predecessor at Clairvaux. Peter, according to his *Vita*, invited the two kings to meet him at the Cistercian abbey of Mortemer, south-east of Rouen, on Ash Wednesday, 6 February, and there he is said to have reconciled them, and to have ashed both of them.[50] This striking ritual, only mentioned in the *Life*, occurred during a truce which the two kings had agreed from at some point in January until the end of Easter.[51] Its only effect on following events may be Louis's delay in renewing hostilities until July.[52]

It is not hard to see how the Cistercians with their strong constitutional networks must have appeared to popes as good go-betweens for Anglo-French negotiations, whilst those same networks made them acceptable to the two kings. Most papal legates, though not all – there were failures in 1187 and 1189 – succeeded in obtaining truces between the two kings, but none of them had a success like the Treaty of Venice of 1177, which was achieved by a group of white monks, including one of those we have observed involved in the events of 1174. It is striking that both Frederick Barbarossa and Alexander III paid tribute to the work of two Cistercians, Hugh of Bonnevaux and Bishop Pons of Clermont, in bringing about the peace between emperor and pope.[53] Legates are certainly the most significant group of intermediaries found in the second Henry's reign. Why was this? The overwhelming motivation for popes to try to create peace was their desire to strengthen support for the Christian states in the Holy Land. The point is stressed, for example, in the letter which Alexander III sent to the archbishop of Rheims in the autumn of 1173 telling him of the appointment of the three Cistercians as legates.[54] To them all other strife seemed a distraction, and it is not surprising to find that on at least one occasion a papal legate lost patience. Right at the end of Henry's life, Cardinal John of Anagni threatened excommunication on Philip of

---

[48] Y.M.-J. Congar, 'Henri de Marcy, abbé de Clairvaux, cardinal-évêque d'Albano et légat pontifical', *Studia Anselmiana* xliii, 1958, 1–90.

[49] Robert of Torigni, 263, who lays stress on reconciling Henry and the young Henry. Alexander's own letter 1102 to the archbishop of Rheims dated 21 July 1173, *PL* 200, cols 962–3 makes clear that his hope was for peace between the two kings and the sons of King Henry. The letter also names additional people, who did not act, with the archbishop of Rheims and the archbishop of Sens and the three Cistercians. Later the prior of Mont-Dieu was added as another possibility: ep. 1107, *PL*, 200, cols 965–6. For the careers of Peter and Pons see Newman, *Boundaries*, 250.

[50] Vita of Peter of Tarentaise, *Acta Sanctorum*, Maii, ii, para. 37, 334. Newman, *Boundaries*, 208, has a misprint, calling the abbey Montmer. The episode is not in Eyton, *Itinerary*, 178, but can be fitted in with Henry's known movements.

[51] Benedict i, 63–4: Eyton, *Itinerary*, 178.

[52] Warren, *Henry II*, 132, who does not pick up the Mortemer episode.

[53] Newman, *Boundaries*, 208.

[54] Ep. 1102, cited n. 49 above.

France and his then ally, Prince Richard. Philip is said to have replied that he was not frightened, that the pope had no business intervening in a case which only concerned him and rebels against his kingdom, and that the legate only spoke that way because he loved pounds sterling.[55] This has a certain ring of truth, besides suggesting some of the difficulties which ever were to affect popes trying to make peace. Excommunication, or the threat of interdict used, according to Benedict in 1177 by Cardinal Peter, was not necessarily effective if a ruler believed that his cause was just, as John was to show not many years later.[56]

Now to the contents of some of these treaties. Here there is only time to consider three different cases, each of which raises more general issues and also involves the third aspect being reviewed, namely procedures to ensure that a treaty was kept. The cases are the complex negotiations involving peace and a marriage treaty of February 1173, the treaty with William of Scotland first negotiated in 1174 and reiterated in 1175, and the arbitration of Henry in the dispute between Castille and Navarre of 1177.

At the end of February 1173 Henry held a great court at Limoges, at which he tried to settle a number of disputes which had disturbed Aquitaine for some years.[57] There was hostility between Raymond V, count of Toulouse, also known as Raymond of St Gilles, who had been married since 1154 to King Louis's sister, Constance, widow of Eustace of Boulogne, and the king of Aragon, who also controlled the county of Barcelona which straddled the Pyrenees. This involved Henry because he claimed overlordship over Toulouse, but the issue was also involved with a plan to conclude a marriage treaty with the count of Maurienne, involving his daughter, who was also his likely heir, and the young prince John. The count, whose main lands lay in the area now known as Savoy, also had land around Narbonne, concerning which he seems to have had quarrels with the count of Toulouse. At Limoges, Henry made peace between the king of Aragon and the count of Toulouse, and the count did homage to Henry for his county, and, according to some accounts to both the young Henry and to his brother Richard, as count of Poitou.[58] Although in some respects a diplomatic triumph, bringing definition to hitherto uneasy relationships, there were within the marriage treaty seeds for the surfacing of the stresses between Henry and his eldest son. This was because it served to emphasise the fact that whilst it provided for lands to be allocated to John, Henry had not allocated any lands to support his own heir.[59] Those wider implications can not detain us now, but what needs to be drawn out is that the

[55] Benedict ii, 66–7, his account of negotiations at La Ferté Bernard near Mans, 4–9 June 1189. Excommunication was threatened two years earlier at the beginning of 1187: Benedict ii, 6–7. It may be indicative of the different stances of 'Benedict' and Roger of Howden that the latter omits these two threats from his shorter account: *Chronica Rogeri de Houedene*, ed. W. Stubbs, 4 vols, RS LI, 1868–71, ii, 365, 317–18.

[56] Benedict i, 190. Interdict was to be laid on both England and the continental lands if Richard failed to marry the French princess Alice.

[57] Warren, *Henry II*, 117, sets the scene very briefly, as does J. Gillingham, 'The Angevin Empire', *Richard Coeur de Lion: Kingship, Chivalry and War in the Twelfth Century*, London 1994, 31. J. Dunbabin, *France in the Making 843–1180*, Oxford 1985, 299–305, although not mentioning the marriage alliance, clarifies the background.

[58] Benedict i, 36: Torigni, 255, does not mention homage to the young Henry. The fact that the counts of Maurienne and Toulouse were at odds emerges from the *Vita* of Peter of Tarentaise (itself within Maurienne), *Acta Sanctorum*, Maii ii, 330–3: see Newman, *Boundaries*, 167.

[59] Warren, *Henry II*, 117.

marriage treaty embodied three interesting provisions to ensure that it was observed.[60]

In the first place no less than than fifty-one people attached to the count of Maurienne swore that the count would keep the terms of the settlement, but that if he did not, then they would be ready, at Henry's summons, to hand themselves over to him as hostages, and so to remain until the count returned to observe the treaty in full. Here we find a striking variation upon a very normal theme in treaties, namely the use of hostages, though they are rarely involved in treaties between the two kings of England and France during the period under consideration.[61]

Secondly, four churchmen from the count's own lands swore that if the count reneged they would excommunicate him and put his land under interdict. The four are worth a slight pause. They were the Cistercian Peter of Tarentaise, whom we have already met in the attempt to patch up relations between Henry and his eldest son next year, the bishops of Geneva and Maurienne, and the abbot of the monastery of St Michael of Cluse. This abbey was an old and wealthy foundation, which had by this time links with Cluny.[62] Abbot Benedict acted as the count's emissary to Henry in 1171, and seems to have stayed at court for some time: he was at the famous reconciliation of Henry with the Church at Avranches in autumn 1172.[63] It is therefore not surprising that he should have been named in the treaty for a special role. What that was I must defer for a moment, because we must pause here with the four prelates and their threat of excommunication. Was such a provision novel? Where did it originate?

As far as I am aware, this is the first time that such a provision appears in a treaty between England and other powers: it was not to be the last. It occurs, for example, in the Scots settlement of 1174/75, and the settlement with Galloway of 1186.[64] Its origins probably should be sought in two directions: one native to England, the other to southern France. The native strand seems to start in one of the *conventiones* made during the Anarchy, that between the earls of Chester and Leicester, whence it made its way into the treaty between Stephen and Duke Henry, which ended the contest.[65] The rationale behind the threat was that breaking a promise solemnly made was sinful, the same logic that lay behind the church's claim to jurisdiction over wills: as the agreement of the two earls puts it, the bishops of Lincoln and Chester would do justice upon the breaker of the agreement 'as for broken faith'.[66] The other tradition of using church law to compel adhesion to

---

[60] Benedict i, 36–41. Delisle and Berger, *Recueil* ii, 2–4, give the treaty from Benedict, but not the subsequent reiteration of the treaty in England.

[61] See n. 22 above. The earliest parallel known to me is in the Treaty of Dover, 1103, between Henry I and Robert II, count of Flanders, in which the pledges bound themselves to pay indemnities to Henry if the count reneged, and if they could not pay to become Henry's prisoners in the Tower of London: A.L. Poole, *From Domesday Book to Magna Carta 1087–1216*, Oxford 1951, 118 and note, for the text; Ganshof, *Moyen Age*, 131–2.

[62] Torigni, 213 for Abbot Stephen of Cluse, a Cluniac monk, becoming abbot of Cluny.

[63] Torigni, 250, 254. The count's initiative is obscured in Warren, *Henry II*, 117, who has Henry seek the alliance. Also at Avranches was the former abbot of Cluse, Stephen, abbot of Cluny (see n. 62).

[64] For the first see below, and for 1186, Benedict i, 348–9; Howden ii, 309 omits this detail.

[65] F.M. Stenton, *The First Century of English Feudalism*, Oxford 1932, 285–8 and trans. 249–55 (whence repeated in *EHD* ii, 930–2); *Regesta* iii, 97–9.

[66] Stenton, *First Century*, 252. The phrase has slipped out of *EHD* ii, 932. E. Vodola, *Excommuni-*

promises about peace is the rich tradition of the Peace and Truce of God movements, which would surely have been familiar to the count of Maurienne.[67] Besides
these, there was another tradition, found in the struggles between successive popes
and emperors, though this might not, perhaps, have been so congenial to Henry
II.[68] I shall look forward to hearing whether this rather speculative suggestion
commends assent, for I have never seen the problem addressed.[69]

The third aspect of the Maurienne agreement which attracts attention is the
subsequent provisions made when envoys of the count came to England to adhere
to the treaty (they form an interesting group, headed by the marquess of Montfer-
rat, and including named castellans, knights and burgesses). The issue then addressed was what could be done to ensure that John would receive what the treaty
granted to him if the count did in fact have a legitimate male heir, when he would
expect not to inherit Maurienne itself. A number of places, including some mountain valleys, had been listed, of which the most significant seems to have been
Roussillon, on the face of it not an obvious place for the count to have interests.[70]
The guarantee worked out was that if these places could not be passed on to John,
then the witnesses would see that equivalent land would be provided 'according to
the judgement of the abbot of Cluse and of Reginald archdeacon of Salisbury, or of
other legitimate assigns of the King'.[71] The choice of these two particular people is
not hard to explain: the abbot had been deeply involved in these particular negotiations, whilst Reginald FitzJocelin was one of Henry's most trusted servants, deeply
involved in the Becket dispute, for instance. This seems to be the first use of named
persons to see to the settlement of a difficult issue left hanging in a treaty. Others
which I have noticed were the 'internal' quarrel between the archbishop of York
and the bishop of Ely about who had hit whom, which was assigned to the
archbishop of Rouen and the bishops of the French kingdom, the Castille Navarre
arbitration to be discussed in a moment, and the Treaty of Ivry, 1177, and its
renewal by Henry and Philip Augustus in 1180.[72] Certainly, there can be no doubt
that the practice of 'mixed' commissions appointed by each side had a very
significant future before it.[73] Where does this practice come from? I think one can
find many charters where a donor promises to provide equivalent land if his
original gift fails for some reason, but I do not as yet know of charters in which
individuals are named to see that this is done fairly.[74] The matters involved in these

---

cation in the Middle Ages, Berkeley, Los Angeles, and London 1986, does not mention the English
examples, nor does he discuss excommunication in peace treaties.

[67] Excommunication was *the* threat here: e.g. the Council of Charroux of 989, cited P. Contamine
(trans. M. Jones), *War in the Middle Ages*, Oxford 1984, 271.

[68] Vodola, *Excommunication*, 20–7 on this from Gregory VII to Urban II.

[69] Ganshof, *Moyen Age*, 132, mentions, without comment, a provision in an agreement between
Philip Augustus and the counts of Boulogne and Flanders involving excommunication by local
prelates in case of infraction.

[70] No doubt further work on the count's family would explain this.

[71] Benedict i, 36–41.

[72] Benedict i, 119: here it is Howden ii, 99, who mentions the 'external' arbitrators. Dr Chibnall
pointed out in the discussion that failing recourse to the pope it was a logical provision; Delisle and
Berger, *Recueil* ii, 60–2, 128–30.

[73] E.g. R.R. Davies, 'Frontier Arrangements in Fragmented Societies: Ireland and Wales', *Medieval
Frontier Societies*, ed. R. Bartlett and A. MacKay, Oxford 1989, 84–7; G.W.S. Barrow, 'Frontier and
Settlement: Which Influenced Which? England and Scotland, 1100–1300', same volume, 12.

[74] A search of R.C. Van Caenegem, *English Lawsuits from William I to Richard I*, 2 vols, *Selden*

negotiations of 1173 are packed with interesting questions, even though one of their main purposes, a marriage, was never put into effect.

My second case is the agreement made to end the war with Scotland. Here I want to direct attention briefly to the guarantee.[75] Here we find that the Scots bishops bound themselves to put an interdict on Scotland should William the Lion break the faith he had promised – a provision very like that made in the marriage treaty of 1173 – but there is something more besides: the Scots nobles committed themselves to act with Henry II to take action to bring William back into line. Here there is surely a significant advance on the provision of the marriage treaty that named people should hand themselves over as hostages if the agreement were breached; a far more energetic role was taken, one perhaps more natural for people who had become the king of England's men just as William had ordered them.[76] We may note that the peace made with Roland of Galloway twelve years later in 1186 involved the Scots king and his nobles swearing to compel Roland to keep the terms which had been agreed.[77]

The third and final case to be examined is, like the Maurienne treaty, one scarcely mentioned in the secondary literature, namely Henry II's arbitration over a complex and long-standing dispute between the kings of Castile and Navarre in 1177.[78] One reason that this case made its way to Henry must be that in the previous year Alphonso VIII of Castile had married Henry's daughter Eleanor, but it is interesting that the voluminous record made by 'Benedict' provides that if Henry were to die before the case were finished then it should be taken to the king of France. If there were but world enough and time, as someone once remarked, I should love to pause over the details: but alas time, and no doubt your patience, run out. But having used the trope which classical and medieval rhetoricians called *praeteritio*, I cannot resist drawing attention to one detail. The huge embassies from the two competing countries each included a champion, 'of wondrous strength and boldness' ready to do or die, if the matter were put to the test of battle, which transports us back into the same world as that of Louis VI by the Epte in

Society CVI–VII, 1990–91, suggested by Professor Gillingham, was fruitless, though the index, *sub* perambulations, shows many cases where settlement involved this procedure. Another parallel may be in the provision of *Leges Henrici Primi*, ed. L.J. Downer, Oxford 1972, 9.4, 104–5, where some cases may be heard 'in the boundary courts of feudal equals' (*vel certis agendorum locis adiacens*). R.R. Davies, 'Kings, Lords and Liberties in the March of Wales', *TRHS*, 5th ser. xxix, 1979, 46, n. 26, draws attention to this passage.

[75] Benedict i, 94–9; Diceto i, 396–7. There is a useful translation in *EHD* ii, 413–16.

[76] Benedict i, 94–5, 'facere ligantiam et fidelitatem et hominium Henrici regis . . .'.

[77] Benedict i, 348–9; cf. Warren, *Henry II*, 604.

[78] Benedict i, 138–43, 144–54; Howden ii, 151–4 and Diceto i, 415–16, 418–20 are much briefer. Warren, *Henry II*, 143, n. 2, merely has a footnote. K. Norgate, *England under the Angevins*, 2 vols, London 1887, ii, 190, has a sentence. The involvement of John of Oxford, one of Henry's most trusted diplomats, is noted by C. Harper-Bill, 'John of Oxford, Diplomat and Bishop', *Medieval Ecclesiastical Studies in honour of Dorothy M. Owen*, ed. M.J. Franklin and C. Harper-Bill, Woodbridge 1995, 91. The longest modern treatment is in J. Gonzalez, *El Reino de Castilla en la epoca de Alfonso VIII*, 3 vols, Madrid 1960, 802–11 (with a useful map between 802 and 803), but this does little more than summarise the documents printed earlier, themselves taken from Benedict, without his connecting narrative, 440–4, 456–8, 459–61. D.W. Lomax, 'Los "Magni rotuli pipae" y el medievo hispánica', *Annuario de Estudios Medievales* i, 1964, 544, draws attention to expenses settled by the Exchequer at this time. I am grateful to Dr S. Barton for drawing these two studies to my attention. Professor Gillingham pointed out that English historians in earlier periods did discuss the case, but I have not followed this up.

1109.[79] In fact, matters were settled quite otherwise, after an elaborate presentation of their case from each side, first verbally and then, three days later, in written form. The double pleading was, apparently, necessary because neither king nor the barons of the court could understand what the Spaniards were saying (it is not clear whether it was their Latin pronunciation which was the trouble or their various forms of Spanish: I suspect it was the former). At the end Henry followed the advice of the court, which included ecclesiastical as well as secular lords, and ordered that each side should return to the other what they had taken. Gerald of Wales comments upon this in words which at the end of this discussion seem to resound. Having explained how the Navarre team included Peter of Cardona, a man of formidable eloquence, he went on

> whereupon the king, relying upon wise counsel, resolved to walk by a middle course, and was careful to take away any strife in the transaction; so that something being given up, and something being retained, neither party might be injured by any great loss, but, as he was a judge selected by both sides, so, if it were possible, that each might be indemnified.[80]

The resonance, I sense, is that of the language of compromise found in those local agreements which have attracted the attention of historians recently.[81] This language of compromise and accommodation (never easy to speak and mean) is not frequent around the making of treaties in the last years of the second Henry, but it can be found in 1170, about an agreement between Henry and Louis VII, and 1186, the settlement of the quarrel about the dower of Queen Margaret, widow of the young Henry.[82] What the arbitration of 1177 also shows us is Henry at a peak in his international prestige, being called upon to settle a difficult problem in his world. In the following years his skills as arbitrator or mediator were called upon four times more. In the former role he succeeded in reconciling Philip Augustus with his mother over her dowry in 1180 and four years later arbitrated with less success between Philip and the count of Flanders about the young king's claim to Vermandois.[83] In 1182, on the other hand, he deployed his influence as mediator between the emperor and Henry the Lion, by then the king of England's son-in-law, and again between Philip Augustus and the count of Flanders.[84] Here we see methods still used today being created before our eyes, so to say.

Looking back over the methods which have come before us, we can easily recognise two very different things. On the one hand some of the methods, notably the use of hostages and oaths, were very old: they would not have seemed very strange to Alfred, to Julius Caesar, or to Solomon.[85] Others, like turning witnesses into treaty enforcers, and boosting their power with excommunication, were new,

---

[79] Benedict i, 138, 'mirae probitatis et audaciae . . .'.

[80] *De Principis Instructione*, II.xxx, *Giraldi Cambrensis Opera*, ed. J.S. Brewer, J.F Dimock and G.F. Warner, 8 vols, RS XXI, 1861–91, viii, 218. I quote the trans. of J. Stevenson, *Church Historians of England*, 5 vols in 8, London 1853–58, 5/i, 177.

[81] See n. 37 above.

[82] Benedict i, 6 and i, 343.

[83] Diceto ii, 6, 'ad arbitrium regis Anglorum concordiam inierunt.'; Benedict i, 311–12.

[84] Benedict i, 287 and 284. See J.W. Baldwin, *The Government of Philip Augustus: Foundations of French Royal Power in the Middle Ages*, Berkeley, Los Angeles, and London 1986, 16–20.

[85] R. Abels, 'King Alfred's Peace-Making Strategies with the Vikings', *Haskins Society Journal* iii, 1992, 23–34.

reflecting a different world in which bonds between kings and their nobles were coming to involve defined obligations, and where the one weapon which the church had, to deprive fighters of the medicine for their ills here below and of the hope of heaven, still seemed to have a certain power. Often we know that particular agreements did not hold: war recommenced, but this should not disguise the fact that most of the time in the twelfth century peace held. Perhaps the fact that it did owed a lot to those other aspects of the situation which I have deliberately excluded from consideration in a single paper, but part of the maintenance of peace was related to the skill of go-betweens, the flexibility of settlements to deal with a variety of situations, and the range of means developed to provide that whatever had been agreed should be done. Perhaps most was owed to the go-betweens, and their clerks (a group who leave small trace in the evidence) with their trained minds and sometimes wide experience. It was they, one must deduce, who did most to help the process forward, working, like their fellows in other aspects of law and administration, to see that what was done should be done as effectively as possible, so that as little ambiguity and cause for further dispute were created as possible.

SHERIFFS, LORD-SEEKING AND THE NORMAN SETTLEMENT OF THE SOUTH-EAST MIDLANDS

Richard Abels

'In the twenty-first year of King William's reign', observed Henry of Huntingdon, as he looked back from his vantage point in the third decade of the twelfth century, 'there was hardly a nobleman of English descent left in England, but all were reduced to servitude and mourning, so that it was a disgrace to be called an Englishman.'[1] Though perhaps a touch melodramatic, the archdeacon's assessment of what the Norman Conquest meant for the fortunes of the native aristocracy is among the very few things upon which modern scholars studying the period can agree.[2] Indeed, Henry's lament could be generalized to extend to the fate of lesser native landowners. The Domesday Book surveys of the south-east midland counties of Circuit III (Middlesex, Hertfordshire, Buckinghamshire, Cambridgeshire and Bedfordshire) read like obituaries for the Anglo-Saxon landholding class. Native-born tenants-in-chiefs in Hertfordshire, for example, accounted for only forty-one hides valued at £55 at the time of the Inquest, just under 4% of the county's total hidage assessment and 3% of its valuation,[3] while another twenty-five Englishmen held about thirty hides as tenants of Norman lords. Nearly half of them were tenants on lands that had once belonged to them freely.[4] Of the county's 224 anonymous sokemen recorded in Domesday Book as holding 'tempore regis

---

[1] Huntingdon, 209. Cf. Orderic ii, 266–7.

[2] Even the idea that it was shameful to be known as an Englishman seems to be borne out by the fashion adopted by surviving Anglo-Scandinavian landholders of providing their children with good continental names. Ann Williams, *The English and the Norman Conquest*, Woodbridge 1995, 96, 199–200, 204, 207.

[3] Even these modest figures overstate the case for continuity, since Edgar the Ætheling, Edward the sheriff of Wiltshire and Deorman, who among them held all but six of the forty-one hides, had acquired their lands in the county after the Conquest. Though Edward of Salisbury's name suggests that he was of English descent, the supporting evidence is slight. See E.A. Freeman, *The History of the Norman Conquest of England*, 6 vols, Oxford 1870–79, ii, 797; Williams, *English*, 105–6. In any event, Edward's main holding, the £22 manor of Great Gaddesdon, belonged by right to St Albans, whch had only leased it to his antecessor, Wulfwynn (*Domesday Book* i, 139). There is no way of determining whether Deormann was a kinsman of his *antecessor*, a king's thegn named Alwine Horne, but it is worth noting that he did not succeed to Alwine's lands in either Bedfordshire or Middlesex (*Domesday Book* i, 128v, 215–215v).

[4] Richard Abels, 'An Introduction to the Hertfordshire Domesday', *The Hertfordshire Domesday*, ed. Ann Williams and G.H. Martin, London 1991, 33–5. Typical is the case of Thorkil, a man of Esger the Staller, who in 1066 freely held two hides in Digswell, Broadwater Hundred, and three hides and one virgate in Bengeo, Hertford Hundred. Twenty years later Thorkil still held in Digswell, but now as the tenant of its new lord, Geoffrey de Mandeville, Esger the Staller's successor in numerous counties. Geoffrey chose to reward a different follower, a priest, with Thorkil's land in Bengeo (*Domesday Book* i, 139v). Similarly Godwine continued to hold 'Sele' from Geoffrey de Bec but not Roxford (*ibid.* 139v, 140v).

Edwardi' (TRE), a mere forty-five remained in 1086, their reduced social and tenurial circumstances reflected in their placement by the scribe among the peasant complement of their former estates.[5] Analyses of the other counties of Circuit III confirm the findings from Hertfordshire.[6] Even if Domesday Book underestimates the tenurial presence of Englishmen by omitting the names of tenants of undertenants, as Dr C.P. Lewis has persuasively argued,[7] it is impossible to avoid the conclusion that the Norman Conquest was an unmitigated catastrophe for thegn and sokeman alike, though the precise dimensions of the disaster may have differed from region to region.

On this much, at least, there is a consensus. How this enormous redistribution of land occurred and whether it constituted a 'tenurial revolution' are matters that have yet to be resolved to everyone's satisfaction. The nine-hundredth anniversary of Domesday Book in 1986 seems to have given new life to the classic questions and arguments about the consequences of 1066. For Peter Sawyer, the Normans simply stepped into the tenurial shoes of Anglo-Saxon predecessors, claiming not only their antecessors' lands but those of their men as well. If the Domesday compilers had more consistently entered the information they had on pre-Conquest lordship, Sawyer reasons, we would better appreciate how little the Conquest changed things, at least tenurially.[8] Nonsense, responds Robin Fleming. When one

---

[5] Many of the missing sokemen may simply have been 'reclassified' as *villani*. See Abels, 'Introduction to Hertfordshire', 16–17.

[6] In Bedfordshire ninety lesser tenants-in-chief and undertenants either bore English names or are explicitly said to have held their lands before 1066. Together they accounted for only 9% of the county's hidage (107 out of 1,200 hides) and under 8% of its annual revenues (£79 out of £1,037). Richard Abels, 'An Introduction to the Bedfordshire Domesday', *The Bedfordshire Domesday*, ed. Ann Williams and G.H. Martin, London 1991, 23, 40–1. In Buckinghamshire about four dozen Englishmen held 141 hides (6% of the county's assessment) worth £114 (5% of total value) in 1086. As in Hertfordshire, the Buckinghamshire figures are skewed by the presence of four men who weathered the Conquest particularly well: Edward of Salisbury, the sheriff of Wiltshire, held 26 hides and a virgate worth £23 10s (*Domesday Book* i,150v); Ælsige, the son-in-law of Wulfweard White, received as wedding gifts from Queen Edith three estates totalling 10 hides valued at £8 (*Domesday Book* i,153); Alric the Cook's 20-hide manor of Steeple Claydon, which also had belonged to Queen Edith, brought him £16 a year (*Domesday Book* i, 153); and Leofwine of Nuneham Courtenay retained four of his pre-Conquest holdings in-chief, 16 hides in all, an additional hide as an undertenant of Roger d'Ivry, and the lordship of five burgesses who were also his in 1066 (*Domesday Book* i,143,151v, 153). Cambridgeshire: 56 hides and 3 virgates out of 1297 hides (4%); £58 out of £1847 (3%). See A. Williams, *The English*, 86–9, 117–18. Middlesex: four tenants-in-chief and 11 undertenants, with 37½ hides, about 4.5% of the county's TRW hidage. For population and hidage totals, see H.C. Darby, *Domesday England*, Cambridge 1977, 336, 359.

[7] C.P. Lewis, 'The Domesday Jurors', *The Haskins Society Journal* v, 1993, 17–44. That Domesday Book omitted some English holders is certain. Though Godwine Frambolt, a king's thegn, retained none of the four small estates he held in Bedfordshire TRE (*Domesday Book* i, 215v [Wymington], 216v [Carlton and Hinwick]), a landowning family bearing the surname 'Frambald' figures in county records of the thirteenth century. G.H. Fowler, *Bedfordshire in 1086: an Analysis and Synthesis of Domesday Book*, Quarto Memoirs of the Bedfordshire Historical Record Society i, Aspley Guise 1922, 104. Norman undertenants were also omitted in this way. Burston, Cottesloe Hundred, Buckinghamshire, is listed twice in Domesday Book, first under the heading of Walter Giffard, with Turstin holding from him, and then later in a struck out entry in the brief of Turstin fitzRolf. In the latter, we find Reginald holding from Turstin (*Domesday Book* i,147, 151). If it had not been for the compiler's error, we would not know about Reginald's tenancy.

[8] Peter Sawyer, '1066–1086: a Tenurial Revolution?' in *Domesday Book: a Reassessment*, ed. Peter Sawyer, London 1985, 71–85.

looks more deeply into the matter, aided by careful statistical analyses, charts and maps, one discovers that, on a loose estimate, 'something like a fifth of all land in secular fees descended to Normans by antecessorial inheritance'.[9] About a third came from later territorial grants often based on hundreds, and the remainder from what Fleming terms 'private enterprise'.[10] David Roffe has answered Fleming by refining Sawyer's argument to take better account of pre-Conquest overlordship by the holders of 'sake and soke', which he defines as full rights over land 'indicative of and synonymous with tenure by book'.[11] The grant of a manor by right of an antecessor conferred title to all lands dependent upon it. This, for Roffe, determined the contours of many Norman baronies, which reproduce pre-Conquest estates in both form and composition. Hence, Sawyer was right about continuity, though for the wrong reasons.[12] C.P. Lewis's pronouncement that the argument is close to being settled is perhaps a shade premature.[13] I, for one, however, am more persuaded by Fleming's interpretation than by either Sawyer's or Roffe's, in part because, like her, I appreciate the chaos and disorder that attended the Norman settlement. On the other hand, my study of the descent of land within the south-east Midland counties of Domesday Circuit III (the only circuit to identify on a regular basis the personal lords of pre-Conquest holders) also persuades me that, in theory, the Norman lords were doing precisely what Sawyer and Roffe contend, pursuing the 'rights' that they could claim through their antecessors.[14] But the varieties of Anglo-Saxon lordship created so many overlapping claims that the pursuit of real or assumed rights led to numerous disputes. Before 'stepping into their predecessors' shoes', they had to find out what this meant.[15] Whether the result was

9   Robin Fleming, *Kings and Lords in Conquest England*, Cambridge 1991, 211.
10   Fleming, *Kings and Lords*, 107–231. See also Robin Fleming, 'The Tenurial Revolution of 1066', *ANS* ix, 1987, 87–102.
11   David Roffe, 'From Thegnage to Barony: Sake and Soke, Title, and Tenants-in-Chief', *ANS* xii, 1990, 166; *idem*, 'Domesday Book and Northern Society: a Reassessment', *EHR* cv, 1990, 328–36.
12   Roffe, 'From Thegnage to Barony', 157–76. Sawyer's emphasis upon the tenurial importance of pre-Conquest commendation and Roffe's upon soke rights might have been influenced, to a degree, by the information included in the county returns of the Domesday circuits they focused upon, respectively Circuit III and Circuit VI (Yorkshire, Derbyshire, Nottinghamshire, Lincolnshire and Huntingdonshire).
13   Lewis, 'Domesday Jurors', 17. Cf. Williams, *English*, 71–6.
14   Abels, 'Introduction to Hertfordshire', 20–35; 'Introduction to Bedfordshire', 29–49. (I would like to thank Editions Alecto for permitting me to use material and maps prepared for these works in the present paper.)
15   Although it falls outside the geographical scope of this paper, the dispute between William de Chernet and Picot over 2 ½ virgates of land in (South) Charford, Hampshire, recorded in Hugh de Port's *breve* (*Domesday Book* i, 44v), is (in the words of E.A. Freeman) 'one of the most instructive passages in all Domesday' concerning such matters (*The Norman Conquest of England*, 5 vols, Oxford 1867–79, v, 493–4). It tells how William, as the tenant of Hugh de Port, brought a claim to these lands against its TRW holder, Picot (who is often assumed, but on unexplained grounds, to have been the same man of that name who was sheriff in Cambridgeshire). William contended that the land ought to have been in his holding, *per hereditatem sui* [i.e. Hugh de Port's] *antecessoris*. Two other TRE holders in the vill had held their lands from Hugh's antecessor Ælfwine of Oakley. Picot responded that Vitalet had been a free man and had held his land in alodium. William, probably calling upon the clout of his lord, then sheriff of Hampshire, called upon witness *de melioribus et antiquis hominibus totius comitatus et hundredi*. Picot responded by marshalling the testimony 'de uillanis et vili plebe, et de praepositis', who were willing to prove by oath or ordeal that the TRE holder, Vitalet, had been a free man who 'could go with his land to whomever he wished'. William's witnesses refused to allow Picot's to give their testimony, citing the authority of

'continuity' or tenurial 'revolution' is debatable. But one clear arena in which continuity of Anglo-Saxon administrative practice certainly led to revolutionary tenurial changes was in the activities of William's sheriffs. The manner in which the sheriffs of these counties obtained their lands in Domesday Book is a clear example of an alternative method of acquiring lands that has few pre-Conquest precedents. What I plan to do in this paper is purposely to 'miss the point' (to paraphrase Dr Roffe on Sawyer and Fleming) and consider merely the mechanisms whereby control over land passed from English into Norman hands in the counties that comprise Domesday Book's third circuit, focusing upon a single, perhaps atypical group, William the Conqueror's sheriffs. First, I will examine in some detail how land was generally redistributed in these counties 1066–1086, and then examine how William's sheriffs, in particular, went about acquiring their Domesday holdings. What I will propose is that William's sheriffs in these counties – Picot in Cambridgeshire; Ansculf de Picquigny in Buckinghamshire; Ralph Taillebois and Hugh de Beauchamp in Bedfordshire and Buckinghamshire; and Ilbert of Hertford and Peter de Valognes in Hertfordshire – were well positioned, as well as dispositioned, to profit from their office and the turmoil of the times. They did not transform the office of sheriff. Indeed, they performed the same duties as had their English predecessors, but in a radically different social and legal climate. As a result they emerged as 'enterprisers' par excellence, though perhaps more along the lines of jackals than lions, since their favourite 'targets of opportunity' were unprotected monastic establishments, lordless lesser thegns and, especially, the royal sokemen with whom they dealt so often in their official capacity.

Domesday Book essentially provides 'snapshots' of the shires at two points in time, 1066 and 1086, and the picture that emerges from its folios is misleadingly static. The 'before and after' picture may be most deceptive in terms of the disappearance of native landowners. TRE: Now you see them; TRW: Now you don't.[16] As both Robin Fleming and Ann Williams have demonstrated, the massive redistribution of land was not the result of a single catastrophe but of successive waves of confiscations and steady encroachment.[17] The virtual disappearance of the native Anglo-Saxon landholding aristocracy in Circuit III probably took place over a decade or more, and much of the displacement occurred according to the forms of law. William I regarded himself as the Confessor's kinsman and legitimate heir, as is evidenced by his choice of the 'day that King Edward was alive and

---

the laws of King Edward: 'sed testes Willelmi noluerunt accipere legem nisi regis E. usque dum diffiniatur per regem [Willelmi]'. There is much that is uncertain about this, including the law to which William's witnesses appealed (perhaps a variation on II Cnut 23, that no man may vouch to warranty unless he has trustworthy [*treowe*] witnesses). What is indisputable, though, is that TRW right to the land depended upon a holding of fact concerning the quality of the TRE holder's tenure and his relationship to his pre-Conquest lord. Clearly, a Norman lord could claim by hereditary right from his named antecessor, and this included thegnland and lænland. Equally clear is that the authority of existing English law was recognized, though it could be overridden by an order from the king. Domesday Book does not explain the outcome of the suit. Although the entry appears under Hugh's lands, the main text says that Picot holds the lands of Vitalet, a free man who held the land from King Edward in alodium.

16 Domesday Book's temporal terms of reference 'TRE' (*Tempore Regis Edwardi*) and 'TRW' (*Tempore Regis Willelmi*) are 'the day when King Edward was alive and dead', i.e. 5 January 1066, and the time of the Domesday survey, i.e. 1086.

17 Fleming, *Kings and Lords*, 145–214; Williams, *English*, 7–70.

dead' as a point of reference in Domeday Book.[18] In confiscating the lands of rebels and malefactors he saw himself as exercising his legal rights as king. Edward the Confessor had done no differently in 1051 when he confiscated the lands of Earl Godwine and his sons.[19] But William's interpretation of the king's rights over the lands of his subjects would have amazed his predecessors. In 1067 William, we are told by the Peterborough chronicler, returned to England from the continent and 'gave away every man's land',[20] just about the same time that he issued writs to the city of London assuring its burgesses 'that every child shall be his father's heir after his father's day', and to a number of abbeys confirming their lands and privileges.[21] The contradiction may only be apparent. One does not seek a warrant for that which is unchallenged and secure. From the references scattered throughout Domeday Book, it appears that no possession was legally safe TRW unless the holder could produce either a writ or a king's agent, a 'liberator', to warrant it.[22] In Bedfordshire, for instance, a native landholder Almaer held a half virgate from the king in Sharnbrook, which his father had had before him. His title, however, did not derive from his father's tenure but from a writ through which King William returned the land to him.[23] Similarly, Edward, a burgess of Bedford, had William's writ granting him a half hide in Hinwick which his father had held freely TRE.[24] The manor of Tewin in Hertfordshire provides still another example. The TRE holder, a king's thegn named Healfdene, continued to hold these 5 ½ hides in 1086, but as a tenant of the sheriff Peter of Valognes. King William, we are told, had given the manor to Healfdeane and his mother 'for the soul of Richard his son', probably around 1075, and there was a writ to that effect. If Peter is to be believed, the king subsequently changed his mind and gave the land as a gift to the sheriff.[25] Most dramatically, a royal priest named Earnwig lost a hide in Harrowden, Bedfordshire, that his father had held before him because he was unable to produce either livery or writ placing him in seisin of the property in question. The hundred concluded that he had occupied the hide against the king.[26]

'Feudal' assumptions (*pace* Susan Reynolds) and the Normans' refusal to comprehend the character and complexities of Anglo-Saxon lordship and land tenure

---

[18] George Garnett, 'Coronation and Propaganda: Some Implications of the Norman Claim to the Throne of England in 1066', *TRHS*, 5th series xxxvi, 1986, 91–116, esp. 101–7.

[19] F.M. Stenton, *Anglo-Saxon England*, 3rd edn, Oxford 1971, 622–4.

[20] *Anglo-Saxon Chronicle* E, *s.a.* 1067. Cf. *Domesday Book* ii, 360b (Stanham, Suffolk): reference to land placed in pledge *quando redimebant anglici*.

[21] *Regesta* i, nos 12–19. For the London writ, see T.A.M. Bishop and P. Chaplais, *Facsimiles of English Royal Writs to AD 1100*, Oxford 1957, pl. 14.

[22] E.g. *Domesday Book* i, 36 and 50. See Freeman, *The Norman Conquest* v, 526–33; Bishop and Chaplais, *English Royal Writs*, xi; James Campbell, 'Some Agents and Agencies of the Late Anglo-Saxon State', in *Domesday Studies*, ed. J.C. Holt, Woodbridge 1987, 214–15.

[23] *Domesday Book* i, 218.

[24] *Domesday Book* i, 218. Cf. *Domesday Book* i, 218v (Turvey). In both these cases the writ may have been issued because the holdings were being granted in alms, releasing the land from secular services.

[25] *Domesday Book* i, 141–141v.

[26] *Domesday Book* i, 211. Earnwig the priest also held land in Lancashire under Roger of Poitou and was styled 'Roger of Poitou's man' in the Lincolnshire Domesday (fo. 352). He held a house in Lincoln from Earl Morcar, a small estate at Widme in alms from King Edward and land at Ingham and Fillingham, all in Lincolnshire (fo. 371). His father, Earnwig Catense, had held an extensive estate in Yorkshire (*Domesday Book* i, 374).

undoubtedly facilitated the transfer. As is well known, King William commonly, though not invariably,[27] transferred intact the estates of a thegn to a single tenant-in-chief, who would then be regarded as his antecessor's legal heir, one of the key reasons that the Domesday commissioners bothered to inquire into the identity of the pre-Conquest holder.[28] The estates of most of the greater Anglo-Saxon land-owners in Circuit III, with the notable exceptions of the very greatest, Earl Harold and Archbishop Stigand, descended intact, or very nearly so, to a designated successor. As Eudo fitzHerbert's men explained, in contesting Robert d'Oilly's right to hold a half hide in Thurleigh, Bedfordshire, the land in question had belonged to Wulfgeat, a king's thegn, 'all of whose lands King William gave' to Eudo.[29] In that manner, Count Eustace of Boulogne obtained the lands of Æthelweald of Stevington, Ralph Taillebois of Eskil of Ware, William de Eu of Ælfstan of Boscombe, Geoffrey de Mandeville of Esger the Staller and Count Alan of Eadgifu the Fair.[30] As Domesday Book makes clear, these barons not only took possession of the lands owned by their 'antecessors' but also claimed the estates of their men, whether or not those men held that land as dependent tenures. Many of the disputes that are recorded in Domesday Book involve attempts to comprehend and disentangle the various threads of Anglo-Saxon overlordship, whether personal, tenurial or jurisdictional.[31] It was one thing to know what lands one's antecessor had owned, and quite another to identify what rights he had enjoyed over them. Hugh de Beauchamp's quarrel with William de Warenne over the latter's possession of a hide and a virgate holding in Easton, Beds., is illuminating in this respect. Authgi, a man of Hugh de Beauchamp's antecessor, Eskil, held this

---

[27] E.g. Godwine Frambolt and Leofwine Cild each had properties in Bedfordshire TRE and each had four successors TRE (*Domesday Book* i, 211, 214v, 215, 215v, 216v). Archbishop Stigand represents an extreme case. His extensive holdings in Circuit III were scattered among Count Gilbert, Ralph de Limesy, Rothais wife of Richard fitzGilbert, Adelaide wife of Hugh de Grandmesnil, Richard Puignant, Ralph de l'Isle, Walkelin bishop of Winchester, Robert bishop of Chester, the abbey of St Albans and Archbishop Lanfranc. See Abels, *Introduction to Bedfordshire*, 43–4; *Introduction to Hertfordshire*, 33.

[28] R. Welldon Finn, *An Introduction to Domesday Book*, London 1963, 28. For references to claims *per heridatem*, see *Domesday Book* i, 46v (Worthy, Hampshire), 175 (Bartley, Worcs.); *Domesday Book* ii, 44b (Chardford, Essex).

[29] *Domesday Book* i, 215. One searches in vain for the other lands of this king's thegn. If he is the same man as the Buckinghamshire Wulfgeat, then Eudo also lost out to Hugh de Beauchamp (*Domesday Book* i, 150v).

[30] The king, not Count Alan, succeeded, however, to Eadgifu's great estate of Exning in Cambridgeshire (*Domesday Book* i, 189), while Earl Hugh had possession of Mentmore in Bucks. (*Domesday Book* i, 146v).

[31] *Domesday Book* i, 211v. Cf. 213 (Easton); 213v (Colmworth). The Norman barons' essential indifference to the peculiarities of Old English lordship left its mark on the Inquest. The Domesday commissioners on inquest in Circuit III tended to ignore soke unless it happened to belong to the king (and was thus a source of royal revenue) or was involved in a dispute over land. In other circuits, of course, they ignored pre-Conquest commendation. In fact, outside of Circuits III, VI, and VII the compilers tended to omit any systematic description of pre-Conquest lordship and overlordship. The tenurial implications of pre-Conquest *commendatio* have also generated dispute among historians. See, especially, Frederic Maitland, *Domesday Book and Beyond*, Cambridge 1897, reprinted 1987, 66–74; Carl Stephenson, 'Commendation and Related Problems in Domesday', *EHR* lix, 1944, 289–310; Barbara Dodwell, 'East Anglian Commendation', *EHR* lxiii, 1948, 289–308. My own view is that commendation was revocable, and that the Domesday phrases about 'giving and selling' and about receding with one's land to another lord are synonymous with and refer to rights of free disposal and bequest.

land and could sell to whom he would, but Eskil retained in his manor of Colmworth soke-rights over a separate virgate holding that Authgi also had in the vill. King William confirmed Authgi's right to hold his land and commended him by writ to the sheriff Ralph Taillebois 'that he might serve him during his life'. Ralph was Eskil's designated successor, and the writ may provide some insight into how he and other Norman lords became the lords of their antecessors' men. Some time later, however, the Englishman withdrew his commendation from Ralph and turned to William de Warenne, whose man he was on the day that he died. Accordingly William was seised of his lands, including the virgate in Easton held TRE by Authgi's man Blæc. While Hugh de Beauchamp, Ralph Taillebois's heir, did not contest William de Warenne's possession of Authgi's hide and virgate, he did pursue the virgate of sokeland as lord of the manor of Colmworth and was supported in his claim by the testimony of 'all the sworn men of the shrievalty'.[32] Despite this, the virgate is entered in William de Warenne's *breve*, one of the few disputes in the 'county' – the land lay physically in Huntingdonshire – that the sheriff Hugh de Beauchamp lost.[33] Apparently, personal commendation (*tantum commendatio*), in and of itself, did not, in all cases, confer superior legal title to another's sokeland, at least in the eyes of the hundred juries of the Domesday Inquest.[34] Norman barons, however, *acted* as if it did, if it was in their interest to do so. In many cases they reinterpreted what had been non-tenurial relationships between their antecessors and their men for their benefit, and thus simplified the complexities of Anglo-Saxon lordship and overlordship. Their real antagonists were not the Englishmen whose lands they absorbed into their own estates, but other Normans who might have a claim to the same land.

Though a careful study of Old English lordship and tenure might demonstrate that full rights to property came only with 'sake and soke', and not with commendation or even soke alone, Normans like William de Warenne were not interested in or deterred by such niceties. As far as he was concerned, Authgi had done him homage and was his man on the day that he died. That was sufficient claim for him. Hugh de Beauchamp behaved in precisely the same way toward other commended men of Eskil of Ware, claiming them as his through his antecessor Ralph Taillebois.[35] Few Norman lords enjoyed the success of William de Eu, who held the lands of all nine of his antecessor Ælfstan's men in Bedfordshire and Hertfordshire, Geoffrey bishop of Coutances, who snatched up the properties of all but four of the twenty nine clients of his antecessor Burgræd, or Count Alan, who made good his claim upon the holdings of sixty-seven of Eadgifu the Fair's ninety-eight commended men and all but five of those who held either 'from' or 'under' her in Cambridgeshire, Hertfordshire and Buckinghamshire.[36] Nor did many lose out as thoroughly as the abbots of Ely, who saw the lands of most of their commended

---

[32] *Domesday Book* i, 211v. Cf. *Domesday Book* ii, 102 (Ovington, Essex), 102v (Colne, Essex), 25 (Hanningfield, Essex). Cf. *Domesday Book* ii, 148v (Stalham, Norfolk), 153v (Kilverstone, Norfolk). None of these, however, is an unambiguous text. See Stephenson, 'Commendation', 239–310.

[33] But note also *Domesday Book* i, 211v (Tilbrook, Hunts.).

[34] Roffe, 'From Thegnage to Barony', 163, citing *Domesday Book* ii, 71v; *Domesday Book* i, 208.

[35] *Domesday Book* i, 213–213v. Hugh held the lands of four of Eskil's other seven men in the county. Ralph's widow held two of the remaining three (fo. 218). The seventh 'man' was a woman, Ælfgifu, whose three virgates in Holme passed to William de Eu (fo. 212).

[36] He acquired twenty-seven of thirty-nine lands and estates of men commended to her and twenty-eight of thirty-two subtenancies. In Hertfordshire, he did nearly as well, assuming

men and even the thegnlands of undertenants of the abbey pass into the hands of men like the sheriff Picot and Hardwin de Scalers. Most were like Bishop Remigius, who managed to acquire the lands of three of Bishop Wulfwig's six men in Bedfordshire, though he was compensated for the loss by securing not only the property that Alwine deule had held as the bishop's man but also those that he had held as a king's man.[37] In short, the Normans pursued whatever 'rights' and claims they might have upon their antecessors' men and their lands, whether it entailed *commendatio*, *soca*, sake and soke, dependency of tenure or some combination. The result was a ripple effect. One great lord who rebelled could cost dozens of lesser men their lands. And even if a native landholder scraped past the Scylla of forfeiture, he was liable to be sucked under by the Charybdis of extortion or illegal encroachment by powerful and greedy neighbors.

Even this makes the transfer of men and land from Anglo-Saxon overlords to Norman successors in the south-east midlands shires seem more orderly than it probably was. Greed and conflicting interests guaranteed that the process was rarely neat.[38] Though Stenton thought it 'remarkable proof of the Conqueror's statesmanship that this tenurial revolution never degenerated into a scramble for land',[39] many barons, particularly ones with merely local interests, were scrambling for all they were worth to get what they could. The new lords jealously pursued their interests at each other's expense as well as that of their natural prey, their English neighbours. Whatever order there was to this 'land rush' came from the personal friendships and familial alliances that bound together the predatory newcomers and moderated their competition, and from a general acceptance that legal 'right' based on the principles of antecessorial inheritance and royal grant ought to govern the descent of property. Bedfordshire Domesday, despite its lack of a *Clamores* section, notes in passing twenty-eight disputes over land. In fifteen cases the claimant sued upon grounds of continuity of tenement, asserting either that the land had lain TRE in one of his other estates, or that either he or his 'antecessor' had once been seised of it.[40] Many of these suits revolved around boundary disputes and most involved modest amounts of land, in some cases no more than a few acres of arable, meadow, or woods.[41] As might be expected, the sheriff of Bedfordshire, Ralph Taillebois, was a notable transgressor.[42] William

possession of seven of ten holdings of her men. However, William fitzAnsculf, Jocelyn the Breton and Odo of Bayeux succeeded to the lands of her three men in Buckinghamshire.

[37] *Domesday Book* i, 210 (Easton and Tempsford, as the Bishop's man), 210v (Clifton, as a king's man). His lord for his holding in Chicksands (fo. 210v) is not named in the text.

[38] As Robin Fleming has shown with an appropriately intricate chart, the men of the greater lords in Buckinghamshire rarely passed as a body to a single Norman lord. Fleming, *Kings and Lords*, 119, fig. 4.4.

[39] Stenton, *Anglo-Saxon England*, 626.

[40] Fowler, *Bedfordshire in 1086*, 81.

[41] *Domesday Book* i, 215 (Pavenham) and 215v (Wymington). The Pavenham case is especially interesting, because it appears to have arisen from a boundary dispute. Ranulf brother of Ilger held 5 hides in Pavenham. He claimed, and the Half Hundred concurred, that he had been wrongfully dispossessed of twelve acres of land by Gilbert fitzSalomon and four acres of meadow by Hugh de Grandmesnil. Gilbert's manor of Felmersham borders on Pavenham to the north, while Hugh's steward Ivo held a manor (possibly from Hugh's wife Adelaide) in Milton Ernest, which also adjoins Ranulf's holding.

[42] *Domesday Book* i, 210 (Easton, against William de Caron), 212 (Sandy, against Eudo the steward), 214 (Clophill, against Nigel d'Aubigny), 217v (Houghton Conquest, against Adelaide,

Espec, on the other end of the scale, was by his own account victimized by great and small alike. Not only was he preyed upon by Ralph Taillebois, Eudo the Steward and William de Warenne, but he even lost land to an Englishman, a burgess of Bedford named Godwine, from whom he claimed a virgate and a quarter in Biddenham, again citing illegal dispossession.[43]

As the case of Authgi reminds us, Englishmen who held their land freely in 1066 expected to be able to withdraw with it to a more satisfactory lord. Authgi, actually, was joined in his defection from the lordship of Ralf Taillebois by twenty sokemen in Tilbrook, Beds., which like Easton lay physically in Huntingdonshire.[44] These twenty men had held among them five hides, and 'they belonged in such a way to the king's soke and sake that they could give and sell their land to whom they wished and withdraw to another lord without the leave of him under whom they were' [*ita de soca & saca regis fuerunt quod dare & uendere terram suam cui uoluissent potuerunt, & recedere ad alium dominum sine licentia eius sub quo fuerunt*]. Hugh claimed the land against William on the grounds that his antecessor, the sheriff Ralph Taillebois, was seised of it by the king, and was supported in this assertion by the jurors of Stodden Hundred. The attractive power of William's great Huntingdonshire lordship of Kimbolton had taken all of Swineshead and a small part of Keysoe out of Bedfordshire. Apparently, the sokemen of Tilbrook also felt its pull. It probably helped that William de Warenne was willing to permit them, as he did Authgi, to continue in their tenures as undertenants. Warenne's success was due to the pre-Conquest freedom of the sokemen to change lords, his own flexibility in cutting a deal with them and, not least, to geography. In Tiscott, Hertfordshire, five sokemen held TRE land in what was to become Robert d'Oilly's manor. Not one was commended to Robert's antecessor Wigot of Wallingford on the day that King Edward was alive and dead and each could sell his land. Soon after the Conquest one of the sokemen paid King William nine ounces of gold for his land, apparently either redeeming the property or purchasing a

---

wife of Hugh de Grandmesnil). Hugh de Beauchamp, Ralph's successor, claimed that he was encroached upon in Tilbrook (211v).

[43] *Domesday Book* i, 218. Among William Espec's holdings in 1086 was an estate in Chawston assessed at 7 hides and 1 virgate, which represented the property of 12 sokemen TRE. Hugh de Beauchamp (*Domesday Book* i, 213v) and Eudo the steward (fo. 212) also held land in the vill, the former having acquired one hide that belonged to two sokemen, and the latter, one hide and one virgate once held by two king's men. Perhaps because of the vill's complex tenurial pattern in 1066, there was great uncertainty twenty years later over who properly held what. William's men claimed by right of 'antecessor' 1 ½ acres of meadow from the men of Eudo the steward and another 7 acres of fields from Hugh de Beauchamp's undertenant, Rhiwallon, who, they said, had dispossessed William of the land. Eudo, in turn, claimed that one of these 7 acres actually belonged to him by right. *Domesday Book* i, 215. The jurors offered no judgement concerning the justice of these claims. William Espec also impleaded one of the most powerful magnates in the realm, William de Warenne, over 2 ½ virgates in Dean. William Espec complained that, though he had been seised of this land 'through the king and his deliverer', William de Warenne had dispossessed him of it 'without the king's writ'. To add insult to injury, William de Warenne had also taken away two horses from William Espec's men and had not yet given them back. The jurors of Stodden Hundred confirmed William Espec's story, but it apparently did the plaintiff little good. The priory of Huntingdon was to receive William de Warenne's estate in Dean, including the disputed land. Fowler, *Bedfordshire in 1086*, 102.

[44] *Domesday Book* i, 211v. For Willam de Warenne's holding of the manor of Kimbolton and its sokeland in Huntingdonshire, which straddled the borders of the two counties, see *Domesday Book* i, 205v. Abels, 'Introduction to Bedfordshire', 5–6.

confirmation of title. Still fearful for the safety of his tenure, he turned for protection to Wigot, one of the few Anglo-Saxon magnates to enjoy William's favor. We do not know what the other four sokemen did, but we know what happened to their land. When Wigot died, Robert snatched the lands of all five, presumably on the grounds that one of them had been commended to his antecessor.[45] Sigar, one of Esger the Staller's commended men in Cambridgeshire, played his cards with considerably more finesse, managing to retain four of six lands as an undertenant of Geoffrey de Mandeville. In the process, however, he lost his main estate in Haslingfield and a lesser holding in Sawston to another of Geoffrey's men, Roger. His balance sheet stood at £7 8s retained and £12 lost.[46] Sigar, obviously, 'cut a deal'. Some Norman lords, most notably Countess Judith, Hugh de Beauchamp, and Geoffrey, bishop of Coutances, were more amenable than their fellows to the idea of English undertenants. Native landowners held seven of the thirty-three subtenancies in Countess Judith's fief,[47] while twenty-three survivors managed to retain seven subtenancies from Hugh de Beauchamp, and twenty others shared four holdings under Geoffrey, bishop of Coutances.[48] Countess Judith's English tenants in Bedfordshire are of particular interest because of their geographical concentration. They are largely found in a single vill, Sutton in Wenslow Hundred, with the result that Sutton stands out as a pocket of continuity in the Bedfordshire countryside. In 1086 seven and a half of the vill's nearly eleven plowlands were still in the hands of men with patently English names. In part, this reflects the success of one of Countess Judith's six English tenants in the vill, a man named Alwine, who not only survived but profitted from the changing conditions. Twenty years before he and Edward had held jointly two plowlands in Sutton. Not only did he retain this land as a 'de rege' tenure after the Conquest,[49] but added to it an additional two plowlands that had belonged to ten of his former neighbors. Some of this land he held in chief[50] and some as an undertenant of Eudo fitzHubert,[51] in one case, and of Countess Judith[52] in another.

Alwine's success may be the exception that proves the rule. From the last *breve* we learn that one of Alwine's holdings in Sutton had been placed into the king's administration (*in ministerio regis*) by Ralph Taillebois when he was sheriff.[53] Alwine's main tenancy in the vill is also entered in the last *breve*, and since this *breve* is a compendium of the tenures of the king's minor agents and almsmen, it is difficult to escape the conclusion that Alwine had at some time been a king's

[45] *Domesday Book* i, 137v.

[46] *Domesday Book* i, 197.

[47] *Domesday Book* i, 217v: Alwine in Sutton and Clifton; Leofgar, Sweting, Godwine, Godric, and Thorkil, all in Sutton.

[48] Hugh de Beauchamp: 7 sokemen at Stanford (*Domesday Book* i, 212), 11 sokemen at Salph (fo. 213), Ælfric the priest at Riseley (fo.213), Leofgeat at Thurleigh (fo. 213), Leodmær at Astwick (fo. 213v), Northmann at Cople (fo. 214), Branting at Cople (fo. 214); the bishop of Coutances: 6 'Englishmen' (jointly with two 'Frenchmen') at Easton (fo. 210), Thorgils 'anglicus' at Sharnbrook (fo. 210), 7 sokemen at Sharnbrook (210), and Alweald at Rushden (fo. 210).

[49] *Domesday Book* i, 218v.

[50] *Domesday Book* i, 218v.

[51] *Domesday Book* i, 212.

[52] *Domesday Book* i, 217v.

[53] *Domesday Book* i, 218v.

reeve.[54] If so, his personal relationship with the king's sheriff might explain why he was able to prosper at the expense of his neighbors. Even so, Alwine's fortunes were not uniformly favourable. Despite accepting him as her undertenant in both Sutton and Clifton, Countess Judith felt no qualms about dispossessing him of two plowlands in Stratton and four bovates in Holme, which she then used to enfeoff a Frenchman, Fulcher of Paris. In a tenurial version of 'musical chairs', Alwine appears to have made good this loss by obtaining from the king one-and-a-half plowlands in Holme that had belonged to two other men TRE.[55]

Enterprising Englishmen, especially ones in the king's employ, could also benefit from the distress of their neighbours. Osgeat, a royal reeve, claimed a half hide at Turvey, Beds., on the basis of his relationship with its TRE owner, a sokeman whom King Willam had commended to him 'with his land . . . so that as long as he [the sokeman] lived he should provide food and clothing for him'.[56] This looks very much as if the property in question was exchanged for an annuity, the sokeman perhaps also retaining a life interest. If so, we are witnessing here a secular version of the 'corrody' system widely practiced by religious establishments both before and after the Conquest. We cannot even begin to guess how common such arrangements were. Given the unsettled tenor of these times, it is certain that all survivors anxiously sought protection. Besides, all free men were obliged under Anglo-Saxon law to have a lord to whom they were answerable for wrongdoing. What must have ensued was a scramble to find patrons among the foreign magnates at the same time that the new lords were seeking to lay claim to all the lands and men that their antecessors had. The more fortunate native landowners struck deals by which they retained at least some of their lands as undertenants, or, as in the case of the English Domesday jurors recorded in the *Inquisitio Eliensis* and *Inquisitio Comitatus Cantabrigiensis*, as undertenants of Norman tenants. (Baldwin, an antecessor and tenant of the sheriff of Buckinghamshire Ansculf, retained not only two of his holdings in that shire but gained a third that had belonged TRE to two of his own men.[57]) The majority probably eventually sank into the peasantry. No doubt the conquerors aggressively pressed their lordship upon their English neighbors, hoping thereby to consolidate and expand their sphere of influence, and one would suspect that these offers were often made in a manner that could not be easily refused. In this way the patterns of pre-Conquest lordship were preserved, to a degree, in the Norman baronies that emerged.

But what determined these patterns? If *commendatio* among the Anglo-Saxons

---

[54] It is tempting to identify him with Alwine the king's reeve who held land in Tempsford, Edworth, and Holme (*Domesday Book* i, 218v), though it is curious that the scribe, having written 'Aluuinus prefectus regis' in these three entries, should have then omitted the designation in describing Alwine's tenures in Sutton and Beeston. The name Alwine, of course, was extremely common in eleventh-century England.

[55] *Domeday Book* i, 217v, 218v. This assumes that 'Aluuinus praefectus regis' and 'Aluuinus' in *Domesday Book* i, 218v were the same man.

[56] *Domesday Book* i, 218v.

[57] Baldwin was a king's thegn commended to Archbishop Stigand TRE. The lands he retained *de* William TRW were: *Domesday Book* i, 149 (Chiceley & land in Lamua Hundred: 5 hides in all); 62v (? Curridge, 2 hides and 3 virgates from Ralph de Mortimer). Those lost: 148v (Ellesborough, 1 ½ hides); 61 (Hodcott, Berks.: 6 ½ hides), 61v (Pangbourne, 6 hides 1 virgate). His holding in Hardmead (fo. 149) had belonged TRE to two men commended to him and a third commended to Toki. Baldwin may also have been William fitzAnsculf's tenant for lands in Worcester and Surrey.

was a bond entered into voluntarily, as was at least theoretically the case, what led men to select one lord over another? Geographical proximity is one answer.[58] Because of the information it preserves concerning pre-Conquest commendation, the county surveys of Circuit III permit us to draw up a rough gazetteer of Anglo-Saxon personal lordship and landholding on the eve of the Conquest. From this some general conclusions may be drawn about lord-seeking in the south-east midlands in 1065. Great 'national' magnates, such as Archbishop Stigand and Earl Harold, had large followings that did not necessarily conform to any geographical rationale. They attracted to their lordship landowners of all stripes, but most prominently the elite of the shire.[59] The lord-man relationship in such cases was essentially social and political in character, a sort of treaty between a great magnate and a member of the local gentry. Having such men in as many hundreds as possible was to the lord's advantage, since a thegn who possessed five hides of land could appear in the hundred courts on his lord's behalf.[60] For the client's part, the protection of a great lord could prove decisive in disputes with other local powers or with their patrons. In short, political considerations rather than geographical convenience shaped the landed followings of the great men of the realm. The clientele of a local thegn was a different matter entirely. For small landowners geographical proximity was often the decisive factor in choosing a lord. Many sokemen and lesser thegns sought patrons within the hundreds in which they held land, which is not at all surprising in the light of the personal services they proffered and expected. An especially interesting example of this, one which provides information about two levels of commendation, is to be found in the vill of Steppingley in Bedfordshire. The vill's manor was held TRE by a thegn named Almær. This Almær had commended himself to 'Ælfric of Flitwick', a wealthy local thegn who held a manor bordering Steppingley to the east, and was, in turn, the lord of two sokemen who held land in Steppingley.[61] In the case of Almær, his lord, and his men, we have a nice illustration of the geographical or territorial principle. In some cases, however, a lord could be too close for comfort. Most of Bedfordshire's vills were under divided lordship, and in many of these lesser men who 'could take their land to any lord they would' chose not to commend themselves to the landowner who dominated their village. Instead they placed themselves under an outside power, probably in an attempt to counterbalance the influence of their powerful and dangerous neighbour. Six sokemen in Dean, for example, commended them-

---

[58] Fowler, *Bedfordshire in 1086*, 106 and map 4.

[59] Queen Eadgyth, for instance, had four 'men' in Bedfordshire, one of whom, Alsige of Bromham, ranked among the shire's greatest landowners. Alsige: *Domesday Book* i, 209v, 213v; Moding: 213v; Algar: 216v; Wælhræfn: 209v; Ketilbert: 218v (and in 1086). Wulfweard White, who held the great manor of Toddington (212) and enjoyed an estate that stretched over at least ten shires, was also the queen's man (in fact, he was her steward), though he is not so described in the Beds. folios. See *Domesday Book* i, 147, 153. Similarly, Earl Leofwine Godwineson held only the four hide manor of Puttenham in Hertfordshire, but his influence ensured that more than a dozen men of the county sought his lordship, a mixed group that included burgesses, thegns, sokemen, a huntsman and even a housecarl (*Domesday Book* i, 132, 134, 136, 136v, 140).

[60] *Gethynctho* 3, ed. Felix Liebermann, *Die Gesetze der Angelsachsen*, 3 vols, Halle 1903–16, i, 456.

[61] *Domesday Book* i, 214v. 'Ælfric of Flitwick' presents us with a bit of a problem, since, according to Domesday Book, the lord of Flitwick TRE was a man named 'Alwine' (*Domesday Book* i, 216). 'Alwine' may be an error, or Ælfric may have been Alwine's overlord. Ælfric was a great landowner in the hundred and elsewhere in the county TRE.

selves to Burgræd (and eleven others to the king) rather than placing themselves under the vill's major landowner, Godric, King Edward's rapacious sheriff of Berkshire and, perhaps, Buckinghamshire.[62] Burgræd's lordship was so desirable (or, alternatively, he was so persuasive in pursuing clients) that the sokemen who held land in Higham Ferrers' (Northants) berewicks in Rushden, Irchester, and Raunds all commended themselves to Burgræd rather than to the manor's lord, Countess Gytha, the wife of Earl Ralph of Hereford.[63] In Risely, Hertfordshire, on the other hand, a small landowner named Wulfnoth thought it more prudent to 'bow' to Godric, who held a single plowland in that vill, than to the lord of the vill's manor, Burgræd. Another landowner in that vill, Alwine, preferred the lordship of Stori, one of Earl Tostig's commended men, whose only holding in Bedfordshire according to Domesday Book was a plowland in Easton that he held jointly with a sokeman, while a third sought protection from Earl Harold.[64]

Though the geography of lordship TRE in the south-east midlands was as tangled as one of Robin Fleming's charts of antecessors, it does reveal a certain logic that derives from what men expected from their lords in the years before and, probably, also immediately after the Conquest. The common thread, it seems to me, was the hundred and its court. A local thegn such as Burgræd may not have enjoyed the national prominence or influence of an Ælfstan of Boscombe or an Esger the Staller, but within his particular locale he was obviously a man to be reckoned with. Little could have taken place in the hundred courts of Stodden and Willey without Burgræd's approval (see Map 2). Although the evidence is not as certain as one might wish, it is likely that juridical considerations entered into one's choice of a lord, and that hundred boundaries as well as simple geographical proximity helped determine the lordship pattern found in pre-Conquest Bedfordshire, Hertfordshire and the other shires of Circuit III (see examples in Maps 1–8). Hundred courts were especially important for lesser landowners, for it was here that they defended title to their land, secured their inheritances, assembled before the sheriff and hundredman in their tithings, answered criminal charges brought against them and rendered their military service to the king.[65] The lord also profitted from the arrangement; he not only increased his prestige in county society but secured for himself (and his men) the oath-helpers necessary to pursue a plea to its successful conclusion. With its monthly meetings, the court of the hundred provided local magnates with a regular opportunity to confirm their social status by playing the role of patron to their neighbours. If Patrick Wormald is correct about the post-Conquest origins of Oswaldslow and other such franchises, the hundred

---

[62] *Domesday Book* i, 210, 218v. Since the TRE holders of Dean and nearby Riseley were both king's thanes named Godric whose holdings passed to Bishop Remigius (fo. 210), it is all but certain that the same man held both lands. The identification of this Godric with the sheriff of Buckinghamshire and Berkshire is based on another entry for Riseley (fo. 213) where we read that Wulfnoth held two virgates in the vill and was the 'man' of 'Godric the Sheriff'.

[63] *Domesday Book* i, 225v.

[64] *Domesday Book* i, 216v.

[65] H.R. Loyn, 'The Hundred in the Tenth and Early Eleventh Centuries', in H. Hearder and H.R. Loyn, eds, *British Government and Administration*, Cardiff 1974, 1–15; *idem, The Governance of Anglo-Saxon England, 500–1087*, Stanford, CA, 1984, 140–8; Abels, *Lordship and Military Obligation*, 179, 182–4.

court and the sheriff played an even more central role in the public lives of these lesser landowners than has been commonly believed.[66]

Of course, there was not one or even two 'principles' of lord-seeking in the south-east midlands in 1065. Many of the individual decisions undoubtedly were made on the basis of personal motives. Wealth and proximity, of course, were important factors, but so were hereditary affinities between lords and men, ties of kinship, friendships, enmities, property disputes, and the like. This is precisely the 'human dimension' that is missing from the Exchequer Domesday. Still, the desire to find a patron within one's hundred might well explain why Norman lords were able to absorb with so little apparent difficulty the lands not only of the men commended to their predecessors in the vill, but of their neighbours' as well. The importance of the hundred court for such men did not diminish with the Conquest. The Norman barons, like their English antecessors, also profitted from collecting tenants within their hundreds, especially when it came to inquests over the rightful possession of land.[67] As Robin Fleming has demonstrated, it could be quite benefi-cial to a lord to have a man or two among the jurors in 'the real-world, hard-ball politics that must have operated at every court in the tenth and eleventh centuries, including the ones that produced Domesday Book'.[68] In 1086, Abbot Simeon of Ely guarded his abbey's remaining demesne and thegnlands by packing the hun-dred juries of the Isle of Ely with his own men.

In building up their holdings, the new lords must have depended heavily upon the knowledge of local Englishmen, just as King William himself relied upon the administrative expertise of native-born sheriffs for the first years of his reign.[69] However incomplete and self-serving the Norman understanding of Anglo-Saxon institutions of lordship and tenure, clearly *someone* had disclosed to them the tenurial arrangements of their antecessors and pointed to the men in the shire who had 'bowed' to them TRE. Their knowledge about tenurial conditions on the day that King Edward was alive and dead and their service on the juries of the Domesday inquest made men like Alan of Richmond's tenants Colsveinn,[70] his son Almær cild[71] and Ordmær of Badlingham[72] as valuable to the count as any of his Norman tenants.

Among those most successful in placing their men on such juries were the

---

[66] Patrick Wormald, 'Lordship and Justice in the Early English Kingdom: Oswaldslow Revisited', in *Property and Power in Early Medieval Europe*, ed. W. Davies and P. Fouracre, Cambridge 1996, 114–36.

[67] Loyn, *Governance*, 196–7; W.L. Warren, *The Governance of Norman and Angevin England, 1086–1272*, Stanford, CA, 1987, 44–7, 60–2.

[68] Robin Fleming, 'Oral Testimony and the Domesday Inquest', *ANS* xvii, 1995, 108, and, gener-ally, 101–22.

[69] For William I's reliance upon English royal *servientes*, see Campbell, 'Some Agents', 210–18; Williams, *English*, 98–125; W.L. Warren, 'The Myth of Norman Administrative Efficiency', *TRHS*, 5th series xxxiv, 1984, 113–32.

[70] *Domesday Book* i, 194v (Whaddon, Meldreth and Melbourn).

[71] *Domesday Book* i, 195 (Kingston, Toft, Bourn, Caldecote, Longstowe, Hatley St George), 195v (West Wratting, Balsham).

[72] *Domesday Book* i, 195v (Badlingham; but cf. Swaffham). Ordmær's service as a Domesday juror for Staploe Hundred, Cambridgeshire, is made even more remarkable by the fact that he had been less than ten years before a member of a jury from that same hundred that had been heavily fined for perjury. Fleming, 'Oral Testimony', 107–9. The favour of both Count Alan and Picot the Sheriff, the two most powerful men in the shire, explains Ordmær's remarkable recovery of his reputation.

sheriffs. This was in part the result of their knowledge of how the courts worked. But it also arose from self-interest. The private activities of sheriffs in building up their personal fiefs made them particularly vulnerable to counter-claims. Considering the importance of William's sheriffs in the local administration of Conquest England, surprisingly little has been written about them (or, for that matter, their Anglo-Saxon predecessors).[73] Yet their activities were critical in overseeing and facilitating the massive redistribution of land that took place between 1066 and 1086. This was well understood by their contemporaries and the monastic and ecclesiastical historians of the next generation who pointed to the sheriffs as being the worst culprits among the many who stole land from their houses in the disturbed times following Hastings. In the words of Henry of Huntingdon: 'The sheriffs and reeves, whose function it was to preserve justice and legality, were fiercer than the thieves and robbers, and more savage to all than the most savage.'[74] A few, such as Eustace of Huntingdon, Picot of Cambridgeshire and Urse de Abetot, sheriff of Worcestershire and Gloucestershire, achieved lasting notoriety. Urse's castle building at the expense of a monastic cemetery so exasperated the elderly Archbishop Ealdred that it provoked a memorable curse, 'If thou hattest Urse, thou be cursed'. But, as Emma Mason observes, 'the castle stood intact until the thirteenth century, while the descendants of Urse's daughter long continued to dominate the region'.[75] One can well imagine the abbot of Ely desperately trying to find some appropriate word-play on 'Picot'. Picot's depredations against the abbey are too well known to be rehearsed; his and the abbot's *brevia* are filled with evidence of his successful filching of the abbey's lands, and of the abbot's forced acquiescence to Picot's (and Hardwin de Scalers') subtenancies.[76] (Picot apparently even aided Bishop Remigius's seizure of Ely's 1 hide and 1 virgate in Histon, where the bishop of Lincoln had a 26 ½ hide manor, and Picot two subtenancies.)[77] The monks of Ely had reason to remember him as 'a hungry lion, a roving wolf, a crafty fox, a filthy pig, a shameless dog'.[78] Picot was precisely the sort of sheriff that King William had in mind when he issued a writ to Archbishop Lanfranc, Geoffrey bishop of Coutances and his other magnates ordering them to summon the sheriffs and inform them that they had to return all the demesne land that they had taken from the abbeys and bishoprics.[79] Of course, thegnland was a different matter, and the king's solution was to regularize the situation by ordering Picot to serve the abbot for these lands.[80]

---

[73] But see William Alfred Morris, *The Medieval English Sheriff to 1300*, Manchester 1927, chs 2–3; Judith Green, 'The Sheriffs of William the Conqueror', *ANS* v, 1982, 129–45, and *English Sheriffs to 1154*, HMSO, London 1990.

[74] Huntingdon, 209: 'Vicecomites et præpositi, quorum erat officium justitia et judicium, furibus et raptoribus atrociores erant, et omnibus sævissimis sæviores.'

[75] Emma Mason, *St Wulfstan of Worcester, c.1008–1095*, Oxford 1990, 123. Urse's son was less lucky, falling foul of Henry I and losing the land and shrievalty he had inherited from his father for having ordered the killing of a royal official. *De Gestis pontificum*, 253. Freeman, *Norman Conquest* iv, 116–17; R.R. Darlington, ed., *The Cartulary of Worcester Cathedral Priory*, Pipe Roll Society, ns lxxvi, 1968, xxv, 26–7.

[76] Edward Miller, *The Abbey and Bishopric of Ely*, Cambridge 1951, 66–70.

[77] *Domesday Book* i, 190v.

[78] *Liber Eliensis*, 211. For the lands he took from Ely abbey, see *Inquisitio Eliensis Breviate*, ed. N.E.S.A. Hamilton, 175–6.

[79] *EHD* ii, no. 38.

[80] E.g. *Inquisitio Eliensis*, fos 113, 135.

Encroachment upon the church was what most blackened the posthumous reputations of William's sheriffs, but their fortunes were not built, by and large, upon stolen ecclesiastical lands but upon property that had belonged TRE to laymen. Picot, like Ilbert in Herfordfordshire, Ralph Taillebois in Bedfordshire and Ansculf de Picquigny in Buckinghamshire, fashioned a large holding in his shrievalty by patching together the lands of an enormous number of sokemen and other minor landowners, and by seeking undertenancies from other barons in the county.[81] For his thirty-two holdings Picot claimed 196 predecessors, 171 of whom had been sokemen. Of these, 115 had been King Edward's men, while thirty-four had either been Ely's commended men or belonged to its soke.[82] The other lords of Picot's predecessors were a veritable who's who of King Edward's court and south-east midland society: Archbishop Stigand, Earls Ælfgar, Waltheof, and Harold, Esger the Staller, Robert fitzWymarc, Eadgifu the Fair, Ælfric Cilt and Wulfmær of Eaton. Picot's holdings as an undertenant in the county were nearly as impressive. He held land from eleven other tenants-in-chief, including two colleagues in the shrievalty, Peter of Valognes and Ansculf de Picquigny.

Picot's holding was unusual in that he lacked any one antecessor who gave his estate shape and cohesion. The closest thing he had to one, not counting the abbey of Ely, was Blæcwine, King Edward's sheriff, whose lands in Girton, Oakington, Landbeach and Waterbeach, about eight hides in all, Picot absorbed into his massive fief.[83] Picot's manor of Bourn is more typical of how he went about assembling his landed estate. This thirteen-hide manor had come to Picot as two manors. Twenty-two men had held lands in the vill TRE, including a king's thegn, who had had three hides in the village under (*sub*) King Edward; two priests, his men; three sokemen of Archbishop Stigand; a man of Esgar the Staller; two men of the abbot of Ramsey; and thirteen men of King Edward, who rendered six cartage-dues and seven escort-services to the sheriff for their two hides. All twenty-two, we are told, could sell, and all their lands ended up in Picot's hands.[84] In a similar way Picot put together the holdings of nineteen royal sokemen and one of Earl Ælfgar's men in Hinxton to make a 15 ½ hide manor.[85] The only thing unusual about Bourn and Hinxton was that there Picot did not seem to have encroached blatantly upon any of his Norman neighbours in building up these estates.

Picot's ability to gain possession over the lands of king's sokemen was due to his position as sheriff. The sheriff's main duties, managing and farming the king's demesne in the county and supervising the payment of dues and renders owed the Crown, meant that he *was* royal authority incarnate to the sokemen who rendered to him cartage, watch and ward, and other renders that they traditionally owed to the king.[86] One of Picot's duties as sheriff was protecting the king's sokemen

---

81 Green, 'Sheriffs', 142–4.

82 *Domesday Book* i, 200–201v. Twenty-four of these Ely men had lands belonging to the abbey's soke; eight held thegnlands that 'could not be separated' from the monks' demesne.

83 *Domesday Book* i, 201–201v.

84 *Domesday Book* i, 200v–201; *Inquisitio Comitatus Cantabrigiensis*, fo. 111b.

85 If, on analogy with the northern shires discussed by David Roffe, these twenty sokemen had a common overlord TRE, one might ask, who was he? The answer, it seems to me, is that these sokemen were, as the text says, the king's men and held freely under him. In fact, there is little evidence throughout the Cambridgeshire Domesday Book (or ICC or IE, for that matter) that the Norman lords of the county were reproducing through their baronies pre-existing sokes.

86 *Inquisitio Comitatus Cantabrigiensis* fo. 79–79b (Swaffham, Staine Hundred).

against the depredations of others. When Aubrey de Vere attempted to add to his manor of Abington by taking possession of the land of a king's sokeman, Picot, acting in his official capacity, pressed the king's claim and obtained custody of the sokeman, his land, 380 sheep and a plow.[87] Picot and other sheriffs, both before and after the Conquest, could and did attach royal sokemen *en bloc* to royal demesne manors in order to increase the king's revenues and their own profits. In Bedfordshire, for example, Ralph and Ivo Taillebois practised on a grand scale what Bondi the Staller had been doing more modestly before the Conquest, increasing the size and revenues of the royal manors of Luton and Houghton Regis by absorbing neighbouring small holdings.[88] And in attaching the manors of Westoning (in Beds.) and King's Walden to Hitchin, Ilbert of Hertford was merely completing on behalf of the king Earl Harold's even more ambitious encroachments upon the sokemen and thegns of the hundred.[89] William's sheriffs, in short, in building up the royal demesne were simply pursuing more vigorously the same policies as earls, stallers and, undoubtedly, sheriffs in previous times.

William's sheriffs were even more aggressive when it came to attending to their own interests. A few Anglo-Saxon sheriffs, notably Godric of Berkshire and Buckinghamshire, had used their position to feather their nests.[90] But, by and large, King Edward's sheriffs had been modest landowners, at least within the shires they tended for their royal lord. Ælfstan sheriff of Bedfordshire,[91] Edmund sheriff of Hertfordshire,[92] Ælfgæt of Middlesex[93] and Alric Godricson of Cambridgeshire[94] are little more than names. Two other sheriffs of King Edward, Ordgar and Blæcwine, appear in Cambridgeshire Domesday as having held land in the shire. Ordgar held his lands on loan from the royal demesne and from Earl Harold.[95] Since Blæcwine's modest possessions all passed to Picot, they too may well have been shrieval lands. The income of King Edward's sheriffs seems to have come largely from what they could get from farming the royal estates.[96] Even after the Conquest, Peter de Valognes derived far more income from farming and the profits of justice than from his landed revenue.[97] But the difference between the TRE and TRW sheriffs in terms of their landed wealth within their shires is clear and dramatic. William's sheriffs were far greater men than their pre-Conquest counterparts.[98] None of King Edward's sheriffs in the south-east midlands, not even

---

[87] *Domesday Book* i, 190, 199v.

[88] *Domesday Book* i, 290–209v, 218v.

[89] *Domesday Book* i, 132–133. Cf. J.H. Round, 'Introduction to the Hertfordshire Domesday', *VCH Hertfordshire*, ed. W. Page, i, London 1902, 271–3.

[90] See, e.g., *Domesday Book* i, 60v (Sparsholt, Berks.); 140 (Oakley, Bucks.). Godric assigned a half hide of the king's demesne lands in Oakley to a girl, Ælfgyth, for as long as he held the office of sheriff, so that she might teach his daughter gold embroidery.

[91] S 1235, as witness to a charter (1053x1066) of Oswulf and Æthelgyth donating land to St Albans abbey.

[92] *Regesta* i, no. 16.

[93] S 1130, 1131. F.E. Harmer, *Anglo-Saxon Writs*, Manchester 1952, nos 86, 87.

[94] *Domesday Book* i, 189. He is named to give perspective to Picot's extortionate demands on the burgesses of Bedford.

[95] *Domesday Book* i, 197 (Chippenham); 199v (Isleham); 200 (Harston, from Earl Harold).

[96] E.g. *Domesday Book* i, 189.

[97] *Domesday Book* i, 132 (borough customs).

[98] The great exception was Mærl-Sveinn, sheriff of Lincolnshire, who possessed extensive lands in Yorkshire, Lincolnshire, Gloucestershire, Somerset, Devon and Cornwall. Williams, *English*, 22–3.

Godric, had anything approaching the landed estates of their Domesday successors. In part, this was because their activities were more closely monitored. Not only did they have an earl looking over their shoulder, but a royal bureaucracy that was at least effective when it came to its own finances. Nor could they run roughshod over even the lesser landowners in their counties, since there then existed intact a social system of patronage that meant that even modest landholders had access to 'friends' with clout. The personal ambitions of the men who replaced them may not have been greater, but the opportunities to cash in on the office certainly were. Their access to and power over royal sokemen and lesser king's thegns help explain the success that these sheriffs had in constructing their patchwork fiefs. Given that the king was far from the shire and the sheriff all too near, he became, in effect, the lord of these sokemen, the man who could protect or ruin them. If an Aubrey de Vere attempted to encroach upon a king's sokeman, Picot would be there to stop him on the king's – and his own – behalf. But if Picot chose to absorb the lands of a few dozen royal sokemen in his holding, there was no one on the scene with the power or interest to stop him. Even when the king did take official notice of Picot's high-handed activities, as when he ordered his sheriff to pull down a mill that he had erected in Cambridge to the detriment of the burgesses' mill, his displeasure seems to have had little effect. Domesday Book reports that the sheriff had three mills in the borough which diminished the pasture and destroyed many houses.[99] Indeed, the borough customs of Cambridge read almost like a legal indictment against Picot: 'In the time of King Edward the burgesses lent their ploughs to the sheriff three times a year, now they are demanded on nine occasions. In the time of King Edward they found neither cartage nor carts; they now do so because of an imposed custom. They also claim back for themselves from Picot the sheriff the common pasture taken away through him and by him. . . . Picot also has £8, a riding-horse, and arms for one man-at-arms from the heriot of lawmen. When Ælfric Godricson was sheriff, he had 20s as the heriot of one of them.'[100] Like Urse, Picot never paid for his transgressions.[101]

Hugh de Beauchamp, Ralph Taillebois's probable son-in-law and successor as sheriff of Bedfordshire and Buckinghamshire, also managed to rise from obscure antecedents to found an important local barony.[102] The fief he inherited from Ralph had at its core the lands of an antecessor, Eskil of Ware, but also included the holdings of 137 sokemen. These men came to Ralph in various ways. He received

---

Mærl-Sveinn's fortunes arose from his close relationship with Harold Godwineson. In many ways his career and activities are closer to that of a 'staller' than a typical TRE sheriff.

99 *Regesta* i, no. 151. Cf. *Domesday Book* i, 189.

100 *Domesday Book* i, 189.

101 Picot, like Urse, even became a benefactor of religion, founding what became Barnwell Priory (*English Episcopal Acta*, i, *Lincoln 1067–1085*, ed. D.M. Smith, London 1980, no. 2, 2–3).

102 Hugh probably succeeded Ralph Taillebois as sheriff of Bedfordshire. He was also sheriff of Buckinghamshire under both William I and William Rufus and served as the latter's almoner, an office that became vested in his family. See G.H. Fowler, 'The Beauchamps, Barons of Eaton', *Proceedings of the Bedfordshire Historical Record Society* ii, 1914, 61–91; Joyce Godber, *History of Bedfordshire 1066–1888*, Luton 1969, 21–2. Despite holding only a single undertenancy in Bedfordshire in 1086 (*Domesday Book* i, 210, Goldington from the bishop of Lincoln), Ivo Taillebois, Ralph's brother or son, also appears to have held the office sometime before 1086. He was particularly active in building up the royal demesne. See *Domesday Book* i, 209 (Leighton Buzzard, Luton), 209v (Houghton Regis).

the lands of some through the king's gift and others through commendation and/or encroachment.[103] The lands of many of these men were in or near vills in which Ralph's 'antecessor' Eskil of Ware had had estates. They had not, however, been Eskil's men and there is no hint that they belonged to his soke. Rather, Hugh simply attached as many minor landholders as he could to the manors or lands that he held. Hugh de Beauchamp's manor of Stotfold was a composite estate that combined Askell's 7 ½ hides with 5 ½ hides held freely TRE by seven sokemen. The manor of Willington provides an even more dramatic example.[104] Here Ralph acquired not only Eskil's three hides but seven additional hides that had belonged to eight sokemen (who may or may not have been Eskil's men). And to this Ralph and his successor added the lands of sixty-five sokemen in the surrounding vills of Great Barford, Cardington, Salph, Goldington, and Cople.[105] Ralph Taillebois obtained the last three named vills from Hugh de Grandmesnil in exchange for Askell's great residential manor of Ware, Hertfordshire. We do not know how he or Hugh de Beauchamp came to hold the lands of twenty-four sokemen in Great Barford and Cardington, but, whatever the means, the result was a compact territorial block stretching across northern Wixamtree and southern Barford Hundreds and grouped around the shire borough (Map 10).[106] Hugh held in demesne his manors nearest Bedford, perhaps to support the retinue that attended him at his seat in the borough's castle.[107] The only reversal that Ralph Taillebois experienced in his quest for sokemen came at the hands of a 'nationally' prominent neighbour, William de Warenne.

As sheriff Ralph took for forfeiture the lands of men unable or unwilling to pay geld or, in the case of royal sokemen and other lesser king's men, rents and services owed the king. Although forfeited land went to the Crown, the sheriff could assume the tenure by acquitting it of its dues, which is precisely how Ralph came to hold a small tenement in Sharnbrook.[108] Across the border in Hertfordshire, the sheriff Peter de Valognes was doing precisely the same thing to a king's sokeman in Libury. According to Domesday, a king's sokeman forfeited to the king 25 acres which he had held freely in this village before the Conquest, because he failed to meet his tax bill. An Anglo-Saxon ruler would have found nothing outrageous about confiscating land that did not acquit its *wara*. But few would have made the demands that William did, a geld of 6 shillings from each hide of land in 1084/85, which comes to a tax rate of close to 30%. It would be remarkable if many native

103 *Domesday Book* i, fo. 211v.

104 *Domesday Book* i, fo. 213, for both Stotfold and Willington.

105 Respectively *Domesday Book* i, fos 213v, 212v, 213, 212v, 213v–214.

106 Hugh had a second block of land stretching almost in a straight line from Houghton Conquest in the west to Stotfold in the east. These lands centred around Aki's (possibly an alternate spelling of Askell/Eskil) TRE manor of Haynes and Eskil's great manor of Stotfold. Hugh's (or more probably, Ralph Taillebois') acquisition of land in the vicinity of Bedford was probably motivated by the location of the sheriff's seat in the castle of the shire borough. Similarly, Ilbert built up a large estate in Bengeo a few miles from Hertford.

107 Godber, *History of Bedfordshire*, 22.

108 *Domesday Book* i, 216v. The land in question was held TRE by Tovi, a housecarl of King Edward. After the Conquest, Tovi refused to pay the rent (*gablum*) on one virgate and the fourth part of a virgate. Ralph accordingly confiscated it, paid the rent, and retained the land as part of his fief. Tovi subsequently lost the rest of his land, which was given to a royal fisherman, Osbern. On the activities of late Anglo-Saxon and early Norman sheriffs, see Morris, *Medieval English Sheriff*, chs 2–3.

smallholders did not succumb to the fate of Libury's unfortunate sokeman. But there is more to the entry. It goes on to say that the sheriff, Peter de Valognes, had acted unjustly in 'taking the land into the king's hands for forfeiture' (actually his own, since it was recorded as part of his fief), because the land had been quit of the payment of geld for as long as that sokeman had held it.[109] Libury, then, is not a case of forfeiture for back taxes, but is another instance of the rapacity of a sheriff.

Any powerful lord could try his hand at encroachment,[110] but sheriffs were more liable than most to succeed. Assuming many of the duties of Edward's earls, they served as the king's eyes and hands in the shires, collecting his revenues, executing his writs, and presiding in his name over the shire and hundred courts.[111] If property was to be transferred more than likely it would pass through their hands, and some might stick to their fingers. They apparently did not have the reputation, as a group, of being trustworthy deliverers of title. Few earned the praise that Roger the sheriff, perhaps Roger Bigod, received in the king's *breve* for Suffolk. 'Thorkel and Edric', we read, 'hold St Laurence's Church with 12 acres. Leoflæd, a certain free woman held TRE. Count Alan claims it as belonging to Earl Ralf's holding, and he recalls Ivo Taillebois as its "liberator". Thorkel and Edric, indeed, cite Roger the sheriff as their warrantor, saying that they had the church through him, and Roger was such a warrantor as any sheriff would rightfully have been in the time of King Edward' (*talis guarant qualis uicecomes esset iuste t.r.e.*).[112] The implicit contrast between the good old days, when sheriffs were honest, and current times is unmistakeable.[113] The more unscrupulous of William's sheriffs, such as Eustace of Huntingdon or Picot of Cambridge, gave substance to the complaint. Quite simply, the sheriff was in an ideal position to encroach upon his defenceless English neighbours, especially on the modest landholders who belonged to the king's soke. Few of William's sheriffs in the south-east midlands resisted the temptation. Ilbert of Hertford's fief, held in 1086 by Geoffrey de Bec, followed the same patterm as Picot's, an amalgamation of the lands of twenty-five separate individuals, seventeen of whom had belonged to the king's soke (Map 9). Even other Norman barons complained about the way Ilbert added to his manors at their expense.[114] Ilbert finally went too far when he attempted to encroach upon the king himself. Despite losing the shrievalty to Peter de Valognes, he retained the manors of (Temple) Dinsley and Wellbury that he held by King William's writ 'for as long as he was sheriff, as the shire testifies'. Apparently, he had not given up the office willingly. He refused to pay to the new sheriff the two cartage-dues and two escort-services that the manors owed in Hitchen. He may have had legal grounds for his resistance. Though the manors had paid these dues TRE, the hundred testified that had been imposed upon them by Earl Harold 'by force and unjustly'.

---

[109] *Domesday Book* i, 141.

[110] See, e.g., *Domesday Book* i, 137.

[111] For the activities of Domesday sheriffs TRE and TRW see J.D. Foy, *Domesday Book. Vol. 38: Index of Subjects*, Phillimore Domesday Book, Chichester 1992, *s.v. sheriff* (pp. 211–14); Robin Fleming, *Law and Custom in Domesday England*, Cambridge forthcoming, Index Rerum, *s.v. sheriff.*

[112] *Domesday Book* ii, 290v. But cf. *VCH Suffolk* i, 396–7, for Roger Bigod's encroachments against small landowners in Suffolk.

[113] Cf. the complaints of tenth- and early eleventh-century homilists against corrupt royal reeves and sheriffs. Morris, *Medieval English Sheriff*, 15–16.

[114] *Domesday Book* i, 140v (Hailey).

In a nice irony, Peter de Valognes and Ralf Taillebois dismissed his claim and attached the lands to the king's manor of Hitchin.[115] By 1086 Ilbert's lands had passed to Geoffrey of Bec. One does not know whether Ilbert ended up like another of King William's rapacious early sheriffs, Froger of Berkshire, of whom the Abingdon chronicler relates: 'In these [encroachments upon the monastery], Froger, then sheriff of Berkshire, was prominent. But God the Judge later punished this mighty man who persecuted the humble, for the royal justice deprived him of the office which he had turned into a tyranny, and he spent the remainder of his life in brutish want despised by all.'[116]

The Domesday Book holdings of Ralph Taillebois, Ilbert of Hertford, Ansculf de Picquigny of Buckinghamshire (represented by the fief of his son), and Picot were all monuments to the enterprise of their builders. Though Ralph and Ansculf were able to build around a core represented by the lands of an antecessor, Eskil and Ulf respectively, these were dwarfed by their acquisitions of the lands of dozens of minor landowners. The sheriffs' fiefs, patchworks of small holdings, have little to do with claims to title on the basis of antecessors and even less to do with pre-Conquest overlordships. Rather, they reflect the opportunities that men with power and office had in the unsettled times between Hastings and Domesday Book. All these men built their fortunes by acquiring the lands of royal sokemen. Other than that, one can make few generalizations. Picot was a predator upon church lands. Neither Ilbert nor Peter of Valognes was, at least in Hertfordshire. The difference may well have been one of circumstance. Picot profitted from the disfavour that Ely fell into because of the monks' complicity in the revolt of Hereward the Wake.[117] The sheriffs of Hertfordshire, on the other hand, had to contend with an aggressive abbot of St Albans in the person of Paul of Caen, nephew of Archbishop Lanfranc.[118] Ralph also may have had a freer hand in Bedfordshire than he did when he acted as sheriff of Hertfordshire, because the latter was the seat of three great barons (Robert, count of Mortain at Berkhamsted; Hugh de Grandmesnil at Ware; and Ralph de Tosny at Flamstead) while in the former he had no serious rivals. The sheriffs of Middlesex during this period, Ralph Bainard (?) and 'Roger' had little land or influence, largely because they were overshadowed by Geoffrey de Mandeville.

Perhaps what motivated men like Ralph, Peter and Picot to engage so freely in self-help was that they did not come from the upper Norman nobility. Judith Green in her study of William the Conqueror's sheriffs was unable to connect any of these men to Odo of Bayeux or William fitzOsbern or to the king's court. The most we can say is that they held land from one another and some were kinsmen through blood or marriage. Ralph Taillebois's son (or younger brother) Ivo was sheriff, at one time or another, of Lincolnshire and perhaps Bedfordshire and Norfolk as well.

---

115 *Domesday Book* i, 132v, 133. Peter de Valognes' holding in Hertfordshire was more typical of the settlement baronage, consisting largely of the lands of a single antecessor, Almær of Bennington, and his men. Peter may have held these lands by royal grant before he replaced Ilbert as sheriff sometime around 1075 (*Domesday Book* i, 140v–141v).

116 *Chronicon Monasterii de Abingdon*, ed. J. Stevenson, 2 vols, RS 2, London 1858, i, 484, 494; trans. *EHD* ii, 901.

117 Peter in his capacity as sheriff of Essex is another matter. In 1077 King William issued a writ ordering him to release the men of Bury St Edmunds whom he had imprisoned. *EHD* ii, no. 40. On the other hand, his holding in Essex does not reveal predation upon monastic lands.

118 Abels, 'Introduction to Hertfordshire', 24.

Hugh de Beauchamp, Ralph's successor in Bedfordshire, in his lands as well as his office, was probably his son-in-law; they may also have been neighbours in Normandy, but it is difficult to trace their origins with certainty.[119] The sobriquets of men such as Ralph and Ivo Taillebois, Picot of Cambridge and Ilbert of Hertford do not lead us back to the fields and manors of Normandy. In short, these men, like their English predecessors and their successors in the reign of Henry I began humbly. If they ended greater, it was because the times were opportune.[120]

A study of the role of the sheriffs and of lord-seeking in the redistribution of land in the south-east midlands between 1066 and 1086 warns us against assuming too readily that the legal forms encountered in Domesday Book were what really directed the process. The sheriffs built their holdings and aided their friends in acquiring their estates using mechanisms and powers of their office that had been exercised by their Anglo-Saxon predecessors. The new circumstances, however, enhanced these traditional powers, while the sorts of men whom William appointed to tend his lands and oversee his rights in the countryside shared with other Norman barons an overriding desire to establish themselves and their descendents in the counties. Like their predecessors, William's sheriffs were granted lands from the king's farm to be enjoyed during the term of their office; unlike them, they had an uncanny knack of turning revocable grants into hereditary possessions. They took advantage of their office most notably to snatch the lands of as many sokemen and lesser thegns as they could, with the result that obscure men such as Hugh de Beauchamp were able to become the founders of locally important baronages. There may also have been continuity, of sorts, in the lord-seeking activities of those Englishmen fortunate enough to be able to exercise that prerogative. If the new Norman lords were able to assemble honours from the scattered holdings of their antecessors' and their men, it was in part because lesser thegns and sokemen cooperated with them and perhaps even sought them as lords. Like the office of sheriff, this may have constituted continuity of practice, but the social context had changed so radically that instead of finding shepherds, the surviving English landholders often discovered that they had given themselves to wolves. Nor was this even true continuity in terms of the pattern of lordship and tenure. The Normans ignored the complexities of Anglo-Saxon lordship to their own advantage, devising tenurial dependency where none had existed TRE. And even if the lordship patterns of 1066 were preserved to a degree by the principle of antecessorial inheritance, we ought not to forget that lord-seeking before the Conquest had been a dynamic process. By transforming *commendatio* into an irrevocable tenurial relationship, the Norman barons froze lordship relations as they had been in 'on the day that King Edward was alive and dead'. In short, by using the procedures and forms of Anglo-Saxon law to pursue aggressively the lands and authority over men they claimed by right of their English antecessors, the Normans erected a new tenurial world upon the foundations of the old.

---

[119] Hugh may have come from Tilly-sur-Seules and Ralph from Cristot in the Calvados. L.C. Loyd, *The Origins of Some Anglo-Norman Families*, Harleian Soc. ciii, 1951, 20–1; Green, 'Sheriffs', 133, 138–9.
[120] Green, *English Sheriffs*, 15–16; *idem, The Government of England under Henry I*, Cambridge 1986, 207–8. Cf. Morris, *Medieval English Sheriff*, chs 3–4.

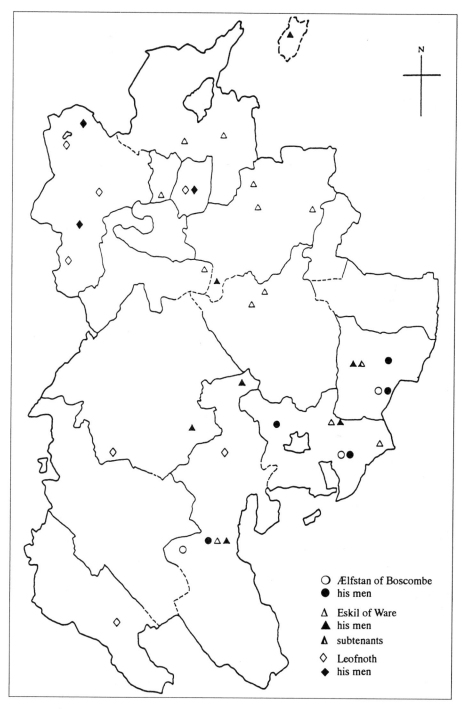

Map 1. The holdings of Ælfstan of Boscombe, Eskil of Ware, and Leofnoth in Bedfordshire in 1066 (from R.P. Abels, 'An Introduction to the Bedfordshire Domesday', The Bedfordshire Domesday, London: Alecto Historical Editions 1991)

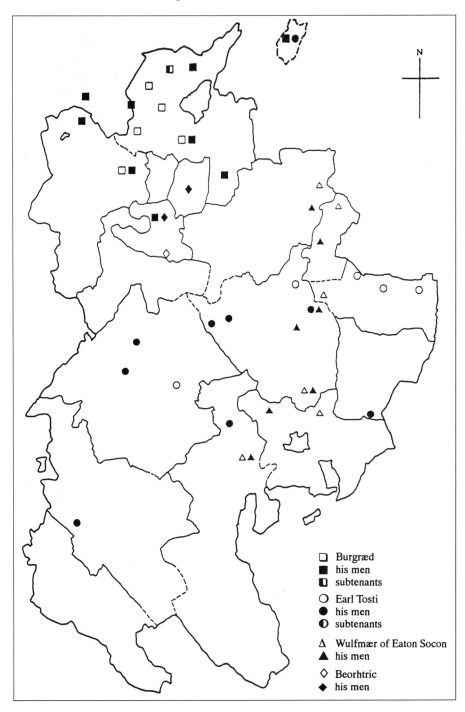

Map 2. The holdings of Burgræd, Earl Tosti, Wulfmær of Eaton Socon, and Beorhtric in Bedfordshire in 1066 (from R.P. Abels, 'An Introduction to the Bedfordshire Domesday', The Bedfordshire Domesday, *London: Alecto Historical Editions 1991)*

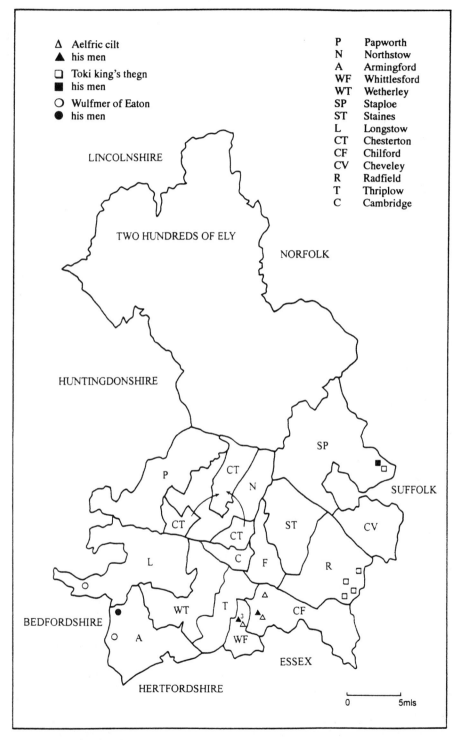

Map 3. *Cambridgeshire in 1066*

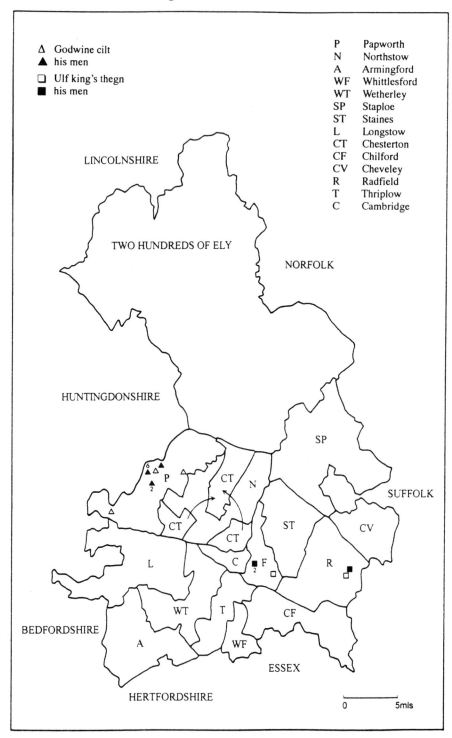

Δ   Godwine cilt
▲   his men
□   Ulf king's thegn
■   his men

P   Papworth
N   Northstow
A   Armingford
WF   Whittlesford
WT   Wetherley
SP   Staploe
ST   Staines
L   Longstow
CT   Chesterton
CF   Chilford
CV   Cheveley
R   Radfield
T   Thriplow
C   Cambridge

LINCOLNSHIRE

TWO HUNDREDS OF ELY

NORFOLK

HUNTINGDONSHIRE

SP

CT

N

SUFFOLK

P

CT

ST

CV

CT

L

C   F

R

WT   T

CF

BEDFORDSHIRE

A

WF

ESSEX

HERTFORDSHIRE

0   5mls

Map 4. Cambridgeshire in 1066

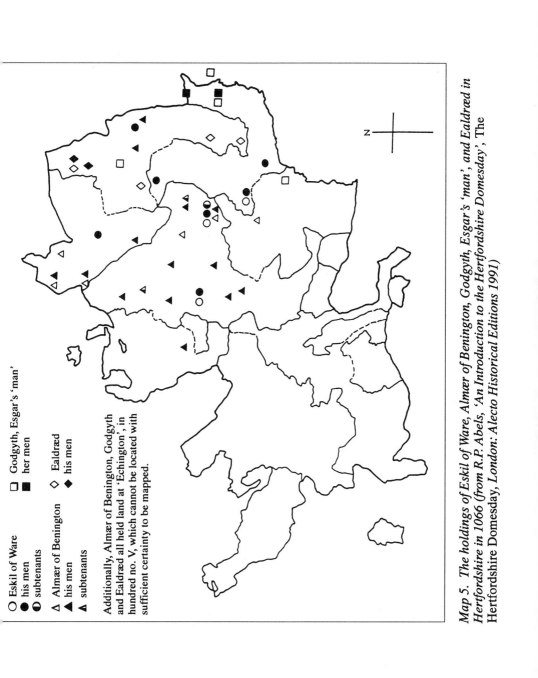

○ Eskil of Ware   □ Godgyth, Esgar's 'man'
● his men   ■ her men
◑ subtenants

△ Almær of Benington   ◇ Ealdred
▲ his men   ◆ his men
▲ subtenants

Additionally, Almær of Benington, Godgyth and Ealdred all held land at 'Echington', in hundred no. V, which cannot be located with sufficient certainty to be mapped.

N

Map 5. The holdings of Eskil of Ware, Almær of Benington, Godgyth, Esgar's 'man', and Ealdred in Hertfordshire in 1066 (from R.P. Abels, 'An Introduction to the Hertfordshire Domesday', The Hertfordshire Domesday, London: Alecto Historical Editions 1991)

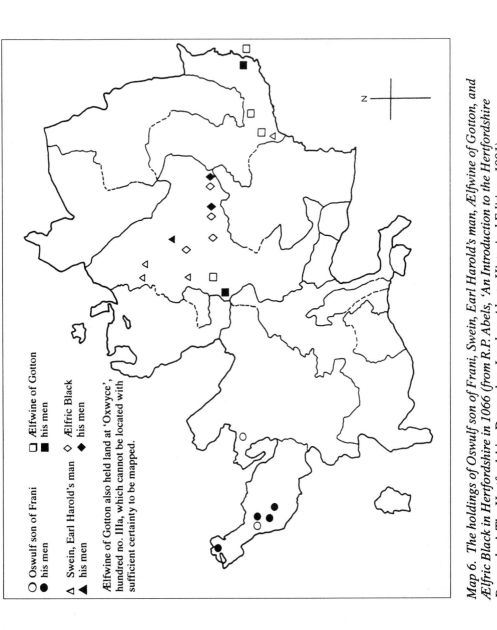

○ Oswulf son of Frani   □ Ælfwine of Gotton
● his men   ■ his men

△ Swein, Earl Harold's man ◇ Ælfric Black
▲ his men   ◆ his men

Ælfwine of Gotton also held land at 'Oxwyce', hundred no. IIIa, which cannot be located with sufficient certainty to be mapped.

Map 6. The holdings of Oswulf son of Frani, Swein, Earl Harold's man, Ælfwine of Gotton, and Ælfric Black in Hertfordshire in 1066 (from R.P. Abels, 'An Introduction to the Hertfordshire Domesday', The Hertfordshire Domesday, London: Alecto Historical Editions 1991)

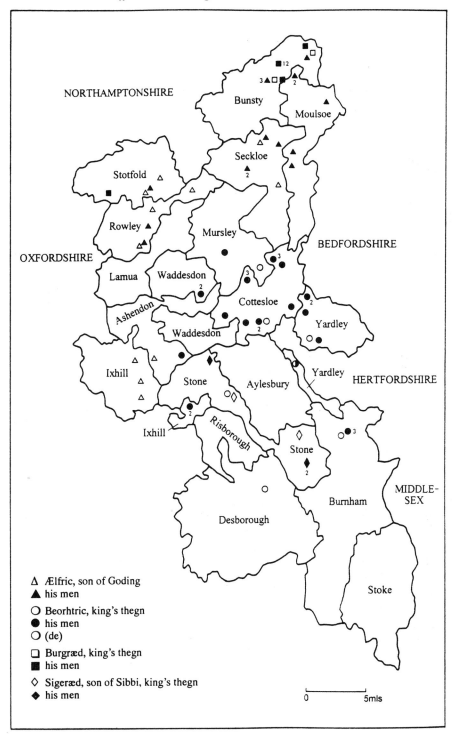

Map 7. Buckinghamshire in 1066

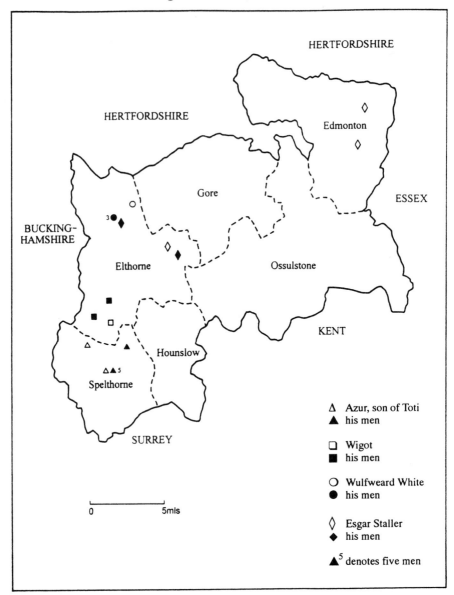

HERTFORDSHIRE

HERTFORDSHIRE

ESSEX

Edmonton

Gore

BUCKING-
HAMSHIRE

Elthorne

Ossulstone

KENT

Hounslow

Spelthorne

SURREY

0   5mls

△   Azur, son of Toti
▲   his men

▢   Wigot
◼   his men

○   Wulfweard White
●   his men

◇   Esgar Staller
◆   his men

▲⁵ denotes five men

Map 8. Middlesex in 1066

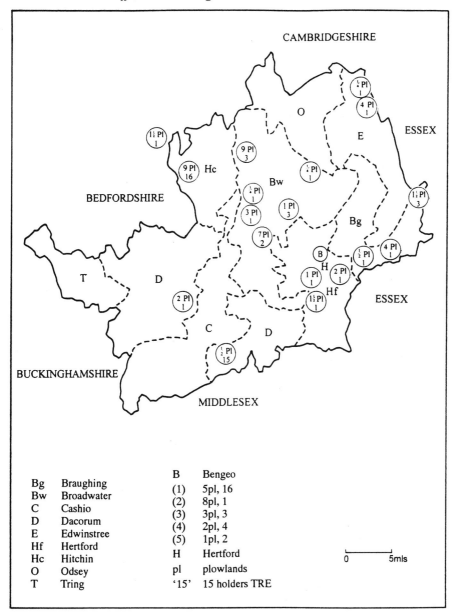

Map 9. The holdings of Ilbert of Hertford in Hertfordshire in 1066 (from breve *of his successor Geoffrey de Bec,* Domesday Book *i, 140–140v)*

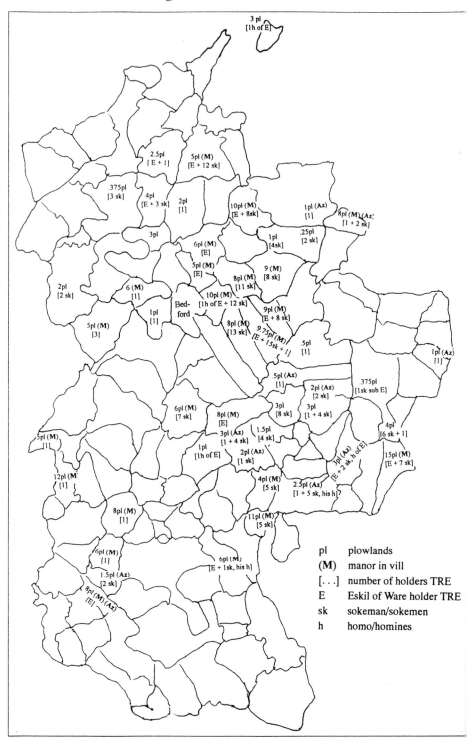

Map 10. The holdings of Hugh de Beauchamp and Azelina Taillebois (Az) in Bedfordshire TRW (representing holdings of Ralph Taillebois)

SUGER AND THE ANGLO-NORMAN WORLD*

Lindy Grant

When, in 1149, Abbot Suger of St Denis wrote to Geoffrey of Anjou, asking him to protect the properties of the abbey of St Denis in Normandy, he claimed that he had always had such protection from Henry I, and moreover, that while Henry had been duke of Normandy, there had been no single treaty or truce, over twenty years of war and diplomacy between Normans and Capetians, in which he, Suger, had not been personally involved.[1] Suger's claims incorporate two of the themes which I want to address in this paper: firstly the extent to which property, privilege and propinquity would force any active abbot of St Denis to take more than a passing interest in the Anglo-Norman world; and secondly, the rather remarkable extent to which Suger involved himself as a Capetian diplomat. The third strand of my investigation will be more diffuse. I will look at Suger's debt to the Anglo-Norman world in matters intellectual and cultural, and at the occasional evidence for indebtedness in the opposite direction.

Carolingian charters show the abbey of St Denis holding immense properties in what would become Normandy.[2] They held a huge swathe in the Tellau, around and to the south of Dieppe and across the Pays de Bray, plus substantial amounts in the Cotentin, though by 1100 these had been whittled down to little more than a couple of churches and associated rights and revenues at Berneval on the north Norman coast. They had properties in the Perche, which had been rationalised in the eleventh century into a priory at St Gauburge. They had many properties too in the Vexin, including some on the edge of the Forest of Lyons, on the Norman side of the river Epte. The abbey also acquired property in England, notably the venerable priory of Deerhurst.

    The abbey had personal connections with the circle of Edward the Confessor and William the Conqueror through the St Denis monk Baldwin, prior of the abbey's Lotharingian cell of Lebraha. Baldwin was sent to England, apparently to look to the abbey's English interests. He was a distinguished doctor, and soon caught the eye of the slightly hypochondriacal Edward the Confessor, who

* I would like to thank Professor David Bates, Dr Marjorie Chibnall, Dr Elizabeth van Houts, Dr John Hudson, Professor Thomas Keefe, Dr Kathy Thompson and Dr Jennifer Ward, for discussing various aspects of this paper with me.

[1] A. Lecoy de la Marche, *Oeuvres Complètes de Suger, recueilliés, annotées et publiées d'après les manuscrits*, Paris 1865, 264.

[2] A.J. Stoclet, 'Le Temporal de Saint-Denis du VIIe au Xe siècle', *Un Village au temps de Charlemagne, Moines et paysans de l'abbaye de Saint-Denis du VIIe siècle à l'An Mil*, ed. J. Cuisenier and R. Guadagnin, Reunion des Musées Nationaux, Paris 1988, 94–105, esp. maps 99–101.

appointed him his personal physician, and then abbot of Bury St Edmunds, though he continued to oversee St Denis's English properties and interests. Baldwin remained in place at Bury after the Conquest; he impressed William quite as much as he had impressed Edward, and he played an important role in the Domesday inquests. The priory of Deerhurst in Gloucestershire and Tainton in Oxfordshire were given almost as personal gifts to Baldwin by Edward. Baldwin continued to administer them after he became abbot of Bury, as part of St Denis's property.[3] He kept in close touch with his mother abbey, and was responsible for St Denis's enthusiastic espousal of the English cult of St Edmund, which issued in an altar, and a series of narrative capitals, in the crypt of the French abbey.[4] It was perhaps at Baldwin's behest that William the Conqueror paid for a new bell tower at St Denis. Sadly, the tower was badly built and soon collapsed.[5]

So Suger's involvement in Anglo-Norman matters was not a new feature of his abbacy. In this, as in most other things, he followed in the footsteps of his predecessors. In this, as in most other things, he did so with a new vigour and determination.

Suger tended to leave the administration of the various priories of St Denis to their priors unless serious problems emerged. Consequently, he had almost no involvement in the affairs of Ste Gauburge.[6] He did take a direct interest in properties which pertained directly to St Denis itself, like Berneval and the Vexin churches. In this section on Suger and the Anglo-Norman properties, I shall concentrate on Berneval, because we know quite a lot about his activities there, and then add some observations about his handling of the Vexin and, briefly, the English properties.

Berneval provided Suger with his own first responsible post, his first role as an obedientiary within the abbey hierarchy. He held the position of *prepositus* there between 1108 and 1109.[7] It was a position of great responsibility. The *prepositus* had total control of the abbey's estates at a local level. He was in charge of extracting all proper returns from the estates, whether in money or kind, for their storage, and their transport to the mother house or other disposal. He judged cases in the local court, and he was often responsible for choosing the mayor of the estate.[8] It is possible that Abbot Adam of St Denis sent Suger to Berneval in the hope that he would be able to reconstitute some of the abbey's lost Carolingian property in the area, for Suger's aptitude for dealing with documents claiming legal tenure was noted early. It turned out to be a baptism of fire, for relationships

---

3 *Monasticon* vi, pt. ii, 1077–78, for Edward's act re. Tainton. For Baldwin, see D.C. Douglas, *Feudal Documents from the Abbey of Bury St Edmunds*, Oxford 1932 (Records of the Social and Economic History of England, vol. viii), esp. lxi.

4 P. Blum, 'The Saint-Benedict Cycle on the Capitals of the Crypt at Saint-Denis', *Gesta* xxi, 1981, 73–87, and 'A St Edmund Cycle in the Crypt at St Denis', paper forthcoming in the *Transactions of the British Archaeological Association Conference* held at Bury St Edmunds in 1994.

5 J.F. Benton, *Self and Society in Medieval France. The Memoirs of Abbot Guibert of Nogent*, Medieval Academy Reprints, Toronto 1984, 228.

6 For the St Gauburge acta see Paris AN LL1158 (Liber Albus, St Denis Cartulary, part ii), 401–19. Suger's consent is invoked in only one act, 418–19, no. xlv, out of 4 issued during his abbacy. The other three are nos i, v, and xii, 401, 402, 406.

7 Suger, 'De Administratione', *Oeuvres Complètes*, 171, 184.

8 See e.g. AN LL1158, 24–5, act of 1169, re. Toury; and *ibid.* 220, act of 1134, re. Laonnois.

between Henry I and Louis the Fat deteriorated into open warfare during this period.

Before Suger's appointment, the abbey had found it impossible to maintain a *prepositus* in residence at Berneval. There had been an 'absence of monks'. As a result, the abbey was quite unable to administer the property, and collect and profit by the revenues that should pertain to it. In the long absence of the monks, others had become accustomed to benefiting from these revenues, and much of Suger's time as prepositor of Berneval was taken up with the pursuit of them through Henry I's Norman courts. In this he had the full and active support of Abbot Adam.

With 'many pleas', Suger managed to free Berneval from ducal exactions, known as *graffiones*.[9] But the key revenue in question was a fish render, a tax on fish landed. We know about this revenue, how it was regained, and how the recuperated revenues were spent, from an act of Abbot Adam of 1108/9, which chronicles everything, including the legal hoops leapt through, in unusual detail.[10] The render was considerable, and in the absence of an abbey prepositor, had been levied and pocketed by the prepositor of the village, the *'prepositus villae'*, named Robert, and now by his son Ralf, who claimed it by hereditary right. The *prepositus villae* was presumably the ducal prepositor. It took Suger and Adam some time to obtain the judgement they wanted. Firstly, their case came before a commission of ducal justiciars, Gilbert de L'Aigle and William the Chamberlain, at Rouen, but without a successful resolution. Abbot Adam and his trusty prepositor then spent a frustrating period travelling round to several places trying to obtain justice. Finally, at St Denis en Lyons, the case came before Walter fitz Ancher de Turre and Gilbert fitz Rainer. This time they won their case.[11]

Abbot Adam used the revenues from the fish render, together with revenues from some other estates, to establish an elaborate commemorative anniversary for the death of the supposed founder of the abbey, King Dagobert. In addition to its detailed account of the recuperation of the render, the act sketches out the complex liturgical choreography of the anniversary service, and institutes a lavish accompanying banquet of roasts, pastries, clarets and spiced wines for the monks.[12]

So Suger's period as *prepositus* at Berneval gave him first hand experience of justice available under Henry I in Normandy. He was clearly impressed: he stresses Henry's reputation as a fount of justice when he praises his kingship in *The Life of Louis the Fat*.[13] The reality of judicial processes in both Normandy and Capetian France in the early twelfth century is clouded in obscurity, and this is one happy instance where we see how it was done in Normandy. It seems unlikely that so clear and enforceable a judgment could have been won from the court of the Capetian king at this stage.

---

9 Suger, 'De Administratione', *Oeuvres Complètes*, 184 'multisque placitis'.
10 R. Barroux, 'Anniversaire de la mort de Dagobert à Saint-Denis au XIIe siècle', *Bulletin philologique et historique du Comité des travaux historiques et scientifiques*, 1942–43, 131–51. For the act itself, 148–51. See also Suger's comments in 'De Administratione', *Oeuvres Complètes*, 185, that he 'helped to arrange (*executere*) the fish render'.
11 Barroux, 'Anniversaire', act of Abbot Adam, 150. I would like to thank K. Thompson for information as to when the Norman justiciars were sitting, which confirms Barroux's dating of this act to 1108/9, see Barroux, 'Anniversaire', 146.
12 Barroux, 'Anniversaire', Act of Adam, 149–50.
13 Suger, *Vie de Louis VI le Gros*, ed. and trans. H. Waquet, 2nd edn, Paris 1964, 98–103.

All the cases in Capetian lands in which Suger was able to get a favourable judgement from the royal court were cases where the Capetian king also had a substantial interest in the property in question, for instance at Monnerville,[14] and Laversine.[15] This was in effect the case at Berneval, which was held by the abbey in feof from the duke, though under the protection, the *tutela*, of the FitzOsberns, at least in the late eleventh century.[16] This is presumably what allowed the abbey to pursue its case in the ducal court. Indeed, the prepositors of the *villa*, the villains of the piece from the abbey's point of view, were probably ducal prepositors.

The difference was that, in Normandy, the defendant turned up. His absence was often the reason for failure of the judicial process in Francia. Moreover, the favourable judgment appears to have been enforceable. There is a striking contrast with an absolutely contemporary experience of the French abbey of Morigny. Their property was burnt; but the perpetrator lived on the lands of Guy de Rochefort, who was in the Holy Land, and 'aut vix aut nunquam ad justiciam poterat adduci'.[17] No appeal to royal justice was possible.

Suger continued to take an interest in Berneval after he became abbot. There were two parish churches (*parrochiales ecclesias*) on the estates at Berneval. Their curacy was held, and claimed as a hereditary right, by Roger the priest and his brother Geoffrey. Suger disputed their claims successfully in the early days of his abbacy, taking the two churches back into 'the lordship of our church', but we do not know how he did so.[18] Since this was essentially an ecclesiastical matter, presumably he pursued his case this time not through the ducal court, but at the court of the diocesan bishop, the archbishop of Rouen. Suger dedicated the restored revenues from the two churches, and any others that might be built in the future, to the treasury of St Denis for the care of old and the acquisition of new linens for the abbey church.[19]

When Suger wrote the *De Administratione* in the late 1140s, he noted rather smugly that he had increased the revenues from Berneval, including census tax, from nothing to almost fifteen *livres*.[20] But Suger wrote the *De Administratione* largely to counter internal criticism of his abbacy. There were complaints, among other things, that he was tyrannical,[21] and that he was wasting abbey revenues on expensive building campaigns and a planned new crusade.[22] It is clear that there were serious problems in the abbey and its properties during the later part of his

[14] The lord of Mereville claimed he held his hereditary right to levy various taxes, to which Suger objected, from the king. 'De Administratione', *Oeuvres Complètes*, 168–9; act of Louis VII of 1144, ind. *Oeuvres Complètes*, 372.

[15] J. Dufour, *Recueil des Acts de Louis VI, roi de France (1108–1137)*, 3 vols, Paris 1992–93, ii, 348–51, no. 409.

[16] AN LL1158, 590, no. ii. In the 1172 inquest, the abbey owed the service of one knight for the estate, see C.H. Haskins, *Norman Institutions*, reprint, New York 1960, 9.

[17] *La Chronique de Morigny*, ed. L. Mirot, Paris 1912, 40–41.

[18] 'De Administratione', *Oeuvres Complètes*, 185.

[19] 'De Administratione', *Oeuvres Complètes*, 185.

[20] 'De Administratione', *Oeuvres Complètes*, 185, see also act of 1137 for the treasury, *Oeuvres Complètes*, 342.

[21] A. Wilmart, ed., 'Le dialogue apologetique du moine Guillaume, biographe de Suger', *Revue Mabillon* xxxii, 1942, 86.

[22] The biography of Suger by the monk William aims to deflect these complaints, William of St Denis, 'Sugerii Vita', *Oeuvres Complètes*, esp. 392, 400.

reign: many of these latent problems came to light under his successor, Odo of Deuil. In some cases, they were problems that Suger, through force of personality, and the manipulation of friends, had kept under control; in others, they were problems that had been festering for some time, which Suger had not, it seems, cared to confront. Berneval was one such.

An act of 1154 in the cartulary shows Matilda, widow of Hugh of Berneval, coming to Abbot Odo at St Denis to make reparation for the exactions and violations which her late husband had visited upon the abbey's settlers, the *hospites*, of Berneval.[23] It may be that the widow was rather easier to bring to heel than her violent husband; it may be that Berneval had been as difficult for the abbey of St Denis to administer in the years since Henry I's death as it had been in the years before his acquisition of the duchy, but that by 1154, north east Normandy was finally stable under Henry II. But Berneval fits a pattern perceptible in the abbey's properties across France: it adds to the impression that, for all that he has the reputation as a great administrator – a reputation largely self-generated – Suger lost his grip on the abbey in his last years, and his heritage to his successor was an institution in some disarray.[24]

By the early twelfth century, the abbey's English possessions included the priory of Deerhurst, and the manor of Tainton in Oxfordshire, both given to Baldwin of Bury St Edmunds. It also claimed property in London, at Rotherfield in Sussex, and at or near Hastings and Pevensey. The claims to these properties are expressed in a set of charters which were copied into the abbey's *Livre des Privilèges* of c.1200. These latter claims seem to have been pursued, with the aid of some elaborate forged Saxon charters, by Baldwin in the later eleventh century. We do not know how effective these efforts had been, or how real was the abbey's control of its English possessions under Suger.[25]

Around 1140, Suger dispatched his eventual successor, Odo of Deuil, to England to take special care of the English properties in the difficult circumstances of the anarchy. Odo was less than a roaring success when he finally succeeded Suger as abbot of St Denis. But Suger thought highly of him, and often sent him on difficult assignments. In 1135, Suger established him as prior of La Chapelle Aude in Berry, which was suffering badly from attacks on its properties by rival monasteries. In the second half of the 1140s, Suger sent Odo to institute reform at two

---

23 AN LL1158, 591, no. iiii.
24 See L. Grant, *Abbot Suger of St Denis*, forthcoming. See also, for problems at the priories of La Chapelle Aude, J. Doublet, *Histoire de l'Abbaye de S.Denys en France*, Paris 1625, 496–7; Chaumont en Vexin, Doublet, *Histoire*, 502–3; Salonne, Doublet, *Histoire*, 498: disputed claims at Tremblay, AN LL1157 (Liber Albus, St Denis Cartulary, i), 464, 466–7; Solesmes, Doublet, *Histoire*, 499; AN LL1158, 224–5, 227–8; and with Hugh de Roucy in the Laonnois, AN LL1158, 173, 175–6: disputes with the canons of St Paul who served the parish of St Denis for the abbey, Doublet, *Histoire*, 506.
25 See H. Atsma and J. Vezin, 'Le dossier suspect des possessions de Saint-Denis en Angleterre révisité (VIIIe–IXe siècles)', in *Fälschungen im Mittelalter*, MGH Schriften, band 33, teil iv, Hannover 1988, 211–36. For Rotherfield, see J. Ward, 'The Lowy of Tonbridge and the Lands of the Clare Family in Kent, 1066–1217', *Archaeologia Cantiana* xcvi, 1980, 125. Rotherfield was given to Odo of Bayeux after the Conquest, and was then aquired by the Clare family. Renders pertaining to the church of Rotherfield were made on the feast day of St Denis, which must mean that the property had belonged to the abbey at some stage. I would like to thank Dr Ward for her help with this question.

venerable monasteries, St Vaast at Arras and Ferrières. It was in between his priorate of Chapelle Aude, and his period as monastic reformer, i.e. around 1140, that Odo was sent to England. Exactly what Odo did in England is unclear. According to Suger's librarian and biographer, the monk William, Odo was deeply loved by the English, who were very sad to see him sail back to St Denis.[26] When William wrote that, he was doing his best to ingratiate himself with Odo, so it may not be true. It is certainly not helpful. When we look later at Suger's diplomatic activity in the 1140s, we should remember that he had always to keep the abbey's English possessions in mind.

The Vexin, where the abbey had many properties, and of which it tried briefly to claim suzerainty, fell entirely within the confines of the diocese of Rouen. The Vexin was run and accounted as a single prepositorship. Suger claims that he increased the revenues from it, which he dedicated to food for the monks, a weekly commemoration of the Virgin, and an anniversary for Louis the Fat, by 114 *livres* and 12 *solidi*.[27] The properties included Morgny, Lilly and Fleury la Forêt in the Forest of Lyons, and Châteauneuf sur Epte, within the Norman Vexin;[28] Cergy, Ableiges, Bercagny and Cormeilles en Vexin in the French Vexin.[29] In the mid 1140s Suger persuaded Louis VII to allow the abbey to take over the collegiate church of Chaumont en Vexin and reform it as a priory.[30]

These properties propelled Suger into close relationships with some of the Franco-Norman border aristocracy, such as Payn of Gisors.[31] Early in his abbacy he had to deal firmly with the depredations of the abbey's advocates in the Vexin,[32] but he often talks of the men of the Vexin in almost the same breath as the men of St Denis.[33]

Above all Suger found himself dealing with the archbishop of Rouen, to whom he had to look for episcopal confirmations of tenure. He was particularly close to Hugh of Amiens, who became archbishop in 1130, all the more so perhaps since Hugh was, as his name implies, a Frenchman rather than a Norman. Like Suger, Hugh was a Benedictine monk, and had been abbot of a house intended, like St Denis, for royal burial. Hugh's cousin Matthew was well known to Suger. He had been prior of St Martin des Champs in Paris, and was then made cardinal bishop of

---

[26] For Odo's career and William's comments on his stay in England, see Wilmart, 'Dialogue apologetique', 102.

[27] 'De Administratione', *Oeuvres Complètes*, 162; Ordinance of 1124, *Oeuvres Complètes*, 328; Ordinance of 1140/1, *Oeuvres Complètes*, 350.

[28] 'De Administratione', *Oeuvres Complètes*, 185.

[29] 'De Administratione', *Oeuvres Complètes*, 162, 164, 184 and Dufour, *Actes*, i, 334–8, no. 163: 'De Administratione', *Oeuvres Complètes*, 184, and act of 1137, *Oeuvres Complètes*, 346: 'De Administratione', *Oeuvres Complètes*, 162, and AN LL1157, 627.

[30] 'De Administratione', *Oeuvres Complètes*, 183–4: acts of Louis VII, AN LL1158, 381, no. ii; also no. i, dated 1145, 9th regnal year, ed. Doublet, *Histoire*, 869, and indic. A. Luchaire, *Etudes sur les actes de Louis VII*, Paris 1885, 152–3, no. 167, who dates it 1146.

[31] Suger bought tithes at Franconville from Payn, probably in 1123, when Payn retired as a monk to St Martin at Pontoise, see 'De Administratione', *Oeuvres Complètes*, 163; Ordinance of 1140/1, *Oeuvres Complètes*, 356. For Payn's career, see J. Green, 'Lords of the Norman Vexin', in *War and Government in the Middle Ages: Essays in Honour of J.O. Prestwich*, ed. J. Gillingham and J.C. Holt, Woodbridge 1984, 58–9.

[32] 'De Administratione', *Oeuvres Complètes*, 162; Ordinance of 1140/1, *Oeuvres Complètes*, 350.

[33] E.g. Suger, *Vie de Louis*, 118, 196, 230.

Albano, and as such was sent as papal legate to France in 1128. Both Hugh and Matthew were Cluniacs. Although Suger sometimes saw the Cluniacs as rivals, he got on well and worked closely with both men in matters both ecclesiastical and more purely political. Hugh played a principal role in the consecration of both the new west and east ends of Suger's abbey church.[34]

In 1124, Suger persuaded Louis the Fat to sign a charter which effectively claimed that the abbey of St Denis had the suzerainty of the French Vexin, which the king held from the saint and the abbey.[35] Louis was faced by invasion by the German Emperor, and much in need of the prayers of St Denis at the time. Louis ignored these dyonisian claims completely as soon as the crisis was past, giving the Vexin to William Clito in 1127, without the slightest reference to the supposed rights of the saint or abbey of St Denis.[36] But Suger continued to press the claim. He mentions it in his *Life of Louis the Fat* and the *De Administratione*, and had it confirmed by a papal bull in 1131.[37]

After this, the French kings seem to have been reluctant to give the abbey more property in the Vexin. Grants of property in the Vexin to the abbey coincide with stages at which the Capetians were threatened by the Norman duke, and much indebted to Suger's abilities as a diplomat, in 1143–44, and then again in 1149–51, as we shall see. At the consecration of the new shrine-choir, in 1144, Louis VII gave the abbey what the king had at Cormeilles-en-Vexin. Permission to reform Chaumont-en-Vexin was given shortly thereafter, but only after Suger had worked hard to persuade the king.[38]

It is interesting that dyonisian encroachment on the Vexin continued after Suger's death. Shortly after he died, the abbey was given the new *castrum* at St Clair sur Epte.[39] This occurs so soon after Suger's death, and seems so much in line with his acquisition of Cormeilles and Chaumont in the mid-1140s, as to raise suspicions that Suger had been angling for it before he died. It looks as though Suger took advantage of the king's relative weakness in the 1140s as he did in the early 1120s, to bolster the abbey's properties in the Vexin, which was in effect the Capetian's front line against Normandy.

Any abbot of St Denis keen to protect its property base was thus drawn inexorably into the Anglo-Norman world. But Suger's political career reinforced and capitalised on this. Suger's political career began early. He was politically active from at least 1106. He was often, as it were, on loan to the Capetian court. His role was twofold: on the one hand, that monastic speciality, recording the deeds of his patron, Louis the Fat; and on the other, acting as roving ambassador and negotiator. These skills were initially honed and were always primarily employed in the difficult area of relationships between the Capetians and the Papacy. Doubtless

---

[34] For Hugh of Amiens, see *PL* vol. 192, cols 1111–1130 and G. Constable, *The Letters of Peter the Venerable*, 2 vols, Harvard 1967, ii, 99–100; for Matthew of Albano, see Constable, *Peter the Venerable* ii, 96–7.

[35] Dufour, *Actes* i, 458–66, no. 220, esp. 465.

[36] R. Barroux, 'L'abbé Suger et la vassalité du Vexin en 1124', *Le Moyen Age* lxiv, 1958, 8–9, n. 24: Orderic vi, 370.

[37] Privilege in *PL* vol. 179, cols 93–5; 'De Administratione', *Oeuvres Complètes*, 161–2; Suger, *Vie de Louis*, 220.

[38] 'De Administratione', *Oeuvres Complètes*, 162, 183–4.

[39] For St Clair-s.-Epte, see AN LL1158, 389.

because he proved so adept a diplomat, he was also a key negotiator in the often strained relations between the Capetians and the Anglo-Normans.[40]

Cartellieri, in his biography of Suger, flatly refused to believe Suger's own claims on this count. He argued that Suger was merely trying to ingratiate himself with Geoffrey of Anjou, and saw Suger's role as almost exclusively that of expert in matters papal. The principal ground for his argument is that Suger is not once mentioned by Orderic Vitalis.[41]

But this is to misunderstand not only much of Suger's career, but also the conduct of negotiators. The reason someone like Suger was so effective was because he was so discreet. Peace was celebrated in great ceremonies which brought together the kings and their respective magnates and great bishops. These are what Orderic, like every other chronicler, records. The forging of the peace was a different matter. It was painfully negotiated, as Robert of Torigni puts it, by 'wise and religious men running backwards and forwards', or as Orderic says, by 'envoys of peace (who) went to and fro and secured the acceptance by all parties of a firm peace'.[42] Such men were not, in the nature of things, named.

We should, I think, take Suger at his word in this case, and accept that he was one of them. Suger's claim that there was no treaty or truce over twenty years between Henry I and Louis the Fat with which he not involved fits well enough with the fact that the long sequence of wars and truces between the two kings did indeed extend over a period of some twenty years, from 1109 to 1128. Moreover, although Louis VII did not like Suger much, he was almost totally dependent on him in his dealings with Norman problems. He would surely have chosen someone else, but for the fact that Suger's expertise, and network of connections in this area, were so developed.

We know far more about Suger's diplomatic dealings under Louis VII than under Louis the Fat, largely because we benefit from two letter collections, Suger's own, covering the years 1144 to his death in January 1151, and St Bernard's.[43] That Bernard's letters should throw so much light on Suger's dealings with Normandy may seem strange. The reason is that much of the diplomacy involved St Bernard's friend and patron, Theobald of Blois.

Theobald, count of Blois and Chartres, Troyes, Meaux and Champagne, was the only one of the great princes of northern France who regularly attended the Capetian court. But if he saw himself as pre-eminent among the Capetian aristocracy, he also felt that he should, according to the *Morigny Chronicle*, 'make war against the king, as if by hereditary right'.[44] There was always an Anglo-Norman aspect to Theobald's rebellions, because his uncle was Henry I. After Henry's death, Theobald made a brief bid for his Anglo-Norman inheritance, but that fell to his younger brother Stephen.[45] Theobald did not support Stephen in his struggles to hold England and Normandy against the Empress Matilda as consistently as might

---

[40] See Grant, forthcoming, where I argue the case for Suger's early contact with the Capetian court.
[41] O. Cartellieri, *Abt Suger von Saint-Denis*, Historische Studien Bd. ii, Berlin, 1898, 31.
[42] Robert de Torigni, *Chronique*, ed. L. Delisle, Paris 1872, i, 255: Orderic vi, 180–1. See also the paper in this volume by Christopher Holdsworth.
[43] For Suger's letter collection, see *Recueil des Historiens des Gaules et de la France*, ed. M. Bouquet *et al.*, 24 vols, Paris 1869–1904, xv, 483–532, and *Oeuvres Complètes*, 239–84, for the letters from Suger.
[44] *Chron. Mor.*, 22, 'velud hereditario bellorum jure, regem cepit infestare'.
[45] Haskins, *Norman Institutions*, 124.

have been expected. He always put his own interests first. Nevertheless, their relationship meant that all wars, whether between the Capetians and the duke of Normandy, or between the Capetians and the counts of Champagne, and thus all diplomacy, was apt to become three-sided. Theobald saw Suger as his 'advocate' with the king.[46]

Trouble broke out for the first time in spring 1109 when Suger was based in Normandy as *prepositus* at Berneval. Since he had already, in that capacity, met Henry I and some of the most important Norman magnates, together, one must assume, with prominent members of the clergy of the diocese of Rouen, he was a natural choice as negotiator. Louis the Fat and Henry I came to blows over Henry's refusal to do homage to Louis, and over that perennial thorn in Capetian flesh, the castle of Gisors. Suger's account of the meeting between the two kings at Planches de Neaufles to try to settle matters, and the subsequent skirmishing, is very full and reveals detailed local knowledge. Everything suggests that it is an eye witness account.[47]

Suger uses the encounter to present his view, presumably also Louis the Fat's view, of the Normandy question. Normandy was a part of Gaul. It had been given by the kings of France as a fief to the Norman dukes, and they, as a result, should do homage for it.[48] The problem, of course, was that the duke of Normandy was now also king of England, and it was, as Suger himself said, 'neither right nor natural that the French should be subjected to the English, or the English to the French'.[49]

In 1116, war between Henry and Louis broke out again. Suger's well-informed account of it concentrates on the Vexin, where, indeed, much of the fighting took place. He deals as discreetly as possible with the disastrous French defeat at Brémule in 1119, and is slightly coy about the French capture of Gasny-en-Vexin in the previous year, assuring us that the French soldiery disguised themselves as travellers, '*viatores*',[50] while Orderic claims that they made their entry disguised as monks, with their swords hidden under their habits in the best Hollywood tradition.[51]

A mutually acceptable treaty with Henry was finally brokered in 1120.[52] It was perhaps in recognition of Suger's role in obtaining it that Louis at last returned to St Denis the crown, which he had retained since his coronation in 1108. He gave it to the saint as '*dux et protector*' of the *regnum*, which suggests a context of war and peace, and handed over to the safekeeping of St Denis property and privileges in the Vexin where so much of the war had been fought.[53] Suger was not yet abbot of St Denis, but, as Dufour has argued, he must have drafted the act recording the gift.[54] Indeed, in the *Life of Louis the Fat*, he ruthlessly appends the return of the crown and the gifts in the Vexin to the list of gifts and concessions which Louis did

46 William, 'Sugerii Vita', *Oeuvres Complètes*, 385.
47 Suger, *Vie de Louis*, 102–12.
48 Suger, *Vie de Louis*, 106–7.
49 Suger, *Vie de Louis*, 10–11.
50 Suger, *Vie de Louis*, 186–7.
51 Orderic vi, 183–4.
52 Orderic, 290–1. A. Luchaire, *Louis VI le Gros, annales de sa vie et de son règne*, Paris 1890, 139.
53 Dufour, *Actes* i, 334–8, no. 163.
54 Dufour, *Actes* i, 337. See also Barroux, 'Vassalité du Vexin', 19–21.

make when Suger was abbot after the imperial invasion of 1124.[55] All of which conspires to suggest, *pace* Cartellieri, that Suger was telling Geoffrey of Anjou the truth.

When we come to Suger's involvement in Anglo-Norman affairs under Louis VII, we are, as I have indicated, much better informed. In 1140, Louis VII married his sister Constance to Eustace, son of Stephen of Blois. It must have looked like an astute move. Eventually, Louis could hope to see his own nephew installed as duke of Normandy and king of England. Louis invested Eustace as duke of Normandy in February 1141, after Stephen's capture at the battle of Lincoln.[56]

But in spring 1141, Geoffrey of Anjou invaded the duchy of Normandy. Stephen's cause did so badly that Hugh of Amiens offered both the dukedom and the kingdom to Stephen's brother Theobald. Theobald refused. He was prepared to let Geoffrey of Anjou take Normandy, provided Stephen were released, and Theobald himself given the rich city of Tours.[57]

It is probably in the context of Geoffrey of Anjou's apparently inexorable absorption of north west France, from the Loire to the English Channel, that we should set the visit of three bishops of the Breton/Angevin/Norman border dioceses, the bishops of St Malo, Rennes and Vannes, together with their metropolitan, the archbishop of Tours, and Archbishop Hugh of Rouen, to St Denis in October 1140 or 1141. They were there ostensibly to view the opening of a reliquary altar given to the abbey by Charles the Bald. The relics turned out to be quite as genuine as Suger had hoped; they came with neat identificatory inscriptions, like museum exhibits. The Bretons were not the only bishops present, but the others – Soissons, Beauvais, Senlis and Meaux – were near neighbours of St Denis; and while one Breton bishop might be accidental, three are suggestive, not to say suspicious. It was a long way to come to inspect the shrivelled arms of SS Vincent and Stephen.[58]

In 1143–44 Louis VII pursued a vicious war against Theobald of Champagne.[59] By the spring of 1144, Geoffrey of Anjou was in control of most of Normandy.[60] What was more, he was now allied with Thierry of Flanders, and had an arrangement with Theobald of Blois. Louis VII was now faced with a potentially formidable hostile alliance of Anjou, Blois, Normandy, Flanders and Champagne.[61]

There had for some time been urgent diplomatic action to end the war between Louis and Theobald. Louis's principal negotiators were Suger and Bishop Jocelyn of Soissons; Theobald's were St Bernard and the ex-Cistercian, Bishop Hugh of

[55] Suger, *Vie de Louis*, 226–8.

[56] Henry of Huntingdon in Bouquet, *Recueil* xiii, 40; William of Newburgh in Bouquet, *Recueil* xiii, 97, 99.

[57] Orderic vi, 548

[58] 'De Administratione', *Oeuvres Complètes*, 201, and E. Panofsky, ed., *Abbot Suger on the Abbey Church of St-Denis and its Art Treasures*, 2nd edn, Princeton 1979, 68–9; Ordinance of 1140/1, *Oeuvres Complètes*, 354 (ed. Panofsky, *Abbot Suger*, 130–31). The only other unexpected episcopal presence was that of the archbishop of Lyons. For the date of the opening of the reliquary, see Panofsky, *Abbot Suger*, 196.

[59] M. Pacaut, *Louis VII et son royaume*, Paris 1964, 43–5.

[60] Haskins, *Norman Institutions*, 129–30.

[61] Pacaut, *Louis VII*, 45–6.

Auxerre.[62] Now it was clear that the peace would have to be three-way, for Louis had also to reach an accommodation with Geoffrey of Anjou. Geoffrey wanted Louis's affirmation of his, or his son's, tenure of the dukedom of Normandy, which Louis had conferred on Eustace of Boulogne. Suger's friend Archbishop Hugh of Rouen played a key role in the necessary diplomacy.[63]

So too surely did Suger. The evidence of his involvement is contained in the cast list of the consecration of the new shrine-choir of St Denis on 11 June 1144.[64] Along with Louis and Eleanor, and the expected Ile de France bishops, there is an extremely heavy Anglo-Norman contingent: Archbishop Hugh of Rouen, of course, but also Rotrou of Evreux, Algare of Coutances, who had gone over to Geoffrey in 1143, and Theobald of Canterbury, who had generally been mildly pro-Angevin.[65] The fact that Theobald of Blois's bishops – Chartres, Reims, Chalons, Meaux and Auxerre – were also present in force adds to the impression that the choir consecration doubled as a surreptitious summit, at which the Norman side of the simultaneous equation was resolved.

It was not the final concord between Louis and Theobald. That took place, again at St Denis, in October of the same year. But we know that peace negotiations were pursued at the consecration of the new choir, because St Bernard wrote to Jocelyn of Soissons that he hoped to see him to prosecute them at a forthcoming appointed celebration, an '*indicta celebritate*', at St Denis. The 'appointed celebration' cannot have been the October concord, because by that time peace negotiations had been finalised.[66]

Louis remained wary of the Angevins in Normandy. Rumours of an intended marriage between one of Louis's daughters and the young duke Henry of Normandy reached St Bernard in 1146. The saint thought the proposed marriage consanguineous, and wrote to both the king and Suger to say so.[67] Bernard either knew, or assumed, that Suger was behind this initiative. It was at this stage that Suger got permission to convert the collegiate church of Chaumont-en-Vexin into a priory of St Denis. He frankly admitted its convenience for himself and his successors travelling to Normandy on business.[68]

Louis worried that Geoffrey of Anjou might take advantage of his absence on Crusade. He wrote to warn Suger, who was left behind as regent, to take special care that the Angevins should not take Gisors. In fact Suger as regent had no trouble from Geoffrey of Anjou: quite the contrary, when Suger faced insurrection led by Louis' bellicose younger brother Robert, Geoffrey wrote to the regent: 'If it

---

[62] *Sancti Bernardi Opera*, ed. J. Leclercq, C.H. Talbot, H.M. Rochais, 8 vols, Rome 1957–77, vols vii and viii, *Epistolae* viii, 88, no. ccxxii; 94, no. ccxxv; 95–6, no. ccxxvi.

[63] Haskins, *Norman Institutions*, 129–30.

[64] 'De Consecratione', *Oeuvres Complètes*, 236–7 (ed. Panofsky, *Abbot Suger*, 118–19).

[65] For Algare see Haskins, *Norman Institutions*, 130, n. 24. For Theobald, see A. Saltman, *Theobald Archbishop of Canterbury*, London 1956, 16–41.

[66] St Bernard, *Epistolae* viii, 94, no. ccxxv. See also, 95–6, no. ccxxvi. The 'Fragmenta ex tertia vita Sancti Bernardi Gaufrido monacho', Migne, *PL* vol. 185, col. 527 makes it clear that the final concord was arranged on the feast of St Denis, i.e. 9 October.

[67] St Bernard, *Epistolae* viii, 330–1, no. ccclxxi.

[68] 'De Administratione', *Oeuvres Complètes*, 183–4.

is necessary, call me to the service of the king, and certainly you will have me ready to do all things which you wish for the service of the king.'[69]

Suger got on rather well with Geoffrey. He was sympathetic to the Angevin cause, and the Angevins courted him. There was a substantial exchange of letters between Suger and Geoffrey and the Empress. Matilda gave flowers from her Imperial crown to the St Denis treasury,[70] and her cousin, King David of Scotland, sent Suger a precious walrus tusk for the attention of one of the abbot's ivory carvers.[71] Pro-Angevin English bishops, Robert of Hereford and Jocelyn of Salisbury, made contact with Suger in 1148.[72] In both cases their letters contain fulsome praise of Suger, followed by a request for some relics of St Denis for their own cathedrals. Jocelyn of Salisbury has been prevented from meeting Suger for important business at St Denis, but Jocelyn has sent his archdeacon, to whom, Jocelyn says, he has committed *viva voce* the other information that Suger has asked for.

In this pro-Angevin stance, Suger was at variance with his king. Louis himself was a supporter of Stephen. He had married off his sister to Stephen's son and heir; and Louis still hoped to see a nephew succeed to the English throne. But the Angevins fought to have Matilda's son Henry, the young duke of Normandy, accepted as the proper successor to Stephen. At the Council of Reims, it was clear that the Angevin cause was winning papal support, and Geoffrey's supporter, Arnulf of Lisieux, wrote in the summer of 1149 to the bishop of Lincoln asking him to consider whether the duke of Normandy should not, by the right of hereditary succession, become king of England.[73]

Stephen desperately needed Louis's support to obtain the succession of Eustace of Blois and Constance of France. Both he and his brother Henry, bishop of Winchester, approached Louis through Suger, hoping perhaps to take advantage of the friendship between Suger and their brother Theobald, and forgetting that Theobald had long since disassociated himself from Stephen's cause. Both thank Suger for his help in Stephen's affairs.[74] Suger had, of course, as we have seen, English possessions to protect.

In fact, Suger was intriguing on behalf of the Angevin cause. Arnulf, bishop of Lisieux, wrote to Suger to report that Arnulf was dealing, as he and Suger had discussed, with Norman business with the Empress and her son, Henry, and with Angevin matters with Count Geoffrey. Finally, Arnulf asked Suger to let him know secretly, as he had promised, 'the day on which the royal response to the complaints of the English shall have been delayed by your efforts'.[75] Suger was playing a very complicated game.

His motivation is unclear. Perhaps seeing the effect of the anarchy on the abbey's English possessions made him very wary of Stephen and Eustace. Perhaps he was impressed by the relative stability that Geoffrey brought to Normandy. Nor

---

[69] Bouquet, *Recueil* xv, 494.

[70] 'De Administratione', *Oeuvres Complètes*, 207 (ed. Panofsky, *Abbot Suger*, 76–77).

[71] William, 'Sugerii Vita', *Oeuvres Complètes*, 384.

[72] Bouquet, *Recueil* xv, 498–9.

[73] *The Letters of Arnulf of Lisieux*, ed. F. Barlow, Camden Society, 3rd series, LXI, London 1939, 6–7, no. 4, 'ut ducem nostrum, cui ius successionis hereditarie regni vestri gubernacula debet'.

[74] Bouquet, *Recueil* xv, 520.

[75] *The Letters of Arnulf of Lisieux*, 9, no. 6, 'diemque, in quem regia responsa postulantionibus Anglorum vestro studio dilata fuerunt'.

is it clear whether he had always been pro-Angevin, or, like his friend Hugh of Amiens, became so after Geoffrey's capture of Normandy in 1144.

The English succession was not the only point at issue between Louis and the Angevins. Once Geoffrey had control of Normandy, he turned his attention south of his Angevin lands, to northern Aquitaine. Between 1149 and 1151, he besieged the marcher baron Gerard de Berlay in his castle of Montreuil-Bellay, on the very border of Anjou and Poitou, controlling the important road from Saumur to Thouars and Parthenay. Louis, naturally, supported Gerard de Berlay. On, presumably, Louis' orders, Suger gave Gerard 4000 s. from the Poitevin issues in spring 1149.[76]

In 1149–50, tension between Louis and Geoffrey erupted in open warfare, and Geoffrey turned to Suger as mediator. Louis' younger brother Robert had acquired the county of Perche through marriage to its widowed countess. From there, he attacked southern Normandy, taking lands from Geoffrey's ally John Talvas in 1149. In the campaigning season of 1150, Geoffrey attacked and regained them.[77] Louis complained to the pope, via St Bernard, of the attack on himself and his brother. Eugenius did not see Robert, who had up to now been nothing but trouble to all, as a natural victim: he wrote to Suger to find out the truth of the matter.[78] Since Eugenius wrote to Suger for clarification, it is clear that Geoffrey attacked Robert before Suger's death. This is important, because Robert of Torigni's account in the *Appendix to Sigebert*, written many years later, places Geoffrey's attack on Robert, and the war which followed, in the spring and summer of 1151, i.e. after Suger's death. It becomes clear, when the evidence for Suger's activities is fitted into the picture, that Robert of Torigni conflated the campaigns of 1150 and 1151. In the meantime, Louis and Robert led a *chevauchée* into Normandy and fired the city of Sées, which belonged to the Talvas family.[79]

Suger was at the heart of the resulting diplomacy. He wrote to Geoffrey and Matilda, promising to mediate, and asking for protection for St Denis's Norman possessions in case of war; to Louis, saying that the king should not attack the man he had made duke of Normandy, without a general council;[80] and to Geoffrey, assuring him that the king would not attack, owing to pressure from Suger and Thierry of Flanders.[81] The principal Angevin negotiator was Bishop Arnulf of Lisieux.[82] Arnulf's single surviving letter to Suger shows the two men dealing with all three areas at issues between Geoffrey and Louis: the English succession question; things pertaining to the count and county of Anjou – Gerard de Berlay,

---

[76] Bouquet, *Recueil* xv, 499. The siege of Montreuil Bellay is a problem. All sources concur that it ended in 1151, but the Tours Chronicle says it lasted seven years, Bouquet, *Recueil* xii, 474; the St Aubin, Angers, chronicle, one year, Bouquet, *Recueil* xii, 481; Robert of Torigny, Appendix to Sigebert, *Chronique*, ed. Delisle i, 251, 253, gives three years.

[77] Robert of Torigni, Appendix to Sigebert, *Chronique*, ed. Delisle i, 254.

[78] Bouquet, *Recueil* xv, 461.

[79] Robert of Torigni, Appendix to Sigebert, *Chronique*, ed. Delisle i, 254.

[80] It is interesting that Suger refers to Geoffrey as duke of Normandy, though Henry had assumed the title of duke in charters by early 1150, see M. Chibnall, *The Empress Matilda: Queen Consort, Queen Mother and Lady of the English*, Oxford 1991, 148.

[81] For this group of letters see *Oeuvres Complètes*, 264–6, 266, 267.

[82] Geoffrey to Suger, Bouquet, *Recueil* xv, 521.

presumably; and things pertaining to Normandy and to the Empress and her son, Duke Henry – the Sées/Perche border problem, perhaps.[83]

Louis and Robert pursued their war against Geoffrey.[84] Louis convened a large army at Mantes, the obvious place to muster for a south Norman campaign, in August. Bishop Peter of Bourges wrote to Suger asking him to convey his apologies to Louis for his absence: he had just got back from Rome and was exhausted by the summer heat. This letter provides more evidence that Robert of Torigni conflated two years' campaigning into one.[85]

In January 1151, Suger died. The war continued. That August, Louis again mustered between Mantes and Meulan to attack Normandy. Geoffrey had now defeated Gerard de Berlay, and could turn his undivided attention to the threat to Normandy. Louis and Geoffrey came to terms. In September 1151, young Duke Henry did homage for Normandy to Louis in Paris, and Geoffrey of Anjou died a few days later.[86]

I shall now turn from the relatively factual realm of politics and diplomacy, to the thoroughly speculative realm of intellectual and cultural influences. I shall start with some observations about Suger's writings, and the context in which he wrote.

The only area in which Suger expanded the intellectual horizons of the abbey of St Denis is in the field of historical writing. The abbey scriptorium under Suger produced strikingly few theological and liturgical manuscripts. They concentrated instead on the compilation of a historical miscellany, B. Maz. 2013, to which, in the 1160s, was added Suger's own *Life of Louis the Fat*. The compilation is at the root of the great tradition of historical writing which developed at the abbey. William of Jumièges, in the version revised by Orderic Vitalis, plays a very large part in it. The other St Denis manuscripts which contain early copies of the *Life of Louis the Fat* also incorporate a great deal of Anglo-Norman material. It is unclear why Anglo-Norman material should have such a high profile at St Denis. Perhaps it was Suger's own choice.[87]

Norman monks, for their part, were interested in legends and history generated at St Denis. The earliest extant version of the legend of how Charlemagne retrieved relics of the true cross and the crown of thorns from Constantinople, and how Charles the Bald then presented them to St Denis, appears in a manuscript written at St Ouen at Rouen, probably in the 1120s.[88] A general history of the French kings,

---

[83] *Letters of Arnulf of Lisieux*, 9, no. 6.

[84] Robert of Torigni, Appendix to Sigebert, *Chronique*, ed. Delisle i, 254.

[85] Bouquet, *Recueil* xv, 705.

[86] Robert of Torigni, ed. Delisle i, 255

[87] For the abbey scriptorium, see H. Stahl, 'The Problem of Manuscript Painting at Saint-Denis during the Abbacy of Suger', in *Abbot Suger and Saint-Denis: a Symposium*, ed. P.L. Gerson, New York 1986, 163–81, and D. Nebbiai della Guarda, *La Bibliotheque de l'abbaye de Saint-Denis*, Paris 1985, 288, 318–19; for historical writing at St Denis see G. Spiegel, *The Chronicle Tradition of Saint-Denis: a Survey*, Brookline, Mass. 1978, 40–1. For B. Maz. MS 2013 and the other St Denis-related manuscripts containing early copies of the *Life of Louis the Fat*, and Norman material, see E.M.C. van Houts, *The Gesta Normannorum Ducum of William of Jumièges, Orderic Vitalis and Robert of Torigni*, 2 vols, Oxford 1992, i, civ–cvi.

[88] Paris, B. Maz. MS 1711, see E.A.R. Brown and M. Cothren, 'The Twelfth-Century Crusading Window of the Abbey of Saint-Denis', *Journal of the Warburg and Courtauld Institutes* xlix, 1986, 14, n. 63.

compiled at St Denis under Suger, the *Abbrevatio Gestarum Franciae Regum*, was used by Robert of Torigni at Bec around 1139–40.[89]

The clearest evidence that Suger himself knew the writings of his Anglo-Norman contemporaries is that he incorporates Geoffrey of Monmouth's *Prophesies of Merlin* into *The Life of Louis the Fat*.[90] Henry of Huntingdon saw a copy of the prophesies at Bec-Hellouin in 1139, and Orderic Vitalis inserted it into his *Historia Ecclesiastica* in 1135 or 1136.[91] Since *The Life of Louis the Fat* was in circulation by 1142,[92] Suger had access to this incantatory nonsense at a surprisingly early stage.

Both Suger and Orderic Vitalis use the prophesies of Merlin in the context of a very similar treatment of Henry I. Apart from this striking example, there are just enough other correspondences between Orderic Vitalis and *The Life of Louis the Fat* to raise a suspicion of interaction, if not quite complicity. Both Orderic and Suger give exactly the same reason why Philip I was buried at Fleury, rather than St Denis – that he thought he was not good enough to rest with his ancestors; a sentiment which is not echoed in the *Morigny Chronicle*.[93] In their accounts of the 1116–20 wars, both make much of the taking of Gasny, for instance, though this may just be because it was a good story.[94] Orderic knows rather a lot about the attack of the Montmorency on St Denis in 1101/2.[95] There is often an intriguing consensus in who or what was worth mentioning, and who was a thoroughly bad hat, between Suger's and Orderic's account of events in Capetian territories. This may mean no more than that there was a general consensus about current affairs among well-informed Benedictine monks; but Suger and Orderic are often closer to each other in selection and comment, than either to the Morigny Chronicler. Suger and Orderic may have drawn on the same oral traditions; and drafts of some of Suger's earlier chapters may have been in circulation on the Neustrian scriptorium network long before the book achieved its final form. We might speculate here on the role of Bec, and of Bec's priory close to St Denis at Conflans Ste Honorine, in the dissemination of either or both manuscripts and oral traditions.

In fact, both the structure and the content of *The Life of Louis the Fat* owe far more to Norman historical writing than to obvious French precedents. The obvious models for *The Life of Louis the Fat* ought to have been Einhard's *Life of Charlemagne*, and Helgaud's *Life of Robert the Pious*.[96] *The Life of Louis the Fat* could hardly be more different. It has neither their Suetonian bipartite structure, nor their emphasis on their subject's piety and ecclesiastical foundations. *The Life of Louis the Fat* is loosely chronological in structure, though its marked absence of dates distinguishes it from annals-based history. Its main subject is Louis the Fat at war,

[89] University of Leyden MS lat. 20; see van Houts, *Gesta Normannorum Ducum* i, cix. See also Spiegel, *Chronicle Tradition*, 43–4.

[90] Suger, *Vie de Louis*, 98–9.

[91] Orderic vi, 380–1, n. 5.

[92] *Chron. Mor.*, 69.

[93] Suger, *Vie de Louis*, 84–5; Orderic vi, 154–5; cf the account of Philip's death in *Chron. Mor.*, 10–11.

[94] Suger, *Vie de Louis*, 186–7. Orderic vi, 183–4.

[95] Orderic vi, 156; Suger, *Vie de Louis*, 14–19.

[96] *Einhard's Life of Charlemagne*, ed. H.W. Garrod and R.B. Mowat, Oxford 1915: Helgaud de Fleury, *Vie de Robert le Pieux*, ed. R.-H. Bautier and G. Labory, Sources d'Histoire Médiévale, CNRS Paris 1965.

firstly gaining control of his barons, and then leading *tota Francia* in a great set-piece stand against the German invasion of 1124. The text it seems to have most in common with, both in structure and content, and to some extent in language, is William of Poitiers's *Gesta Guillelmi*.

There is an Anglo-Norman context, too, for Suger's account of the administration of his abbey, the *De Administratione*. In a general sense, this belongs as a text-type to a broad genre of lives of bishops and abbots, ultimately based on the *Liber Pontificalis*, in which a prelate's recuperation of the rights and revenues of his church is followed by an account of his building campaigns and embellishments, which were what much of the recuperated revenues were spent on. Eleventh- or twelfth-century French examples include Andrew of Fleury's *Life of Abbot Gauzelin*, and the *Acts of the Bishops of Le Mans*.[97] Within this extensive genre, the text which is closest to Suger's is an account of the administration of Glastonbury Abbey by Henry of Blois.[98] Suger and Henry share the distinction of writing their accounts themselves, instead of leaving it to an admiring acolyte in the usual manner.[99] Both write with the express intention of protecting their recuperations against future loss: Suger writes 'for the memory of posterity' (*'posteritati memoriae'*); Henry, 'for the memory of those to come' (*'futurorum memoriae'*). Both hope that those reading their accounts will pray for their souls.[100] The texts share a systematic quality: the estates are dealt with in groups rather than in continuous prose. There are two differences between the texts. The first is that Henry of Blois does not go on to describe how he spent all these newly generated revenues on rebuilding and embellishment. He must have intended to. He did plenty of it at Glastonbury, and it is, after all, the section of text which transmutes what might otherwise be condemned as base avarice into the proper provision for the House of God. The second difference is that Henry is able to talk about the recuperation of whole manors, where Suger always talks about the recuperation of specific revenues and privileges. Presumably that reflects the more fragmented way in which French estates had been alienated.

Much has been made in the past about the architectural influence of Normandy on St Denis. Here I am less convinced. It is true that rib vaulting infected the Ile de France from Upper Normandy, but the west end of St Denis was by no means the first, nor the only, Ile de France building to employ this useful new technology in the 1130s. The twin-towers of Suger's west facade are always regarded as a Norman import. St Etienne at Caen is often mentioned. But none of the relevant Norman twin-towered facades were connected with a massive narthex and upper chapel arrangement in the manner of Suger's St Denis. It seems rather that Suger

---

97 André de Fleury, *Vie de Gauzelin, Abbé de Fleury*, ed. and trans. R.-H. Bautier and G. Labory, Sources d'Histoire Médiévale, CNRS Paris 1969: *Actus Pontificum Cenomannis in Urbe Degentium*, ed. G. Busson and A. Ledru, Archives Historiques du Maine II, Le Mans, 1901, see esp. bishops Hoel, pp. 393–5; Hildevert of Lavardin, pp. 415–16, 418–21; Guy, p. 441; Hugh, pp. 449–53.

98 Adam de Domerham, *Historia de rebus gestis Glastoniensibus*, ed. T. Hearne, Oxford 1727, 2 vols, ii, 305–15. I would like to thank Dr John Hudson for bringing this text to my notice.

99 See article by S. Keynes in this volume on the probably mid-twelfth-century 'ghosted' autobiography of Bishop Giso of Wells.

100 'De Administratione', *Oeuvres Complètes*, 155 (ed. Panofsky, *Abbot Suger*, 40–1): Adam de Domerham, *Historia*, 305–6.

wanted a modern and structurally sound version of the twin-towered Carolingian west front, with porch area between, which he had just had dismantled.[101]

The impact of Suger's new church on the ecclesiastical architecture and sculpture of the Anglo-Norman world was surprisingly uneven. In Normandy itself, that impact was purely architectural, and very delayed, but at last, between the late 1160s and the 1180s some of the grandest abbey churches in the duchy, notably Fécamp, Mortemer and St Etienne at Caen, responded to Suger's choir at St Denis.[102] The English reaction, curiously, was faster and largely sculptural. Zarnecki has pointed to the influence of Suger's west front, in particular on Henry of Blois's work at Glastonbury and elsewhere, and at Bury St Edmunds.[103] Suger's reputation as a great builder had certainly spread among the English clergy. When Bishop Jocelyn of Salisbury wrote to Suger in 1148, he praised the abbot as a modern Solomon, adding 'We have looked with admiration at that Temple which you have built' – 'templum quod aedificastis aspeximus'.[104]

At the intersection of architecture and literature, it is arguable that Suger's experiences at St Denis lay behind the famous cart cult, which took fire, particularly in Normandy, in the mid-1140s. In the *De Consecratione*, Suger gives a vivid description of the people of Pontoise and St Denis harnessing themselves to carts to help with the construction of the west end of the abbey church in the late 1130s. Suddenly, around 1145, we hear of a rash of similar outbursts of popular piety, most of them in Normandy. In that year, Suger's old friend, Archbishop Hugh of Rouen, wrote to Bishop Thierry of Amiens, describing cart cults at the cathedral of Rouen and elsewhere across Normandy. Hugh tells Thierry that this new manifestation has spread from the cathedral of Chartres – the only non-Norman site mentioned. This is corroborated by Robert of Torigni. A similar manifestation is recorded in a letter of the abbot of the Norman abbey of St Pierre sur Dives. It is also mentioned in several Norman chronicles, including the *Annales Uticenses*, the annals of Mont St Michel and the *Rouen Chronicle*.[105]

Perhaps we might speculate that Hugh's focus on this new type of popular piety was inspired by Suger's account of the building of St Denis in the *De Consecratione*. Hugh, Geoffrey of Leves – who as bishop of Chartres was a close associate of Theobald of Champagne – and Thierry of Amiens all took part in the great consecration of the shrine-choir in June 1144. It is tempting to suggest that Suger's famous short treatise on the consecration of his new shrine choir was written for distribution at the final concord between Louis and Theobald on 9 October 1144,

---

[101] See his description of the previous building in 'De Administratione', *Oeuvres Complètes*, 187 (ed. Panofsky, *Abbot Suger*, 44–5).

[102] L. Grant, 'Architectural Relationships between England and Normandy, 1100–1204', in *England and Normandy in the Middle Ages*, ed. D. Bates and A. Curry, London 1994, 125: L. Grant, 'The Choir of Saint Etienne at Caen', in *Medieval Architecture and its Intellectual Context: Studies in Honour of Peter Kidson*, ed. E. Fernie and P. Crossley, London 1990, 113–25.

[103] *English Romanesque Art*, ed. G. Zarnecki, Arts Council of Great Britain, London 1984, 143, 148, 183, 185: G. Zarnecki, 'Henry of Blois as a Patron of Sculpture', in *Art and Patronage in the English Romanesque*, ed. S. Macready and F.H. Thompson, Society of Antiquaries, Occasional Papers, new series, VIII, London 1986, 160–2.

[104] Bouquet, *Recueil* xv, 498–9.

[105] 'De Consecratione', *Oeuvres Complètes*, 220–1 (ed. Panofsky, *Abbot Suger*, 92–5), for Suger's account. For the Norman texts see V. Mortet and P. Deschamps, *Recueil de textes relatifs à l'histoire de l'architecture en France au Moyen Age, xiie–xiiie siècles*, Paris 1929, 63–7, and 65, n. 1.

just four months after the great consecration itself. It makes generous reference to the Cistercians, and mentions gifts to St Denis from Louis and Theobald, whose political demands were resolved over the two meetings.[106] In this case, Hugh of Rouen and Geoffrey of Chartres would have received their complimentary copies at the great concord of October 1144: giving them a convenient few months to digest the full dramatic possibilities of the cart cult.

This paper has been rather episodic, and perhaps adds up to saying no more than that Suger, like any abbot of St Denis, had much contact with the Anglo-Norman world. But I think that the Anglo-Norman perspective does throw fresh light on Suger and his abbey.

For one thing, it brings home the extent to which Suger was only really able to push the abbey's claims in the Vexin at stages when the French kings were seriously beholden to his diplomatic expertise in their attempts to deal with the dukes of Normandy, almost as if handing properties or privileges in the war zone to the abbey of St Denis might propitiate their patron saint. Neither king was interested in buttressing the abbey's position in the Vexin when the area was not in serious dispute.

Secondly, Suger may have been abbot of the burial house of the kings of France, but he saw himself, as his diplomatic dealings with his fellow clergy reveal, as belonging to an ecclesiastical élite, supra-regional and supra-national, and not a little arrogant in their ability to stitch things up for, or even despite, their notional masters. Both these points should warn us that there was not always a total identity of interest between the king of France and the abbot of St Denis.

For St Denis is always presented as an institution quintessentially and centrally Capetian and Parisian, and its abbot as a pillar of the Capetian realm. I am not really trying to marginalise them, but I think it is important to point up the extent to which they were, from certain perspectives, on the edge. St Denis was perilously close to the war-zone of the Vexin. Conversely, the abbey's and the abbot's web of connections stretched across the no-man's land of the Vexin into Normandy, as well as back towards Paris. Suger's Anglo-Norman network meant a vastly expanded horizon, both for himself and for his institution. Bright light on Suger's relations with the Anglo-Norman world casts long shadows across the Vexin, and, for once, leaves Capetian Paris in the dark.

---

[106] 'De Consecratione', *Oeuvres Complètes*, 229, 231 (ed. Panofsky, *Abbot Suger*, 106–7, 110–11).

'AND THEY PROCEEDED TO PLOUGH AND TO SUPPORT THEMSELVES': THE SCANDINAVIAN SETTLEMENT OF ENGLAND[1]

D. M. Hadley

This paper considers aspects of the Scandinavian impact on Anglo-Saxon England between the later ninth and the mid-tenth century, once the Scandinavian raiders began to settle. It is based on the premise that a number of issues have become confused in the study of this subject. I hope to demonstrate this by examining four aspects of the Scandinavian conquest and settlement: the numbers of Scandinavians involved in the settlement of Anglo-Saxon England; the distinctive nature of the regions in which they settled, especially that of the so-called Danelaw; the nature of the relationships which the Scandinavian settlers forged with the native population; and the general question of continuity. Commonly, hypotheses about one of these aspects of the settlement are used to draw conclusions about the others. However, while these issues are certainly related, the nature of the relationship is far from clear-cut. Consequently, this paper will examine the preconceptions inherent in studies of the Scandinavian settlement and suggest new ways to approach the subject and to integrate the diverse types of evidence we have for the period.

The Scale of the Scandinavian Settlement and the Problems with the Place-Name Evidence

From the 870s viking raiding apparently turned to settlement: in 876, according to the Anglo-Saxon Chronicle, the viking leader Halfdan 'shared out the land of the Northumbrians, and they proceeded to plough and to support themselves'. Further divisions of land among the members of viking armies took place in parts of Mercia the following year and in East Anglia in 880.[2] The period of Scandinavian overlordship and the nature and extent of their settlement are not well-documented. Nevertheless, the impact of the Scandinavians is traditionally deemed to have been

---

[1] I would like to thank Prof. Christopher Harper-Bill for inviting me to present this paper to the Battle Conference. In preparing this article for publication I have benefited from the help and advice of Dr Lesley Abrams, Dr Steven Bassett, Dr John Blair, Dr Simon Loseby, Prof. Pauline Stafford and Prof. Chris Wickham.

[2] *EHD* i, *s.a.* 876, 877, 880. For this, and subsequent events, see F.M. Stenton, *Anglo-Saxon England*, 3rd edn, Oxford 1971, 252–68, 320–63; for the northern sources see, P.H. Sawyer, 'Some Sources for the History of Viking Northumbria', in *Viking Age York and the North*, ed. R.A. Hall, *Council for British Archaeology Research Report* xxvii, 1978, 3–7; A.P. Smyth, 'The Chronology of Northumbrian History in the Ninth and Tenth Centuries', in *ibid.*, 8–10.

wide-ranging and long-lasting chiefly on the grounds that the society of the regions in which they took control and settled in the late ninth and early tenth centuries apparently became so very different from that of other parts of Anglo-Saxon England. At a later date, the regions of Scandinavian settlement in northern and eastern England were characterised to varying degrees by Scandinavian place-names, by Scandinavian names for legal and administrative offices and institutions, by a distinctive legal and administrative organisation, by large numbers of free peasants (according to Domesday Book), and by the prevalence of large multi-vill estates (called sokes) which survived into the eleventh century and beyond.[3] All of these aspects of the society of northern and eastern England have at some point been directly attributed to the Scandinavians, and used as an index for the nature and extent of their settlement. Studies that have made such a connection between the peculiarities of the region and the Scandinavian settlement have generally been underpinned by a belief in large numbers of Scandinavian settlers, and have tended to emphasise the Scandinavian identity, and the unique racial composition, of northern and eastern England. The pre-conceptions that fostered such an interpretation of the available evidence are apparent: the notion that freedom had Germanic roots and was bolstered by a second wave of Germanic settlement; a belief in racial characteristics; the myth of the pioneering, independent spirit. These ideas all played a part in forming earlier twentieth-century interpretations of the Viking Age, and are most extensively expounded in the voluminous writings of Sir Frank Stenton.[4] To Stenton – who argued for a massive settlement of Scandinavians – the Danish element, although it varied across the region, was everywhere the dominant strain: it was no accident that 'a social organisation to which there is no parallel elsewhere in England occurs in the one part of the country in which the regular development of native institutions had been interrupted by a foreign settlement'.[5] The Scandinavian settlement, hence, not only overturned the existing political system but fundamentally altered the basis of social and economic organisation.

During the 1960s and '70s Viking Studies were dominated by arguments over the numbers involved in the conquest and settlement of England, and the old notion of a mass invasion was called into question. Little purpose would be served by rehearsing these arguments at any length; put briefly, the consensus reached by the end of the 1970s was that although the viking armies were perhaps not as sizeable as was once thought, they were, nonetheless, not as small as Peter Sawyer had claimed, and in any case the armies alone could not have been responsible for the great impact made by the Scandinavian languages on the place-names, personal names, and speech of Anglo-Saxon England.[6] The linguistic impact, according to

---

[3] For summaries see Stenton, *Anglo-Saxon England*, 502–25; P.H. Sawyer, *The Age of the Vikings*, 2nd edn, London 1971, 152–76.

[4] F.M. Stenton, 'The Free Peasantry of the Northern Danelaw', *Bulletin de la société royale des lettres de Lund*, 1925–26, 73–185; *idem*, 'The Danes in England', *Proceedings of the British Academy* xiii, 1927; cf. P. Stafford, 'The Danes and the Danelaw', *History Today*, Oct. 1986, 17–23, at 18–19.

[5] Stenton, *Anglo-Saxon England*, 519.

[6] The literature on this subject is enormous, but the main outlines of the debate can be traced through the following: Stenton, *Anglo-Saxon England*, 502–25; R.H.C. Davis, 'East Anglia and the Danelaw', *TRHS*, 5th ser. v, 1955, 23–39; P.H. Sawyer, 'The Density of the Danish Settlement in England', *University of Birmingham Journal* vi, no. 1, 1957, 1–17; P.H. Sawyer, *The Age of the Vikings*, London 1962, 120ff; K. Cameron, *Scandinavian Settlement in the Territory of the Five*

many linguists and historians alike, could be accounted for only by a secondary peasant immigration, albeit an unrecorded event.[7]

Given the pre-eminence traditionally accorded the linguistic evidence, it is appropriate to begin my analysis by addressing the limitations of the evidence. Even if we are forced to accept the conclusions of the linguists concerning the relationship between linguistic change and the numbers of people who spoke a particular language a number of important issues remain unresolved.[8] For example, the context in which Scandinavian place-names were coined is obscure: the renaming of existing settlements, and the foundation of new settlements following colonisation doubtless account for the great density of Scandinavian place-names, but it is difficult to offer more than a handful of unequivocal examples of either process.[9] The argument that some Scandinavian place-names were coined following a period of colonisation rests primarily on an evaluation of the nature and quality of the land on which they are located. The generation of distribution maps of Scandinavian place-names in their topographical and geological context – as pioneered by Kenneth Cameron – has fostered interpretations of their significance based on what is, in truth, a rather simplistic binary division of the landscape into areas of primary settlement and areas of secondary settlement on so-called marginal lands.[10] Certainly, upland, wolds, woodland and so on, may not have been as intensively or extensively settled as were some river valleys, but that does not warrant their description as marginal: such land provided important resources for river valley settlements, to which much was undoubtedly annexed. Recent work by Alan

---

Boroughs: the Place-Name Evidence*, Nottingham 1965; *idem*, 'Scandinavian Settlement in the Territory of the Five Boroughs: the Place-Name Evidence, Part II, Place-Names in Thorp', *Mediaeval Scandinavia* iii, 1970, 35–49; *idem*, 'Scandinavian Settlement in the Territory of the Five Boroughs: the Place-Name Evidence, Part III, the Grimston Hybrids', in *England Before the Conquest*, ed. P. Clemoes and K. Hughes, Cambridge 1971, 147–63; Sawyer, *Age of the Vikings*, 2nd edn, 154–71; N. Lund, 'The Settlers: Where Do We Get Them From – and Do We Need Them?' in *Proceedings of the Eighth Viking Congress*, ed. H. Bekker-Nielsen *et al.*, Odense 1981, 147–71; N.P. Brooks, 'England in the Ninth Century: the Crucible of Defeat', *TRHS*, 5th ser. xxix, 1979, 1–20.

[7] F.M. Stenton, 'The Historical Bearing of Place-Name Studies: the Danish Settlement of Eastern England', *TRHS*, 4th ser. xxiv, 1942, 1–24; H.R. Loyn, *Anglo-Saxon England and the Norman Conquest*, London 1962, 54, 61; Cameron, *Scandinavian Settlement*, 10–11.

[8] For discussion of the interaction of languages see U. Weinreich, *Languages in Contact: Findings and Problems*, New York 1953; Sawyer, *Age of the Vikings*, 2nd edn, 154–5, 169–71.

[9] An oft-cited example of a place renamed with a Scandinavian place-name is Derby (formerly *Northworthig*). For this, and other examples of the complete or partial replacement of Old English place-names with Scandinavian names, see G. Fellows Jensen, *Scandinavian Settlement Names in the East Midlands*, Copenhagen 1978, 12, 37, 43, 60, 67, 292–4. For recent overviews of the debate about the context of place-name formation see C.D. Morris, 'Aspects of Scandinavian Settlement in Northern England: a Review', *Northern History* xx, 1984, 1–22, at 8–9, 12–16; G. Fellows Jensen, 'Scandinavian Settlement in Yorkshire – Through the Rear-View Mirror', in *Scandinavian Settlement in Northern Britain*, ed. B.E. Crawford, London 1995, 170–86.

[10] Cameron, *Scandinavian Settlement*; *idem*, 'Places-Names in Thorp'; *idem*, 'Grimston Hybrids'. Cameron states that the Danes came 'as colonists, developing virgin land and establishing new settlements' on the basis of an analysis of the distribution of Scandinavian place-names on geological drift maps: *Scandinavian Settlement*, 12. cf. M. Gelling, *Signposts to the Past*, London 1978, 226, who prefers to substitute 'disused' for 'virgin' in describing the land settled by the Danes. This neatly circumvents the problem created by evidence for Romano-British or early Anglo-Saxon settlement in those areas where Cameron argued for Danish colonisation; they were not regions which had never been settled but they were disused at the time of the Scandinavian settlement.

Everitt and Harold Fox has explored this issue in various regions, and Fox has suggested that when land on the wolds or in upland locations was severed from the river valley settlement to which it was attached that this could provide a context for the formation of new place-names.[11] A significant number of Scandinavian place-names are located on the Leicestershire wolds which, Fox has argued, represents not the colonisation of 'an unused void' but the intensification of settlement between the ninth and eleventh centuries in a region previously characterised by woodland and pasture, as a result of which territorial organisation was transformed and new place-names were coined: the preponderance of Scandinavian place-names was due to Scandinavian naming elements being in common usage at the time. This is not to say that the wolds were necessarily settled by Scandinavians or that Scandinavians were responsible for coining those names. It may be true that an influx of new settlers was broadly responsible for increasing pressure on available land and resources; although it should be noted that similar transformations in land-use have been noted in regions for which there is no suggestion of Scandinavian settlement.[12]

Place-names were formed in multifarious contexts, and the great emphasis placed on the topographical and geological context should not be permitted to overshadow the estate context. The Scandinavian place-name element *thorp* is widely agreed to carry the meaning of a 'secondary settlement, an outlying farmstead or a small hamlet dependent on a larger place'.[13] It is not difficult to see why this should have become a widely used generic term for settlements in such a context; such an interpretation carries at least as much conviction as the uncorroborated claim that they represent 'colonisation in the strict sense'.[14] Furthermore, changes to the composition of estates doubtless provided an important catalyst to place-name transformation.

Even if we had a better understanding of the context in which place-names were coined their distribution cannot be used as a guide to the locations of peoples: we should not be tempted to divide the countryside into areas of English and Scandinavian settlements on the basis of place-name evidence alone, because this depends on assumptions about 'ethnic' separation and continuity that are difficult to sustain. We cannot assume that any settlement with a Scandinavian name ever contained only people of Scandinavian descent, or that English-named settlements never experienced an influx of Scandinavians: the Scandinavian place-name Ingleby (farmstead/village of the English) is a stark reminder of the fallacy of such

[11] A. Everitt, 'River and Wold: Reflections on the Historical Origin of Regions and Pays', *Journal of Historical Geography* iii, 1977, 1–19; *idem*, 'The Wolds Once More', *Journal of Historical Geography* v, 1979, 67–78; *idem*, *Continuity and Colonisation: the Evolution of Kentish Settlement*, London 1983; H.S.A. Fox, 'The People of the Wolds in English Settlement History', in *The Rural Settlements of Medieval England*, ed. M. Aston, D. Austin and C. Dyer, Oxford 1989, 77–101; cf. Fellows Jensen, 'Scandinavian Settlement in Yorkshire', 181–3.

[12] Fox, 'The Wolds', 85–96.

[13] Cameron, 'Place-Names in Thorp', 35; cf. A.H. Smith, *English Place-Name Elements*, English Place-Name Society xxv–xxvi, Cambridge 1956, 214–16. It has been argued that some place-names formed with *thorp* may have developed from an Old English word *throp*, but the sheer number of them in the Danelaw argues for most of them deriving from a Scandinavian word; Gelling, *Signposts*, 226–8.

[14] Cameron, 'Place-names in Thorp', 43.

assumptions, not least because Ingleby (Derbys.) is the site of a cremation cemetery at which Scandinavian-style artefacts have been found.[15] Similarly, the fact that Scandinavian lords took over estates without causing the name of the estate centre to have changed demonstrates that it is not appropriate to make a simple connection between Scandinavian place-names and places of Scandinavian settlement.[16] Conversely, regions with few or no Scandinavian place-names may nevertheless have experienced a significant influx of Scandinavians, to judge from the occurrence in these same areas of large numbers of Scandinavian names for landscape features.[17] Furthermore, the fact that stone sculpture displaying Scandinavian motifs is commonly located at sites with Old English place-names similarly points up problems in associating Scandinavian settlement with Scandinavian settlement names; not all the patrons of such sculpture were necessarily of Scandinavian origin, but some surely were.[18] Used in isolation, place-name distribution maps are too blunt an instrument with which to identify the location or movements of peoples. We must question Cameron's attempts to plot the movement of Scandinavian settlers on the basis of place-name distribution: he has argued that 'the Danish-named villages near the Bain . . . could well have been established by settlers entering the country by the Wash, then following the Witham as far as the Bain'. As Sawyer observed, 'settlements along a river do not prove that the settlers came up that river'.[19]

We must also remember that the linguistic evidence has few clear chronological parameters. Most Scandinavian place-names are not recorded until two centuries after the onset of settlement, and minor names and landscape features generally much later. Scandinavian place-names continued to be coined into the twelfth century, and whatever the correlation between the numbers of Scandinavians and the dissemination of Scandinavian terminology, the linguistic impact of the Scandinavian settlers is unlikely to have been confined to the late ninth or early tenth centuries.[20] Furthermore, linguistic evidence alone cannot identify precisely when place-names were coined and historical probability has to be brought into the equation. It is alarming that while few would now attempt to use place-name evidence to establish a chronology of settlement in the earlier Anglo-Saxon

---

[15] *The Place-Names of Derbyshire*, ed. K. Cameron, EPNS xxvii–xxix, Cambridge 1959, 639.

[16] G.R.J. Jones, 'Early Territorial Organisation in Northern England and its Bearing on the Scandinavian Settlement', in *The Fourth Viking Congress*, ed. A. Small, Edinburgh 1965, 67–84, at 77, 83; P.H. Sawyer, *Kings and Vikings: Scandinavia and Europe AD 700–1100*, London 1982, 106. Old English place-names often became 'scandinavianised' in pronunciation and spelling: Morris, 'Scandinavian Settlement', 7–8.

[17] G. Fellows Jensen, *Scandinavian Settlement Names in Yorkshire*, Copenhagen 1972, 118; K. Cameron, 'Early Field-Names in an English-Named Lincolnshire Village', in *Otium et Negotium*, ed. F. Sandgren, Stockholm 1973, 38–43, at 41; Lund, 'The Settlers', 156–67. On regions with documentary and sculptural evidence for Scandinavian settlement, but where there are few Scandinavian place-names, see V.E. Watts, 'Place-Names of the Darlington Area', in *Darlington: a Topographical Study*, ed. P.A.G. Clark and N.F. Pearson, Durham 1978, 40–3; C.D. Morris, 'The Pre-Norman Sculpture of the Darlington Area', in *ibid.*, 44–51; *idem*, 'Scandinavian Settlement', 8.

[18] G. Fellows Jensen, 'Place-Names and the Scandinavian Settlement in the North Riding of Yorkshire', *Northern History* xiv, 1978, 19–46, at 38; Morris, 'Scandinavian Settlement', 10–11.

[19] Cameron, *Scandinavian Settlement*, 19; Sawyer, *Age of the Vikings*, 2nd edn, 168.

[20] G. Fellows Jensen, 'Lancashire and Yorkshire Names', *Northern History* xix, 1983, 231–7; *idem*, 'Scandinavian Settlement in Yorkshire', 178.

centuries, it is still felt appropriate to do so in the aftermath of the Scandinavian settlements.[21] Therefore, in spite of the certainty of some accounts, chronologies of settlement or of colonisation have to be regarded with suspicion.

The question of who coined place-names is difficult to answer but is crucial to an understanding of their meaning. Presumably it was not the inhabitants of a settlement but others who gave it its name; this, however, opens up the possibility that any given settlement may have been known by more than one name – the names given by neighbouring communities and local lords were not necessarily identical. It is the latter that are more likely to have entered the written record, which blurs still further the long-held connection between place-names and the scale of the Scandinavian settlement. The replacement of Old English place-name elements with cognate Scandinavian words also clouds the issue; a scandinaviani-sation of the existing place-name corpus presents a somewhat different proposition from the wholesale replacement of place-names, or from the coining of place-names for new settlements.[22] One final point concerns the nature of land-holding. Attitudes to land in the Scandinavian homelands were seemingly rather different from those that obtained in Anglo-Saxon England, and it is notable that place-names formed with *by* in Scandinavia have a much lower incidence of personal names as their first element than is the case in England.[23] Consequently, the incidence of Scandinavian personal names in the Danelaw suggests contact with natives and adaptation to local attitudes to land. Together with the fact that a person bearing a Scandinavian name was not necessarily of Scandinavian origin, this dictates that this group of place-names cannot be taken in isolation as an index of ethnically Scandinavian activity.

In sum, although it may be true on a very broad level that the large numbers of Scandinavian place-names and of Scandinavian words for landscape features are the result of a significant influx of Scandinavians, when we attempt to move from such generalisations to specific examples of the nature of the Scandinavian settle-ment monocausal explanations are proven to be inadequate. Eastern and northern England was not a blank canvas; the population was too dense, the settlement of the region was too extensive, 'the cultural, social and economic structures too coherent',[24] and, even if the settlers are to be numbered in thousands rather than hundreds, the Scandinavian settlements were proportionately too small for us to continue to believe that the society and place-names of whole regions were rapidly overwhelmed. The valuable work of place-name scholars must now be revised; the institutional context, especially that of estate structures, offers a more satisfactory

---

[21] Although some place-name elements (topographical ones, in particular) are considered likely to have been earlier than others, it cannot be assumed that all examples of a particular type of place-name were therefore earlier than all examples of another. Renaming and regional variation are two important reasons why place-name and settlement chronologies cannot be finely calibrated: Gelling, *Signposts*, 106–29.

[22] This problem has been extensively considered in respect of field-names: Lund, 'The Settlers', 162–5.

[23] P. Wormald, 'Viking Studies: Whence and Whither?' in *The Vikings*, ed. R.T. Farrell, 1982, 128–51, at 144–8. On the incidence of personal names in place-names of England and Scandinavia see K. Hald, *Vore Stednavne*, Copenhagen 1965, 109–13; Fellows Jensen, *East Midlands*, 15–17, 27–8.

[24] Stafford, *The East Midlands in the Early Middle Ages*, Leicester 1985, 121.

perspective on place-name formation. Meanwhile, questions about the interaction of groups of peoples and about the construction of ethnic and cultural identities must also be considered. The place-name distribution map needs a new overlay.

The Distinctive Nature of the Danelaw and the Scandinavian Influence

Despite the problems in utilising place-name evidence it still dominates most interpretations of the Scandinavian impact. It is important to note that of the characteristic features of the region it is only the linguistic evidence that is now used to support a case for large numbers of Scandinavian settlers. Many of the other peculiarities of the region have been attributed to terminological differences.[25] In recent years the emphasis has been much more on continuity: elements of the estate structure, social organisation, and parochial system – to take just a few examples – have all been ascribed pre-viking origins in a number of studies, and the Scandinavian contribution to their form has been down-played.[26] For example, 'multiple-estates' comparable to the sokes of northern and eastern England and relatively free peasants analogous to the sokemen of the region have been identified widely in other parts of Britain and in continental Europe; this has rendered as untenable the supposed singularity of the social and estate structures of regions settled by the Scandinavians, and the traditional belief in ethnic influences behind their emergence.[27] This approach neatly circumvents the numerical question, because it is implicit in such studies that no matter how many Scandinavians there were, the basic institutions of the region survived. However, new problems emerge to be resolved; and, despite my critique of place-name scholarship, it is possible to go too far in minimising Scandinavian immigration and influence. It has become increasingly fashionable to speak of a swift assimilation of the Scandinavians into native society, but this tends to minimise the number of Scandinavian settlers, to underplay the Scandinavian contribution to the society of the Danelaw and to avoid the crucially important question of why integration might have been so rapid.[28]

[25] J.M. Kaye, 'The Sacrabar', *EHR* lxxxiii, 1968, 744–58; Stenton, *Anglo-Saxon England*, 504–5; Sawyer, *Age of the Vikings*, 2nd edn, 153–4; Stafford, 'The Danes', 21–3; *The Anglo-Saxons*, ed. J. Campbell, Oxford 1982, 201.

[26] Davis, 'East Anglia'; G.R.J. Jones, 'Basic Patterns of Settlement Distribution in Northern England', *Advancement of Science* lxxii, 1961, 192–200; *idem*, 'Early Territorial Organisation'; *idem*, 'Early Territorial Organisation in Gwynedd and Elmet', *Northern History* x, 1975, 3–25; *idem*, 'Celts, Saxons and Scandinavians', in *An Historical Geography of England and Wales*, ed. R.A. Dodgshon and R.A. Butlin, Cambridge 1978, 57–79; C.D. Morris, 'Northumbria and the Viking Settlement: the Evidence for Land-Holding', *Archaeologia Aeliana* 5th ser. v, 1977, 81–103; *idem*, 'Viking and Native in Northern England: a Case-Study', in *Proceedings of the Eighth Viking Congress*, Bekker-Nielsen, 223–44; A.K.G. Kristensen, 'Danelaw Institutions and Danish Society in the Viking Age: *Sochemanni*, *Liberi Homines* and *Konigsfreie*', *Mediaeval Scandinavia* viii, 1975, 27–85; R.K. Morris, *Churches in the Landscape*, London 1989, 133–9; D.M. Hadley, 'Conquest, Colonisation and the Church: Ecclesiastical Organisation in the Danelaw', *Historical Research* lxix, 1996, 109–28.

[27] Stafford, 'The Danes', 22.

[28] D. Whitelock, 'The Conversion of the Eastern Danelaw', *Saga-Book of the Viking Society* xii, 1941, 159–76; *The Place-Names of the West Riding of Yorkshire*, ed. A.H. Smith, vols xxx–xxxvii, Cambridge 1962, xxxvi, 63; D.M. Wilson, 'The Vikings' Relationship with Christianity in Northern England', *Journ. BAA* xxx, 1967, 37–46; *idem*, 'Scandinavian Settlement in the North and West of

Similarity of language or the readiness of the pagan belief-system to admit the Christian God into its pantheon may well explain *how* integration was facilitated but this does not explain *why* it happened. Moreover, we must take care not to regard the Scandinavians as an undifferentiated mass; we must seek to draw a distinction between the behaviour of the leaders of the armies, their followers and the peasants who apparently followed in their wake. Finally, it is also necessary to state that many studies of continuity – given the scanty documentary evidence – involve great leaps of faith, based on back-projection from late evidence, bolstered by models generated for other parts of Anglo-Saxon England, which are themselves open to critical revaluation. Before we allow the pendulum to swing fully towards integration and continuity we need to explore the pre-conceptions and use of evidence of the proponents of this model.

A number of recent studies have sought to reconstruct aspects of the socio-economic and ecclesiastical organisation of parts of Anglo-Saxon England in the seventh to ninth centuries,[29] and a few such studies have attempted to apply the methodology to the Danelaw in order to demonstrate continuity through the period of Scandinavian conquest and settlement. Christopher Morris, for example, has used the evidence of the *Historia de Sancto Cuthberto* to argue that the basic pattern of settlement in pre-viking Northumbria was the multi-vill estate and that this had implications for the Scandinavian conquest of the region. Ælfred, son of Brihtulf, who fled from somewhere west of the Pennines during the reign of Edward the Elder, was given a number of estates by Bishop Cutheard, so that he 'should render full service from them'; when he died in battle against a viking army under Ragnald, the latter granted a number of estates to his followers Scula and Onlafbal, and these estates seem to have coincided to some extent with those held by Ælfred. As Morris observes, 'it would seem to be a clear example of take-over by a Scandinavian of a native estate as a going concern'.[30] This assessment echoes the work of Jolliffe and G.R.J. Jones on the essential antiquity of the estate structure of northern England; Jones has argued that the estate structure depicted by Domesday Book owes its origins to pre-viking, or even to pre-Anglo-Saxon, patterns of organisation.[31]

However, although models that draw on late evidence to uncover earlier patterns of organisation are appealing to students of a region lacking in substantive Anglo-Saxon documentation, caution must be urged since it is possible to make a case for elements of both continuity and discontinuity. It is certainly striking that many of the most important estate centres of Domesday Book can be demonstrated to have performed this role centuries earlier, and similarly many of the major churches of

the British Isles – an Archaeological Point-of-View', *TRHS*, 5th ser. xx, 1976, 95–113, at 96–8; D.A. Hinton, *Archaeology, Economy and Society: England from the Fifth to the Fifteenth Century*, London 1990, 71.

[29] On the territorial organisation of the earliest Anglo-Saxon centuries see J. Campbell, *Essays in Anglo-Saxon History*, London 1986, 95–6, 110–16; S.R. Bassett, 'In Search of the Origins of Anglo-Saxon Kingdoms', in *The Origins of Anglo-Saxon Kingdoms*, ed. idem, Leicester 1989, 3–27; J. Blair, *Early Medieval Surrey*, Stroud 1991, 12–34.

[30] Morris, 'Viking and Native', 223–7.

[31] J.E.A. Jolliffe, 'Northumbrian Institutions', *EHR* clxi, 1926, 1–42; G.R.J. Jones, 'Early Territorial Organisation'; *idem*, 'Multiple Estates'.

the region have their origins in the pre-viking period.[32] This pattern, which is widespread and somewhat remarkable for a region once thought to have experienced such a calamitous history, provides the starting point from which to explore continuity. The gap between the pre-viking period and Domesday Book can be narrowed in a few cases. Bakewell (which architectural evidence suggests had a pre-viking church), Ashford and Hope (Derbys.) were the centres of large estates before the middle of the tenth century: no later than 911 one Uhtred bought 60 *manentes* of land from the vikings at Ashford and Hope, and in 949 probably the same Uhtred acquired land with which to endow a monastery at Bakewell.[33] Although the charters do not name any dependencies it is not unlikely, to judge from the size of assessment, that the tenth-century estates included the berewicks of the respective Domesday manors.[34] This assumption is supported by the example of Howden (Yorks.): a charter of 959 names the dependencies of Howden and these do, indeed, correspond to the berewicks of the Domesday manor.[35] Similarly, although the Domesday berewicks of Sherburn-in-Elmet (Yorks. – which has some evidence for a church and a royal centre in the ninth and early tenth centuries respectively) and Southwell (Notts. – also the site of a pre-viking church) are not named, later evidence makes it clear that they must have included those places named as their dependencies in charters of the mid-tenth century.[36] This leads one to enquire whether many more of the large sokes of Domesday Book existed as such in the tenth century, or perhaps even earlier. It is tempting to posit that the estate of Ripon (Yorks.) outlined in tenth and eleventh-century sources was descended from the 30 hides of land granted there to Bishop Wilfrid in the seventh century, and that the Domesday estate of Repton (Derbys.) is the remnant of the 31 *manentes* 'called *Hrepingas*' granted to the abbot of Breedon-on-the-Hill (Leics.) in the late seventh century.[37] The place-names of these estates lend support to the case for continuity. It has long been recognised that place-names in which a personal-name is combined with *tun* reflect changes in patterns of land-holding in the later Anglo-Saxon period. In southern England, where charters of the ninth and

---

[32] See above, n. 26; cf. D.M. Hadley, 'Multiple Estates and the Origins of the Manorial Structure of the Northern Danelaw', *Journal of Historical Geography* xxii, 1, 1996, 3–15.

[33] R. Cramp, 'Schools of Mercian Sculpture', in *Mercian Studies*, ed. A. Dornier, Leicester 1977, 191–234, at 218–25; F.M. Stenton, *Types of Manorial Structure in the Northern Danelaw*, Oxford 1910, 74–6; *Anglo-Saxon Charters II: Charters of Burton Abbey*, ed. P.H. Sawyer, London 1979.

[34] *Domesday Book*, fos 272d–273a.

[35] *Early Yorkshire Charters*, ed. W. Farrer and C.T. Clays, 12 vols, Edinburgh 1914–65, i, 12–15; M.H. Long, 'Howden and Old Drax', in *Yorkshire Boundaries*, ed. H.E.J. le Patourel, M.H. Long and M.F. Pickles, Yorkshire Archaeological Society 1993, 125–34; *Domesday Book*, fo. 304c.

[36] On Sherburn see *Early Yorkshire Charters*, i, 18–23; M.H. Long, 'Sherburn', in *Yorkshire Boundaries*, ed. Le Patourel *et al.*, 117–24; *Domesday Book* fo. 283a; W. Farrer, 'Introduction to the Yorkshire Domesday', in *VCH County of York* ii, London 1912, 210; on the possibility of an early church see E.W. Crossley, 'All Saints' Church, Sherburn-in-Elmet', *Yorkshire Archaeological Journal* xxi, 1910, 195–6; R.A. Smith, 'Anglo-Saxon Remains', in *VCH County of York* ii, London 1912, 98–9. On Southwell see *Early Yorkshire Charters*, ed. Farrer, i, 5–10; Stenton, *Types of Manorial Structure*, 78–80; on Southwell as the ninth-century resting-place of St Eadburh see D.W. Rollason, *Saints and Relics in Anglo-Saxon England*, Cambridge 1989, 120.

[37] On Ripon see *Early Yorkshire Charters*, ed. Farrer, i, 21–3; *Bede's History of the English People*, ed. B. Colgrave and R.A.B. Mynors, London 1969, v, 19; *EHD* i, no. 114; *Domesday Book*, fo. 303d. On Repton see *Felix's Life of St Guthlac*, ed. B. Thorpe, London 1956, 2–4, 84–7; *EHD* i, *s.a.* 757; Rollason, *Saints and Relics*, 121–9; A. Rumble, '*Hrepingas* Reconsidered' in *Mercian Studies*, ed. Dornier, 169–71.

tenth centuries are more abundant, it can be seen that some estates came to be named after the person to whom they were granted, and that the emergence of such place-names can be linked to the break-up of larger territories.[38] It is perhaps significant then that such place-names are rare among the dependencies of the estates referred to above, reflecting the continuing integrity of the estates through the later Anglo-Saxon period.[39] Scandinavian place-names are also equally rare on such estates, which in turn suggests that changes to the estate structure are, indeed, an important part of the explanation for the distribution and coining of Scandinavian place-names.[40]

It is also striking that many of the larger Domesday estates of the Danelaw are mirrored by the parochial geography; that is to say, outlying members of the estate are commonly located within the parish of the church at the estate centre.[41] A number of studies have argued that the parochial geography of a region can reveal the extent of secular territories which existed in the seventh and eighth centuries when the parishes of the earliest so-called minster churches were defined.[42] Despite recent critical appraisal of this model, few would seek to deny that pastoral care had become territorialised by the ninth and tenth centuries.[43] Admittedly, there is a danger here of conflating evidence, but it is striking that there is such a coincidence of parishes and Domesday estates, of important churches and manors, and of important pre- and post-viking churches and estate centres. It provides persuasive evidence of some wider form of institutional continuity. This superficial impression, however, requires examination in greater depth.

To ascribe any significance to the configuration of parish boundaries and the location of churches it is necessary to make a case for some semblance of continuity in ecclesiastical life through the Scandinavian settlement, a notion that is traditionally rejected. The evidence for the survival of ecclesiastical life is disparate. The community of St Cuthbert clearly survived and retained many of its estates, even if it moved location. Indeed, the wanderings of the community have been re-interpreted by David Rollason as a series of strategic moves undertaken by a community which retained its power and influence throughout the various moves described.[44] The careers of successive archbishops of York demonstrate that

---

[38] Gelling, *Signposts*, 177–8.

[39] D.M. Hadley, 'Personal Names and Place-Names', forthcoming.

[40] Saywer, *Kings and Vikings*, 103–4. It is notable that the Scandinavian-named appurtenances of the Domesday manor of Howden were not those named in the tenth-century charter, and were thus later acquisitions, newly founded settlements or places which had not previously been identified separately: Long, 'Howden', 125–7.

[41] D.M. Hadley, 'Danelaw Society and Institutions: East Midlands' Phenomena?', unpublished Univ. of Birmingham Ph.D. thesis 1992, ch. 5; D.R. Roffe, *Introduction to the Derbyshire Domesday Book*, London 1990, 12–14; D.M. Hadley, *Early Medieval Social Structures: the Northern Danelaw c.800–1100*, Leicester forthcoming, ch. vi.

[42] Bassett, 'In search', 18–21; Blair, *Surrey*, 31–4; C.C. Taylor, *Dorset*, London 1970, 49–72; J. Croom, 'The Fragmentation of the Minster *Parochiae* of South-East Shropshire', in *Minsters and Parish Churches*, ed. J. Blair, Oxford 1988, 67–82.

[43] D. Rollason and E. Cambridge, 'The Pastoral Organisation of the Anglo-Saxon Church: a Review of the "Minster Hypothesis" ', *Early Medieval Europe* iv (1), 1995, 87–104; cf. J. Blair, 'Ecclesiastical Organisation and Pastoral Care in Anglo-Saxon England', *Early Medieval Europe* iv (2), 193–212.

[44] D. Rollason, 'The Wanderings of St Cuthbert', in *Cuthbert: Saint and Patron*, ed. *idem*, Durham 1987, 45–61, at 50.

collaboration with Scandinavian leaders was possible; indeed, the support given by Archbishop Wulfstan to Olaf Sihtricson and Eric Bloodaxe seems to have been rather more than compromise born of fear.[45] The large corpus of so-called Anglo-Scandinavian stone-sculpture indicates that many churches were in use for burial through the period of Scandinavian settlement.[46] The survival of pre-viking buildings to their full height at Wearmouth and Jarrow does not suggest decades of abandonment.[47] The veneration of the cult of St Edmund (a martyr at the hands of a viking army) within the Danelaw by the early tenth century, and the late ninth- and early tenth-century coinage bearing the names of Christian saints, indicate a tolerance for, if not an actual promotion of, Christianity.[48] Archbishop Oda of Canterbury was apparently born of Danish parentage in the late ninth century and had become bishop of Wilton by 929; this may indicate that Christianity was thriving in the eastern Danelaw, as does the existence of numerous small religious foundations by the middle of the tenth century in that region.[49] A passage in the early twelfth-century *Libellus Æthelwoldi* states that at the time of the Scandinavian conquest there was a monastery at Horningsea (Cambs.) under a priest called Cenwold and 'later the people of the place who gathered together from paganism in the grace of baptism gave this minster five hides at Horningsea and two in Eye'. This, and the fact that Cenwold's successor was said to have been a follower of Athelstan, suggesting that he remained in post for many years, indicate, as Dorothy Whitelock put it, that 'there was thought to have been little, if any, breach of continuity at this church'.[50] The failure of any contemporary chronicler to mention the complete cessation of ecclesiastical life at any community, and the knowledge that in the case of Lindisfarne, for example, ecclesiastical life could survive an assault, also serve as reminders of how tenacious ecclesiastical communities could be.[51] Finally, there is a general absence of evidence for pagan practice.[52] This all provides a context for at least moderating traditional views concerning the disintegration of ecclesiastical organisation and for accepting that the widespread coincidence of pre-viking churches with later mother churches serving immense parishes is indeed suggestive of some level of continuity in ecclesiastical organisation.

However, it would be rash to press this evidence too far, and any argument for continuity has to be tempered. We cannot ignore the disruption to the dioceses of the region, or the loss of most of the early books and charters of the Danelaw.[53] The churches of the Danelaw tended to have very small landed endowments according

---

[45] *EHD* i, *s.a.* 943, 947–8; D. Whitelock, 'The Dealings of the Kings of England with Northumbria in the Tenth and Eleventh Centuries', in *Anglo-Saxon England*, ed. P. Clemoes, London 1959, 70–88, at 71–3.

[46] Below, 91–2.

[47] R. Cramp, 'Monastic Sites' in *The Archaeology of Anglo-Saxon England*, ed. D.M. Wilson, Cambridge 1976, 223–41.

[48] *Medieval European Coinage, i: The Early Middle Ages (5th–10th Centuries)*, ed. P. Grierson and M. Blackburn, Cambridge 1986, 319–23.

[49] Whitelock, 'The Conversion', 169–175.

[50] Whitelock, 'The Conversion', 169.

[51] D. Dumville, 'Ecclesiastical Lands and the Defence of Wessex in the First Viking Age' in his *Wessex and England from Alfred to Edgar*, Woodbridge 1992, 29–54, at 31–6.

[52] Whitelock, 'The Conversion', 159–64; see below, 89–91.

[53] Wormald, 'Whence and Whither', 137–41.

to Domesday Book, and few had sizeable communities.[54] We must also look beyond the Scandinavians for explanations of the fate of the Church between the ninth and eleventh centuries. There is some evidence to suggest that Northumbrian kings were seizing church lands in the ninth century,[55] and it has been argued that the kings of Wessex seized ecclesiastical land with which to endow their followers during the wars against the Scandinavians.[56] Furthermore, virtually nothing can be said about the exercise of pastoral care and the composition of ecclesiastical communities during the ninth and tenth centuries, and therefore any continuity in the structure of ecclesiastical organisation may have been accompanied by substantial transformations to individual communities. In sum, I would suggest that the ecclesiastical organisation of the Danelaw demonstrated great tenacity through the period of Scandinavian settlement, but this should not be allowed to obscure the evidence for disruption, not all of which should be attributed to the Scandinavian settlement.

Turning our attention to the estate structure of the region, a good case can be made for change in the tenth and early eleventh centuries. For example, the estates of Howden, Barrow-on-Humber, Barton-on-Humber (Lincs.), and Sutton-by-Retford (Notts.) had clearly gained members between the tenth century and 1086, and the archbishop of York's estates at Ripon, Otley and Sherburn lost members in the later tenth century.[57] Although it is common to explain the complex and interlocking pattern of estates as the product of the fragmentation of once larger estates, in some parts of the region such a supposition leads to the projection of estates that extend across almost the whole of a county.[58] This seems questionable. Rather, the complex spatial distribution of the Domesday estate structure, which was characterised by the intermingling of members of different estates, may be suggestive of both fragmentation of larger estates and amalgamation of lands. The fact that the estate structure and the parochial geography often do not coincide may also indicate change, as does the fact that some estates include dependencies which bear place-names incorporating personal names; it begs one to consider whether this is a sign of places which had formerly constituted separate estates.[59] A number of studies have noted that berewicks of Domesday estates tend to have Old English

---

[54] J. Blair, 'Secular Minster Churches in Domesday Book', in *Domesday Book: a Reassessment*, ed. P.H. Sawyer, London 1985, 104–42; R. Fleming, 'Monastic Lands and England's Defence in the Viking Age', *EHR* c, 1985, 247–65, at 249.

[55] *The Anglo-Saxons*, ed. Campbell, 135.

[56] Fleming, 'Monastic Lands'; Dumville, 'Ecclesiastical Lands'. For the history of ecclesiastical endowments in the later tenth and eleventh centuries see Blair, 'Secular Minster Churches', 118–19; Hadley, 'Ecclesiastical Organisation', 111–13; R. Fleming, 'Domesday Estates of the King and the Godwines: a Study in Late Saxon Politics', *Speculum* lviii, 1983, 987–1007.

[57] On Howden compare the charter of 959 (*Early Yorkshire Charters* i, ed. Farrer, 13–15) with the Domesday estate (*Domesday Book*, fo. 304c); on Barton and Barrow see D. Roffe, *Introduction to the Lincolnshire Domesday*, London 1992, 10; on Sutton see G.T. Davies, 'The Anglo-Saxon Boundaries of Sutton and Scrooby, Nottinghamshire', *Trans. of the Thoroton Society* lxxxvii, 1983, 13–22; on the archbishop's estates see *EHD* i, no. 114.

[58] For an example of estate projection taken to its extreme see M.W. Bishop, 'Multiple Estates in Late Anglo-Saxon Nottinghamshire', *Trans. of the Thoroton Society* lxxxv, 1982, 17–47; cf. Hadley, 'Multiple Estates', 5–6.

[59] Hadley, 'Multiple Estates', 5–8; cf. D. Roffe, 'Great Bowden and its Soke', in *Anglo-Saxon Landscapes in the East Midlands*, ed. J. Bourne, Leicester 1996, 107–20; Stenton, *Types of Manorial Structure*, 44–6.

place-names, whereas Scandinavian place-names tend to be associated with sokeland and separate manors.[60] This can be explained in the following ways. Berewicks are generally located closer to the manorial centre and the inhabitants of the berewicks tended to be more closely involved in the economy of the manor, being less free and owing labour services, whereas the inhabitants of sokeland tended to be the freer sokemen who owed few, if any, labour services, and are often located at great distances from the manor.[61] Some of the smaller manors of the Danelaw seem to have been the product of the fragmentation of larger estates; and there is evidence in Domesday Book to suggest that many such manors continued to be held on limited terms from a greater lord, and that as a result the survey sometimes found it difficult to determine what should be enrolled as a manor and what as sokeland.[62] The relationship of such holdings to major manorial centres may have been more fluid than that which bound berewicks to the corresponding manorial centre. This leads to the conclusion that land closely, and presumably continuously, associated with the manorial centre was unlikely to acquire a new name, whereas changes to the estate structure – the annexation of land to form separate manors, the imposition of a sub-tenant, or even the acquisition of new land – might lead to the coining of new place-names. Since this happened at a time when Scandinavian naming-elements were current, the proliferation of Scandinavian place-names ensued. In sum, whether or not one is swayed by the evidence for continuity through the period of Scandinavian control, it is clear that the ecclesiastical and estate structures of the Danelaw owed much to events of the *post-viking* period. What was once cited as evidence for the immediate Scandinavian impact should be seen rather in a wider context, as the product of periods of both continuity and continued evolution.

It is similarly difficult to sustain older arguments concerning the association of the Scandinavians with the peculiar social structure of the region. The debate about the free peasants of the Danelaw (*sochemanni* and *liberi homines*) hinges on the distribution of these peasants, who according to Domesday Book are largely limited to the east and north of England. Stenton's argument that this distinctive group within rural society were the descendants of the rank and file of the viking armies has received much criticism.[63] First, R.H.C. Davis observed a similarity between socage tenure, Kentish tenure by gavelkind and the tenure of the '*ceorl* who sits on *gafolland*' named in the treaty of Alfred and Guthrum.[64] All three forms of tenure appeared to have their origins in freehold land held under payment of tribute to the king. The significance of this association was that the '*ceorl* who sits on *gafolland*' existed before c.890, which means that, by analogy, socage tenure was not an innovation, and the necessity of explaining it, and by extension sokemen, by reference to the Scandinavians was removed. Secondly, to make any sense the

[60] Sawyer, *Kings and Vikings*, 106–7; Hadley, *Danelaw Society*, ch. vii.

[61] D. Roffe, 'The *Descriptio Terrarum* of Peterborough Abbey', *Historical Research* lxv, 1992, 1–16.

[62] D. Roffe, 'Domesday Book and Northern Society: a Reassessment', *EHR* cv, 1990, 310–36, at 330–1.

[63] F.M. Stenton, 'The Free Peasantry'; *idem*, 'The Danes', 145. This was in spite of the caution urged by Maitland in the immortal phrase 'we must be careful how we use our Dane'; F.W. Maitland, *Domesday Book and Beyond*, Cambridge 1897, 139.

[64] Davis, 'East Anglia', 33–5; cf. *The Kalendar of Abbot Samson of Bury St Edmunds*, ed. R.H.C. Davis, Camden 3rd ser. lxxxiv, 1954, xlv–xlvi.

connection between sokemen and Scandinavians requires large areas to have been depopulated or otherwise vacant, but it now seems unlikely that there were many areas devoid of settlement in the Danelaw on the eve of the Scandinavian settlement.[65] It is as plausible to believe that the free peasants were of Anglo-Saxon descent but that the Scandinavian settlement in some way either altered or preserved their status; we might do as well to ask what happened to the free peasants of the rest of Anglo-Saxon England.[66] To further this debate here would necessitate examining the nature of the Anglo-Saxon peasantry and the ways in which the structure of society changed through the later Anglo-Saxon centuries, and that is not possible within the confines of this paper. But it is notable that recent accounts of the peasantry of the Danelaw pay less attention to the Scandinavian influence than to factors such as forms of agrarian exploitation and the nature of the landscape.[67] The prevalence of free peasants in the Danelaw is also doubtless accounted for by the paucity of ecclesiastical estates, since ecclesiastical estate management had a great levelling effect on peasant status, and by the fragmented pattern of landholding, since it must have proved difficult to exploit dispersed estates intensively or to impose labour services on the peasant population of such estates.

Two final observations are pertinent at this juncture. Recent work by David Roffe has revealed the extent to which some of the complexities of the Danelaw counties presented by Domesday Book can be explained by reference to experiments in scribal practice, so we need to be wary of using the survey at face value as a straightforward guide to the peculiarities of the region.[68] Secondly, it is erroneous to treat the Domesday record as a guide to interpreting the Scandinavian impact without considering the developments in the region during the later tenth and earlier eleventh centuries. It may seem an obvious point, but so many assessments of the Scandinavians in England take the Domesday record as a major part of their evidence that it appears that this point can become somewhat obscured.

Ethnicity and Identity in the Danelaw

Many interpretations of the Scandinavian impact on Anglo-Saxon society have been informed by a fairly simplistic understanding of such matters as ethnicity and identity, which is further confused by the traditional correlation of numbers and impact. As always there are two extremes. At one extreme the Scandinavian element is believed to have overwhelmed native society and culture, and it has been further argued that the Danelaw was characterised by the presence of two distinct ethnic groups – Danish and English – and that they long continued to be recognisable groups within the region. Stenton spoke of 'two races in pre-Conquest England' and argued that 'all lines of investigation – linguistic, legal and economic – point to the reality of the difference between Danes and English in the

[65] P.H. Sawyer, *From Roman Britain to Norman England*, Oxford 1978, 132–67; Morris, 'Scandinavian Settlement', 13–15.

[66] *The Anglo-Saxons*, ed. Campbell, 164; Sawyer, *Age of the Vikings*, 2nd edn, 171.

[67] Stafford, *East Midlands*, 158–61; T. Williamson, *The Origins of Norfolk*, Manchester 1993, 94–5, 116–21.

[68] D. Roffe, 'Northern Society'.

tenth century'.[69] To Henry Loyn the Scandinavians were 'an important recognisable element' in the population and 'a distinct community living under separate laws'.[70] At the other extreme Julian Richards has seen fit to ask what it was about the viking character that meant that in some areas 'they disappeared', and Sawyer has stated that apart from their settlements and their influence on language, names and the terminology of law and administration 'the Scandinavians do not seem to have made a distinctive mark on England' – a fact which he associated with their lack of numbers.[71]

However, this correlation between numbers, impact and the ethnicity or identity of the Scandinavian settlers is too simplistic to be useful. Most statements about the ethnic composition of the Danelaw were written within an older historical tradition and do not stand up to comparison with more recent studies of ethnicity and identity in the early medieval period.[72] It was a feature of earlier writing on the early middle ages to assume that national and ethnic groups were internally homogeneous, historically continuous entities that could be objectively defined by their cultural, linguistic and racial distinctiveness, and that such groups manifested themselves in the archaeological record in the form of sharply delineated distributions of artefacts.[73] Such views have, however, been subject to extensive critical reappraisal. We would not now define ethnicity as a concrete or objective fact, but rather as a subjective process by which individuals and groups identified themselves and others within specific structures and circumstances such as contact with external forces, a developing awareness of common interests and competition for access to resources. Ethnic identity was not static but rather dynamic, situational and heterogeneous, and as such one should neither expect nor predict a simple one-to-one correlation between ethnic groups and language, culture and religion, artefacts and racial characteristics. We must question, if not reject, the definition of an ethnic group as being characterised by a distinct language, culture, territory or religion (they may be, of course, but these characteristics are not *necessary*) but rather as a community bound together primarily by a shared and subjective sense

---

[69] Stenton, 'The Danes', 41, 46. It has also often been claimed that there was a clear distinction between Danes and Norwegians; A. Mawer, 'Redemption of the Five Boroughs', *EHR* xxxviii, 1926, 551–7; Stenton, *Anglo-Saxon England*, 358–9.

[70] H. Loyn, *The Vikings in Britain*, London 1977, 113.

[71] J. Richards, *Viking Age England*, London 1991, 9; Sawyer, *Age of the Vikings*, 2nd edn, 172–3.

[72] There is a vast literature on this subject: R. Wenskus, *Stammesbildung und Verfassung*, Cologne 1961; P. Geary, 'Ethnic Identity as a Situational Construct in the Early Middle Ages', *Mitteilungen der anthropologischen Gesellschaft in Wien* cxiii, 1983, 15–26; *Theories of Race and Ethnic Relations*, ed. J. Rex and D. Mason, Cambridge 1986; H. Wolfram, 'Einleitung oder Uberlegungen zur Origo Gentis', in *Typen der Ethnogenese unter besonderer Berucksichtigung der Bayern*, ed. H. Wolfram and W. Pohl, I, Vienna 1990. P. Amory, 'Names, Ethnic Identity and Community in Fifth- and Sixth-Century Burgundy', *Viator* xxv, 1994, 1–30; *idem*, 'The Meaning and Purpose of Ethnic Terminology in the Burgundian Laws', *Early Medieval Europe* ii (1), 1993, 1–28; S. Reynolds, 'What do we mean by "Anglo-Saxon" and "Anglo-Saxons"?', *Journal of British Studies* xxiv, 1985, 395–414; S. Shennan, 'Introduction' in *Archaeological Approaches to Cultural Identity*, ed. S. Shennan, London 1989, 1–32; most recently see the various contributions to *Cultural Identity and Archaeology*, ed. P. Graves-Brown, S. Jones and C. Gamble, London 1996.

[73] Shennan, 'Introduction'; S. Jones and P. Graves-Brown, 'Introduction: Archaeology and Cultural Identity in Europe', in *Cultural Identity*, ed. Graves-Brown, Jones and Gamble, 1–24; S. Jones, 'Discourses of Identity in the Interpretation of the Past', in *ibid.*, 62–80.

of common interests *vis-à-vis* others.[74] Furthermore, greater attention has been paid recently to the self-identification of peoples and to their behaviour rather than to the labels imposed by external commentators which it is now recognised are not necessarily identical.[75] Nothing here is, of course, new; these ideas have been applied to many regions of early medieval Europe. But the Scandinavian settlement of Anglo-Saxon England has not been systematically reconsidered in this light. Such reconsideration proves instructive, not least because we are forced to reconsider the appropriateness of the questions we have hitherto asked of our evidence: we cannot continue to ask whether this or that site is 'Scandinavian' or 'native', or to use place-name evidence to plot the locations and movements of peoples, or to argue over whether this or that feature of the society and culture of the Danelaw is Scandinavian without re-examining the nature of 'ethnicity' and identities and adopting a more complex perspective on the ways in which peoples interacted.

We must begin by considering the behaviour of the Scandinavians in England once they began to settle and the ways in which they were perceived. One of the main regions of Scandinavian settlement – in eastern and north-eastern England – subsequently came to be known as the Danelaw. It is difficult to be sure what the Danelaw was, but, especially in the late ninth and early tenth centuries, there are good reasons to question the traditional emphasis placed on 'ethnic' factors. There is, I would suggest, in spite of traditional interpretations, no good evidence that the Scandinavians who settled in what became known as the Danelaw retained a 'Danish' or a 'Norwegian' ethnic consciousness or that there was a clear cultural division between, on the one hand, 'Danes' and 'Norwegians' and, on the other, 'Anglo-Saxons'. Nor is this an issue that hinges on numbers. It is difficult to argue from the documentary evidence that the Scandinavian settlers were perceived as, or long remained, a distinctive group within the Danelaw, or that the characteristics of the Danelaw, although undoubtedly owing much to Scandinavian influence, can only be understood by positing such a distinction.[76] The first problem, as is well known, is that it is anachronistic to use the term 'Danelaw' when describing the events of the late ninth and earlier tenth centuries; the term is first used in a law-code compiled in 1008, and in legal codes of the eleventh and twelfth centuries to distinguish a region in which Danish as opposed to Mercian or West Saxon law was thought to prevail.[77] The idea of the Danelaw was developed by twelfth-century jurists, who when recording regional differences tended to associate them with Danish influence. This, as Pauline Stafford has observed, may have resulted from no more than a recognition that certain regional differences coincided with an area known to have once been under some form of Danish control.[78] In fact, it is not now thought that the law of the region was entirely or even largely of Scandinavian creation, but rather that it exhibited a Scandinavian influence which may have been largely terminological; many of its supposed legal peculiarities can, in

---

74 Jones, 'Discourses'.
75 Amory, 'Ethnic Terminology'.
76 Reynolds, 406–12.
77 D. Whitelock, *History, Laws and Literature in 10th–11th Century England*, London 1981, xiii–iv, 23–4, 72–85; *The Laws of the Kings of England from Edmund to Henry I*, ed. A.J. Robertson, Cambridge 1925, 2.2, 2.3, 3.3, 17.1, 21.2, 21.4, 39.2, 42.2.
78 Stafford, 'The Danes', 19.

fact, be paralleled elsewhere.[79] Certainly, the 'Danelaw' was identified as a separate unit and from the mid-tenth century the region was legislated for separately, but the employment of ethnic terminology to identify these differences cannot be taken as a guide to the racial or ethnic composition of the region, either real or perceived. Patrick Amory's work on similar issues on the continent between the fifth and the ninth centuries is worth citing. He has observed that ethnic labels were often applied inconsistently and came to be used as territorial identifiers, and that increasingly ethnicity was defined by territorial origin and adherence to a particular law-code rather than by blood or descent alone; he has commented that 'law was not so much a result as the major determining factor' of the new ethnic identities forged in the Carolingian period.[80]

It is not certain where the concept of the 'Danelaw' originated: whether it was generated by the inhabitants of those regions to which the label was applied or whether it was formulated externally. But it is difficult to envisage the inhabitants of the 'Danelaw' having a long-lasting and coherent sense of a regional or ethnic identity – not least because the Danelaw was not seemingly a fixed area. The extent of the region known as the Danelaw varied throughout the eleventh and twelfth centuries, and it is unknown what, if anything, constituted the 'Danelaw' before then.[81] There is little to suggest that at an earlier date anyone thought of the region as being composed of a distinctively Danish population. Certainly Edgar legislated (962x963) that 'there should be in force among the Danes such good laws as they best decide on' and there are a number of references in the Anglo-Saxon Chronicle to 'Danes' in England but these references have little to reveal about the numbers of people of Danish descent in England. Such references to Danes from the mid-tenth through to the eleventh century are now assumed to refer to recent arrivals – to the Danish merchants and nobles who arrived from the mid-tenth century, for example – rather than to the descendants of Danish immigrants of the late ninth century. To the chroniclers the subjects of the kings of England were, in fact, considered to have been English; Danes were invaders, and enemies – as Reynolds has put it, 'recent Danes' – people who had come recently from Denmark and who might be going back there, rather than the descendants of earlier hordes of immigrants.[82] The argument that the descendants of the Danish settlers of the late ninth century did not continue to be regarded as such does not depend on decisions about the scale of Scandinavian immigration. Indeed, most of our evidence concerning the 'Danelaw' reveals nothing about the numbers of settlers and it is unhelpful to use the existence of the Danelaw in this context. The extent of the Scandinavian influence on law has little to tell us about the numbers of Scandinavians who settled; this is one aspect of Danelaw society in which it is reasonable to suppose that a small number of Scandinavian rulers might have a disproportionate effect.

It is also worth noting that the term 'Danelaw' is much less frequently used to describe the area than many modern accounts imply – geographical terms or shire names are more common. It may, as Reynolds has commented, suggest that the

---

[79] O. Fenger, 'The Danelaw and the Danish Law', *Scandinavian Studies in Law* xvi, 1972, 85–96; Kaye, 'The Sacrabar'; Sawyer, *Age of the Vikings*, 2nd edn, 153–4; Stafford, 'The Danes', 19.
[80] Amory, 'Ethnic Terminology', 23.
[81] H.M. Chadwick, *Studies on Anglo-Saxon Institutions*, Cambridge 1905, 198–201.
[82] Reynolds, 409.

Danishness of such areas was not their most obvious characteristic.[83] Stafford has also commented on the absence of what she calls 'an ethnic voice' in the disputes of the later tenth century; regional grievances seem to be more prominent.[84] Although 'ethnic' differences have been seen behind the activities of Swegn (who in 1013 acquired the submission of England north of Watling Street before ravaging southwards),[85] and ethnic loyalties have been sought as an explanation for the conflicts of Edward the Confessor's reign[86] and for the allegedly incomplete unity of England in 1066,[87] it is difficult to sustain these old notions. It is hard to envisage that Scandinavian settlers, however many there were, could have maintained a completely separate identity for almost two centuries. In practice, social mixing and inter-marriage make it probable that it would soon have been difficult to distinguish people of exclusively English or Danish descent. Thus, my first major observation concerning the construction of ethnic identity in the Danelaw is that the mere existence of the 'Danelaw' is not a very sound basis for any argument concerning the ethnic affiliations of the inhabitants of the regions which were thus known. I would not wish to claim that no one in the Danelaw ever felt themselves to be 'English' or 'Danish'. Nevertheless, it is important to stress that the evidence we have for such feelings is less substantive than is sometimes supposed.[88]

My second point about the ethnic identity of the peoples of the Danelaw concerns the question of whether the Scandinavians who came to England arrived with a common sense of identity. It is unlikely that even the smaller war-bands were composed exclusively of people who thought of themselves as Danes, or of people from the same region. The few well-known viking leaders operated all over the place and their war bands are likely to have been ethnically mixed; their ability to attract allies and followers from the regions they raided is well-known,[89] as is their capacity to change sides in a conflict: 'the vikings were not united against anything or anybody, and were as pleased to fight other vikings as they were to fight Christians or Muslims if the prospects of booty were good'.[90] The fact that the Danish territories did not yet constitute a consolidated kingdom does not, in itself, preclude the possibility that those who came to England developed some sense of group solidarity; it is precisely when peoples come into contact with other peoples that they begin to forge such common identities. Certainly, the creation of a great army in the 860s which seems to have drawn together a multiplicity of viking leaders and their war bands created a common purpose, and one which was seemingly maintained despite the departure of particular leaders along with part of

---

[83] Reynolds, 408.

[84] Stafford, 'The Reign of Æthelred II: a Study in the Limitations on Royal Policy', in *Ethelred the Unready*, ed. D. Hill, Oxford 1978, 17–21.

[85] D. Whitelock, introduction to *EHD* i, 48; W.E. Kapelle, *The Norman Conquest of the North*, London 1979, 14–15; Stenton, *Anglo-Saxon England*, 384–5; Reynolds, 410–11; cf. the remarks of P. Stafford, *Unification and Conquest*, London 1989, 65–6.

[86] F. Barlow, *Edward the Confessor*, London 1970, 89, 92–3, 102, 191–2; Kapelle, *The Norman Conquest of the North*, 28–9, 47.

[87] Kapelle, 12–15; R.A. Brown, 'The Norman Conquest', *TRHS*, 5th ser. xvii, 1967, 109–10, 116–20; cf. Reynolds, 406–7.

[88] Reynolds, 411.

[89] N. Lund, 'Allies of God or Man? The Viking Expansion in a European Context', *Viator* xix, 1989, 45–59.

[90] Lund, 'Viking Expansion', 47.

the army.[91] However, it is arguable that the ultimate origin of viking leaders and their followers became irrelevant after settlement began and feelings of ethnic identity and military solidarity were overlaid by those of political solidarity. The way in which the Anglo-Saxon Chronicle describes the West Saxon conquest of the Danelaw may be deceptive in this respect; it repeatedly involved defeating the armies of burhs and it has often been supposed that these must correspond to divisions of the great army and that the Scandinavian settlers kept their military formation, and hence their separate identity.[92] However, it is not certain that this was the case; the burghal groupings could as easily be re-groupings in the face of West Saxon expansionism, in which case they are as likely to have been manned by the local populations, whether of East Anglia, parts of Mercia or Northumbria who were unlikely to have been any more well-disposed towards rule by a southern king than were the Scandinavian settlers. Such a division between conquerors and conquered would have been difficult to maintain once settlement began, and I would suggest that, although there may have been many who recognised themselves as being of Scandinavian or native descent, by the fourth and fifth decades of the tenth century – some sixty to seventy years after the initial Scandinavian settlement – there were doubtless many who were unable to say so clearly where their ancestry lay. By that time the notionally divergent interests of the native population and the Scandinavian settlers must have been thrown into confusion by subsequent conquest of the region by the kings of Wessex and of Dublin. Given the political context, and the fact that links were seemingly not maintained with Scandinavia, it is difficult to envisage a separate Scandinavian identity being long sustained, certainly among the leaders of the Scandinavian settlers. If the situation after the Norman Conquest is in any way comparable we can see that it was the great lords who maintained strong links with Normandy who retained their Norman identity longest: lesser men with little or no property in Normandy quickly became known as 'English'.[93] Further, it has been suggested that a truly united nation of English and Normans was forged in the context of a conscious sense of difference from the other inhabitants of Britain.[94] These observations are, once again, not prejudiced by the numbers of Scandinavian settlers, and it does not help to confuse the numerical issue with that of the common identities formed in the region.

The emphasis on the supposed 'particularism of the Danes' tends to treat them as an undifferentiated mass;[95] but there is no good reason to assume that the Scandinavian leaders – men such as Ivarr, Halfdan, Guthrum, Guthfrith or Ragnald – felt a greater affinity with the peasant hordes who apparently followed them, simply because they spoke the same language or came from the same region. Men like these are likely to have behaved in the same way as other leaders of the Middle Ages: they created a basis of support for themselves which involved rewarding followers, and which cannot easily be said to have been limited to pan-Scandinavian interests. For example, Ragnald granted estates in the North not only to his own

---

[91] Brooks, 8–11.
[92] Stenton, 'The Danes', 5–7.
[93] A. Williams, *The English and the Norman Conquest*, Woodbridge 1995, 1–6, 187–219.
[94] J. Gillingham, 'Conquering the Barbarians: War and Chivalry in Twelfth-Century Britain', *Haskins Society Journal* iv, 1992, 67–84; Williams, 5–6.
[95] Stenton, 'The Danes', 46.

followers but also to native lords, and the basis of the authority of Guthfrith as king of one group of vikings was the support lent to him by the community of St Cuthbert.[96] Landed estates, administrative units, strongholds, and trading centres were manipulated by the elites of whatever origin, and so were peasants, whether native or from Scandinavia. There is no necessary reason why one group should have been treated differently from the other, or that they should have long remained distinguishable. The power base of rulers in the Danelaw depended on commanding the support of, or subjugating, other powerful figures and little to do with marshalling the support of peasants. Admittedly, for the peasantry themselves issues of identity may have been rather different. Primarily their identities would have been forged within the communities and estates within which they lived and worked. Native peasants may well have reacted unfavourably to newcomers, although we will never know the details. If any case can be made for the existence of separate ethnic identities in the Danelaw it is at that level; but this is to pose another irresolvable problem. A more important observation to offer in summary is that it is the belief in a mass invasion that has formed the basis for the argument that there was a distinctive Danish identity in parts of Anglo-Saxon England, yet the documentary evidence does not readily support the idea of either a mass invasion or of a distinctive Danish ethnic identity. Neither can we uphold older views about the Scandinavian nature of the society and institutions of the Danelaw, which was another form of evidence traditionally used to support the argument for a mass invasion. Those distinctive aspects of the regions settled by Scandinavians owe their form to the activities of the elite; and as such they should be kept separate from the discussion concerning the density of the settlement.

My third observation about ethnic identity in the Danelaw is that although the linguistic impact of the Scandinavians who settled in England was undoubtedly great, and this may well be indicative of great numbers of people who spoke Old Norse languages, it cannot be demonstrated from this evidence alone that they retained any separate ethnic consciousness. Admittedly, the fact that people spoke different languages would initially have made them distinctive from one another; but the simple correlation between language, on the one hand, and ethnic or cultural identity, on the other, does not pay sufficient regard to the logistics of conquest and settlement and to the needs of the newcomers to form a *modus vivendi* with the native population. No matter how many Scandinavians there were, they were still in the minority, and in such circumstances it is difficult to imagine, and is indeed unlikely, that they maintained a separate existence which was not in any way reliant on interaction with the native population. As Scandinavian leaders took over estates and had them cultivated they must have relied on native labour, and perhaps also native estate administrators. It is, in any case, not clear how long the Scandinavian languages remained in active use in England; Old English did remain the dominant language even if much was borrowed from the languages of the newcomers.[97] Personal names are no reliable guide to descent, still less of ethnic consciousness or of cultural characteristics; the very fact that, at a later date, the same family might have members some of whom bore Old English names and

---

96 Morris, 'Northumbria and the Viking Settlement', 83–4.
97 R.I. Page, 'How Long did the Scandinavian Language Survive in England? The Epigraphical Evidence', in *England before the Conquest*, ed. Clemoes and Hughes, 165–80.

others Scandinavian names urges caution.[98] A more interesting line of enquiry would be to consider why native families began to employ the personal names of the newcomers; a similar situation obtained after the Norman Conquest and one can but conclude that, as well as simply starting a new fashion in nomenclature, these conquests encouraged people to align themselves or, strictly, their children, self-consciously with their new overlords.[99] Naming processes may have more to reveal about class and professional allegiances than ethnic identities.[100]

Fourthly, there is the question of the paganism of the vikings: to what extent and for how long did this distinguish them from the indigenous population? It is well-known that viking armies commonly found allies among the peoples they were raiding; their paganism did not prevent alliance with lay lords or even ecclesiastics.[101] Certainly, the latter may have preferred to deal with Christians and alliance between pagan vikings and Christians often led to baptism into the Christian faith; but ultimately the importance of the alliance lay in the advantages that viking leaders and their followers could offer, which was commonly to add their weight to one side in some power struggle. Paganism was, hence, not an insurmountable obstacle to interaction between vikings and natives. There is some evidence from the Danelaw that has been used to identify a level of active paganism: a number of burials accompanied by grave-goods have been discovered which have been cited as examples of 'pagan' burial practice; and the clearly secular motifs on the monumental sculpture of the region, including depictions of armed warriors and scenes from pagan mythology, have also sometimes been identified as further evidence for pagan practice. However, this evidence is ambiguous. Many of the accompanied burials were located within Christian churchyards, and there are, in any case, very few identified examples. Accompanied Viking Age burials have been discovered at less than thirty sites in northern and eastern England; and at some of these sites a pagan viking burial has been inferred only on the basis of the discovery of artefacts in Christian cemeteries.[102] Perhaps there were many more examples of accompanied burials which have not been discovered precisely because they were located at sites which continued to be used for burial afterwards. This burial evidence, especially its dearth, has given rise to various interpretations: the rapid conversion of the Scandinavian settlers; proof that there were, after all, few Scandinavian settlers; the use of pre-existing burial grounds by settlers who had yet to renounce paganism; the acceptance of Christianity which,

---

98 F.M. Stenton, *Documents Illustrative of the Social and Economic History of the Danelaw*, British Academy 1920, cxiv–xv; O. von Feilitzen, *The Pre-Conquest Personal Names of Domesday Book*, Uppsala 1937, 18–26; E. Ekwall, 'The Proportion of Scandinavian Settlers in the Danelaw', *Saga-Book of the Viking Society* xii, 1937–45, 19–34; Davis, 'East Anglia', 29; D. Whitelock, 'Scandinavian Personal Names in the *Liber Vitae* of Thorney Abbey', *Saga-Book of the Viking Society* xii, 1937–45, 127–53; G. Fellows Jensen, *Scandinavian Personal Names in Lincolnshire and Yorkshire*, Copenhagen 1968.

99 C. Clark, 'Clark's First Three Laws of Applied Anthroponymics', *Nomina* iii, 1979, 13–19; Williams, 206–7.

100 Amory, 'Names', 3.

101 Lund, 'Viking Expansion', 50–1.

102 At Brigham (Cumbria) a Viking burial has been identified on the basis of the discovery of a ring-headed cloak-pin in the churchyard, and at Heysham (Lancs.) a similar deduction was drawn from the discovery of a weapon in the churchyard: Richards, 111; cf. Wilson, 'Scandinavians in England', 396–7.

however, entailed a reluctance to give up traditional burial practices; or syncretistic practice.[103] Any, or all, of these interpretations may be valid in particular instances; however, there are a number of additional observations that should be made. It is dangerous to deduce religious belief, as much as 'ethnic' origin, on the basis of burial practice alone. The problem concerning viking burial is reminiscent of the debate about Anglo-Saxon burial in the post-Conversion period; studies of the earlier period have become cautious in their interpretations of burial evidence, and the recent recognition that clothed-burial, of which small knives and buckles are the visible remnants, was a feature of the burial practice of the mid to late Anglo-Saxon period, serves to remind us that the association of grave items with paganism is simplistic.[104] It is also worth noting that not all regions of Scandinavia were characterised during the Viking Age by accompanied burials; therefore, not all the Scandinavian settlers necessarily arrived in England with a tradition of accompanied burial.[105]

Burial customs may have been slower to respond to Christian influence than other aspects of personal behaviour, especially if the Church concentrated its efforts on securing baptism – a process which is less archaeologically visible than burial practices.[106] Whatever the personal beliefs and practices of the Scandinavians who settled in England, and whatever the speed and readiness with which they converted to Christianity and transformed their personal beliefs and practices to conform to Christian ideals (and there may have been a marked difference in the response of Scandinavian rulers and any peasant immigrants who followed in their wake), it is undeniable that at a very early date the leaders underwent a process of Christianisation and were prepared to work with and accept the guidance of ecclesiastics. We might think here again of the mutually beneficial relationship between successive archbishops and viking leaders at York, the promotion of the interests of the viking Guthfrith by the community of St Cuthbert, and the readiness with which Scandinavian rulers issued coinage in their name, which also bore the names

103 J. Graham-Campbell, 'The Scandinavian Viking-Age Burials of England: Some Problems of Interpretation', in *Anglo-Saxon Cemeteries*, ed. P. Rahtz, BAR Brit. Series, Oxford 1980, 379–82; M. Biddle and B. Kjolbye-Biddle, *Repton 1986: an Interim Report*, Repton 1986; M. Biddle, 'A Parcel of Pennies from a Mass-Burial associated with the Viking Wintering at Repton in 873–4', *British Numismatic Journal* lvi, 1986, 25–30; Wilson, 'Scandinavians in England'; *idem*, 'Scandinavian Settlement'; J. Graham-Campbell, 'Pagans and Christians', *History Today* xxxvi, 1986, 24–8; M. Biddle and B. Kjolbye-Biddle, 'Repton and the Vikings', *Antiquity* lxvi, 1990, 36–51; R. Hodges, *The Anglo-Saxon Achievement*, London 1989, 153–4.
104 J. Blair, *Anglo-Saxon Oxfordshire*, Stroud 1994, 70–3; cf. D.M. Hadley, 'The Historical Context of the Inhumation Cemetery at Bromfield, Shropshire', *Transactions of the Shropshire Archaeological and Historical Society* lxx, 1995, 146–55.
105 E. Roesdahl, 'The Archaeological Evidence for Conversion', in *The Christianisation of Scandinavia*, ed. P. Sawyer, B. Sawyer and I. Wood, Alingsas 1987, 2–3.
106 If the Anglo-Saxon Church had attempted to suppress the burial of artefacts then it is surprising that this is not mentioned in contemporary or later accounts of the early Church in England: D. Bullough, 'Burial, Community and Belief in the Early Medieval West', in *Ideal and Reality in Frankish and Anglo-Saxon Society*, ed. P. Wormald *et al.*, Oxford 1983, 177–201, at 185–6. The gradual decline in grave-goods has been noted at Shudy Camps (Cambs.) and Winnall II (Hants); A. Boddington, 'Models of Burial, Settlement and Worship: the Final Phase Reviewed', in *Anglo-Saxon Cemeteries: a Reappraisal*, ed. E. Southworth, London 1990, 177–99; A. Meaney and S.C. Hawkes, *Two Anglo-Saxon Cemeteries at Winnall, Winchester, Hampshire*, Society for Medieval Archaeology, Monograph 4, 1970, 50.

of Christian saints.[107] This distinction between private conversion and public Christianisation is important in explaining the apparently contradictory nature of the documentary and archaeological evidence. Evidence from Scandinavia following the Christianisation of those lands indicates that the reception of Christianity was not even. Churchyard burials, burials with grave-goods and votive offerings in rivers have been discovered in the same locality, and they are believed to be contemporaneous; it suggests that different groups of people – even within the same village – responded to Christianity in different ways and that burial practices did not change uniformly.[108] This also serves as a reminder that the burial evidence should not be used too readily to represent paganism in general; it was the product of a particular context, that of transition from one form of religious expression to another, which involved a concomitant transition in behaviour and social structure. In such a context it would not be surprising to find that Scandinavian newcomers to England concerned themselves with a variety of burial practices.

The sculptural evidence has also given rise to much debate, not least because even where it makes explicit reference to pagan symbols it very clearly belongs to a Christian milieu. Stone sculpture production was an ecclesiastical preserve in England, but little known in Scandinavia, and most examples of the so-called Anglo-Scandinavian sculpture are located in and around Christian churches. Other factors complicate our interpretation of this sculptural evidence: for example, it is not known who produced or patronised this art form, but it is found in some locations which were continuously associated with surviving native lords or religious communities, at York and Chester-le-Street, for example, so the Scandinavian stylistic influence cannot be attributed solely to Scandinavian patrons.[109] In any case, the overtly pagan symbols – such as the heroic scenes involving Sigurd and Weland on sculptural fragments from Lancashire and Yorkshire[110] – are found on only a small percentage of the total corpus of Anglo-Scandinavian sculpture, and are depicted alongside Christian iconography.[111] Recent attempts to establish a chronology for this sculpture have tended to suggest that it can be assigned to a much shorter period of production than was allowed for by older chronologies which attempted to identify steadily evolving processes of production spread over a much wider time-span. The recognition that the same workshop could produce radically different designs and that late viking styles (Mammen or Ringerike) are not represented has resulted in the ascription of most Anglo-Scandinavian sculpture to the late ninth or early tenth century.[112] The sculptural evidence can be

---

[107] *Medieval European Coinage*, ed. Grierson and Blackburn, 319–23.

[108] L. Ersgard, 'The Change of Religion and its Artefacts: an Example from Upper Dalarna', *Papers of the Archaeological Institute* ns x, University of Lund 1993–94, 79–94; I. Wood, 'Christians and Pagans in Ninth-Century Scandinavia', in *The Christianization of Scandinavia* (as n. 105), 36–67.

[109] R. Cramp, 'The Pre-Conquest Sculptural Tradition in Durham', *Medieval Art and Architecture at Durham Cathedral*, Transactions of the British Archaeological Association, 1980, 1–10; J. Lang, 'Recent Studies in the Pre-Conquest Sculpture of Northumbria' in *Studies in Medieval Sculpture*, ed. F.H. Thompson, London 1983, 177–89; R.N. Bailey, *Viking Age Sculpture in Northern England*, London 1980.

[110] J. Lang, 'Sigurd and Weland in Pre-Conquest Carving From Northern England', *Yorkshire Archaeological Journal* xlviii, 1976, 83–94; cf. *idem*, 'Illustrative Carving of the Viking Period at Sockburn on Tees', *Archaeologia Aeliana*, 4th ser. i, 1972, 235–48.

[111] Lang, 'Pre-Conquest Sculpture', 187.

[112] Lang, 'Pre-Conquest Sculpture', 185–6.

interpreted in a similar vein to the burial evidence; it was the product of a period in which peoples with different belief systems came into contact with each other, and represents the fusion of Scandinavian style and a native tradition, rather than the 'overwhelming of one by the other'.[113] Whatever else the Scandinavians perpetrated they did not destroy this native form of artistic and cultural expression; as Richard Bailey has remarked, 'stone carving did not just continue into the viking period but was *enthusiastically* taken up' both at existing centres of production and at new locations.[114]

I have already stated the case for continuity in ecclesiastical organisation through the period of Scandinavian settlement, and the burial evidence, sculpture and coinage could be interpreted as proof of the success of the ecclesiastical network and its provisions for pastoral care in accommodating the settlement of pagan Scandinavians. It seems fair to conclude that both the Christian Church and the Scandinavian settlers adapted themselves to each other, apparently relatively rapidly, although there may have been regional and class differences in this response. It should not be supposed that the transition from 'paganism' to Christianity was swift, and the evidence we have suggests an on-going period of adaptation and transition. In any case, paganism is not an easily definable belief-system, and there is much to debate over what it was to be a Christian in the ninth century: we may have been too hasty to draw a clear distinction between paganism and Christianity.[115] Christianity may, in the long run, have been less a factor which distinguished the native population from the Scandinavian settlers, than a force for their integration.

My final point about Scandinavian identity in the Danelaw concerns the issue of whether we can see in the material culture of the region any evidence for the Scandinavian settlers establishing or retaining a separate cultural identity in the Danelaw. The excavation of settlements provides us with little to go on. Despite extensive excavations at both urban and rural sites – such as York, Thetford (Norfolk), Ribblehead (Yorks.), Simy Folds (Co. Durham) – which have been dated to the later ninth or early tenth century, little has been discovered that can be said to have been especially Scandinavian, and even if it had it would be quite another matter to argue that the possessors of such artefacts were of Scandinavian extraction.[116] The search for 'typically Scandinavian' monuments has recently been labelled as a 'wild goose chase', and we ought to remember that any attempt to identify Scandinavian settlements has to explain how they fitted into the surrounding countryside; settlements, whether rural or urban, did not exist in isolation.[117] In recent years large amounts of metalwork incorporating Scandinavian motifs have

---

113 Morris, 'Viking and Native', 233.

114 Bailey, *Viking Age Sculpture*, 81.

115 Wood, 52–3.

116 A. King, 'Gauber High Pasture, Ribblehead', in *Viking Age York*, ed. Hall, 21–5; D. Coggins *et al.*, 'Simy Folds: an Early Medieval Settlement Site in Upper Teesdale', *Medieval Archaeology* xxvii, 1983, 1–26; S. Dickinson, 'Bryant's Gill, Kentmere: Another "Viking Period" Ribblehead?' in *The Scandinavians in Cumbria*, ed. J. Baldwin and I. White, Edinburgh 1985, 83–8; B.K. Davison, 'The Late Saxon Town of Thetford: an Interim Report on the 1964–6 Excavations', *Medieval Archaeology* xi, 1967, 189–207; R.A. Hall, *Viking Age York*, London 1994.

117 J. Bradley, 'The Interpretation of Scandinavian Settlement in Ireland', in *Settlement and Society in Medieval Ireland*, ed. J. Bradley, Kilkenny 1988, 49–78, at 60.

apparently been uncovered, especially through the use of metal detectors.[118] Until these finds are more widely available for inspection it is difficult to comment on the significance of their stylistic form and distribution; they may have much to reveal about aristocratic taste and it would be pertinent to investigate the extent to which there was an inter-mixing of Scandinavian and native motifs, as on the stone sculpture of the region, and the extent to which its distribution coincides with that of the sculpture.[119]

Towards a Solution

To sum up thus far. It is difficult to uphold traditional ideas concerning the long-term binary division of society into Scandinavian and English in the regions in which Scandinavians settled. Nor is it easy to identify very much about the society of those regions that can be said to have been especially Scandinavian. The ethnicity paradigm is not only difficult to maintain (and generally used in an outdated manner), but it tends to divert our attentions from what the native popula- tions and the newcomers had in common, and how they proceeded to forge a *modus vivendi*. Furthermore, many assessments of the impact of the Scandinavian settlement have regarded the numerical question, the distinctiveness of the region and the level of continuity as being directly related to each other. So often discus- sions of the latter have been used to uphold inferences about the former; but as I have demonstrated, neither the distinctiveness of the society and institutions of the region nor the degree of continuity can be used as an index of the numbers of Scandinavians who came to England. To cite Niels Lund, 'it is misleading to arrange "numbers", "influence" and "permanent effects" co-ordinately: the lat- ter two are the premises, the first is the conclusion drawn from these'.[120] Such an equation overlooks the fact that estate structures, the ecclesiastical network, trading networks, the legal and administrative structure and most of the documentary evidence is only indicative of the activities and the practices of the elites of the region. For the activities of the masses only the linguistic evidence – given the present state of the archaeological record – has much to offer. Furthermore, tradi- tional correlations between numbers and effects have often had little to say about the probability that both pre-viking variations and developments in the period following the West Saxon conquest of the region must also have played a part in creating the society of northern and eastern England.

For much of this paper I have argued that a major dynamic in the history of the regions settled by the Scandinavians was the integration of the Scandinavian settlers into native society, and the adaptation of Scandinavians and natives to each other's way of life. This requires further justification. In spite of the fact that they

---

[118] R.A. Hall, 'Vikings Gone West? A Summary Review', in *Developments around the Baltic and the North Sea in the Viking Age*, ed. B. Ambrosiani and H. Clarke, Stockholm 1994, 32–49, at 38.

[119] For published information on the metalwork see R. Bailey, 'An Anglo-Saxon Strap-End from Wooperton', *Archaeologia Aeliana*, 5th ser. xxi, 1993, 87–91; D. Haldenby, 'An Anglian Site on the Yorkshire Wolds', *Yorkshire Archaeological Journal* lxii, 1990, 51–62; *idem*, 'An Anglian Site on the Yorkshire Wolds', *Yorkshire Archaeological Journal* lxiv, 1992, 25–40; M. Beresford and J. Hurst, *Wharram Percy Deserted Medieval Village*, London 1990.

[120] Lund, 'The Settlers', 167.

came as pagans, from a non-monetary economy, with no extensive tradition of stone-sculpture production, it is striking how quickly the Scandinavian leaders came to forge alliances with ecclesiastics, to issue coinage and to influence the iconography of stone sculpture. Along with the evidence to suggest that they took over estates as going concerns and the indications of some basic level of continuity in the secular and ecclesiastical institutions of the region, this indicates that the Scandinavian rulers quickly came to terms with existing media in exercising control in the regions where they settled. Furthermore, our evidence reveals to us something of the on-going processes of adaptation. To take as an example the stone sculpture with its mixture of traditional Christian motifs, Scandinavian ornamentation, secular figures and pagan scenes: it represents either the patronage of a Scandinavian lord trying to record his presence and to legitimate his authority by establishing links with the past and with native traditions; or it was the product of native patronage, by a lord seeking to express newly formed allegiances, and perhaps to understand something of the society of the newcomers; or perhaps it was encouraged by someone whose origins were less certain but who was aware that his existence was something to do with the arrival at an earlier date of Scandinavian settlers. All three influences doubtless played a part in forging the material culture and society of the region; the stone sculpture, as much as the coinage, changes to the corpus of personal- and place-names, or the adoption of particular burial practices, were a product of their time, a period when two groups of peoples with different belief-systems worked out a common means of existence. Analogy with other periods and regions of post-Roman Europe dictates that elites have a habit of behaving like elites, and when two societies come into contact it is not surprising to find that the leaders of the newcomers adopt the forms of control utilised by those they have conquered, and associate themselves with existing centres of power and replicate modes of behaviour.[121] On the basis of what is known of Viking-Age Scandinavia and of other Germanic peoples, Patrick Wormald has argued that the emergence of 'royal' dynasties in parts of Scandinavia caused a great deal of competition for power and led to the exile or departure of disaffected followers or off-shoots of the various dynasties, who went off in search of somewhere to rule.[122] Western sources refer to some of the leaders of the viking armies as kings, but it is rarely possible to say whether their title derived from their having a kingdom to rule.[123] Once divorced from their Scandinavian background it is not perhaps surprising that they should have been readily converted to Christianity, as they sought to establish themselves in an unstable environment, especially since the Church could offer models for kingship and the exercise of power. This would have been especially important in the face of the concerted efforts of the house of Wessex to conquer the areas of Scandinavian settlement, not to mention the context of rivalries with other Scandinavian rulers and native lords.

It was also in the interests of the Church for such a situation to obtain; by promoting the interests of a handful of Scandinavian rulers they echoed a well-worn policy for instilling order into a turbulent situation.[124] The expansionist

---

121 Amory, 'Names', 3, 13–19.
122 Wormald, 'Whence and Whither', 144–8.
123 Brooks, 7–8; Lund, 'Viking Expansion', 52–4.
124 Wormald, 'Whence and Whither', 145–6; cf. I. Wood, 'The Conversion of the Barbarian Peoples', in *The Christian World*, ed. G. Barraclough, London 1981, 85–98.

policies of the house of Wessex left no doubt that an independent kingdom of Northumbria was not part of their agenda, but if individual ecclesiastics were in any doubt about this the transfer of relics out of the region combined with the seizure of ecclesiastical land and isolated events such as Eadred's burning of the church at Ripon would have served to focus their minds.[125] The West Saxons did not behave as if they faced a solely Scandinavian problem in the north; it was a regional problem that confronted them – a resurgent northern power constantly being reinforced by the arrival of new forces. The complex situation in the Danelaw must – as Pauline Stafford has observed – have meant that the distinction between neighbour and subject was blurred in the tenth century, and the balance between active and passive hostility, alliance, invasion, subjection, and so on, varied.[126] Cultural, ethnic, regional and local identities and concerns were by no means static and everyone who wanted to take control of any part of the Danelaw in the late ninth and early tenth centuries had to take account of, and where possible exploit, these ever-changing allegiances and identities.

Other developments in the regions of Scandinavian settlement doubtless fostered the integration of peoples. Urban expansion, the extension of trading networks, the striking increase in the quantity and quality of pottery-production, the creation of a new improved silver currency to replace the debased copper-based currency of mid ninth-century Northumbria, the proliferation of stone sculpture and transformations in the countryside which lead to the creation of nucleated villages and open-field systems in some regions in the decades following the Scandinavian settlement, are all attested by archaeological evidence. It is difficult to avoid the conclusion that the Scandinavian settlement itself was the cause or the catalyst for most of them.[127] But it is equally difficult to believe that only those of Scandinavian descent could have produced or experienced these developments. Indeed, they must stem from, and must have contributed to, the forging of a truly Anglo-Scandinavian society.

In conclusion, it is clear that the evidence available for the Scandinavian settlement in England requires sensitive handling and that the difficulties of drawing together the testimony of contemporary and later documentary sources, of archaeological and architectural evidence, and of linguistic evidence are made all the greater by confusing the issues to which they relate. I would not seek to deny that great damage was done by successive viking armies, and this has not been an attempt to 'white-wash' the vikings. My point is simply that in highlighting the destructiveness of the vikings, and the differences between Scandinavian and English society, we have not sufficiently addressed the very real issue of how and why the Scandinavians did eventually integrate themselves into native society and

---

[125] D.W. Rollason, 'Relic-Cults as an Instrument of Royal Policy c.900–1050', *Anglo-Saxon England* xv, 1987, 91–103, at 95–7; Fleming, 'England's Defence'; Dumville, 'Ecclesiastical Lands'; D. Whitelock, 'The Dealings', 70–8.

[126] Stafford, *Unification*, 114.

[127] Hinton, 72–4, 82–97; Hodges, 154–62, 166–77; J. Hurst, 'The Wharram Research Project: Results to 1983', *Medieval Archaeology* xxviii, 1984, 77–111; P. Hayes, 'Relating Fen Edge Sediments, Stratigraphy and Archaeology near Billingborough, South Lincolnshire', in *Palaeoenvironmental Investigations*, ed. N.R.J. Feiller, 1985, 245–69; M. Harvey, 'Planned Field Systems in Eastern Yorkshire: Some Thoughts on their Origins', *Agricultural History Review* xxxi, 1983, 91–103; D. Roffe, 'The Lincolnshire Hundred', *Landscape History* iii, 1981, 27–36; Hall, 'Vikings', 33–8.

culture. Much work remains to be undertaken. The field of Viking Studies has been prone to extremes, and perhaps it is now time to forge a middle ground, as, I would argue, did the Scandinavian settlers and the native population of parts of England in the course of the late ninth and early tenth centuries.

ANGLO-SAXON WOMEN AND PILGRIMAGE*

Patricia A. Halpin

The Late-Antique period provides various accounts of pilgrimage undertaken by women, most notably that of Egeria, whose valuable travel itinerary describes her three-year journey through the Holy Land in the late fourth century. In the later Middle Ages, Chaucer, Margery Kempe and the records of women among the crusading pilgrims provide descriptive passages, detailed itineraries and vivid images of female pilgrims. The early Middle Ages, however, especially pre-Conquest England, suffer from a paucity of these straightforward accounts by and about women. Studies of Anglo-Saxon pilgrimage have concentrated on kings, noblemen, clerics, and the laity as a whole.[1] Rarely are English women accounted for in the scholarship, yet they do appear in the sources – as pilgrims and as the impresarios of shrines both at home and abroad – and they deserve our attention.

There was a long tradition of female pilgrimage upon which Anglo-Saxon women could reflect and which they could emulate. Constantine's mother, the empress St Helena, made the first or at least the most renowned pilgrimage to the Holy Land. By the end of the fourth century she was credited with the discovery of the True Cross, and was an important figure in Anglo-Saxon England. In addition to church dedications and Bede's mention of her discovery of the cross, there was a literary and homiletic tradition focusing on St Helena's devotion to the True Cross and the sites she supposedly visited in the Holy Land.[2] Women including SS Paula

* I would like to thank the members of the Battle Conference for inviting me to present this paper. I am most grateful to Robin Fleming and Mary Frances Smith for their valuable comments and suggestions.

[1] For a record of Anglo-Saxon pilgrimage to the Continent, see W.J. Moore, *The Saxon Pilgrims in Rome and the Schola Saxonum*, published dissertation, Fribourg 1937; R.A. Aronstram, 'Penitential Pilgrimages to Rome in the Early Middle Ages', *Archivum Historiae Pontificae* xiii, 1975, 65–83; V. Ortenberg, *The English Church and the Continent in the Tenth and Eleventh Centuries: Cultural, Spiritual and Artistic Exchanges*, Oxford 1992, 148–53.

[2] Bede, *Historia Ecclesiastica Gentis Anglorum*, ed. and trans. B. Colgrave and R.A.B. Mynors, OMT, Oxford 1969 (hereafter *HE*), V.16; 'The Hodeoporicon of Saint Willibald by Hugeberc of Heidenheim', in *The Anglo-Saxon Missionaries in Germany*, ed. C.H. Talbot, New York 1954, 161, 165; Ælfric's 'Inventio Sanctae Crucis', *Ælfric's Catholic Homilies: the Second Series*, London 1979, 174–9; J.W. Drijer, *Helena Augusta: the Mother of Constantine the Great and the Legend of her Finding the True Cross*, New York 1992; P.O.E. Gradon, *Cynewulf's Elene*, Methuen's Old English Library Series, London 1958, repr. New York 1966; *The Old English Finding of the True Cross*, ed. and trans. M. Bodden, Woodbridge 1992. For the convent or parish church of St Helen, see *Chronicon Monasterii de Abingdon*, ed. J. Stevenson, RS ii, 2 vols, London 1858, i, 7–8, ii, 269–70; A. Thacker, 'Æthelwold and Abingdon', in *Bishop Æthelwold: His Career and Influence*, ed. B.A.E. Yorke, Woodbridge 1988, 59–60; L. Butler, 'Church Dedications and the Cults of the Anglo-Saxon Saints in England', in *The Anglo-Saxon Church*, ed. H.M. Taylor, Council for British Archaeology, London 1986, 44; A.M. Pearn, 'Origin and Development of Urban Churches and

and Mary of Egypt were also remembered in England for their pilgrimages to the Holy Land and were venerated by Anglo-Saxon women.[3] Mary of Egypt's cult may have been brought to England as early as the seventh century, and the success of her cult in England is attested by her appearance in most calendars and by the existence of two vernacular *vitae* for her.[4] In his *vita* of the tenth-century saint, Edith of Wilton, Goscelin of Canterbury compared Edith, her mother Abbess Wulfthryth, and their priest to the fourth-century pilgrims St Paula, her daughter Eustocia and St Jerome.[5] There was even a home-grown pilgrim-saint, Pega, the anchorite sister of St Guthlac. By the early twelfth century Pega had acquired legendary status as a pilgrim to Rome where she prayed for herself and her people before she died.[6] Through their *vitae* and litanies, these female pilgrim-saints served as potent models for English women.

Three main avenues existed for women wishing to express their peregrine yearnings. First there was pilgrimage to Continental holy sites, particularly Rome and Jerusalem. But numerous centres closer to England, including St Vaast, Fulda and Corvey, were popular destinations for Anglo-Saxon pilgrims. A whole pilgrimage culture and economy developed around these pilgrimage shrines including hospices, monasteries and established routes. Second, there was pilgrimage around the network of English shrines both local and supraregional. Architectural and textual evidence including the *Secgan*, or 'list of the resting-places of saints', suggests the existence of a wealth of shrines in England by the eleventh century.[7] Finally, there is what might be described as 'virtual pilgrimage', that is petitioners transcending earthly time and space through devotional texts and art. Women who never reached Continental centres or even the major shrines within England could recreate the gospel events and transport themselves spiritually to the holy places in the presence of Christ through meditative texts, art and liturgical dramas while remaining in their own churches.

Travel accounts, in addition to memorial books, wills, charters, and chronicle and archaeological evidence, make it clear that there was an established tradition of Anglo-Saxon pilgrimage to the Continent of which women were a part. The success of Roman pilgrimage, in particular, is evidenced by the foundation in the early eighth century of the *Schola Saxonum*, a pilgrim community with its own

Parishes: a Comparative Study of Hereford, Shrewsbury and Chester', unpublished Cambridge dissertation, 1986, 84.

[3] For St Paula in Anglo-Saxon England, see M. Lapidge, *Anglo-Saxon Litanies of the Saints*, London 1991, 76–7, 229; N.R. Ker, *Catalogue of Manuscripts containing Anglo-Saxon*, Oxford 1957, no. 315; E.D. Hunt, *Holy Land and Pilgrimage in the Later Roman Empire, AD 312–460*, Oxford 1982, 82, 87, 171–84.

[4] For the cult of Mary of Egypt in Anglo-Saxon England, see *Ælfric's Lives of the Saints*, ed. W.W. Skeat, 4 vols, EETS os lxxvi, lxxxii, xciv, cxiv, Oxford 1881–1900, ii, 2–53; Ortenberg, *The English Church and the Continent*, 99, 115, 257–8; M. Clayton, *The Cult of the Virgin Mary in Anglo-Saxon England*, Cambridge 1990, 272; C. Wolfe, 'The Audience of Old English Literature', unpublished Cambridge dissertation, 1994, 80; V. Ortenberg, 'Aspects of Monastic Devotions to the Saints in England ca. 950 – ca. 1100: the Liturgical and Iconographical Evidence', unpublished Cambridge dissertation, 1987, 280.

[5] A. Wilmart, 'La Légende de Saint Edith en prose et vers par le moine Goscelin', *Analecta Bollandiana* lvi, 1938, 73 (hereafter *Vita Edithe*).

[6] Orderic ii, 344–5.

[7] D. Rollason, 'Lists of Saints' Resting-Places in Anglo-Saxon England', *Anglo-Saxon England* vii, Cambridge 1978, 61–93.

church, priest, hospices and cemetery, all of which were financed by the Peter's Pence or 'Romscot', the tax levied in England and shared between the *Schola* and St Peter's.[8] Pilgrimage from Anglo-Saxon England to Continental sites was such a regular occurrence that chroniclers ignored the journeys of the majority of travellers, noting only those of the very great. As a result, pre-Conquest sources offer little direct information about women pilgrims in Rome and elsewhere on the Continent. More often, we see shadows of women next to better-documented male saints, churchmen and noblemen. For safety, pilgrims often travelled in large, fluid groups of merchants, ambassadors, ecclesiastics and other pilgrims.[9] Charlemagne's late eighth-century letter to King Offa suggests mixed parties of Anglo-Saxon merchants and pilgrims along Continental pilgrimage routes.[10] And on his way to Rome in 1027, Cnut met with King Rudolf of Burgundy and negotiated an understanding which protected English convoys of merchants and pilgrims travelling to Italy.[11] Throughout the Anglo-Saxon period numerous churchmen including Abbot Ceolfrith, St Willibald and Archbishops Sigeric and Ealdred are recorded as leaving for Rome in large organized parties.[12] It is likely that women – religious, noble, common and servile – accompanied these men as Bede claims had been the tradition since the seventh century.[13] Trips made to Rome and Jerusalem by kings, nobles and other dignitaries, like the one undertaken by Earl Tostig in 1061, which must have included among their ranks women other than the Earl's wife – other wives, attendants and female servants – were similarly composed of various travellers.[14] Continental memorial books such as the Brescia, Bremen, St Gall, and Pfafers *Libri Vitae* record Anglo-Saxon women's names, some of which can be identified.[15] The inclusion of these women's names in the memorial books generally, though not always, indicates their presence at these particular communities; kinsmen or others who wished to admit these women into the corporate memory of

8   Moore, *The Saxon Pilgrims*, 109–10; H. Loyn, 'Peter's Pence', *Friends of Lambeth Palace Library Annual Report*, 1984, 10–20, repr. in his *Society and Peoples: Studies in the History of England and Wales c.600–1200*, Westfield Publications in Medieval Studies vi, London 1992, 241–58.

9   For large parties of Continental pilgrims, see D.F. Callahan, 'Jerusalem in the Monastic Imagination of the Early Eleventh Century', *The Haskins Society Journal: Studies in Medieval History* v, 1994, 119–27, and E. Joranson, 'The Great German Pilgrimage of 1064–65', in *The Crusades and Other Historical Essays presented to Dana C. Munro by his former students*, ed. L.J. Paetow, New York 1928, 4, 10, 11, 40.

10   *EHD* i, 417.

11   *Councils and Synods with Other Documents Relating to the English Church: AD 871 – 1204*, ed. D. Whitelock, M. Brett, and C.N.L. Brooke, Oxford 1981, i, *871–1066*, 509–10; *ASC, s.a.* 1031 (DEF) [1027].

12   Bede, *Historia Abbatum* in *Venerabilis Bedae Opera Historica*, ed. C. Plummer, 2 vols, 1896, i, 34, 401; 'The Hodoeporicon of St Willibald by Hugeberc of Heidenheim', 157; V. Ortenberg, 'Archbishop Sigeric's Journey to Rome in 990', *Anglo-Saxon England* xix, 1990, 197–246; *ASC, s.a.* 990 (F), 1058 (D), 1061 (D); *John of Worcester* ii, 554; *Historians of the Church of York and its Archbishops*, ed. J. Raine, RS lxxi, 3 vols, 1879–94, ii, 353–4; F. Barlow, *The English Church 1000–1066*, 2nd edn, London 1979, 88–90.

13   *HE*, V.7.

14   *ASC , s.a.* 1061 (D); *Vita Eadwardi*, 34.

15   *The Liber Vitae of the New Minster and Hyde Abbey, Winchester: British Library Stowe 944*, ed. S. Keynes, Early English Manuscripts in Facsimile xxvi, Copenhagen 1996, 50–2; S. Keynes, 'King Æthelstan's Books', in *Learning and Literature in Anglo-Saxon England: Studies presented to Peter Clemoes*, ed. M. Lapidge and H. Gneuss, Cambridge 1985, 198–201.

these communities may also have enrolled them. The Brescia *Liber Vitae*, for instance, contains the names of King Burgred and Queen Æthelswith, a couple known to have made their way to Rome in the late ninth century, and their inclusion within the memorial book presumes their actual presence at this northern Italian monastery.[16] Furthermore, the Exeter guild statutes, along with a number of wills and charters, include women, some by name, who left with their husbands for the Continent on pilgrimage.[17] At least twenty-two Anglo-Saxon women, some with their intended destination specified, are recorded as having made arrangements for or having actually gone on pilgrimage abroad.

The challenges facing unarmed and vulnerable pilgrims were typical to any traveller, but other problems and dangers were particular to the period, especially threats from the Vikings, Magyars and Saracens. And women, of course, faced additional threats of abandonment, abduction and rape. Wills made by pilgrims including those of Siflæd, of Ketel and his stepdaughter, and of Ulf and Madselin, suggest that the likelihood of returning safely was not taken for granted.[18] This uncertainty appears justified by the grim and gruesome accounts throughout the period of pilgrims succumbing to disease and exposure, drowning, falling from cliffs, dying in avalanches and even worse happenings.[19] Such vulnerability, along with complaints about improper wanderings by wayward pilgrims, led, from the eighth century, to increasing institutional opposition to pilgrimage in general, and to female pilgrimage in particular. The vows of chastity and ascetic practice, which for the most part seem to have been adequate insurance for women pilgrims of the late Antique period, no longer placated the anxieties of churchmen.[20] In his letter to the Anglo-Saxon abbess Bugga, written sometime before 738, Boniface cautions her against a trip to Rome at that time because of the danger of Saracens.[21] Later, while archbishop of Mainz, a different danger concerned Boniface. He wrote to the archbishop of Canterbury to complain about the 'scandal and disgrace' of matrons and veiled women who frequently journeyed to Rome, only to fall into trouble and harlotry along the pilgrimage trail.[22] Boniface further recommended to the Council of Clovesho in 747 that women be forbidden to make the journey.[23] Alcuin shared Boniface's concern about women pilgrims; while an avid fan of St Peter's city and

---

[16] Keynes, *The Liber Vitae of New Minster and Hyde Abbey*, 51–2.

[17] Whitelock, *Councils and Synods* i, no. 16, 57–60; *Anglo-Saxon Wills*, ed. D. Whitelock, Cambridge 1930, 34, 39; P.H. Sawyer, *Anglo-Saxon Charters: an Annotated List and Bibliography*, Royal Historical Society Guides and Handbooks viii, London 1968, 1206 (hereafter S).

[18] Whitelock, *Anglo-Saxon Wills*, 38, 34, 39.

[19] For dangers along the pilgrimage route, see 'The Hodoeporicon of St Willibald', 153–77; *ASC*, s.a. 667 (E), 1052 (C), 1061 (D); *Le 'Liber Pontificalis': texte, introduction et commentaire*, ed. L. Duchesne, 2 vols, Paris 1886–89, ii, and vol. iii, C. Vogel, Paris 1957, 53–4, 100, 110–11; S. Keynes and M. Lapidge, *Alfred the Great: Asser's 'Life of King Alfred' and Other Contemporary Sources*, Harmondsworth 1983, 82; *HE*, IV.1 and V.7; *Vita Edithe*, 278–80; A. Celli-Fraentzel, 'Contemporary Reports on the Mediaeval Roman Climate', *Speculum* vii, 1932, 96–8, 100–101; G.B. Parks, *The English Traveller to Italy i: The Middle Ages [to 1525]*, Stanford 1954, 20, 56, 57.

[20] For the freedom of movement of women religious in the early church, see J.E. Salisbury, *Church Fathers, Independent Virgins*, London 1991, 83–96.

[21] *The Letters of St Boniface*, ed. E. Emerton, New York 1940, 56–7.

[22] Emerton, *Letters of Saint Boniface*, 140.

[23] Emerton, *Letters of Saint Boniface*, 140.

a pilgrim himself, he was troubled by women's tendency to succumb to poverty and disgrace.[24]

Boniface and Alcuin were not alone, but were manifestations of a vocal, though often overlooked, corporate concern for the vulnerability of pilgrims, especially women, and about the doubtful advantages and true motives of the exercise itself. Since the Church's early days, various ecclesiastics including Augustine, Gregory of Nyssa, and even Jerome, Paula's spiritual adviser and fellow pilgrim, questioned the necessity of all Christians to take physical and moral risks in venturing to holy sites.[25] Gregory viewed biblical descriptions of New Testament sites as symbols of salvation that lay in Christ. But the physical remains of the Holy Land were important to Gregory only as signs of the inner spirituality which should be part of all Christians everywhere. This discomfort expressed by some Church Fathers concerning pilgrimage to the Holy Land gradually came to dominate the thinking of early medieval churchmen. Bede's terse remark about the monk Oftor's leaving his studies at Canterbury for a pilgrimage to Rome certainly seems to question the true value of such a journey.[26] By the eighth or ninth century, ecclesiastical and royal prohibitions against wandering penitents and unwise pilgrims, and the increased emphasis on claustration, particularly for women religious, were creating powerful obstacles to women's pilgrimage.[27]

In spite of official warnings and prohibitions, however, it is clear that women continued to leave England for holy sites abroad. While references to English nuns specifically on Continental pilgrimage do not survive for the Anglo-Saxon period, we do not hear much about nuns anyway, and it seems fair to surmise that they continued to clog the roads to Rome, as did their lay counterparts. In her letter to Boniface requesting advice on a desired pilgrimage to Rome, Eangyth refers to councils enjoining stability. However, she seems to dismiss those who blindly adhered to canon law and placed greater weight on the opinions of a respected personal advisor such as Boniface than the canons of the Church.[28] There was a

---

[24] A friend of Alcuin's, Æthelburga, had to abandon her plans to go to Rome because of the unstable political situation in Mercia after the deaths of both her father King Offa and her brother. Alcuin's reaction to her news makes it clear that he shared Boniface's misgivings about women pilgrims (*Alcuini sive Albini Epistolae*, ed. Ernst Dummler, Monumenta Germanica Historica, Epistolae IV, *Epistolae Karolini Aevi*, Tomus II, Berlin 1895, 300); D.B. Schneider, 'Anglo-Saxon Women in the Religious Life: a Study of the Status and Position of Women in Early Medieval Society', unpublished Cambridge dissertation, 1985, 231.

[25] For the following discussion, see Hunt, *Holy Land Pilgrimage*, 86–101.

[26] *HE*, IV.23. Bede also relates the story of the priest, Wigheard, who was sent to Rome to be consecrated archbishop under King Oswiu of Northumbria, but died from the plague along with most of his companions in Rome (*HE*, IV.1).

[27] Emerton, *Letters of Saint Boniface*, 36–40. The Council of 813 warned against injudicious pilgrimages to Rome and Tours, and other later conciliar legislation required that penitents not wander around but stay where their own priest could keep an eye on them. The Council of Friuli in 796/7 decreed that permission should never be given to an abbess or nun to visit Rome or 'other venerable places' and attributed this desire to the inspiration of Satan in the form of an angel (G. Constable, 'Opposition to Pilgrimage in the Middle Ages', *Studia Gratiana* xix, 1976, 123–46). Patristic literature, early monastic rules and Continental canons mandated strict enclosure, especially of women (J.T. Schulenburg, 'Strict Active Enclosure and its Effects on the Female Monastic Experience (ca. 500 – 1100)', in *Medieval Religious Women: Distant Echoes* I, ed. J.A. Nichols and L.T. Shank, Kalamazoo, MI, 1984, 51–86).

[28] S. Hollis, *Anglo-Saxon Women and the Church: Sharing a Common Fate*, Woodbridge 1992, 146–7.

long history of Anglo-Saxon women religious travelling to the Continent and evidence of this continues throughout the period. At least nineteen references survive for individual Anglo-Saxon nuns and laywomen or groups of women seeking sanctuary or retiring at Continental religious communities. Furthermore, despite their own writings against female pilgrimage, both Boniface and Alcuin personally acted as tour guides in Rome for a nun and a laywoman, respectively.[29] Clearly there was a disjunction between these churchmen's public pronouncements and their private relationships. Laywomen of every status, including King Alfred's sister, Æthelswith, the Exeter guild wives, and Eadburgh, the former Mercian queen who died penniless in Pavia, left England, though accompanied by male relatives.[30] And narrative and testamentary records as late as the 1060s make it clear that women were still trekking to these sites regardless of the official pronouncements and real physical dangers.[31]

These women who travelled to Rome and Jerusalem – the locus of the biblical narratives and sacred treasures – achieved pilgrimage *par excellence*. And though hundreds more women doubtless made the journey than are recorded, they were, in fact, the exception. The majority of pious women, for either logistical reasons and responsibilities to their religious communities or kinsmen, or out of respect for the official prohibitions, never made it to Continental shrines. These women could, however, fulfil their yearnings for peregrination with visits to the renowned network of curative shrines within England. Indeed, some of these shrines were being promoted as better than the more famous Continental sites. In Byrhtferth's *Life of Bishop Ecgsine*, for example, a foreign penitent who failed to find release from his iron fetters at other sanctuaries in Europe is miraculously freed at the saint's shrine at Evesham.[32] The curative power of Swithun's relics is also related in an account from his *vita* of how a rich thegn had been healed at the saint's shrine at Old Minster, Winchester, after failing to find relief in Rome.[33] A letter of introduction by King Æthelstan for a visiting Breton anchorite-pilgrim suggests that such a network of shrines, which attracted foreigners and had support for travellers, was established within England by the early tenth century.[34] And women were part of

---

[29] In the same year that he wrote to Archbishop Cuthbert, or very close to it, Boniface met with Abbess Bugga in Rome where they visited the shrines together (Emerton, *Letters of Saint Boniface*, 177–8). In a letter dated to 745, the Cardinal-Deacon Gemmulus informs Boniface that he is caring for some monastic women who arrived in Rome with recommendations from him (Emerton, *Letters of Saint Boniface*, 114). Alcuin likely acted as an escort to King Æthelwald Moll's daughter, Æthelthryth, c.782 (Ortenberg, *The Anglo-Saxon Church and the Continent*, 103 and n. 37).

[30] *ASC, s.a.* 888; Whitelock, *Councils and Synods* i, no. 16, 57–60; Keynes and Lapidge, *Alfred the Great*, 72, 113.

[31] S 1521; Whitelock, *Anglo-Saxon Wills*, 34, 39.

[32] *Vita Sancti Ecgwini* in *Vita Quorundam Anglo-Saxonum*, ed. J.A. Giles, London 1854, 387–90; Goscelin, *Miracula Ivonis* in *Chronicon Abbatiae Ramesiensis*, ed. W.D. Macray, RS lxxix, London 1886, lxvii–lxviii; A. Thacker, 'Saint-Making and Relic Collecting by Oswald and his Communities', in *Saint Oswald of Worcester: Life and Influence*, ed. N.B. Brooks and C. Cubit, London 1996, 263–4.

[33] 'Sancti Swithuni Wintoniensis episcopi translatio et miracula auctore Lantfredo monacho Wintoniensi', ed. E.P. Savage, *Analecta Bollandiana* iv, 1895, ch. 16, 397; R.N. Quirk, 'Winchester Cathedral in the Tenth Century', *Arch. Journ.* cxiv, 1957, 41; *Symeonis Monachi Opera Omnia*, ed. T. Arnold, RS lxxv, 2 vols, London 1882–85, i, 81.

[34] C. Brett, 'A Breton Pilgrim in England in the Reign of King Æthelstan', in *France and the British Isles in the Middle Ages and Renaissance: Essays in Memory of Ruth Morgan*, ed. G. Jondorf and

this native devotional phenomenon in all capacities: as pilgrims, patrons, donors, guardians of shrines and as saints.

Three *Libri Vitae* containing Anglo-Saxon names survive in English manuscripts. Memorial books for Durham, Thorney, and New Minster Winchester, like similar lists from the Continent, record both lay and religious women, some of whom are identifiable, and all of whom wanted to be remembered by members of the host communities.[35] Whether all the women memorialized in these pages were actual pilgrims seeking intercession from these three communities' patron saints is difficult to establish, but numerous women are recorded among the healed at various English shrines. An anonymous crippled woman who dragged herself by her hands to St Cuthbert's shrine at Durham was cured, and afterwards walked to Rome to pray.[36] At Christ Church Canterbury, moreover, the only miracle whose context can safely be assigned to a period soon after Dunstan's death is the cure of three blind women.[37] According to the *vitae* of both Swithun and Æthelwold, women were among the numerous pilgrims attracted to the sumptuous shrines and rebuilt churches of England's tenth-century reform, and the accounts suggest such visitors enjoyed close access to the desired relics.

Swithun's curative power seems to have attracted many of lowly status. After his second translation, the interior of the Old Minster Winchester was said to have been covered with the crutches and stools of cured cripples.[38] Lantfred reports that on one occasion Old Minster, Winchester, became so crowded with the diseased clustered around Swithun's shrine that the throngs of pilgrims had to be cleared out of the church periodically to make way for the clergy.[39] In addition to a blind woman from Bedfordshire, Lantfred reports pilgrim parties ranging from sixteen to over one hundred people from all parts of England who petitioned the saint.[40] Among those whose prayers were answered by the saint was a manacled woman who was made invisible and carried through the crowd to the shrine of the saint where she was found by its custodian within the locked chamber holding the saint's reliquary.[41] And in 'Swithun's honor' the woman was freed from her bonds by her master.[42] Likewise, three blind women from the Isle of Wight journeyed to Swithun's shrine, where the whole party was cured of its afflictions after a night

D.N. Dumville, Woodbridge 1991, 43–70; Rollason, 'Lists of Saints' Resting-Places', 91; D. Rollason, 'The Shrines of Saints in Later Anglo-Saxon England: Distribution and Significance', in *The Anglo-Saxon Church*, ed. L.A.S. Butler and R.K. Morris, Council of British Archaeology 60, 1986, 36.

[35] *Liber Vitae Ecclesiae Dunelmensis*, ed. J. Stevenson, Surtees Society cxxxvi, 1923; *The Oldest English Texts*, ed. H. Sweet, EETS lxxxiii, London 1885, 153–66; C. Clark, 'British Library Additional MS 40,000 ff. 1v–12r', *ANS* vii, 1984, 55; *The Liber Vitae of the New Minster*, fos 28v–29r.

[36] *Symeonis Monachi Opera Omnia*, xxxviii, 81–2.

[37] *Memorials of Saint Dunstan Archbishop of Canterbury*, ed. W. Stubbs, RS lxiii, London 1874, 131; A. Thacker, 'Cults at Canterbury: Relics and Reform under Dunstan and his Successors', in *St Dunstan: His Life, Times and Cult*, ed. N. Ramsay, M. Sparks and T. Tatton-Brown, Woodbridge 1992, 224.

[38] 'The Life of Saint Swithun', in *Ælfric's Lives of Saints*, no. xxi, 468–9.

[39] M. Lapidge, 'The Saintly Life in Anglo-Saxon England', in *The Cambridge Companion to Old English Literature*, ed. M. Lapidge and M. Godden, Cambridge 1991, 243.

[40] Lantfred's '*Translatio et miracula S. Swithuni*', in Lapidge, 'The Saintly Life in Anglo-Saxon England', 245–6.

[41] Quirk, 'Winchester Cathedral in the Tenth Century', 42–3.

[42] 'Life of St Swithun', 468–9.

vigil next to the saint's remains.[43] Among St Æthelwold's posthumous miracles at his Old Minster shrine were the cures of a small girl and a blind boy, both of whom had been taken to the saint's tomb by their mothers.[44] Æthelwold's cures are typical of miracle stories dating from the late tenth century for their attention to lay people and those of humble status.[45] Edith of Wilton's reputation for curative miracles likewise facilitated the spread of her cult among the lower levels of society, and both Edith and her mother Abbess Wulfthryth were credited with a number of domestic cures.[46] Three women, all nuns at Wilton, found relief at Edith's tomb, and included among the miracles at Wulfthryth's tomb were the healing of a paralytic woman and a Wilton sister suffering from dysentery.[47] At one point, however, when sickness killed off a number of sisters at Wilton and with no alleviation in sight, the nuns complained that their patron saint seemed to pay more attention to the needs of strangers – pilgrims – than to those of her own house-hold.[48] A story from the *Vita Wulfhilde* shows how two other women's communities could profit from the sufferings of a single pilgrim. Wulfhild, who had been abbess of Horton as well as Barking, made one poor woman, blind and crippled, seek a cure for the two afflictions at both houses. Given back her sight at Horton, the woman then had to crawl to Barking to gain the use of her legs.[49]

Architectural changes to Anglo-Saxon churches, including the construction of porticus, chapels, and ring crypts, provided pilgrims with better access to and visibility of the shrines they petitioned. Corridor crypts at Christ Church, like those at Brixworth, Repton, and Old Minster, Winchester, allowed for the easier circula-tion of larger numbers of pilgrims without causing overcrowding or the disruption of services, and provided space for invalids to be laid beside the relics.[50] Abbot Eadnoth of Ramsey's placement of St Ivo's sarcophagus half within and half outside the church wall at *Slepe* provided greater access to pilgrims who sought cures from the spring at the sepulchre.[51] The new tomb chamber built by Bishop Æthelwold for St Swithun's relics was probably similarly designed to make the sarcophagus more accessible and visible to pilgrims.[52]

Archaeological and narrative evidence also shows a concerted attempt on the part of English religious communities to replicate in design and decoration the sacred space of famous Continental churches. The creation of a sacred interior

[43] 'Life of St Swithun', 450–3.
[44] *Wulfstan of Winchester: The Life of St Æthelwold*, ed. M. Lapidge and M. Winterbottom, Oxford 1991, caps 44 and 45.
[45] D. Rollason, *Saints and Relics in Anglo-Saxon England*, Oxford 1989, 187.
[46] S.J. Ridyard, *Royal Saints of Anglo-Saxon England: a Study of West Saxon and East Anglian Cults*, Cambridge 1988, 151.
[47] *Vita Edithe*, 9, 10, 11.
[48] *Vita Edithe*, 297; Ridyard, *Royal Saints*, 151.
[49] '*La Vie de sainte Vulfhilde par Goscelin de Cantorbery*', ed. M. Esposito, *Analecta Bollandiana* xxxii, 1913, xi; S. Millinger, 'Humility and Power: Anglo-Saxon Nuns in Anglo-Norman Hagiogra-phy', *Distant Echoes*, 127, n. 39.
[50] Quirk, 'Winchester Cathedral in the Tenth Century', 60; H.M. Taylor, 'Corridor Crypts on the Continent and in England', *North Staffordshire Journal Field Studies* ix, 1963, 17–18; Rollason, *Saints and Relics*, 54.
[51] Goscelin, *Vita sancti Ivonis* in *Acta Sanctorum*, June 11, 1698 edn, 291; Goscelin, *Miracula sancti Ivonis*, lix–lxxxiv, 115; Thacker, 'Saint-Making and Relic Collecting by Oswald's Communi-ties', 259.
[52] Quirk, 'Winchester Cathedral in the Tenth Century', 56–9.

landscape allowed women to experience the flavour of holy sites along the Continental pilgrimage roads, while remaining within England and often within their own local churches. Excavations at Old Minster, Winchester, for example, have revealed the supports for a *ciborium*, similar to the house-like structure that covered the tomb of Christ within the circular church of Anastasis in Jerusalem.[53] Pictorial evidence in the *The Benedictional of Æthelwold*, the *Tiberius Psalter*, and the *Sacramentary of Robert of Jumiéges* clearly suggests English familiarity with architecture in Jerusalem.[54] Particularly influential were plans for circular churches like that holding Christ's tomb, the use of western sanctuaries, and centrally placed altars dedicated to the cross. In the *Historia Ecclesiastica*, Bede includes Adomnan's account of the pilgrim Arculf's description of the round church at Anastasis.[55] St Willibald's observation of the cross-shaped Bethlehem church was recorded in the account of his pilgrimage to the Holy Land by the Anglo-Saxon nun Hugeberc.[56] At St Augustine's Canterbury, Goscelin records that Abbot Wulfric built the rotunda on the model of that at Saint-Benigne in Dijon, which he may have visited on his journey to Rheims in 1049, which, like its model at Cluny, was based on the plan of Jerusalem churches.[57] Eadmer, moreover, specifically describes the crypt or Roman *confessio* at Christ Church as a replica of that at St Peters, Rome.[58] Evidence for corridor crypts, of a style derived from Gregory the Great's modification of St Peter's shrine, suggests the direct influence of Roman churches on Anglo-Saxon shrines.[59]

In addition to the topographical significance of some of the ecclesiastical architectural designs, the sheer splendor of the interior of pilgrimage churches served to overawe visitors and reflect the power of the saints whose remains they contained. Bishop Wulfstan and Abbot Æthelwold were among those churchmen who advocated the beautification of holy spaces in order that the beholder could see something of the 'Paradise of God'.[60] Visitors to Old Minster Winchester would have been captivated by the silver-gilt and gem-covered shrine, which Wulfstan the

---

[53] B. Raw, *Anglo-Saxon Crucifixion Iconography and the Art of the Monastic Revival*, Cambridge 1990, 46.

[54] Raw, *Crucifixion Iconography*, 46–7.

[55] *HE*, V.16–17.

[56] 'The Hodoeporicon of Saint Willibald', 167.

[57] Goscelin, *Historia Translationis S. Augustini episcopi Anglorum Apostoli*, in *PL* clv, 32–3; *ASC*, s.a. 1049 (E); Ortenberg, *The Anglo-Saxon Church and the Continent*, 236; Raw, *Crucifixion Iconography*, 44–5.

[58] For a discussion of Eadmer's statements, see R. Willis, *The Architectural History of Canterbury Cathedral*, London 1845, 25–6; Taylor, 'Corridor Crypts', 38–9: the columns supporting the Repton crypt were described as 'twisted candy', similar to those in the interior of St Peters (H.M. Taylor, 'Repton Reconsidered: a Study of Structural Criticism', in *England before the Conquest: Studies in Primary Sources presented to Dorothy Whitelock*, ed. P. Clemoes, Cambridge 1971, 351–85; Rollason, *Saints and Relics*, 54–9).

[59] Taylor, 'Corridor Crypts', 38–9; H.M. Taylor, 'The Anglo-Saxon Cathedral Church at Canterbury', *Arch. Journ.* cxxvi, 154–8. St Peter's design was replicated in numerous English churches down to the mid-eighth century; surviving crypts at seventh-century Hexham and Ripon, almost certainly influenced by the travels of Bishop Wilfrid, are of the Continental and possibly Roman type (Taylor, 'Corridor Crypts', 17–18; E. Gilbert, 'Saint Wilfrid's Church at Hexham', in *Saint Wilfrid at Hexham*, ed. D.P. Kirby, Newcastle upon Tyne 1974, 81–113; H.M. Taylor, 'English Architecture in Bede's Time', in *Bede and his World: the Jarrow Lectures*, Cambridge 1994, 58).

[60] *Wulfstan's Canons of Edgar*, ed. R. Fowler, EETS, os cclxvi, Oxford 1972, 2nd edn, 4–5; *Chronicon de Abingdon* i, 344; Theophilus, *The Various Arts*, ed. C.R. Dodwell, London 1961, bk 3

Cantor described as being adorned with more than 300 pounds of precious jewels and finely engraved scenes of Christ's life.[61] Wulfstan believed pilgrims would be awed upon entering the cathedral, and he drew special attention to the elaboration of the colonnaded alley and adjacent maze-like chapels which would bewilder visitors by their intricacy.[62]

In the same manner images, whether in sculpture, painting or metalwork, manifested the meaning of the cults, defining the actual presence of the community of saints. Unfortunately, so much material evidence has been lost or damaged that, as historians, we must rely largely on limited contemporary descriptions to grasp the visual culture of Anglo-Saxon England. As Charles Dodwell has noted, these records are often narrowly focused on certain aspects of objects, especially their material worth, and we hear little about manuscript illuminations, mural paintings, textile figural imagery, three dimensional effigies or personal meditative icons.[63] As a result of this lacuna, there has been a tendency to underestimate the mnemonic, emotive and didactic power of images and objects on their beholders.

Sanctuary ornamentation, like the carvings and sculpture of the tenth-century New Minster tower, was intended to remind the pilgrim that she was walking on holy ground and constantly surrounded by the intercession she sought.[64] Bejewelled images of the four saintly Ely ladies were placed by Abbot Byrthnoth on either side of the high altar near which they were buried.[65] These images, along with those of three Glastonbury abbots placed over their tombs, recalled the portraits on early Christian funerary tombs which made visible the saints who lived on in the relics sometimes hidden from view.[66] Bede made this connection of the intersection of heaven and earth clear when he explained that the panel paintings which covered the inside of Wearmouth-Jarrow church ensured that all who entered the church, both literate and illiterate, would be surrounded by the faces of Christ and his saints, if only in images.[67] Many of the statues and paintings mentioned in the records suggest the idea of the community of saints: the rows of figures and saints on the Breedon and Fletton friezes; the carved images on Æthelwold's retable at Abingdon and Harold's altar at Waltham; and the rows of angels and saints under the arcading of the reliquary Hedda Stone at Peterborough.[68]

Prologue, 62–3; R. Gameson, *The Role of Art in the Late Anglo-Saxon Church*, Oxford 1995, 261–3.

[61] *Wulfstan the Cantor's 'Narratio metrica de Sancto Swithuno'*, in *Frithegodi monachi breviloquium vitae beati Wilfredi et Wulfstani cantoris narratio metrica de Sancto Swithuno*, ed. A. Campbell, Zurich 1950, 66; C.R. Dodwell, *Anglo-Saxon Art: a New Perspective*, Manchester 1982, 41, 198–200 and nn. 114–16.

[62] *Narratio metrica de Sancto Swithuno* ii, 66; Dodwell, *Anglo-Saxon Art*, 41 and n. 169; Quirk, 'Winchester Cathedral in the Tenth Century', 44.

[63] Dodwell, *Anglo-Saxon Art*, 1–23.

[64] R.N. Quirk, 'Winchester New Minster and its Tenth-Century Tower', *Journ. BAA* ii, 1961, 3rd ser., 35.

[65] *Liber Eliensis*, ed. E.O. Blake, Camden 3rd ser. xcii, London 1962, II.6.

[66] *The Early History of Glastonbury: an Edition, Translation and Study of William of Malmesbury's 'De Antiquitate Glastione Ecclesie'*, ed. J. Scott, Woodbridge 1981, 86; Raw, *Crucifixion Iconography*, 17; Dodwell, *Anglo-Saxon Art*, 93; R. Gameson, 'Ælfric and the Perception of Script and Picture in Anglo-Saxon England', *Anglo-Saxon Studies in Archaeology and History* v, 1992, 94.

[67] *Historia Abbatum*, VI, 369–70; P. Maeyvaert, 'Bede and the Church Paintings of Wearmouth-Jarrow', *Anglo-Saxon England* viii, 1979, 63–77.

[68] Raw, *Crucifixion Iconography*, 16–17.

Statues, like that of St Swithun at Sherborne, and the numerous talking, bleeding, and writhing crucifixes recorded at various communities, directly interacted with worshippers, and served as links between earth and heaven.[69] All these images acted as direct channels of divine power for the pilgrims who venerated them.

Women, both lay and religious, were important patrons of the cult of the saints and pilgrimage churches. As custodians of shrines and procurers of relics for themselves or religious communities, they helped to foster this sense of the saints' intercessory powers and presence in these churches. Oswen, an anchoress at Abingdon, is recorded as watching over the relics of St Edmund in the tenth century.[70] At Croyland, another anchoress, Pega, is credited with establishing her brother St Guthlac's shrine and fostering his cult in the ninth century. In one instance, Pega even cured a blind man at the shrine by means of some salt consecrated by Guthlac prior to his death.[71]

Communities of religious women, including Nunnaminster, Wilton and Barking, were also custodians of shrines and pilgrimage centres. Though often not as wealthy or prestigious as the pilgrimage centres at male foundations, women's communities obeyed the Benedictine *ordo* to accommodate guests, the poor and pilgrims.[72] Susan Ridyard has noted that it was primarily through the initiative of the Winchester nuns themselves, by their record of St Edburga's miracles in the vicinity of her tomb, and by their arrangement for her translation to the shrine beside the high altar of the church, that her cult at Nunnaminster became popular.[73] Edburga's cult became a celebrated, if local cult, especially among the poor. In fact, two of her five healing miracles involve poor women.[74] Wilton, a beneficiary of royal patronage, especially in the tenth-century reform period, profited as the guardian of the relics of its patron saint, Edith. Edith's sumptuous golden shrine within the chapel she had built and dedicated to St Denys was the *locus* of various miracles which benefited both lay and religious petitioners. Her mother, and abbess of the community, Wulfthryth, both fostered her daughter's cult and acquired major relics for the community. Among the relics she procured, and which became a focus of pilgrimage, was a nail of the Passion, and also the relics of St Ivi.[75] Wilton also attracted foreign pilgrims to its curative shrines, including an epileptic dancer from Kolbec, who had wandered through Europe in search of miraculous assistance before finding his cure at Edith's shrine.[76] Barking, too, became a desired

---

[69] *The Waltham Chronicle: An Account of the Discovery of Our Holy Cross at Montacute and Its Conveyance to Waltham*, ed. and trans. L. Watkiss and M. Chibnall, OMT 1994, 18, 20, 46; Raw, *Crucifixion Iconography*, 18.

[70] *Three Lives of English Saints*, ed. M. Winterbottom, Toronto 1972, c.14, 82, 1.9 – 83, line 21; Ridyard, *Royal Saints*, 64.

[71] *Felix's Life of Saint Guthlac: Introduction, Text, Translation and Notes*, ed. B. Colgrave, Cambridge 1956, 160, 162, 168.

[72] *The Rule of St Benedict, the Abingdon Copy*, ed. J. Chamberlain, Toronto 1982, c. 53; H. Mayr-Harting, 'The Venerable Bede, *The Rule of St Benedict*, and Social Class', in *Bede and his World: the Jarrow Lecture*, Cambridge 1994, I, 3; W. Levison, *England and the Continent in the Eighth Century*, Oxford 1949, 38.

[73] See S. Ridyard, 'The Life, Translations and Miracles of the Blessed Virgin Eadburg', in *Royal Saints*, fos 101v and 105.

[74] Ridyard, *Royal Saints*, 119–20, 253–310.

[75] *Vita Edithe*, 74, 273–4; Ridyard, *Royal Saints*, 145–6.

[76] *Vita Edithe*, 292. This account is said to have been related and recorded in the vernacular, in the presence of Abbess Brihtgifu (Ridyard, *Royal Saints*, 40).

destination, particularly for local pilgrims in search of curative miracles. In addition to the poor woman forced to trek between Horton and Barking, Bede mentions the story of a local blind woman who left for the nunnery with the intention of praying before the Barking relics, but was restored her sight after praying for intercession within the sacred bounds of the nuns' cemetery.[77] Bede also records Abbess Æthelhild's healing of a nobleman, a guest at Barking's hostel, by means of a miraculous patch of soil associated with St Oswald.[78]

As patrons of churches and shrines, Anglo-Saxon women followed in the legendary tradition of St Helena, creating sacred space for the contemplation and the veneration of relics.[79] An eleventh-century woman, Gytha, is credited with the establishment of Nether Wallop, a church which contains the remains of a wall painting above the chancel that served to remind viewers that they were in the presence of the risen and glorified Christ.[80] At Wilton, Edith, who is described by Goscelin as having lived 'a pilgrim's life on earth', was credited with the construction and ornamentation of an oratorium dedicated to St Denys that was shaped like a cross and decorated with scenes from the Passion.[81] Likewise, in the *Vita Edwardi Regis* Queen Edith is praised for her construction of a stone church at Wilton so that the tomb of the community's patron-saint, Edith, could be adequately venerated.[82] At Abingdon, an Ælfhild was remembered for building a chapel in the mid-tenth century dedicated to St Vincent.[83] Queen Margaret, the granddaughter of Edmund Ironside, who spent her formative years at Edward the Confessor's court, was also praised for initiating the construction of the church of St Andrew, where the apostle's relics attracted so many pilgrims from the south that the queen was moved to provide a ferry and hostels. The eleventh-century *vita* compares Margaret's church to those in Jerusalem and Rome, and remarks that it had a tower that served as a landmark to guide pilgrims.[84]

Women's patronage also included devotional gifts, which were key facilitators in the pilgrims' approach to the Divine. Devotional art not only supplied a channel for private spirituality for female pilgrims, but by its very production and donation for the glory of God, women patrons could, according to contemporary clerics, expect spiritual benefits, in particular redemption and salvation. Ælfgifu Emma, in the tradition of St Helena, was noted for her generosity to various churches and religious communities.[85] To Ely, Emma presented decorated silk coverings for the

---

77 *HE*, IV.10.
78 *HE*, III.11.
79 Hunt, *Holy Land Pilgrimage*, 36–8.
80 R. Gem and P. Tudor-Craig, 'A "Winchester School" Wall-Painting at Nether Wallop, Hampshire', *Anglo-Saxon England* ix, 1981, 115–36; P. Tudor-Craig, 'Nether Wallop Reconsidered', in *Early Medieval Wall Painting and Painted Sculpture in England*, ed. S. Cather, D. Park and P. Williamson, British Archaeology Reports ccxvi, British Series, 1990, 89–97; Raw, *Crucifixion Iconography*, 13–14.
81 *Vita Edithe*, 45, 86–7.
82 Barlow, *The Life of Edward the Confessor*, 46–7.
83 *Chronicon de Abingdon* i, 91–2; *Anglo-Saxon Charters*, ed. A.J. Robertson, 2nd edn, 1956, no. xlii; A. Thacker, 'Æthelwold and Abingdon', 60–1.
84 M.O. Anderson, 'St Andrews before Alexander I', in *The Scottish Tradition: Essays in Honor of Ronald Gordon Cant*, ed. G.W.S. Barrow, London 1974, 5; M.O. Anderson, 'The Celtic Church in Kinrimund', *The Innes Review* xxv, no. 2, 1974, 72; R.G. Cant, 'The Building of St Andrews Cathedral', *The Innes Review* xxv, no. 2, 1974, 77.
85 Hunt, *Holy Land Pilgrimage*, 36.

tombs of the saints, and for the tomb of Ely's most important saint an especially magnificent covering of silk, bordered with gold and decorated with gems.[86] Susan Ridyard suggests that Emma may have been influential in the benefactions to Ely by the men in her life – Æthelred, Cnut, and Edward the Confessor – and her own generosity to the abbey receives special attention in the *Liber Eliensis*.[87] But Emma's gifts were not limited to this one community: she contributed twenty pounds of silver to Sherborne for the repair of the roof through which rain fell upon the tomb of St Wulfsige, and at Winchester there was a contest between Emma and Bishop Ælfwine, who 'vied with each other in making embellishments for the church of St Swithun from their treasures'.[88] Queen Emma also vigorously participated in the spread of relics throughout England. The *Abingdon Chronicle* credits the queen with the gift of a 'Greek' shrine for St Vincent, which held a collection of relics.[89] Eadmer notes that Emma exchanged an embroidered cope and many pounds of silver with the bishop of Benevento for the arm of St Bartholomew, which she then donated to Canterbury, thus initiating his cult there.[90] The *Anglo-Saxon Chronicle*, moreover, mentions that on the death of her son Harthacnut, Emma gave the head of St Valentine to New Minster Winchester for the benefit of his soul.[91] Among the treasures of which Edward the Confessor deprived his mother in 1043 was the head of St Ouen, which she had purchased when in Normandy after Æthelred's death.[92] She had already given Ouen's trunk to Canterbury.[93]

Queen Emma is a particularly well-documented patron. But as a very active queen, indeed the 'relic queen', she stands out in the surviving records. The majority of ecclesiastical inventories omit the names of benefactors, particularly those women of humble status and their equally modest gifts. If, however, the wealth of evidence for Emma's generosity and for that of a few other noble women is any indication of the patronage practices of Anglo-Saxon women, then it is clear that women were essential to the material culture of pilgrimage. Women of noble and thegnly status are remembered by chroniclers for the gold and gem-covered reliquaries they donated to religious communities including Abingdon, Evesham, Ramsey and Rochester.[94] We also have evidence for such gifts in women's wills. In her will, Ælfgifu made provisions for 'her shrine with her relics' to be bequeathed to the Old Minster, Winchester.[95] Hagiographical evidence for Queen Margaret describes how upon her marriage to King Malcolm III, she took a miraculous

---

[86] *Liber Eliensis*, II.50.

[87] *Liber Eliensis*, II.79; Ridyard, *Royal Saints*, 194.

[88] 'The Life of St Wulfsin of Sherborne by Goscelin', ed. C.H. Talbot, *Revue Bénédictine* lxix, 1959, 81; *Annales Monasterii de Wintonia: AD 519–1277* in *Annales Monastici*, ed. H. Luard, London 1864–69, ii, 25.

[89] *Chronicon de Abingdon* i, 433; Dodwell, *Anglo-Saxon Art*, 25.

[90] *Eadmer, Eadmeri historia novorum in Anglia*, ed. M. Rule, RS lxxxi, London 1884, 107–10.

[91] *ASC, s.a.* 1041 (F).

[92] *De gestis pontificum*, 419–20.

[93] *De gestis pontificum*, 419.

[94] *Registrum Roffense*, ed. J. Thorpe, London 1769, 199; *Historia Rameseiensis*, 194; *Chronicon de Abingdon* i, 429; *Chronicon Abbatiae de Evesham*, ed. W.D. Macray, RS xxix, 1863, 46; Dodwell, *Anglo-Saxon Art*, 23, 197.

[95] Whitelock, *Anglo-Saxon Wills*, 20.

reliquary with her to Scotland.[96] The palm-length shrine was made of gold and formed in the shape of a cross, which, when opened, revealed a fragment of the True Cross and an ivory carving of Christ.

In addition to being an example of a female donor of devotional objects, Margaret's reliquary was representative of the popularity of the cult of the True Cross that flourished in Anglo-Saxon England. From the earliest days of the Church, the cross had been the object of veneration, and pieces of it were desired as relics. Its power lay in the belief, as set out in *The Dream of the Rood*, that devotion to the cross or crucifix would ensure entry to heaven.[97] The discovery of the True Cross was ceremoniously linked through legend with St Helena, and Helena's feast day, the Day of the Invention of the True Cross, was celebrated in England by the eighth century.[98] The extraordinary popularity of the legend of the cross in England may lie in the belief that Helena was of British origin.[99] Barbara Raw has examined the various ways in which Christ's death on the cross was portrayed in the art, literature and theology of tenth- and eleventh-century England.[100] Raw has looked at the cross's function in Anglo-Saxon society, particularly in redemption history and devotional practice, and she has shown how devotion to the cross was expressed in church dedications, homiletic literature, liturgical ceremony, poems, art, and meditative prayers like those added to the Vespasian Psalter.[101]

When one looks more closely at the culture of pilgrimage in Anglo-Saxon England, however, particularly women's pilgrimage, it is apparent that crucifixion iconography and theology played an essential role both in pilgrimage and women's spirituality. For pilgrims, the cross was both the instrument of Christ's death and the ultimate symbol of his Resurrection and redeeming power. Pilgrimage to Jerusalem, particularly Golgotha, with its relics of the True Cross, produced an opportunity to relive the Crucifixion event, the epitome of Christian theology. Crucifixes, like reliquaries, devotional texts and images, provided a focus for contemplation by women about death, redemption and salvation. At Nunnaminster, for example, there was a tradition of personal devotion around the theme of the Crucifixion. A devotional work, once in the possession of this women's house, includes a group of prayers, each of which concentrates on a different aspect of Christ's Passion.[102] The text includes prayers from the Good Friday 'Veneration of the Cross' liturgy, similar to that in the *Regularis Concordia*, a text known to have

---

[96] *Genealogia regum Anglorum auct. Aelredo, abbate Rievallensis abbatiae* in *PL* cxcv, col. 715; Dodwell, *Anglo-Saxon Art*, 197 and n. 106.

[97] Raw, *Crucifixion Iconography*, 62.

[98] J. Chance, *Woman as Hero in Old English Literature*, Syracuse, NY, 1986, 46; R. Morris, *Legend of the Holy Rood*, EETS, os xlvi, London 1871, 3–17; Ælfric's 'Exaltation of the Holy Cross', in *Ælfric's Lives of the Saints* i, 144–59; C. Wolfe, 'The Audience of Old English Literature', unpublished Cambridge dissertation, 1994, 74–5.

[99] Bodden, *The Old English Finding of the True Cross*, 2 n. 3, 54, 55.

[100] Raw, *Anglo-Saxon Crucifixion Iconography*.

[101] Butler, 'Church Dedications and the Cult of Anglo-Saxon Saints in England', 44; *Ælfric's Catholic Homilies*, ed. Godden, 174–9; Raw, *Crucifixion Iconography*, 2, 166–7.

[102] *An Ancient Manuscript of Nunnaminster, Winchester*, ed. W. de Gray Birch, Hampshire Record Society v, London 1889, 67–78; *The Making of England: Anglo-Saxon Art and Culture AD 600–900*, ed. L. Webster and J. Backhouse, Cambridge 1992, 210.

been in the possession of women's communities.[103] Pilgrimage and devotion to the True Cross was linked directly through iconographical depictions such as the *navis crucis*, an image of the cross as a ship. The idea of the cross as a vehicle for salvation is suggested in *The Dream of the Rood* as well, and it is found in an eighth-century Anglo-Saxon manuscript illumination in which a stylized crucified Christ is shown above the hull of a ship holding several passengers.[104] The devotional function of the crucifix is clear as well in Goscelin's description of the wall paintings at Edith of Wilton's church, which portrayed scenes of Christ's passion 'as she had pictured them in her heart'.[105] According to Goscelin, contemplation of Christ's death on the cross could allow man to pass through the door to the unseen world where Christ had preceded him. In this way the paintings may have been intended to make Wilton nuns and other worshippers aware that the way to the Holy Land was through the cross, which was both an instrument of Christ's death and a bringer of eternal life.[106] Women, then, were clearly participants in the devotional practices associated with the True Cross.

It was this environment that facilitated the third type of pilgrimage available to Anglo-Saxon women – virtual pilgrimage. Using various aspects of material culture, women could be conveyed to the holy sites abroad without ever having to leave home. In particular, the cult of the cross and the art it spawned served to channel women's spirituality and allowed them to envision the gospel events of the Holy Land while remaining in their own churches. Women's gifts to churches and religious communities fostered this cult of the cross in Anglo-Saxon England, allowing worshippers – including women – to meditate upon past events in the Holy Land without even going there. In their wills, Wulfwaru and Wulfgyth included gifts of crosses to the communities of Bath Abbey and Christ Church respectively.[107] In another case, a Leofgifu left a crucifix to Ramsey, while a Countess Goda donated silver crucifixes to Rochester.[108] Queen Margaret's hagiographer describes the jewel-encrusted cross she presented to the abbey church at Dunfermline and the giant cross St Andrews received from her, which was so large that thieves were unable to steal it.[109] Chronicle evidence by Orderic Vitalis describes how Countess Godgifu bestowed all her treasures on Coventry with the order that goldsmiths there were to rework all the gold and silver into venerable art objects including crucifixes for the church.[110] Countess Judith and her husband Earl Tostig commissioned a figure of Christ on the cross clothed in gold and silver for Durham.[111] And Tovi the Proud and his wife Gytha were remembered by the

---

[103] *Regularis Concordia: the Monastic Agreement of the Monks and Nuns of the English Nation*, ed. T. Symons, NMT, London 1953, VI.35, 34–6.

[104] E.A. Lowe, *Codices Latini Antiquiores: a Paleographical Guide to Latin Manuscripts prior to the Ninth Century*, ix, Oxford 1950, 52, pl. 1424; B.F. Huppe, *The Web of Words: Structural Analysis of the Old English Poems Vainglory, the Worker of Creation, the Dream of the Rood and Judith*, Albany 1970, pl. 3, facing p. 42; S. McEntire, 'The Devotional Context of the Cross before AD 1000', in *Sources in Anglo-Saxon Culture*, ed. P. Szarmach, Kalamazoo, MI, 1986, 350–1.

[105] *Vita Edithe*, 86–7.

[106] Raw, *Crucifixion Iconography*, 16.

[107] Whitelock, *Anglo-Saxon Wills*, 21, 32.

[108] *Historiae Rameseiensis*, 199; *Registrum Roffense*, 119; Dodwell, *Anglo-Saxon Art*, 23.

[109] D. McRoberts, 'The Glorious House of St Andrews', in *The Scottish Tradition: Essays in Honor of Ronald Gordon Cant*, London 1974, 104.

[110] Orderic, ii, 183; Dodwell, *Anglo-Saxon Art*, 66.

[111] *Symeonis Dunelmensis monachi opera omnia*, 95; Dodwell, *Anglo-Saxon Art*, 119.

chronicler at Waltham for the great stone crucifix they gave to the community, and which bore the dedication of the Cross. This cross was described as a masterpiece of gems, gold and silver, and Gytha commissioned the decoration of the figure of Christ with a crown and head-band made of gold and precious stones, an act reminiscent of Helen's decoration of the holy rood in Cynewulf's *Elene*.[112] These crucifixes, like the magnificent cross pictured in the frontispiece of the New Minster *Liber Vitae*, with its donors, Emma and Cnut, and described as having a compartment for relics, were sumptuous objects which played instructional, liturgical and devotional roles. Individually or in great clusters, as recorded at Glastonbury, Beverly, Peterborough and Durham (the last collection a gift by Judith and Tostig), these crosses must have presented an awesome spectacle to pilgrims.[113] As Ælfric reminded his audience in one of his homilies, these great crosses were more than just instruments of Christ's suffering, they were a memorial to his victory over death and man's sin.[114]

Devotion to the True Cross and the whole concept of pilgrimage, particularly penitential pilgrimage, must be viewed within the larger European atmosphere of apocalyptic anxiety and preoccupation with sin, judgment and redemption. In the later Anglo-Saxon period redemption history and millenarianism played an increasingly dominant role in religious belief and practice. The idea that man's existence in this transitory world was itself a pilgrimage is found in various churchmen's writings of the period. The Last Judgment and redemption appear as frequent themes in Anglo-Saxon vernacular literature, homilies, ecclesiastical correspondence and art. The iconography and design of many reliquaries, weavings, wall-paintings, and crucifixes served to remind women of their own sin and to provide hope for redemption. The central register from the New Minster's *Liber Vitae* depicts Peter hitting a devil on the head with a key in order to rescue a soul. The saved soul is presented to an angel on the left holding the open *Book of Life*, while on the right, a winged demon takes away two condemned souls, a man and woman.[115] Another Winchester work from the mid-eleventh century, *The Tiberius Psalter*, a devotional work which played an important part in the role of private prayer, shows the harrowing of hell; a group, including a woman, is saved by Christ.[116] The account of the Wenlock monk's admonitory vision of Judgment, which Boniface sent to an Anglo-Saxon abbess, includes women among the saved and damned.[117] The monk's vision included an unknown woman who was released from the pit of purgatory by the celebration of mass in her name, and two former queens, Cuthburga and Wiala, who suffered for their sins in torturous, flaming, penitential pits. Additional evidence for women's search for redemption is found at Bath on the eighth-century lead funerary burial cross of a nun, Eadgyfu.[118] The inscription asks God that Eadgifu be granted salvation for her sins through the

[112] *The Waltham Chronicle*, 10–12; Dodwell, *Anglo-Saxon Art*, 119; Bodden, *The Old English Finding of the True Cross*, 92; J.N. Garde, *Old English Poetry in Medieval Christian Perspective: a Doctrinal Approach*, Cambridge 1991, 177.

[113] Gameson, *The Role of Art*, 129.

[114] *Catholici Homilies* II.xviii, ed. Godden, 175–6.

[115] E. Temple, *Anglo-Saxon Manuscripts 900–1066: a Survey of Manuscripts Illuminated in the British Isles*, London 1976, 95–6, ill. 248; Gameson, *The Role of Art*, pls 7a and b.

[116] Gameson, *The Role of Art*, pl. 13b.

[117] Emerton, *Letters of Saint Boniface*, 25–31, 189–91.

[118] E. Okasha, *Handlist of Anglo-Saxon Non-Runic Inscriptions*, Cambridge 1971, 51–2.

redeeming power that springs from Christ's death in Jerusalem, and from the cross itself. Finally, an illustration in the early eleventh-century *Paris Psalter* shows a woman in the embrace of a man, who has been struck by an arrow from a demon's bow, on account of her lust and wantonness.[119] Thus, in both material and written culture, women participated in the western European preoccupation with sin, judgment and redemption.

It was within this climate of heightened anxiety that the tenth-century cult of All Souls took hold. The Cluniac phenomenon was, however, a dramatic expression of long existing European practice in which individuals and their kinsmen sought spiritual benefits from religious communities. In the eighth and ninth centuries, Anglo-Saxon communities, including Christ Church and St Augustine's, Canterbury, were already spiritual remission factories.[120] Women's charters and wills demonstrate their fixation with sin, personal penitence and redemption. Provisions in these documents reflect the donor's wish to obtain intercession from saints through the prayers of the living, and especially through offertory masses. Beornthryth, Werburh and Eahlburg and their respective spouses provided gifts to Christ Church or St Augustine's in exchange for the commemoration of their souls through prayers, masses or the singing of psalms.[121] Individual women, too, including an abbess and nun, gave gifts to Christ Church with similar expectations of spiritual benefits.[122] Finally, in her tenth-century will, Æthelgifu includes specific instructions for female attendants to sing psalms for her soul.[123]

Women may have had a particular devotion to the redemptive cross, since they could imagine themselves in the role of either the Virgin Mary or Mary Magdalene, both of whom had strong cults in Anglo-Saxon England.[124] There was both an artistic and literary tradition in Anglo-Saxon England of the Virgin Mary as an intercessor during Judgment. The Marian apocrypha, which describes the Virgin Mary's power to release damned souls after Judgment, is found in several anonymous English texts.[125] Furthermore, on the eleventh-century North Elmham ivory and in the New Minster refoundation charter and *Liber Vitae*, Mary is depicted with St Peter as a Last Judgment intercessor.[126] Two of the four manuscripts that contain drawings of Mary as an orant figure beneath the cross also include a prayer

---

[119] R.M. Harris, 'An Illustration in an Anglo-Saxon Psalter', *Journal of the Warburg and Courtauld Institutes* xxvi, 1963, 255–7; C. Neuman de Vegvar, 'Images of Women in Anglo-Saxon Art IV: First Target of a Demonized Eros in the Paris Psalter', *The Old English Newsletter*, 1993, no. 1, vol. xxvii, 44–6; B. Colgrave, ed., *Paris Psalter*, Early English Manuscripts in Facsimile viii, Copenhagen 1958.

[120] See R. Fleming, 'History and Liturgy at pre-Conquest Christ Church', in *The Haskins Society Journal: Studies in Medieval History* vi, Woodbridge 1994, 66–83.

[121] S 1188, 1195, 1198; F.E. Harmer, *Select English Historical Documents*, Cambridge 1914, no. 9; Fleming, 'History and Liturgy at pre-Conquest Christ Church', 70–1, 72, 74.

[122] S 123, 125, 1197; Fleming, 'History and Liturgy at pre-Conquest Christ Church', 73–4.

[123] *The Will of Æthelgifu; a Tenth-Century Manuscript*, ed. and trans. D. Whitelock, Oxford 1968, 12.

[124] For the cult of the Virgin Mary in Anglo-Saxon England, see M. Clayton, *The Cult of the Virgin Mary in Anglo-Saxon England*, Cambridge 1990. For the cult of Mary Magdalen, see Lapidge, *Anglo-Saxon Litanies*, and J.E. Cross, 'Mary Magdalen in the Old English Martyrology: the Earliest Extant "Narrat Josephus" Variant of her Legend', *Speculum* xxxiii, 1978, 16–25.

[125] Clayton, *The Cult of the Virgin Mary*, 253–7, 263.

[126] Clayton, *The Cult of the Virgin Mary*, 159, 175–6, 255.

Fig. 1. The Lady Gunhild. Anglo-Saxon (?), c.1075. Obverse and reverse of cross. (National Museum, Copenhagen)

Fig. 2. Crucifixion. Weingarten Gospels. (New York, Pierpont Morgan Library, M.709, fo. 1v)

Fig. 3. Frontispiece to the Liber Vitae *of New Minster,
Winchester. King Cnut and Ælfgifu presenting altar cross. (BL
MS Stowe 944, fo. 6r, by permission of the British Library)*

to Mary, which links her intercession specifically to her presence beneath the cross of Christ the Redeemer.[127]

Old English private poetry and prayer books, like these 'visual homilies', addressed similar themes of death, judgment and redemption. While not the spontaneous outpourings of piety found in later mystical poetry, poems of the late Anglo-Saxon period, particularly *Resignation* and *The Dream of the Rood*, reveal the movement towards the expression of more intimate needs of the individual petitioner rather than those of the universal church.[128] Collections of prayers and private devotions which facilitated personal meditation are also found in the *Portiforium of Wulfstan*, the *Regularis Concordia*, the *Book of Cerne*, and the *Book of Nunnaminster*.[129] The Nunnaminster work, thought to have belonged to King Alfred's wife, contains a series of prayers on the theme of salvation history, including a detailed recollection of Christ's sufferings in which each detail of the crucifixion is recited in a series of prayers.[130] The eighth-century Mercian *Royal Prayerbook*, believed to have been used by a woman, also includes litanies to saints and prayers similar to those in the *Regularis Concordia* for the Good Friday 'Veneration of the Cross' ceremony.[131] The *Harley Prayerbook*, also of Mercian origin and dating to the early ninth century, includes litanies to Continental female saints with both communal and personal petitions.[132] There are indications that many of these devotional prayers in search of redemption and salvation were recited in front of contemplative visual aids including decorated panels, reliquaries, and crucifixes.[133] Thus private texts, like women's personal meditative objects, played a contemplative function in women's sphere of private spirituality.

The pilgrimage themes illustrated and expressed in the communal and private objects and devotional texts used by women facilitated their vicarious pilgrimage experiences. Sometimes this vicarious pilgrimage experience took the form of liturgical dramas set within both monastic and public spheres. These religious reenactments aimed at transporting viewers and participants to biblical events, drawing them closer to Christ the Redeemer. Amalarius of Metz's *Liber Officialis*, which was known in England in the late Anglo-Saxon period and referred to by Ælfric, contained his interpretation of the mass as a dramatic ritual which recreated the events of salvation history.[134] Amalarius hoped that both the clergy and lay congregation would recall past gospel events and actually feel present at all the events of Christ's life, particularly his Passion and Resurrection. While Anglo-Saxon practice tended to concentrate more on the meditative rather than the

---

127 Raw, *Crucifixion Iconography*, 102.
128 *The Dream of the Rood*, ed. M.F. Swanton, Exeter 1987; *The Anglo-Saxon Poetic Records: The Exeter Book III*, ed. G.P. Krapp and E.K. Dobbie, New York 1936, 215–18; B. Raw, *The Art and Background of Old English Poetry*, London 1978, 123, 126, 130, 132.
129 *The Portiforium of Wulfstan*, ed. A. Hughes, 2 vols, London 1858–60, ii, 18–23; *Regularis Concordia*, ed. Symons, 11–13; Webster, *The Making of England*, 210–21; Raw, *Crucifixion Iconography*, 56–7.
130 *An Ancient Manuscript of the Eighth and Ninth Centuries*, ed. Birch, 39–57; Raw, *Crucifixion Iconography*, 58.
131 Lapidge, *Anglo-Saxon Litanies*, 75, 212–13; Webster, *The Making of England*, 209–10.
132 Lapidge, *Anglo-Saxon Litanies*, 75, 210–11; Webster, *The Making of England*, 208.
133 Raw, *Crucifixion Iconography*, 57–8.
134 *Amalarii episcopi opera liturgica omnia*, ed. J.M. Hughes, G.P. Krapp and E.K. Dobbie, Vatican City 1948–50, 138–40; Raw, *Crucifixion Iconography*, 183–4.

historical value of such dramas, some English religious practices suggest a similar spirit. The *Regularis Concordia* includes the Palm Sunday procession description, which commemorated Christ's entry into Jerusalem, complete with chanting children along the Christ-actor's path.[135] For Easter Day, this text also includes a type of 'virtual Resurrection' ceremony with a ceremonially buried and discovered cross of Christ, impersonations by religious as angels and the women at the tomb, and specific chants sung to aid in the recreation of the past gospel events.[136] These interactive ceremonies venerating Christ's redemptive powers, like the devotional objects and private and communal prayers, provided a spiritual, if not physical, pilgrimage for both laity and enclosed monastics.

Four objects associated with noble women played a similar role as these interactive ceremonies as aids to transport their owners spiritually. These four pieces internalized and personalized the public liturgical dramas in such a way that women could be constantly reminded of their search for redemption. The first of these examples is the frontispiece of the New Minster *Liber Vitae*. The depiction of Ælfgifu Emma's presentation of the giant cross to the Winchester altar is accompanied below by an inscription of her name and title. Below her a monk holds the New Minster *Liber Vitae* which corresponds to the heavenly one held by Christ. Since there would be no question of her identity at Winchester, the inclusion of her name in the presence of Christ, Mary and St Peter meant to include her in the most prominent way possible with Cnut at the head of the list of names of the memorial book.[137] Both in text and image, Emma is present in two realms, the earthly corporate memory of the Winchester community and in the heavenly company of Christ and the saints. Through her gifts to the community, and, in turn, their continued prayers for her soul, her niche in Paradise was assured. The combined emotive power of text and image is also expressed by Gunhild's ivory crucifix. The ornate Anglo-Saxon crucifix decorated with elaborate Crucifixion and Last Judgment scenes was carved, according to its inscription, for and upon the request of Gunhild – who is simultaneously referred to as Helena – shortly before her death in 1076.[138] Gunhild's personalized devotional crucifix is intriguing for its incorporation of inscribed meditative texts on the True Cross and an iconography that includes female figures among the blessed and damned in its Last Judgment depiction. Together the words and images provided a link to Christ's death in Jerusalem for its female beholder.

Two other objects, a Gospel book and an embroidered alb, provide examples of the personal devotion of women through the depiction of themselves as redemptive sinners seeking salvation from Christ. The first, the alb Edith of Wilton made, had, according to her *vita*, golden figures of Christ and the apostles embroidered around the hem. While this design is similar to others of the period, Edith included herself in the picture. She is portrayed as the penitent Mary Magdalene in the presence of

---

[135] *Regularis Concordia*, IV.36, 35.

[136] *Regularis Concordia*, IV.46, 44; B. Raw, 'Biblical Literature: the New Testament', 230.

[137] Gameson, *The Role of Art*, 82–3, pl. 6.

[138] 'May those who believe in the crucified Christ be mindful in prayer of Liutger, who carved me at the request of Helen, who is also called Gunhild' (J. Beckwith, *Ivory Carvings in Early Medieval England*, London 1972, 57–8, 127); Gameson, *The Role of Art*, 251 n. 103. For another view on the identity of this Gunhild, see *ASC*, s.a. 1044 (D) (1045). I would like to thank Ann Williams for directing my attention to this source.

Christ, embracing his feet.[139] A similar theme is found in the fourth devotional object commissioned by a woman. The eleventh-century Weingarten Gospel Book illumination shows Judith, its patron, as a penitent Mary Magdalene next to the Virgin Mary, grasping the base of a cross holding Christ reminiscent to that described in the *Dream of the Rood*.[140] Judith's inclusion of herself as a perpetually redemptive sinner in this biblical scene allowed her to imagine herself actually in Jerusalem at the crucifixion. Judith appears as more than the traditional donor present at a biblical event. She is depicted simultaneously as herself and as Mary Magdalene, grasping the base of the cross and sharing the Virgin Mary's grief. For both Edith and Judith, their meditative objects played a similar role, though in different contexts. For Edith of Wilton, a cloistered nun who never saw the Holy Land, such objects, including her alb, her Passion wall-paintings, her mother's Nail of the Passion, and her community's devotional texts, allowed her to visit, intellectually and spiritually, a location she would never see in person. Judith, however, is known to have gone on pilgrimage with her husband. Her Gospel Book allowed her to revisit the holy sites again and again while remaining at home. These representations by Anglo-Saxon women imagining themselves participating in events from the life of Christ, or simply in his company, became an increasingly frequent motif in later medieval art. More importantly, however, the pictures show how their patrons could remain prostrate at the feet of Christ, bridging the gap between the human and divine through the medium of the picture, even if they were unable to do so in fact.[141] These objects were part of what had to have been a much larger corpus of religious objects which provided a focus for meditation, lifting women in their churches to a higher plane of prayer. Furthermore, these four works of art reflect the convergence of two trends within late eleventh-century religious thought. First was the growth of internalized spirituality so often associated with twelfth-century women mystics. This individualized form of devotion grew more popular within a church that was becoming increasingly uncomfortable about encouraging women, particularly monastic women, to make actual journeys to the holy sites abroad. The objects also visually reflected the growing opinion, especially of some churchmen, towards pilgrimage that the true pilgrimage should be with the heart rather than the feet, and that forgiveness and spiritual fulfillment were not necessarily achieved simply by visiting holy sites mentioned in the biblical narratives. While we lack written reflections by the women themselves, describing their religious experiences and motives, contemplative objects like Gunhild's crucifix, Judith's Gospel Book, and Edith's alb, and the meditative images in their chapels and abbeys, seem to anticipate the twelfth-century use of religious images to capture the direct inspiration of the spirit.

This desire to transcend spiritually place and time through devotional images and texts was expressed by the fourth-century pilgrim Egeria. Through her language and description of the places and people she encountered, she hoped her female audience's careful reading of her journey through the Holy Land would

---

139 *Vita Edithe*, 79.
140 Weingarten Gospel Book, New York, Pierpont Morgan Library, MS 709 (Weingarten Gospel Book), fo. 105v; E. Temple, *Anglo-Saxon Manuscripts 900–1066: a Survey of Manuscripts Illuminated in the British Isles* ii, London 1976, 142, ills 285, 289.
141 Raw, *Crucifixion Iconography*, 24.

contribute to their spiritual growth.[142] Though no such accounts or itineraries by Anglo-Saxon women survive, those of churchmen from the eighth-century Arculf to the tenth-century Archbishop Sigeric were popular throughout the period.[143] Bede considered such works as Adomnan's account of Arculf's pilgrimage useful for the majority of people who were unable to make such a journey and could only know of the holy places from what they learned from books.[144] An early twelfth-century abbot claimed that if unable actually to go on a pilgrimage, those who read and reflected upon the accounts of other pilgrims should receive the same reward from God as those who actually travelled to holy places.[145] The abbot was among a number of writers advocating vicarious pilgrimage through pilgrim narratives. Though pilgrimage had yet to reach its height in popularity, especially with the Crusades, such thoughts, reminiscent of the misgivings expressed by Gregory of Nyssa and Jerome, were reinforced by the opinions of contemporary churchmen. In the mid-eighth century, Boniface's successor, Bishop Lull, excommunicated the Anglo-Saxon missionary abbess, Switha, and two of her nuns, for their violation of the requirement of *stabilitas*.[146] Condemned to a life-long penance of bread and water, Switha and her subordinates were chastised for their blatant disregard of canonical regulations regarding enclosure. Centuries later, Archbishop Anselm favored enclosure over pilgrimage for monastics. The Anglo-Norman period would see an acceleration of this trend, and twelfth-century women mystics, too, expressed concern for the welfare of pilgrim-nuns.[147] For laywomen, and especially nuns restricted from pilgrimage by increased demands for stricter enclosure, objects, images, texts and the various semi-dramatic liturgical ceremonies facilitated their escape from earthly time and space to the realm of the divine while never leaving their community, their private chapel or local church.[148] Countess Goda, for instance, had a private chapel at Lambeth, and among her gifts to Rochester were a shrine and a Gospel Book.[149] These women could, in essence, experience a virtual pilgrimage. On a deeper level – and facilitated by Old English and Latin devotional writings and personal meditative objects and images – women could internalize the mystical and redemptive experience. Spiritual interiorization was

---

[142] J. Wilkinson, *Egeria's Travels to the Holy Land*, Warminster 1981, 95, 101, 103, 110, 113, 123, 144.

[143] *Adomnan, De locis sanctis*, ed. D. Meehan, *Scriptores Latini Hiberniae* iii, Dublin 1958; A. Grabois, 'Anglo-Norman England and the Holy Land', *ANS* vii, 133.

[144] Bede himself used Adomnan for his own compilation *On the Holy Places* (*HE*, V.15).

[145] Daniel the Abbot, *The Pilgrimage of the Russian Abbot Daniel in the Holy Land*, annotated by C.W. Wilson, Palestine Pilgrim Text Society iv, 1895, repr. New York 1971; 'Daniel the Abbot', in *Jerusalem Pilgrimage 1099–1185*, ed. J. Wilkinson, London 1988, 121.

[146] *Die Briefe des heiligen Bonifatius und Lullus* in *Monumenta Germaniae Historica: Epistolae Selectae*, ed. M. Tangl, 2nd edn, Berlin 1955, i, 128; C. Fell, 'Some Implications of the Boniface Correspondence', in *New Readings of Women in Old English Literature*, ed. H. Damico and A.H. Olsen, Bloomington, IN, 1990, 36–7.

[147] Constable, 'Opposition to Pilgrimage', 132–3, 140.

[148] Wulfstan, *Narratio metrica de Sancto Swithuno*, 69–70 lines 141–70. In his account of the re-dedication of the church at Ramsey in 991 by St Oswald, then bishop of York, the abbey's chronicler describes the mixture of the organs and voices together among the assembled people (*Vita Sancti Oswaldi* in *The Historians of the Church of York and its Archbishop*, ed. J. Raine, i, 464–5); M. Berry, 'What the Monks Sang: Music in Winchester in the Late Tenth Century', in *Bishop Æthelwold: His Career and Influence*, 157–9.

[149] *Registrum Roffense*, 119; Dodwell, *Anglo-Saxon Art*, 193 and n. 60.

not new to women's religious lives in the twelfth century, but little attention has been focused on this aspect for Anglo-Saxon women or their contribution to the twelfth-century explosion of such means of veneration – that is, the attention to the private visionary experience and the growth of mysticism, especially for women.

Pilgrimage did not end with the Norman Conquest, but it did decline at least temporarily with the general unrest in England. In addition to the dangers women faced because of the Norman invaders, social and political conditions in Europe during the mid and late eleventh century contributed to a decreasing number of pilgrims leaving England for Rome. Rome itself was frequently a theological battleground in this period, and the history of the *Schola Saxonum* in this period is one of steady decline. Furthermore, religious aspirations in the West tended to shift further east towards Jerusalem, especially as crusading zeal increased. Despite the many obstacles, official denouncements, and various catastrophes awaiting them along the pilgrimage route, women continued to travel to holy sites. Indeed, the latest evidence for Anglo-Saxon women on pilgrimage – the will of a laywoman, Madselin, and charter for another, Leofgifu, both dating from the time of the Conquest – shows that these women were part of this intensified movement towards Jerusalem.[150]

Almost without exception, the voices in early medieval pilgrim narratives, chronicles and miracle stories are those of clerical men. Occasionally, however, women emerge from the shadows. If we look at pilgrimage and Anglo-Saxon women together, women clearly emerge as participants in pilgrimage culture. And through their devotional prayers and endowments, English women were essential to the promotion of saints' cults and the relic culture of western Europe throughout the Anglo-Saxon period and beyond. But if we look indirectly at Anglo-Saxon women through the material culture of devotional art and texts, women are even more visible as pilgrims of the heart. These glimpses reveal that from the conversion of England up through the Norman Conquest, Anglo-Saxon women, both lay and religious, and from all social levels, in search of miraculous assistance, relics, redemption, salvation and a deepened spirituality, participated in pilgrimage in all its forms – on the Continent, throughout England, and within their private chapels surrounded by their devotional objects.

---

[150] S 1029; Whitelock, *Anglo-Saxon Wills*, 39.

WILLIAM MALET AND HIS FAMILY

Cyril Hart

Ask the average historian of medieval England what he or she knows about William Malet, and the answer will probably be: 'He buried Harold after Hastings – didn't he?' The query at the end of the reply might arise from some subconscious reservation on the matter. After all, the prime evidence comes from the *Carmen de Hastingae Proelio*, a suspect text, which does not mention Malet by name:[1]

Carmen line 587   ... quidam, partim Normannus et Anglus,
              Compater Heraldi, iussa libenter agit.
         Corpus enim regis cito sustulit et sepeluit;
              Imponens lapidem, scripsit et in titulo:
         'Per mandata ducis, rex, hic, Heralde, quiescis,
              Vt custos maneas littoris et pelagi.'

The unlikely claim about an inscribed stone looks as if it was invented to enable the poet to make his sardonic remark about Harold's corpse being left guarding the seashore. So why accept the rest of the story? This contrived account, maybe by Guy of Amiens, was softened somewhat by William of Poitiers, who having supplied William Malet's name, then went on (using a phrase from the *Carmen*):[2]

> Dictum est illudendo, oportere situm esse custodem littoris et pelagi, quae cum armis ante vesanus insedit.

Orderic Vitalis repeated the Poitiers version:[3]

> ... ad tumulandum prope littus maris quod diu cum armis seruauerat Guillelmo agnomine Maleto uictoris iussu traditus.

At least three-quarters of early English history – and the history of the Malets is no exception – is based not on fact but on supposition. It is the art of the possible, in which the evidence behind many a confident assertion hardly stands up to

---

[1] *Carmen*, 38. The date and place of authorship, and the identity of the writer, remain uncertain (see the discussion in *ANS* ii, 1979, 1–20; *The Waltham Chronicle*, ed. and trans. Leslie Watkins and Marjorie Chibnall, Oxford 1994, xliv–xlv; 48 n. 2; *The Battle of Hastings*, ed. Stephen Morillo, Woodbridge 1996, 45). The *Carmen* was written (so it has been claimed) within two years of the battle, but there is nothing to suggest that the poet witnessed the events he commemorated; had he done so, surely he would have made much of the fact. Most likely, then, he was writing from hearsay. With so much in doubt, it seems unprofitable to agonise over the exact meaning of *compater* in the poem, and the precise nature of William Malet's alleged connection with Harold.
[2] *Gesta Guillaumi*, 204. William is thought to have been writing c.1075. A new edition by Marjorie Chibnall is awaited.
[3] Orderic ii, 178.

critical scrutiny. At the extreme end of this spectrum we have Henry Ford's nihilistic conclusion that 'history is bunk'. Yet somewhere in between pure romanticising and total rejection of historical evidence there must be a sensible, defensible stance and in dealing here with the early Malets, that is the position I shall strive to adopt. Such evidence as I have found will be paraded as fully, fairly and faultlessly as I can manage. At the end of it all, it is for the readers to decide whether or not the results have justified the effort.

There seems to me to be little reason to doubt that Harold's body was identified and buried (in the first instance) by the sea and that in spite of the *Carmen's* reluctance to name him, the person chosen by the Conqueror to supervise the ceremony was in fact William Malet. Later on, in the process of reconstructing the family tree, we shall need to examine the implications of the claim that William was 'half Norman, half English'. Subsequent events show him to have been a faithful servant of the new king who stood high in his favour. He founded a family of which branches survive in England and in France to the present day. We shall be concerned here with only its first three generations.

In order to set the stage for the next events in William Malet's recorded career, a brief review is necessary of what little is known of developments in Northern England in the four years after Hastings. Our main authorities are independent accounts in Book IV of the *Historia Ecclesiastica* of Orderic Vitalis and ASC 'D',[4] representing to some extent the 'Norman' and 'English' versions of events. As to their factual content, both accounts appear in the main to be reliable, though they are vague on chronology and naturally each shows some bias in its interpretation of sources. There are few points of conflict between them for the years under review. Orderic's account, modelled partly on that of William of Poitiers, is the fuller; it was written in Latin at St Évroul c.1125. The vernacular account in ASC 'D' was written perhaps at Worcester c.1095. It is supplemented by 'John' of Worcester, a Latin text compiled at Worcester c.1120,[5] which attempts to supply a chronology. This version may have been seen by Orderic; if so, he used it only sparingly. Many modern commentators have sought to conflate these accounts, with varying degrees of accuracy and success.[6] What follows is my own attempt at a revision.

---

4 For ASC 'D', I have used the following editions: *The Anglo-Saxon Chronicle. Collaborative edn, vol. 6; MS D*, ed. G.P. Cubbin, Cambridge 1996; *The Anglo-Saxon Chronicle*, trans. M. Swanton, London 1996; *The Anglo-Saxon Chronicle*, trans. Dorothy Whitelock, London 1961. There is room for still further analysis of the sources for the conquest of the North, particularly the relation of ASC 'D' to the Worcester Latin Chronicle (n. 5 below).

5 A new edition of this section of the Worcester chronicle has been promised by Dr P. McGurk. Meanwhile, I have worked from photo-copies of the chief MSS. As I have reservations concerning the current vogue of ascribing this text to 'John' of Worcester, I prefer to cite it simply as 'the Worcester Latin Chronicle'. This Worcester version was used extensively in 'Simeon' of Durham's *Historia Regum*, but 'Simeon' had little of value to add to it for the years in question. 'Simeon's' account is available in a copy made at Hexham c.1154: *Symeonis Monachi Opera Omnia: Vol. II, Historia Regum*, ed. Thomas Arnold, London, RS LXXV, 1885; hereafter, SD. I have not seen *Symeon of Durham*, ed. David Rollason, Stamford 1996.

6 See the account in E.A. Freeman's *Norman Conquest* iv, Oxford 1871, 202–4, 768–778. This was Freeman at his best. In the main, his treatment has been followed by Stenton and by subsequent commentators. For a good recent account, see W.E. Kapelle, *The Norman Conquest of the North*, London 1979. This has carried the analysis of events a good deal further in some important directions, but I find myself at odds with several of its conclusions. It is likely to be a long while before anything approaching a definitive interpretation of the sources is achieved.

The Conqueror soon established a precarious foothold in parts of England south of the Thames, but the rest of his newly-won kingdom must still have been in turmoil when he departed for Normandy in March 1067. His audacity takes the breath away. True, he took with him as hostages Earls Edwin, Morcar and Waltheof; but their absence seems to have made for more anarchy in England, rather than less.

In the North, the situation remained particularly confused and precarious. William had been crowned in London on Christmas Day 1066 by Ealdred, the northern archbishop, but there is no evidence that any part of Yorkshire (let alone Northumbria) had been brought under royal control before the Conqueror's return to England from Normandy nearly a whole year later. Even then, King William took his time before events forced him to attend to affairs in the North. He spent Easter 1068 at Winchester and had his queen crowned in London that Whitsun, after which Edwin and Morcar returned to their earldoms.

Meanwhile in Yorkshire and Northumbria there had been much infighting between various local factions, some of whom were for the new king, but the majority against. After Morcar's return to Northumbria, he established contact with the Scots under King Malcom, to whom had fled the Ætheling Edgar, the most prestigious of the English royal pretenders. The Danes ruled by Swein Estrithson were also approached. Alarmed at these developments, during the late summer or autumn of 1068 (unfortunately we have no precise date) the Conqueror moved north and occupied York, pre-empting the build-up of any organised and effective opposition. There he erected his first castle, on the mound at Clifford Tower to the south of the walled city, occupying the peninsula between the Ouse and the Foss. Initially the castle was put in the charge of Robert, son of Richard, but he was killed in February 1069 and it appears that William Malet was then appointed castellan in his place.[7]

Just where William Malet had spent the two-and-a-half years following his burial of Harold is a mystery one would dearly like to solve. He was close to the Conqueror and may have been in Normandy with him for most of 1067, or he may have gone to East Anglia, or he may have remained in the South; we do not know.[8] What appears to be the least likely option however is that he had been involved in northern affairs for a very long period of time before the Conqueror made him castellan of York.

One suspects that William Malet found his appointment uncongenial, sited as it was in the midst of a hostile population far from the Conqueror's power base in England and still further from Malet's Normandy fief. No sooner had he been given charge of the defences of the city, than the Ætheling Eadgar appeared at York with a large force of Northumbrians. Malet sent an urgent request for help to the king, who made a rapid march to relieve the garrison. This achieved, the Conqueror spent just eight days there, during which (according to ASC 'D') he ravaged the

---

[7] The choice may have been influenced by William Malet's possession of a similarly-sited castle and motte at Graville at the mouth of the Seine, the *caput* of his fief in Normandy.

[8] He may have spent most of this time at court as a royal official. He witnessed a royal charter of privileges for Peterborough in 1067, and was present at the coronation of Queen Mathilda at Westminster at Whitsun 1068, when he witnessed as *princeps* another royal charter, for the collegiate church of St Martin-le-Grand, in a position after the earls but before Arfast the Chancellor. *Regesta* i, nos 8, 22.

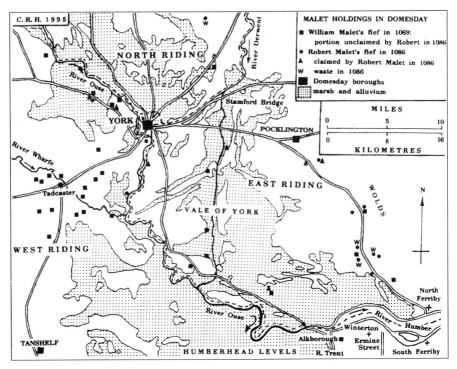

Map 1. Malet lands in Domesday: the environs of York

city, dishonoured the cathedral in some way and initiated the construction of a second, subsidiary castle, hastily built of wood it seems, at Baile Hill on the opposite bank of the Ouse. Having entrusted the completion of this to William fitz Osbern, earl of Hereford, the Conqueror left for Winchester to keep the Easter feast.[9]

The two castles, both upgraded rapidly into typical motte-and-bailey form, now controlled all navigation, preventing a hostile fleet from penetrating up-river to the city bridge spanning the Ouse.[10] In attempting to reconstruct events in the North one should always bear in mind certain fundamental features of the walled city of York, by far the largest urban centre north of London. The hub of the north-eastern communications system by road and by water, it was both an important strategic centre and a great international trading port. The River Ouse was its umbilical cord (Map 1).

William Malet may have received the sheriffdom of Yorkshire a few months

---

9 Fitz Osbern soon rejoined him; both were at Winchester on 13 April. *Regesta* i, no. 26.

10 The stratagem of placing two fortifications on opposite banks of a river to control its traffic was an old one, having been employed for instance in the campaigns of Edward the Elder early in the previous century. We still know very little concerning the defences of York in William Malet's time; in particular the exact course of the city wall in relation to the castles is unknown. It seems likely that the Foss was dammed in order to fill the moat surrounding the eastern castle. See R.A. Hall, 'Sources for pre-Conquest York', in *People and Places in Northern Europe*, ed. I. Wood and N. Lund, Woodbridge 1991, 90–1.

prior to his installation as chief custodian of the city defences. At the earliest, this appointment to the shrievalty can hardly have been made before the late autumn of 1068; at the latest, his sheriffdom is unlikely to have begun long after he became castellan. It seems that he was the first Norman sheriff and very probably the earliest Norman fiefs within the shire were established during his short term of office. Certainly his own extensive Yorkshire properties were acquired during this period.

Unlike many of his more noble contemporaries, William Malet was not made the successor to one or more powerful English or Danish landowners, each having estates scattered over a number of shires. Instead (as with some other Norman sheriffs) his early endowment was restricted to his home shire, where it was built up piecemeal by the allocation of relatively small properties which had been in the possession TRE of numerous thegns of modest estate. Typically, these were individual smallholdings within divided vills and none of them was the head of a major soke.[11]

We find from Domesday that William's estates had been concentrated in three sharply-differentiated groups centred respectively on York and its environs, on the Northumbrian border, and within the large wapentake of Holderness.[12] The core of each of these groups is listed in quite separate sections of the Yorkshire Domesday.

Taking first the properties surrounding York (Map 1), one notes that most of these are described in the section of the Survey which is devoted to claims over disputed territory within the three Ridings.[13] It is not possible to identify every one of these properties precisely, because one important sub-group is referred to rather vaguely by the name of its pre-Conquest *antecessor*. We are told that William succeeded to all the properties of Northmann, son of Maelcolumban in the East Riding, and held them for as long as he had land within the shire.[14] Unfortunately, several thegns called Northmann held properties in Yorkshire TRE, and we can identify for certain only two of these estates, lying in the North Riding, as having been in the possession of William's *antecessor*.[15]

Setting this problem to one side, those estates in the vicinity of York which can be identified as having once belonged to William Malet comprise thirty properties, assessed altogether at over ninety carucates. In addition, William had held nine dwellings occupied by named tenants in York city itself.[16] One might assume that all these estates were acquired from William's *antecessores* by forfeiture, but such was not the case. Sand Hutton near York was bought by William from one Sprottr

---

[11] For the eighty-two major Domesday sokes of Yorkshire, see C.R. Hart, *The Danelaw*, London 1993, 251–9, where I list twenty-two within the West Riding, twenty-seven in the North Riding and thirty-three in the East Riding, none of which are known to have been in the possession of William Malet.

[12] The point was first made by Judith Green, 'The Sheriffs of William the Conqueror', *ANS* v, 1982, 129–145, esp. 142.

[13] North Riding: DB Yorks. CN 3–4. East Riding: DB Yorks. CE 13, 15, 17, 19–23, 26, 30. West Riding: DB Yorks. CW 2–3, 25–32. These and all subsequent Domesday references (except for Lincolnshire) identify holdings by the numbering adopted in the Phillimore edition. It has been noted that half the *clamores* section of the Yorkshire Domesday is concerned with lands formerly in the possession of William Malet; see the account in the little-known but very useful monograph by F.W. Brooks, *Domesday Book and the East Riding*, East Yorks. Local Hist. Soc. 1966, 47–9.

[14] DB Yorks. CE 23.

[15] Estates at Kirby Hall and Susacres: DB Yorks. CW 26; 25 W 21, 26.

[16] DB Yorks. C 12.

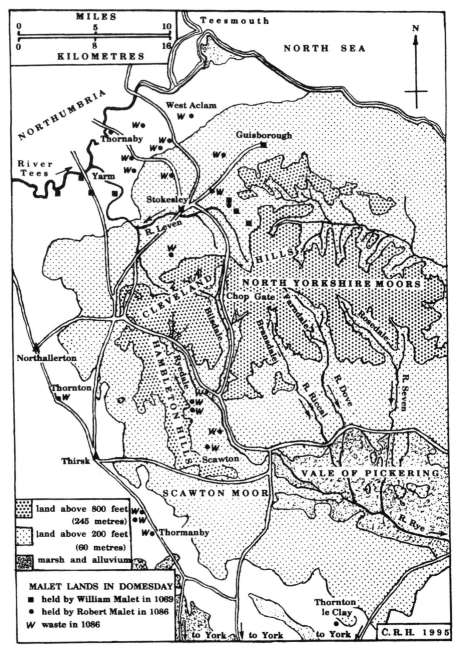

Map 2. Malet holdings in Domesday: Teeside and the Yorkshire Moors

for ten silver marks.[17] One cannot tell how many other estates were acquired in similar fashion. This list of properties in the region surrounding York is completed by a number of estates in the Domesday fief of William Malet's son Robert, whose activities we shall be considering in more detail presently.[18] Although there is no specific mention of it in the body of the Survey, one is tempted to assume that the whole of Robert's Yorkshire fief of 1086 had once been in the possession of his father. We shall have to consider other factors in this equation before deciding whether or not such an assumption can be justified.

It will be seen from Map 1 that all these holdings were strategically placed. There was a group scattered along the road leading north-westwards from North Ferriby which was the major route taken by those travelling from London to York via Ermine Street. A remarkable concentration of estates surrounded Tadcaster to the western side of the Vale of York, at the meeting-place of two Roman roads giving access to York from the Midlands. Other estates were sited on or near to roads leading north-eastwards and north-westwards from the city. The significance of these dispositions will be discussed in due course.

Turning now to William's Teeside properties (Map 2), we discover that the core of these derived from an *antecessor* called Havathr.[19] His estates are not named individually in the main text of Domesday, but they can be identified from entries in the *Recapitulatio* or Summary which concludes the account of the shire. They comprised eight properties, amounting in all to twenty-eight carucates.[20] By the time of the Domesday Survey these were in a variety of hands; none were claimed at that time by William's son Robert Malet. None of these eight properties are described as waste in Domesday, as are practically all the remaining estates in this area which had once belonged to William. This second group of properties, amounting in all to over sixty carucates, formed part of Robert Malet's Domesday fief.[21] As with his estates in the region of York, we shall have to consider presently whether or not Robert held his Teeside properties by descent from his father.

Whatever the process by which these Teeside estates fell into the Malets' hands, it may be surmised that whoever held them would be in a commanding position as far as repelling descents on York overland from Northumbria is concerned (Map 2). Yarm and Thornaby were sited beside the two most easterly crossings (whether by bridge or by ferry) of the River Tees. Further south, Stokesley, Thornton and Thormanby commanded the major road routes to York, while a group of estates north of Scawton controlled the alternative approach from the north via passes across the Cleveland Hills into Bilsdale and Ryedale. One cannot discount these strategic implications.

The third grouping of Malet estates in Yorkshire was sited in the Holderness peninsula and received the attention of a special section which concluded the

---

[17] DB Yorks. CN 4.

[18] Estates at North Cave (7½ carucates), South Cave (a large integral vill of 24 carucates), and smaller estates at Drewton, Kettlethorpe, Hotham, Houghton, Sancton and Burnby: DB Yorks. 11 E 1–9. The South Cave estate is sometimes confused with another of the same name in the Suffolk fief of the Malets.

[19] DB Yorks. CN 3. Note that these estates were virtually frontier posts, defending the northernmost limits of Norman penetration at this time.

[20] Estates at Little Ayton, Easby, Battersby, Low Worsall, Kirk Leavington, Yarm, Castle Leavington and Stokesay: DB Yorks. 1 N 22–4, 118, 120–3; 29 N 8.

[21] DB Yorks. 11 N 1–23.

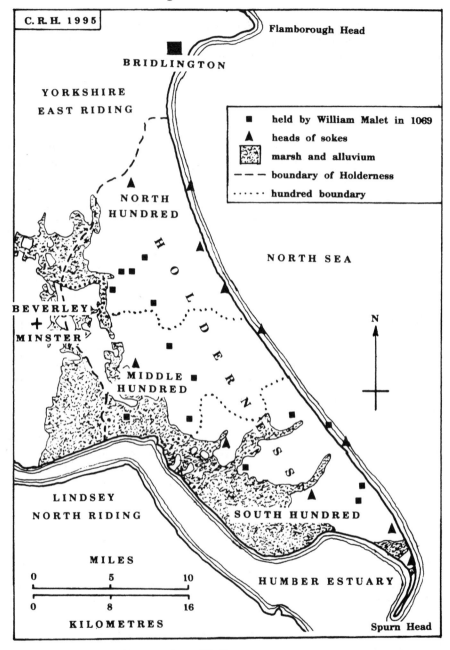

Map 3. Estates of William Malet in Holderness

clamores of the Yorkshire Domesday (Map 3).[22] Eighteen smallish estates are listed, comprising ninety carucates scattered throughout the three hundreds of Holderness. The list is introduced by the following statement:[23]

> The men of Holderness, having been sworn, testify that William Malet had the lands noted below because they saw them held in possession in the same William's hand, until the Danes seized him; but concerning this (i.e. his right), they have not seen the king's writ or seal.

The first point to note about William's estates in Holderness is that they must have come into his possession after Archbishop Ealdred had succeeded in obtaining from the Conqueror confirmation of privileges which had been granted by the Confessor to the ancient collegiate church of Beverley, a dependency of York Minster. King William's writ established *inter alia* the rights and endowments of Beverley in all its twenty-one berewicks in Holderness.[24] The Malet lands were so disposed as to avoid scrupulously any encroachment on this territory. As with all the other major ecclesiastical foundations possessing estates in Yorkshire (St Peter and Holy Trinity of York, St Wilfred of Ripon and St Cuthbert of Durham), Ealdred had secured from the Conqueror as a price of his loyalty that their properties should remain inviolate. Evidently they were thought to be a stabilising element; hopefully their population would remain loyal to the crown. It would have been William Malet's responsibility, in his capacity as sheriff, to ensure that this policy of non-interference was strictly implemented.

Considering the turmoil in the county, it may seem surprising that there was also no encroachment by William on any of the eleven smaller sokes in Holderness. However, two of these belonged to the archbishop.[25] Harold's small soke of Cleeton is likely to have lapsed to the crown, and five of the remaining eight sokes may have stayed nominally in the possession of Earl Morcar until his final defection in 1071.[26] There was every reason in 1069 not to provoke him. It was therefore the smaller landowners of Holderness, all (as the Domesday *clamores* show) with Danish names, whose properties were seized by William Malet and became part of his Yorkshire fief.[27] Apart from the ecclesiastical lands of York and Beverley, practically the whole of Holderness passed eventually to Drogo de Beuvrière, but

---

[22] DB Yorks. CE 35–52. For the earlier tenurial history of Holderness, see M. Harvey, 'Regular Field and Tenurial Arrangements in Holderness, Yorkshire', *Journal of Historical Geography* vi, 1980, 3–16; 'Planned Field Systems in Eastern Yorkshire: Some Thoughts on their Origin', *Agricultural History Review* xxix, 1981, 91–103. More work on this important topic is needed.

[23] DB Yorks. CE 34.

[24] W. Farrer, *Early Yorkshire Charters* i, 1914, no. 8, dated 1066–9. F.E. Harmer, *Anglo-Saxon Writs*, Manchester 1952, 432–3; Hart, *The Danelaw*, 257–9 and map. DB Yorks. CW 39.

[25] Partington and Swine.

[26] Easington, Hornsea, Kilnsea, Mappleton and Withernsea.

[27] One is reminded of a statement by Gaimar that the Conqueror sent a message to Archbishop Ealdred at York, that all the thegns who came to him should have safe conduct and receive back their inheritance, but when they arrived he imprisoned them and gave their lands to the Normans. This could have happened before William Malet was made sheriff, but it is doubtful how much credence to give to the story. *L'Estoire des Engleis, by Geffrei Gaimar*, ed. A. Bell, Anglo-Norman Text Society, Oxford 1960, lines 5380–5401.

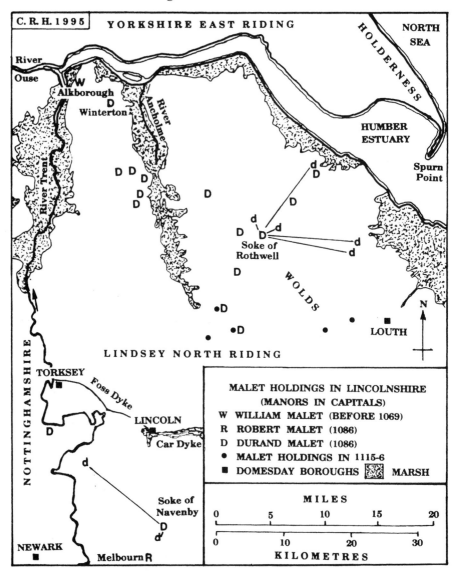

Map 4. Malet holdings in Lindsey

this occurred after William Malet's period as sheriff, and therefore after the Conqueror's harrying of the North.[28]

William Malet's Yorkshire fief could hardly have come to him before he was made sheriff, and the most likely time for its acquisition is directly after the Conqueror had built the second castle at York. It could be argued that the disposition of his estates shows a strategical motive, with concentration on the major road communications and on the Holderness peninsula (which would have made a suitable base for a seaborne force intent on capturing York). Parties of knights from the York garrison could have been billeted on these estates, in the hope of providing an effective initial deterrent to invading forces and to act as a communications network. Some such explanation of the choice of estates for his fief appears likely, but of course this is no more than supposition, incapable of proof. Against such a theory, one notes that when the expected attack from the North materialised it was the Conqueror himself and not William Malet's tenants in Holderness who warned him of the presence of hostile ships in the estuary of the Humber. Alternative explanations for the selection of Malet estates are possible. Holderness, for example, was the richest agricultural region of Yorkshire, with the earliest and most extensive development of strip cultivation in common fields, and the highest taxable resources and population density.

Whatever the circumstances underlying its acquisition, it is certain that William's fief was quite short-lived. A number of Domesday entries tell us that he held estates for 'as long as he held land in Yorkshire', or 'as long as he was sheriff of York', or 'as long as he held the castle at York', or 'until the castle was attacked' or 'before the castle was taken'.[29] We have seen already that his lands in Holderness were held only 'until the Danes seized him'. All these refer to the attack on York which occurred in the early autumn of 1069. We are told that a huge force of Danes appeared in 240 ships at the mouth of the Humber, where they were joined by the Ætheling Eadgar and the Northumbrian earls, with a large section of the local population. According to Orderic, the Conqueror sent warning of this event to York, offering to come to its aid, but William Malet replied that he was confident he could hold out in the city for a whole year, if necessary.

His confidence was disastrously misplaced. According to the Worcester Latin Chronicle, which gives the most circumstantial account, Archbishop Ealdred died on 11 September and the Normans buried him in his cathedral on 19 September. The following day, or the day afterwards, the occupants of the two forts set fire to the adjacent houses, for fear that the Danes might use their timber to fill up the moats and so overwhelm them. The fire spread rapidly to destroy the city and cathedral. Then the Danes arrived and the garrison made a foolish sally, exposing itself to the superior forces of the enemy. The chronicler says that more than three thousand Normans were killed, leaving the castles undefended. The lives of William Malet, his wife and two children were spared. The exact circumstances attending this unusual act of clemency are not given in the chronicles, but it is evident from subsequent events that they were taken as hostages. Hearing that the

---

[28] For a preliminary review of the later tenurial history of Holderness, see B. English, *The Lords of Holderness 1086–1260*, Oxford 1979, repr. 1991 for Hull Univ. Press.

[29] DB Yorks. CE 15, 20–1, 23, 35; CN 3. For the later history of the Malet Domesday fief in Yorkshire, see Farrer, *Early Yorkshire Charters* iii, 434–466 (nos 1822–1860).

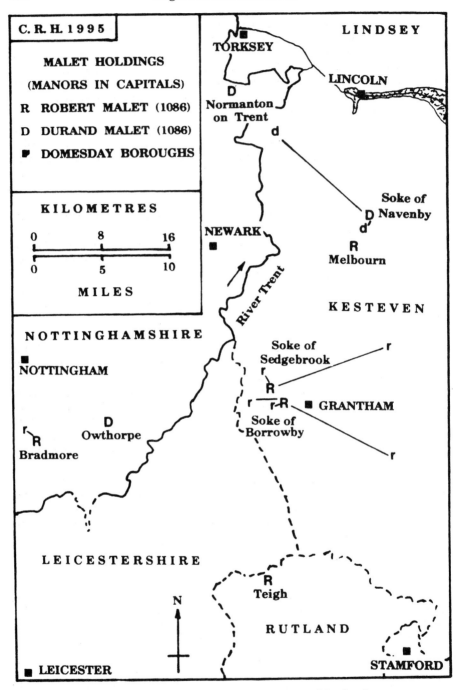

Map 5. Malet holdings in Kesteven, Nottinghamshire and Rutland

Conqueror was marching towards them, the Danes fled across the Humber to the Lindsey shore, carrying with them great booty.

The sequel is well known. The Conqueror embarked on an extensive and ruthless harrying of Yorkshire and Northumberland, depopulating and destroying most of the villages. Those inhabitants that were not put to the sword died of famine. Such was the devastation that two decades later the Domesday Survey still describes most of the territory as 'waste'.

To return to William Malet and his family, the Danes appear to have taken him with them when they crossed the Humber into Lindsey. The Conqueror is said to have made a pact with the Danish army which allowed them to forage freely along the coast, so long as they returned eventually to Denmark when the winter was over. There is no specific reference, but it seems that the release of the Malets was part of the deal.

We hear no more of William Malet in relation to Yorkshire, where a new sheriff, Hugh son of Baldric, was appointed. There was nothing left in the devastated shire worthy of William's attention; he had not proved a good general or effective governor, and it is doubtful if he ever returned there. Yet in spite of the catastrophe at York, he remained high in the Conqueror's favour. He is next encountered as the possessor of a vast fief in East Anglia, far greater than his Yorkshire possessions. Before discussing this, we need to take a look at Domesday's account of lands held by the Malets in Lindsey and adjacent shires (Maps 4 and 5).

The only estate which William Malet is known for certain to have held in this region was five carucates at Alkborough in the north-western corner of the North Riding of Lindsey, where the Trent runs into the Humber.[30] His name is given in the Alkborough entry as the *antecessor* to Ivo Taillebois, the Lincolnshire sheriff in 1086, whom we shall encounter again later. J.H. Round concluded from this entry that William held the estate TRE and was established therefore in England before the Norman Conquest.[31] His opinion was repeated as a fact by F.M. Stenton in his great introduction to the Lincolnshire Domesday, a view followed by most later commentators.[32] However, many Domesday entries refer to Norman *antecessores* who were given estates after the Conquest but who died or were dispossessed before the Domesday Survey, and it seems likely that William Malet's holding at Alkborough falls into this category. It will be shown that Ivo came into possession of it not by William's forfeiture, but by inheritance. The holding formed a convenient *pied à terre* for travellers from London along Ermine Street to York, resting before a ferry passage across the Humber. Presumably it was acquired by William

---

[30] *The Lincolnshire Domesday and the Lindsey Survey*, ed. C.W. Foster and T. Longley, with an introduction by F.M. Stenton, Lincoln Record Society xix, 1924 reprinted 1976, entry Li DB 14/28. All subsequent references to Lincolnshire properties use the numbering of this edition, prefaced by Li DB for Domesday entries and LiS for Lindsey Survey entries.

[31] J.H. Round, *Feudal England*, London 1895, 330.

[32] Li DB p. xlii. C.P. Lewis claims also that holdings at Elsham and Rothwell and a small soke at Linwood in Lindsey were all in William Malet's possession before the Conquest ('The French in England before the Norman Conquest', *ANS* xvii, 1994, 123–144, esp. 144). Just possibly, the William who had once shared ownership of these estates with one Grinchel may have been William Malet, because Durand Malet also held there in 1086 (Linwood, Rothwell and Middle Rasen). Even so, one need not conclude that William Malet was their pre-Conquest tenant. He may have held them in 1068–9 until he left York. Alfred of Lincoln held them in chief in 1086 (Li DB 27/7–8, 14).

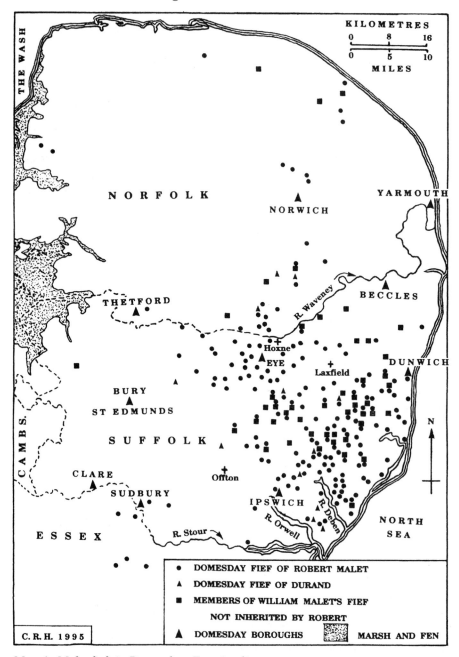

Map 6. Malet fiefs in Domesday: East Anglia

during his sheriffdom of Yorkshire, and it may have been passed on to Ivo soon afterwards.

The remaining properties of the Malets which appear in the Lincolnshire Domesday comprise a set of estates mostly north of Lincoln held by Durand Malet in 1086,[33] and a smaller set in Kesteven held in the same year by Robert, the son of William Malet.[34] Durand's Lindsey estates had nearly all been the property of one Rolfr TRE and included the soke of Rothwell. He held also from Earl Edwin a small property at Winterton.[35] His small manor at Owthorpe in Nottinghamshire had once been in Rolfr's possession; another at Normanton-on-Trent may have been in his own hands TRE.[36] Presumably he is the Durand who preceded Robert Malet at Sutton near Guildford in Surrey[37] and possibly he is the Durand who held both TRE and TRW in Suffolk and Norfolk. Ralph and Walter Malet who held of William Meschin lands in the Lindsey Wolds in 1115–16 may have been Durand's descendants.[38] His place in the family pedigree will be considered presently.

The Domesday entries for all Robert Malet's Lincolnshire holdings, including two small sokes near Grantham, name Godwin and Azor as his *antecessores*. The same individuals preceded him in estates at Bradmore in Nottinghamshire and Teigh in Rutland,[39] and we shall encounter them again in connection with his properties in Suffolk and Norfolk. It is to these holdings that we now direct our attention.

We start this section of our survey by picking up the story of William Malet and his family after they had been released by the Conqueror from Danish hands in the Humber estuary in the autumn of 1069. No sooner had William been relieved of his appointment as sheriff of Yorkshire than he appears to have been appointed to similar duties in Suffolk. An early Latin writ of King William addressed to Bishop Æ(thelmær) of Elmham, Abbot B(aldwin) of Bury St Edmunds and W(illiam) Malet in favour of Bury survives in a late copy in the Bury archives.[40] Æthelmær was the brother of Archbishop Stigand, and both were deposed on 11 April 1070 after an enquiry by the papal legate. Although William Malet is not addressed as sheriff in this writ, one concludes from it that he was acting in Suffolk in that capacity just before Bishop Æthelmær's deposition.[41]

---

[33] Li DB 44/1–19; 70/12. There is no evidence that Durand held in Lincolnshire TRE. His Lincoln-shire holdings were all lost (like those of his kinsman Robert) in the reign of William Rufus.

[34] Li DB 58/1–8; 72/20, 35.

[35] Winterton, next to Alkborough, was sited at the end of Ermine Street and provided another *pied à terre*, much sought after by those using the Humber Ferry. See Hart, *The Danelaw*, 344.

[36] DB Notts. 9/69; 26/1. However, there is no firm evidence in Domesday or other surviving sources that Durand held Normanton before the Conquest.

[37] DB Sr 28/1. We do not know why or when this estate passed to Robert.

[38] Li S 3/5; 7/7; 18/8, 9. On the revised date of Li S, see J. Tait, 'The Lindsey Survey and an Unknown Precept of King Henry I', *BIHR* lix, 1986, 212–15.

[39] DB Notts. 25/1, 2; DB Rut 10. I have been unable to identify the Malet who held a single virgate at Rushden on the Beds/Northants border (DB Beds 22/2).

[40] J.H. Round, *Feudal England*, 429–30. *Regesta* i, no. 44 (edited there as no. IV) . D.C. Douglas printed another version, which he thought superior, in which William's name is replaced by that of his son Robert. It seems to me that the evidence of the *Regesta* text is to be preferred, but this issue needs more attention. D.C. Douglas, *Feudal Documents of the Abbey of Bury St Edmunds*, British Academy, London 1932, cxxxix, n. 2; 47–8.

[41] Perhaps he succeeded Northmann, to whom four slightly earlier Suffolk writs of the Conqueror in OE are addressed (*Regesta* i, nos 40–43). DB shows that Northmann was the sheriff before

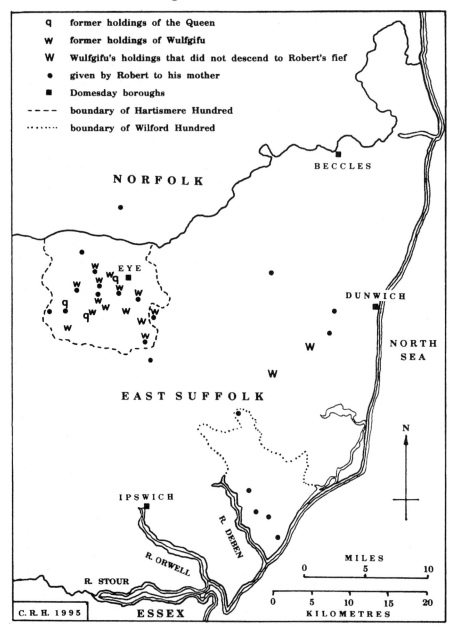

Map 7. Some Domesday holdings and lordships of Robert Malet's mother

William was given a huge fief in Suffolk, Norfolk and Essex, the great bulk if not all of which is listed in Little Domesday Book (Map 6). It was by far the largest to be granted out by the Conqueror in East Anglia, and the most concentrated of all the Norman fiefs in England. How was room made for him? Was Eadric of Laxfield, his *antecessor*, who must have been one of the greatest landholders in England towards the end of the Confessor's reign, deprived by the Conqueror of his vast East Anglian holdings in order that William could be endowed with them, or did Eadric die conveniently without heirs, just at the right moment? This second possibility was ruled out decisively many years ago, by Professor Douglas's surprising but conclusive demonstration that Eadric (who was nicknamed *cecus*, 'the Blind') held a tiny estate of only one virgate at Hartham in Wiltshire, both TRE and in 1086.[42] Eadric seems to have been displaced in East Anglia to provide William Malet with his fief.

Let us note from the outset that the descent of William's lands and lordships as given in Little Domesday is enormously complex and that so far there has been no adequate summary of the matter by modern commentators. For a large number of his holdings, important links in the chain of descent are omitted in the Survey and for many others such information as it does offer is ambiguous. Handling of this material is further complicated by the fragmentation of East Anglian estates into numerous smallholdings, each with its own individual peculiarities of obligations and tenure. After much detailed analysis, three conclusions have emerged which, taken together, clarify the situation greatly. It is not profitable to display the arguments in detail, for that would take up too much time and space. One can only invite readers to accept the results on trust. Those unwilling to do so are faced with many hours of nit-picking among the Domesday entries before they can hope to work it all out satisfactorily for themselves.

First, whenever Little Domesday mentions 'Robert Malet's *antecessor*' without naming him, the individual referred to is Eadric of Laxfield. Secondly, William Malet's *antecessor* in Norfolk, Suffolk and Essex was always this same Eadric.

William Malet's time (DB Sf 6/91; 7/36). He was preceded by Toli, who was also sheriff of Norfolk (DB Sf 4/15; 7/31, 67; 31/53; DB Nf 1/229; 14/35; 47/4). Nor(th)man(n) (or a later namesake) is also called 'the Sheriff' in two other DB entries, apparently relating to 1086 (63, 6/29), but further entries show beyond doubt that Roger Bigot was the sheriff of Norfolk and Suffolk in 1086 (see n. 47). No Suffolk writs survive that are addressed to Norman as sheriff after 1070 and his Domesday title appears to have been an 'honorary' one. The situation is complicated further by a dispute about the priest of Ashfield recorded under the bishop of Bayeux's Domesday fief (DB Sf 16/34). A certain 'Norman' claimed to have a writ from the King, ordering him to transfer to the possession of Ralph of Savenay all the free men of Walter of Dol which Hubert of Port had given to the bishop of Bayeux after Walter's forfeiture (in 1075). One such freeman was Snaring, the priest of Ashfield, the possession of whom was being disputed between Roger Bigot (Ralf of Saveney's lord) and Earl Hugh at the time of the Domesday Survey. The Domesday commissioners arranged for this dispute to come to judgement, but the outcome is not recorded. Norman appears to have acted as the king's agent over this, but he could not have been entirely disinterested, as his son Hugh held 23 freemen at Ashfield of Earl Hugh (DB Sf 4/6). Understandably, modern commentators have glossed over the problem of Norman's alleged second shrievalty. I think he may have acted as deputy to Roger Bigot and perhaps to Robert Malet also. Both were often away from the county, at court or in Normandy.

[42] Douglas, *Feudal Documents*, xc–xciii, based on entries in the Feudal Book of Abbot Baldwin. See DB Wilts 67/53. Douglas pointed out that several other East Anglian notables were established on thegnlands in Wiltshire TRE. The reason for this is obscure, but some general administrative decision seems to have been involved and the matter is important. It does not seem to have been pursued further. More research is badly needed.

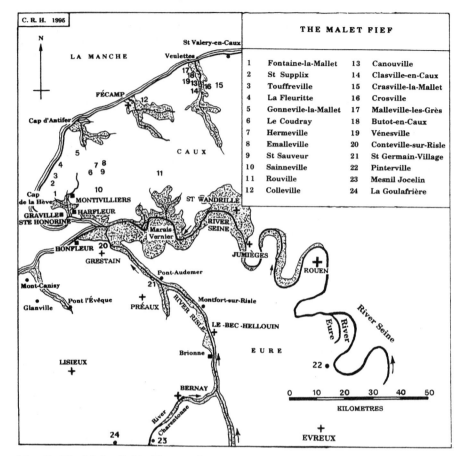

Map 8. The Malet fief in Normandy

Thirdly, Robert Malet never inherited Eadric's lordships and estates directly, but always through his father William Malet. Note that between them, these three criteria do not imply that *all* of William Malet's East Anglian fief passed on to his son Robert; nor do they rule out the possibility that *some* of Robert's East Anglian fief was acquired from *antecessores* other than Eadric.

Note, too, that so far we have not considered the possibility that Robert was already in possession of some lands and lordships in East Anglia before his father arrived there from Yorkshire. To anticipate here what will be dealt with in more detail later, William Malet is known to have had two sons and a daughter. Only two of these, presumably the youngest, were taken captive with their mother and father by the Danes at York.[43] Robert, his oldest child, was already able to witness Norman charters with his father before the Conquest, and so old enough, it seems, to hold estates in his own right in England and/or Normandy soon afterwards. He

---

[43] William belonged to the small group of 'companions of the Conqueror', but the family tradition that he and his three (*sic*) sons all fought at Hastings cannot be sustained.

may have commuted between fiefs in the two countries. Godwin, son of Ælfhere, who preceded Robert in some of his estates near Ipswich and Sudbury, is possibly identical with the Godwin who was the *antecessor* of his holdings in Lincolnshire and Nottinghamshire which have been described already.[44] These may have come to Robert after his father's death, but possibly he acquired them earlier.

Wulfgifu, another of Robert Malet's *antecessores*, held a compact group of lordships (some of only a few acres) in Hartismere Hundred. Some she may have acquired TRE, others as late as 1075. A few had once belonged to Archbishop Stigand. Mostly she was his sub-tenant, but in the case of Occold we are told that Stigand gave the property to her, and that she held it later of the queen.[45] This may provide the clue to the descent of her estates, for it seems that Stigand surrendered them with his other Suffolk properties after his forfeiture of the archdiocese on 11 April 1070. If Roger Bigot, who appears to have been sheriff of Suffolk at the time, dealt originally with Stigand's forfeited holdings on behalf of the crown, he managed to retain a number of them in his own possession.[46]

He was followed as sheriff in 1072 or perhaps a year or two later by Robert Malet, who may have handled the disposal of the remainder of Stigand's Suffolk estates and lordships. It appears that most of them came into the queen's hands, and that she had passed some of them directly on to Wulfgifu.[47] By the time of Domesday, nearly all of these holdings were in the possession of Robert Malet's mother Esilia. It could be that Robert arranged this transfer with the queen during his sheriffdom, presumably some time after his mother had been widowed in 1071–2. She was still holding them in 1086 (Map 7).

The descent of Wulfgifu's estates was not, however nearly as straight-forward as

---

[44] *Goduinus Alferi filius; Goduinus filius Alferi; Goduinus Alfies sone.* DB Sf 6/1 (Edwardstone), 6/2 (Chilton), 6/12 (Thorpe Hall), 6/26 (Belstead) (wrongly translated as 'son of Alsi' in the Phillimore edition), DB Sf 6/27 (Brantham), DB Sf 6/112 (Playford), DB Sf 6/113 (*Neccemara*, unlocated but near Rushmere St Andrew), DB Sf 6/114 (Kesgrave), DB Sf 6/116 (Rushmere St Andrew), DB Sf 6/120 (Tuddenham), DB Sf 6/307 (Bedfield). He is to be differentiated from the *Goduuini Algari filius* who held at Darsham, a manor of Eadric which descended to William Malet (DB Sf 7/36). The Godwin of Sutton who had held of Robert's baron, Walter of Caen, at Sutton (DB Sf 6/165), Capel St Andrew (DB Sf 6/166), Shottisham (DB Sf 6/167), Bromeswell (DB Sf 6/168) and Bredfield (DB Sf 6/169), a compact group of estates east of the Deben, also appears to have been another person.

[45] DB Sf 77/1. She also held at Stoke Ash and Rishangles by commendation to Stigand (DB Sf 6/213; 222). The soke of other properties at Rishangles, Thorndon and Braiseworth was hers by gift from Stigand (DB Sf 6/222–3; 225). See also, for Braiseworth, DB Sf 6/228.

[46] DB Sf 7/4, 52, 60, 75, 124. Entries in Little Domesday show that Roger Bigot had two spells as sheriff of Suffolk, with Robert Malet's tenure of the office sandwiched between them (DB Sf 1/103, 105). Roger's first spell (which apparently followed that of William Malet, already referred to) lasted at least until 1072. He is entitled *vicecomes* in the Ely land pleas of 1072–5 (*Inquisitio Comitatus Cantabrigiensis*, ed. N.E.S.A. Hamilton, London 1876, 194; hereafter ICC and IE). Robert was sheriff in 1075 during the revolt of the earls, but Roger was back again as sheriff of Suffolk in 1086, see the introduction to the king's holding in the Suffolk Domesday: *terra regis de regione quam Rogerus Bigotus seruat*, and many subsequent entries e.g. DB Sf 1/122 f. It is very likely that he was sheriff of Norfolk in the same year, for DB Nf 9/86 mentions Roger the Sheriff, and no other Roger is known who could fit the description. See further, A. Wareham, 'The motives and Politics of the Bigod Family, c.1066–1177', *ANS* xvii, 1994, 223–242, esp. 224, 229. Wareham assigns Roger's first tenure of the Norfolk sheriffdom to 1081–87.

[47] E.g. Yaxley and Wickham Skeith (DB Sf 6/229–30); perhaps also a half-acre strip at Bedingfield (DB Sf 6/232).

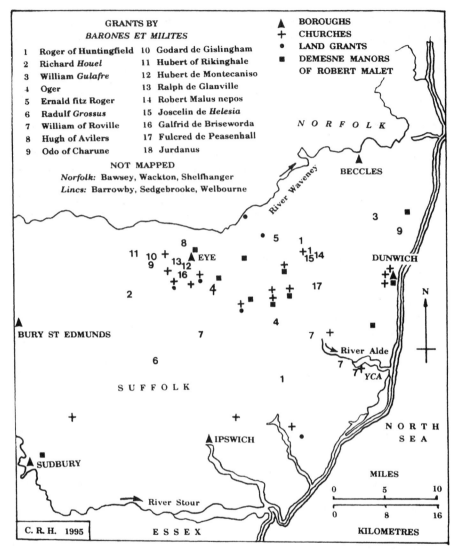

Map 9. *Foundation endowment of Eye Priory*

may appear from this account. At least one of her holdings came to her by virtue of her commendation to Eadric of Laxfield.[48] Others may have been given to her after the forfeiture of Walter of Dol in 1075.[49] Still others were tenanted by her of Robert Malet and the queen's holding jointly, presumably also by commendation.[50] It seems that she held ten acres at Morston by her commendation to one Brihtmær

---

[48] 20 acres at Great Glemham (DB Sf 3/102).
[49] *Caldecota* (DB Sf 2/212); Thornham Magna (DB Sf 6/215).
[50] Finningham (DB Sf 6/209; see also DB Sf 6/231).

(not, apparently, the man of that name who was Robert Malet's reeve).[51] Two properties at Finningham and Mellis were held by Wulfgifu jointly with one Leofric, possibly a relative.[52] Leofric also held estates in his sole right and became one of Robert Malet's *antecessores*. Finally, the route by which Wulfgifu acquired some of her holdings is not revealed in Domesday.[53] In spite of all these supposedly different origins, the end-result was an unusually integrated group of estates and lordships.

One would like to know more about Wulfgifu and Leofric. The reason why I have gone into their holdings in some detail is that they were concentrated to a remarkable extent in Hartismere Hundred, where Eye was destined to become the *caput* of the Malet honour. It is well known that the great bulk of Malet lands in Suffolk with which the honour was endowed had been in the possession of Eadric of Laxfield TRE. There is however no evidence known to me that Eye was the centre of administration of these estates in Eadric's day. Certainly there is no indication of this in Little Domesday and unfortunately we know little about Eadric except what is contained in the Survey.[54] His lands lay mostly within the five-and-a-half hundreds of Wicklaw, a franchise of the queen before it was granted to Ely Abbey in 970. Laxfield, the village from which he took his name, was well within the five-and-a-half hundreds.[55] It seems that his group of holdings had been created as a tenancy within the Wicklaw franchise, possibly before it was given to Ely.[56] Eye was a long way away from its centre of gravity.

So far, we have not established any clear-cut instance of Robert Malet holding land or lordships in East Anglia before William Malet's arrival there in the winter of 1069–70; nor have we uncovered any evidence to show unequivocally that either William Malet or his son Robert held estates anywhere in England before the

---

[51] DB Sf 39/4. 'Holding by commendation' is a new concept which I hope to develop elsewhere. As with 'soke', the term 'commendation' had a spectrum of meanings according to time and place. See further, the article by Professor R. Abels in this volume.

[52] Finningham (see n. 50) and Mellis (DB Sf 6/227). Unfortunately, Leofric is a common name in Little Domesday, but the Leofric who was associated with Wulfgifu was probably the same person as the Leofric who was Robert Malet's mother's *antecessor* at Hemingstone (DB Sf 6/8), and he was probably identical with the Leofric who preceded Robert at Great Glemham (DB Sf 3/95, 6/49) and Bedingfield (75/5) (in both of which Wulfgifu also held). He was also, perhaps, the Leofric, Robert's *antecessor* at Westhorp, next to Finningham (DB Sf 6/58), at Rushmere St Andrew (DB Sf 6/116; 21/69), and at Sternfield (DB Sf 7/138) and Farnham (7/139), both near Great Glemham. He may have been the Leofric *Cobbe* ('the Fat') who was Robert's predecessor at Darsham (DB Sf 7/36), and/or the Leofric *Coccus* ('the Cook'), Robert's predecessor at Minsmere DB Sf (6/107). Wulfgifu and her son (un-named) held jointly at *Caldecota* (6/212, unlocated).

[53] Thornham Magna (DB Sf 6/214–5); Gislingham (DB Sf 6/216); Thornham Parva (DB Sf 6/218); a manor of two carucates at Kelsale (DB Sf 7/3).

[54] Eadric of Laxfield does not appear in known pre-Conquest charters of Eastern England; see C.R. Hart, *The Early Charters of Eastern England*, Leicester 1966. Perhaps he was the Eadric who appears in two charters of the Conqueror; see Douglas, *Feudal Documents* xciii, n. 1.

[55] P.H. Sawyer, *Anglo-Saxon Charters*, London 1968, no. 779. Hart, *The Danelaw*, 47. It became one of Robert's demesne manors, being perhaps his administrative centre.

[56] Eadric's lands stood in much the same relationship to the lordship of the Wicklaw Hundreds as did those of his contemporary, Ælfric son of Wihtgar, to the eight-and-a-half hundreds of Thingoe, a franchise of the queen which was granted to the abbey of Bury St Edmunds. Just as Eadric's lands formed part of the endowment of the honour of Eye, so were those of Ælfric used to endow the honour of Clare; see Hart, *The Danelaw*, 69 and R. Mortimer, 'The beginnings of the Honour of Clare', *ANS* iii, 1980, 119–41.

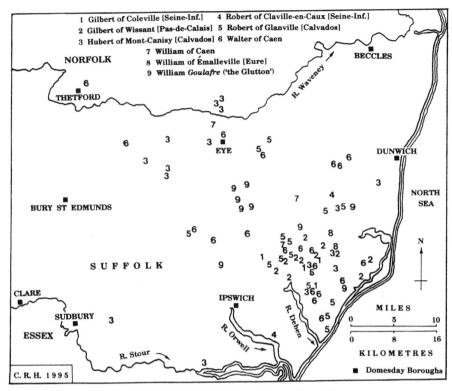

1 Gilbert of Coleville [Seine-Inf.]   4 Robert of Claville-en-Caux [Seine-Inf.]
2 Gilbert of Wissant [Pas-de-Calais]   5 Robert of Glanville [Calvados]
3 Hubert of Mont-Canisy [Calvados] 6 Walter of Caen
7 William of Caen
8 William of Émalleville [Eure]
9 William *Goulafre* ('the Glutton')

C. R. H. 1995

■ Domesday Boroughs

Map 10. Some tenants of Robert Malet: holdings and lordships

Norman Conquest. If there is any indication at all that the Malets were in England in the Confessor's time, it lies in the account given in Little Domesday of one Durand, who did not hold in chief in East Anglia but was in possession of a number of sub-tenancies in 1086 which are shown on Map 6. We need to bear in mind from the outset of this part of our investigation that none of the persons named 'Durand' in Little Domesday is given the by-name 'Malet'.

In all, Durand's Domesday holdings in Suffolk and Norfolk amounted to around seven carucates (= 840 *ware* acres), most of which he appears to have acquired TRE. A further three carucates, which he had held TRE, had become alienated by the time of Domesday. His properties lay in thirteen vills, a few of which he farmed directly as manors; in the remainder he had forty-five free men commended to him. Several entries show that TRE Durand himself had been commended equally between King Harold and Eadric of Laxfield and he had held a few individual properties directly from each of them. In 1086 his chief Suffolk property, comprising nearly half his total geld liability in the shire, was at Stowlangtoft, held of the abbey of Bury St Edmunds. However, one Domesday entry describes Durand as 'of Offton', and it is probable that this was his original base, although he had no recorded holding there in 1086. The main manor at Offton had been in the hands of Archbishop Stigand TRE (DB Sf 7/60). Durand (or his parents) may have held there before Stigand's acquisition.

It will be seen from Map 6 that Durand's Domesday holdings in East Anglia were closely intermixed with those of Robert Malet. He held forty acres at Cransford directly from Robert Malet and he held in three other vills (Kenton, *Ingoluestuna*, Bredfield) where Robert himself also had properties belonging to his fief. The coincidence is remarkable, but in isolation this does not establish conclusively that Durand was related to Robert.[57]

We have not yet finished with Durand, for a man with this name held a number of estates in Cambridgeshire in 1086 as an under-tenant of Hardwin de Scales, a despoiler of Ely.[58] One might assume that he was identical with the Durand who held TRE and in 1086 in Suffolk, but here once again caution is necessary before identifications are made.

The estates of the Cambridgeshire Durand were mostly in the south of the shire, nearer to the Essex than the Suffolk border. In the Essex Domesday we find a small fief of two properties, formerly in the possession of free men, but held in chief in 1086 by Adam, son of Durand *malis operibus*.[59] Now Alexander Rumble, the editor of the Phillimore Domesday of Essex, an onomastic scholar of note, very properly pointed out that that this is a Latinisation of OFr *malesouvres*, accepted by

[57] Durand held forty acres at Cransford of Robert Malet in 1086 (DB Sf 6/128). Previously this had been held from Eadric of Laxfield by Godric the priest. One wonders if it was once the glebe of Cransford. Robert Malet held other Cransford properties (DB Sf 6/44, 52, 55, 137).

In 1086 Durand held from Roger Bigot the sheriff shares in thirty-one acres at Norton, seventy-three acres at Kembroke, fourteen acres at '*Leofstanestuna*' and twenty-five acres at *Kuluertestuna* (unlocated). In all four places TRE he had been under the commendation of Norman, perhaps the man of that name who had once been sheriff (DB Sf 7/84, 111, 118, 121; see n. 41). All these are in Suffolk. In Norfolk in 1086, Durand held from Roger Bigot nine-and-a-half free men on fifty-nine acres at Shelton and six-and-a-half free men on eighty-six acres at Wacton (DB Nf 9/214, 216). It is not stated how he became seized of these holdings. In 1086 Durand held four carucates at Stow Langtoft (DB Sf 14/77) and two freemen with eighty acres at Kenton (DB Sf 14/119), both of the abbot of Bury St Edmunds. It is not absolutely clear if he had held these of the abbey TRE, but this appears probable. In 1086 he held of the bishop of Bayeux eighty acres at Helmingham as a manor, which he had held TRE as a free man under the commendation of Eadric of Laxfield (DB Sf 16/25). He had held also from Eadric, by similar tenure, one carucate and eighty acres at *Aluredstuna* (unlocated), but he had lost this holding by 1086. Several other small holdings over which Durand had held the commendation TRE had been alienated to Hervey of Bourges by 1086. These included three acres at Little Bealings which had been farmed by Hardekin, a free man; eighty acres farmed by eleven free men at *Dernford* (unlocated) and one carucate and sixteen acres farmed by fourteen free men at *Ingoluestuna* (unlocated; DB Sf 67/12, 17–18). In all three entries, Durand himself is described as a free man, half under the commendation of Eadric and half under the commendation of (King) Harold. A fourth holding which had been alienated to Hervey by 1086 was twelve acres at Bredfield, farmed TRE by a free man under the commendation of Durand of Offton (DB Sf 67/23). Durand had also held thirty acres at Battisford TRE, apparently directly under the king, which were in the hands of one of King William's *vavassores* in 1086 (DB Sf 74/3).

[58] One hide at Weston Colville, half a hide (three virgates in IE) at Babraham, one hide at Hinxton, half a hide at Ickleton, one hide + one virgate at Melbourn, three-and-one-third virgates at Orwell and one virgate at Eversdon (DB Cambs 26/6, 11, 14–15, 31, 34, 37; IE 22, 36, 40–1, 67, 78, 85). According to IE, a small part of this was held by Durand of the king's fee. The Durand who in 1072–5 shared ownership with one Walter (as under-tenants of Hugh II de Montfort-sur-Risle, the Conqueror's constable) of twenty-six sokemen on twenty-six acres at Marham on the edge of the Norfolk marshland may have been the same person (IE 186, 195). This holding had been seized by Hugh from Ely after the fenland uprising of 1070–1. It is not impossible that Durand was given all these under-tenancies after the mission of William Malet which followed the uprising.

[59] A manor of half a hide at Willingale, formerly held by five *liberi homines*, and a smallholding at Stebbingford (House), formerly held by a free man named Godric (DB Ess 63/1, 2).

Tengvik as a recognised Norman by-name which later became Anglicised as Malzor. The name *malesouvres* means 'evil deeds', in much the same way (according to some etymologists) as the diminutive OFr *malet*. I have searched Domesday without discovering another example. We are dealing with a unique by-name as far as Domesday is concerned; it does not appear again in England until a century later. The possibility has to be considered that the Domesday scribe, encountering Durand *malet* (perhaps abbreviated as *mal'*) in his *breve*, extended it mistakenly to *malis op(er)ib(us)*. For two different Durands with such similar by-names to be holding estates in the eastern counties would be a most odd coincidence.

The name 'Durand', itself continental in origin, may not have been uncommon in Normandy, but it was rare in England before the Norman Conquest.[60] The fundamental question (which in spite of much investigation, I am unable to answer for certain) is whether or not the Durand who held TRE and in 1086 in East Anglia was identical with the Durand who held TRE and in 1086 in Nottinghamshire, the Durand who held in 1086 in Cambridgeshire, the Durand *malis operibus* whose son held in 1086 in Essex and the Durand Malet who held in 1086 in Lincolnshire. Should certain of these identities be established beyond all doubt, then we have at last pinned down one of the Malets as being settled in England before the Conquest. As matters stand at present, such certainty has not in my view been established; all one can say is that this looks to be a distinct possibility. An immediate *caveat* is necessary: whatever the extent of his English possessions, we remain ignorant of Durand Malet's precise relationship to the rest of the family.[61]

William Malet's great East Anglian fief is shown on Map 6. It was obtained *en bloc* by the transferrence of the bulk of Eadric of Laxfield's holding. During his brief period of tenure, William chose for the centre of his fief Eye near the Norfolk border, which had been no more than a large rural manor when he acquired it. There he created a deer park. More importantly, he took advantage of the weak position of the East Anglian see, following the deposition of Bishop Æthelmær, to open a Saturday market at Eye in direct opposition to one held on the same day which had long been established at the nearby episcopal centre of Hoxne.[62] He built a motte-and-bailey castle there and installed twenty-five burgesses, turning Eye into a small but prosperous borough.[63] There is no evidence of a mint.

This enterprising move placed William in command of the internal trade of East Suffolk. Indeed, William's fief at Eye shows one way in which new patterns of trade developed under Norman rule. In spite of maritime encroachment his other borough, at the seaport of Dunwich, also prospered exceedingly, whereas the much larger rival port of Ipswich, having lost most of its Scandinavian trade, declined alarmingly in population at this time. There is no direct proof, but it seems likely that William attempted to establish a fresh trade route between England and Normandy, with ships plying between Dunwich and the port of Harfleur, sited on the

---

[60] Lewis, 'French in England', 141.

[61] A pedigree constructed a century ago by the Malet family places Durand Malet as William's brother. This is plausible, but unsupported by conclusive evidence. The Durand, cleric of St Edmunds and of Abbot Baldwin, who appears in the Suffolk Domesday and in Douglas, *Feudal Documents*, 11, 24, 38 was almost certainly not a Malet.

[62] DB Sf 6/191; 18/1. The new bishop changed his market to a Friday but lost much trade.

[63] For the topography of the borough and its castle, see Brown, *Eye Charters* ii, 3 and map.

north bank of the Seine estuary beside the *caput* of his Norman fief at Graville-Ste-Honorine.[64]

All this activity was brought to an abrupt halt towards the end of 1071 when William Malet was sent by the Conqueror on a mission into the southern fenland bordering on the Wash.[65] Freeman, who was of the opinion (rightly, I think) that this had to do with the revolt at Ely in which Hereward 'the Wake' played a part, bewailed that the author of the *Gesta Herewardi* made no reference to William in his account of the fighting. It seems to me unlikely however that William Malet was involved actively in the campaign. He had failed as a military commander at York, and one doubts if the Conqueror would have used him in the same capacity in the fenland. An administrative assignment appears more likely.

Among the rebels were a number of prominent Northumbrians including Earl Morcar and the powerful thegn Siward Bearn, who had previously been William Malet's opponents in the battle for York. When they were captured, the Conqueror held them in prison for the rest of his reign, though whether they spent all their captivity in England or in Normandy is uncertain.[66] It could well be that William Malet was entrusted by the Conqueror with the arrangements for their imprisonment (as was Robert Malet after a later uprising), but there is no proof of this. Whatever his precise role, it is evident that William Malet died in the course of his duties – perhaps in Normandy.[67]

The bulk of William's East Anglian fief descended forthwith to his son Robert. Clearly Robert regarded himself as the rightful successor to everything in England that had been his father's.[68] Nevertheless a substantial part of William's fief became alienated. By 1086 we find some of his former holdings in the possession of no less

---

[64] For a 'little Anglo-Saxon colony' at Harfleur in the late 11th century, see Jacques de Maho, 'L'Apparition des seigneuries châtelaines dans le Grand-Caux à l'époque ducale', *Archéologie Médiévale* vi, 1976, 1–111, esp. p. 33 n. 114. See also E. Hall and J.R. Sweeney, 'The "licentia de nam" of the Abbess of Montivilliers and the Origins of the Port of Harfleur', *BIHR* lii, 1979, 1. See also n. 79 below. Wissant too may have been part of this supposed trading network. Gilbert of Wissant was one of Robert Malet's most important Suffolk tenants (DB Sf 6/30, 143, 239, 244, 281, 286–7). Emma, daughter of Beatrix Malet, married Manasses, *comte* de Guisnes, whose Norman fief included the port of Wissant (see pedigree 2).

[65] Freeman surmised that William's mission was connected with the terminal stages of the insurrection at Ely (*Norman Conquest* iv, 473). J.H. Round suggested instead that the relevant phrase in Little Domesday, '*quando iuit in maresc*', resulted from a mistake by the scribe, who misread *Eueruic* i.e. York in his source (see Round's letter of 26 August 1884 in *The Academy*, and *Feudal England*, 430). This idea has often been repeated, but there are *two* Domesday entries which mention William's mission in the marsh (DB Nf 1/197; 35/16). The scribe could hardly have misread his sources for *both* of them. Round's supposition therefore falls.

[66] See Hart, *The Danelaw*, 631. Morcar was in Normandy in 1086, with Roger de Beaumont as his gaoler. F. Lot, *Etudes critiques sur l'abbaye de Saint-Wandrille*, Bibliothèque de l'École des Hautes Études civ, Paris 1913, no. 41 and correction on p. 207.

[67] Many entries in Little Domesday refer to East Anglian properties in William's hands 'on the day in which he went on the king's service', or 'at the time of his death'. The most specific entry relates to a manor at Chediston, Suffolk: '*ex hoc erat sesitus Willelmus Malet quando ivit in servitium regis ubi mortuus est*' (DB Sf 7/15). Note the verb used was *mortuus*, not *occisus*. I know of no evidence that his death occurred in England.

[68] A sokeman at Instead under William's lordship was claimed by his son Robert '*putans esse de feodo patris sui*' (DB Sf 75/4); a free man at Fritton who had been held wrongly by Robert was surrendered to the king '*quam modo tandem cognouit eum non esse de feodo patris sui*' (DB Nf 66/60).

than fourteen different successors – Count Alan, Earl Hugh, Roger Bigot, Roger of Poitou, Odo of Bayeux, Eudo the Steward, Roger of Rames, Walter Giffard, Walter of St Valery, Humphrey the Chamberlain, William of Warrenne, Robert son of Corbution, Drogo de Beuvrière and St Benedict of Hulme.[69] Further examination however shows that in many cases these alienated holdings represent only part of William's possessions in individual vills.

Thus, taking Great Glemham as an example, seven freemen there who had commended themselves to William Malet had their allegiance transferred to Roger Bigot (though Robert Malet retained their soke). At the same vill, the commendation of Wulfric had been shared between Eadric, William's predecessor, and the abbot of Ely TRE. William obtained the whole commendation of Wulfric's successor, together with the soke (presumably in 1069–70), but by 1086 this was in the possession of Eudo the Steward.[70] A similar sequence of events occurred with a manor at Great Glemham held by Starling TRE; later, William Malet had shared Starling's commendation with Ely, but by 1086 the manor was held without encumbrance by Walter Giffard. In spite of these losses, Robert still retained a number of holdings in Great Glemham in 1086.[71] Similar events, if on the whole less complicated, occurred in several other divided vills after William's death.

It is important to examine carefully these *minutiae* of tenure, because some modern commentators have concluded that a proportion of William's fief was forfeited on his death. I do not think that this was really the case. What happened, in my view, was that the opportunity was taken by the sheriff (at that time, Roger Bigot) to review William's tenures and where appropriate to pass them on to others who were thought to have better claims. The revision highlights vividly the chaos in land tenure which had resulted (especially in the Danelaw) from the Norman occupation. I would suggest that such reassessment may have been the custom whenever a tenant-in-chief died during the two decades following the Conquest. A similar process on a much grander scale occurred, of course, in 1086 when the Domesday commissioners adjudicated in disputed claims. It is noteworthy that the sections of Domesday devoted to *clamores* and *invasiones* were characteristic of the Danelaw shires, where minute division of vills had been the rule, rather than the exception.

Having inherited the core of his East Anglian fief from his father, Robert manipulated its components in various ways. He made use of local knowledge by appointing Brihtmær, a sub-tenant of Eadric of Laxton TRE, as his reeve.[72] We have noted already that he obtained additional lands from one Godwin, and that he set up a collection of estates which once belonged to Wulfgifu and Leofric as a fief for his widowed mother.[73] The Gilbert who held many sub-tenancies on Robert's

---

[69] DB Sf 3/39–40, 94–5, 98–102; 4/42; 7/8, 14–17, 26, 33, 36, 131, 133, 138–40, 143; 8/42; 16/6, 15, 30; 26/13; 28/6; 31/20; 38/6; 45/2; 51/2; 52/1; 67/15–17, 19–24, 28–31; 75/4; 77/4. DB Nf 8/12; 9/211; 17/52; 30/2. A few of these passed through Robert's hands before they were finally lost to his fief.

[70] DB Sf 7/144; 28/6.

[71] DB Sf 6/45, 49–51, 56; 45/2.

[72] DB Sf 4/17. Not all the entries in the Suffolk Domesday relating to individuals called Brihtmær are to be ascribed to Robert's reeve, but there is a good case for assuming the identity in the case of properties held by Brihtmær of Eadric of Laxfield TRE.

[73] In 1086 she was in dispute about some of these with Odo of Bayeux (DB Sf 77/4).

estates was just possibly his brother.[74] Many men, formerly free, were assimilated into the manorial structure of his father's holdings, being reclassified as villeins in Little Domesday. It is notable that the king and the earl retained between them the soke of many of Robert's commended men. Other holdings (mostly commendations) were obtained which had formerly been held by men commended to the king, to Earl Gyrth and to King Harold, or to Godric, *antecessor* of Swein of Essex, or to Ælfsige, nephew of Earl Ralph, or (in a few cases) by men holding sub-tenancies from thegns such as Ulf, son of Manni Swart.

Evidently much activity involving modifications of tenure was going on throughout Robert's honour (as his fief should properly be called). It is well known that he established as undertenants in Suffolk and Norfolk a number of people from his Norman estates. The English holdings of some of these men are illustrated on Map 10. We have three sets of information concerning them. Firstly, various Domesday entries; secondly, details in the foundation charter of their grants to the priory which Robert established at Eye; thirdly, references in Norman charters to their family holdings as sub-tenants of the Malet fief in Normandy.

We have reached the stage where a brief excursion into Normandy is necessary. This is merely a preliminary exploration, in largely uncharted territory, but I have attempted to plot some of the early Malet holdings there on Map 8. Since we do not have a Domesday Survey of the Duchy, the list is likely to be far from complete. Moreover, it has not proved possible at the present time to date precisely the origins of such tenures as we know about.

The greater part of the Malet fief, lying in the Caux region of Normandy, appears to have been created towards the end of the fourth decade of the eleventh century by hiving off some of the properties belonging to a much larger fief which became centred on Montivilliers, held by the Giffards.[75] However, from an early date the Malet family interests had reached far outside the Caux. They held properties in the department of Eure south of the River Seine, intermixed with the monastic endowments of St Pierre de Préaux, Le Bec-Hellouin and Bernay along the valleys of the River Risle and its tributary the Charentonne. They had other interests near Caen, the history of which I have not explored in detail.

William Malet I and his son Robert were already important members of Duke William's court well before the Norman Conquest, witnessing ducal charters of the abbeys of Jumièges,[76] Le Bec-Hellouin, Préaux (near Le Bec), St Florent (at Saumur in the Loire Valley)[77] and Fécamp. Their fief had for its *caput* a great fortified château at Graville-Ste-Honorine, in a commanding position on the north bank of the Seine estuary. The site is now buried under the suburbs of Le Havre. Its

---

[74] DB Sf 6/19–21, 29–30, 34–7, 40, 52, 83, 92, 100, 279, 283. The Gilbert of these Domesday entries is more likely, however to have been Gilbert of Colville, an honorial baron. Other possibilities are Gilbert Blund and Gilbet de Wissant, both Domesday sub-tenants of William Malet.

[75] J. de Maho, 'Seigneuries châtelaines', 35–6, 42, 47, 83–5. The *caput* of the Giffard fief was established at Montivilliers in 1030–5, and the Malet fief based on Graville-Ste-Honorine must have originated very soon afterwards. William Malet I subscribed (as a sub-tenant) to a *pancharta* of the abbey of Montivilliers, dated a few years before 1066. (Fauroux p. 361, no. 173). In England after the Conquest Rohese daughter of Walter Giffard married Richard fitz Gilbert, who held the Honour of Clare in Suffolk.

[76] *Willelmi Mallet et Rotberti filius eius* subscribed to a *pancharta* of the abbey of Jumièges, dated 1060–66 (Fauroux pp. 417–19).

[77] For Robert Malet and St Florent temp. King William I, see *Cal. Docs France*, no. 1110.

immense oval *motte*, still visible in part as late as 1870, measured some 85 x 60 metres in diameter, being fed with water via numerous channels running through the marsh which separated it from the estuary. To the east lay the nascent port of Harfleur, whose early post-Conquest trade has been touched on already; it was dominated by the Malets and the Giffards.[78] It was from Harfleur that the Malets maintained contact with their English possessions across the Channel. Small boats could also sail inland from the same port, upstream through the marshes to reach the Malet estates further along the Seine, the Risle and the Charentonne.

Although the Malet fief in Normandy was probably more or less complete by the time of the Conquest, early accounts of it are scarce. Such evidence as has been assembled so far for its dependencies varies a good deal in quality and antiquity from *ville* to *ville*.[79] The earliest known records showing Malet lordship of a group of *villes* north of Graville-Ste-Honorine come from a century or more after the Norman Conquest of England. All the evidence known to me for La Fleuritte and Emalleville, for example, is that in c.1220 and in 1503 they were *fiefs de haubert* held of the lord of Graville. Similarly, we know that the churches of Hermeville, St Supplix, Le Coudray, St Sauveur and Fontaine-la-Mallet were given by Guillaume Malet to the priory at Graville at the beginning of the thirteenth century. Two *fiefs de haubert* at Sainneville were held by the same Guillaume of the Honour of Clare, showing that at least one Malet holding was a sub-tenancy. For Gonneville-la-Mallet the evidence is even more indirect; the local tenant named Pierre Vaste who presented to the living there in 1236–44 was probably descended from Guillaume Vaste who witnessed a charter of Mathieu de Graville in 1159. Another witness to this charter was G. de Touffreville, and Touffreville was a Malet tenancy in 1503.

Further along the Normandy coast the Malets possessed a solitary holding at Colleville, near to the great abbey of Fécamp.[80] In the late twelfth century Eustace de Colevilla held a fee in Colleville of the Malets, lords of Graville-Ste-Honorine. A century later the abbot of Le Bec-Hellouin (a house to which the Malets were benefactors) was patron of the church of Colleville, and as late as 1503 Colleville was still part of the lands of Admiral Louis Malet, *sieur* de Graville. In Suffolk, Gilbert of Coleville's tenancy of Malet estates at the time of Domesday is shown on Map 10.[81] The de Colevilles do not appear in the foundation charter of Eye Priory, but in c.1210 William de Coleville held four knights' fees of the honour of Eye, so the family had a long-lived English as well as a Norman connection with the Malets.[82]

---

[78] For a saltpan at Harfleur held by William Malet in 1066–71, see *Cal. Docs France*, no. 319.

[79] The most useful set of sources for the early tenacies of Malet estates in Normandy appears in L.C. Lloyd, *The Origins of Some Anglo-Norman Families*, ed. C.T. Clay and D.C. Douglas, Leeds, 1951. This may be supplemented by lists in J. de Maho, 'Seigneuries châtelaines', 1–114. Except for a few charters quoted specifically, the following attempt to reconstruct the Malet tenancies depends entirely on evidence provided in these two works. Much more research is needed, especially for the family estates in the Eure. Some of this deficiency will be made good in a forthcoming paper by Dr K. Keats-Rohan. Unfortunately, no cartulary survives for Bernay.

[80] In 1085 Robert Malet witnessed a charter on behalf of Fécamp, in the presence of the Conqueror (*Cal. Docs France*, no. 116).

[81] He held in Clopton, Bromeswell, Stokerland and Rendlesham (DB Sf 6/127, 180, 236, 272). He may have been the Gilbert who held many other Malet tenancies.

[82] Thomas Hearne, *Black Book of the Exchequer* i, 301–2; on the date, see Hubert Hall, *Red Book of the Exchequer*, RS CIC, 1896, i, lvi and lxii.

Still further along the coast a group of *villes* in the valley of the River Durdent, just south of its estuary at Veulettes, were dependent on the Malet fief of Canoueville (itself subject to Graville),[83] where there was another great château protected by a pre-eleventh-century fortification, 50 metres in diameter.[84] Its dependencies included Clasville-en-Caux, Crasville-la-Mallet, Crosville, Malleville-les-Grès, Vénesville and Butot-en-Caux. Between 1040 and 1066 a *vavasseur* named Raoul gave his land at Butot to the church of St Pierre de Préaux (just to the south west of Pont-Audemer on the River Risle) on becoming a monk there, with the consent of his lord, William Malet (I) of Graville.[85] Robert of Clasville held of Robert Malet in Suffolk in 1086.[86] The prior of Graville (a Malet foundation) was patron of the church of Clasville. Pierre de Canouville presented to the cures of Crosville and Vénesville in 1236–44. Crasville was a Malet holding in 1503 and probably at a much earlier period.

The cases of Conteville and Auvilliers are a little more involved. In his foundation charter of Eye Priory (discussed in more detail below), Robert Malet confirmed to the priory the gift by Osbert de Cuncteville of the land he held of Robert at Occold, a village near to Eye. This Osbert cannot be identified in Domesday for the Survey does not name the tenants of the Malet holdings in Occold. Turning to the other side of the Channel, in 1121 William Malet (II) gave Conteville to the abbey of St Mary of Le Bec-Hellouin, just as he and his predecessors had held it.[87] A later confirmation shows that the gift included the manor and church.

There are no less than four Contevilles in Normandy. One, near to the Malet fiefs of Malleville and Butot, belonged to the abbey of Fécamp as early as 1025; moreover it had no church and cannot therefore have been the *ville* given to Bec. Conteville in Calvados is hardly a contender for identification with the *ville* donated by William, for it lies a long way from the rest of the known early holdings of the Malets. Similarly the third Conteville, an ancient *ville* with a *motte*, is sited between Forges-les-Eaux and Aumale on the eastern border of the Duchy, far outside the usual limits of Malet territory. However, Lloyd pointed out that this Conteville lies only 10 km south-east of Auvilliers and he noted that Hugh de *Avilers* was a tenant of Robert Malet at Brome, Suffolk and Shelfhanger, Norfolk, parts of which he used to endow Robert's foundation of Eye.[88] Hence he deduced that both Auvilliers and Conteville near Aumale were early Malet tenancies.

---

[83] Walter de *Conoville* witnessed the foundation charter of Eye Priory in 1086–7. Raoul de Canouville witnessed a charter of Mathieu de Graville in 1159 and 40 years later he gave his son and namesake the *seigneurie* of Malleville. By c.1220 this Raoul held Canouville of the lord of Graville as two *fiefs de haubert*. The William de Malavill' who held of Robert Malet at Wantisden and Blaxhall in Suffolk in 1086 (DB Sf 6/30, 33) is perhaps just as likely to have originated from Malleville-les-Grès as from Emalleville north of Saint-Sauveur, as has previously been thought.

[84] De Malo, 'Seigneuries châtelaines', 83–4.

[85] *Cal. Docs France* no. 319. After William's death, Robert Malet confirmed his gift and remitted to Préaux the castle ward owed by the tenant of Butot to Canoueville. See also *Cal. Docs France* no. 324, for Robert's confirmation to Préaux of a house at St Germain-Village (near Conteville).

[86] Holdings at Swefling and Stratton (DB Sf 6/46, 110). He may have held also at Badingham (DB Sf 6/306). The Avilers still held Shelfhanger, as a royal serjeanty, in the fourteenth century.

[87] *Cal. Docs France* no. 372. The gift was made for the souls of William (II) and his wife, who is unnamed in the charter. I suggest that the 'predecessors' mentioned in the charter were William Malet I and his son Robert, who was probably the brother of William Malet II. See later for the fate of William II.

[88] Lloyd, *Anglo-Norman Families*, 31–2.

If Lloyd's identifications had been correct we should have expected these two places to recur in later records of the Malet fief, but as far as I can determine, this is not the case. Moreover, Lloyd's solution fails to take full account of the known history of the fourth *ville* with this place-name, Conteville-sur-Risle on the south bank of the Seine beside the Marais Vernier. It was this *ville* which gave its name to the *vicomté* of Herluin, the Conqueror's stepfather. It is said to have been connected at a later date with the abbey of Grestain, Herluin's foundation. Moreover, its manor is said to have been given by King Richard I to the abbey of Jumièges in 1195. However the early charters of Le Bec-Helouin and Saint-Pierre de Préaux suggest very strongly that it was Conteville-sur-Risle (near to Saint Germain-Village and Préaux) which was given by William Malet II to Le Bec.

Hugh de Avilers, Robert's tenant in Suffolk, may well have come from Auvilliers near Aumale, but there is no evidence that Auvilliers was part of the Malet fief in Normandy. Moreover, we have seen that the Conteville given to Le Bec was almost certainly not the place of that name near to Aumale.

Our last known early Malet holding in the Seine-Inferieure is Rouville north of Bolbec, 14 km east of Emalleville. William of Ro(u)ville gave tithes at Glemham and *Clachestorp* (near Sudbourne in Loes Hundred, Suffolk) and sokemen at Pettaugh to Robert Malet's priory, founded at Eye. Robert held land at the first two places according to the Suffolk Domesday, but no tenant named William held there in 1086. Rouville was a Malet holding in the twelfth century.

Finally, mention must be made of a late eleventh-century charter by which Robert Malet and his wife Emmelina gave land in Pinterville (arr. Louviers, Eure) to the abbey of St-Taurin at Evreux for the support of their son Hugh as a monk.[89] More Malet properties in the Eure will be discussed later.

Before leaving Normandy, a brief mention may be made of the end of the Malet fief there. I have referred already to various members of the fief in 1503, when it was held by Louis Malet, *sieur* de Graville, admiral of France. Malets continued to hold the *berceau du lignage* at Graville-Sainte-Honorine and its dependencies until well into the sixteenth century. Meanwhile, a distinguished branch of the family had been founded in Jersey – reputedly in the eleventh century – which still survives. Turstin Malet, who witnessed two early charters of the Abbaye aux Hommes and the Abbaye aux Dames at Caen, appears to have come from a cadet branch of the family but nothing more is heard of it.[90] Another branch which reached Rouen at an early date emigrated to Geneva in 1530 as Hugenot refugees. Several other cadet branches are still established to this day in various châteaux in the south of France. All claim ancestry from Rollo of Normandy![91]

We return now to Robert Malet and his East Anglian fief. He was sheriff of

---

[89] *Cal. Docs France* no. 316. Emmelina appears to have been Robert's second wife.

[90] Lucien Musset, *Les Actes de Guillaume le Conquérant et la reine Mathilde pour les abbayes Caennaises*, Mémoires de de la Société des Antiquaires de Normandie, XXXVII, Caen 1987, no. 25 (pp. 134–4), dated 1079–1101, and no. 27 (pp. 136–40), dated 1109–1113. It is noteworthy that Walter of Caen, a large Domesday landholder in East Anglia, was Robert Malet's tenant in many vills which were members of the honour of Eye.

[91] See further Michael Edward, *Anne Malet de Graville: une femme poète du XVIe siècle*, Paris 1913. A brief sketch of the subsequent history of the various French branches of the Malets is contained in a pamphlet by Lady Matilde Malet, printed privately for those attending the Eleventh Malet Family Dinner held at London on 13 July 1933 (copy at Cambridge University Library, no. 9494 c. 48).

Suffolk (and perhaps Norfolk also) in 1075 when there was a second uprising against the Conqueror, centred once more on the fenland surrounding the Wash.[92] According to the version in the Worcester Latin Chronicle, a plot to revolt against the Conqueror was hatched at Exning (near Newmarket, Cambs.)[93] following the marriage of Earl Ralph Wader of East Anglia to the sister of Roger, earl of Hereford.

The two earls were joined, reluctantly it was said, by Waltheof, earl of Northumbria, who had held also the East Midlands earldom of Northampton, Bedford, Cambridgeshire and Huntingdon. Between them, Ralph and Waltheof had once ruled practically the whole of the Danelaw. The crucial question facing anyone seeking to understand Waltheof's involvement in the revolt is the extent to which he may still have been in charge of the four East Midland counties in 1075.[94] But however widespread the fenland estates of the conspirators, the nature of their rebellion was very different from that of 1071; significantly, it is doubtful if the 1075 revolt had much support from the peasantry. Earl Roger was prevented by Worcestershire magnates from bringing his troops to the aid of Earl Ralph, who had concentrated his forces near Cambridge. An attempt to secure aid from Denmark was unsuccessful. Earl Ralph retired to his fief in Brittany and the king's forces, led by his two half-brothers, then mounted a three months' siege against Ralph's newly-wedded wife, holed up in the family castle at Norwich.

[92] Our best authority for this revolt of the earls is the Worcester Latin Chronicle, which should however be used with caution. Its information is supplemented by ASC 'D', Orderic and the letters of Lanfranc, who was the Justiciar at the time and acted as the Conqueror's viceroy during the latter's absence in Normandy. Accounts in the *Liber Eliensis* and the *Gesta Herewardi* confuse some events during this revolt with the one by Hereward four years previously (LE lvi, 186–8). The importance of the fenland element in the uprising has been insufficiently stressed in the past, because of a failure to recognise that (as far as the evidence permits of a judgement) Holland was then still a part of the East Anglian earldom. See, for instance the account by F.M. Stenton, *Anglo-Saxon England*, Oxford, 2nd edn 1947, 602–4, followed by D.C. Douglas, *William the Conqueror*, London 1964, 231–3. It seems probable that it was not until after the revolt had been crushed that Ivo Taillebois was given effective charge of Holland, which was joined to Kesteven and Lindsey to form Lincolnshire. For all this, see Hart, *The Danelaw*, 181–8. Not only was Ivo made sheriff of the new county, he was also made responsible for the delivery of some of Ralph's landholdings in East Anglia to Count Alan of Brittany (DB Sf 1/122f). His family was joined in marriage to the Malets.

[93] Part of Exning had been in the hands of Edeva (= Eadgifu) the Fair, alias the Rich (DB Cambs 14/68), who held widely in Cambridgeshire, Essex, Suffolk and Norfolk. Much has been written on Edeva, a member of one of the really great pre-Conquest families in Eastern England. I think she was the *Ædgeua comitissa* who had held in Suffolk (DB Sf 4/17). Some if not all of her properties passed to Earl Ralph Wader and after his forfeiture many of her estates were surrendered to Count Alan of Brittany. She may have been the widow of Ralph de Gael, the Staller, Ralph Wader's father and predecessor in the East Anglian earldom. Eadgifu is an English name but both ASC 'D' and the Worcester Latin Chronicle state that Ralph Wader had a Breton mother. Perhaps Eadgifu was Ralph de Gael's *second* wife. He may have divorced his first wife, putting her away (with the Conqueror's consent) into the monastery of St Benet of Hulme (DB Nf 8/8, 17/24; see C. Johnson in *VCH Norfolk* ii, 1906, 11). ASC 'D' says that the Conqueror approved the marriage of Ralph Wader but the Worcester Latin Chronicle claims that the king opposed the union. Stenton rejected this Latin version, wrongly I think. It supplies a motive for the revolt.

[94] It appears likely to me that Waltheof *did* keep overall control of these four shires until his defection, in the same way that Ralph had retained control of Holland. For a rather different view, see now C.P. Lewis, 'The Early Earls of Norman England', *ANS* xiii, 1991, 207–24, esp. 221.

Subsequently, Earl Ralph's wife was allowed to join her husband in Brittany. Earl Waltheof was executed and Earl Roger banished.

Robert Malet's part in all this does not appear in the narrative sources, but he surfaces in a letter of Lanfranc to the Conqueror announcing the surrender of Norwich Castle.[95] It was then occupied by Bishop Geoffrey of Coutances, William de Warrenne and Robert Malet, together with 300 men-at-arms, supported by *ballistarii* and many engineers. It is evident that Robert, the sheriff and largest local landholder loyal to the king, must have played a key part in the suppression of the revolt. What, if anything, did he stand to gain?

Modern commentators have claimed that after Ralph's banishment, his East Anglian earldom was dismembered.[96] Certainly we hear no more of an earl bearing this title for a further sixty years, but there is ample evidence that the perquisites, if not the power of the earldom, were retained and passed on by the king to others.[97] The issue is important for our assessment of Robert Malet's wealth and influence. Domesday shows that in the case of Suffolk not all of these perquisites were obtained by the sheriff. He acquired some of Ralph's holdings, but not their jurisdiction. Nevertheless Robert was positioned to gain a great deal of power, with no counterbalancing authority from a local earl left to restrain him. Nationally too he became a more important figure; from this time onwards he was an intimate of the king, often at court and witnessing many of his charters.[98]

We do not know for how long Robert Malet held the shrievalty of Suffolk, which was in the hands of Roger Bigot at the time of the Domesday Survey. Robert was undoubtedly heavily involved in the great Survey, checking his own rights of tenure and challenging those of his neighbours to which he might have some claim. He held the most extensive of all the fiefs in East Anglia, comprising 511 holdings and lordships, including well over fifty-six churches and interests in two boroughs.[99] In addition his properties in Lincolnshire and adjacent shires were not

---

[95] *Regesta* i, no. 82.

[96] D.C. Douglas, *William the Conqueror*, London 1964, 296. Lewis, 'Early Earls', 221–2.

[97] A large number of Domesday entries for Robert Malet's Suffolk fief record that 'the soke belongs to the king and the earl' (*in soca regis et comitis; rex et comes socam*) e.g. DB Sf 6/3,7, 8, 10, 13, to quote only the first few. The description of a holding of twenty-five freemen in Huntingfield ends: *de tota hac terra liberorum ho(minium) iacet soca et saca in blideburh ad opus regis et comitis* (DB Sf 6/82). In three other cases the soke of Robert's holdings is shared between the abbot of Ely and Earl Hugh in 1086 (at *Manuuic*, Ashfield and Thorpe Hall: DB SF 6/19–21). Perhaps the unnamed earl who shared with the king jurisdiction over many other Domesday estates belonging to Robert Malet was also Hugh, *vicomte* of the Avranchin, who was made earl of Chester in 1071–76. Hugh held a substantial Suffolk fief in his own right in 1086 (DB Sf 4/1–42). In many entries of Hugh's fief, he is said to share the soke either with the king or with the abbot of Ely. The last entry for his fief relates to Framlingham, and records that the soke belonged to Ely (St Etheldreda) in 1086, but previously it was held by Hugh's *antecessor* (DB Sf 6/42). 'Soke' in these particular entries may refer to hundredal jurisdiction. The matter deserves further investigation. Certainly Hugh held one of the greatest of all the English fiefs.

[98] For example, Robert Malet witnessed a royal writ of 1082, notifying the gift of two carucates at Covenham in Lindsey to the church of St Calais and another of 1078 x 1087 notifying the gift by Bishop Walchelin of Winchester of Alton Priors, Wiltshire, to the king's cook. *Regesta* i, nos 147, 270. He accompanied the Conqueror on a visit to Fécamp in 1085, the last recorded occasion of Robert's presence in Normandy (*Cal. Docs France* no. 116, an original charter).

[99] R. Welldon Finn, *The Norman Conquest and its Effects on the Economy, 1066–86*, London 1971, 260. For several other churches on Robert's estates, existing at the time of Domesday but not recorded therein, see the foundation charter of Eye Priory. My own count of Robert's Domesday

negligible and he seized the opportunity offered by the Survey to lay claim to many of the Yorkshire estates of his father which had been laid waste by the Conqueror's harrying of the North, and had remained barren ever since. In this he was not totally unsuccessful, for a few of them became absorbed into his honour of Eye.[100]

Robert was one of the first Norman magnates to found a priory in England, endowed with estates of his English fief. He chose for its site Eye in Suffolk, the *caput* of his honour, and placed his new foundation under the supervision of the Benedictine abbey of St Mary of Bernay, some 55 km south-west of Rouen, which had been established about 1026.[101] The undated *pancharta* purporting to record the endowments of Eye Priory was probably constructed some time after its foundation but its contents seem to be reliable.[102] Most of the endowments it records appear to date from after the Domesday Survey but before the death of the Conqueror, who is said to have approved of the priory's establishment. If we assume that the returns for Little Domesday, when Robert's fief was *inbreviatus*, were completed by the spring of 1086 and recall that the Conqueror died early in September 1087, we have the most likely outside dates for Robert's foundation. The king's permission to create the priory might have been obtained at any time in 1086.

It is quite possible that the review of the tenancies of his fief necessitated by the Domesday Survey was the factor which triggered Robert Malet to set up his foundation. The *pancharta* claims that some at least of the records of the land endowments were laid by their donors upon the altar of the church of St Peter of Eye; presumably this was the pre-existing mother church of the estate. It seems that there was a foundation ceremony; if so, it should be dated as far from the date of the Domesday Survey as is practicable, to allow for changes in tenure of the estates forming the endowment. The names of individual donors are given in the *pancharta*; only rarely are they identical with those of the respective Domesday tenants. The kalends of August, established by Robert as the date of the beginning of the four days' annual fair at Eye which he granted to the monks, may have commemorated the date of the endowment ceremony.[103] Let us postulate 1 August 1087 for this event, with the reservation that at our present state of knowledge a date up to two or three years later is not impossible.[104] Greater precision may be achieved in the future by deeper analysis of all the relevant evidence.

holdings shows him in possession of the soke and/or commendation over 1,397 freemen and sokemen in East Anglia. Altogether, his honour in 1086 extended into nine shires and was worth almost £600 a year.

100 Barf in Birdforth, Hutton Sessay, Thornton le Moor, Bustardthorpe and Acaster (William Farrer in *VCH Yorks.* ii, 168). At some stage, the whole of the Malet fee in Lincolnshire was also annexed to Eye.

101 Robert's Normandy fief included properties quite near to Bernay (Map 10). The family priory founded at Graville-Ste-Honorine in 1206 was also made subject to Bernay.

102 The only surviving text of the foundation charter is that entered in a late thirteenth-century cartulary entitled the 'Liber Albus' *al.* 'Registrum Malet' from the Audley End estate archives, deposited at the Essex Record Office (D/DBy Q 19, no. 1, fos 17–18b). This has now been edited superbly in two volumes by Mrs Vivien Brown for the Suffolk Record Society: *Eye Priory Cartulary and Charters*, 2 vols, Woodbridge 1992–94. (Foundation charter text and translation I, 12–16; comment II, 88–90).

103 The market commenced on one of the the patronal festivals of St Peter's, the mother church of Eye (1 August is the feast of St Peter's Chains, commemorating his escape from prison).

104 According to the surviving text of the foundation charter, the priory was founded and endowed

By any measure the foundation charter is an extraordinary document which deserves to be better known. It mentions Robert's castle at Eye and the honour bestowed on him by the Conqueror, and records the honorial baronage, knighthood and sokemen. It is of great value for the additional information it supplies about many Domesday vills and their tenants. It tells of schools and inns, fairs and tithes, deer and their park, sheaves of corn, sheepskins and cheeses, large eel and herring fisheries, and churches and chapels unrecorded in Domesday. Robert granted to his foundation various properties including the church of St Peter, a fishpond and the tithes of a market in Eye and a fair at Dunwich for three days commencing on the feast of St Leonard (6 November, the saint's day of the mother church of Dunwich), together with all the churches of Dunwich (three are named in Domesday) and their tithes, and *scolae* (? schools) in the town. He gave the tithes of all his demesne manors (ten of those listed are in Suffolk and three in Lincolnshire, one in Essex and one in Yorkshire), and twenty-six Suffolk churches.[105] He also gave all his fisheries at Upwell and Outwell, Cambs., and at Ely, and all his tithes of woodland in money, pannage and swine. Finally, he refers to his jurisdiction over an unknown number of his knights, sokemen and peasantry and orders them to make gifts to the monastery according to their means. The location of churches and estates given to Eye Priory at its foundation by Robert and his tenantry is shown on Map 9.

In conformity with current custom when religious foundations were being established in England or Normandy, Robert persuaded or coerced nineteen of his tenants, all named and described as *barones et milites*, to support his endowment with their own donations. In most cases a tenant would grant the church on one or more of his estates, with its glebe and two-thirds of its tithes; often other land was given also. Several of these churches are not mentioned in Little Domesday Book, and the Eye charter is the earliest record of their existence. The charter ends with twenty-one named witnesses, all it seems from Robert's Suffolk estates.

Of outstanding interest is the church of St Botolph at *Yca*, given with its appurtenances by William of Ro(u)ville, who came from one of the members of the Malet fief in Normandy. *Yca* does not occur in Little Domesday Book, being included perhaps under Sudbourne. Nearby were Glemham and the lost *Clakestorpe* in Eyke; two-thirds of the tithes from both of these holdings were also given by William to Eye Priory.[106] There is no reasonable doubt of the location of the church of *Yca* at Iken on a marshy spur on the south bank of the River Alde in

---

by Robert *assensu domini mei Willielmi regis Anglie pro anima ipsius et uxoris ejus Matildis reginae, pro memetipso, et pro animabus patris mei Willielmi Malet et matris mei Hesiliœ*. This is not absolutely unequivocal evidence that the Conqueror was still alive at the time of the foundation, but it is very difficult to see how reference to Rufus could have been avoided in the charter, if he were on the throne at that time. However, this supposes the text to be strictly contemporary and authentic. Mrs Brown points out that some of the individual gifts recorded in the charter could not have been made before Robert was re-established in his honour by Henry I. She dates the charter 1086 – 1105/6 and suggests that it paraphrases original charters in the possession of the monastery, relating to individual endowments. With this I would agree.

[105] Interestingly, Robert's demesne estates in Suffolk were spread within the territory between Eye and Dunwich, which is where the new trading pattern was concentrated. See Map 10.

[106] Robert Malet had two Domesday holdings at *Clachestorp*, one of which was tenanted by Walter de *Risbou al. Risboil* from some unidentified place in Normandy (DB Sf 6/274, 284). Whether the place-name *Eike* may be related etymologically to *Icanho* is a matter for place-name scholars to determine, but there is no doubt as to their topographical proximity.

Suffolk. Note also the proximity of Iken to Sudbourne, the administrative centre of a franchise over five-and-a-half hundreds given to Ely Abbey on its foundation in 970.[107] Here at last we have firm evidence for the location of St Botolph's famous seventh-century monastery of *Icanho*, and proof that his church, with its dedication, survived long after the Danish settlement.[108]

Only three of Robert Malet's tenants who made gifts to Eye Priory can be identified in Little Domesday. They are William *Goulafré* ('the Glutton') who held at Uggeshall, Barham, Winston, Debenham, Thorpe Hall, Boyton, Rushmere, Sternfield, Aspall, Oakley, Thrandeston, Kenton and Martley,[109] Walter the Cross-bowman *(Arbelestarii)* who held Shottisham (including *Halgestou*) and sixteen acres in Eye[110] and Richard *Houel al. Houerel* who held at Wyverstone.[111] The remaining fourteen donors to Eye Priory who are named in its foundation charter do not appear in the Domesday Survey, but most if not all of their donations can be identified as Domesday holdings of the Malet fief.

Two of the most interesting tenancies recorded in the charter are those of Ralph of Glanville and Hugh of Mont-Canisy, each of whom is said to have placed his gift of a *hospitium* (? inn) at Yaxley, Suffolk on the altar of the church of St Peter of Eye. These two men are not to be found in Domesday, but the Survey records that the Malet fief included two holdings by unnamed tenants at Yaxley.[112] Moreover, Ralph and Hugh are likely to have been related to Robert of Glanville and Hubert of Mont-Canisy, both substantial Domesday undertenants of Robert Malet (Map 10).[113] Glanville and Mont-Canisy are neighbouring *villes* near the Calvados coast

---

107 Hart, *The Danelaw*, 47, 577, 595. Such franchises were often of ancient origin.

108 For *Icanho* and St Botolph, see ASC 'A' *s.a.* 654 and H.P.R. Finberg, *The Early Charters of the West Midlands*, Leicester 1972, 202, 204, 207. There is more than a hint in the wording of William of Ro(u)ville's donation that he had in mind the establishment of a small monastic cell at *Yca*. The phrase in the charter recording the donation is vaguely worded, and may be corrupt, but I think it very possible that William was seeking to restore some of the prestige to be associated with an ancient foundation. One is reminded of the similar motivation underlying Gilbert of Ghent's foundation of a priory on the site of an ancient monastery at Bardney in Lincolnshire in 1087, populating it with monks from Charroux in Aquitaine. (Hart, *The Danelaw*, 242).

109 DB Sf 6/10–11, 14–15, 25, 65–66, 138–141, 206, 271, 293; 7/8. The Goulafrés continued to hold this barony, one of the largest of the honour of Eye, until at least the mid-thirteenth century when they had four knights' fees. Dr K. Keats-Rohan has identified their Norman holding as la Goulafrière near Montreuil-l'Argillé, Eure.

110 DB Sf 6/176, 191, 238.

111 DB Sf 6/57, 211; 14/151. He occurs also in the 'Feudal Book of Abbot Baldwin' I, 10; see Douglas, *Feudal Docs*. The Hovels held Wyverstone as subtenants of the Mountchesneys (of Mont-Canisy) until well into the thirteenth century.

112 DB Sf 6/196, 229. Note that Hubert of Mont-Canisy was also a Domesday tenant of Robert Malet at Yaxley (n. 112 below). The Mountchesneys held twelve knights' fees of the honour until after 1300.

113 Robert of Glanville held from Robert Malet at Creeting St Peter, Great Glemham, Benhall, Burgh, Bawdsey, Hollesley, Charsfield, Boulge, Dallinghoo, Stradbroke and Horham, all in Suffolk (DB Sf 6/3, 5, 51, 54, 124, 157, 160, 179, 181, 291, 308–9), and Honing in Norfolk (DB Nf 17/51). Robert held also from William de Warenne at Burgh, Boulge, Debach, '*Torstanestuna*' and Bred-field (DB Sf 16/16–20). Hubert of Mont-Canisy held in chief at Wyverstone (DB Sf 57). He held also from Robert Malet at Bromeswell and Staverton (DB Sf 6/190, 260) and almost certainly at Edwardstone, Belstead, Brantham, Wantisden, Benhall, Wyverstone, Westhorpe, Rickinghall (Superior and Inferior), Theberton, Yaxley, Sutton and Walsham le Willows all in Suffolk (DB Sf 6/ 1, 26–7, 30, 53, 57–8, 62, 109, 190, 196, 235, 248–9, 260, 280, 299, 302), and Thorpe Parva and Frenze in Norfolk (DB Nf 7/9, 11). He had a house in York (DB Yorks. C19). See also Map 7.

and one wonders if they were in fact part of the Malet fief in Normandy. Overall, the substantial degree of change in the Malet tenancies might suggest that the foundation charter dates from as much as a decade after Domesday. As we shall see however, this does not appear to have been the case, for within a very few years of the Survey most if not all of the honour of Eye had been forfeited by Robert Malet. A safer conclusion appears to be that the charter in its surviving form is a later compilation incorporating some anachronistic statements, but based mostly on genuine materials.

It has long been known that, soon after the death of William the Conqueror, Robert Malet fell out of favour with his son and successor King William Rufus.[114] Recently Christopher Lewis has established that things were worse than that; it seems that Robert actually surrendered his honour early in the reign and it was given to Count Roger the Poitevin.[115] There is no need to cite the evidence in detail, for it is displayed in Lewis's paper; sufficient to note that Robert's forfeiture occurred before 1094 and Lewis thought (mistakenly, it seems) that Durand Malet may have fallen with him, losing his Lincolnshire estates to Roger the Poitevin.[116] Some, if not all, of Robert's honorial baronage in East Anglia became tenants of the new lord and Robert's endowment of Eye Priory was alienated, at least in part.

The precise date and extent of the fall of the Malets under Rufus, and the reason underlying it, have not as yet been established. Lewis thinks that Robert retired to his Normandy fief and that (to quote) 'Malet's eclipse after 1087 must surely have been due to his preference for Robert Curthose over William Rufus and ultimately to his willingness to risk (and lose) Eye for the sake of Graville-Sainte-Honorine'.[117] I am not so sure. Certainly the revenue of the honour of Eye was worth several times as much as that of the Graville fief. We have no evidence from charters or from any other source to support the theory that Robert Malet retired to Normandy to side with Robert Curthose against William Rufus, likely though that hypothesis may appear. We do not even have unequivocal proof of the continuity of Robert's tenure of the Malet fief in Normandy, although that too appears to be very likely. Finally, we have no proof that Rufus confiscated the *whole* of Robert's honour. The reality of the situation may have been much less clear-cut.

The complete hiatus in the evidence for Robert's activities after the foundation of Eye Priory comes to an abrupt end with the death of William Rufus. Henry I was

---

[114] F. Barlow, *William Rufus*, London 1983, 151 n. 279, noted that Robert witnesses none of the known writs and charters of Rufus.

[115] C.P. Lewis, 'The King and Eye: a Study in Anglo-Norman Politics', *EHR* civ, 1989, 569–87. See also V. Chandler, 'The Last of the Montgomerys: Roger the Poitevin and Arnulf', *BIHR* lxii, 1989, 1–14. Count Roger already held a large fief scattered all over East and West Suffolk at the time of Domesday; his many *antecessores* included the king, the bishop and the abbeys of Ely and Bury St Edmunds (DB Sf 8/1–82). Lewis thought that the *whole* of Robert's honour was given by William Rufus to Roger, but the evidence he offers to support such a view is insufficient. Conceivably Robert retained a part of it, either in chief or as Roger's tenant. It has to be remembered that the foundation endowment of Eye Priory, substantial though it was, represented only a small fraction of the holdings of the honour of Eye.

[116] Lewis thought that Durand forfeited his estates at the same time as Robert Malet, but later evidence shows that the gifts of Roger the Poitevin of the manors of Wellingore to the monks of Charroux and Navenby to Lancaster were both properties that had been royal demesne manors, rather than the lands that Durand had possessed at these places; see Vivien Brown, *Eye Cartulary* ii, 8, n. 33, and David Roffe, 'The *Descriptio Terrarum* of Peterborough Abbey', *BIHR* lv, 1992, 2 n. 7.

[117] Lewis, 'The King and Eye', 584–5.

crowned on 5 August 1100, just three days after his brother was shot in the New Forest. Robert Malet witnessed Henry's coronation charter at Westminster.[118] Lewis has suggested, very plausibly, that either Robert was present with Henry in the New Forest at the time of William Rufus's death, or he was summoned from Normandy and arrived immediately afterwards.[119]

In the past historians have been led astray by Orderic Vitalis, who tells us that Robert Malet, as a consequence of his taking Robert Curthose's side in the civil war of 1101, was disseised and banished by Henry I in 1102. If that is what really happened, then Robert was very quickly reinstated. In fact, as Hollister has demonstrated so ably from charter evidence, Orderic's account is very unlikely to be true.[120] By contrast, it seems that Robert was an intimate of King Henry from the outset of the reign and was soon made his master chamberlain, being probably the first to hold that post. In addition he was reappointed sheriff of Suffolk[121] and appears to have been restored to full possession of his honour of Eye, which he continued to hold until his death. His establishment of Eye Priory was also restored in full, with all its endowments.

The early restoration of Robert's position in East Anglia after the death of Rufus is illustrated by his presence at the formal foundation of Norwich Cathedral Priory, which occured no later than 3 September 1101 and possibly before 21 April in that year.[122] He witnessed the foundation charter and two other charters of a similar date, this time with a William Malet whom I shall designate (not without trepidation) as William II. These charters survive only in cartulary texts but there seems no reason to doubt them in any respect.

Robert witnessed English royal charters regularly from 1103 until 13 February 1105 when he attested as *camerarius* a charter dated at Romsey *in transitu regis*, as the king was awaiting his crossing to Normandy for a campaign that would see the burning of Bayeux and the capture of Caen. It seems likely that Robert accompanied the king on this venture and it is generally held that he is heard of no more thereafter. Some have assumed that he died at the battle of Tinchebray (28 September 1106) but there is no evidence whatever to back this supposition. If the suggested dating of another Norwich charter to late August or early September 1107 is to be accepted it seems that Robert lived at least until that date, for the surviving copy of the charter carries his attestation (assuming that this relates to the same individual).[123]

If we reject the account by Orderic of events in 1101–2, I see no reason why we need assume that Robert forfeited either his Normandy fief or his English honour at any time after the accession of King Henry I. It seems possible that both passed

---

[118] *Regesta* ii, no. 488.
[119] Lewis, 'The King and Eye', 582.
[120] C. Warren Hollister, 'Henry I and Robert Malet', *Viator* iv, 1973, 115–32, to which readers are referred for details of charters witnessed by Robert during the reign of Henry I.
[121] Hollister suggests, on the strength of *Regesta* ii, no. 672, that Robert was replaced as sheriff of Suffolk by 5 June 1104.
[122] *Charters of Norwich Cathedral Priory*, i, ed. Barbara Dodwell, London, Pipe Roll Society 1974, pp. 2–4 (no. 3) and pp. 61–3 (nos 112–13). Nos 3 and 113 were witnessed by Robert and William Malet II. Three later royal writs for Norwich in this cartulary are also witnessed by Robert Malet (nos 13, 77–8).
[123] *Regesta* ii, no. 834; Dodwell, *Charters of Norwich Priory*, 9, no. 13.

intact to his heir William Malet II who was in all probability his brother.[124] If so, it is not known at what date Robert was succeeded by William Malet II, who was deposed by King Henry and stripped of his English possessions at the Whitsun court held at New Windsor in 1110.[125] However, other interpretations of the evidence are possible; the matter is complicated and an unequivocal solution appears doubtful.[126]

William Malet II appears to have spent the rest of his life in Normandy. Evidently he held the Graville fief, for records survive of his grants to the abbey of Le Bec-Hellouin. In the first of these dated 1117, a very informative charter for the history of the Malets, he gave to the abbey a church and manor called the *Mesnil Joscelin* situated near *Rosteria* (? Roussière) on the River Charentonne, on the occasion of his son William (III) becoming a monk there, and for his own soul and the souls of his wife and children, his parents and his brother Robert, who had given the mill there to the abbey before 1077.[127] The second of William II's gifts to Le Bec was the *ville* (including manor and church) of Conteville-sur-Risle in 1121. The original charter survives, with a confirmation by Henry I which shows that William Malet's loss of the honour of Eye did not affect his continued tenancy of the Graville fief in Normandy.[128]

Throughout this review so far, I have deliberately taken what might be termed the 'minimalist' position regarding the Malet family tree. There are many reasons for this cautious approach, the most compelling being the fact that there is usually only one witness – whether a chronicle, charter or narrative source – for each piece of information that goes to make up the overall picture. More often than not, each surviving historical source is one or more stages removed from the original, so that it is correspondingly difficult to ensure that there has been no forgery and no significant damage to the text in the process of transmission. Moreover, one cannot always be sure whether two independent records of different but contemporary events which involve identical names – particularly William and Robert – are concerned with the same person, or two different individuals. Finally, it is unsafe to assume that every individual carrying the name Malet was a member of the same family, however extended the family may have been. These constraints should be borne in mind when assessing the validity of the pedigrees with which our study concludes. Minimalist as they are, they still involve many assumptions, not all of which can easily be identified, much less discussed. One can only offer what seems to be the best possible reconstruction, using such evidence as has survived.

It is with William Malet II that we are brought back to the starting point of our review, for the tradition at Le Bec links him to the illustrious family of Crispin, of

---

[124] See n. 126 below. Hollister, 'Henry I and Robert Malet', 119, and Brown, *Eye Cartulary*, 11 take a different view.

[125] ASC 'E' *s.a.* 1110; Huntingdon, 237.

[126] See the discussion by Vivien Brown in *Eye Cartulary* ii, 11 n. 54 and 23–4.

[127] Chanoine Porée, *Histoire de l'Abbaye de Bec*, Evreux 1901, I, 334 n. 4, quoting Paris, Bib. Nat. Lat. 13905, ff. 21v and 116; see also Bib. Nat. Lat. 12884, ff. 165v and 175v. According to Porée the gift of the *Mesnil Jocelin* had first been made by Robert Malet and it was confirmed in 1130 by a Gilbert Crispin, whom he identifies as William's *parent*. It is hazardous to translate *parent* in this context any more closely than 'older relative'. See further, Brown, *Eye Cartulary* 10–11, n. 49, where she locates the *Mesnil Joscelin* at La Trinité-de-Reville, 17 km SW of Bernay and E of Roussière.

[128] *Cal. Docs France* no. 1121.

'the first nobility of Normandy', close to the Conqueror and benefactors to the abbey, from whom sprang Gilbert the famous abbot of Westminster, who ruled that foundation so successfuly during the thirty-two years following his appointment as abbot in 1085.[129] A curious document in the Le Bec archives is entitled 'The Miracle whereby Blessed Mary succoured William Crispin senior, wherein is an account of the noble family of the Crispins'. It was written perhaps by a cousin of Abbot Gilbert named Milo Crispin, precentor of Le Bec, and relates that Gilbert Crispin, the head of the family, had three sons and two daughters, of whom the younger daughter named Esilia was the mother of William Malet (II). The information appears to be reliable. Reinforced by notices of the family in the letters of Anselm, archbishop of Canterbury (a former abbot of Le Bec), a pedigree can be constructed which runs thus:

Pedigree 1. The Crispin connection: a provisional solution

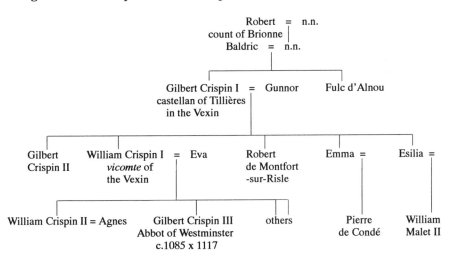

For the next stage of our pedigree we return to the Eye cartulary, which has a charter by Beatrix, sister of Robert Malet, by which she grants to the priory the *villula* called *Radingefeld* (Redlingfield, Suffolk), for her soul and for those of her father and mother and her brothers Robert Malet and Gilbert Malet.[130] The charter has every appearance of being based on a genuine original. It is undated but should probably be assigned to 1087 x c.1092. There are difficulties here, for a Gilbert Malet is not found as a landowner in English or Norman sources at this time; conversely, Beatrix does not name her brother (William Malet II). It will be recalled that the Worcester Latin Chronicler mentioned only two children accompanying William Malet I and his wife when they were captured in 1069. He

---

129 J. Armitage Robinson, *Gilbert Crispin, Abbot of Westminster*, Cambridge 1911, 13–18.
130 Essex Record Office D/DBy Q 19, no. 1, f. 59. Brown, *Eye Cartulary* i, 16. For her family, see T. Stapleton, 'Some Observations upon the Succession to the Barony of William of Arques', *Archaeologia* xxxi, 216–37; J.H. Round, *Geoffrey de Mandeville*, London 1892, 397–8.

may of course have been mistaken, or the facts may have suffered in transmission, or the Malets may have had two or more grown-up children no longer under parental care, but in the absence of evidence to the contrary it seems reasonable to take the chronicler's account at its face value.

Wherever Robert was at this time, he was too old to have been a child still living *en famille*. So I suggest that the two unnamed children of the chronicler's account were Beatrix and William (II). It seems to me unlikely that Beatrix would have excluded any brothers and sisters, alive or dead, from the list of those in her family whose souls were to be prayed for by the community at Eye.[131] If so, there seems to be no way of reconciling Beatrix's charter with the Worcester chronicler's account without introducing a modification of one or the other of these two texts. Most reluctantly therefore, I suggest that the cartulary text should be amended by substituting the name of William (= *Guillaume*) for Gilbert. We are then left with the following core pedigree:

Pedigree 2. The Malets in England and Normandy: a provisional solution

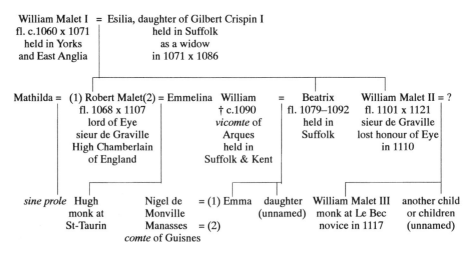

Durand Malet, who was of the same generation as Robert, cannot be placed safely in the pedigree at our present state of knowledge; he held in Lincs. and Notts. in 1086. I have found no evidence of any progeny of Robert Malet by his first wife Mathilda, about whom very little is known.[132] His only known child was a son called Hugh, by his second wife Emmelina; he became a monk at St-Taurin. As we have seen, upon Robert's death it is probable that the bulk of the honour of Eye passed to his brother William II, but one at least of his possessions appears to

---

131 Mrs V. Brown has suggested that the surviving version of the charter's list may be truncated. There seems to be no answer to this problem that does not involve suggesting modification to the surviving sources in some form or another.

132 Brown, *Eye Cartulary* ii, 10 n. 40, quoting late copies of a charter from the secular Goldingham Cartulary preserved in the Essex Record Office, D/DEx, M25, fo. 2r and fo. 42r. The charter, which is in French and spurious in its surviving form, seems to contain genuine elements. It is said to have been sealed by the great seal of King William I.

have descended to his sister Beatrix. This was Redlingfield, which Beatrix gave to Eye Priory; it had been held of Roger by her husband William of Arques in 1086 (DB Suffolk 6/192).

It is known that Robert Malet was the uncle of the Countess Lucy, a substantial heiress who married a series of Lincolnshire magnates, but in spite of considerable research by a number of scholars during the past century and a half, as yet neither the origins of Lucy nor her exact relationship to Robert have been ascertained with certainty.[133] However, a recent paper by Dr Katharine Keats-Rohan offers some prospect of light at the end of this very dark tunnel.[134] She claims that there is 'no doubt' that Countess Lucy was the daughter of Robert Malet's sister by her marriage to Thoraldr the sheriff of Lincoln. Although I do not share her conviction, she does provide a fresh interpretation of the evidence in favour of this identification, which has long been suspected. Whether or not this issue should now be regarded as solved, only time will tell. I rather suspect that further evidence will be required before a final verdict can safely be delivered. We are making progress, but we are not there yet.

Dr Keats-Rohan does not name Lucy's mother but so far I have seen no evidence to establish beyond all doubt that Robert had more than one sister, the Beatrix who added to the endowment of Eye. Taking once more the minimalist approach, one might suggest that Thoraldr, who died in or before 1079, could have been her first husband. The following provisional pedigree is based on this supposition:

Pedigree 3. The Malets and Countess Lucy: a provisional solution

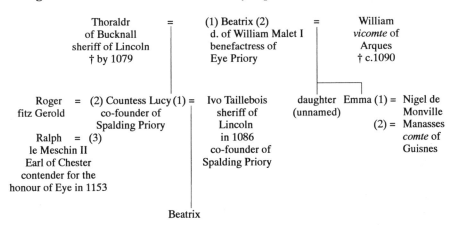

```
    Thoraldr          =    (1) Beatrix (2)        =       William
    of Bucknall            d. of William Malet I         vicomte of
 sheriff of Lincoln        benefactress of                 Arques
    † by 1079              Eye Priory                     † c.1090


  Roger   = (2) Countess Lucy (1) =  Ivo Taillebois   daughter  Emma (1) =  Nigel de
fitz Gerold    co-founder of           sheriff of     (unnamed)            Monville
               Spalding Priory          Lincoln                    (2) =  Manasses
  Ralph   = (3)                         in 1086                           comte of
le Meschin II                        co-founder of                        Guisnes
Earl of Chester                     Spalding Priory
contender for the
honour of Eye in 1153

                         Beatrix
```

---

[133] The prime evidence is an original Cotton charter dated 1152 which records the grant by Henry II (as Duke of Normandy) to Ranulph le Meschin II, Earl of Chester (third husband of the Countess Lucy) of *totum honorem de Eia, sicut Robertus Malet avunculus matris sue melius et plenius unquam tenuit. Et feudum Alani de Lincoln ei dedi qui fuit auunculus matris sue.* (Regesta iii, 180). J.G. Nichols, 'The Descent of the Earldom of Lincoln', *Memoirs of Annual Meeting of the Archaeological Institute of Great Britain, held at Lincoln, July 1848*, London 1850, 253–78, esp. 255. Most modern historians have avoided like the plague the terrible topic of Lucy's family connections.

[134] K.S.B. Keats-Rohan, '*Antecessor noster*; the Parentage of Countess Lucy made Plain', *Prosopon: Newsletter of the Unit for Prosopographical Research* no. 2, May 1995. The new analysis offered by Dr Keats-Rohan turns on the precise meaning of the terms *heres, antecessor* and

If accepted, this hypothethetical pedigree would explain many known facts concerning the fate of the earldom of East Anglia and the descent of Malet estates in Lincolnshire and Suffolk. In particular, the dower which Lucy brought with her to her first marriage would seem to have reached her from her father's family rather than from the Malets (*via* her mother). It was not until her third marriage that restoration of the honour of Eye, surrendered by William Malet II in 1110, was sought by the family. It was planned to give it to her husband after it had been alienated from the family for forty-three years, but for some reason the grant did not take effect. Exploration of this interesting topic must be left to others.

For the rest, the Malet pedigree has been pruned somewhat and I hope that the family connection with the Crispins is established more clearly. I hope too that the accompanying maps will illustrate more precisely the importance of the landed interests of the Malets in England and Normandy and the comings and goings of both lords and tenants between the two fiefs. Unexpectedly, our survey has also highlighted the reorientation of the external trade of the Eastern Danelaw from Scandinavia to Normandy, with the Malet borough of Dunwich threatening to take over from Ipswich (temporarily, as it transpired) as the major seaport along the Suffolk coast.

As might be expected, huge gaps in our knowledge remain. The fundamental questions that prompted this review remain unanswered. Sadly, we must leave the mystery of the origins of William Malet I no nearer to a solution than when we started. In particular, no hard evidence has been found that any member of the family was resident in England before the Norman Conquest, nor has any source been uncovered to illustrate the connection (if any) between the family and Harold before the battle of Hastings. The challenge remains for others to continue the story from here.[135]

predecessor in early charters. I am grateful to Sir James Holt for bringing this paper to my notice. See also N. Summer, 'The Countess Lucy's Priory? The Early History of Spalding Priory and its Estates', *Reading Medieval Studies* xiii, 1988, 81–103.

[135] It should be noted that although the honour of Eye passed out of the hands of the Malets in 1110, the family continued to hold widely in England and to exert great influence at court. Ralph and Walter Malet (descendants perhaps of Durand Malet) were still holding of William Meschin in the Lincolnshire Wolds and elsewhere in the North Riding in 1115–16 (Li S 3/5; 7/7; 198/8, 9). A (? second) Ralph Malet was sheriff of Wiltshire in 1154–5. A Robert Malet was steward of the royal household in 1136; he was with King Stephen in Normandy in 1137 but had defected to the Empress by 1141. Presumably this was the Robert who occurs with reference to Warminster (Wilts.) in 1129–30; the same man may have been ancestor to the family which held the honour of Curry Malet (Somerset) in 1140 (below; see also Sanders, *English Baronies*, 39); perhaps he was the Robert Malet who held in Cambridgeshire in 1150 (W. Farrer, *Feudal Cambridgeshire*, Cambridge 1920, 109). A Hugh Malet granted land to Woburn Abbey, Bedfordshire in 1140–3 (*Regesta* iii, no. 961). A Gilbert Malet was steward of the royal household in 1175, with interests in Somerset. By 1195 a William Malet, son of Gilbert, had reached Shepton Mallet in Somerset, an estate held by the family for many centuries thereafter. I am grateful to Dr Robert Bearman for some of these references; he is collecting the charters of the honour of Curry Malet as part of his forthcoming volume on West Country *acta*. For the later history of the family in England, see Arthur Malet, *Notices of an English Branch of the Malet Family*, London 1885; privately printed, with some errors, but a good family history for its date. *The Conquest of England from Wace's Roman de Rou*, trans. Sir Alexander Malet Bart., London 1860 contains unreliable pedigrees of the family.

Acknowledgements

This paper has passed through the hands of many scholars, all of whom have offered helpful advice. I am indebted in particular to Mrs Vivien Brown, Professor Harper-Bill, Sir James Holt and to Dr Melissa Malet. Much helpful feedback came from members of the Conference. The paper was completed largely in its present form before I became aware of the considerable research on the Malet family which has been undertaken by Dr Katharine Keats-Rohan, who has kindly sent me a copy of her own forthcoming paper, a formidable and impressive contribution to English prosopography. She has established many facts that I had missed, and proved me wrong on others. Clearly our different approaches have resulted often in different conclusions. Neither of us can be right on every point at issue. With this in mind, I have reduced to what I regard as the absolute minimum the amendments to my paper arising from her researches. For the rest, it is best for readers to compare the two papers and form their own opinions.

THE MEMORY OF 1066 IN WRITTEN AND ORAL TRADITIONS

Elisabeth van Houts

The anonymous author of the *Battle Abbey Chronicle*, writing in the 1170s,[1] records that on his deathbed the Conqueror bequeathed the amulets he used to wear to Battle Abbey.[2] He does not explicitly say that these were the amulets which William had had with him at Hastings and which, according to William of Poitiers,[3] the duke had worn around his neck, but I assume that this was the case. Since he founded Battle in atonement for the bloodshed and out of gratitude for God's victory it seems reasonable to assume that that is where the relics he had worn on that very day ended up.[4] No precise description of the objects has survived, but we know that they were of metal, that they were precious, and that they joined others hanging round a larger relic shrine. Within a decade of the bequest, however, the monks of Battle parted with this souvenir and the chain of events which then unfolded illuminates the way in which medieval traditions, oral and written, emerged.

As part of a fund raising expedition aimed at rich post-Conquest England the monks of Saint-Germer at Fly, a small Benedictine house just a few miles across the border of the French Vexin, pursued King William Rufus through England and Wales in their quest for money to buy a new chasuble for their church. After several attempts to shake them off, Rufus became fed up and directed them to Battle Abbey with an order for Abbot Henry (1096–1102) to pay them. Henry protested poverty to the king but in vain, whereupon he felt obliged to convert the Conqueror's amulets into cash. With the money thus acquired the monks of Fly

---

[1] *The Chronicle of Battle Abbey*, ed. E. Searle, Oxford 1981, consists of two separate chronicles whose interdependence has been explained in different ways. Searle argues that both were written after 1155, that the first one (London BL MS Cotton Domitian A ii, fos 8–21v, ed. Searle, 32–66) was the earlier text, while the second and longer chronicle (fos 22r–130, ed. Searle, 66–334) was written in the late 1170s. Other scholars (A. Gransden, *Historical Writing in England c.550 to c.1307*, London 1974, 272, 277–9, and M. Brett in his review of E. Searle's edition in *Medium Aevum* l, 1981, 319–22), however, prefer a reversed order of origin. To establish their date two other points have to be taken into account. Martin Brett (p. 322) and I (cf. van Houts, *ANS* x, 1987, 165) have pointed out the existence of a now lost text entitled 'De constructione ecclesiae Belli', which may well lie behind either or both chronicles. Secondly, the paleography of the manuscript suggests that perhaps the text of the first chronicle may have been copied earlier in the twelfth century (C. Kaufmann in *English Romanesque Art 1066–1200*, London,1984, p. 91, no. 13, and illustration of the initial on p. 17) than Searle (pp. 26–7) suggests when she argues in favour of a date in the late twelfth century and a thirteenth-century hand; see also below notes 57–9.

[2] *Battle Chronicle*, 90, 102–6, 128.

[3] *Gesta Guillelmi*, 180–2: 'Appendit etiam humili collo suo reliquias, quarum favorem Heraldus abalienaverat sibi, violata fide quam super eas jurando sanxerat.'

[4] *Battle*, 90, states that most of the relics hanging on the Battle shrine had come from King William's predecessors, the Anglo-Saxon kings.

purchased purple cloth out of which the chasuble was made. About one year later lightning destroyed it, but not the one lying on top nor the one underneath it. The miraculous loss of the garment was seen, both at Fly and at Battle, as an act of punishment by God. A written account of the misfortune was published apparently at Fly, and about two decades later during the abbacy of Abbot Warner (1125–38) but before 1133,[5] Abbot Odo of Fly and his monk Richard, who was the man who had originally approached William Rufus, came to Battle to offer a public apology.[6] It was witnessed by the Battle Abbey chronicler, as a young monk, who wrote in his account that he relied upon what he heard on that occasion rather than on the earlier Fly text.[7] Sceptics may argue that the amulets had disappeared for other reasons and the chronicler's story was invented to explain the loss, but it was confirmed at the time by the French historian Guibert of Nogent, a former monk of Fly, in his autobiography.[8]

We do not know who orchestrated the public apology and it is possible that it was motivated on the French side by political considerations. It took place after the defeat of King Louis VI of France at the battle of Brémule in 1119 and it may represent an attempt to achieve reconciliation, by bringing monks from a French house to a prestigious royal monastery in England. It is, however, on the attitude of the Battle community that I wish to focus here. I link the apology with the death in 1124, at the age of eighty-four, of perhaps the last survivor within the community of the generation of monks who had experienced the Conquest themselves, Abbot Ralph of Caen.[9] I link it with the efforts to collect and record 1066 memorabilia which followed Abbot Ralph's death – efforts which resulted in the copying of the *Ship list* of William the Conqueror, the earliest surviving copy of the *Brevis Relatio* and the first version of a foundation history of Battle Abbey.[10] The monks of that time, it seems to me, were acutely aware that fifty or sixty years after the Conquest they were losing touch with the past. In that climate the loss of a relic dating from the Conquest seemed a much more serious matter than it had seemed to Abbot Henry in the late 1090s. There is a pattern here, or so I maintain, which can be traced elsewhere. First comes the epic event, a moment of triumph or disaster according to one's point of view. About two generations later comes the realisation that aspects of the event which were once common knowledge are common knowledge no longer; hence the urge to collect information and pass it on, usually by oral communication to younger people, but sometimes in writing. About two

---

5   In that year Abbot Odo of Saint-Germer at Fly became abbot of Beauvais (Brett, 321).

6   There may have been a political reason for the public apology, which followed not very long after the defeat of King Louis VI of France at the hands of Henry I at Brémule in 1119. Saint-Germer at Fly lies only a few kilometres into the French Vexin and its monks may have wished to renew ties with a potentially rich English abbey, and through it, perhaps, with King Henry I.

7   *Battle Chronicle*, 106.

8   *Guibert de Nogent, Autobiographie*, ed. E.-R. Labande, Paris 1981, 188–91 who says that the sum of money involved was 15 marks but that the value of the garment had been only half of that. Brett, 321, suggests that the earlier Fly text may have been Guibert of Nogent's autobiography. I think it more likely that Guibert himself used that text.

9   *Battle Chronicle*, 130–2, and R.W. Southern, *Saint Anselm: a Portrait in a Landscape*, Cambridge 1990, 372–6.

10   E.M.C. van Houts, 'The Ship List of William the Conqueror', *ANS* x, 1987, 159–83. With regard to the *Brevis Relatio* it is significant to point out that its author elaborates William of Poitiers' story of William the Conqueror denying his belief in magic: see below, nn. 57–8.

generations later still come the first attempts at detached historical analysis, such as the account which the Battle chronicler set down in the 1170s.

Likewise at Waltham Abbey, about a century elapsed before crucial information about the true burial place of its one time patron, King Harold, was written down, though that information had been collected orally about fifty years previously. In this case the writer was an elderly canon, who composed his history of the abbey in about 1177 in order to ensure that the memories of his community would not be forgotten if Henry II carried out his threat to close it down. Almost incidentally, he included a number of stories going back to the Norman Conquest, some of which had been told to him in the 1120s by the sacristan Turketil, then about eighty years old. Turketil had witnessed King Harold's visit to Waltham on his way back from his victory at Stamford Bridge after he had been told of the Norman invasion,[11] and he was probably the source of the story, undoubtedly true, that King Harold's remains had been buried in a proper tomb in Waltham by two canons who had brought them back from the battlefield.[12] The anonymous author who recorded these stories c.1177 was probably unaware of the Norman accounts which claimed that Harold had been buried on a hilltop in Sussex, but he evidently knew of other rumours in circulation to the effect: 'that Harold dwelt in a cave at Canterbury and that later, when he died, was buried at Chester'.[13] It was to kill off such unfounded speculation that the Waltham canon put the record straight in writing.

At Westminster, meanwhile, in the late 1130s, Osbert of Clare took up the cause of King Edward's sanctity as yet another means of preserving in a positive and very personal way the memory of 1066. On evidence which was distinctly meagre, as Frank Barlow has pointed out, he waged a tireless campaign for almost thirty years. Like the chroniclers of Battle and Waltham, Osbert claims to be using oral information from people who witnessed, shortly after Edward's death in 1066, miraculous events attributed to his holiness. Edward's canonisation was granted in 1161 and was followed two years later by his solemn translation to a new tomb in Westminster Abbey. King Edward's death, an event which had led to the Norman challenge to the English throne and hence, indirectly, to the bloodbath of 1066, was thereby transformed: having been a fateful tragedy for the English in 1066 it became for Osbert and the Westminster community in the 1160s a triumph of saintly commemoration.[14]

In Normandy, the main fourth generation contribution to the analysis of 1066 took place in the form of Wace's *Roman de Rou*.[15] Wace was a canon of Bayeux Cathedral, and had been educated at Caen. In the 1150s and 1160s he began to translate and adapt the already considerable body of Latin historiography into Anglo-Norman verse. He collected oral stories for the pre- and post-Conquest

---

[11] *The Waltham Chronicle*, ed. L. Watkiss and M. Chibnall, Oxford 1994.
[12] *Waltham Chronicle*, 45–6 and 56–7. The two versions regarding Harold's burial need not be mutually exclusive. It is quite possible that after the battle Harold was buried temporarily by William Malet (*Gesta Guillelmi*, 204, and *Carmen*, lines 583–96, pp. 36–9) before his remains were collected by the Waltham canons for a proper burial. William of Malmesbury records gossip suggesting that both stories already circulated in his time (*De gestis regum*, 306–7).
[13] *Waltham Chronicle*, 56–7.
[14] *Vita Eadwardi*, 150–63.
[15] Wace and E.M.C. van Houts, 'Wace as Historian', *Family Trees and the Roots of Politics: the Prosopography of Britain and France from the Tenth to the Twelfth Century*, ed. K.S.B. Keats-Rohan, Woodbridge 1997, 103–32.

history of Normandy and built these around the centrepiece of his work, the longest narrative account of the Conquest. I have argued elsewhere that although several stories are clearly anachronistic and of little historical value, his list of the Conqueror's companions is based on what we now would call an oral history project. Most of the people he lists had connections with Bayeux Cathedral or the abbeys at Caen. I believe Wace to have combed through the archives of those institutions and supplemented this material with stories collected orally from his contemporaries, both men and women, about their grandfathers and great grandfathers. The most striking of them is the story of William Patric, who shortly before the Conquest witnessed Duke William in the company of Earl Harold riding through his village of La Lande Patry on his way to Brittany.[16] The duke's expedition is well recorded in contemporary chronicles but without the charming eyewitness account passed on by William Patric's grandson and name-sake to Wace.[17]

Abbot Ralph and Sacristan Turketil, on whom the chroniclers of Battle and Waltham relied, were exceptionally old in the 1120s, and had been grown men at the time of the Conquest. There must, however, have been others still alive at the same period who had been teenagers in 1066. Among those who undoubtedly had stories to tell would have been, on the Norman side, Robert of Beaumont and William of Evreux, who died in their late sixties in 1118, and, on the English side, Edgar the aetheling, who died in about 1125.[18] But from, say, 1130 onwards it was up to the children of the 1066 generation to pass on the stories. Robert of Beaumont's twin sons Waleran and Robert, for example, who died respectively in 1165/66 and 1168, may well have informed Wace about their father's deeds.[19] William the Conqueror himself died in 1087, but several of his children survived until the mid-1130s and may as pensioners have told their stories about their father to third-generation historians.[20] Such details concerning age and longevity should be borne continuously in mind when we discuss the transfer of stories from one generation to the next. We need to tread carefully, however, because although the reconstruction of a chain of informants may help to assess how memories are formed, it cannot guarantee that particular memories are accurate.

So far I have concentrated on stories of 1066 which were passed on two generations later by oral means and not written down until the fourth generation. Some stories, however, were written down in the second generation. The first accounts of the Conquest to be written down in England, all of them brief and all of them written by monks, took the form of additions to the *Anglo-Saxon Chronicle*: the contributions made by Eadmer of Canterbury, John of Worcester, Simeon of Durham and William of Malmesbury are the most significant. In recent years Richard Southern, James Campbell and Antonia Gransden have argued that one effect of the Conquest was to turn English monks back to their Anglo-Saxon past in an attempt to salvage what they could of it.[21] They sought to link that past with the

16 Wace ii, 205–6 (lines 8585–8602); van Houts, 'Wace as Historian', 103–32.
17 The expedition is mentioned by William of Poitiers (*Gesta Guillelmi*, 106–115) and *The Bayeux Tapestry*, ed. D. Wilson, London 1985, plates 18–24.
18 *Gesta Guillelmi*, 192, 260; D. Crouch, *The Beaumont Twins: the Roots and Branches of Power in the Twelfth Century*, Cambridge 1986, 3; *Jumièges* ii, 98; Orderic vi, 146–8, 180; N. Hooper, 'Edgar the Ætheling: Anglo-Saxon Prince, Rebel and Crusader', *Anglo-Saxon England* xiv, 1985, 197–214.
19 Crouch, *The Beaumont Twins*, 78–9, 95–6.
20 F. Barlow, *William Rufus*, London 1983, 441–5.
21 R.W. Southern, 'Aspects of the European Tradition of Historical Writing', 4. The Sense of the

present by interpreting the defeat of the English by the Normans as God's punishment for English sins. In effect, they presented a theological rationalisation of the
collective national shame, a common enough literary reaction to defeat in battle;
historians on the losers' side reacted in much the same way after the battle of
Fontenoy in 841.[22] The English monks who first attempted to chronicle the events
of 1066 pay some attention to King Harold and his brothers, who were all three
killed at Hastings, and also to members from the English resistance such as Eadric
the Wild, Hereward and Earl Waltheof, but on the whole they are surprisingly silent
about individual disasters. In an age of liturgical commemoration, when monasteries were normally scrupulous in recording deaths in memorial books, obituaries or
other documents, why did no English monk write down the names of the victims of
1066?[23] All we have is a handful of names preserved by accident in *Domesday
Book*, in charters, or in later cartulary chronicles.[24] Perhaps, this is due to the fact
that monks were writing history. Janet Coleman, in her study on ancient and
medieval memories, has argued that the rule of St Benedict aimed at brainwashing
monks into forgetting their families and personal histories and that they were thus
conditioned to disregard individuals.[25] However, complete disassociation from
one's own family is impossible for most of us. In my view, English monks in the
two generations which followed the Conquest experienced a very deep sense of
loss and shame, which had a national dimension, an institutional dimension and a
personal dimension as well; it comes through in their brief accounts, which unsur-
prisingly are all pervaded by gloom. However, by introducing the theme of national sin and divine punishment, and by depersonalising their subject matter, they
contrived to anaesthetise to some extent the trauma from which they were suffering.

A few fragmentary remarks about 1066 are to be found in sources which predate
the monastic versions of the *Anglo-Saxon Chronicle* which I have been discussing,

Past', *TRHS*, 5th ser. xxiii, 1973, 243–63; J. Campbell, 'Some Twelfth-Century Views of the
Anglo-Saxon Past', *Essays in Anglo-Saxon History*, London 1986, 209–28; A. Gransden, *Historical
Writing in England c.550 to c.1307*, London 1974, 105–6, 136, 167–8.

[22] J. Nelson, *Charles the Bold*, London 1992, 117–20; I am grateful to Stuart Airlie for pointing out
this parallel.

[23] For a recent study on commemoration, see P.J. Geary, *Phantoms of Remembrance: Memory and
Oblivion at the End of the First Millennium*, Princeton 1994. More than a decade ago Cecily Clark
(*ANS* vii, 1984, 50–65 at 55) already pointed out that in England only Thorney Abbey, Durham
Cathedral and Hyde Abbey at Winchester possessed memorial books, a relatively small number
compared with other European countries.

[24] During the discussion after my paper Robin Fleming suggested, plausibly, that after 1066 some
monasteries, instead of commemorating fallen Anglo-Saxon friends, 'forgot' about them for purely
political reasons: if the abbots acknowledged the existence of the fighters at Hastings as their
tenants, they risked losing their lands on the charge of treason. In fact, as George Garnett in his
'Coronation and Propaganda: Some Implications of the Norman Claim to the Throne of England in
1066', *TRHS*, 5th ser. xxxvi, 1986, 90–116 at 104–5, has pointed out, the Normans were ambivalent
in their accusations of treason and used them as pragmatic means to acquire land. On the one hand
William as the new king promised security of tenure for the English, while at the same time he
confiscated monastic lands of, e.g., Abingdon and Bury St Edmunds on the grounds that their
tenants had fought at Hastings. The surviving documentation does not distinguish between those
who fought, stayed alive and subjected themselves to the Normans, those who fought but remained
rebellious, and those who were killed, as different categories of 1066 veterans.

[25] J. Coleman, *Ancient and Medieval Memories: Studies in the Reconstruction of the Past*, Cambridge 1992, 155–91.

and those which reflect the English point of view are bleaker still. The earliest such source is the *Life of King Edward*, written at the request of his wife Queen Edith in the years 1065–7. The queen lost three of her brothers in the battle of Hastings and her mother Gytha and other relatives were obliged to flee to Flanders to escape the wrath of the Normans,[26] yet the battle is only hinted at in the *Life*. The catastrophe was too appalling and too recent, I suggest, for an author to face it. The various entries in the *Anglo-Saxon Chronicle*, all condemning the invasion, are equally brief. Version 'D' may have been written as contemporary comment on events immediately after the Conquest, but due to interpolations it is difficult to distinguish what was written when in the only copy available, written after 1100. Version 'E' copied at Peterborough is based on Canterbury material up to 1120 and, here too, it is impossible to tell what the annalist wrote in 1066. In both versions, therefore, revisions date from a time when England was firmly under Norman control.[27] Amongst this meagre harvest, the E-version of the *Anglo-Saxon Chronicle* is unique in expressing the anguish and frustration of the English; it seems to have been focussed on the aetheling, who pops up here, there and everywhere without being able to rally effective groups of resistance fighters around him.[28] The most evocative expression of grief comes in a poem written by the skald Thorkill Skallason for his master Earl Waltheof, after he had been executed for treason in 1076. It is written in Old Norse but may have been based on an Old English version used much later by William of Malmesbury.[29] The most intriguing aspect of this poem is its theme of Waltheof's betrayal by William the Conqueror, which neatly reverses the official Norman charge of treason against the earl: 'William crossed the cold channel/ and reddened the bright swords, / and now he has betrayed/ noble Earl Waltheof. It is true that killing in England/ will be a long time ending.' Thorkill may here be revenging Waltheof's death by hinting at the fact that it was Waltheof's wife Judith, William's niece, who betrayed her husband.[30]

The shortage of information about the Conquest in English sources which date from the decades immediately following it, a shortage which I have attributed to the traumatic effects of shock, can to some extent be made good by looking, as I have done elsewhere, at Continental sources. Most of them express horror and moral indignation at the bloodbath and loss of life. English authors would surely have expressed the same sentiments had they been less stunned.[31]

There is, however, one exception to the rule of the *tabula rasa* of post-Conquest personal commemoration in England, and that is the *Gesta Herewardi*, a story

---

[26] *Vita Eadwardi*, 88; see also 110 for a section that was probably written in 1067 (p. xxxii). Countess Gytha fled the country after the fall of Exeter in 1067 (*ASC* 'D').

[27] On the different versions of the *ASC*, see *English Historical Documents* ii: 1042–1189, 107–9 (introduction) and 110–203 (text of all versions).

[28] See entries under the years 1066–69, 1074, 1085 (1080), 1086 (1087), 1091, 1093, 1097. I am grateful to David Bates for discussing Edgar's role with me.

[29] Two sections of this poem have survived in Old Norse as part of the saga of Harold Hardrada (*King Harald's Saga: Harald Hardradi of Norway from Snorri Sturluson's Heimskringla*, trans. M. Magnusson and H. Pálsson, Harmondsworth 1966, 157–8); cf. *De gestis regum* ii, 311: 'Siquidem Weldeofus in Eboracensi pugna plures Normannorum solus obtruncaverat, unos et unos per portam egredientes decapitans.' The suggestion of an underlying verse was first launched by F.S. Scott, 'Earl Waltheof of Northumbria', *Archaeologia Aeliana*, 1952, 159–213 at 179.

[30] Orderic Vitalis, who used information from the monks of Crowland, is the sole source for Judith's role: '. . . et per delationem Iudith uxoris suae accusatus est' (Orderic ii, 320).

[31] E.M.C. van Houts, 'The Norman Conquest through European Eyes', *EHR* cx, 1995, 832–53.

which has been unfairly neglected by modern historians.[32] The Latin text, as we have it now as part of the Peterborough cartulary, was written between 1109 and 1131 by a clerk at Ely, probably called Richard. He used a now lost Old English biography by Hereward's chaplain Leofric which he claims to have combined with the reminiscenses of several of Hereward's companions, two of whom he names as Siward of Bury St Edmunds and Leofric the Black.[33] Bearing in mind that 1066 veterans survived well into the twelfth century, as I stressed, I have absolutely no doubt that Richard of Ely consulted these elderly eyewitnesses. Hereward's adventures cover two distinct phases. During the first, which lasted from c.1062 to 1067, he fought as an exiled mercenary for a variety of masters in Cornwall, Ireland and Flanders. The stories of his adventures in this period, and particularly the Flemish ones, generally interpreted as fiction, may have more historical content than has been supposed.[34] During the second phase, Hereward led the uprising in the Fenland and the siege of Ely in 1071, and his *Gesta* contains the fullest account we have of these events: the kernel of it is substantially corroborated by details from the *Anglo-Saxon Chronicle*, John of Worcester and documentary texts.[35] Hereward's biography is based on a series of eyewitness reports which Richard of Ely linked together as best as he could. The linking is clumsy, but I take that to be a sign of authenticity, for no forger would have produced something so full of 'contradictions'. I see the *Gesta Herewardi* very much as an attempt to cope with the trauma of defeat, not by theological rationalisation and depersonalisation, but by romanticising heroic behaviour and honourable surrender, through the medium of epic narrative. Its personal nature may be partly due to the original version having been written in the vernacular, the language in which most of the oral stories must have been told, and by a secular priest. Richard, the author of the Latin text, must have been bi-lingual if he was able to translate the original Old English into Latin and supplement it with vernacular reports.[36] He may himself have been a member of the secular clergy attached to Ely rather than a monk and have felt freer on that account to tell the story of an Anglo-Saxon defeat in personal terms.

If he were a secular clerk, Richard may be compared profitably with two other secular clerks who were responsible for later off-shoots of the *Anglo-Saxon Chronicle*. Archdeacon Henry of Huntingdon extended the chronicle into the 1150s, rewriting and revising his text continuously.[37] His struggle to reconcile the

---

[32] Ed. T.D. Hardy and C.T. Martin in *Gaimar, Lestorie des Engles*, London 1888, ii, 339–404; it was translated by M. Swanton, *Three Lives of the Last Englishmen*, New York 1984, 45–88.

[33] Ed. Hardy, 339–41.

[34] See my forthcoming article on 'Hereward in Flanders c.1062–1067', *Anglo-Saxon England*.

[35] For recent evaluations of Hereward's role in the Fenland, see the uncritical study by J. Hayward, 'Hereward the Outlaw', *Journal of Medieval History* xiv, 1988, 293–304, and the much more stimulating discussions in C. Hart, 'Hereward the Wake and his Companions', *The Danelaw*, London 1992, 625–48, D. Roffe, 'Hereward the Wake and the Barony of Bourne: a Reassessment of a Fenland Legend', *Lincolnshire History and Archaeology* xxix, 1994, 7–10, and A. Williams, *The English and the Norman Conquest*, Woodbridge 1995, 49–50.

[36] Particularly instructive is the insertion in two places of almost identical lists of Hereward's companions. The author presumably had two lists which he gave integrally rather than amalgamating them. Some of the individuals have been identified by Hart and Williams. It seems to me that all are historical persons of whom only the most important as landholders can now be traced and identified.

[37] *The Archdeacon Henry of Huntingdon's* Historia Ecclesiastica, ed. D.E. Greenway, Oxford 1996; N. Partner, *Serious Entertainments: the Writing of History in Twelfth-Century England*, Chicago

demands of a military society full of wordly vanity with God's plan pervades his brief account of the Norman Conquest. Yet, I am convinced that his secular background enabled him to be much more forthcoming about the actual organisation of the Conquest. His views on the vital role of William fitz Osbern as the brain behind the logistics of the invasion and battle predate the same opinion of Canon Wace of Bayeux. The archdeacon is, however, the first historian to focus his thoughts on the military aspects and achievements of the Conquest. He too thought that moral lessons needed to be learnt, but not in the form of one nation repenting its sinful past, but, as John Gillingham recently argued, by soldiers and other groups of the population each contemplating their own past. Henry of Huntingdon's contemporary was Gaimar, who in 1137–8 translated the *Anglo-Saxon Chronicle*, not like the others into Latin, but into Old French.[38] Though he does not contribute much new material to the topic of the Norman Conquest, he includes the longest account of Hereward outside the *Gesta Herewardi*, albeit in a slightly different version.[39] Both Ian Short and Ann Williams have pointed to the irony of the fact that a French clerk appropriated the language of the conquerors in order to present them with a history grafted upon the *Anglo-Saxon Chronicle*. This, they feel, is a sign that by the third generation some grandchildren of the Conquest were prepared to learn the history of their new country from an English perspective. Henry's and Gaimar's place in society as secular clerks meant a much more intimate contact with the people in England and the effects of the Conquest on the common population than, I believe, the monk historians had. It also meant closer contact with women and their view of the past. Gaimar wrote in response to a request from a lay woman, Constance, wife of Ralph fitz Gilbert, who may have had access to members of Hereward's family. Henry of Huntingdon was almost certainly married, and one just wonders to what extent his wife's views influenced his account of the Conquest. The down to earth tone, attention to the practical side of life and the willingness to move away from the abstract theological moralisations are surely due to a non-monastic environment.

Thus far I have concentrated my analysis on England and the historians writing in that country and I have shown how initial shocked silence was followed by two parallel perceptions of the past: oral stories which were more personal and emotional, but circulating at the same time as abstract writings theorising about national guilt. But what was the historiographical development like in Normandy? How did historians writing in the duchy perceive the past during the first four generations? The literature generated by contemporaries, that is the first generation of the Norman Conquest, is not surprisingly dominated by the Norman view. William of Jumièges added a brief account of the Norman Conquest to his history of the dukes of Normandy but firmly declined the possibility of writing about England after 1070; instead he promised a future sequel about William the

and London 1977, 11–48; D. Greenway, 'Henry of Huntingdon and the Manuscripts of his *Historia Anglorum*', *ANS* ix, 1987, 103–26 and 'Authority, Convention and Observation in Henry of Huntingdon's *Historia Anglorum*', *ANS* xviii, 1995, 105–22; Williams, *The English and the Norman Conquest*, 177–80.

[38] *Gaimar, Lestoire des Engleis*, ed. A. Bell, Oxford 1960; A.D. Legge, *Anglo-Norman Literature and its Background*, Oxford 1963, 27–36, 276–8; Williams, *The English and the Norman Conquest*, 181–2.

[39] I. Short, 'Patrons and Polyglots: French Literature in Twelfth-Century England', *ANS* xiv, 1991, 229–50 at 243–4.

Conqueror's son Robert Curthose.[40] William of Poitiers wrote a biography of the victorious duke which contains the Norman story of the Conquest, concentrating on the invasion, battle and subsequent campaigns in England.[41] He highlights the careers of the Conqueror's eleven main advisers, but is silent on the 3000 to 5000 participants in the Conquest. His account of the raids in Northern England shows a particular degree of detail not easily matched elsewhere. Although his story has survived incomplete we can reconstruct its last chapters through the *Ecclesiastical History* of Orderic Vitalis, who copied the end but supplemented it with his own comments.[42] Some aspects of this mixture, normally attributed to Orderic, may in fact have come from William of Poitiers. One of the central characters of the immediate post-Conquest period was Earl Morcar. He had been captured in 1071 during the siege of Ely and brought to Normandy where he was entrusted to the care of Roger of Beaumont.[43] The following fifteen years were spent in Normandy, where in 1086 he witnessed one of Roger's charters for Saint-Wandrille.[44] In 1087 he was set free as part of a general amnesty issued by William Rufus.[45] William of Poitiers himself knew the Beaumont family intimately and his sister was the abbess of the Beaumont foundation of Saint-Léger at Préaux,[46] so it is not at all improbable that he had access to Earl Morcar's memories, in particular for information about his family and the military campaigns in which Morcar and his brother had been involved. An exchange of some sort between the English Morcar and the Norman William may have generated a certain understanding of the English victims and led to William's surprisingly well informed account with its mild and empathetic flavour.[47] Thus we cannot exclude an oral exchange between Normans and Englishmen for the specific purpose of historical writing in the immediate post-Conquest period.[48] Even Bishop Guy of Amiens in his celebratory poem on the Conquest, which is our most detailed but not necessarily most trustworthy account of the battle, may have consulted some English informants for his intriguing story about the English negotiators before their surrender.[49] Like William of Poitiers, his occasional empathy for the English position could emerge alongside vituperations against the English leader Harold. The passionately negative terms in

---

[40] *Jumièges* ii, 164–73, 182–5.

[41] *Gesta Guillelmi*.

[42] Orderic ii, pp. xviii–xxi and 208–58.

[43] Orderic ii, 258.

[44] F. Lot, *Études critiques sur l'abbaye de Saint-Wandrille*, Paris 1913, no. 41 and p. 207.

[45] ASC 'E' *s.a.* 1087; Barlow, *William Rufus*, 65.

[46] *Gesta Guillelmi*, vii.

[47] *Gesta Guillelmi*, 256–8. Details on the background of Edwin and Morcar could come either from William or Orderic. In Orderic ii, 258, the author, in the first person, refers back to his earlier remarks on the brothers' parents (p. 216). Since this is the last but one sentence of the section which Orderic specifically attributes to William of Poitiers, I take it that William is the author. If this is the case the discrepancy between his account of Edwin's death (namely six months after Morcar was taken to Normandy) and that as told by the *ASC* and 'Florence' of Worcester (that Edwin's death occurred either before Ely or at an early stage of the Ely siege) must be due to another informant than Morcar.

[48] In this context we have to be reminded that in 1067 several aristocratic Englishmen were in Normandy as the Conqueror's hostages, and they presumably exchanged views with their Norman 'hosts' (*Gesta Guillelmi*, 244: Archbishop Stigand, Edgar the ætheling, Earls Edwin, Morcar and Waltheof. Orderic (ii, 198) and 'Florence' of Worcester (*s.a.* 1067) add Aethelnoth of Canterbury).

[49] *Carmen*, lines 653–752, pp. 42–9.

which he denounces him have recently been characterised by Giovanni Orlandi as typical of an immediate victorious response in writing to a battle.[50] The other contemporary source for the Norman Conquest is the Bayeux Tapestry, which alone gives a glimpse of a more positive portrait of Harold, before he acceded to the throne, carrying one of his men on his shoulders during the Breton campaign. But this may simply be an artistic trick to emphasise his later arrogance and fall in terms of sharp contrast. The overwhelming reaction of the first generation Normans was one of legitimisation and justification, which were in fact abstract moralisations to bury any sense of guilt or shame.

This tendency to moralisation did not stop with the death of the survivors of 1066. If anything the theorising and moralising became much stronger. The most important representative of the next generation was Orderic Vitalis, a monk of mixed Anglo-Norman background who worked in Normandy. He interpolated William of Jumièges' *Gesta Normannorum Ducum* with details of King Harold's brothers Tostig and Gyrth, the battle and in general a revision of William's text aimed at toning down some of the more explicit pro-Norman sentiments.[51] Orderic not only fitted the account of 1066 more firmly into a Norman context but he also expressed empathy with the English losses. At the same time he began his *Historia Ecclesiastica*, in which he transformed a local history of his monastery into a large scale chronicle of western Europe. For his account of the Norman Conquest he used William of Poitiers' biography and some passages from his own interpolated version of the *Gesta Normannorum Ducum*.[52] He also wove the famous condemnation of William the Conqueror's harrowing expeditions in the North into this account.[53] Even at an early stage of Orderic's career, in 1114–15, he bears witness to the fact that some people on the Continent had refused to accept land or spoils from England on the grounds that they had been gained at the expense of too much bloodshed. He puts into the mouth of Guitmund of La Croix-Saint-Leufroi words to this effect.[54] It has long been thought that Orderic put forward these sobering thoughts because of his English origin. But some pure blooded Normans certainly shared his ideas. Canon John of Coutances, the author of the biography of Bishop Geoffrey of Coutances written at about the same time, defended his father Peter, who had been Geoffrey's chamberlain, against implicit accusations of greed for English spoils. Having set out Peter's acquisitions for the new cathedral of Coutances he assures his readers: 'that the venerable bishop had not, as some people think, acquired all this from the copious abundance of England's bounty,

---

50 G. Orlandi, 'Some Afterthoughts on the *Carmen de Hastingae Proelio*', *Media Latinitas: a Collection of Essays to Mark the Occasion of the Retirement of L.J. Engels*, ed. R. Nip, H. van Dijk and E.M.C. van Houts, Turnhout 1996, 117–28.

51 *Jumièges* ii, 158–72, and i, pp. lxxiii–lxxv, where the suggestion is made that some of the interpolations are based on William of Poitiers' biography.

52 Orderic ii, p. xvii.

53 Orderic ii, 232.

54 Orderic ii, 272–8, esp. 272: 'After carefully examining the matter I cannot see what right I have to govern a body of men whose strange customs and barbarous speech are unknown to me, whose beloved ancestors and friends you have either put to the sword, driven into bitter exile, or unjustly imprisoned or enslaved. Read the Scriptures, and see if there is any law to justify the forcible imposition on a people of God of a shepherd chosen from among their enemies.' It is interesting to note that neither Guitmund, nor for that matter Orderic, minded Guitmund's acceptance in c.1088 of the bishopric of Aversa in Norman occupied Italy!

. . . but that most of the above mentioned lands had been acquired before the English war.'[55] As a good historian he then proceeds to give evidence by pointing out that the cathedral was dedicated in 1056 and that the English war did not take place until nine years later. However, John's indignation that some thought the bishop enriched himself at the expense of the English sounds a little hollow if we read the next paragraph where he lists the 'precious ornaments, embroideries and goldwork with smaragds and gems' which the bishop had brought over from England after the Conquest.[56] Like the young Orderic and John of Coutances, the anonymous Norman author of the *Brevis Relatio*, written probably at Battle between c.1114 and 1120, makes moral comments with regard to that English war. He contrasts the haughty Harold, who did not recognise that God is on the side of the humble, with William, a paragon of humility, by developing the bible quotation 'ante ruinam exultatur cor'.[57] The author also develops William of Poitiers' story of the Conqueror inadvertently putting on his hauberk back to front and laughing the matter off, saying it was not a bad omen. Here he has Duke William say: 'If I believed in magic I would not today engage in battle. But I have never put faith in magicians nor loved witches. In all I have ever undertaken I have always commended myself to my Creator.'[58] This emphasis on God's predisposition as opposed to the workings of magic may well be an attempt of the Battle monks – mourning at that very moment the loss of William's amulets – to temper the thought that the relics did swing the outcome of a battle in favour of the Normans.[59] These three Norman historians all wrote within a decade after the Battle of Tinchebrai, fought on Norman soil in 1106 almost forty years to the day after the battle of Hastings.[60] The theme of God and not military prowess or magic deciding the outcome of battles had a curiously topical value.

An entirely different approach to the story of the Conquest can be found in the so-called 'Hyde chronicle', written probably in Normandy towards the end of the reign of Henry I by someone, perhaps a chaplain, attached to the Warenne family.[61]

[55] *De statu hujus ecclesiae ab anno 836 ad 1093*, ed. *Gallia Christiana*, ix Instr, cols 217–24 at 220: 'Venerabilis quidem et memorandus episcopus non, ut aliqui putant, de copiosa abundantia Anglice superfluitatis omnia haec operabatur . . . terrasque praescriptas ex maxima parte ante bellum Anglicum acquisivit.' For the authorship, see L. Delisle, 'Notice sur un traité inédit du douzième siècle intitulé: miracula ecclesiae Constantiniensis', *Bibliothèque de l'Ecole des Chartes*, 2e ser. iv, Paris 1847–48, 339–52 at 368: 'ego Johannes, praedicti Petri camerarii filius'; M. Chibnall, 'La Carrière de Geoffroi de Montbray', *Les Evêques normands du XIe siècle*, ed. P. Bouet and F. Neveux, Caen 1995, 279–93 at 282.

[56] *De statu*, ed. *Galla Christiana*, col. 220: '. . . illic ornamenta pretiosa, et brodaturas, et aurifrisas cum smaragdis et gemmis parabat'.

[57] *Anonymi auctoris Brevis relatio de origine Willelmi Conquestoris*, ed. J. Giles, *Scriptores rerum Gestarum Willelmi Conquestoris*, Publications of the Caxton Society iii, London 1845, 1–21 at 6.

[58] *Anonymi auctoris Brevis relatio*, 'Si ego in sortem crederem, hodie amplius in bellum non introirem. Sed ego nunquam sortibus credidi, nec sortilegos amavi. In omni enim negotio quicquid agere debui, creatori meo me semper commendavi.'

[59] My new edition of the *Brevis Relatio* (forthcoming in the *Camden Miscellany* of the Royal Historical Society, xxxiv (1998) argues in favour of a Norman author writing at Battle Abbey.

[60] None of the Norman historians draws the parallel, but William of Malmesbury did, *De gestis regum* ii, 475: 'Idem dies ante quadraginta circiter annos fuerat, cum Willelmus Hastingas primus appulit; provido forsitan Dei judicio, ut eo die subderetur Angliae Normannia, quo ad eam subjugandam olim venerat Normannorum copia.'

[61] *Chronica monasterii de Hida juxta Wintoniam ab anno 1035 ad annum 1121, Liber monasterii de Hyde*, ed. E. Edwards, RS XLV, 1866, 284–321; C.P. Lewis, 'The Earldom of Surrey and the

Although there is no doubt about the author's Norman point of view, he is remarkably well informed about the family of King Harold, much more than was Orderic, with the result that the account of 1066 is set in a much more 'English' context than any of the other Norman chronicles. The author clearly knew a great number of sources, including English ones, considering his frequent references to oral and written testimonies which he, unfortunately, does not identify. His sources require further investigation but suggest a Flemish or northern French link with the community of Saint-Omer, which offered shelter to King Harold's mother Gytha, and which was the home of Gundreda of Warenne. The details on the two families of Harold and Warenne introduce a personal element in an account that is far less moralising than that of Orderic or the author of the *Brevis Relatio*. The chronicler's exceptional military information on the battles of Eu and Brémule suggests that he might have been William of Warenne's chaplain. His Latin style is poor and suggests that it came from the pen of someone who was better versed in vernacular French. As such his work prepares us for the writings of Wace, another secular clerk, to whom I briefly referred above.

Wace single-handedly transformed the writing on the Norman Conquest from a series of moralisations to a triumphant account of the achievements of the Norman soldiers. He used the Latin sources with great ingenuity but left out all moralising justifications and legitimisations. Like Henry of Huntingdon, he paid attention to the logistical organisation of the Conquest, and in the process he unwittingly introduced certain anachronisms, and like the author of the *Gesta Herewardi*, he commemorated the names of those who took part in the Conquest. Not only did he list William the Conqueror and his twelve leaders, whom William of Poitiers had compared with Caesar and his senate; he added more than 130 names of local Norman lords, whose achievements had not yet been recorded in writing. Their deeds had survived in oral tradition, which was the single most important source for Wace's reconstruction of the actual Conquest.[62] Wace was not interested in the Norman nation or the collective Norman memory; he was a local historian writing the history of the Cotentin soldiers based on interviews and historical archival research. In fact he put into practice what two English chroniclers described as the task of an historian. The Waltham chronicler and Walter Map stipulated that memories handed down from father to son and from son to grandson constitute valid alternatives in cases where primary eyewitness accounts had been lost.[63] Any information handed down along a recognisable chain of informants within a period of one hundred years, so Walter Map says, is admissable evidence for 'our own time'.[64] Thus, according to this rule, the historians of the fourth generation were the last to be able to record the memories of 1066 and employ them as substitute

---

Date of Domesday Book', *Historical Research* lxiii, 1990, 329–36; J. Gillingham, 'Henry of Huntingdon and the Twelfth-Century Revivial of the English Nation', *Concepts of National Identity in the Middle Ages*, ed. S. Forde, L. Johnson and A.V. Murray, Leeds 1995, 75–101, esp. Appx 'The Hyde Chronicle' on 90–91.

62 For Wace's critical attitude to oral sources, see Peter Damian-Grint, 'Truth, Trust and Evidence in the Anglo-Norman *Estoire*', *ANS* xviii, 1995, 63–78 at 71–2.

63 *Waltham Chronicle*, 18: 'Nam ut primi patres qui afuerunt filiis suis reliquerunt . . . ab illis didicimus.'

64 *Walter Map, De nugis curialium. Courtiers' Trifles*, ed. M.R. James, C.N.L. Brooke and R.A.B. Mynors, Oxford 1983, 122–4: 'Nostra dico tempora modernitatem hanc horum scilicet centum annorum curriculum, cuius adhuc nunc ultime partes extant, cuius tocius in his notabilia sunt satis

eyewitness accounts. At the same time, Henry II's lawyers, for the same reasons, stopped people pursuing land claims going back beyond the Conquest. Officially no one could go back beyond the reign of Henry I. In fact, as Paul Brand has shown, some people ignored this order and put in claims well into the thirteenth century.[65]

My study of the formation of oral and written memories of 1066 clearly shows the circulation of stories about the Conquest through several generations into the reign of Henry II. The stories were local, centered on specific aspects of the Conquest and were quite personal. This oral tradition for a time ran parallel to a written tradition which attempted to cope with the past by seeing the defeat of 1066 in terms of God's punishment for the sins of the English nation. By the reign of Henry II the theme of 'national guilt' had evaporated and made place for more discussion of military matters. Tales of military defeat and resistance survived. But what strikes the modern historian most is the almost total amnesia in the long term of individual loss and grief. The psychological reason of trauma is as likely an explanation for the complete lack of a memorial to the English dead of 1066[66] as other explanations, which blame the fear of abbots of association with the memory of rebels or the lack of patronage for literary activity in general. In Normandy the situation was different. The written memories concentrated first on the victorious leader, his legitimisation of the use of force and the justification of military action. The second and third generation continued and expanded the moral justification of their actions. Meanwhile oral tradition kept alive the memories of fighters lower down the social scale. These were rescued by Wace and incorporated in his vernacular *Roman de Rou*, which became a memorial for those who had fought at Hastings. What my study also shows is that it is not enough to study the history of the Norman Conquest purely in terms of questions about the continuity of Anglo-Saxon customs. The modern emphasis on the long-term survival of Old English modes of justice and administration after 1066 could easily create the impression that the Conquest was just a mere hiccup in the course of English history.[67] The very fact that the English were so traumatised that they could not bring themselves to write down their memories proves how deeply shocked they remained for a very long time.

est recens et manifesta memoria, cum adhuc aliqui supersint centennes, et infiniti filii qui ex patrum et suorum relacionibus certissime teneant que non viderunt.'

[65] P. Brand, 'Time Out of Mind: the Knowledge and the Use of the Eleventh- and Twelfth-Century Past in Thirteenth-Century Litigation', *ANS* xvi, 1994, 37–54.

[66] E.M.C. van Houts, 'The Trauma of 1066', *History Today* xlvi, no. 10 (October), 1996, 9–15.

[67] See N. Vincent's review of Ann Williams's book in the *Times Literary Supplement*, 10 November 1995, p. 31.

THE ABBEY OF ABINGDON, ITS *CHRONICLE*
AND THE NORMAN CONQUEST

John Hudson

According to its first editor, writing in the second half of the 1850s, the *Abingdon Chronicle*

> is not, it does not profess to be, a record of the facts which lie on the surface of history; of battles lost, of treaties broken, of invasions repulsed, of thrones overturned. These it leaves to the general historian. It affords materials, rarer and far more precious, to illustrate the advancement of society; the origin and growth of these various ranks and conditions of life which now constitute the English people. It shows how our forefathers acted, and were acted upon; how they were disciplined and educated by the pressure of the times in which they lived; how their interests, at first independent, gradually became harmonized and identified. . . . The tale which it tells is worth reading; it is the history of a nation's progress, socially and morally, from barbarism to civilization.[1]

The editor is equally confident in his assessment of the Norman Conquest. 'Tested by its results', it was the greatest revolution within the period covered by the *Chronicle*:

> It struck deep and spread wide. It radically and permanently affected the condition of the English people. It touched them at home and abroad; in the cottage, and the castle, and the monastery; in the state and in the church; as individuals, and in their social condition. It was well for England that it should undergo this great change, and many were the advantages which ultimately resulted from it. And it is by such results that we ought to judge. If the metal is to be refined, let it pass through the furnace.[2]

This editor was Joseph Stevenson. He is an example of the type of editor now sometimes patronisingly referred to as a Victorian clergyman, but in fact an immensely prolific and respected editor and translator of a great range of texts.[3] Knowles called him the 'last and one of the most learned of the self-taught editors, [who] lived on into the age of Stubbs and Tout, . . . it is to his initiative, in the last resort, that we owe the Rolls Series'.[4] Born at Berwick in 1806, he was schooled at

---

[1] *Chronicon Monasterii de Abingdon*, ed. J. Stevenson, 2 vols, RS ii, 1858 (henceforth *CMA*), ii, p. lxxxv.
[2] *CMA* ii, p. xxi.
[3] For Stevenson, see his entry in the *Dictionary of National Biography* and M.D. Knowles, 'Great Historical Enterprises. IV. The Rolls Series', *TRHS* 5th Ser. 11, 1961, 137–59.
[4] Knowles, 141. Knowles, 145–6, gives a further interesting insight into the early history of the

Durham under James Raine the elder. In the early 1830s, instead of joining the Presbyterian ministry as originally intended, he worked at the Tower on the public records and at the British Museum on an edition of Rymer's *Foedera*. His career in the archives continued through his appointment as vicar of Leighton Buzzard in 1849, and as already mentioned, he was fundamental in the establishment of the Rolls Series in the mid-1850s. He travelled to archives in France, and following resignation of his benefice, took up an appointment at the PRO. Conversion to Catholicism in 1863 forced another change of position, and he retired to Birmingham where he worked for the Historical Manuscripts Commission. In 1872, following the death of his wife, he was ordained priest. In the same year Gladstone gave him a small pension on the civil list, which he used for making transcriptions of English documents in the Vatican Library. In 1877 he became a Jesuit, and he continued in his scholarly works until his death in 1895.

In 1893, at the age of eighty-six, he received the honorary degree of Doctor of Laws from the University of St Andrews.[5] The list of honorands is headed by his patron, Gladstone, and by the Marquis of Salisbury. The Senate minutes cited Stevenson as one 'who has spent a long life in historical study of the most valuable kind, including matters relating to the history of Scotland'. The local paper, the *St Andrews Citizen*, also reported the ceremony. Listing the honorands' achievements, Professor Scott Lang noted that 'Mr Stevenson had published "The History of Mary Queen of Scots" by her secretary; a history printed by Mr Stevenson from the original manuscripts for the first time, with illustrative papers from the archives of the Vatican.' Yet the *Citizen*'s report records none of the 'applause' which followed some other citations of honorands, let alone the 'loud applause' which greeted the achievements, for example, of Demetrios Bikelas for having 'written the first book in Greek upon Scotland, in which, among other things, he described Scotland and extolled out national poet, Burns'.[6]

Calls for a new edition of the *Abingdon Chronicle* could already be heard before the First World War, as in Stenton's *The Early History of the Abbey of Abingdon*,

---

Rolls Series. With Stevenson, the earliest contributor was the Reverend F.C. Hingeston, who edited John Capgrave's *Chronicle* and his *Liber de illustribus Henricis*. Knowles writes that 'Hingeston, a young Fellow of Exeter College, had been recommended by Stevenson, and the correspondence shows him visiting Leighton Buzzard as the accepted suitor of Stevenson's eldest daughter, a circumstance that may have affected the elder man's judgment.' The two resulting volumes were poor, but still more disastrous was his attempt to edit royal and historical letters of Henry IV's reign. One volume appeared, but was badly received and meanwhile, records Knowles, Hingeston 'had been tactless enough in 1860 to throw over Stevenson's daughter, and the outraged father took it very ill'. The second volume of the letters was printed but never published, and there ended Hingeston's involvement with the Rolls Series.

5 University of St Andrews, *Minutes of the Senatus*, ns 4 (April 1892–1899), 96, for 14 October 1893; *St Andrews Citizen*, 25 November 1893, 5.

6 On Bikelas, see R.J. Macrides, 'The Scottish Connection in Byzantine and Modern Greek Studies', University of St Andrews, St John's House Papers 4, 1992, 8–11. Last year, 1995, was marked by no great centenary celebrations for Stevenson. Yet in recent years, his influence upon undergraduates has surreptitiously become immense; if your students look at the title pages of the useful Llanerch translated volumes of, for example, William of Malmesbury's *History of the Kings* or Gerald of Wales *On the Instruction of Princes* they will find that the translator was Joseph Stevenson.

and have been repeated thereafter.[7] The essential problem is that Stevenson based his text on the later of the two manuscripts of the *Chronicle*, to which he referred as its 'improved' form. This is BL MS Cotton Claud. Bvi, from the thirteenth century. He then added passages which appeared only in the earlier manuscript, BL MS Cotton Claud. Cix, thus providing a conflated text such as existed in neither manuscript.[8] Curiously, this opened him to the very criticism which he levelled at Kemble for his methods in editing Anglo-Saxon charters:

> Where more than a single copy of a charter existed, he thought that he was justified in framing for himself a text gleaned from these several sources, without enabling his reader to separate the variations of diction and spelling derived from each. Thus his text is an eclectic text, such possibly as is found in no single manuscript.[9]

Editing from a later text is generally undesirable in itself. However, the nature of the Abingdon manuscripts may explain Stevenson's choice. For the Anglo-Saxon period the later manuscript provides not just more material but better versions of the Anglo-Saxon charters, with boundary clauses and fuller witness lists. The compiler had presumably gone back to the original charters, and therefore Bvi really can be referred to as not just a later but also in some ways an 'improved' version.[10]

Nevertheless, the mixture of conflation and primary reliance on the later text does produce serious problems. Particularly for the Anglo-Saxon period, one struggles to reconstruct the earlier text from Stevenson's edition because the version he used was considerably rearranged and greatly expanded: 494 of the pages of volume one of his edition are taken up with the *Chronicle*, 249 pages of volume two [i.e. a ratio of 2 to 1]; the equivalent section of the earlier manuscript are 31 folios and 41.5 folios respectively [i.e. a ratio of 3 to 4], of the later 116.5 folios and 58.5 folios [again 2 to 1].[11] Even in the Norman and Angevin sections, his method of editing leads to some confusion in the narrative.[12] Sections absent from the earlier version have gained a spurious authority through their appearance in the printed edition.[13] In addition, there are places where he indicates that the narrative

---

[7] F.M. Stenton, *The Early History of the Abbey of Abingdon*, Reading 1913, 1 n. 1 commented that 'In 1858 little work had been done upon Old English diplomatic, and it would not be expected that the editor's criticism of the land-books in the series should have value at the present time. It is more serious that he cannot be trusted implicitly to give the exact reading of his texts . . . The whole plan of the edition, by which the latest MS was adopted for the text, is faulty.' See also J. Gillingham, 'The Introduction of Knight Service into England', *ANS* iv, 1982, 57; *The Anglo-Saxon Chronicle: A Collaborative Edition. Volume 10: The Abingdon Chronicle, A.D. 956–1066*, ed. P.W. Conner, Cambridge 1996, xxxiii. D.D. James, 'A Translation and Study of the *Chronicon Monasterii de Abingdon*', unpublished Ph.D. dissertation, Rice University 1986, rests on Stevenson's edition.

[8] *CMA* i, pp. xv–xvi

[9] *CMA* i, p. x.

[10] Note *CMA* i, pp. vii–viii; S.D. Keynes, *The Diplomas of King Æthelred 'the Unready'*, Cambridge 1980, 10–13. I am very grateful to Simon Keynes for lending me his unpublished work on Abingdon, which has been extremely helpful on this and other textual points.

[11] BL MS Cotton Claud. Cix fos 105r–135v; 136r–177r; BL MS Cotton Claud. Bvi fos 3r–119r; 119v–177v.

[12] See below, pp. 187–8; also e.g. *CMA* ii, 166–90, which follows Bvi's arrangement; the form of Cix gives a much clearer account of events affecting Tadmarton and Chaddleworth.

[13] See below, pp. 193–4, on 'Abbot Adelelm's list of knights'.

in the earlier manuscript has stopped, but then gives supposed alternative readings from it in footnotes.[14] There are also some incorrect transcriptions and many problems with the index.[15]

How then should a new editor proceed?[16] The *Chronicle* in the earlier manuscript, Cix, was written by a scribe who was also responsible for an Abingdon version of John of Worcester, preserved in a Lambeth Palace manuscript.[17] Following the end of the text of the *Chronicle* in Cix there is various other material, some of it in later hands, but also some in that of the main scribe; the latter includes the Abingdon surveys and Domesday related material which D.C. Douglas published in 1929.[18] Precise dating of the manuscript is difficult. Patrick McGurk dates the scribe's work to the late twelfth century on palaeographical grounds, and states that 'this late date stands in the way of any attempt at identifying the scribe . . . with the compiler of the Abingdon chronicle and [the John of Worcester] Abingdon entries.'[19] Some may doubt whether the hand of a scribe of the end of the 1160s can be distinguished with certainty from an even later twelfth-century hand, so what of internal evidence? One of the scribe's entries in the manuscript after the main text of the *Chronicle* relates to the *Cartae Baronum*, so he was certainly active beyond 1166.[20] In the Lambeth manuscript, the scribe's last entry in its list of archbishops of Canterbury is Thomas Becket. This might be taken as firm evidence that the scribe was active between 1162 and 1170, but for the fact that another manuscript of John of Worcester reveals that late twelfth-century Abingdon scribes need not be consistent in their extending of episcopal lists.[21] One writ in MS Cix gives Henry I the title 'rex Anglie' spelt out in full. This form is more appropriate to the reign of John and after, and hence was more likely to slip into the mind of a thirteenth than a twelfth-century scribe, but again this is not definitive proof.[22] If the scribe were writing so late, it is perhaps odd that Richard I's charter for Abingdon appears not in his hand but that of another.[23] As yet I cannot improve upon the general ascription of the manuscript to the later twelfth century.

We do not know the name of the composer of the version of the *Chronicle* in the earliest surviving manuscript, or of the man who later expanded and modified it. Such anonymity is not unusual amongst monastic chronicles. Even when the chronicle is generally accompanied by the name of an 'author', as in the case of

---

14 E.g. *CMA* ii, 223 n. 2.

15 Faulty transcription (or mis-print): e.g. *CMA* ii, 4 (3 lines up), should read *terram*. Problematic index entries: e.g. Anskill/Anskitill; Chively/Civella.

16 See below, p. 189, on other sources for the history of Abingdon. As already stated, the text of the *Chronicle* is contained in two manuscripts. The number of manuscripts, and the fact that their structure and contents differ, are in line with other monastic chronicles of the period. Some have only one manuscript, some two or more. In the latter cases the form of the chronicle often differs between manuscripts; see e.g. *Liber Eliensis*, ed. E.O. Blake, Camden Soc. 3rd Ser. 92, 1962, xxiii–xxvii; *The Chronicle of Hugh Candidus*, ed. W.T. Mellows, Oxford 1949, xvii–xix.

17 *The Chronicle of John of Worcester*, ed. R.R. Darlington and P. McGurk, OMT 1995, ii, p. xlv.

18 D.C. Douglas, 'Some Early Surveys from the Abbey of Abingdon', *EHR* xliv, 1929, 618–25.

19 *John of Worcester* ii, p. xlv.

20 Cix fo. 190r–v.

21 *John of Worcester* ii, pp. xlv, lvii.

22 Cix fo. 164v (*CMA* ii, 162); see also fo. 167v (*CMA* ii, 189) for a writ of Henry II where the title is 'Henricus rex angl' et dux Normann' et aquitanie et comes andegau'.'

23 Cix fos 177v–178r.

Hugh Candidus at Peterborough, that 'author's' role is not exactly clear.[24] Stenton suggested that the Abingdon chronicler must have been at the monastery by 1117, for he wrote in the first person plural of an event under Faritius.[25] Such usage is good if not definitive evidence, and demands no impossible longevity. The chronicler might indeed have had a life almost exactly contemporary with that other childhood resident of Abingdon, Earl Robert of Leicester.[26] The chronicler may well have become attached to the sacristy, for Richard the sacrist becomes something of a hero in the later stages of the text.[27] The writing of the first version must have been complete before 1170, for it refers to Henry II consistently as 'Henricus junior', a style inappropriate after the coronation of Henry the Young King. Continuations of the text, in contrast, use the name 'Henricus Secundus'.[28] The earlier version of the text does not mention the death of Walkelin on 31 October 1164, making this a plausible *terminus ante quem*.[29]

The *Chronicle* is split into sections, generally with titles, and into books. Usually sections contain an incident, a report of a gift, or a charter. The earlier manuscript is divided into two books, with the division coming not at, but a few years after the Norman Conquest, with the appointment in 1071 of the first post-Conquest abbot, a monk from Jumièges.[30] The later manuscript has a division between books one and two at the time of tenth-century reform,[31] and – as we shall see – is rather confused in its division around the time of the Norman Conquest.[32] It reinforces certain stages in its text by illustrations of kings, whereas the only illustration in Cix is of Abbot Faritius, perched within an initial A.[33]

Thus key new abbots, not political events, are crucial to the structuring of the narrative, especially as revealed by Cix.[34] The *Chronicle* is essentially a record of the abbey, its buildings, its possessions, and its rights. The story it tells is given added coherence by the presence of certain heroes. In Cix the two leading figures are revealed by the regular, indeed the almost invariable, writing of their names in capital letters; they are the dedicatee of the abbey, Mary, and the early twelfth-century abbot, Faritius. In contrast, the great tenth-century reformer, Aethelwold, is only occasionally picked out in such a way.[35]

Some historians have rather casually referred to the *Abingdon Chronicle* and various other twelfth-century texts as forming a genre referred to as 'monastic

---

[24] *Hugh Candidus*, xvii.
[25] Stenton, 4; *CMA* ii, 49.
[26] *CMA* ii, 229.
[27] *CMA* ii, 201–8.
[28] E.g. *CMA* ii, 234, 297.
[29] *CMA* ii, 226. The later version ends with Richard I's confirmation charter to Abingdon; *CMA* ii, 245–9. This charter also appears in Cix fos 177v–178r, but in a different hand from the *Chronicle* text.
[30] This is rather unclear from Stevenson's edition, see *CMA* i, 487, 494, ii, 1; cf. Cix fos 135v–136r.
[31] *CMA* i, 120–1.
[32] See below, pp. 187–8.
[33] Cix fo. 144; see e.g. Bvi fo. 119v for William I.
[34] Cf. Part Three of the *Ramsey Chronicle* does end with Hastings; *Chronicon Abbatiæ Rameseiensis*, ed. W. Dunn Macray, RS lxxxiii, 1886, 179–80.
[35] Cf. fos 115r and 115v. For other abbots being honoured with capitals, see e.g. fo. 165 for Vincent. Capitals are also used, for example, to pick out names of kings and places in Anglo-Saxon charters; e.g. fo. 120v for Edgar. Outside the charters, Ine in particular seems to be honoured with capitals; e.g. fo. 105r. See also e.g. the capitalisation of Saint Peter's name on fo. 107r.

charter chronicles'.[36] Yet how much do these texts have in common, besides their monastic provenance? Certainly they are all concerned with lands and rights.[37] They record foundations and founders, benefactions and benefactors, the deeds of abbots, and their buildings. Indeed, they can provide a 'mirror for abbots', judging incumbents by the degree to which they fulfilled their oath of office not to disperse their abbey's lands, but to resume those which their predecessors had given away.[38] The villain favoured his kin over obligations to the monks and the saint, the hero defended and extended the rights of the church.[39] He was also likely to pursue his ends through royal aid, re-emphasizing the special, lofty position of his church.

Yet if there are similarities of purpose, differences of form and content are too great to allow these texts to be grouped as a genre. Many are accounts of an abbey's history over several centuries, by an anonymous and apparently otherwise insignificant author. However, Henry of Blois' description of his abbacy at Glastonbury is an autobiography, a *De administratione* to parallel that of Suger.[40] Differing use is made of documents. The longer of the Battle Abbey chronicles contains no charters, although it paraphrases many.[41] The main post-Conquest section of the *Ramsey Chronicle*, in contrast, is made up almost entirely of charters or brief sections intended to resemble charters; yet to these is appended a short tract on Abbot Walter containing no charters.[42] Hugh Candidus' *Chronicle* has only very limited charter material, and after the Conquest it is notably more concerned with the miraculous than either the Ramsey or the Abingdon chronicles.[43] As for structure, some are split into books, some, like Battle, are not; some are split into titled chapters, some, like that of Peterborough, are not.

Perhaps the chronicle most similar to that of Abingdon is the *Liber Eliensis*. Like the later version of the Abingdon text it is broken into three books, with the first division again coming with tenth-century reform, but the second with the establishment of Ely as a bishopric.[44] Yet despite general similarities of structure, content and purpose, there are still differences. The proportion of the Ely text devoted to documents increased chronologically; at Abingdon, particularly in the later version of the text, charters are most predominant in the Anglo-Saxon period. The difference stems in part from Ely's greater use of pre-existing narrative sources, notably the *Libellus Aethelwoldi* for the tenth century.[45] And as with some

---

[36] Others have associated these various texts with the growing desire for written evidence and with the events and aftermath of Stephen's reign, although the *Ramsey Chronicle* is unusual in spelling out such a link; A. Gransden, *Historical Writing in England c. 550 to c. 1307*, London 1974, 269; *Ramsey*, 4.

[37] In some cases, for example the *Battle Chronicle*, freedom from the local bishop is another central theme.

[38] *The Pontifical of Magdalen College*, ed. H.A. Wilson, Henry Bradshaw Soc. 39, 1910, 81.

[39] Particularly in the twelfth century, a good abbot might well be responsible for the future protection of the monks' interests by granting the convent its own endowment.

[40] Henry's work is printed in *Adami de Domerham Historia de Rebus Gestis Glastoniensibus*, ed. T. Hearne, 2 vols, Oxford 1727, ii, 304–15; for Suger, see Lindy Grant's essay in this volume, and note also Simon Keynes' essay on Giso of Wells.

[41] Note the presence of surveys in the shorter of the Battle chronicles; *The Chronicle of Battle Abbey*, ed. E. Searle, Oxford Medieval Texts 1980, 48ff.

[42] *Ramsey*, 200–336.

[43] E.g. *Hugh Candidus*, 75, 106–8.

[44] *Liber Eliensis*, 65, 237–8.

[45] *Liber Eliensis*, ix–xviii, xxxiii–xxxiv, li–liii, 72–117.

of the other chronicles from monasteries dedicated to local rather than supra-national saints, the miraculous is more prominent at Etheldreda's Ely than Mary's Abingdon.[46]

The presentation of the Norman Conquest both in the printed text and the manuscripts illustrates many of the points already made.[47] Let us begin by outlining the account as it appears in the earlier manuscript, Cix. We begin after the Confessor's death with the death of Abbot Ordric, and Harold's appointment of Abbot Ealdred. Then are mentioned Halley's comet, the coming of the king of Norway, Harold's victory at Stamford Bridge, and William's invasion and victory.[48] Ealdred and others took an oath of loyalty to the king. The narrative then turns to local Abingdon matters relating to estates and the plundering of the church's ornaments. Next comes mention of rebellions against William and the imprisonment of Bishop Aethelwine of Durham and Abbot Ealdred of Abingdon. Book One of the *Chronicle* ends with further description of the state of England.[49] Book II then gets under way with the appointment of Abbot Adelelm, and two royal writs confirming Abingdon's rights and protecting it from exactions. The impact of these writs is then described, before the narrative turns to the endowment of military tenants with lands.[50] Following this, there is a return to the history of individual estates, although punctuated for example with mention of Abbot Adelelm accompanying Robert Curthose to Scotland in 1080. A further Danish threat is recorded, before we come to the death of Adelelm.[51]

Bvi brought various changes to this text, and confuses the account in various ways. Following the description of events from the appearance of the comet until Hastings, it brings its Book II to an end with a short recapitulatory section on gifts and charters for the church.[52] The *incipit* to Book III is then followed by a return to the Confessor's time, and Edward's charter concerning Chilton which had already appeared earlier in both manuscripts. This version, like that which appeared earlier in Cix, but not that in Bvi, omits the boundaries and the names of those witnessing, stating only 'his testibus quorum nomina in superiori carta nominantur'.[53] There follows another short section stating that the previous two books had dealt with gifts and charters from the old kings of the English and their men, and that the text will now move onto the liberties and gifts given by the Norman kings. Next comes a section headed 'About the death of king Edward', which contains a description of William's coronation drawn from the Worcester chronicle, followed by criticism of William's rule.[54] The narrative then follows a more logical order, and confusion only returns at the point where the two volumes of Stevenson's edition split the text. After describing the arrival of Abbot Adelelm from Jumièges, and before

---

[46] E.g. *Liber Eliensis*, 264–76.
[47] See also below, appendix.
[48] Cix fos 134v–135r.
[49] Cix fo. 135r–v.
[50] Cix fo. 136r–v.
[51] Cix fos 136v–137v.
[52] Bvi fo. 117r–v.
[53] Bvi fos 117v–118r = *CMA* i, 488–9; already printed *CMA* i, 455–6 (= Cix fo. 132v, Bvi fos 110v–111r).
[54] Bvi fo. 118r; *John of Worcester* ii, 606. Note that this is not one of those passages of the Worcester chronicle unique to the Abingdon version.

William I's confirmation charter, is written 'Here begins book two of the history of this church of Abingdon.'[55] The division of the earlier manuscript Cix into two books has inappropriately crept into Book III of the later manuscript, Bvi. Finally Bvi gives the account of the reading of royal letters in the county court of Berkshire before providing the text of William's writ prohibiting exaction of tolls and customs.[56] The narrative of the dispute therefore is inappropriately linked solely to William's confirmation of the abbey's customs.

In addition to confusion, Bvi also introduces some new sections into the account of these years. These are a statement of William's claim [i 483]; the description of William's coronation and rule [i 490]; a different version of the flight and dispossession of the priest Blacheman [i 490]; a dispute concerning a mill at Cuddesdon [i 491–2]; a list of knights holding from Abingdon [ii 4–6]; and a story concerning Robert d'Oilly [ii 12–15].[57] The list of knights will be discussed later. However, it may well be significant that the accounts concerning both Cuddesdon mill and Robert d'Oilly, whilst both concerned with disputes, are quite unusual within the *Chronicle* in dealing with the miraculous. The style of parts of the Robert d'Oilly story also seems distinctive, perhaps in its vocabulary, certainly in the way it uses Biblical quotation. One may wonder whether the compiler of the later version drew on separate notes or texts concerning miraculous events.

Stevenson's printed version adds still further confusion. Halley's comet first appeared on p. 482 of volume one of his edition, in a section present in both manuscripts which dealt with events from the death of Abbot Ordric in late January 1066 to Harold's death at Hastings on 14 October. There then follow three and a half pages edited solely from the earlier manuscript, but some of which also appear in the later manuscript.[58] This section takes us to the end of Book One of the earlier manuscript, the *explicit* of which is printed only in a footnote.[59] He then resumes the text as it appears in the later manuscript, Bvi. First comes one paragraph which takes us to the end of Book Two of this version.[60] Then come six pages giving the start of Book Three of Bvi. They include passages already printed solely from Cix; these passages therefore appear twice in the printed version, although only once in either manuscript.[61] The volume then ends just after the beginning of Book Two in MS Cix, although this is unclear in the printed version.[62] Volume two follows the order and contents of Bvi.

Whatever the problems of manuscripts and editions, the *Abingdon Chronicle* remains a most interesting local source for the history of the Norman Conquest. In this context, J.H. Round became almost civil about Freeman:

> To the interest and importance of the Berkshire portion of the Conqueror's great survey Mr. Freeman bore striking witness when he selected it for

55 *CMA* ii, 1; Bvi fo. 119v.
56 Bvi fos 119v–120r
57 Bvi fos 117r–v, 118r, 118v–119r, 120v–121r, 122v–123v. Robert d'Oilly's experience should probably be dated to the abbacy of Reginald, 1084–97 (see *CMA* ii, 24–5).
58 *CMA* i, 483–7; cf. 490–4. Cix fo. 135r–v; Bvi fo. 118–119v
59 *CMA* i, 487 n. 1.
60 *CMA* i, 487.
61 *CMA* i, 488–94.
62 See Cix, fo. 136r.

special treatment as typifying the effect of the Conquest on this country in practice. He analysed its evidence so fully that in dealing with the subject one is forced to traverse, to some extent, his footsteps. There was, however, an external reason for this choice of Berkshire, namely the existence of that chronicle of the local Abbey of Abingdon, which helps us to illustrate the Domesday text, and which is specially rich in that personal detail that Mr. Freeman valued most of all.[63]

Likewise according to Stevenson, the *Abingdon Chronicle* 'sets before us the whole system introduced by the Normans, not in its theory, but in its application, not as an idea, but as a reality'.[64]

But how trustworthy is the *Chronicle* as a source for the Conquest and its aftermath? In undertaking a new edition of the *Chronicle*, I am helped by the availability of a fuller corpus of material than Stevenson possessed. There is an edition/calendar of the two main Abingdon cartularies. These give only two pre-Conquest charters – both dubious –, but do provide additional texts of many of the *Chronicle*'s Anglo-Norman and Angevin documents, some further documents from this period, and many charters from the thirteenth century and beyond.[65] There has also been considerable archaeological investigation of Abingdon and the area of its estates.[66] However, neither the cartularies nor archaeology can add much to our knowledge of Abingdon and the Norman Conquest. Here it is the evidence of Domesday Book which is vital, for example with regard to values, hidation, and disputes.[67]

With the help of Round and Stenton's work for the *Victoria County History*, we can also use Domesday to test the accuracy of the *Abingdon Chronicle*'s account of the Conquest and its aftermath. We find many occasions on which *Chronicle* and survey agree.[68] Some differences are minor or readily explicable. For example, the *Chronicle* records that a knight called Hermer, whose hands had been chopped off by pirates, received land in Denchworth which had previously provided food for the monks. Domesday records Hermer as holding seven hides in Goosey 'in dominico uictu monachorum'. These seem simply to be different descriptions of the same land; Denchworth and Goosey are neighbouring settlements.[69]

---

[63] *VCH, Berkshire* i, 285; E.A. Freeman, *The History of the Norman Conquest*, 6 vols, Oxford 1867–79, iv, 32–47.

[64] *CMA* ii, p. xxiv.

[65] *Two Cartularies of Abingdon Abbey*, edd. G. Lambrick and C.F. Slade, 2 vols, Oxford Hist. Soc. ns 32 and 33, 1990–2; no. L70 is a writ of the Confessor, whilst no. C360 contains a supposed charter of Cenwulf. Knowledge of diplomatic practice, of pre-Conquest Abingdon, and of the twelfth-century perception of that past will be greatly increased by the appearance of Susan Kelly's edition of Abingdon material in the British Academy's *Anglo-Saxon Charters* series.

[66] See e.g. M. Biddle, G. Lambrick, and J.N.L. Myres, 'The Early History of Abingdon, Berkshire, and its Abbey', *Medieval Archaeology* xii, 1968, 26–69; C.J. Bond, 'The Reconstruction of the Medieval Landscape: the Estates of Abingdon Abbey', *Landscape History* i, 1979, 59–75; T. Allen, 'Abingdon', *Current Archaeology* xi, 1990, 24–7.

[67] See below, pp. 192–3, 198. Also N. Hooper, 'Introduction', *The Berkshire Domesday*, Alecto Historical Editions, London 1988.

[68] E.g. *Domesday Book* i, fo. 59r, *CMA* ii, 7 on forest at Winkfield.

[69] *CMA* ii, 6 'de uictualio monachorum'; *Domesday Book* i, fo. 59r. Elsewhere the *Chronicle* provides information which does not appear in Domesday Book, but this need not lead us to distrust the *Chronicle*; see below, p. 195, on Nuneham Courtenay.

In some instances, however, Domesday Book does raise the possibility that the chronicler made errors – although one must also allow that Domesday Book need not always be a true record. Some problems concerns names. Thus Domesday records that 'Henry [de Ferrers] holds Kingston [Bagpuize] himself and Ralph from him. Stanchil held TRE . . .'. In contrast, both manuscripts of the *Chronicle* record that a rich man named Thurkill, with Earl Harold witnessing and advising, did homage to Abingdon and its abbot concerning himself with his land at Kingston. Thurkill died at Hastings, and Henry de Ferrers usurped the land. Conceivably the difference of names reflects pre-Conquest tenurial arrangements between Thurkill and a Stanchil, but Round concluded that 'it would seem possible, at least, that the monks made a mistake'.[70]

Other possible errors concern tenure and dating.[71] Domesday Book records that Abingdon had 60 hides at Barton. 'Of these 60 hides Reginald holds one manor, Shippon, from the abbot, in pledge. Ednoth the Staller held it before 1066, but it was not then in the abbey. Earl Hugh gave it to the abbot.' In contrast the *Chronicle* records that Ednoth had held of the abbey; perhaps this was untrue, perhaps lies were told to the Domesday Commissioners, or perhaps the contrast reflects conflicting perceptions of the pre-Conquest situation.[72] The *Chronicle* goes on that Hugh acquired Ednoth's lands, but when he learnt that these hides belonged to the abbey, he gave them to the church in a ceremony on 31 March 1090. In return he received £30 and various spiritual benefits, and the transaction was recorded in writing. Domesday shows that Hugh had already given the land by 1086; either the *Chronicle* has simply got the date wrong, or the two differing accounts conceal further dispute, negotiation, or transactions.[73]

Bearing in mind these cautions, let us examine the *Chronicle*'s presentation of the Norman Conquest and the Conquest's impact upon the abbey of Abingdon. To begin with the narrative of national events: we are told of the coming of the comet; the invasion of the king of Norway and his defeat; William's arrival. At this point only the later of the manuscripts, Bvi, spells out William's claim based on Edward's leaving him the kingdom as his relative, although Cix had already traced William's descent in the context of Ethelred's marriage to Emma, daughter of Count Richard of Normandy.[74] Harold's defeat at Hastings is blamed on his overconfidence. The manuscript accounts then diverge, although both emphasize the oaths of loyalty sworn to William. As already mentioned, the later manuscript draws on the Worcester chronicle for an account of William's coronation, and then

70 *Domesday Book* i, fo. 60v; *CMA* i, 484, 490–1; Round in *VCH, Berkshire* i, 294.

71 See also above, n. 57, on Robert d'Oilly; below, p. 191, on the dating of the Danish threat.

72 It is conceivable that the confusion may arise from pre-Conquest arrangements involving soke ; see D. Roffe, 'From Thegnage to Barony: Sake and Soke, and Title and Tenants-in-Chief', *ANS* xii, 1990, 157–76, and also Richard Abels' essay in this volume.

73 *Domesday Book* i, fo. 58v; *CMA* ii, 19–20; Round in *VCH, Berkshire* i, 295 suspected 'that Eadnoth had been assisted by [Harold] to encroach on the rights of the abbey'. I find nothing to support Round's suggestion that Domesday Book 'even suggests that the land has been mortgaged in order that the abbot might raise the £30 for the earl'. *The Charters of the Anglo-Norman Earls of Chester*, ed. G. Barraclough, Record Society of Lancashire and Cheshire cxxvi, 1988, no. 2 states that the letter 'laying down the conditions for completion, evidently preceded the actual transaction, but probably by no more than a few weeks'. See also below, pp. 195–6, concerning Sparsholt.

74 *CMA* i, 483, 430–1.

adds its own comments on William's failure to keep his promises, and his depositions of prelates.[75]

Thereafter the *Chronicle*'s account focuses primarily on local matters, but continues to show awareness of other events, especially when they touch upon Abingdon. The disorder and the castle-building of the early post-Conquest years are mentioned.[76] Abbot Adelelm participated in Robert Curthose's expedition to Scotland in 1080.[77] Almost all of the abbey's knights were ordered to join an expedition to Wales.[78] William's dispute with his brother Odo is included because it led to Abingdon's loss of an estate.[79] A threat of Danish invasion, almost certainly that of 1085, is also recorded, although it appears before the death of Adelelm in 1083.[80]

As for an overall view of the Conquest, the *Chronicle* takes no very firm line. The earlier manuscript referred to William having 'usurped the kingdom for himself', and the later was critical of his kingship.[81] Oppressions, such as the loss of treasures, were recorded.[82] However, there is no great sense of tragedy for the nation or for the monastery. This must, above all, reflect Abingdon's relations with the king.[83]

Before Hastings, Abingdon had quite close connections with Harold. As earl, he had helped the abbey regain control of lands at Leckhamstead.[84] As king he appointed Ealdred abbot.[85] The Abingdon version of the *Anglo-Saxon Chronicle* is critical of Harold, as of the Godwin family generally, in the crisis of the early 1050s, but ends its obituary of Edward with the lines

> Yet the wise ruler entrusted the realm
> To a man of high rank, to Harold himself,
> A noble earl who all the time
> Had loyally followed his lord's commands
> With words and deeds, and neglected nothing
> That met the need of the people's king.[86]

Such close relations help to explain the support Harold enjoyed from Abingdon

---

[75] See above, p. 187. On William I and Stigand, see *CMA* i, 463.

[76] See below, p. 198, for instances of Domesday values which fell after the Confessor's time, but in some cases rose again by 1086.

[77] *CMA* ii, 9–10. Note the comment of J. Le Patourel, *The Norman Empire*, Oxford 1976, 208. The chronicler may be allowing later twelfth-century English views to colour his impression of events of 1080.

[78] *CMA* ii, 10.

[79] See below, p. 195.

[80] The *Abingdon Chronicle* makes no mention of the Domesday Survey, unless its reference to a royal enquiry concerning knight service is in fact a confused memory of 1086, *CMA* ii, 3; note that Florence of Worcester, *Chronicon ex chronicis*, ed. B. Thorpe, 2 vols, London, 1848–9, ii, 18, includes 'how many enfeoffed knights' as one of the questions asked in 1086.

[81] *CMA* i, 431, and above, pp. 190–1.

[82] See also below, n. 136.

[83] A combination of local conditions and relations with the king determined the attitude of most of the monastic histories to the Norman Conquest; see e.g. *Chronicon Abbatiæ de Evesham*, ed. W. Dunn Macray, RS xxix, 1863, 88–90.

[84] See *CMA* i, 475; F.E. Harmer, *Anglo-Saxon Writs*, Manchester 1952, 122–3, 131, 427–8. Note also Hooper (as n. 67), 12–13, 18.

[85] Note *CMA* i, 482. The *Chronicle* makes no attempt to avoid calling Harold 'rex'; *CMA* i, 483.

[86] *ASC* 'C', *s.a.* 1052, 1065; cf. its critical tone with regard to Tostig in 1066.

tenants at Hastings.[87] In the wake of William's victory, Abingdon suffered along with other monasteries from royal demands and depredations.[88] Not surprisingly, the abbey and its tenants became involved in the rebellions of the early 1070s. Abbot Ealdred incurred the king's anger, and was imprisoned first in the castle of Wallingford and then transferred into the hands of the bishop of Winchester, in whose custody he remained until his death.[89] Ealdred's fate was central to the *Chronicle*'s somewhat ambiguous judgement of him: after recounting his restoration of certain estates to the church, the *Chronicle* concluded that just as Ealdred had succeeded concerning these lands, so too might he have succeeded concerning others alienated from the church's demesne, had he not incurred William's anger.[90]

William's determination to secure the abbey's loyalty must have encouraged him in his selection of Adelelm, a monk of Jumièges, as Ealdred's successor. His appointment marked, if not an end to trouble affecting the abbey,[91] at least a major shift in its fortunes. In the earlier manuscript of the *Chronicle*, Book II begins with the appointment of Adelelm, and William I's sending of a writ to Lanfranc, Robert d'Oilly and others of the realm of England:

> Know that I have granted to St Mary of Abingdon and to Adelelm abbot of this place the customs of their lands . . . as Abbot Adelelm can show by writ or charter that the church of St Mary of Abingdon and his predecessor had these customs by gift of King Edward.[92]

This is immediately followed by another writ of William concerning tolls, and then by a description of the reading of these writs in the court of Berkshire, and their effect in ending officials' oppressions.[93] William also granted a more specific confirmation of Adelelm's acquisition of lands at Hill and Chesterton in Warwickshire.[94]

Royal favour may also be apparent in changes in hidation, but these were enjoyed by almost all lords in Berkshire. For Abingdon, Domesday records a reduction from slightly over 500 hides to approximately 320, with particularly drastic cuts at, for example, Chieveley from 27 to 7.5 hides, and at Uffington from

---

[87] Note *CMA* ii, 3 on Abingdon thegns falling in the battle, and below p. 193; see also Freeman iv, 33ff.

[88] *CMA* i, 485, 491; also A. Williams, *The English and the Norman Conquest*, Woodbridge 1995, p. 45.

[89] CMA, i 485–6, 493; Williams, 55. The versions given by Cix and Bvi differ; that in Cix is very closely related to an Abingdon addition to the Worcester chronicle; Florence of Worcester ii, 9 n. 2.

[90] *CMA* i, 484.

[91] See below, p. 195, concerning Winkfield and Nuneham Courtenay. For Adelelm's presence at great ecclesiastical councils, see *Councils and Synods with Other Documents relating to the English Church*, edd. D. Whitelock *et al.*, Oxford 1981, 604, 615. Despite the fact that the relevant passage precedes the capture of Ealdred in the text, it was probably into the hands of Adelelm that Bishop Aethelwine of Durham was placed following the fall of the Isle of Ely in 1071. He remained imprisoned at Abingdon until his death; *CMA* i, 485–6, Williams, 55. The chronological disorder may stem from the Abingdon manuscript of the Worcester chronicle, see above, n. 89.

[92] *CMA* i, 494, ii 1 (= *Regesta* i, no. 49, Bates, no. 4).

[93] *CMA* ii, 1–2 (= *Regesta* i, no. 201, Bates, no. 6). The use of the plural 'imperialibus mandatis', and the description of events suggests that both of the writs were read in the shire court.

[94] *CMA* ii, 8 (= *Regesta* i, no. 200, Bates, no. 5). *De Abbatibus*, *CMA* ii, 284, recalled that Adelelm bought Chesterton and Hill from the king. The *De Abbatibus* ends in the time of Abbot Hugh (1189/90–c. 1221).

40 to 14.[95] The exact timing of the change in hidation is uncertain, although interestingly one instance occurred before the death of King Edward: Beedon's hidation was reduced from 10 hides to 8 between 1066 and 1086, but Domesday notes that it had once been 15 hides before the Confessor reduced it to 11.[96]

Lords might benefit from reduced hidations, but new burdens were also imposed. The *Chronicle* recounts that the knights of the abbey served the king in Wales, and stresses castle-guard duties at the royal fortress of Windsor. It also records that Adelelm at first relied on stipendiary knights, but later allotted lands to his kinsmen [*pertinentibus*] to be held in return for service, specifically lands of thegns who had fallen at Hastings. These grants it relates to a royal recording of the knight service owed by churches, whilst the shorter chronicle *De Abbatibus* criticises Adelelm as excessively generous to his relatives.[97] However, Domesday and even the *Chronicle* itself do not fully support the more specific allegations, all of which concern lands in Oxfordshire, mostly granted to Robert d'Oilly. No previous tenant is mentioned for the two hides he and Roger d'Ivry held at Arncott. However, the hide they received at Sandford had previously been held by Siward, a tenant who 'could not withdraw from the church'. Land granted to Robert at Tadmarton was regained, although at some cost.[98] Of these lands, both Arncott and Tadmarton, but not Sandford, are some distance from the core of the abbey's estates. In general, Domesday evidence supports the idea that there was no great reduction in the church's demesne but rather lands previously held by tenants were again alienated.[99]

I do not here wish to enter into the whole question of the introduction of knight service and of quotas, which have been dealt with in earlier conferences by Professors Holt and Gillingham. Rather, my sole detailed argument will be a destructive one. The above comments on military service, and on Adelelm's grants, appear in both manuscripts of the *Chronicle*. However, it is only the later version which includes the text sometimes referred to as 'Abbot Adelelm's list of knights'. This section intrudes rather awkwardly into the narrative. It is made up of two lists, one headed 'These are the knights holding from Abingdon', the other 'These are the names of those who hold small portions which belong to the chamber of the lord

[95] *Domesday Book* i, fos 58v, 59r. Oxfordshire Domesday does not give TRE hidages.

[96] J.H. Round in *VCH, Berkshire* i, 286 n. 5 suggests that 'possibly xi. is an error for x.' The benefits of the new hidation may not have been passed on to the tenants of the church, for a post-Conquest Abingdon document survives which uses almost entirely the TRE hidages; Douglas, 621. However, it is also possible that some of the beneficial hidations were withdrawn, perhaps by Henry I; *VCH, Berkshire* i, 287. For reductions in Berkshire starting before the Conquest, see also *Domesday Book* i, fo. 60v (Stanford).

[97] *CMA* ii, 3–4, 10, 283–4; such are common concerns of monastic chronicles, see e.g. Hugh Candidus, 84–5. See above, n. 80, for a suggestion that the supposed enquiry may in fact be a mistaken memory of the Domesday survey; but note also the arguments of Gillingham, 'Introduction of Knight Service', esp. 57. Hooper, 13 points out the number of men holding small portions of land in 1086, and suggests that such men were likely to have been burdened with the service of less than one knight, fulfilled by payment of scutage. Abingdon knights also travelled overseas on royal business, *CMA* ii, 6–7.

[98] *Domesday Book* i, fo. 156v; *CMA* ii, 25, 283–4; see also below, p. 197. For the meadow at Oxford, see *CMA* ii, 12–15, 25. On Whitchurch, see below, p. 196.

[99] E.g. Bayworth, Beedon, Seacourt; *Domesday Book* i, fo. 58v. The gift to the mutilated knight Hermer, above, p. 189, is a somewhat exceptional case because of its charitable nature and limited duration.

abbot.'[100] It is one amongst several Abingdon lists relating to land-holding and services, but has received particular attention as relevant to 'the introduction of knight service'.

Historians have attributed a variety of dates to the document. For example, Richardson and Sayles stated that 'This list cannot be much later, if it is not earlier, than the year 1100.'[101] Approached carefully, however, the 'document' in fact proves impossible to date from the names within it. Checking the names and holdings against Domesday Book in several cases provides a good fit,[102] and in others a partial one.[103] Elsewhere, however, the correlation is poor. None of those listed as holding small portions turn up in the relevant Domesday entries. Among the larger tenants, Hugh de Bocland and Henry fitzOini, for example, are tenants of Henry I's time, not William I's.[104] But the problems do not stop here. Herbert fitzHerbert and Raerus de Aure among the larger tenants, and Peter de Aldebiri and Richard Gernun de Wateleia among the smaller, look suspiciously like the tenants of the same name mentioned in the *Cartae Baronum* of 1166, whilst the list's Baldwin de Columbers who owed one knight for Fawler may well be the *Cartae's* Baldwin de 'Flagesflore'.[105] No John fitzRobert appears in the *Cartae* but one was present in Abingdon documents of the late twelfth and early thirteenth centuries.[106]

Abbot Adelelm's 'list of knights' thus turns out to be an untrustworthy amalgam, quite possibly made up of two different lists and certainly constituted of a bewildering range of entries. Its purpose remains unclear to me, and will have to be analysed within the full range of Abingdon lists and surveys. What its later influence upon historians does illustrate very well is the authority conferred by uncritical inclusion within a Rolls Series edition of a chronicle.

Let us move from disputes between historians concerning knight service to disputes involving Abingdon concerning its lands and rights. Their nature reflects the pattern of settlement in Berkshire and Oxfordshire, neither of which were counties dominated by one or a few lay magnates. The substantial majority of the abbey's lands were in Berkshire, where the king was the dominant land-holder, with Abingdon the second most important.[107]

---

100 *CMA* ii, 4–6. The 'list of knights' is preceded by a sentence which neatly concludes the previous section, rather than leading on to the list: 'Itaque de his sat dictum: quare stilus ad historiam inchoatam uertatur' – *CMA* ii, 4.

101 H.G. Richardson and G.O. Sayles, *The Governance of Mediaeval England from the Conquest to Magna Carta*, Edinburgh 1963, 79; see also their n. 5. My conclusion fits that of J.H. Round, *Feudal England*, London 1895, 221; cf. his comments and use of the list at p. 306.

102 Warin; Hubert; Walter de Riparia; Walter Giffard; Gilbert Marshall. Note also Gilbert de Columbers, although the list also attributes to him a holding at 'horduuelle' (furthermore there was a *Cartae Baronum* tenant of same name; clearly the particular difficulty that two men, living a century apart, had the same name further hampers the dating of the list).

103 Rainbald; Reginald of St Helena; Anskill; Gilbert; there may be another instance if Stenton in *VCH, Oxfordshire* i, 381 and n. 2 was right to argue that 'it is highly probable that the [Domesday] tenant named Wenric . . . was identical with Gueres de Palences' who appears at the head of the list of knights.

104 Again, another Hugh de Bocland appears in the *Cartae Baronum*.

105 *Liber Rubeus de Scaccario*, ed. H. Hall, 3 vols, RS lxxxxix, 1896, i, 305–6. Note also the number of English toponyms among the smaller tenants, strongly suggesting a date later than the eleventh century.

106 *Abingdon Cartularies*, nos L205, L256.

107 Hooper (as n. 67), 26. Round wrote in *VCH, Berkshire* i, 288 that among lay barons 'the most

It is useful to divide the disputes in the years shortly after the Conquest into certain types. Some arose from disloyalty to the king, reflecting the emphasis in both versions of the *Chronicle* upon oaths of loyalty to William and the earlier connections with Harold.[108] Prominent are disputes relating to the lands of a rich priest named Blacheman who left the country with Harold's mother. According to the *Chronicle* he had been a man of the church of Abingdon and held lands in Chilton, Sandford and Leverton. The *Chronicle* leads us to believe that all these lands were held of the church, but Domesday states that he held Chilton 'in alodio' from Harold, and could go where he wished, and that he held Leverton 'in feudo'; only Sandford does it specify that he held from the church. Abingdon's rights in Blacheman's lands thus sound restricted. If so, it is unsurprising that the abbot had difficulties in regaining the lands after Blacheman's flight led the king to confiscate them.[109]

The king also became involved in other types of dispute. Leofwin sold Nuneham Courtenay to Abbot Adelelm, and Odo of Bayeux, who was controlling England in William's absence, confirmed the sale. However, William and Odo later quarrelled, and Odo was placed in captivity. According to the *Chronicle*, the king turned against all whom Odo had favoured, and took Nuneham Courtenay away from Abingdon, giving it to another. Domesday reveals this to have been Richard de Courcy, although it mentions no Abingdon interest in the land and no dispute concerning it, stating only that a certain Hakon held it TRE.[110]

Conflicts with royal officials were common. Froger sheriff of Berkshire tyrannised the abbey before suffering what the *Chronicle* saw as a divinely ordained collapse in his fortunes.[111] William I's writ concerning tolls was aimed against officials imposing burdensome customs.[112] Trouble notably arose over woods and forest. As we shall see, Abbot Adelelm dealt very forcibly with the reeve Alfsi who harassed the tenants of the church.[113] However, nothing could be done to resist four hides at Winkfield being taken into the royal forest, especially since the royal official in this case was Walter fitzOter, the powerful guardian of Windsor castle and of all the royal forest of Berkshire.[114]

A further set of cases, some straddling the Conquest, related to land tenure. According to the *Chronicle* it had been the custom among the English that monks might dispose of their moveables and patrimonies as they liked. Thus, the *Chronicle* states, Godric Cild's patrimony of Sparsholt passed to Abingdon and remained

---

conspicuous figure is that of Henry de Ferrers.' R.V. Lennard, *Rural England*, Oxford 1959, ch. 3, made famous the lack of a dominant magnate in Oxfordshire.

[108] See above, p. 191.

[109] *CMA* i, 474, 484, 490; *Domesday Book* i, fos 59r, 156v; Hooper, 12–13; also *CMA* ii, 283 for the account in *De Abbatibus*. Again the situation may reflect arrangements concerning soke.

[110] *CMA* ii, 9; *Domesday Book* i, fo. 159r; discussed by Stenton, *VCH, Oxfordshire* i, 394–5. Note that *CMA* ii, 52–3 has William de Courcy give Abingdon the church of Nuneham Courtenay, one hide there, and certain other rights. *De Abbatibus*, *CMA* ii, 284 recalled that Adelelm bought Nuneham from the king.

[111] *CMA* i, 486, 494.

[112] *CMA* ii, 1–2.

[113] See below, p. 197.

[114] *Domesday Book* i, fo. 59r; *CMA* ii, 7. For the later history of Winkfield, see *CMA* ii, 29–30, 87, 132 (where the account of the earlier history of the woods differs somewhat from that given at *CMA* ii, 7).

in the fee of the church to the time of writing. Domesday, however, reveals greater complexity. The entry for Fawler, one of the three manors making up the pre-Conquest estate known as Sparsholt, states that

> the shire confirms that Edric, who held it ['in alodio' from King Edward], delivered it to his son [presumably Godric], who was a monk in Abingdon, to hold it at farm, and to give him thence the necessities of life as long as he lived, and that after his death he should have the manor. And so the men of the shire do not know what pertains to the abbey. For they never saw the king's writ or seal concerning it. But the abbot witnesses that in the time of King Edward he [Godric] transferred [*misit*] the manor to the church where he was, and he has the writ and seal of King Edward, with all his monks witnessing.

The abbey managed to retain this land, but not Whitchurch in Oxfordshire over which a similar dispute had arisen.[115]

Leases dating from before the Conquest caused particular problems.[116] The *Chronicle* claimed that Blacheman's lands were held 'ad firmam', but this did not stop the king confiscating them.[117] Henry de Ferrers seized part of Fyfield which Godric, a former sheriff, had held from Abingdon for only three lives. Godric was *antecessor* of Henry in other lands, including another part of Fyfield which he had held of the king, and this may have encouraged Henry to assert a right to lands Godric held only by lease.[118]

This case could also be included amongst another set of disputes, those with acquisitive lords. Here Abingdon was protected by the absence of locally dominant magnates, but the position of men such as Henry de Ferrers remained strong. He may have been sheriff of Berkshire at some point after the Conquest, whilst in 1086 his gains possibly enjoyed some protection by his acting as a Domesday Commissioner on circuit v.[119] Another interesting instance appears in Domesday Book, although not the *Chronicle*. In the time of King Edward, Alfyard's sons had held Lyford from the abbot. They could not go elsewhere without permission, yet still they commended themselves to Walter Giffard without the abbot's order. Such a case might well have been to the lasting loss of the abbey, but a solution, perhaps a compromise, was found, for Domesday records that in 1086 Walter Giffard held the land from the abbot. Yet this entry may hide a continuing conflict, for the *Chronicle* records that in the time of Abbot Faritius (1100–1117), the Domesday Walter's son, also called Walter, was refusing to do service and perhaps homage.[120]

What then of the conduct of disputes? In the *Chronicle*, the immediate post-Conquest period and Stephen's reign are unusual in the amount of direct action taken during cases. Abbot Adelelm in the early days of his abbacy reputedly went

115 *CMA* i, 477, ii 284; *Domesday Book* i, fo. 59r; *VCH, Berkshire* i, 296–7; Williams, 102.

116 See also Ann William's essay in this volume.

117 See above, p. 195.

118 *CMA* i, 484–5, 491; *Domesday Book* i, fo. 60v.

119 J.A. Green, *English Sheriffs to 1154*, London 1990, 26. Circuit v consisted of Cheshire, Staffordshire, Shropshire, Worcestershire, Herefordshire, and Gloucestershire. The chronicler also recorded Henry, perhaps wrongly, as the despoiler of their estate of Kingston Bagpuize; see above, p. 190.

120 *Domesday Book* i, fo. 59r; Williams, 75 and n. 18, takes this to show that the land was 'thegnland'. The two Walters mentioned by Domesday may be different men, I.J. Sanders, *English Baronies*, Oxford 1960, 62. *CMA* ii, 133–4.

nowhere unless guarded by a band of armed knights.[121] In minor conflicts, he was very capable of looking after himself. Alfsi, reeve of the royal vill of Sutton, troubled the men of the abbey by exacting carting services, and by cutting brushwood from woods at Bagley and Cumnor. Adelelm intervened in person. When the reeve was employing the abbey's oxen to cart some lead which he had acquired for the king's use, the abbot struck him with a stick which 'by chance' he was holding; the lead was scattered, the oxen taken back. On a second occasion, Adelelm seized the loads from Alfsi's carts, and forced him to flee by horse through the river Ock.[122]

Characteristic also of this early post-Conquest period, but primarily in the later manuscript, is the intervention of the supernatural in disputes.[123] Some men of the bishopric of Lincoln desired to destroy the sluice of Cuddesdon mill, against the wishes of Abbot Ealdred of Abingdon. The men were armed, and led by a royal chaplain, the guardian of the bishopric during an episcopal vacancy. The abbot confronted these men with his own band of laymen and monks, together with the relics of St Vincent the martyr. The abbot swore on the relics to the justice of his case, and then beneath the feet of his enemies the earth began to shake violently and grow soft, so that their horses' feet were caught up. A mighty wind whipped their spears from their hands, and shattered them against one another. Not surprisingly, the morale of the men of the bishopric collapsed and they promised that, if allowed to leave, they would never renew the conflict.[124]

Other disputes proceeded in more sedate ways. As we have seen, cases were processed before the Domesday commissioners, and the shire court of Berkshire heard the royal writs forbidding unjust exactions. The *Chronicle* mentions in this context the help which Adelelm received from two monks, who were brothers, Sacolus and Godric, and also Alfwi, priest of the royal vill of Sutton; these men were blessed with those vital skills of the court, eloquence and memory. In addition Abingdon enjoyed the aid of many other English pleaders or 'causidici'.[125]

A writ was only one form of royal intervention in Abingdon disputes. Persuaded by Robert d'Oilly, Adelelm unwisely gave him land at Tadmarton, but afterwards repented of the deed. Only by the king's decision could the land be regained, and even then Robert's animosity had to be assuaged by an annual payment of £10.[126] Royal involvement stemmed not only from the abbey's initiative. The king being absent in Normandy, Alfsi the bruised reeve complained to the queen about his rough treatment at the hands of Abbot Adelelm. To prevent further proceedings the abbot hurriedly made a payment in compensation for anything he had done to the official, but at the same time obtained a decision from the royal gathering that the abbey should suffer no similar exactions in future, and enjoy perpetual freedom.[127]

Here – at least according to the *Chronicle* – we have a triumph for the abbey and abbot, although the payment of compensation may suggest an element of

---

[121] *CMA* ii, 3.

[122] *CMA* ii, 10–11; see also below, p. 197. Note also Abbot Reginald's use of anathema *CMA* ii, 15–16.

[123] See above, p. 195, on the fate of Froger, which is mentioned in both MSS. See above, n. 57, for dating *CMA* ii, 12–15 to Abbot Reginald's time.

[124] *CMA* i, 491–2. On Vincent's relics at Abingdon, see *CMA* ii, 156.

[125] *CMA* ii, 2.

[126] *CMA* ii, 7–8, see also 12–15, 25, 283.

[127] *CMA* ii, 10–11.

compromise. For the abbacy of Faritius, 1100–1117, the *Chronicle* would provide a tale of almost uninterrupted success. In the early post-Conquest period, fortunes were rather more mixed. Successes included the dispute concerning Blacheman's estates, the clash at Cuddesdon mill, and the tolls exacted from the abbey. Compromises were probably reached over the lands at Lyford held by Walter Giffard and at Tadmarton by Robert d'Oilly. Failures occurred in the loss of lands at Nuneham Courtenay, Winkfield, Fyfield and possibly Kingston Bagpuize.[128]

Why the mixed fortunes of the abbey, compared with the golden age of Faritius? The latter enjoyed particularly close connections with his king and patient, Henry I, whereas Ealdred had a difficult relationship with William I. It may also be that in the Conqueror's reign the extent of royal justice, and the protection it offered churches, was more limited than under Henry.[129] The type of miraculous settlement of land disputes which features in MS Bvi tends to characterise situations in which decisive judicial action was unavailable. As the chronicler states, the problems also reflect the disorder of the country; the depredations Abingdon suffered at the hands of local officials and of influential and favoured laymen are typical of the stories told in monastic chronicles.[130]

What then of the overall fate of Abingdon's estates? Fairly few gifts were made to the abbey in the abbacies of Ealdred and Adelelm, an exception being that of lands in Warwickshire from Turkill of Arden.[131] But if new acquisitions were few, Domesday Book does record an overall rise in the income derived from existing estates by 1086. In Berkshire, this amounted to about 10%, in the less extensive lands in Oxfordshire about 15%. There was also a rise in the value of the very small amount of land Abingdon held in Warwickshire, a fall in Gloucestershire.[132] Let us concentrate on the core of Abingdon estates, those in Berkshire. The values of Abingdon lands rose less than those of the more limited estates of Winchester Cathedral, but did better than those of Salisbury Cathedral, Glastonbury Abbey or Henry de Ferrers. However, the overall rise in value was largely made up of a few big increases in income, for example from £30 to £50 at Cumnor, at £20 to £40 at Barton.[133] In other estates, there was a fall in value after the Conquest, sometimes followed by a partial recovery.[134] The evidence is insufficient to indicate whether the general increase in Abingdon values reflected good management or other factors, perhaps beyond the abbey's control.

If Abingdon maintained its material prosperity across the Conquest, what of its spiritual affairs, especially with the arrival of a monk from Jumièges as abbot? The

---

[128] *Domesday Book* i, fo. 169r adds an unsuccessful claim for South Cerney in Gloucestershire; see also *CMA* i, 462–3.

[129] See the suggestions in J.G.H. Hudson, *Land, Law, and Lordship in Anglo-Norman England*, Oxford 1994.

[130] E.g. *Liber Eliensis*, 188–9, 202, 210–11.

[131] *CMA* ii, 8, *Domesday Book* i, fos 239r, 241v. Note also Leofwine's gift of Nuneham Courtenay which did not survive the fall of Odo of Bayeux, above, p. 195. Domesday, although not the *Chronicle*, presents Abingdon's control over Blacheman's estates at Chilton and Leverton as new acquisitions. For another grant before the death of the Conqueror, see *CMA* ii, 15–16; see also above, p. 190 concerning lands at Shippon.

[132] *Domesday Book* i, fos 166r, 239r, 241v.

[133] *Domesday Book* i, fo. 58v.

[134] See e.g. Beedon, Farnborough, Fawler; *Domesday Book* i, fos 58v, 59r, 59r.

Chronicle gives little evidence on such matters,[135] but according to the *De Abbatibus* Adelelm prohibited the commemoration of Sts Aethelwold and Edward, condemning them as English rustics. One day, sitting at table with his relatives and friends, he smilingly derided Aethelwold and his works, saying that churches of English rustics should be destroyed. After dinner, he went to the privy, but there gave out a wretched cry. His household rushed to him, but found him dead.[136]

Less impassioned supporting evidence for trouble in the monastery comes from a letter of Lanfranc. Although the archbishop condemns the monks, his lenience towards them and his admonition of Adelelm may suggest that the latter too was at fault:

> Archbishop Lanfranc to his beloved son and friend, Abbot Adelelm, greeting and blessing. These monks have come to me as their own accusers, saying that they have sinned gravely against you, and that they are to blame for leaving the monastery. I indeed have expatiated to them at length on their folly, rebuking them in the harsh and bitter words their condition merited.

The monks agreed to amend their lives, and asked that Lanfranc intervene for them.

> In these circumstances I entreat you as a brother (if my entreaties carry any weight with you) that out of love for God and me you forgive them wholeheartedly whatever injury they have done you and whatever offence they have committed against their monastic profession, and that you receive them back into the positions that they held before their offence: show them henceforth such fatherly love that God may show mercy to you.[137]

Clearly Abingdon was not immune from the troubles which afflicted Malmesbury, Glastonbury, Peterborough, and other houses as they came to terms with abbots from abroad.[138]

By the time of Adelelm's death, Abingdon had become freshly integrated into new sets of royal, local, and ecclesiastical relationships. The closeness of ties to the king had been reasserted within years of the Conquest.[139] It was an essential theme of the *Chronicle*, and one to be symbolised by the illustrations of kings in the later manuscript of the text. Connections with its neighbours continued to include both conflict and co-operation, just as it had with their pre-Conquest predecessors. Two of the next three abbot's would, like Adelelm, be former monks of Jumièges, and his immediate successor was the Conqueror's chaplain.[140] Threatened in the time of Abbot Ealdred, the security and prosperity of the abbey of Abingdon were again assured.

---

[135] Note, however, *CMA* ii, 11 on Adelelm's turning late in life to ecclesiastical affairs, including the renovation of the church.
[136] *CMA* ii, 284. The same text relates the despoliation of Abingdon treasure by a Jumièges sacrist and monks following the Conquest; *CMA* ii, 278.
[137] *Lanfranc's Letters*, no. 28.
[138] Williams, 47–8, 133–5.
[139] Note also *CMA* ii, 12 for the visit of the future Henry I.
[140] *The Heads of Religious Houses: England and Wales 940–1216*, edd. D. Knowles *et al.*, Cambridge 1972, 24–5.

APPENDIX

The *Abingdon Chronicle* and the Norman Conquest: a Concordance

This concordance shows the relationship of Stevenson's edition to the two manuscripts of the *Chronicle*. For ease of use, it is arranged according to the headings which Stevenson, like other Rolls Series editors, placed in the margin of his text.

Page	Heading	Printed from	Other manuscript
i 482	Death of King Edward	Bvi fo. 117r	= Cix fos 134v–135r
482	Death of abbot Ordric, and succession of Ealdred	Bvi fo. 117r	similar to Cix fo. 135r[141]
482–3	Political events	Bvi fo. 117r	= Cix fo. 135r
483	Arrival of William the Conqueror	Bvi fo. 117r–v	part = Cix fo. 135r
483–4	Of abbot Ealdfred	Cix fo. 135r	cf. Bvi fo. 118r (= *CMA*, i 489–90)
484–5	Concerning Kingestune and Fifhide	Cix fo. 135r	= Bvi fo. 118r–v (= *CMA*, i 490–1)
485	The church at Abingdon plundered of its ornaments	Cix fo. 135r–v	= Bvi fo. 118v (= *CMA*, i 491)
485	Concerning abbot Aldred	Cix fo. 135v	v. similar to Bvi fo. 119r (= *CMA*, i 493)
485–6	Political incidents which occurred at this period	Cix fo. 135v	v. similar to Bvi fo. 119r (= *CMA*, i 493)
486–7	Unhappy state of England	(i) Cix fo. 135v (to '. . . depredari debeat.')	v. similar to Bvi fo. 119r–v (= *CMA*, i 493–4)

End of Cix Book I (*CMA*, i 487 n. 1)

| | | (ii) Bvi fo. 117v ('Hucusque . . . ambiguum') | not in Cix |

End of Bvi Book II

---

[141] See *CMA* i, 482 n. 3.

Start of Bvi Book III

Page	Heading	Printed from	Other manuscript
488–9	Charter of Cildatun	Bvi fos 117v–118r	not in Cix here[142]
489–90	Death of King Edward the Confessor AD 1066[143]	Bvi fo. 118r	not in Cix, but cf. fos 134v–135r (= *CMA*, i 482–4)
490	Oppressions exercised by William	Bvi fo. 118r	not in Cix, but cf. fo. 135r (= *CMA*, i 484)
490–1	Concerning Kingestun and Fifhide	Bvi fo. 118r–v	= Cix fo. 135r (= *CMA*, i 484–5)
491	The church of Abingdon plundered of its ornaments	Bvi fo. 118v	= Cix fo. 135r–v (= *CMA*, i 485)
491–2	Of the dispute concerning Cuddesdune	Bvi fos 118v–119r	not in Cix
493	Of Abbot Aldred	Bvi fo. 119r	v. similar to Cix fo. 135v (= *CMA*, i 485)
493	Political incidents	Bvi fo. 119r	v. similar to Cix fo. 135v (= *CMA*, i 485–6)
493–4	Unhappy state of England	Bvi fo. 119r–v	v. similar to Cix fo. 135v (= *CMA*, i 486–7) [*end of Cix Book I*: '. . . debeat.'] and Cix fo. 136r [*start of Cix Book II*: 'Ut . . . transmisit'].

Start Bvi 'Book II'

Page	Heading	Printed from	Other manuscript
ii 1	King William's mandate in favour of Abingdon	Bvi fo. 119v	= Cix fo. 136r
1–2	The effect of this writ[144]	Bvi fos 119v–120r	= Cix fo. 136r
2	King William's charter of exemption from tolls and customs[145]	Bvi fo. 120r	= Cix fo. 136r

[142] This charter of Edward the Confessor has appeared earlier in both MSS; C. ix f. 132v; Bvi ff. 110v–111r; = *CMA* i, 455–6.
[143] NB Bvi has already mentioned the death of Confessor at f. 117r.
[144] Order of this and following section reversed in Cix.
[145] Order of this and preceding section reversed in Cix.

Page	*Heading*	*Printed from*	*Other manuscript*
3	Condition of England at this period	Bvi fo. 120r	= Cix fo. 136r
3–4	Abbot Athelelm's arrangements	Bvi fo. 120r–v	= Cix fo. 136r–v
4–6	The military tenants of Abingdon	Bvi fos 120v–121r	not in Cix
6–7	Incidents connected with the military tenants of Abingdon	Bvi fo. 121r	= Cix fo. 136v
7	Incidents connected with Winkfield	Bvi fo. 121r	= Cix fos 136v–137r
7–8	Incidents connected with Tadmarton	Bvi fo. 121r–v	= Cix fo. 137r
8	Incidents connected with Chesterton	Bvi fo. 121v	= Cix fo. 137r
9	Incidents connected with Nuneham	Bvi fo. 121v	= Cix fo. 137r
9–10	William's military expeditions into Scotland and Wales	Bvi fos 121v–122r	= Cix fo. 137r–v
10–11	Incidents connected with Sutton	Bvi fo. 122r	= Cix fo. 137v
11	Troops levied against the arrival of the Danes	Bvi fo. 122r–v	= Cix fo. 137v
11	Death of Abbot Athelelm	Bvi fo. 122v	= Cix fo. 137v
12	Of the visit of Prince Henry to Abingdon	Bvi fo. 122v	= Cix fos 137v–138r
12–15	Of the sickness and recovery of Robert D'Oyley	Bvi fos 122v–123v	not in Cix
15	Of Abbot Rainald	Bvi fo. 123v	= Cix fo. 138r
15–16	Of the Abbot's residence at Westminster	Bvi fo. 123v	= Cix fo. 138r
16	Of the death of William the Conqueror	Bvi fos 123v–124r	= Cix fo. 138r

GISO, BISHOP OF WELLS (1061–88)

Simon Keynes

Giso was born in the town of Saint-Trond, in the diocese of Liège and the arch-diocese of Cologne, in what was then a part of (Lower) Lotharingia, in the king-dom of Germany, and in what would now be described as a place near Maastricht in Belgium. It is not known under what circumstances or for what reasons he came to England; but he did so presumably in the 1040s or 1050s, perhaps as a minor cleric in the entourage of a greater man, or as one in search of a better life, and presently entered into the service of King Edward the Confessor. When Duduc, bishop of Wells, died, on 18 January 1061, Giso was appointed in his place; and he remained in that office for the next twenty-seven years, until his own death in 1088. I carry no brief for Giso, and am not about to argue that he has been unduly neglected, or that he deserves recognition as the personification of everything that is good, or bad, or foreign, in the eleventh-century church, or that he was a pivotal figure in the politics of his age. My sole purpose is to draw together the material which can be brought to bear on the career of a minor player in a major league, in the hope that the subject will prove to be of some intrinsic interest.[1] All that needs to be said by way of advertisement is that Giso was a royal priest who gained preferment from King Edward, who had dealings with King Harold, and who soon came to terms with King William; as such, he is one among the many in England whose activities spanned the Norman Conquest, and whose experiences reveal what different effects the events of 1066 had upon those who lived through them. If Giso stands apart from others, it is because his activities have left their trace in a delightful variety of writs, diplomas, and other forms of written record;[2] to which

[1] I should like to thank Julia Barrow, David Bates, David Dumville, John Hudson, John Insley, Michael Lapidge, Nigel Ramsay and Warwick Rodwell for their guidance in various respects, and Christopher Harper-Bill for his editorial indulgence. I should also like to express my gratitude to Mrs Frances Neale, Archivist, Wells Cathedral Library, for her kindness when I visited Wells in August 1993, and for the trouble taken in supplying photographs of various items from the cathedral archives. In references to charters, S = P.H. Sawyer, *Anglo-Saxon Charters: an Annotated List and Bibliography*, London 1968, and Pelteret = D.A.E. Pelteret, *Catalogue of English Post-Conquest Vernacular Documents*, Woodbridge 1990. KCD = *Codex Diplomaticus Ævi Saxonici*, ed. J.M. Kemble, 6 vols, London 1839–48. Anglo-Norman charters are cited by their number in *Regesta Regum Anglo-Normannorum 1066–1154*, ed. H.W.C. Davis, *et al.*, 4 vols, Oxford 1913–69, and in *Regesta Regum Anglo-Normannorum: the Acta of William I, 1066–1087*, ed. D. Bates, Oxford, forthcoming. In references to papal charters, *PUE = Papsturkunden in England*, ed. W. Holtzmann, 3 vols, Berlin 1930–52. Great Domesday Book (GDB) and Little Domesday Book (LDB) are cited from *Domesday Book*, ed. J. Morris, 35 vols, Chichester 1975–86, in the form *DB [county abbreviation]*, followed by section number.
[2] It is true that there is a 'complete absence' of *acta* for Giso's episcopate, and that the series of episcopal charters for Wells begins with Bishop John of Tours (1088–1122); see *EEA* x: *Bath and Wells 1061–1205*, ed. F.M.R. Ramsey, London 1995, xxxix. It is arguable, however, that some of the

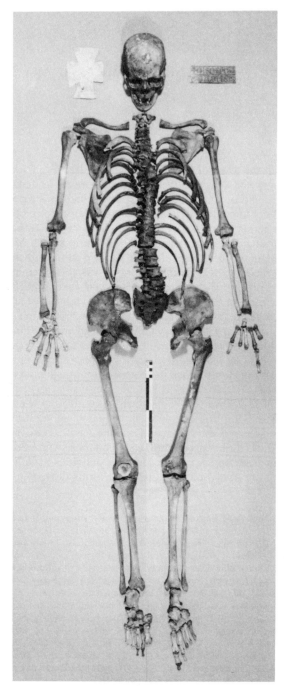

Fig. 1. The bones of Bishop Giso, with mortuary cross and lead name-plate (courtesy of Dr Warwick Rodwell)

one should add the remarkable text generally known as Giso's autobiography, and the service-book regarded in various quarters as the 'Sacramentary of Bishop Giso' (BL Cotton Vitellius A. xviii), which is held to reflect his distinctive liturgical interests. It is also the case that we have the unusual advantage of being able to gaze upon bones which are presumed to be those of Giso himself, reassembled at Wells in 1979 (Fig. 1);[3] so while we could never claim to reconstitute his flesh, at least we have something on which to hang his clothes.

The Lotharingian Connection

Giso owed his opportunities, directly or indirectly, to the closeness of the connections which had developed, throughout the tenth and eleventh centuries, between the kingdom of England and the German empire.[4] It is, however, against the background of Cnut's reign, in particular, that we should view the presence of a significant number of German ecclesiastics at the English royal court in the central decades of the eleventh century.[5] The fact that Cnut had taken 'Lambert' as his baptismal name may signify that he developed a personal devotion to St Lambert of Liège,[6] and might in some way help to account for his seemingly benevolent disposition towards Lotharingian clergy. More significantly, Cnut attended the coronation of the emperor Conrad II (1024–39), at Rome, in 1027, and was pleased to boast to his own people how he had been honoured by the emperor with numerous gifts.[7] The story is told, in a different context, of two decorated books

documents considered in more detail below are episcopal acts of one kind or another. For the diplomatic context, see J. Barrow, 'From the Lease to the Certificate: the Evolution of Episcopal Acta in England and Wales (c.700–c.1250)', *Die Diplomatik der Bischofsurkunde vor 1250*, ed. C. Haidacher and W. Köfler, Innsbruck 1995, 529–42.

3   See W. Rodwell, 'The Anglo-Saxon and Norman Churches at Wells', *Wells Cathedral: a History*, ed. L.S. Colchester, West Compton 1982, reprinted with a supplementary bibliography, 1996, 1–23, at 21; W. Rodwell, *Wells Cathedral: Excavations and Discoveries*, 3rd edn, Wells 1987, 14–18; and W. Rodwell, *et al.*, *The Archaeology of Wells Cathedral: Excavations and Structural Studies 1978–1993*, forthcoming. See also below, n. 81.

4   For recent reviews of the evidence, see R. Deshman, '*Christus rex et magi reges*: Kingship and Christology in Ottonian and Anglo-Saxon Art', *Frühmittelalterliche Studien* x, 1976, 367–405, at 390–404, and V. Ortenberg, *The English Church and the Continent in the Tenth and Eleventh Centuries*, Oxford 1992, 41–94.

5   For Cnut's relations with the German empire, see M.K. Lawson, *Cnut: the Danes in England in the Early Eleventh Century*, London 1993, 108–9 and 136–8, and L. Abrams, 'The Anglo-Saxons and the Christianization of Scandinavia', *Anglo-Saxon England* xxiv, 1995, 213–49, at 227–9.

6   For Cnut's baptismal name, see Adam of Bremen, *Gesta Hammaburgensis ecclesiae pontificum*, bk II, ch. 52, Schol. 37 (*Adam von Bremen, Hamburgische Kirchengeschichte*, ed. B. Schmeidler, Scriptores Rerum Germanicarum, Hannover and Leipzig 1917, 112); F.J. Tschan, *Adam of Bremen: History of the Archbishops of Hamburg-Bremen*, New York 1959, 91, n. *a*. The entry 'Obitus Landberti piissimi regis' which stands against 11 Nov. in the calendar in the Leofric Missal (*The Leofric Missal*, ed. W.E. Warren, Oxford 1883, li) clearly relates to Cnut, as noted by J. Gerchow, 'Prayers for King Cnut: the Liturgical Commemoration of a Conqueror', *England in the Eleventh Century*, ed. C. Hicks, Stamford 1992, 219–38, at 235–6; it is interesting that Cnut should have been known by this name in the circle of the 'Lotharingian' Leofric.

7   See Cnut's second letter to the English people (1027), ch. 5 (*The Chronicle of John of Worcester* ii: *The Annals from 450 to 1066*, ed. R.R. Darlington and P. McGurk, Oxford 1995, 512–18, at 514); see also *The Liber Vitae of the New Minster and Hyde Abbey, Winchester*, ed. S. Keynes, Early English Manuscripts in Facsimile 26, Copenhagen 1996, 36–7. The manuscript which contains the

which had been produced under the auspices of a certain Earnwig at Peterborough, probably c.1020, of which one (a sacramentary) was given to King Cnut and of which the other (a psalter) was given to Queen Emma.[8] Sooner or later the king had occasion to send both of the books to Cologne, 'so that he might place the grace of his remembrance among those people', but in 1054–5 it so happened that a person in Cologne presented them as a parting gift to Ealdred, bishop of Worcester, who gave them in turn to his protégé Wulfstan (bishop of Worcester, 1062–95).[9] Sadly, neither the sacramentary nor the psalter survives; but the story is given some substance by the fact that a gospel-book produced probably at Christ Church, Canterbury, c.1000, appears to have found its way from England to Cologne during the course of the eleventh century, perhaps during the reign of Cnut or perhaps during the reign of Edward the Confessor.[10] The development of a special relationship between Cnut and the German emperor found further expression in the pact of friendship made between them at Bamberg on 18 May 1035,[11] which led in turn to the marriage, in June 1036, between Cnut's daughter Gunnhild and Conrad's son Henry,[12] soon to come into his own as Henry III (1039–56). In July or August 1036, a churchman at Conrad's court informed a bishop elsewhere in the German empire that envoys from England had just reached Gunnhild (Chunegunda), telling her of the plotting against her brother Harthacnut;[13] and although Gunnhild died on 18 July 1038,[14] there is reason to believe that relations between the English and German establishments continued to develop thereafter. The emperor Henry III marked the accession of Edward the Confessor in 1042 by sending ambassadors, bearing gifts.[15] In 1054 Edward himself sent Ealdred, bishop of Worcester since 1046 (and formerly a monk of the Old Minster, Winchester), to Cologne, 'on the

---

Heliand in Low German (BL MS Cotton Calig. A vii), written in England in the late tenth century, was for some reason described by Cotton's librarian, Richard James, as 'Liber quondam Canuti Regis'; see N.R. Ker, *Catalogue of Manuscripts Containing Anglo-Saxon*, Oxford 1957, no. 137.

[8] *The Vita Wulfstani of William of Malmesbury*, ed. R.R. Darlington, Camden Society 3rd ser. 40, London 1928, 5; J.H.F. Peile, *William of Malmesbury's Life of St Wulstan, Bishop of Worcester*, Oxford 1934, 7. The story is discussed to good effect by T.A. Heslop, 'The Production of *de luxe* Manuscripts and the Patronage of King Cnut and Queen Emma', *Anglo-Saxon England* xix, 1990, 151–95, at 159–62.

[9] *Vita Wulfstani*, ed. Darlington, 16; Peile, *Life of St Wulstan*, 23.

[10] New York, Pierpont Morgan Library, MS M. 869 (Arenberg Gospels), known to have been at the church of St Severin, Cologne, by the early twelfth century. See E. Temple, *Anglo-Saxon Manuscripts 900–1066*, London 1976, no. 56, and *The Golden Age of Anglo-Saxon Art 966–1066*, ed. J. Backhouse, *et al.*, London 1984, no. 47.

[11] For references, see *Die Regesten des Kaiserreiches unter Konrad II., 1024–1039*, ed. H. Appelt, Regesta Imperii 3.1.1, Graz 1951, 109 (no. 225c).

[12] Wipo, *Gesta Chuonradi II. imperatoris*, ch. 35 (*Die Werke Wipos*, ed. H. Bresslau, Scriptores Rerum Germanicarum, Hannover and Leipzig 1915, 54); Adam of Bremen, *Gesta Hammaburgensis ecclesiae pontificum*, bk II, ch. 56 (ed. Schmeidler, 116–17; Tschan, *Adam of Bremen*, 93); and *Die Regesten des Kaiserreiches unter Konrad II.*, ed. Appelt, 116 (no. 238c). According to the monk Hemming, Gunnhild was accompanied 'ad Saxoniam' by Brihtheah, bishop of Worcester (1033–8), and by a certain Hearlewine (*Hemingi Chartularium Ecclesiæ Wigorniensis*, ed. T. Hearne, 2 vols, Oxford 1723, i. 267).

[13] For this letter, see W.H. Stevenson, 'An Alleged Son of King Harold Harefoot', *EHR* xxviii, 1913, 112–17, at 115–16.

[14] Wipo, *Gesta Chuonradi II. imperatoris*, ch. 37 (ed. Bresslau, 57). Gunnhild's death in 1038 is also registered in *Annales Sangallenses Maiores* (*ibid.*, 94), *Chronicon Herimanni Augiensis* (*ibid.*, 100), and *Chronicon Suevicum Universale* (*ibid.*, 102), from the last of which it emerges that she was known as 'Elifdrud'.

king's business', charged (it seems) with the task of making necessary arrangements for the return of the ætheling Edward the Exile from Hungary to England.[16] In the event, Ealdred stayed overseas for nearly a year, as the guest of the emperor Henry III and of Heriman, archbishop of Cologne, doubtless taking advantage of the opportunity to deepen his experience of foreign ways in matters of both church and state.[17] It is not likely that Ealdred would have returned to England empty-handed, and one suspects that the experience he gained on this expedition, as on his other journeys abroad, influenced the manner in which he conducted his activities in the 1060s, at Beverley, Southwell, and York. We may also imagine, perhaps, that so well-connected a prelate as Ealdred would have attracted a following whereveɪ he went, and that when he returned to England in 1055, as on other occasions, he would have been accompanied by persons hoping to gain advancement though his influence and support. It is all the more striking, against this background, that an English chronicler, taking a commendable interest in continental affairs, should have erred in reporting the death of 'the emperor Cona', in the annal for 1056;[18] for while it was Henry, of course, who had died in that year, the mistake suggests that where German emperors were concerned, the chronicler's thoughts remained with Conrad.[19]

It was doubtless in connection with contacts of this kind that churchmen came from Germany to the royal court in England, in a process which would soon gather a momentum of its own. A short register of the persons concerned may help to give an impression of their separate careers, and to convey a sense at the same time of their collective identity.[20] WYTHMAN, described simply as 'Teutonicus natione', was appointed abbot of Ramsey in 1016, but proved unable to control his monks. He resigned four years later, and set out on pilgrimage to Jerusalem; yet he returned to Ramsey, and passed the rest of his life there as a hermit.[21] DUDUC,[22] described by Giso as a 'Saxon' and by John of Worcester as a Lotharingian,[23] was

---

[15] *Vita Ædwardi regis*, bk I, ch. 1 (*The Life of King Edward who Rests at Westminster, attributed to a Monk of Saint-Bertin*, ed. F. Barlow, 2nd edn, Oxford 1992, 16).

[16] ASC, MSS CD, *s.a.* 1054; John of Worcester, *s.a.* 1054 (ed. Darlington and McGurk, 574–6).

[17] For Bishop Ealdred, see F. Barlow, *The English Church 1000–1066*, 2nd edn, London 1979, 86–90; M. Lapidge, 'Ealdred of York and MS Cotton Vitellius E. XII' (1983), reptd in his *Anglo-Latin Literature 900–1066*, London 1993, 453–67; and V. King, 'Ealdred, Archbishop of York: the Worcester Years', *ANS* xviii, 1996, 123–37.

[18] ASC, MSS CD, *s.a.* 1056.

[19] Cf. *Hemingi Chartularium*, ed. Hearne, i, 267.

[20] For Lotharingians in England, see E.A. Freeman, *The History of the Norman Conquest of England: its Causes and its Results*, 6 vols, Oxford 1867–79, ii, 2nd edn, 1870, 79–81 and 582–7 (Note L: 'The Lotharingian Churchmen under Eadward'); J. de Sturler, *Les relations politiques et les échanges commerciaux entre la duché de Brabant et l'Angleterre au moyen âge*, Paris 1936, 72–3; Barlow, *English Church 1000–1066*, 16–17, 46, and 82–4; Ortenberg, *English Church and the Continent*, 57–9; and esp. J. Barrow, 'English Cathedral Communities and Reform in the Late Tenth and the Eleventh Centuries', *Anglo-Norman Durham*, ed. D. Rollason, M. Harvey and M. Prestwich, Woodbridge 1994, 25–39, at 33–4. For the more unusual names, see E. Förstemann, *Altdeutsches namenbuch*, 2 vols in 3, Bonn 1900–16, i, cols 413 (Duduc), 644 (Giso); and T. Forssner, *Continental-Germanic Personal Names in England in Old and Middle English Times*, Uppsala 1916, 61–2 (Duduc), 117 (Giso), 149–50 (Hereman), 209 (Regenbald).

[21] *Liber benefactorum* of Ramsey abbey, in *Chronicon Abbatiæ Rameseiensis*, ed. W.D. Macray, RS LXXXIII, 1886, 120–5 and 160–1; see also Barlow, *English Church 1000–1066*, 103, n. 1.

[22] For Duduc, see Barlow, *English Church 1000–1066*, 75 and 224.

[23] John of Worcester, *s.a.* 1060 (ed. Darlington and McGurk, 586).

accorded first place among the royal priests at the court of King Cnut, in a charter dated 1033.[24] It cannot have been long afterwards that he was appointed to succeed Brihtwig Merehwit as bishop of Wells, since he was consecrated bishop on 11 June, probably in the same year.[25] He features regularly, as a witness, in the charters of King Edward,[26] and seems to have been the leader of the delegation sent by the king to attend the synod convened at Rheims in 1049;[27] he died, as already remarked, on 18 January 1061. HERMAN,[28] described (again by John of Worcester) as a native of Lotharingia,[29] would appear to have served, in the early 1040s, first in the household of Harthacnut and then in the household of Edward the Confessor, prior to his appointment as bishop of Ramsbury in 1045.[30] He was a leader (with Ealdred, bishop of Worcester) of the delegation sent by King Edward to attend the synod convened at Rome in 1050;[31] soon afterwards, he tried to move his see to Malmesbury abbey, but on failing to achieve his purpose he left the country, and became a monk at Saint-Bertin, where he remained for three years (1055–8).[32] He was back in England by 1058, initially, it seems, as bishop of Ramsbury;[33] but after the death of Ælfwold, bishop of Sherborne, in the early 1060s,[34] Herman was

---

[24] S 969 (*Charters of Sherborne*, ed. M.A. O'Donovan, Anglo-Saxon Charters 3, Oxford 1988, no. 20). The evidence of witness-lists is best displayed in tabular form, so that a series of attestations in the name of one person can be judged on its own terms and as part of a larger pattern (for example, in relation to the appearances or non-appearances of other persons over the same period), and so that the evidence of one charter can be judged at a glance in relation to the evidence of charters preserved in other archives. The material for all categories of witnesses is assembled in S. Keynes, *An Atlas of Attestations in Anglo-Saxon Charters c.670–1066* (1993), copies of which are available, in experimental (pre-publication) form, from the compiler. For the attestations of royal priests in the eleventh century, see *Atlas of Attestations*, Table LXVIII.

[25] Brihtwig Merehwit died in 1033 (ASC, MS E, *s.a.* 1033), on 12 April (below, Appendix IV, §1)

[26] For the attestations of the bishops during the reign of Edward the Confessor, see *Atlas of Attestations*, Table LXXII.

[27] ASC, MS E, *s.a.* 1046 (for 1049): 'And King Edward sent there Bishop Duduc and Wulfric, abbot of St Augustine's, and Abbot Ælfwine [of Ramsey], so that they might inform the king of whatever was there decided in the interests of Christendom.' Cf. ASC, MS D, *s.a.* 1049. According to the *Liber benefactorum* of Ramsey abbey (ed. Macray, 170–1), an account of the proceedings at Rheims was drawn up, on the king's instructions, in English, and a copy placed in the king's treasury under the care of Hugelin, *cubicularius*. See Barlow, *English Church 1000–1066*, 301–2, and S. Keynes, 'Regenbald the Chancellor (*sic*)', *ANS* x, 1988, 185–222, at 190, n. 36.

[28] For Herman, see Barlow, *English Church 1000–1066*, 82, 182, 220–1, and 224; and J. Barrow, for the *New DNB* (forthcoming).

[29] John of Worcester, *s.a.* 1045 (ed. Darlington and McGurk, 542).

[30] Herman's appearance among the witnesses to Harthacnut's confirmation of S 982 militates against the supposition that he accompanied Edward from Normandy to England in 1041; cf. *Life of King Edward*, ed. Barlow, xlviii–xlix. Herman otherwise attests, as priest, S 993 (Harthacnut, 1042) and S 999 (Edward, 1043).

[31] ASC, MS C, *s.a.* 1049–50; MS D, *s.a.* 1050; MS E, *s.a.* 1047 (for 1050); see also Barlow, *English Church 1000–1066*, 301–2.

[32] John of Worcester, *s.a.* 1055 (ed. Darlington and McGurk, 578); and William of Malmesbury, *Gesta Pontificum Anglorum* II. 83 (*Willelmi Malmesbiriensis Monachi De Gestis Pontificum Anglorum Libri Quinque*, ed. N.E.S.A. Hamilton, London 1870, 182–3) and V. 264 (*ibid.*, 420).

[33] In Herman's absence, the bishopric of Wiltshire (Ramsbury) had been assigned to Ealdred, bishop of Worcester; and it was when Ealdred set out on his expedition to Jerusalem, in 1058, that the bishopric was restored to Herman. See John of Worcester, *s.a.* 1058 (ed. Darlington and McGurk, 584).

[34] Cf. *Life of King Edward*, ed. Barlow, xlviii–xlix and 133–5 (on Herman and Goscelin of Saint-Bertin). William of Malmesbury (*Gesta Pontificum Anglorum* II. 83, ed. Hamilton, 183)

seemingly permitted to transfer his see from Ramsbury to Sherborne. In 1075 he moved again, from Sherborne to Old Sarum; and it was as 'bishop of Berkshire and Wiltshire and Dorset' that he died, on 20 February (or 21 March) 1078.[35] **LEOFRIC**,[36] who was apparently of 'British' (perhaps Cornish) origin,[37] is said to have been 'brought up and educated among Lotharingians',[38] and presently became Edward the Confessor's 'chancellor';[39] he was appointed bishop of Devon and Cornwall in 1046, and, upon re-establishing his see at Exeter, in 1050, ejected the nuns from St Peter's and introduced canons living according to Lotharingian customs.[40] He died on 10 February 1072. **REGENBALD**,[41] who is presumed from his name to have been of German origin,[42] is known to have been at Edward's court by 1050, and sooner or later was accorded what amounted to episcopal status. It would appear that he held office as the king's chancellor in the early 1060s, and one might suppose that this office would have given him some responsibility for recruitment of clerics to serve in the royal household, and even some influence in the matter of episcopal appointments. He remained in office for a short while after the Norman Conquest, and was still flourishing, at Cirencester, in 1086. **WALTER**,[43]

---

remarks that Herman's return to England (in 1058) was occasioned by news of Bishop Ælfwold's death; but this may be no more than an assumption on William's part, and it seems more likely that Herman's return was actually connected with Bishop Ealdred's imminent departure for Jerusalem (see previous note). A Bishop Ælfwold, presumably of Sherborne, attested S 1027 (dated 1059), S 1036 (dated 1062), and S 1026 (? early 1060s); see also Keynes, 'Regenbald the Chancellor', 202, n. 102.

35 For the day of Herman's death, see further below, 253.

36 For Leofric, see *Leofric Missal*, ed. Warren, xix–xxvi; Barlow, *English Church 1000–1066*, 83–4; F. Barlow, 'Leofric and his Times', in F. Barlow, *et al.*, *Leofric of Exeter*, Exeter 1972, 1–16; D. Blake, 'The Development of the Chapter of the Diocese of Exeter, 1051–1161', *Journal of Medieval History* viii, 1982, 1–11; P.W. Conner, *Anglo-Saxon Exeter: A Tenth-Century Cultural History*, Woodbridge 1993; *EEA* xi: *Exeter 1046–1184*, ed. F. Barlow, Oxford 1996, xxxii; and R. Gameson, 'The Origin of the Exeter Book of Old English Poetry', *Anglo-Saxon England* xxv, 1996, 135–85. See also the texts cited below, n. 116.

37 John of Worcester, *s.a.* 1046 (ed. Darlington and McGurk, 542). Leofric is said to have had a brother, Ordmær, to whom he entrusted the advowson of his Cornish estates; see *Exeter 1046–1184*, ed. Barlow, 2.

38 William of Malmesbury, *Gesta Pontificum* II. 94: 'apud Lotharingos altus et doctus' (ed. Hamilton, 201).

39 John of Worcester, *s.a.* 1046 (ed. Darlington and McGurk, 542).

40 William of Malmesbury, *Gesta Pontificum* II. 94 (ed. Hamilton, 201). A fragment of a manuscript of the Romano-German Pontifical, written in Germany in the eleventh century (BL MS Cotton Vitell. E xii, fos 116–52), was supplemented in the second half of the century by a group of texts which appear to have originated in the circle of Archbishop Ealdred, but which were written by an 'Exeter' scribe (fos 153–60); see Lapidge, 'Ealdred of York', 465–6. If the German manuscript was brought to England from Cologne, by Bishop Ealdred, the supplementary material would seem to have been added by a scribe in Ealdred's circle who subsequently moved with the book to Exeter; alternatively, the German manuscript may have been acquired by Leofric, and the supplementary material acquired on Leofric's behalf from Worcester or York.

41 For Regenbald, see Keynes, 'Regenbald the Chancellor'.

42 He has been described as 'the Lotharingian Regenbald' (*EEA* vii: *Hereford 1079–1234*, ed. J. Barrow, Oxford 1993, xxxii), which is not an unreasonable assumption.

43 For Walter, see Barlow, *English Church 1000–1066*, 83 and 218; *Hereford 1079–1234*, ed. Barlow, xxxii–iii; J. Barrow, 'A Lotharingian in Hereford: Bishop Robert's Reorganisation of the Church of Hereford 1079–1095', *Medieval Art, Architecture and Archaeology at Hereford*, ed. D. Whitehead, British Archaeological Association Conference Transactions xv, 1995, 29–49, at 30–1; and J. Barrow, for the *New DNB* (forthcoming).

described (yet again by John of Worcester) as 'Walter of Lotharingia', served as chaplain to Queen Edith, and became bishop of Hereford in 1060.[44] He met his end in 1079, when trying to rape a seamstress, who killed him with a pair of scissors.[45] GISO,[46] also said by John to be from Lotharingia, makes no appearance as a priest in Edward's charters, but was clearly serving in that capacity when he was appointed bishop of Wells, in 1061.[47] He died in 1088. ROBERT 'of Lorraine',[48] who would appear to have served as a priest at the Confessor's court from about 1050, succeeded Walter as bishop of Hereford in 1079, which office he held until his death on 26 June 1095. According to William of Malmesbury, Robert was responsible for bringing a copy of the world chronicle of Marianus Scotus to England, presumably c.1080; he was also credited with the introduction of the abacus to England, and was the author of a tract on computus, well-known for its passing reference to the Domesday survey.[49] Besides these men, there were others, like Regenbald, who did not become bishops. ALBERT 'of Lorraine' is known to held land at Chalgrave, in Bedfordshire, during the reign of Edward the Confessor, though it is not clear whether or not he was at this stage a royal priest; but he certainly prospered, as a priest, during the reign of William the Conqueror, and is found, for example, on the royal estate at Windsor.[50] Another of the Confessor's priests, called BERNARD, is presumed from his name to have been of German origin, and had interests in Huntingdon.[51] Finally, ADALARD, described as 'a native of Liège who had been a student at Utrecht', was brought by Earl Harold to his church at Waltham in Essex, where he was encouraged to establish 'the rules, ordinances, and customs, both ecclesiastical and secular, of the churches in which he himself had been educated'.[52] Two or three Lotharingians in eleventh-century

---

[44] John of Worcester, *s.a.* 1060 (ed. Darlington and McGurk, 586).

[45] William of Malmesbury, *Gesta Pontificum* IV. 163 (ed. Hamilton, 300).

[46] For Giso, see E.A. Freeman, *History of the Cathedral Church of Wells*, London 1870, 30–4; William Hunt, in the *Dictionary of National Biography* XXI, London 1890, 399–400; J. Armitage Robinson, *The Saxon Bishops of Wells*, British Academy Supplemental Papers 4, London 1918, 51–2; F.E. Harmer, *Anglo-Saxon Writs*, Manchester 1952, 270–86 and 561; Barlow, *English Church 1000–1066*, esp. 82–3 and 224; E.U. Crosby, *Bishop and Chapter in Twelfth-Century England: a Study of the* Mensa Episcopalis, Cambridge 1994, 48–52; *Bath and Wells 1061–1205*, ed. Ramsey, xxi; and J. Barrow, for the *New DNB* (forthcoming).

[47] See further below, 227.

[48] For Robert, see F. Barlow, *The English Church 1066–1154*, London 1979, 63–4 and 258–9; *Hereford 1079–1234*, ed. Barrow, xxxiii–iv; Barrow, 'A Lotharingian in Hereford'; and J. Barrow, for the *New DNB* (forthcoming).

[49] See *Chronicle of John of Worcester*, ed. Darlington and McGurk, xix, with n. 6, and *EHD* ii, no. 198.

[50] J.H. Round, 'Ingelric the Priest and Albert of Lotharingia', *The Commune of London*, London 1899, 28–38, at 36–8; and Barlow, *English Church 1000–1066*, 157. For the estate at Chalgrave, see *DB Beds.* 49.1; he also had interests in Middlesex (*DB Mx* 7.1). For Windsor, see *DB Berks.* 1.1. In William's reign (if not in Harold's), Albert acquired further property in Bedfordshire (*DB Beds.* 49.2–3), and estates at Addington, Surrey (*DB Sur.* 34.1), at Upleadon, Heref. (*DB Heref.* 18.1), and at Newington, Kent (*DB Kent* 13.1); he also held land from the king at Upton, Warwicks. (*DB War.* 1.8), and three churches in Rutland (*DB Rut.* R21), which were given by King William I or II to Westminster abbey (*Regesta* i, no. 381).

[51] GDB 208r (*DB Hunts.* D1). Bernard *capellanus* occurs among the priests who attested King William's charter, dated 1068, in favour of Ingelric and the church of St Martin-le-Grand, London (*Regesta* i, no. 22; *Acta of William I*, ed. Bates, no. 181).

[52] *The Waltham Chronicle: an Account of the Discovery of Our Holy Cross at Montacute and its Conveyance to Waltham*, ed. L. Watkiss and M. Chibnall, Oxford 1994, 26–8, 36, 58 and 66; see

England might amount to no more than a coincidence; five or ten begins to look like a conspiracy.

It would be interesting to establish direct links between any of these men and particular churches in the kingdom of Germany, and one hopes that further evidence may yet be uncovered.[53] It remains unclear, however, what it was that attracted the Lotharingians to England, and whether they would have felt part of a distinctive group. At least we may imagine that they brought with them the benefits of a Lotharingian education,[54] and familiarity with imperial ways,[55] as well as the basic tools of their trade.[56] The majority of the Lotharingians became neighbours in the west:[57] Duduc at Wells (from 1033 to 1061); Herman initially at Ramsbury (in 1045), and later at Sherborne (in the 1060s); Leofric initially at Crediton (in 1046), and at Exeter from 1050; Walter at Hereford (in 1060); Giso at Wells (in 1061);

---

also *ibid.*, xlvii. Freeman's stirring discussion of the foundation of Waltham (*Norman Conquest* ii, 438–45) is brilliantly suffused with all of his familiar prejudices; A. Williams, *The English and the Norman Conquest*, Woodbridge 1995, 129–30, is more carefully measured.

[53] For an impression of the range of diplomatic and liturgical sources which would have to be examined in this connection, see J.-L. Kupper, *Liège et l'église impériale XIe–XIIe siècles*, Bibliothèque de la Faculté de Philosophie et Lettres de l'Université de Liège 228, Paris 1981, 21–3 (charters and necrologies, etc., in manuscript), 30–6 (editions of charters, etc.) and 36–7 (editions of necrologies, etc.). The obit (26 June) of Robert, bishop of Hereford, was registered in the necrology of the cathedral church of Saint-Lambert, Liège: see A. Marchandisse, *L'Obituaire de la cathédrale Saint-Lambert de Liège (XIe–XVe siècles)*, Académie Royale de Belgique, Commission Royale d'Histoire, Brussels 1991, 89; H. Wellmer, 'Le nécrologe de la cathédrale Saint-Lambert de Liège', *Le moyen âge*, 4th ser. xxiii, 1968, 421–38, at 437, n. 48; and A. Marchandisse, 'L'obituaire de la cathédrale Saint-Lambert à Liège', *Le moyen âge*, 5th ser. iv, 1990, 411–20.

[54] C. Renardy, 'Les écoles liégeoises du IXe au XIIe siècle: grandes lignes de leur évolution', *Revue belge de philologie et d'histoire* lvii, 1979, 309–28; A. Peden, 'Science and Philosophy in Wales at the Time of the Norman Conquest: a Macrobius Manuscript from Llanbadarn', *Cambridge Medieval Celtic Studies* ii, 1981, 21–45, at 25–6; A. Joris, 'Espagne et Lotharingie autour de l'an mil', *Le moyen âge*, 5th ser. ii, 1988, 5–19, at 12–14; *Hereford 1079–1234*, ed. Barrow, xxxi–ii; Barrow, 'A Lotharingian in Hereford', 29 and 31–2; and *Bath and Wells 1061–1205*, ed. Ramsey, lxix–lxx.

[55] For the movement of personnel in the eleventh century between the imperial court (and chapel) and the cathedral church of Saint-Lambert, Liège, see Kupper, *Liège et l'église impériale XIe–XIIe siècles*, 344–5. See also T. Reuter, *Germany in the Early Middle Ages c.800–1056*, London 1991, 238–9, and B. Guillemain, 'Les origines des évêques en France aux XIe et XIIe siècles', *Le istituzioni ecclesiastiche della 'societas christiana' dei secoli XI–XII: Papato, Cardinalato ed Episcopato*, Miscellanea del Centro di Studi Medioevali 7, Milan 1974, 374–402, with discussion, 403–7, at 404–5.

[56] The influx of Lotharingian priests into England, and other kinds of contact between England and the German empire, would naturally find reflection in the importation of manuscripts from Germany. Striking examples are the fragment of the Romano-German Pontifical in BL MS Cotton Vitell. E xii, fos 116–52, which most probably came from Cologne (Lapidge, 'Ealdred of York', 454 and 462–5); extracts from the Romano-German Pontifical in BL MS Cotton Tib. C i, to be associated, perhaps, with Bishop Herman (N.R. Ker, 'Three Old English Texts in a Salisbury Pontifical, Cotton Tiberius C I', *The Anglo-Saxons*, ed. P. Clemoes, Cambridge 1959, 262–79, at 263); the exemplar of CCCC 163, a mid-eleventh-century English manuscript of the Romano-German Pontifical (Lapidge, 'Ealdred of York', 463); and the exemplar of the 'Cambridge Songs' (*ibid.*, 464). For the Romano-German Pontifical, see also J.L. Nelson and R.W. Pfaff, 'Pontificals and Benedictionals', *The Liturgical Books of Anglo-Saxon England*, ed. R.W. Pfaff, Old English Newsletter Subsidia 23, Kalamazoo, MI, 1995, 87–98, at 96–8. Barlow, *English Church 1066–1154*, 145, remarks, however, on the failure of the 'Lotharingian' bishops to bring in a copy of the *Decretum* of Burchard of Worms.

[57] As noted by Barlow, *English Church 1000–1066*, 77.

Regenbald at Cirencester, before and after the Conquest; and Robert at Hereford from 1079. It is also of interest that so much of the information about the 'Lotharingian' bishops should come from the Worcester chronicle; and since Robert 'of Lorraine', bishop of Hereford, was a close friend of Wulfstan II, bishop of Worcester, it would not be difficult, if pressed, to imagine how information and gossip about the Lotharingians might have passed down the line to Florence and John.[58] Yet what is so obviously striking about the Lotharingian priests is that their path of advancement led from their training in Germany to an English bishopric, via service in the royal household. Interestingly, it was in the reigns of Cnut, Harthacnut and Edward the Confessor that the king's priests came to be included, for the first time since the early tenth century, among the witnesses to royal charters, as if the priests, as a group, had gained for themselves a kind of recognition which for some reason they had not enjoyed before.[59] It is a matter of further interest, under these circumstances, that it was the seal of one or other of the German emperors, in the first half of the eleventh century, which served (directly or indirectly) as the model for the seals of Cnut (so it would seem) and Edward the Confessor.[60] And of course it is scarcely surprising that 'German' influence in eleventh-century England should find expression in many other ways, ranging from the introduction of new liturgical forms to the dissemination of 'foreign' cults, a revived enthusiasm for the regulation of the canonical life, and the development of new opportunities for continental craftsmen to practise their respective skills.

The question remains whether we should give any of this a political spin. The German or more specifically Lotharingian priests in England during the Confessor's reign would have had to compete for preferment with native Englishmen, and with Normans; and if the Normans, as a group, owed their advancement to friendship with the king himself, it may be that we should regard the proliferation of Lotharingians as a reflection, in some sense, of competing interests rooted more deeply in the Anglo-Danish past.[61] Freeman regarded the 'German appointments' as 'clearly parts of a system', finding in them 'an attempt of Godwine and the patriotic party to counterbalance the merely French tendencies of Eadward himself', and holding on racial, linguistic, and cultural grounds that a Lotharingian 'would be more acceptable to Godwine and to England than a mere Frenchman'. From Freeman's decidedly Eurosceptic point of view, the results of the policy were not, however, wholly satisfactory, for while he had no reason to believe that any of the Lotharingian prelates were actually traitors to England, he regretted that they did not, as a class, 'offer the same steady resistance to French influences as the men

---

[58] One should add, in this connection, that Wulfstan's successor Samson, bishop of Worcester (1096–1112), had been sent by his brother Odo, bishop of Bayeux, to be educated at Liège: see Orderic iv, 118. The 'Lotharingian' details in the Worcester chronicle are perhaps more likely to have been contributed by Florence, who was active in the late eleventh and early twelfth centuries, than by John, who was active in the 1120s; cf. my review of *Chronicle of John of Worcester*, ed. Darlington and McGurk, in *Speculum* lxxii, 1997.

[59] For royal priests and clerks in the eleventh century, see Barlow, *English Church 1000–1066*, 119–25, 130–7 and 156–8; see also Keynes, 'Regenbald the Chancellor', 187–95, and Keynes, *Atlas of Attestations*, Table LXVIII.

[60] Harmer, *Anglo-Saxon Writs*, 94–101; see also Keynes, 'Regenbald the Chancellor', 216–17.

[61] Cf. F.M. Stenton, *Anglo-Saxon England*, 3rd edn, Oxford 1971, 463–4; Barlow, *English Church 1000–1066*, 109, n. 6 (with reference to Freeman's view that Edward advanced Normans while the house of Godwine favoured Lotharingians).

who had been born in the land'.[62] Freeman's notion that Harold and the secular clergy stood for 'steady and clear-sighted patriotism' against the supposedly 'monkish' party of Edward and his Norman friends was an extension of the same argument.[63] Of course, the factions and tensions which animated the course of domestic politics during the reign of Edward the Confessor are best not reduced to such simplistic terms; but even so, there were doubtless some men at Edward's court who thought in this way, and one can see where Freeman's notions are coming from. The point is that when Giso arrived in England, and entered into service as a priest in the royal household, he would have found himself in a potentially 'interesting' situation – and it is far from clear where his loyalties would lie.

The Autobiography of Bishop Giso

The most valuable source of information on the career of Bishop Giso is the brief text which purports to have been written by Giso himself, and which is known, somewhat loosely, as his autobiography. The text survives only in the form in which it is embedded in an anonymous historical tract, itself accorded no title in the single manuscript in which it is found, but dignified by its first editor as the *Historiola de Primordiis Episcopatus Somersetensis*.[64] It is necessary, for all the obvious reasons, to form at least some impression of the nature of the *Historiola*, and of the circumstances in which it was written; certainly, it would be hazardous to make any use of Giso's autobiography without pausing to examine the work in which it is embedded. The *Historiola* is preserved in a fourteenth-century register of the cathedral priory of Bath,[65] yet all the internal indications are that its author was a canon of Wells. One should add that it was used, at Wells, by the compilers of the *Historia Minor* and the *Historia Major*, seemingly produced in the late fourteenth and the early fifteenth century respectively.[66] It is not so clear precisely when the *Historiola* was produced. Since the narrative is brought to an abrupt end with the consecration of Reginald as bishop of Bath, on 23 June 1174, it might well be supposed that the *Historiola* was compiled some time between c.1175 and

---

[62] Freeman, *Norman Conquest* ii, 79–81.

[63] Freeman, *Norman Conquest* ii, 442–3; cf. W. Stubbs, *The Constitutional History of England* i, 6th edn, Oxford 1897, 264–5.

[64] *Ecclesiastical Documents*, ed. J. Hunter, Camden Society 8, London 1840, 3–41.

[65] London, Lincoln's Inn, MS 185, fos 96r–99r. See G.R.C. Davis, *Medieval Cartularies of Great Britain: a Short Catalogue*, London 1958, no. 25, and *Two Chartularies of the Priory of St Peter at Bath*, ed. W. Hunt, Somerset Record Society 7, 1893, pt II, 105 (no. 532). I am grateful to Guy Holborn, Librarian, Lincoln's Inn Library, for his good offices when I examined the manuscript in November 1991, and for supplying printouts from a microfilm.

[66] These texts are printed in J.A. Robinson, 'The Historia Minor and the Historia Major, from the Wells Liber Albus II', in T.F. Palmer, *Collectanea i: a Collection of Documents from Various Sources*, Somerset Record Society 39, 1924, 48–71. The *Historia Minor* (printed *ibid.*, 54–6) depends initially on the *Historiola*, and extends its coverage thereafter into the second half of the fourteenth century. The *Historia Major* (*ibid.*, 57–71) is the more ambitious production, drawing in part on the works of William of Malmesbury and in part on the *Historiola*, but extending its coverage into the first quarter of the fifteenth century. Both works would be of some help in establishing the text of the *Historiola*.

c.1190,[67] perhaps sooner rather than later within that period. This was the view taken by Joseph Hunter, who named, edited and translated the *Historiola* in 1840;[68] and it is also the view adopted in turn by the majority of modern commentators, from J. Armitage Robinson (Dean of Wells) to Frances Ramsey (in her capacity as editor of the episcopal acta for Wells, 1061–1205).[69] Antonia Gransden has, however, suggested that the *Historiola* was produced in the early thirteenth century, by a compiler who used not only Giso's autobiography but also a separate account of the episcopate of Bishop Robert (1136–66), presumably written in the mid-1170s.[70] The matter would have to be pursued against the background of the complex relationships between the churches of Wells, Bath and Glastonbury in the late eleventh, twelfth, and early thirteenth centuries, which lies some way beyond the scope of this paper and a long way beyond the reach of someone who professes to be a historian of Anglo-Saxon England. It must suffice, therefore, to glide serenely over the surface, in the manner of a fenland skater, with one's hands held loosely behind one's back.

The history of the church of Wells would have afforded interested parties ample opportunity for the development and expression of different views about an increasingly distant past. The see had been created in the early tenth century, when the large south-western diocese over which Asser had presided was divided into three separate bishoprics, of Sherborne (Dorset), Crediton (Devon), and Wells (Somerset). The church of St Andrew at Wells, which stood immediately to the south of the present cathedral, was developed as the episcopal see, and was later extended by Bishop Giso with a cloister, refectory, and dormitory, required for the conventual life of his canons. Giso's work was undone by Bishop John de Villula (1088–1122),[71] who was consecrated bishop of Wells in July 1088,[72] but who seems promptly to have removed the episcopal see to Bath abbey,[73] and who

---

67 Reginald died on 26 December 1191, as elect of Canterbury.

68 *Ecclesiastical Documents*, ed. Hunter, 5.

69 J.A. Robinson, 'Effigies of Saxon Bishops at Wells', *Archaeologia* lv, 1914, 95–112, at 102; J.A. Robinson, 'The First Deans of Wells', in his *Somerset Historical Essays*, London 1921, 54–72, at 60; Robinson, 'The Historia Minor and the Historia Major', 48; C.A.R. Radford, 'The Church in Somerset Down to 1100', *Proceedings of the Somersetshire Archæological & Natural History Society* cvi, 1962, 28–45, at 38–9; *Gesta Stephani*, ed. K.R. Potter and R.H.C. Davis, Oxford 1976, xxxiv–xxxv; *Bath and Wells 1061–1205*, ed. Ramsey, xxxii–iii.

70 A. Gransden, 'The History of Wells Cathedral, c.1090–1547', *Wells Cathedral*, ed. Colchester, 24–51, at 28 and 33–4. Cf. A. Gransden, *Historical Writing in England c.550 to c.1307*, London 1974, 273 and 284.

71 For Bishop John, see Barlow, *English Church 1066–1154*, 66–7.

72 *Bath and Wells 1061–1205*, ed. Ramsey, no. 1.

73 The diploma of King William II granting Bath abbey to Bishop John, 'for the increase of the bishopric of Somerset, so that he may establish his episcopal see there', is preserved at Wells Cathedral in its original form (Cathedral Charters, no. 3: F.H. Dickinson, 'Charter of William the Second, Granting Bath to Bishop John de Villula', *Somersetshire Archæological and Natural History Society's Proceedings* xxii, 1876, 114–19, with folding plate; *Wells Cathedral*, ed. Colchester, 26 (Plate 14)). The main text, beginning with a distinctive chrismon, is in the hand of one scribe, and is dated 27 January '1090', i.e. 27 Jan. 1091. The long witness-list, arranged in the manner of a pre-Conquest diploma, was added in a smaller register of script, perhaps by a different scribe; about twenty of the sixty-five witnesses have what appear to be autograph crosses added against their names. The 'second' scribe inserted a note in available space between the text and the witness-list, to the effect that the grant itself had been made at the instigation of Archbishop Lanfranc, in a meeting held at Winchester in 1088, and that the charter was confirmed (in Jan. 1091)

destroyed the conventual buildings at Wells.[74] It seems, however, that the canons of Wells may have managed to retain some interest in episcopal elections.[75] Robert of Lewes, bishop of Bath (1136–66), was responsible for further building work on the old cathedral of Wells, and for introducing a new constitution, establishing prebends for the dean and chapter in the manner of other well-regulated churches.[76] During the episcopate of Reginald de Bohun, bishop of Bath (1174–91), work started on the building of a much larger church at Wells, on a site to the north of the pre-Conquest and Anglo-Norman cathedral, setting in motion a process which continued during the thirteenth and fourteenth centuries.[77] Bishop Savaric (1192–1205) united the church of St Peter's, Bath, with Glastonbury abbey;[78] and while the monks of Glastonbury strove to maintain their independence, the canons of Wells were keen to give Savaric all the help that they could, perhaps to ease the pressure on themselves.[79] The situation changed, however, in 1206, when Jocelin, a native and a canon of Wells, was elected bishop by the prior and convent of Bath, and simultaneously by the dean and chapter of Wells.[80] For a while he continued to

at Dover. Cf. E.A. Freeman, *The Reign of William Rufus and the Accession of Henry the First*, 2 vols, Oxford 1882, i, 136–9, and ii, 483–90 ('The Bishopric of Somerset and the Abbey of Bath'); *Regesta* i, nos 314–15; and below, n. 163.

[74] *Historiola*, ed. Hunter, 21–2.

[75] See Gransden, 'History of Wells Cathedral', 34–5, and *Bath and Wells 1061–1205*, ed. Ramsey, xxx–xxxvi.

[76] For Bishop Robert, see C.M. Church, *Chapters in the Early History of the Church of Wells, AD 1136–1333*, London 1894, 1–36; Rodwell, 'The Anglo-Saxon and Norman Churches at Wells', 12–14; Gransden 'History of Wells Cathedral', 25–8; and *Bath and Wells 1061–1205*, ed. Ramsey, xxi and xxv–xxvii. Bishop Robert's statute establishing the prebendal system at Wells is *Bath and Wells 1061–1205*, ed. Ramsey, 34–6 (no. 46). Robinson ('First Deans of Wells', 56–60) regarded an appended clause in the transmitted text as a spurious addition, and adduced what appear to be strong reasons for supposing that the statute (in its received form) was promulgated in 1159 x 1166, formalising arrangements made c.1140. Ramsey accepts the appended clause at face value, taking the view that the statute was issued at Stephen's Easter court in 1136, on which occasion the see was granted to Robert (*Regesta* iii, no. 46). The arrangements were confirmed by Pope Hadrian IV in 1158 (*PUE* ii, 287 (no. 101)). According to the compiler of the *Historia Major*, Bishop Robert 'distinxit eciam prebendas ecclesie Wellensis que fuerunt primitus in communi, et de novo fundavit in ea duas prebendas, videlicet Yatton et Hywysch in marisco, cui annexuit ecclesiam de Compton episcopi' (ed. Robinson, 62–3).

[77] For Bishop Reginald, see Church, *Chapters in the Early History of Wells*, 37–87; and *Bath and Wells 1061–1205*, ed. Ramsey, xxi–xxii. See also J.H. Harvey, 'The Building of Wells Cathedral, I: 1175–1307', *Wells Cathedral*, ed. Colchester, 52–75, and J.H. Harvey, 'The Building of Wells Cathedral, II: 1307–1508', *ibid.*, 76–101.

[78] For Bishop Savaric, see Church, *Chapters in the Early History of Wells*, 88–126; Gransden 'History of Wells Cathedral', 28–31; and *Bath and Wells 1061–1205*, ed. Ramsey, xxii. See also J.P. Carley, *Glastonbury Abbey: the Holy House at the Head of the Moors Adventurous*, Woodbridge 1988, 25–8.

[79] The details are recounted in the mid-thirteenth-century chronicle of Glastonbury abbey attributed to Adam of Damerham, preserved in Cambridge, Trinity College, MS R. 5. 33, fos 21–51: see *Adami de Domerham Historia de Rebus Gestis Glastoniensibus*, ed. T. Hearne, 2 vols, Oxford 1727, ii, 303–502, and J. Crick, 'The Marshalling of Antiquity: Glastonbury's Historical Dossier', *The Archaeology and History of Glastonbury Abbey*, ed. L. Abrams and J.P. Carley, Woodbridge 1991, 217–43, at 222 and 236–8. For a mid-fourteenth-century version of the same story, see J.P. Carley, *The Chronicle of Glastonbury Abbey: an Edition, Translation and Study of John of Glastonbury's Cronica sive Antiquitates Glastoniensis Ecclesie*, Woodbridge 1985, 184–98.

[80] For Bishop Jocelin, see Church, *Chapters in the Early History of Wells*, 127–238; and Gransden, 'History of Wells Cathedral', 31–5. The announcement of his election in 1206, by the prior and

be styled bishop 'of Bath and Glastonbury', but eventually he asked the pope for permission to change his style to bishop 'of Bath and Wells', claiming that the church of Wells was anciently, by apostolic privilege, a cathedral. It was probably at about this time, in the early thirteenth century, that the mortal remains of the former bishops of Wells were translated from the old cathedral into the new church, and placed under stone effigies, as if to emphasise the status which the church of Wells had once enjoyed.[81] In 1220 Pope Honorius III ordered a papal legate to investigate the claims made for the church of Wells, and, should they prove to be genuine, to grant Bishop Jocelin's request.[82] Jocelin was concerned thereafter to establish that the canons of Wells had long enjoyed the right to participate in the election of the bishop of Bath; and it is perhaps to his initiative that we owe the existence and particular form of the earliest surviving Wells cartulary.[83] It was, however, as bishop of Bath that he died, in 1242; but the case had been made, and it came to pass, under Bishop Roger (1244–47), in 1245, that the bishop of Bath would henceforth be designated the bishop 'of Bath and Wells'.

It does not require much exercise of the imagination to see how this bewildering course of events would generate a variety of pretexts for the preparation of a work concerning the early history of the church of Wells. The need might have been felt, at Wells, to create an historical identity for the church, and more particularly to

convent of Bath, survives at Wells in its original form (Wells, Cathedral Library, Charter 41), bearing what are evidently the autograph signatures and autograph crosses of the entire community of Bath. See *Wells Cathedral*, ed. Colchester, 27 (Plate 15), printed (from an Inspeximus taken in 1242) in C. M. Church, 'Roger of Salisbury, First Bishop of Bath and Wells, 1244–1247', *Archaeologia* lii, 1890, 89–112, at 104–5, and in Church, *Chapters in the Early History of Wells*, 400–2. An announcement in similar form was made at the same time by the dean and chapter of Wells. In this case the original does not survive, but it too was 'inspected' in 1242, and is printed thence in Church, 'Roger of Salisbury', 105–6, and Church, *Chapters in the Early History of Wells*, 402–4.

[81] The bones were placed in oaken boxes encased in stone tomb-chests, each surmounted by a recumbent effigy of a bishop and identified by means of an inscribed strip of lead set into the side of the chest. Five of the surviving effigies are 'older' (c.1200) than the two others (c.1240); it is presumed that the two 'later' effigies were made when the time came to replace the original covers on the tombs of Duduc and Giso, which in the first instance had been retained. Five of the surviving inscribed strips appear to have been made in the early thirteenth century, and relate to bishops named 'Sigarus' (Sigar), 'Eilwinus' (Ælfwine or Æthelwine), 'Burhwoldus' (Burhwold), 'Dudico' (Duduc), and 'Giso' (Giso); the sixth, naming Bishop 'Levericus' (? Leofric), is a 'later' replacement, probably made when the strips were removed from the tomb-chests in the early fourteenth century, reformed into name-plates, and placed inside the boxes. The name-plates came to light when the boxes were opened in 1913; a lead mortuary cross was found at the same time, in the box believed to contain the bones of Bishop Giso. A detailed examination of the bones in 1978–80 revealed that all of the bishops were over sixty years old at death. See Robinson, 'Effigies of Saxon Bishops at Wells'; W. Rodwell, 'Lead Plaques from the Tombs of the Saxon Bishops of Wells', *Antiquaries Journal* lix, 1979, 407–10; and the references cited above, n. 3. For what it may be worth, Sigar, abbot of Glastonbury in the early 970s and bishop of Wells 975–97, is said elsewhere to have been buried at Glastonbury: see William of Malmesbury, *De antiquitate Glastonie ecclesie*, ch. 67 (*The Early History of Glastonbury: an Edition, Translation and Study of William of Malmesbury's 'De Antiquitate Glastonie Ecclesie'*, ed. J. Scott, Woodbridge 1981, 138).

[82] *Calendar of Entries in the Papal Registers Relating to Great Britain and Ireland. Papal Letters, i: AD 1198–1304*, ed. W.H. Bliss, London 1893, 70.

[83] The 'Liber Albus I' was put together c.1240, with later thirteenth- and fourteenth-century additions. See Historical Manuscripts Commission, *Calendar of the Manuscripts of the Dean and Chapter of Wells*, 2 vols, London 1907–14, i, p. ix and 1–304, esp. 6–70, and Gransden, 'History of Wells Cathedral', 29 (Plate 16) and 36.

affirm its special distinction as the former episcopal see of Somerset, whether simply for the gratification of the church's corporate ego, or in implicit but harmless competition with the pretensions of some other church. Or the need might have been felt to explain why the see had been transferred from Wells to Bath, whether in order to promote its return to Wells, or for the sake of explaining the status quo, or even in connection with the proposed removal of the see from Bath to Glastonbury. Perhaps it was work on the building of a new church at Wells, set in motion by Bishop Reginald in the decade 1175–85, that prompted a canon of Wells to compile a history of the bishopric of Somerset, in the fervent hope that Wells would soon regain its status as the episcopal see. Or it may have been thirty or forty years later, in the early thirteenth century, that a canon of Wells was encouraged by Bishop Jocelin to put together a history of the see from its foundation to a convenient point in the more recent past, intended to show that the see had been established for good reason at Wells, and moved for no good reason to Bath. On a more mundane level, there would have been cause, at Wells, to produce an account of the church's endowment intended to indicate which estates were for the bishop and which were for the support of the canons, perhaps to protect the canons against any threat of encroachment by the bishop of Bath, or the bishop of Bath and Wells, or more generally to safeguard the canons' interests against others. The point is, of course, that the *Historiola* deals directly and indirectly with issues which were highly contentious in the late twelfth and early thirteenth centuries; so, clearly, we should be on our guard.

The author's purpose, as declared at the beginning of the *Historiola*, was to make known to contemporaries, and to posterity, under what circumstances the see of Somerset had been transferred, in the first instance, to Wells, and removed, some time later, from Wells to Bath. The implication seems to be that the matter was of current concern, and the author clearly felt that the truth needed to be told (or invented, and then told). He begins by explaining that the see of Somerset was originally at Congresbury, and this leads him to tell, at length, the pleasantly romantic tale of King Ine and the fair Æthelburh, of which I shall spare you the details, but which ended happily enough with their marriage at *Tideston*, now called Wells; so the queen persuaded the king to give the town to Bishop Daniel, who promptly removed his seat from the wilds of Congresbury to the fleshpots of Wells. One should observe, in this connection, that Ine, king of Wessex (688–726), did indeed have a wife called Æthelburh; but Daniel, in his incarnation as bishop of Congresbury and first bishop of Wells, is a figment of the author's fevered imagination, suggested presumably by Bishop Daniel of Winchester (c.705–744) or conceivably by Bishop Daniel of Cornwall (c.956–959x963). The author appears to be woefully ignorant of the actual circumstances of the establishment of a see at Wells in the early tenth century; and for the succession of bishops in the later tenth and eleventh centuries, he is able to provide what amounts to little more than an incomplete list of garbled names in a jumbled order.[84] 'Sigarus' (Sigar) and 'Alwynus' (Ælfwine) flourished in the last quarter of the tenth century;

---

[84] The list was evidently derived directly or indirectly from the episcopal list for Wells (and Bath) in Cambridge, Corpus Christi College, MS 140, from Bath: R.I. Page, 'Anglo-Saxon Episcopal Lists, Part III', *Nottingham Medieval Studies* x, 1966, 2–24, at 20. Cf. William of Malmesbury, *Gesta Pontificum* II.90 (ed. Hamilton, 194), and *Handbook of British Chronology*, 3rd edn, ed. E.B. Fryde, *et al.*, London 1986, 222.

'Brithelmus' (Brihthelm) flourished in the 960s, and was succeeded by Cyneweard, who is not mentioned; 'Burthwoldus' is not recorded among the bishops of Wells, but was conceivably created from a reference to Buruhwold, bishop of Cornwall in the 1010s;[85] 'Liowyngus' (Lyfing) is in the correct place; Æthelwine and Brihtwine are represented by 'Brithtumus, Elwynus'; Brihtwig Merehwit is represented by 'Brithwynus'; and 'Duduco' (Duduc) and 'Gyso' (Giso) are correct. There was evidently a connection between the list of the tenth- and eleventh-century bishops of Wells in the *Historiola*, and the inscribed strips of lead identifying the bishops commemorated by the stone effigies placed in the new church;[86] though it would be difficult to determine whether the effigies were identified in accordance with the rather garbled information contained in the *Historiola*, or whether the *Historiola* and the effigies were different parts of a single plan and were intended, in that sense, to complement each other.

The author of the *Historiola* introduces Bishop Giso's autobiography in a way which clearly suggests that it had a separate existence as a written document (see Appendix IV). The text begins (§1) with the death of Bishop 'Brythcri Merechyyt' (Brihtwig Merehwit), on 12 April '1030', and his burial at Glastonbury (of which he had been abbot).[87] Duduc, here called a Saxon, was consecrated on 11 June; and we are told that some years later, during the reign of King Edward, he gave to his church the possessions which he had obtained before he became bishop, namely the monastery of St Peter, Gloucester, and land at Congresbury and Banwell, and the charters to go with them. Shortly before his death Duduc gave other things to the church, including vestments, relics, vessels for the altar, and a number of books. He died on 18 January in a year unspecified, after holding office for 26 years, 7 months and 7 days. At this point, apparently in 1060, Earl Harold seized the estates and goods which Duduc had bequeathed to Wells, and Archbishop Stigand persuaded King Edward to give him the monastery in Gloucester (§2). Enter Giso (§3), who styles himself 'a Hasbanian from the town of Saint Trond'; in other words, he was an inhabitant of the Hesbaye (a region of rich agricultural land in Lower Lotharingia, in the diocese of Liège),[88] and within that region came from the town of Saint-Trond (St Truiden),[89] not to be confused with the abbey of Saint-Trond.[90] He was appointed bishop of Wells in 1060, and was presently consecrated at Rome. On returning to Wells (§4), Giso found the church to be

---

85 According to the author of the *Historia Major* (ed. Robinson, 59), Burhwold succeeded Ælfwine as bishop of Wells; he was commemorated in the martyrology of the church, and was named on a tomb in the church. A fragment of stone bearing part of an inscription ('[v]old[v]') was found in association with one of the episcopal tombs at Wells; see Robinson, 'Effigies of Saxon Bishops at Wells', 102, and Fig. 13.
86 See Gransden, 'History of Wells Cathedral', 33, and above, n. 81. The strips identify 'Sigarus', 'Burhwoldus', 'Eilwinus', 'Dudico' and 'Giso'; the name-plate for 'Levericus' presumably replaced one which represented Lyfing.
87 Brihtwig Merehwit attests two charters dated 1033 (S 969–70); see Keynes, *Atlas of Attestations*, Table LXVI. He died in the same year: 'In this year Merehwit, bishop of Somerset, died, and he is buried in Glastonbury' (ASC, MS E, *s.a.* 1033). According to William of Malmesbury, *De Antiquitate Glastonie*, ch. 67 (ed. Scott, 138), Brihtwig died in 1034.
88 Kupper, *Liège et l'église impériale XIe–XIIe siècles*, 83–4, and map, 91.
89 J.L. Charles, *La Ville de Saint-Trond au moyen âge: des origines à la fin du XIVe siècle*, Bibliothèque de la Faculté de Philosophie et Lettres de l'Université de Liège 173, Paris 1965.
90 For a detailed account of the abbey of Saint-Trond, with full bibliography, see *Monasticon Belge*, VI: *Province de Limbourg*, Liège 1976, 13–76; see also E.G. Millar, *The St Trond Lectionary . . .*

small, served by only four or five clerks without any communal facilities. We are then treated to a narrative of Giso's activities as manager of the church's estates, full of incidental information and useful details. The emphasis is on measures taken for the good of the clerks, and on Giso's dealings with the established powers, on their behalf. The king gave him an estate at Wedmore, and Queen Edith added some of her own property, at Mark and Mudgley. Giso tried without success to recover some land at Winsham from a certain Ælfsige, who held it in lordship (§5).[91] He also considered taking similar action against Earl Harold; but following the death of King Edward, in '1065', Harold promised to restore what he had taken, and to give more, though in the event was prevented from doing so by his death at the battle of Hastings (§6). The victorious King William soon restored Winsham to the church of Wells (§7), and promised to add the monastery of Oswald (presumably St Oswald's, Gloucester) as soon as he could (§8). Giso then purchased land at Combe from a certain Atsere, and earmarked it for the support of the clerks, together with Worminster and Litton (§9). He also obtained land at Kilmington from Æthelnoth, abbot of Glastonbury, but soon lost it (§10).[92] Giso then describes how he set about the reform of the community, and how the clerks chose one of their own number, called Isaac, to manage their affairs (§11). To judge from Giso's further remarks (§12), the account of the lands assigned to the canons was to be supplemented, at a later date, by an account of the lands which pertained to the bishop, so that the one party would not encroach upon the rights of the other. The autobiography ends with Giso's solemn condemnation of anyone who presumes to take anything away from the canons (§13).

The rest of the *Historiola* covers events from Bishop John's removal of the see from Wells to Bath (1088) to the consecration of Bishop Reginald (1174); but it is very far from being a straightforward history of the see. The unifying theme is the loss and then the recovery of revenues from unspecified lands belonging to the canons of Wells. We are told how Bishop John appropriated a part of the revenues, gave them to his steward Hildebert,[93] and then demolished the communal buildings set up by Giso for the canons. Hildebert's son, John the Archdeacon, asserted a claim to the lands, and to the provostship of the canons, and held on to the lands during the episcopate of Godfrey (1123–35). But John the Archdeacon subsequently relented, telling his brother and heir Reginald not to claim the lands; and with Reginald's help, Bishop Robert (1136–66) recovered the lands for the canons. Reginald was made precentor of Wells, and was given the whole of the manor of Combe (St Nicholas) as a prebend. Bishop Robert instituted other reforms; but

with an Account of the Abbey to 1180 Based on its Monastic Chronicle, Oxford 1949, and G. Boes, *L'abbaye de Saint-Trond des origines jusqu'à 1155*, Tongres 1970.

91 This action is duly registered in P. Wormald, 'A Handlist of Anglo-Saxon Lawsuits', *Anglo-Saxon England* xvii, 1988, 247–81, at 268–9 (no. 151).

92 The form is *Kulmetone* in the *Historiola*, and *Kylmyngton* in the 'Historia Major' (ed. Robinson, 61); it could be either Kilmington in Devon, or Kilmington in Wiltshire. See further below, 230.

93 Presumably the Hildebert who held land at Evercreech and at Yatton from Bishop Giso in 1086 (GDB 89v (*DB Som.* 6.10,14)), and who also held land at Clevedon and Milton from Matthew of Mortagne (GDB 98r (*DB Som.* 44.1,3)). The author of the *Historiola* identifies the brothers John (the Archdeacon) and Reginald (the Precentor) as Hildebert's sons. According to a charter of Bishop Robert, Reginald was the nephew of Bishop John, which implies that Hildebert was Bishop John's brother, or that he married the bishop's sister; see *Bath and Wells 1061–1205*, ed. Ramsey, xl–xli, and no. 46.

about twenty years after the recovery of the lands (and so apparently in the late 1150s), the nephews of Reginald laid claim to the lands in a lay court, until Reginald himself persuaded them to drop their claim. A settlement was reached at Bath, duly recorded in a chirograph, festooned with the seals of all the parties concerned, and presently confirmed by Pope Alexander III. The *Historiola* ends with a reference to the death of Bishop Robert (1166), and, after a vacancy of several years, the consecration of Bishop Reginald (1174). There is no mistaking that the author's purpose, whatever he might have said at the beginning, was to describe the extended dispute over certain unspecified lands belonging to the canons, and its successful resolution in the 1160s. He does not name the lands concerned, and he does not supply a text of the chirograph; so we are left to draw our own conclusions.

Giso's autobiography must obviously be judged in the context of the work in which it has been so fortuitously preserved. There is a certain crudeness about the manner in which the text was incorporated in the *Historiola*; and it is reassuring, in a way, to observe the difference between the compiler's garbled allusion to the name of Duduc's immediate predecessor, and Giso's marginally more accurate statement. On this basis, it certainly looks as if the text is an intrusive element in a work compiled by another hand. The autobiography is also replete with information of the kind that generates confidence in its authenticity. It is interesting, for example, to read here that King Cnut gave Congresbury and Banwell to his priest Duduc, and that Duduc subsequently gave these estates to the bishopric of Wells; for the estates are known from reliable and seemingly independent evidence to have been given by King Alfred to his priest Asser,[94] and whatever may have been their history in the tenth and early eleventh centuries, it is striking that they should have retained their association and that they should have seemed to be an appropriate endowment for a royal priest on the make. Nor is it at all unlikely that Earl Harold should have seized, or come into possession of, both Congresbury and Banwell on Duduc's death, in January 1061; certainly, both estates were duly registered among Harold's holdings in Somerset during the reign of King Edward.[95] There is also reason to believe that Giso managed to establish a good relationship with Harold as king, in 1066, which would accord with the suggestion that Harold was only prevented by his death from making amends. Several other points of detail in the autobiographical tract are found to accord perfectly well with the evidence of Domesday Book. For example, the statement that Stigand managed to acquire Duduc's monastery in Gloucester, if understood to refer to St Oswald's and not to St Peter's, is supported by the record of Stigand's holdings in

[94] Asser, *Vita Ælfredi regis Angul-Saxonum*, ch. 81. See D. Whitelock, 'The Genuine Asser' (1968), reptd in *From Bede to Alfred: Studies in Early Anglo-Saxon Literature and History*, London 1980, [XII] 3–21, at 13–14; S. Keynes and M. Lapidge, *Alfred the Great: Asser's 'Life of King Alfred' and Other Contemporary Sources*, Harmondsworth 1983, 97 and 264; and S. Keynes, 'On the Authenticity of Asser's *Life of King Alfred*', *Journal of Ecclesiastical History* xlvii, 1996, 529–51, at 545. It seems appropriate that Alfred should have given these estates to Asser: for if Asser was in the habit of passing between St David's and Wessex, it may have been his practice to cross the mouth of the Severn from (say) Penarth to Weston-super-Mare, and to recover from the crossing at Congresbury or Banwell.

[95] See further below, 230.

Gloucestershire;[96] the wicked Ælfsige, who had managed to retain an episcopal estate at Winsham, in defiance of the order of a local court, is duly registered in Domesday Book as the holder of Winsham TRE;[97] similarly, Atsere, from whom the bishop purchased Combe during the reign of King William, is registered as the holder of that estate TRE;[98] and Isaac, named here by Giso as the head of the community, is mentioned in Exon Domesday, as 'provost (*prepositus*) of the canons'.[99] Autobiographies, however short, do not survive for many other persons who flourished in the eleventh century; and it is no surprise that historians in general have been disposed to take this remarkable text at face value.[100]

I have to confess, however, that in certain respects I find the text rather troublesome. Few would deny anyone the right to make mistakes over dates, but it must be said that the control of chronology is not exactly what might be expected of an author who had lived through these events. '1030', for the death of Brihtwig, is perhaps no more than a copyist's error, and can be quietly corrected to 1033.[101] The formulation for the length of Duduc's episcopate – 26 years, 7 months, and 7 days – is more difficult to explain. If calculated from 1030, it would be a nonsense; and if calculated from a corrected '1033', it would bring us to 18 January 1060, which was apparently the date intended, but which is probably one year short of the truth. The statement that Giso was consecrated at Rome on Easter Day, 15 April, is correct for 1061. One might add that '1065', for the death of King Edward, is correct, if we assume that Giso followed the practice of some of the mid-eleventh-century chroniclers, who began their year with the Annunciation, on 25 March – on which reckoning an event in January 1066 would have fallen in the year '1065'. Harold's death, on the '21st' day after his victory over King Harald of Norway, is reckoned from 23 September as a date for the battle of Stamford Bridge, which is perhaps a reasonable approximation (Gate Fulford took place on 20 Sept., Stamford Bridge on 25 Sept.). The problem which remains is essentially how to reconcile Giso's apparent belief that Duduc died in January 1060 with modern received wisdom that Duduc died in early 1061,[102] and how to reconcile Giso's statement that he succeeded Duduc in 1060 with the fact that Giso was consecrated at Rome on Easter Day in 1061. We could argue, albeit against the *Anglo-Saxon Chronicle*, that Duduc died and Giso succeeded in 1060, and that Giso did not trouble to explain that he had to wait for a year or so before he could go to Rome for his consecration. Or we could emend '1030' to '1033', '27th' to '28th', and '1060' to '1061', blaming everything on the copyist instead.[103] A more ingenious way to

---

[96] See Barlow, *English Church 1000–1066*, 75, n. 5, and M.F. Smith, 'Archbishop Stigand and the Eye of the Needle', *ANS* xvi, 1994, 199–219, at 208–9.

[97] GDB 89v (*DB Som.* 6.12).

[98] GDB 89r (*DB Som.* 6.2).

[99] Exon DB 78v.

[100] The Giso text has been described with good reason as 'the first self-contained autobiography written in England' (Gransden, *Historical Writing in England c.550 to c.1307*, 87; see also *ibid.*, 91 and 284).

[101] For the date of Brihtwig's death, see above, n. 87.

[102] ASC, MS D, registers Duduc's death at the end of an annal, dated 1060, covering events of 25 Mar. 1060 – 24 Mar. 1061; ASC, MS E, registers Duduc's death at the beginning of an annal, dated 1061, covering events of 1 Jan. – 31 Dec. 1061.

[103] It should be noted, however, that the compiler of the *Historiola* states that Giso occupied the see for about twenty-eight years, which indicates that he was calculating from 1060.

resolve the problem would be to imagine that Giso thought that Brihtwig had died in 1034,[104] in which case the stated length of Duduc's episcopate would bring us to January 1061; and then to suppose that since Giso placed Edward's death in '1065', he must have calculated his year from the Annunciation, in which case '1060' might relate to his appointment in the opening months of the year which we call 1061, bringing Duduc's death and Giso's succession back into a natural and seemingly 'correct' relationship. The less charitable explanation is that the dates '1060', for Duduc's death, and '1065', for Edward's death, were lifted unthinkingly from one or other of the chronicles which began the year with the Annunciation, and that the calculation of the length of Duduc's episcopate was made on this basis by someone blissfully unaware of the horrendous complications, and who knew that Giso had been consecrated on 15 April (Easter Day), but had not troubled to find out from an Easter Table that 15 April was Easter Day in 1061. And, of course, it is always possible that Giso miscalculated, or got himself in a terrible muddle. In short, the chronological difficulties can be explained in so many different ways that, in the end, they prove nothing; it is a matter of how devious, or how ingenious, one is prepared to be, in order to maintain faith in the text.

There are various other considerations which need to be raised in connection with the authenticity, or otherwise, of this work. In the first place, it might be thought mildly suspicious that Giso should have written separately of the lands which belonged to the canons, as a foretaste (*prelibatio*) of his promised account of the lands which belonged to the episcopal see (§12); and we can only register our disappointment that the promised account of the bishop's lands has not been preserved, if indeed it was ever written. Secondly, certain seemingly innocuous but in this context arguably distinctive turns of phrase are common to the autobiography and to the surrounding text, suggesting either that the author of the *Historiola* was consciously or sub-consciously echoing Giso, or that the autobiography, and the rest of the *Historiola*, were put together by one person. Note, for example, that Duduc 'fell asleep in the Lord' (*obdormiuit in Domino*), which is the expression also used of Bishop Giso himself, and, later, of Bishop Robert.[105] Note also that Duduc is described as *natione Saxo*, a formula echoed in the descriptions of Bishop John as *natione Turonensis* and of Bishop Godfrey as *natione Thetonicus*. And note that Giso's interest in places of burial, for Brihtwig and Duduc, is echoed by the similar details provided by the author of the *Historiola* for their successors.[106] Thirdly, some of the incidental information in the autobiography conflicts with independent and seemingly reliable evidence, and some of the details are at variance with the separate charters preserved in the Wells archive. For example, one might infer from §4 that Mark and Mudgley were acquired from Queen Edith during the lifetime of King Edward, though this would conflict with the evidence that Mark was not acquired until after the king's death;[107] and the remark in §9

---

[104] See above, n. 87.

[105] The same phrase is used of Duduc, Giso and Robert in the *Historia Minor* and in the *Historia Major*, derived from the *Historiola*; that it was infectious is suggested by the fact that it is also used in the *Historia Minor* of Bishop Ralph of Shrewsbury (d. 1363) and in the *Historia Major* of Bishop Reginald (d. 1191).

[106] Again, it should be noted that the place of a bishop's burial is a theme which runs through the *Historia Minor* and the *Historia Major*.

[107] Appendix I, no. 15.

which might be taken to imply that Worminster and Litton were acquired during the reign of King William seems to conflict with the evidence that both properties already belonged to the church during the reign of King Edward.[108]

None of these three considerations is fatal to the authenticity of Giso's autobiography; but a fourth, arising from the first, is more difficult to explain away. The autobiography implies that Giso had made a formal and systematic division of the church's property between himself as bishop, on the one hand, and the canons, on the other; and, as we have seen, Giso chose to focus his attention on the acquisition of those estates which had been earmarked for the support of the canons, including Wedmore (§4), Winsham (§7), and Combe (§9). There is no difficulty at all in believing that Giso had re-organised the estates of the church of Wells in such a way that some were held by the bishop and some were held by the canons, though it is likely that the estates held by the canons were held in common and were not (yet) divided up into separate prebends. The difficulties only arise when we try to reconcile statements in the autobiography with the evidence of the Wells charters and with the evidence of Domesday Book. Needless to say, both of these other forms of evidence present their own difficulties of interpretation. Land acquired for one purpose may soon have been put to another, just as land assigned to one party may have been transferred on second thoughts to a different party. According to a writ of King Edward the Confessor, the estate at Wedmore was given to Giso 'for the maintenance of his clerks';[109] and according to a writ of King William, the estate at Winsham was given to the church of Wells 'for the maintenance of the canons'.[110] Yet according to a charter of King William, probably drafted by Giso himself, land at Banwell was restored to the church 'for the demesne of the episcopal see and for the maintenance of the brethren';[111] so the formula 'for the maintenance of . . .', in the Wedmore and Winsham writs, may in itself signify no more than that the land was intended for the church. It is the case, however, that the account of the 'Terra Gisonis' in Domesday Book sustains what would appear to be a meaningful distinction between land held by the bishop and land held by the canons. Of course, all of the 'Terra Gisonis' was (by definition) held by the bishop, whether in lordship, or from the bishop by other named parties.[112] The canons, for their part, are said to have held 14 hides of the 50 hides at Wells, and are registered as holders of separate estates of 4 hides at Wanstrow and of 8½ hides at Litton. If the evidence of Domesday Book is to count for anything, it would follow that the estates at Wedmore, Winsham, and Combe were held by the bishop in 1086, and had not yet been earmarked for the support of the canons. It is conceivable that the revenues from some of the land said to have been held by the bishop 'in lordship' had in fact been assigned to the canons, and that the holdings in Wells, in Wanstrow, and in Litton, registered specifically as the canons' property in 1066 and 1086, were held by them in common, as it were in their own right. It is also conceivable that arrangements made between the bishop and the canons were

---

[108] For Worminster, see Appendix I, no. 9. For Litton, see Appendix I, nos 7 and 9, and GDB 89v (*DB Som.* 6.17).

[109] Appendix I, no. 8.

[110] Appendix I, no. 13.

[111] Appendix I, no. 14.

[112] For what is intended to be merely a convenient summary of the Domesday account of the 'Terra Gisonis', see Appendix V.

flexible, and that whatever may have been true when Giso wrote his account of the canons' estates, perhaps in the mid-1070s, would not necessarily have remained true in 1086. One must emphasise, however, that the Domesday commissioners dealt with the estates of secular cathedrals in ways which suggest that they were quite capable of maintaining meaningful distinctions between the lands of the bishop and the lands of the canons, if there were meaningful distinctions to be made;[113] and one certainly imagines that all the parties concerned would have been interested in getting details of this nature correct.

A fifth and final consideration is perhaps decisive. The apparent discrepancies between the statements in Giso's autobiography, and other evidence bearing on the organisation of the estates of the bishopric of Wells, would be the more suspicious if the arrangements set out in the autobiography are found not merely to be in conflict with Domesday Book but also to be in accord with arrangements known to have obtained at a later date. We have seen that it was Bishop Robert, probably in the 1140s, who put the prebendal system at Wells on what would appear to have been a new and formal footing.[114] Prebends for the canons were established (no doubt in some cases in continuation of existing arrangements) at Wedmore (with Mudgley and Mark), at Litton, at Whitchurch (in Wells), at Dulcote and Chilcote (in Wells), at Worminster, at Wanstrow, and at Winsham; and Combe (St Nicholas) was established as a special prebend for Reginald the precentor, for the rest of his life, in memory of all the good things done by his late uncle, Bishop John, though it was decreed that after Reginald's death his special prebend was to be divided into five. When the deep-rooted dispute over unspecified lands of the canons, as described in the *Historiola*, flared up again in the late 1150s (or thereabouts), it was settled by the production of a chirograph, which is described with loving attention to detail, but not actually quoted. It so happens that the part of the chirograph retained at Wells was copied in the mid-thirteenth-century cartulary ('Liber Albus I'), and again in the late-fifteenth-century cartulary ('Liber Albus II');[115] and it

---

[113] In Devon, for example, a distinction was made between estates held by the bishop of Exeter (*DB Dev.* 2.1–4, 9–24) and four estates earmarked for the supplies of the canons (*DB Dev.* 2.5–8); but it should be noted that one of the bishop's set of estates was 'for the supplies of the canons' (*DB Dev.* 2.22). In Herefordshire, the lands of the bishop or bishopric of Hereford are described in a way which implies that they were considered to be in the collective ownership of 'the church' or 'the canons' of Hereford, though it is apparent that this overarching notion concealed some finer distinctions (*DB Heref.* 2.4–57). In Middlesex, the bishop of London's major holdings (e.g. *DB Mx* 3.1,12) are quite distinct from the holdings which were in the lordship of the canons of St Paul's (e.g. *DB Mx* 3.14–30). In Sussex, a similar kind of distinction was maintained between the estates of the bishop of Chichester (*DB Sx* 3.1–9) and land held by the canons 'in common' (*DB Sx* 3.10). For discussion of these and related matters, see K. Edwards, *The English Secular Cathedrals in the Middle Ages*, 2nd edn, Manchester 1967, 11–12; Barlow, *English Church 1000–1066*, 239–42; J. Barrow, 'Cathedrals, Provosts and Prebends: a Comparison of Twelfth-Century German and English Practice', *Journal of Ecclesiastical History* xxxvii, 1986, 536–64, esp. 555–60; Barrow, 'English Cathedral Communities', 33–4; Barrow, 'A Lotharingian in Hereford', 34–42; Crosby, *Bishop and Chapter in Twelfth-Century England*; and below, 251. See also J. Hudson, *Land, Law, and Lordship in Anglo-Norman England*, Oxford 1994, 234–6; and G. Garnett, 'The Origins of the Crown', *Proceedings of the British Academy* lxxxix, 1996, 171–214, at 193–5.

[114] See above, 215, and n. 76. *Bath and Wells 1061–1205*, ed. Ramsey, 34–6 (no. 46), calendared in HMC, *Dean and Chapter of Wells* I, 33–4. See also Crosby, *Bishop and Chapter in the Twelfth Century*, 56–9.

[115] 'Liber Albus I', fo. 36v (no. cxxi), and 'Liber Albus II', fos 15v and 102v; calendared in HMC, *Dean and Chapter of Wells* i, 39–40.

reveals that the estates in dispute were Winsham, Worminster, Mudgley, and Mark, with the service of a certain Rainer of Wanstrow. The autobiography of Bishop Giso deals with the aquisition of land at Wedmore, Mark, and Mudgley (§4), Winsham (§5 and §7), Combe (§9), and Worminster and Litton (§9), and with the assignment of these estates to the canons; according to Domesday Book, the canons held 14 hides in Wells (perhaps including the land at Worminster), and two estates lying further afield at Wanstrow and Litton; in the mid-twelfth century, there were prebends for the canons in various parts of Wells, and at Wedmore (with Mudgley and Mark), at Winsham, at Combe, at Worminster, at Litton, and at Wanstrow. It could be said, therefore, that the information on the canons' estates, in the autobiography, seems to accord not so much with the situation in 1086 (represented by Domesday Book) as with the conditions which had come to prevail by the middle of the twelfth century, when Bishop Robert divided up the canons' estates into separate prebends; and since several of the estates in question were under dispute in the late 1150s and early 1160s, one can well understand why the need might have been felt to put this information together.

The suspicion must arise, under these circumstances, that Giso's autobiography was fabricated by a canon of Wells during the course of the twelfth century, in order to provide an account of the circumstances in which the canons' estates had been acquired; for unless we are to suppose that the detailed arrangements made by Bishop Giso were concealed in the Domesday account of the 'Terra Gisonis', it has to be admitted (alas) that the arrangements described in the autobiography bear much closer comparison with the arrangements known to have obtained during the episcopate of Bishop Robert. The act of fabrication would then provide a ready explanation for some of the other difficulties presented by the text. Even so, the autobiography would be not so much a product of wilful deception, as the product of wishful thought. It may have been drawn up on the basis of genuine material preserved at Wells, perhaps in the form of a memorandum composed by Giso himself, or in the form of a record, composed by another person, of what Giso had done for his church; and if similar kinds of text are needed to establish a literary context, they are ready to hand in the form (for example) of the various records of the activities of Bishop Leofric on behalf of the church of Exeter,[116] the account by Henry of Blois of his activities on behalf of the abbey of Glastonbury,[117] and the

---

[116] An account of the removal of the see from Crediton to Exeter, in Latin, was entered in the late eleventh century at the beginning of the Leofric Missal (Oxford, Bodleian Library, MS Bodley 579 (S.C. 2675), fos 2r–3v). See *Leofric Missal*, ed. Warren, 1–2; Gransden, *Historical Writing in England c.550 to c.1307*, 90–1; and Conner, *Anglo-Saxon Exeter*, 215–25. Copies of a vernacular memorandum were entered in the late eleventh century at the beginning of two gospel-books at Exeter (one in a detached quire now bound with the 'Exeter Book', and the other in Oxford, Bodleian Library, MS Auct. D. 2. 16 (S.C. 2719), fos 1–2); see Ker, *Catalogue of Manuscripts*, nos 20, art. 6, and 291, art. a. The text is printed, with translation, in *Anglo-Saxon Charters*, ed. A.J. Robertson, 2nd edn, Cambridge 1956, App. I, no. 1 (226–30); see also M. Swanton, *Anglo-Saxon Prose*, London 1993, 24–6. The most recent account, including text and translation, is Conner, *Anglo-Saxon Exeter*, 226–35.

[117] The 'Scriptura Henrici abbatis', also described as a *breuis libellus*, is accorded pride of place at the beginning of the mid-thirteenth-century Glastonbury chronicle preserved in Cambridge, Trinity College, MS R. 5. 33, fos 21–51, on which see above, n. 79. The 'Scriptura' is printed in *Adami de Domerham Historia de Rebus Gestis Glastoniensibus*, ed. Hearne, ii, 305–15.

potted autobiographies of Bede and Orderic Vitalis.[118] Giso's autobiography may have taken its place in the *Historiola* as part of a narrative covering the dispute over the canons' lands which had been formally settled in the early 1160s; and in view of the rather abrupt ending, with the election and consecration of Bishop Reginald in 1173–74, it may be that the compiler was intent upon protecting the canons' interests in the event of any renewed challenge, from whatever quarter it might come. It is also possible, however, that the *Historiola* stops at this point for no better reason than lack of material or ideas, and that its compiler's purpose had been to put together some account of the history of the bishopric of Wells in connection with the revival of the self-consciousness and prospects of the church under Bishop Jocelin, in the early thirteenth century. Of course it could still be argued that Bishop Robert's statute establishing the prebends amounted to little more than the creation of separate prebends from lands hitherto held by the canons in common, and on this basis that the autobiography dates from an earlier period. Yet what I find so difficult to believe is that Giso himself should have made such a point of dividing the bishop's lands from those of the canons, and such a display of recording his act in the interests of both parties, while at the same time failing to ensure that the arrangements were properly registered in the Domesday survey; and, again, that Giso himself should have had the foresight not only to make arrangements which would anticipate the arrangements formalised by Bishop Robert in the 1140s, but to set down a separate account of the lands which pertained to the canons, which would prove so pertinent in the context of a later dispute. Why, you may ask, should a canon of Wells resort to such subterfuge? Perhaps the object of the exercise was to lend distinction to the arrangements which obtained in the twelfth century, by associating them with the renowned Bishop Giso, and with the period when the episcopal see was still at Wells. Perhaps the idea was, at the same time, to provide interested parties with a narrative covering all of the estates which belonged to the canons, in the absence of more helpfully explicit documentation. And perhaps the intention was to protect the interests of the canons in the most effective way possible, by casting the record in the words of the bishop himself. The notion that Bishop Giso's autobiography may not be quite what it seems, or what we should like it to be, is certainly a disappointment; but I hasten to add that I, for one, am not inclined to abandon the autobiography entirely, as a work of fiction. It would not be difficult to imagine that a canon of Wells came across an autobiographical text, of some kind, in the archives of his church, and that he was able to adapt this text for purposes of his own; for quite apart from the fact that some of the detailed information can be corroborated by reference to other sources, one cannot but fail to be struck by the way in which the autobiography seems so effectively to capture the dogged persistence and unflagging energy of Bishop Giso, as he set about the task of reconstruction and reform.

---

[118] Bede, *Historia Ecclesiastica* V. 24; Orderic, *Historia Ecclesiastica* XIII.45 (ed. Chibnall, vi, 550–6).

Bishop Giso and King Edward the Confessor

We may turn now to consider the corpus of documentary evidence which bears on the activities of Giso in his capacity as bishop of Wells. The purpose of Appendix I is to bring together, into a single sequence, charters which would normally find themselves placed in different categories (writs, diplomas, miscellaneous vernacular records, and a papal privilege), and in different volumes of editions which necessarily respect the political divide in 1066. It is by any standards a most interesting series of texts, and one which we owe in large part to the importance attached by Giso himself to the evidence of the written word.[119] Vernacular writs may have flown around in the eleventh century, but they did not hang about for long. The onus appears to have been on the 'beneficiary' of a writ to retrieve it from the officials to whom it was addressed, and to preserve it thereafter as evidence of the oral declaration which had been made to the local court; and Giso was certainly one of those who made the effort, as it were, to save the hard copies of his own e-mail. Royal diplomas may have come to be regarded in some quarters as antiquated mumbo-jumbo, but they too could be made to serve a useful purpose, particularly if, like Giso, you were able and empowered to write them up for yourself. Much would depend thereafter on the inclination, or otherwise, of the compilers of cartularies to copy one kind of document or another; but fortunately Giso's successors did not let him down.[120] And while it must be admitted that charters, and the finer points of estate management in the eleventh century, are not to everyone's taste, the material from Wells is sufficiently rich and varied to take on a life of its own. The most appealing aspect of the material is perhaps the view it gives of Giso's activities, from the early 1060s to the early 1080s: not just how he dealt with Edward, Harold, and William, in his determination to advance the interests of his church, but with whom he associated in the brave new world of Anglo-Norman England.

Nothing is known of Giso's career as a royal priest, during the reign of King Edward the Confessor. He is called 'my priest' in the king's writ announcing his appointment to a bishopric,[121] 'king's priest' by the author of the *Vita Ædwardi regis*,[122] and 'king's chaplain' by John of Worcester;[123] but he does not attest any charters. It should be emphasised that the writ announcing Giso's appointment, drafted no doubt under the watchful (or perhaps the indulgent) eye of Regenbald the chancellor, gave him a mandate beyond the wildest dreams of any ecclesiastical land-tycoon. The bishopric was granted to him 'as fully and as completely as ever

---

[119] For an interest in record-keeping as 'the hallmark of the progressive bishop', see M. Gibson, *Lanfranc of Bec*, Oxford 1978, 153–4, and H. R. Loyn, 'The Beyond of Domesday Book' (1987), reptd in his *Society and Peoples: Studies in the History of England and Wales, c.600–1200*, London 1992, 350–73, at 361.

[120] The compiler of 'Liber Albus I', in the early 1240s, deemed the writs worthy of preservation, though for some reason an apparent distinction was made between a group of four entered on fo. 14rv in the main sequence of royal charters (Appendix I, nos 1, 3, 7, 11) and a group of five others seemingly added as an afterthought on fos 17v–18r (nos 4, 8, 10, 15, 18). The diplomas of Edward and William, and the vernacular record concerning Combe, were not included in 'Liber Albus I', and are preserved only in the later 'Liber Albus II' (Appendix I, nos 9, 14, 16), with copies of a few other pre-Conquest charters (S 527, 709, 579, 380, 262).

[121] Appendix I, no. 1.

[122] *Vita Ædwardi regis*, bk I, ch. 5 (ed. Barlow, 54).

[123] John of Worcester, *s.a.* 1060 (ed. Darlington and McGurk, 586).

Bishop Duduc or any bishop had it before him, in all things; and if any land here has been taken away from the bishopric, it is my will that it be restored or that it be held on such conditions as may be agreeable to him, according to such arrangements with him as can be devised'.[124] With a writ like that, who needs charters? It is no less important to emphasise what additional support Giso gained from his attendance upon the pope in April 1061.[125] He went to Rome, of course, in company with Walter, bishop-elect of Hereford, because he could not be consecrated in England by the somewhat irregular Archbishop Stigand;[126] and he returned not only smelling of canonical roses, but also bearing a magnificent papal privilege, inscribed on a sheet of parchment bigger than almost any Anglo-Saxon charter. The privilege of Pope Nicholas II, issued on 25 April 1061, is still extant in its original form, and, most happily, is still preserved in Wells Cathedral Library.[127] It is far from being the first papal privilege for a religious corporation in Anglo-Saxon England, but it is apparently the first document of its kind directed towards an episcopal see, in favour of a newly appointed bishop;[128] as always, one senses that Bishop Giso knew what he was after, and was determined not to leave Rome empty-handed. 'You, dearest brother, when you received consecration as bishop by the ministration of our humility in the very basilica of the patriarch, asked that we should confirm by the writing of our privilege, to your church, and to you, and your successors in perpetuity, all those things which justly and legally pertain to the aforesaid church.' Pope Nicholas goes on: 'We order that neither king, nor duke, nor marquis, nor count, nor viscount, nor any other person, great or small, of whatever station or degree, shall presume, against our privilege, to disturb or to defraud the aforesaid bishopric in its possessions, or you, dearest brother, or your successors.' Alas, it is not known how Godwine the sheriff and all the king's thegns reacted, when Giso pulled the papal privilege out of his bag in the shire court of Somerset.

Four writs of King Edward the Confessor concern Giso in his capacity as bishop of Wells, issued presumably between Giso's return to England in June 1061 and the king's death in January 1066. In one, the king declares to the shire court of

---

124 Appendix I, no. 1.

125 For the expedition to Rome in 1061 (and the troubles on the way home), see *Vita Ædwardi regis*, bk I, ch. 5 (ed. Barlow, 52–6), and *Vita Wulfstani*, bk 1, ch. 10 (ed. Darlington, 16–17); see also E. Mason, *St Wulfstan of Worcester c.1008–1095*, Oxford 1990, 72–5. According to his autobiography, Giso returned to England in the second week after Albs, i.e. Whitsunday (3 June in 1061); the week in question would be 17–23 June, roughly two months after he had received the privilege from the pope on 25 April.

126 See Barlow, *English Church 1000–1066*, 237–8 and 302–7; see also Smith, 'Archbishop Stigand', 202–4.

127 Appendix I, no. 2. For an impression of the appearance of the original document, see the engraved facsimile in G. Hickes, *Dissertatio Epistolaris*, Oxford 1703, which forms part of G. Hickes, *Linguarum Vett. Septentrionalium Thesaurus Grammatico-Criticus et Archæologicus*, Oxford 1705. In the thirteenth century the dean and chapter of Wells claimed to have letters of Pope Nicholas II, addressed to the clergy of Wells, 'stating that he has ordained as priest Giso whom they have elected their bishop' (calendared in HMC, *Dean and Chapter of Wells* i, 116). This is presumably a rather loose reference to the papal privilege obtained by Giso, and should perhaps not be taken as evidence that the canons of Wells had formally 'elected' Giso in 1061; cf. *Bath and Wells 1061–1205*, ed. Ramsey, xxxi.

128 For the wider context, see Barlow, *English Church 1000–1066*, 300–2; Ortenberg, *English Church and the Continent*, 8, n. 22, and 153; and Barrow, 'English Cathedral Communities', 38–9.

Somerset that Giso is to have the bishopric and everything pertaining to it; as before, he insists that Earl Harold and others are to help Giso secure his rights, 'and if anything has been taken illegally away from the bishopric, whether it be in land or in other things, that [you] will help him, for love of me, that it may be restored, as you know, before God, is right'.[129] Another writ suggests that the officials of the shire court may have tried to claim more than was customary in respect of one of the bishop's principal estates; for the king declares that Giso is to discharge the obligations on his land at **Chew** (Somerset), 'now at the same rate as his predecessor did before him', adding 'And I will not permit that any wrong be done to him'.[130] The third writ, evidently later than the first two since it names Tofig, not Godwine, as sheriff, is an announcement to the effect that a certain Alfred has sold to Bishop Giso his land at **Litton** (Somerset), in the presence of the king (and others, including Queen Edith and Earl Harold) at Perrott (Somerset), and expressing the king's will 'that the bishop shall legally possess the land for the bishopric'.[131] Interestingly, the further statement that Giso is to possess the land 'as fully and as completely as ever any bishop held it in all things' suggests that the land had previously belonged to the bishopric; in which case it may be that Alfred had taken possession of an episcopal estate (which may have been leased to him in the first instance) and had to be induced with money, and some heavy pressure, to restore the land to its rightful owner. The fourth writ, in which the king declares that he has given land at **Wedmore** (Somerset) to Bishop Giso, is of particular interest.[132] Wedmore was an ancient royal estate of the West Saxon kings (bequeathed by King Alfred to Edward the Elder), and it was given to Giso 'for my soul and for my father's soul, and for the souls of all my ancestors who established the episcopal see', suggesting (as Dr Harmer observed) that the king was conscious of its special associations.[133] Yet although the grant is said to have been intended 'for the maintenance of his clerks at St Andrews at Wells', the land is seen from Domesday Book to have belonged TRE, and TRW, to the bishop himself.[134] It is possible that Giso had made his case by pleading the poverty of his clerks, and that he subsequently felt under no obligation to assign the land to them in their own right; or he may have altered various arrangements in the early 1060s; or it may be that the land was the bishop's, and that the revenues from it were assigned to the canons, for their support; or perhaps the formula 'for the maintenance of his clerks . . .' did not at this stage have the technical meaning which it would naturally acquire when a formal division was made between the estates of the bishop and the estates of the canons.[135] The particular interest of the Wedmore writ arises, however, from the fact that it specifically authorises the bishop to draw up a *priuilegium*, with the king's permission. Perhaps Giso was empowered to do this in his capacity as a former royal priest, and perhaps it is a sign at the same time that he was left to

---

129 Appendix I, no. 3.

130 Appendix I, no. 4.

131 Appendix I, no. 7.

132 Appendix I, no. 8.

133 Harmer, *Anglo-Saxon Writs*, 273.

134 GDB 89v (*DB Som.* 6.15). Land at Wedmore seems to have been reckoned among the 'members' of the royal estate at Cheddar, and 'William the sheriff' accounted £12 for it in the king's farm every year; yet this land is said to have been held by Bishop Giso from the king 'for a long time (*longo tempore*) before the death of King Edward' (Exon DB 515v and GDB 86r (*DB Som.* 1.2)).

135 Cf. the formula in the Banwell charter, cited above, 223.

make his own more detailed arrangements. Unfortunately, the charter drawn up by Giso for the estate at Wedmore does not survive,[136] and we can but guess under what circumstances the land was later assigned to the canons and became one of their most important prebendal estates.

Although the writs of Edward the Confessor leave one in no doubt that Giso enjoyed the king's support, it is apparent that things did not always go the bishop's way. Giso may have managed to prevail upon Alfred to give up the land at Litton, but he failed in his various attempts to persuade Ælfsige to give up the land at Winsham.[137] It seems that he was inclined, moreover, to attribute his failure to retain possession of an estate at Kilmington to the 'diabolical interference of a certain powerful person'.[138] If the place is identified as Kilmington, Wilts., the person in question might have been the Ælfsige who held the estate in 1066;[139] and if it is identified as Kilmington, Devon, the powerful person would seem to have been none other than Earl Harold's brother, Earl Leofwine.[140] Our attention is drawn inexorably to Earl Harold himself. The claim was made that Bishop Duduc gave the estates at Congresbury and Banwell to the church of Wells, 'strengthened by charters of royal authority and donation', and that the estates were seized by Earl Harold, presumably in the immediate aftermath of Duduc's death on 18 January 1061.[141] The same story, with respect to Banwell in particular, is told in the charter of King William I restoring Banwell to Wells;[142] and there can be no doubt that it was to Earl Harold that both estates belonged 'on the day on which King Edward was alive and dead'.[143] The question remains whether Earl Harold appropriated the land from the church, or whether he was challenging the propriety of Duduc's bequest. We may readily agree with those in the nineteenth century who sought to exonerate Harold from the charge of a gross act of sacrilege,[144] and not merely because Harold needs all the help he can get if he is to go rather up than down on the Day of Judgement. For while we should at least admit the possibility that the estates had passed after Asser's death into the hands of the first bishop of Wells, and had later been taken back into lay control, it seems just as likely that the

---

[136] It is possible, however, that Giso took the opportunity to produce a *priuilegium* in respect of all of the estates of his bishopric, including Wedmore, and that the charter in question is thus none other than the charter which he produced in 1065 (Appendix I, no. 9).

[137] Giso's autobiography (Appendix IV, §5); see Barlow, *English Church 1000–1066*, 149.

[138] Giso's autobiography (Appendix IV, §10).

[139] L. Abrams, *Anglo-Saxon Glastonbury: Church and Endowment*, Woodbridge 1996, 148–9. An estate of 5 hides at Kilmington, which paid geld for 1 hide, was held TRE by a certain Ælfsige, and TRW by St Edward's Church, from Serlo de Burcy (GDB 98r (*DB Som.* 37.7); see also GDB 86v (*DB Som.* 1.9)).

[140] GDB 101r (*DB Dev.* 1.53). Kilmington was later regarded as one of the estates taken away from the church of Wells by Earl Harold ('Historia Major', ed. Robinson, 61).

[141] Giso's autobiography (Appendix IV, §1).

[142] Appendix I, no. 14. According to this charter, it was 'King' Harold who had taken the land from the church; but we may suppose that the draftsman (probably Bishop Giso) simply and naturally accorded Harold the style which he enjoyed at his death.

[143] Congresbury was assessed at 20 hides (GDB 87r (*DB Som.* 1.21)), and Banwell at 30 hides (GDB 89v (*DB Som.* 6.9)). Giso subsequently acquired an interest in 1 hide of pasture which belonged to Congresbury; see GDB 87r (*DB Som.* 1.21) and 89v (*DB Som.* 6.14).

[144] J.R. Green, 'Earl Harold and Bishop Giso', *Somerset Archaeological and Natural History Society Proceedings* xii, 1863–4, 148–57; Freeman, *Norman Conquest* ii, 446–50 and 674–80 (Note QQ: 'The Quarrel Between Earl Harold and Bishop Gisa'); see also Harmer, *Anglo-Saxon Writs*, 275–6.

estates had always remained at the disposal of successive kings; and if Cnut gave Congresbury and Banwell to his Lotharingian priest Duduc, as claimed in Giso's 'autobiography', the estates might well have been regarded as Duduc's personal property and not ancient holdings of the see of Wells. It is conceivable, therefore, as Freeman suggested, that Harold did no more than exercise a right to take possession of estates which in his view should have reverted to King Edward on Duduc's death.[145] Nor is it a surprise, under these circumstances, that both estates should have remained in Harold's (as opposed to the king's) hands. Harold was not likely to forgo a good opportunity to assume possession of a substantial tract (assessed at 50 hides) of verdant Somerset countryside, in what might be regarded as a strategic position giving good access to the Severn estuary;[146] though whether Giso himself would have seen the earl's action in quite the same light is perhaps another matter.

If only to judge from his attestations in the few surviving charters of Edward the Confessor issued between 1061 and 1066, Giso was in regular attendance at meetings of the great and the good in the kingdom.[147] We have seen that on one occasion during this period the king authorised Giso to draw up a *priuilegium* concerning the king's grant of land at Wedmore to the church of Wells; and although a separate *priuilegium* for Wedmore does not survive, the question arises whether there might have been any other instances in which a similar procedure was adopted for the production of a royal charter. A charter in the name of Edward the Confessor, dated 1061 and preserved in the archives of Bath abbey, records the grant of an unspecified amount of land at Ashwick, in Somerset, to Abbot Wulfwold, in a personal capacity (not, it seems, in his capacity as abbot of Bath).[148] The opening part of the text was modelled, directly or indirectly, on an undated charter by which King Edward the Elder granted land at Wellington, (West) Buckland, and (Bishops) Lydeard, in Somerset, to Asser, bishop of Sherborne, in exchange for the minster at Plympton in Devon;[149] and since the estates in question were re-assigned soon after Asser's death to the newly-established bishopric of Wells, the charter came to be preserved at Wells as the title-deed for an important part of the episcopal endowment. It follows that the person who drafted the charter of Edward the Confessor, for Wulfwold, abbot of Bath, used as his model a charter of Edward the Elder for Asser, bishop of Sherborne, which in 1061 would have been preserved at Wells. The operative part of the text is entirely acceptable, and seems distinctive only in so far as the draftsman set his model aside and found other forms of words for the disposition, the reservation clause, and the combined blessing and sanction. The dating clause is more problematic, for while the

---

[145] As Freeman noted (*Norman Conquest* ii, 447, n. 1), the case might be analogous to the custom observed in Oxford, whereby the king was entitled to the property of an *extraneus* who ended his life there without relatives (GDB 154v (*DB Oxon.* 1.13)). See also Barlow, *English Church 1000–1066*, 136. For the suggestion that Congresbury had been a 'comital' manor, see G. Loud, 'An Introduction to the Somerset Domesday', *The Somerset Domesday*, ed. A. Williams and R.H. Erskine, London 1989, 1–31, at 15.

[146] Cf. R. Fleming, 'Domesday Estates of the King and the Godwines: a Study in Late Saxon Politics', *Speculum* lviii, 1983, 987–1007. Harold's mother, and others, used Flatholme, in the Severn estuary, as a place of refuge in 1067.

[147] Keynes, *Atlas of Attestations*, Table LXXII.

[148] Appendix I, no. 5.

[149] S 380 (BCS 610), preserved in Wells, D. & C., Liber Albus II, fo. 290rv.

indiction (14) is correct for 1061, the epacts and concurrents (which should be 26 and 7) are 6 and 1, correct only for 1051. This is not the kind of error which arises from the miscopying of an exemplar with the appropriate figures, and is more likely to be the result of an error on the part of the draftsman, who in this instance took the figures (forgivably) from the wrong line of his Easter Tables. Another irregular feature of the charter is encapsulated in the line which occurs at the top of the witness-list: '+ Ego Giso dei gratia episcopus hanc cartam dictaui.' Claims to the effect that an ecclesiastical witness 'dictated' a charter are not in themselves uncommon, though they have to be treated with all due care and attention.[150] This claim stands out, however, in part because it is explicit and in part because it is not in the middle or at the bottom but at the top of the witness-list; nonetheless, for whatever reason it has been held to throw doubt on the authenticity of the charter itself.[151] The attestations of the king and Archbishop Stigand are followed by the attestations of three bishops, two abbots, four earls, and twelve other laymen, of whom the first two (Brihtric and Ælfgar) are styled *consiliarius* and of whom the rest are styled *minister*.[152] The bounds occur at the end of the text, which may indicate that they had been added on the dorse of the original single sheet, or which may reflect the position of the bounds in the charter of King Edward the Elder. It would certainly be easy to dismiss this charter as a forgery, on the grounds that it was not put together in accordance with 'normal' diplomatic conventions; but the more immediate and arguably the more natural explanation is that the charter was drawn up, exactly as it claims to have been, by Giso, bishop of Wells, acting on behalf of the king (or conceivably on behalf of the abbot of Bath) and using a Wells title-deed as a model. As we shall soon see, the charter bears comparison, in certain respects, with a charter of Edward the Confessor drawn up by Bishop Giso in 1065, which is itself related to a charter of William the Conqueror drawn up apparently by Bishop Giso in 1068. It should also be noted that in a writ addressed by Abbot Wulfwold to Bishop Giso, and others, the abbot announces that the king had given him the land at Evesty 'that my father owned', and the land at Ashwick; and he goes on to announce that he has given both estates to St Peter's monastery at Bath.[153] The writ, which was presumably formulated at Bath, ends with a combined blessing and sanction; and since this feature in a writ is so unusual, one wonders whether it was suggested by the occurrence of such a formula in the charter which served as Wulfwold's title-deed for Ashwick.[154]

The most interesting of all the Wells charters associated with Bishop Giso is the general confirmation of lands to the bishopric of Wells, issued in the name of King

[150] S. Keynes, *The Diplomas of King Æthelred 'the Unready' 978–1016*, Cambridge 1980, esp. 26–8.

[151] Harmer, *Anglo-Saxon Writs*, 39, n. 3, and 430.

[152] For Brihtric and Ælfgar, see Keynes, 'Regenbald the Chancellor', 205, and below, 235 and 246. The layout of the witness-list in the Bath cartulary (Cambridge, Corpus Christi College, MS 111, p. 91) is such that it is difficult to reconstruct the intended order of the thegns. Among them, 'Æilferth' is probably the 'Aluerd/Ailuert' who was one of Roger Arundel's predecessors in Somerset (*DB Som.* 22.14, 19, 24 and 26).

[153] Appendix I, no. 6. To judge from GDB 89v (*DB Som.* 7.14–15), both estates were accounted TRE as part of the abbey's land.

[154] For the occurrence of such formulas in Anglo-Saxon writs, see Harmer, *Anglo-Saxon Writs*, 67–70.

Edward the Confessor, and dated 1065.[155] The charter has been universally condemned as a forgery, in part, no doubt, because it offends against all the rules of
Anglo-Saxon diplomatic, and in part because it offends against Giso's autobiography, other Wells charters, and Domesday Book. The position has not been helped
by the fact that the charter was printed in the *Monasticon* from an early modern
transcript, and was then simply reprinted by Kemble, from the *Monasticon*;[156] the
version of the text in one of the Wells cartularies, which has better readings and
which incorporates an impressive witness-list, has been calendared, but never
published.[157] In terms of its formulation, the Wells charter is a wonderful curiosity.
It has most of the necessary elements (e.g. invocation, disposition, reservation
clause, sanction, dating-clause, witness-list, endorsement), and employs various
turns of phrase which reflect a basic familiarity with the conventions generally
observed by the draftsman of charters during the reign of Edward the Confessor;
but the separate parts of the charter are not exactly in a normal order, as if the
whole had been put together by someone who was not concerned to follow a
particular model, and much of the wording is distinctive, as if the draftsman had
preferred to compose the text from scratch. The charter runs in the name of the
king, though of course that is not to say that it was necessarily drafted in a royal
office or by a royal scribe. After the pictorial and verbal invocation, the king
expresses the pious consideration which lies behind the making of the grant. He
goes on to state that he has been requested by Giso, bishop of Wells, and most
especially by Queen Edith, to confirm the grants of his predecessors, and to give
his permission that everything set down in the many charters of previous kings,
some of which were now disintegrating, should be gathered together 'in the stor-
age-space of a single charter' (*in armariolo unius cartule*) – in modern parlance, on
the hard disk, not on floppies. The king gives the necessary permission, in respect
of whatever the bishop had acquired from the king, and whatever the bishop's
predecessors had acquired from the king's predecessors; and everything belonging
to the church is established 'in perpetual liberty', with the usual reservation of the
three military obligations. The king declares that he makes the sign of the cross on
the charter, with his own hand, and in the presence of the undermentioned witnesses, and that he affixes the 'seal of my image' (*mee ymaginis . . . sigillum*). A
sanction follows, and then a list of witnesses. The list is headed by the king and
queen, followed by the two archbishops, nine bishops (not including Giso), three
abbots, six earls (with Harold in pole position), seven officers of the royal household (four *procuratores*, two *pincernae*, and a *cubicularius*), three grandees styled
p[rinceps], and eleven other laymen, of whom the last seven are styled *m[inister]*.
At this point the text resumes, with a rather charming remark to the effect that
although the estates were fully described in the separate charters, the king (still in
the first person) thinks that it would be not a bad idea (*non infructuosum*) to supply
the basic details. There follows a list of the principal manors belonging to the
bishopric of Wells, each with a sub-set of its own appurtenances; and when the list
is finished, the king reiterates the act of confirmation to the church and to the
bishop, stating finally that the charter was written on his orders by Bishop Giso, on

---

[155] Appendix I, no. 9.
[156] KCD 816. The transcript was probably derived from a copy of the charter made in the 1590s by
Francis Godwin; see further below, 260.
[157] For a provisional edition, see Appendix II.

24 May 1065, on the royal estate called Windsor. The charter ends with the notarial attestation of Bishop Giso himself.

If genuine, this charter would have some claim to symbolic importance as evidence of a meeting of the king's council held at Windsor in the spring of 1065,[158] and a claim to more substantive importance as Bishop Giso's own record of the endowment of the see of Wells, drawn up just four years after he took up his office. If it is a forgery, it would presumably represent a flight of fancy on the part of a medieval canon of Wells. Though decidedly irregular in form, there is nothing in the formulation of the charter which is incompatible with the supposition that it was drawn up in 1065. It does not grant improbable exemptions from worldly obligations; it does not convey any elaborate jurisdictional privileges; and it does not contain any gross historical, linguistic, or diplomatic anachronisms. Yet one cannot deny that it raises numerous problems. The most immediate difficulty is the remark that King Edward sent Bishop Giso to Rome 'three years ago' (*ante hoc triennium*), when 'four' would be more accurate in 1065.[159] It is a curious mistake, whether the charter is genuine or not; and if it is not simply an aberration, one might wonder whether it signifies that the first paragraph had been drafted on an earlier occasion, in 1064, and was re-used unthinkingly when the document was completed at Windsor a year later.[160] Also disturbing is the fact that this is a general confirmation charter, intended to cover all of the lands which belong to the bishopric. It seems to be an unwritten law of Anglo-Saxon diplomatic that charters of this nature are 'continental', or 'post-Conquest'; and the Wells charter is quite explicitly a general confirmation of earlier grants. It was, however, at about this time that King Edward issued a writ authorising Archbishop Ealdred 'to draw up a *priuilegium* for the lands that belong to St John's minster at Beverley',[161] which sounds exactly like a general confirmation, and it was at about the same time that Abbot Brihtric (who may once have served in the royal household) appears to have produced a similar kind of charter in respect of the lands of Malmesbury abbey.[162] The writ appointing Giso as bishop would have given him all the authority he needed to put together a document of precisely this kind; and the writ authorising him to draw up a *priuilegium* in respect of Wedmore is enough to show that Giso

---

[158] Excavations at Kingsbury, Old Windsor, in the 1950s revealed that the site had been occupied at least from the ninth century; see B. Hope-Taylor's note in *Medieval Archaeology* ii, 1958, 183–5. Æthelsige was consecrated abbot of St Augustine's, Canterbury, at Windsor, on 26 May 1061 (ASC, MS E); and Baldwin was consecrated abbot of Bury St Edmunds, at Windsor, on 15 August 1065 (Herman, 'De miraculis S. Eadmundi', ch. 22). See also T.E. Harwood, *Windsor Old and New*, London 1929, 55–74.

[159] KCD 816 (from the *Monasticon*, from the Tiberius transcript) has *biennium*, perhaps no more than a casual misreading of *triennium*. The turn of phrase in the charter, to the effect that the king dispatched Giso to Rome and received him back ('direxi . . . recepi'), is echoed in Giso's autobiography, Appendix IV, §3 ('direxit . . . recepit').

[160] The procedure could be compared, for example, with that which lay behind the production of King William's charter for Ingelric and St Martin's-le-Grand, in 1067–8; cf. Keynes, 'Regenbald the Chancellor', 218. William II's diploma for Bishop John (above, n. 73, and below, n. 163), which may have been drawn up in the first instance at Wells, would provide another analogy for a two-stage production.

[161] Harmer, *Anglo-Saxon Writs*, no. 7.

[162] S 1038; see Keynes, 'Regenbald the Chancellor', 214, n. 174 (and cf. Harmer, *Anglo-Saxon Writs*, 39, n. 3). It is a curious fact that the Malmesbury charter and the Wells charter share a common error in giving the indiction for 1065 as '4', when it should be '3'.

might be trusted to do the job himself. The king's further statement, in the Wells charter, to the effect that he has affixed 'the seal of my image', would have caused many a raised eyebrow in the royal writing office of the tenth century, though it is certainly not without parallel in the second half of the eleventh century (before and after the Conquest), and is perfectly acceptable (in my view) as a sign of 'continental' practices at Edward's court.[163] The position of the witness-list, in the middle of the main text, is most irregular, and one is tempted to suggest that it was inscribed in the first instance on the dorse of a single sheet, when the charter was formally ratified at Windsor, and only transferred to this point in the text by a later copyist.[164] The list itself is entirely acceptable for its given date, in the sense that it accords well with witness-lists in charters of the early 1060s preserved in other archives. It is self-evident that a list of this nature could only have been drawn up by someone who knew exactly who was who at the court of King Edward the Confessor; and while one has to admit the possibility that a forger simply lifted the list from a genuine document in the Wells archive, the fact that the list is in certain respects selectively 'south-western' makes it seem wholly appropriate to the charter in hand. The three abbots are Æthelnoth of Glastonbury, Leofweard of Muchelney, and Sæwold of Bath. The three grandees (styled *princeps*) are Brihtric, Ælfstan, and Ælfgar, all of whom appear to have had Somerset connections.[165] Among the rest, pride of place is accorded to Tofig, sheriff of Somerset, a man of some substance in his county and obviously an interested party.[166] Evorwacer, who bore a German name (OG Eburacar), was a prominent land-owner in Somerset; his land passed after the Conquest into the hands of Serlo de Burcy, though he was survived by his son, Ælfric.[167] 'Eilwi' may well be Alwig, son of Banna, who held lands in Somerset and elsewhere in the south-west, and Wikyng (ON Víkingr) was perhaps the person of that name who held land in Devon.[168] One should also note

[163] The Malmesbury charter (S 1038) was attested by the king, 'impressione sigilli mei'; see also Keynes, 'Regenbald the Chancellor', 216, n. 188, and cf. S. Keynes, *Facsimiles of Anglo-Saxon Charters*, Oxford 1991, nos 20–1. Diplomas of William I for St Martin's-le-Grand (dated 1068) and for St Denis (dated 1069) would appear to have been 'sealed' as well as 'signed'; and the same is true of William II's diploma (issued in 1091) granting Bath abbey to John, bishop of Wells (above, n. 73). There is, indeed, a close relationship in this respect between the formulation of Giso's charter of 1065 and Bishop John's charter of 1091; and one might suggest that the latter was drawn up at Wells using Giso's charter as a model.

[164] Needless to say, there were few rules about procedure when charters were drawn up in circumstances of this kind. Cf above, n. 160.

[165] For Brihtric and Ælfgar, see below, 246, and n. 246. Ælfstan was undoubtedly none other than Ælfstan of Boscombe, who was granted land in Wiltshire by King Edward in 1043 (S 999; *DB Wilts.* 32.13), who features prominently in the witness-lists of the Confessor's charters (Keynes, *Atlas of Attestations*, Table LXXV; but cf. P.A. Clarke, *The English Nobility under Edward the Confessor*, Oxford 1994, 126); and who was among the wealthiest thegns in the kingdom in 1066, with strong interests in Wiltshire and Somerset (*ibid.*, 229–31). For the other office-holders in the witness-list, see Keynes, 'Regenbald the Chancellor', 204–8.

[166] Tofig the sheriff is named in Exon DB as the holder (TRE) of 2 hides at Lopen (*DB Som.* 47.3), and is presumably the Tofig who held a total of about 13 hides of land elsewhere in the county (*DB Som.* 1.28=17.6, 5.35, 22.25, and 47.4–5 and 7–8).

[167] *DB Som.* 8.33, 27.3, and 37.2–4, 6 and 10; see also *DB Dev.* 16.109. Evorwacer otherwise attests the charter drawn up by Bishop Giso for Wulfwold, abbot of Bath (Appendix I, no. 5). For his name, see Forssner, *Continental-Germanic Personal Names*, 85, and O. von Feilitzen, *The Pre-Conquest Personal Names of Domesday Book*, Uppsala 1937, 249.

[168] Alwig's lands passed to Alfred d'Epaignes (Loud, 'Somerset Domesday', 18; Clarke, *English*

the attestation of a certain Osmund *minister* at the end, making his sole appearance in the Confessor's reign; for he is probably to be identified as the Osmund who held Winsham from the bishop TRW, and who is known to have been Bishop Giso's nephew.[169] Giso himself is conspicuous by his absence from the main witness-list, but he makes his sign manual at the end of the text, in what would seem to have been the approved manner.[170]

The irregular diplomatic form of the Wells charter may have worried some commentators, but the principal objection to its authenticity has always been that it is simply incompatible with what else is known of the history of the Wells estates. The survey of these estates incorporated in the body of the charter gives what seem to be acceptable late Old English forms for many of the minor places which were the constituent members of the chief manors.[171] We are faced, however, with the difficult and undeniable fact that several of the estates mentioned in the charter were patently not acquired or recovered by the church of Wells until some time after 1065. The episcopal manor of '38' hides at Kingsbury is said to have included among its appurtenances some land at Combe and at Winsham, as well as Congresbury and Banwell with all their appurtenances.[172] Yet Combe (St Nicholas) was not acquired until Bishop Giso bought it from Azor in 1072;[173] Winsham, which Giso had failed to recover during Edward's reign, was given to the church by King William I;[174] Banwell, which had been appropriated by Earl Harold, was restored by King William in 1068;[175] and Congresbury, also appropriated by Earl Harold, was not recovered until the early thirteenth century.[176] The question here is whether

---

Nobility, 241–2), but he survived as a tenant TRW on Giso's estate at Banwell. For Wikyng, see *DB Dev.* 19.8–9, 22, 26, 38 and 45, and 34.12, 29–30, 52 and 56.

[169] Osmund 'nepos episcopi' held 3 hides in the 'Terra Gisonis' from which the king did not have the geld (Exon DB 78v); Osmund 'nepos episcopi Gisonis' held 10 hides in Abdick Hundred from which the king did not have the geld (Exon DB 81v), evidently with reference to the estate at Winsham. There was an Osmund Stramin in Somerset TRE (*DB Som.* 5.6–7, 22.15; see also 19.41), whose byname suggests that he may have been of German origin (G. Tengvik, *Old English Bynames*, Uppsala 1938, 217).

[170] The position and form of this attestation, followed by a decorated cross, bears comparison with the notarial subscription of Swithgar which occurs at the end of the charter for Earl Harold's church at Waltham (S 1036), dated 1062. One might also compare Giso's attestation in the charter which he drew up for Wulfwold, abbot of Bath (Appendix I, no. 5).

[171] One is hindered in this respect by the absence of a modern work on the place-names of Somerset, which might set these forms in a useful context. See A.G.C. Turner, 'The Place-Names of North Somerset', unpublished Ph.D. thesis, Univ. of Cambridge (1951), esp. 95–115 (Wells-Forum Hundred); see also A.G.C. Turner, 'Notes on Some Somerset Place-Names', *Proceedings of the Somersetshire Archæological & Natural History Society* xcv, 1951, 112–24, and A.G.C. Turner, 'A Selection of North Somerset Place-Names', *Proceedings of the Somersetshire Archæological & Natural History Society* xcvi, 1952, 152–9.

[172] To judge from their respective assessments in GDB, Combe (20 hides), Winsham (10 hides), Congresbury (20 hides), and Banwell (30 hides) were not included in the '38' hides at Kingsbury; cf. below, n. 184. It is appropriate that Combe and Winsham were grouped, with Chard, under Kingsbury Episcopi; but it is especially interesting that Congresbury and Banwell should have been placed with them.

[173] Appendix I, no. 16, and Appendix III; see also below, 244.

[174] Appendix I, no. 13; see also below, 241.

[175] Appendix I, no. 14; see also below, 242.

[176] For Bishop Jocelin's acquisition of Congresbury, see HMC, *Dean and Chapter of Wells* i, 76–7 and 147–8, and the *Historia Major* (ed. Robinson, 65); see also Loud, 'Somerset Domesday', p. 15, n. 3.

Earl Harold, in particular, would have put his name to a charter which (mis)repre-
sented two of his most substantial estates in Somerset as being the property of the
bishop of Wells. But nor is that all. The estate at Wedmore is said to have included
among its appurtenances some land at Mark; yet Mark would appear to have been
given to Bishop Giso by the Lady Edith, 'widow of King Edward',[177] rendering its
inclusion in Edward's charter another sign of wisdom after the event. In the face of
these facts, the most relaxing course of action would be to dismiss the charter out
of hand, as a gross forgery,[178] and to get on with other business; but that, I think,
would be to miss the beauty of a charter which breaks all of the rules for all of the
best reasons. There is no suggestion that this charter is the product of a royal
chancery; rather, it is a *priuilegium* for the bishopric of Wells, produced by Giso,
bishop of Wells. The question is, therefore, by what standards does one judge a
document which was drawn up by the ecclesiastic most directly concerned, who
already had a writ from the king telling the local authorities that any land taken
away from the bishopric should be restored, not to mention a papal privilege telling
everybody to back off. One quite simple solution would be to imagine that the list
of estates conveyed by the charter was updated from time to time, as if in the
manner of a continental *pancarte*;[179] indeed, it might be remarked in this connection that Winsham, Congresbury, and Banwell occur at the end of the list of
appurtenances of Kingsbury, and that Mark occurs at the end of the list of appurtenances of Wedmore, as if they were later additions. But given what we know of
Bishop Giso, another solution would be to accept the charter at face value, as the
product of Giso's determination to secure the endowment of his church. The
inclusion of Winsham, Congresbury, and Banwell seems entirely appropriate (and
one can be sure that Giso enjoyed his little joke). Perhaps Combe was also episcopal property, like Winsham; and perhaps its owner had come to terms with Giso, as
envisaged in King Edward's writ, until he was bought out a few years later.[180] In
the case of Mark, it may be that this was another property which had fallen into the
wrong hands, or that a grant made during Edward's reign did not stick, and had to
be confirmed by Queen Edith after his death.[181] One might add that it is almost as
difficult to believe that the charter could have been fabricated in this form any
length of time after the Conquest. If the idea was to project the church's ownership

---

[177] Appendix I, no. 15; see also below, 239.

[178] Kemble (KCD 816) marked the charter as spurious. Green, 'Earl Harold and Bishop Giso', 153,
n., dismissed it as 'a gross forgery', taking particular exception to the statement that Edward had
sent Giso to Rome 'two years' before 1065 (*ante hoc biennium*), and to the inclusion of Mark,
Banwell, and Congresbury. See also Freeman, *Norman Conquest* ii, 675 ('manifestly spurious',
citing Green); Harmer, *Anglo-Saxon Writs*, 39, n. 3, 270, n. 2, and 488 ff. ('spurious'); H.P.R.
Finberg, *The Early Charters of Wessex*, Leicester 1964, no. 542 (awarded three asterisks); and *Bath
and Wells 1061–1205*, ed. Ramsey, xxiii ('almost certainly spurious') and xci, n. 65.

[179] For *pancartes*, see L. Musset, *Les actes de Guillaume le Conquérant et de la reine Mathilde
pour les abbayes caennaises*, Mémoires de la Société des Antiquaires de Normandie 37, Caen 1967,
25–35, and nos 4, 7, and 8, etc. See also M. Chibnall, 'Charter and Chronicle: the Use of Archive
Sources by Norman Historians', *Church and Government in the Middle Ages*, ed. C.N.L. Brooke, *et
al.*, Cambridge 1976, 1–17, esp. 11–12; and D. Bates, 'The Forged Charters of William the
Conqueror and Bishop William of St Calais', *Anglo-Norman Durham*, ed. D. Rollason, *et al.*,
Woodbridge 1994, 111–24, esp. 112–13.

[180] See below, 244.

[181] See below, 239. The account of this in Giso's autobiography (Appendix IV, §4) might be taken
to imply that Mark, and Mudgeley, were given to Wells by Queen Edith, before her husband's death.

of Combe, Winsham, Congresbury, Banwell, and Mark back into the Confessor's reign, it seems odd that these places should have been tucked away as appurtenances, and not given the proper treatment. The forger would also have shown commendable restraint in not including other estates which are known to have come into the possession of the church, notably the estate at Milverton given by Queen Edith,[182] and the 20 hides at Yatton which were held TRE by John the Dane.[183] In more general terms, the account of the 'Terra Gisonis' incorporated in the charter makes reasonable sense if it originated some time before the estates were described for the purposes of the Domesday survey, and rather less sense if it was put together by a canon of Wells some time after Giso's death.[184] And if the charter was forged by a canon of Wells, why, one might ask, was no attempt made to represent the particular interests of the canons in certain of the episcopal estates?

The charter of 1065 contains a specific and generous acknowledgement of Queen Edith's role in persuading King Edward to confirm the accumulated endowment of the see of Wells;[185] and there is now perhaps good reason to regard this acknowledgement as Bishop Giso's own expression of the gratitude which he felt towards her. It is well known, of course, that Edith was actively engaged in the promotion of good works during her husband's reign, and perhaps especially so in the early 1060s;[186] and it may be significant that her support of a Lotharingian priest at Wells, in the person of Bishop Giso, seems to match her brother's activities at Waltham in Essex.[187] We have seen that Queen Edith is said to have been instrumental in helping Bishop Giso to acquire the estate at Wedmore from the king, and that she then increased the estate by adding land at Mark and Mudgley.[188] Queen Edith also gave an estate at **Milverton**, Somerset, to Bishop Giso towards the end of Edward's reign, perhaps in the latter half of 1065. A writ issued in her name declares that Bishop Giso is to be entitled to the land at Milverton, as fully and completely as she possessed it, 'on the terms that we have agreed on';[189] and

---

182 Appendix I, no. 10; see also below, 238–9.

183 GDB 89v (*DB Som.* 6.14). Other estates which had belonged TRE to John the Dane were held TRW by Matthew of Mortagne: *DB Som.* 44.1; *DB Dor.* 46.1–2; and *DB Glos.* 73.2.

184 The assessments and configuration of the estates in the charter should be compared with the assessments and configuration of the 'Terra Gisonis' in Domesday Book (Appendix V). The '50' hides at Wells included land at Westbury (6 hides), Wanstrow (4 hides), and Litton (8½ hides); by 1086 Wanstrow and Litton had been transferred to the canons, and were assessed separately. The '50' hides at Chew are represented by 30 hides there in 1086. The '38' hides at Kingsbury included the 20 hides at Kingsbury, plus 8 hides at Chard and 2 hides at Littleney; for Combe, Winsham, Congresbury, and Banwell, see above, n. 172. The '15' hides at Wellington perhaps comprised the 14 hides at Wellington, and the additional hide held by Ælfgifu. The '15' hides at (Bishops) Lydeard included the 10 hides (less 1 virgate) at Lydeard, and the 3 hides (plus 1 virgate) at Ash Priors, said to have been held TRE by the bishop in his manor of Lydeard. The '4' hides at Wedmore appear to have grown to 10, or 11, by 1086, in part, no doubt, by virtue of Bishop Osbern's grant of the church (Appendix I, no. 19).

185 It may be that the specific acknowledgement of Queen Edith reflects the common practice, on the continent, of specifying the person who 'intervened' to have a grant made (cf. Reuter, *Germany in the Early Middle Ages*, 127 and 199). I owe this suggestion to Julia Barrow.

186 'His royal consort did not restrain him in those good works in which he was prepared to lead the way, but rather urged speedier progress, and often enough seemed even to lead the way herself' (*Vita Ædwardi regis*, bk I, ch. 6 (ed. Barlow, 62)). See also Barlow, *English Church 1000–1066*, 109, n. 4.

187 See above, 210.

188 Giso's autobiography (Appendix IV, §4); see also above, 219.

189 Appendix I, no. 10.

although the place is not mentioned in the charter of 1065, land at Milverton was in Giso's hands in January 1066, assessed at 1 virgate.[190] It was apparently the same estate which was taken back by Edith some time after Edward's death, whether during the reign of her brother or during the opening years of the reign of King William, perhaps in accordance with whatever terms had been agreed with Giso, or perhaps in more complex (but unknown) circumstances.[191] For an estate at Milverton was in Edith's hands at the time of her death (in December 1075), and passed thereafter into the hands of King William; and although it had paid geld for only half a virgate, there was land for 16 ploughs, indicating that it was quite a substantial property.[192] Edith's continued support for Bishop Giso, after her husband's death, is otherwise reflected in the writ addressed to the hundred at Wedmore, in which she declares that she has given Giso the land at **Mark**, Somerset, 'for his canons at St Andrew's at Wells'.[193] We saw above that Mark was included among the lands confirmed to Bishop Giso in 1065; and while it is by no means clear how we should interpret Edith's request that the hundred court should pronounce a judgement concerning Wudumann, 'to whom I entrusted my horses and who has for six years withheld my rent',[194] one possibility is that she had previously promised the land to Bishop Giso, leaving Wudumann in place as a sitting tenant, and that Wudumann's unsatisfactory behaviour subsequently prompted her to hand over the estate sooner than had been intended. Whatever the case, Bishop Giso certainly had good reason to be grateful to Queen Edith for her support; and it seems especially appropriate, under these circumstances, that it was in Edith's presence, at Wilton abbey, in 1072, that Giso chose to conduct some further business concerning the affairs of his church.[195]

Bishop Giso and King Harold

On his deathbed in January 1066, Edward the Confessor commended Edith and all the kingdom to the protection of Earl Harold, and at the same time commended to Harold 'those men who have left their native land for love of me, and have up till now served me faithfully'.[196] If the reference was to the men who had joined Edward from Normandy, they would doubtless have been grateful for some form of protection; but there is no reason to believe that the Lotharingians at Edward's court, or on the episcopal bench, would have found themselves under any threat from the new regime. It would appear, nonetheless, that Bishop Giso made a point of securing an assurance from the new king that his own interests as bishop of Wells would be protected; and it is to this concern that we owe the existence of a writ which happens to be the sole surviving document, from any archive, issued in

---

[190] An estate at Milverton which paid geld for 1 virgate was held TRE by Bishop Giso and TRW by King William (GDB 89v (*DB Som.* 6.18)); see Appendix V. A title-deed for an estate of 1 hide at Manworthy, in Milverton, was preserved in the Wells archives (S 709). For the suggestion that Edith's grant did not take effect, see Loud, 'Somerset Domesday', 14.

[191] Cf. Barlow, *English Church 1000–1066*, 114–15.

[192] GDB 87r (*DB Som.* 1.26).

[193] Appendix I, no. 15.

[194] Wormald, 'Handlist of Anglo-Saxon Lawsuits', 265 (no. 95).

[195] See below, 244.

[196] *Vita Ædwardi regis*, bk ii, ch. 11 (ed. Barlow, 122–4).

the name of King Harold.[197] The writ is addressed, as usual, to Æthelnoth (abbot of Glastonbury), Tofig (the sheriff), and all the king's thegns in Somerset. The king declares that Bishop Giso is to be entitled to his various judicial and financial rights, 'as fully and completely as ever he was in King Edward's time'; and, as if there might be some difficulty, he insists that everyone should give Giso all the help that they could in protecting and advancing the interests of his church, echoing in this respect the wording of the writs which Giso had previously received from King Edward:[198]

Writ of Edward (1061)	*Writ of Edward (1061x65)*	*Writ of Harold (1066)*
And I pray you all that you will help him to further the rights of God [i.e. the interests of the church] wherever it may be needful and he may require your aid.	And I pray you all that you will help him to speak Christianity [i.e. to declare the rights of the bishop] wherever it may be needful and he may require your aid.	And I pray you all that you will help him with regard to Christianity [i.e. the rights of the bishop] in order to establish and to further the rights of God [i.e. the interests of the church] wherever it may be needful and he may require your aid.

If we may indulge a fantasy that it was Regenbald, or some other member of the royal secretariat, who was responsible for formulating these writs, as opposed to the king himself, we can almost sense the concern felt at the king's court to ensure that Giso would indeed prevail over his adversaries. In truth, however, it would be rash to attach too much significance to such turns of phrase, as expressions indicative of Giso's particular predicament, for it may have been quite normal for bishops (and abbots) to receive such assurances when first appointed, or from a newly established king, and relatively unusual for the writs to be preserved.[199] Nor is it clear what, if anything, can be made of the remark in the autobiography to the effect that on becoming king Harold 'promised not only to restore what he had taken away, but also to give fresh donations'.[200] It seems somewhat out of character, both for Harold to do it and for Giso to say it; and it may be that a canon of Wells had simply put his own construction upon the writ.

---

197 Appendix I, no. 11.
198 Appendix I, nos 1 and 3. For discussion of the operative phrases, see Harmer, *Anglo-Saxon Writs*, 487 (n. to line 10), 488 (n. to line 7), and 491 (n. to line 6).
199 The following writs deserve comparison as a group: S 1083 (Harmer, *Anglo-Saxon Writs*, no. 23), for Baldwin, abbot of Bury St Edmunds; S 1097 (*ibid.*, no. 44), for Regenbald, in his capacity as a royal priest; S 1100 (*ibid.*, no. 47), for Wulfric, abbot of Ely; S 1102 (*ibid.*, no. 50), for Walter, bishop of Hereford; S 1111 (*ibid.*, no. 64), S 1112 (*ibid.*, no. 65) and S 1163 (*ibid.*, no. 71), for Giso, bishop of Wells; S 1159 (*ibid.*, no. 109), for Ælfwine, bishop of Winchester; and S 1156 (*ibid.*, no. 115), for Wulfstan, bishop of Worcester.
200 Giso's autobiography (Appendix IV, §6).

Bishop Giso and King William the Conqueror

Like the majority of his episcopal colleagues (who owed their positions to royal patronage dispensed during the reign of Edward the Confessor, and were close to the heart of the establishment),[201] but unlike the majority of abbots (who presided over religious communities deeply rooted in local society, and perhaps especially conscious of their 'English' identity),[202] Giso had little difficulty in coming to terms with William the Conqueror. The king, for his part, needed to preserve the appearances of continuity from the regime of Edward the Confessor, and, as the controlled and rather less controlled processes of 'settlement' began, he must have seen the advantage of gaining the confidence of those with standing and influence in the localities.[203] Domesday Book sets the position reached by 1086 beside the position in January 1066, and provides an awesome wealth of detail; but other forms of evidence contribute much to our sense of development within the intervening period. The documents which take us directly into the circle of Bishop Giso and his associates, in post-Conquest Somerset, are a case in point, and when brought together afford a remarkable view of a changing, or perhaps an unchanging, world under Norman rule.

The earliest of the documents in question is a writ announcing that King William has granted land at Charlcombe, in Somerset, to Wulfwold, abbot of Bath.[204] The writ, cast in the vernacular, is addressed to Bishop Giso, Eadnoth the staller, Tofig the sheriff, and all the thegns of Somerset. It is as if the shire-court was continuing to function as normal, in the year following the Conquest; and the inclusion of Eadnoth the staller among the persons addressed suggests that at this stage he held a position in Somerset which gave him powers and responsibilities equivalent to those enjoyed by a pre-Conquest earl.[205] Bishop Giso was active soon enough on his own account. In a (Latin) writ addressed to Abbot Æthelnoth, Tofig the sheriff, and all the *barones* of Somerset, the king declares that at the request of Bishop Giso ('me ammonitione et prece Gysonis episcopi') he has granted land at **Winsham**, Somerset, to the church of Wells, 'ad sustentationem canonicorum';[206] this was, of course, the estate which had been in the hands of the Ælfsige who had successfully resisted Giso's previous efforts to recover the land for the church.[207]

[201] See H. Loyn, 'William's Bishops: Some Further Thoughts' (1988), reptd in his *Society and Peoples*, 374–97, at 379; and Barlow, *Edward the Confessor*, 191.

[202] D. Knowles, *The Monastic Order in England: a History of its Development from the Times of St Dunstan to the Fourth Lateran Council 940–1216*, 2nd edn, Cambridge 1963, 103–6.

[203] For unrest in the south-west in the spring of 1068, see Williams, *The English and the Norman Conquest*, 19–21.

[204] Appendix I, no. 12.

[205] For Eadnoth the staller (often called Alnod in DB), see Freeman, *Norman Conquest* iv, 757–61; J.H. Round, 'Domesday Survey', *VCH Somerset* i, 383–432, at 417–18; Loud, 'Somerset Domesday', 17–18; C.P. Lewis, 'The Formation of the Honour of Chester, 1066–1100', *Journal of the Chester Archæological Society* lxxi, 1991, 37–68, at 48–9 and 67–8; Williams, *The English and the Norman Conquest*, 119–21; and Clarke, *English Nobility*, 281–3. Eadnoth was killed in the summer of 1068, defending Somerset against invasion led by Godwine, Edmund and Magnus, sons of the late King Harold (ASC, MS D, *s.a.* 1067; John of Worcester). The bulk of his lands passed to Hugh d'Avranches, earl of Chester. For Harding, son of Eadnoth, see below, 245.

[206] Appendix I, no. 13.

[207] Giso's autobiography (Appendix IV, §§5 and 7). It is said that King William confirmed the grant by a charter (*priuilegium*), apparently with reference to the Latin writ, from which it appears to quote.

Yet it is one thing to see the king dealing at arm's length with the officials of a shire-court in the south-west; it is another to see men from the south-west coming up to town in order to pay their respects at court. One of the most spectacular gatherings in the opening years of the Conqueror's reign must have been the occasion when the king, and numerous representatives of the ecclesiastical and secular powers, assembled at Westminster for the consecration of Queen Mathilda at Whitsuntide (11 May) 1068.[208] The important charter by which King William confirmed the endowment and privileges of the church of St Martin's-le-Grand, in London, for the benefit of his priest Ingelric, is known to have been produced on this auspicious occasion;[209] and it is no surprise to see that Bishop Giso was present among the witnesses. Nor is it a surprise to find that Giso evidently took advantage of the occasion to badger King William into restoring the estate of 30 hides at **Banwell**, Somerset, to the church of St Andrew at Wells.[210] According to the charter which records this act, the king was 'pulsatus . . . piis precibus Gisonis episcopi'; and there could be little doubt that the charter itself, drawn up like Ingelric's in the manner of a pre-Conquest royal diploma, was produced by Bishop Giso.[211] The scathing remark to that effect that 'King Harold, puffed up with avarice', appropriated land which Bishop Duduc had given to God, affords a fair indication of the bishop's point of view, whatever Harold's may have been;[212] and although Harold is accorded his proper dignity, suggesting that Giso would not have subscribed instinctively to the notion that Harold had not been a legitimate king,[213] Giso was clearly intent upon representing William as Edward's natural successor.[214] The witness-list in Ingelric's charter includes a representative selection of bishops, abbots, and prominent laymen, as well as two 'royal chaplains' and several other chaplains presumably of a different kind. The Wells charter contains a larger number of bishops (though Giso himself is left out), a smaller and different selection of abbots, a number of the same laymen, and a good many others; but the chaplains are not represented. As in the case of the charter of 1065, the Somerset or south-western complexion of the witness-list is quite unmistakable. The four abbots are Æthelnoth (of Glastonbury), Leofweard (of Muchelney), Wulfwold (of Bath), and Wulfgeat (probably of Athelney).[215] Among the laymen we find several

---

[208] ASC, MS D, *s.a.* 1067 (covering events of 1067–8).

[209] *Regesta* i, no. 22; *Acta of William I*, ed. Bates, no. 181. For further discussion, see Keynes, 'Regenbald the Chancellor', 218–19, and references.

[210] Appendix I, no. 14.

[211] Note that the opening structure of the text (pictorial and verbal invocations, followed by superscription, itself leading directly into the pious consideration behind the grant) echoes the structure of Edward the Confessor's charter confirming the endowment of Wells in 1065. The wording of the reservation clause echoes the equivalent formula in Edward's charter for Abbot Wulfwold (S 1034), drawn up by Giso in 1061. The form of the attestations of the king and queen clearly echoes the charter of 1065.

[212] Cf. above, 230–1.

[213] G. Garnett, 'Coronation and Propaganda: Some Implications of the Norman Claim to the Throne of England in 1066', *TRHS*, 5th ser. xxxvi, 1986, 91–116, at 99–105; see also Keynes, 'Regenbald the Chancellor', 220, n. 216.

[214] Giso describes Edward as William's *antecessor*, but perhaps simply in the sense of 'predecessor in office'; see Garnett, 'Coronation and Propaganda', 105–7.

[215] Wulfgeat's Somerset credentials are guaranteed by his appearance among the witnesses in the record concerning the dues pertaining to Taunton (Appendix I, no. 17); see *The Heads of Religious Houses, England and Wales 940–1216*, ed. D. Knowles, *et al.*, Cambridge 1972, 26 and 227.

members of the new land-holding classes in the west country, including William de Courseulles, Serlo de Burcy, Roger Arundel ('Derundel'), Walter of Douai ('Waldtere fleminc'), Thurstan (probably Thurstan, son of Rolf), Haimeric, and William de Vauville.[216] Tofig *minister* stands out among these men as a man accorded the dignity of his social status; he was, of course, the sheriff of Somerset. 'Dinni' may be the Dunna who held a substantial estate, TRE and TRW, at Buckland in Somerset,[217] and/or the Dunna who was the *antecessor* of Osbern Giffard in Somerset, Wiltshire, and Gloucestershire. 'Ælfgear de Thorne' is presumably the 'Algar' who held 6 hides at Thorn(falcon) TRE, and who thus survived for at least a while before losing his land to the count of Mortain.[218] The list ends with five men whose names are redolent of the native aristocracy in the south-west: Wulfweard, Harding, Adzor, Brixi, and Brihtric.[219] The natural assumption is that the men named in the witness-list were present together on a single occasion, in which case the men from Somerset must have been matched by a comparable range of men drawn from other parts of the country. It must have been an extraordinary sight as they all converged on Westminster for the queen's coronation in May 1068, and no less extraordinary as they all took word of the proceedings back to their respective homes.

Giso was not affected by the purge of bishops in the spring of 1070,[220] and is duly found among those who officiated at the consecration of Lanfranc, as archbishop of Canterbury, on 29 August of the same year.[221] Two vernacular documents, one from Winchester and the other from Wells, reveal how little his world seems to have changed as he went about his daily business. A document drawn up some time before the Domesday survey, perhaps in the late 1060s or in the 1070s, and subsequently preserved in the archives of the Old Minster at Winchester, shows Giso acting as the first of many witnesses to a formal report on the outcome of an enquiry into the dues which had pertained to the bishop of Winchester's manor at Taunton, in Somerset, 'on the day when King Edward was alive and dead'.[222] The other witnesses are all 'English', present in their capacity as the worthy men of this part of Somerset; and it is interesting to see Giso associated in this context with Wulfweard White, Harding, son of Eadnoth, a certain Brihtric the Bald, and others.[223] The second document records the bishop's purchase of land at **Combe (St Nicholas)**, in Somerset, from Azur, son of Thorod (or Thorth), and was drawn up at Wilton abbey in February 1072.[224] It is necessary to explain, in this connection, that Wilton abbey, said to have been founded in the first half of the ninth century, had long enjoyed a close association with the West Saxon royal family; we may recall, for example, that St Wulfthryth, who had attracted the amorous attentions of King Edgar, became abbess of Wilton in the 960s, and that

---

[216] Their occurrence in Bishop Giso's charter suggests that they already had 'west country' associations; see Williams, *The English and the Norman Conquest*, 21–2.

[217] GDB 99r (*DB Som.* 47.19). See also *Anglo-Saxon Charters*, ed. Robertson, 487.

[218] GDB 92r (*DB Som.* 19.31).

[219] See further below, 244–7.

[220] Gibson, *Lanfranc of Bec*, 113–15; Barlow, *English Church 1000–1066*, 113–14.

[221] Lanfranc's memorandum on the primacy of Canterbury, in *Lanfranc's Letters*, 38–48 (no. 3), at 40; and Gibson, *Lanfranc of Bec*, 115.

[222] Appendix I, no. 17.

[223] See further below, 244–7.

[224] Appendix I, no. 16: for text and translation, see Appendix III.

their daughter was St Edith of Wilton, who died in 984. Edith, daughter of Earl Godwine, had been educated at Wilton; and when her husband, King Edward the Confessor, turned his attention to the building of Westminster abbey, she was moved to follow his example. The old wooden church at Wilton was replaced with one built of stone, and in 1065 the new church was dedicated by (the Lotharingian) Herman, bishop of Wiltshire (at Sherborne).[225] After the Norman Conquest, Wilton abbey appears to have become a refuge for well-connected ladies; and it seems (at least on the basis of the present document) that it was at Wilton that Edith continued to hold court and conduct her affairs. In February 1072 Bishop Giso and his entourage (including some members of the community at Wells) travelled into Wiltshire, apparently for the express purpose of completing whatever previous arrangements had been made for the purchase of the land at Combe.[226] It was a large estate, assessed at 20 hides; and while the fact that Giso secured it for a good price (six marks of gold) might suggest that he was bargaining from a position of advantage, it is possible that the price was brought down by Azur's good will, or by the promise of liturgical commemoration for his family.[227] We cannot tell who was made responsible for drawing up a formal record of the transaction, though the fact that it is dated 1072, 'in the sixth year that King William reigned (*rixode*)' [1071–2], and 'in the eleventh year since Bishop Giso succeeded to power (*feng to rice*)' [Apr. 1071 – Apr. 1072], is fairly suggestive.

The most remarkable aspect of the document recording the purchase of Combe is the picture it gives of the gathering on the upper storey of the stone church at Wilton; for it is as if the surviving members of the Edwardian establishment had gathered in the presence of the Lady Edith for their annual convention. AZUR, son of Thorod (or Thorth), had held the estate at Combe in the reign of King Edward the Confessor.[228] We may be confident that he was the Adzor who had attested King William's charter for Bishop Giso in 1068; but beyond that we must resort to the usual kind of prosopographical speculation. An Azur, styled king's steward (*regis dapifer*), attested the Waltham charter in 1062;[229] an Azur, *filius Tored . teignus .R.E.* ('thegn of King Edward'), held land in Buckinghamshire which was later held by Earl Aubrey;[230] an Azur, bursar of King Edward (*dispensator .R.E.*), held land in Berkshire in 1086 which had been restored to him (at Windsor) by writ of King William;[231] and an Azur held a number of estates TRE, in Wiltshire, Oxfordshire, and Northamptonshire, which passed after the Conquest into the hands of Earl Aubrey.[232] If we may boldly resolve these persons into one, Azur

---

225 *Vita Ædwardi regis*, bk I, chs 6–7 (ed. Barlow, 70–2 and 74).

226 It has been suggested that they came to Edith because she had retained office as a high justiciar for Somerset; see R.W. Eyton, *Domesday Studies: an Analaysis and Digest of the Somerset Survey*, 2 vols, London 1880, i, 50.

227 Cf. S 1426 (*Anglo-Saxon Charters*, ed. Robertson, no. 117): Abbot Ælfwig and the community of Bath leased 30 hides of land at Tidenham, Glos., to Archbishop Stigand in return for 10 marks of gold and 20 pounds of silver; the witnesses included Bishop Giso.

228 GDB 89r (*DB Som.* 6.2). Exon DB names him in this context as 'Atsor filius Torodi'.

229 S 1036, on which see Keynes, 'Regenbald the Chancellor', 201–3 and (for the witnesses) 204–8. For the attestations of thegns in charters of Edward the Confessor, see Keynes, *Atlas of Attestations*, Table LXXV.

230 GDB 143v (*DB Bucks.* 1.7).

231 GDB 62r (*DB Berks.* 41.6).

232 Cf. Clarke, *English Nobility*, 253.

would emerge into the limelight as a prominent member of King Edward's household, who had survived the Conquest (albeit in much reduced circumstances), and who would appear to have retained an association with the Lady Edith at Wilton. The same game can be played with the witnesses, with similar results. HARDING, named first among the secular witnesses, is doubtless the Harding who attested the Waltham charter in 1062, styled *regine pincerna*, and who attested the Wells charter in 1065, styled *pincerna*; he also attested King William's charter for Bishop Giso in 1068. He is presumably the Harding who held an estate in Berkshire in 1086, which he had previously held from Queen Edith, and which had been held TRE by a certain Ælfgifu;[233] he is conceivably the Harding 'of Wilton' who held land at Cranmore, Somerset, from Glastonbury abbey, in 1066 and in 1086,[234] if only because the connection with Wilton suggests an association with the former queen; and he may thus be the Harding who had extensive holdings in Wiltshire (and Leicestershire and Warwickshire) in 1066, and who was still flourishing, though (like Azur) in reduced circumstances, in 1086.[235] Harding, the queen's butler, conceivably 'of Wilton', might by a further leap of faith be identified as Harding (of Merriott), son of Eadnoth the staller (known to have had interests in Somerset, Wiltshire, and Berkshire),[236] who seems for some reason not to have been able to inherit his father's estates, but who acquired interests in Somerset and elsewhere,[237] and who survived into the early twelfth century.[238] Certainly Harding, son of Eadnoth, is found in company with Bishop Giso, Wulfweard White, and others, in the Taunton document;[239] and it is not inherently unlikely that the son of an Edwardian staller should have entered into the service of the queen in the 1060s, and been forced to make his own way thereafter.[240] WULFWEARD WHITE, the next

---

[233] GDB 63v (*DB Berks.* 65.17).

[234] GDB 90v (*DB Som.* 8.32); Exon DB 527r (*VCH Somerset* i, 537).

[235] Six estates in Wiltshire which Harding held TRE passed into the hands of Earl Aubrey (GDB 69r (*DB Wilts.* 23.1–6)); one estate which Harding held TRE was held TRW by the Count of Mortain (GDB 68v (*DB Wilts.* 20.6)); and three other estates which Harding held TRE were still held by him TRW (GDB 74r (*DB Wilts.* 67.60–2)). The majority of these estates are in southern Wiltshire, not far distant from Wilton. The estates in Leicestershire and Warwickshire were held by Harding TRE, but passed thereafter into the hands of Earl Aubrey: *DB Leics.* 10.1–16, and *DB Warwicks.* 14.1, 3 and 6.

[236] For Harding, son of Eadnoth the staller (on whom see above, n. 205), see Freeman, *Norman Conquest* iv, 757–61; Eyton, *Domesday Studies: Somerset* i, 69–70; Williams, *The English and the Norman Conquest*, 119–22; and Lewis, 'The Formation of the Honour of Chester', 48–9 and 67–8. The identification of Harding, the queen's butler, as Harding, the queen's butler, was made by Freeman, followed by Robertson (*Anglo-Saxon Charters*, 489), and myself ('Regenbald the Chancellor', 207, n. 129); but it certainly involves more than the usual amount of wishful thinking.

[237] In 1086 Harding held several small manors in Somerset which had belonged TRE to Tofig the sheriff (*DB Som.* 47.3–8). The Somerset manors passed to Harding's son Nicholas (ancestor of the Meriet family). Other property passed to Harding's son Robert (Robert fitzHarding of Bristol). Harding's daughter became a nun at Shaftesbury.

[238] William of Malmesbury, *Gesta Regum*, bk. iii, ch. 254 (ed. Stubbs, ii, 313). See also Pelteret, nos 107 and 123; and *Two Cartularies of the Benedictine Abbeys of Athelney and Muchelney*, ed. E.H. Bates, Somerset Record Society 14, 1899, 106–8 (no. 126).

[239] Appendix I, no. 17.

[240] The identification obviously requires that someone who held office and land in the 1060s was healthy enough to have survived into the 1120s (when he might have been in his late seventies or eighties). One can but say that Harding, son of Eadnoth, who was remembered as a benefactor of Shaftesbury (K. Cooke, 'Donors and Daughters: Shaftesbury Abbey's Benefactors, Endowments and Nuns c.1086–1130', *ANS* xii, 1990, 29–45, at 32, 35 and 42) is said to have leased land at

of the witnesses at Wilton, had also attested Giso's charter in 1068. He was, of course, the holder (TRE) of a very substantial amount of land widely distributed across southern England (with a concentration in Buckinghamshire); he was the tenant of land on Queen Edith's estate at Keynsham, in Somerset, and had other land in the same shire which was assessed under the king's holding in 1086;[241] and there are further indications that he was, in fact, a member of the queen's household.[242] Wulfweard is followed in the witness-list by ÆTHELSIGE *stiweard* ('steward'), presumably another member of Edith's household and perhaps the 'Alsi' to whom Edith gave land in Buckinghamshire 'after the arrival of King William' and who held other land there by virtue of his marriage to Wulfweard White's daughter.[243] ÆLFWOLD *burthen* ('chamberlain') is evidently the 'Alwold camerarius' who came into the possession of land in Berkshire which Queen Edith had held TRE.[244] BRIHTRIC, here identified as the son of Dodda, was with Harding and Wulfweard another of those who had attested Giso's charter in 1068. It seems likely, by association and backward extension, that he was the Brihtric *p[rinceps]* who had attested Giso's charter in 1065, and the Brihtric *consiliarius* who had attested Giso's charter for Abbot Wulfwold in 1061;[245] indeed, he would appear on the same basis to have been a significant figure at court throughout the Confessor's reign.[246] Brihtric can perhaps be identified in Domesday Book as the Brihtric who had extensive interests in Buckinghamshire, TRE, and who is known to have been one of the queen's men;[247] but if he was the son of Dodda, he should evidently be distinguished from the well-known Brihtric, son of Ælfgar, of Cranborne (Dorset) and Tewkesbury (Glos.).[248] Brixi (Beorhtsige), here identified as the son of Ceolsige, had also attested Giso's charter in 1068, and might be one or other of the men of that name who held land in Somerset and Wiltshire in 1066.[249] Among the other

Beechingstoke, Wilts., from the abbey in the Confessor's reign (GDB 67v (*DB Wilts.* 12.1)); cf. Williams, *The English and the Norman Conquest*, 121, n. 130.

[241] GDB 87r (*DB Som.* 1.28 and 32–5).

[242] For Wulfweard, see J.H. Round, 'Domesday Survey', *VCH Buckinghamshire* i, 207–28, at 216–17; Round, 'Domesday Survey', *VCH Somerset* i, 399–400; Loud, 'Somerset Domesday', 17; Williams, *The English and the Norman Conquest*, 99–100; and Clarke, *English Nobility*, 366–8. See also S 1476 (*Anglo-Saxon Charters*, ed. Robertson, no. 114) and GDB 43v (*DB Hants* 10.1).

[243] GDB 153r (*DB Bucks.* 56.1–3, which regards 'Alsi' as Ælfsige).

[244] GDB 63v (*DB Berks.* 65.15); see also GDB 58r (*DB Berks.* 1.43).

[245] Keynes, 'Regenbald the Chancellor', 205.

[246] Brihtric occurs regularly among the witnesses to royal charters from the early 1040s onwards, sometimes in apparent association with a certain Ælfgar. Brihtric *consiliarius* and Ælfgar *consiliarius* occur as a pair in Giso's charter of 1061 (above, 232), and Brihtric, Ælfstan [of Boscombe], and Ælfgar occur as a group in the charter of 1065 (above, 235). Brihtric's father was perhaps the Dodda who is occasionally found among the witnesses in charters of the 1040s and 1050s, as a *nobilis* with south-western associations. A certain Brihtric the Bald, and Dodda of Curry, occur as witnesses in the Taunton record (Appendix I, no. 17).

[247] Cf. Clarke, *English Nobility*, 133 and 262–4. Brihtric's interests appear to have spread, with Edith's, into Worcestershire (*DB Worcs.* 18.2 and 19.5). It was in this part of the country that a Brihtric tried, unsuccessfully, to claim two estates against the church of Worcester which had been leased to his father Dodda by Bishop Brihtheah (1033–8); one was apparently still held by Dodda fifty years later (*DB Worcs.* 2.24,63).

[248] Cf. Keynes, 'Regenbald the Chancellor', 205, n. 117. For Brihtric, son of Ælfgar, see Ann Williams, 'A West-country Magnate of the Eleventh Century: the Family, Estates and Patronage of Beorhtric, son of Ælfgar' (forthcoming).

[249] GDB 69v (*DB Wilts.* 25.1) and 95r, 96v and 98v (*DB Som.* 24.27, 27.1, and 46.16).

witnesses we find THEODORIC the goldsmith, who was in the service of King Edward the Confessor, and who certainly prospered during the reign of King William;[250] NORTHMAN, 'son of John', presumably the Northman who had attested Giso's charter in 1065, and perhaps the son of John 'the Dane' whose land at Yatton passed to the church of Wells; and ÆTHELRIC *coc* ('cook'), presumably the 'Alricus coquus' who held 20 hides at (Steeple) Claydon, Bucks., TRW, which had belonged TRE to Queen Edith.[251]

In short, the men who had assembled on the upper story of the Lady Edith's stone church at Wilton, on Ember Wednesday (29 February) in 1072, were clearly men of substance, and consequence; and it is interesting to see that they had retained something of their identity as a group. It would appear that as the men witnessed the transaction between Giso and Azur, they could hear the nuns of Wilton in the background, singing the office for the day. It is apparent, moreover, that while they formally acknowledged the new Norman establishment (King William, Queen Mathilda, Robert 'ætheling', and Archbishop Lanfranc), they also spared a passing thought for Leofric, bishop of Exeter, who had died three weeks before the meeting at Wilton, and for the deposed Archbishop Stigand, who had died just one week before.[252] A gathering held at Wilton – with King William's permission – for the express purpose of completing a transaction in the presence of the Lady Edith and various members of her household should not be invested with too much symbolic importance; but here, at least, was a small and select society continuing to go about its business in despite of the political upheavals.[253] Little is known of the Lady Edith after this meeting. She died at Winchester on 18 December 1075, and her body was taken 'with great honour' to Westminster, for burial near her husband.[254]

In addition to his attendance at routine meetings of the king's court and councillors, Bishop Giso was present at the Council of Winchester at Easter (8 April) 1072, when the primacy was settled in favour of Archbishop Lanfranc;[255] at the Council of London in 1075, when further matters of general importance were

---

[250] GDB 36v (*DB Sur.* 36.6), 63r (*DB Berks.* 63.1–5), and 160v (*DB Oxon.* 58.17–19). See also Barlow, *English Church 1000–1066*, 123, n. 4; Keynes, 'Regenbald the Chancellor', 217, n. 189; and *The Waltham Chronicle*, ed. Watkiss and Chibnall, 62.

[251] GDB 153r (*DB Bucks.* 55.1).

[252] Bishop Leofric died on 10 February 1072. Stigand, who had been deposed in 1070, died on 21 or 22 February 1072.

[253] Edith's presence at Wilton in the early 1070s supplies the background for further developments thereafter. Christina, younger sister of Edgar the Atheling and of Margaret (wife of Malcolm III, king of Scotland), came to Wilton, probably in 1086. She brought her niece Mathilda (daughter of Malcolm and Margaret), great granddaughter of King Edmund Ironside, whom she wished to protect from the lustful attentions of the Normans. Mathilda was intended by her father for marriage to Count Alan the Red, lord of Richmond; but in the event Count Alan preferred Gunhilda (daughter of King Harold), who had also taken the veil at Wilton, and abducted her. Gunhilda received two letters from Archbishop Anselm; Mathilda was promptly removed from Wilton by King Malcolm, and later married King Henry I. See G. Bosanquet, *Eadmer's History of Recent Events in England*, London 1964, 126–31; R.W. Southern, *Saint Anselm and his Biographer*, Cambridge 1966, 182–93; and *Life of Edward*, ed. Barlow, 137, n. 31.

[254] ASC, MSS DE, *s.a.* 1075.

[255] *Councils & Synods with Other Documents Relating to the English Church, I: AD 871–1204*, ed. D. Whitelock, M. Brett and C.N.L. Brooke, Oxford 1981, *ii*, *1066–1204*, no. 91, at 604; *Lanfranc's Letters*, 44–9.

discussed;[256] and at the Council of Gloucester at Christmas 1080, when he assisted in the consecration of William of St Carilef as bishop of Durham.[257] A document preserved by Giso in order to protect his own interests serves now to illustrate how he was expected by the king to perform certain administrative functions. In a writ addressed (in the vernacular) to William de Courseulles, apparently in his capacity as sheriff of Somerset, King William insists that *Rom feoh* (Peter's Pence) is to be paid by Michaelmas, and orders the sheriff to publicise the injunction at Bristol and at Montacute.[258] The king adds that the bishop, and William, are to investigate any instances of non-payment, but he reminds the sheriff that neither he nor any of his men is to take a pledge in the land of Bishop Giso, in the bishop's absence. It is customary, and not without good reason, to presume that the writ was issued at about the time (in 1080) when the king promised (in a letter to Pope Gregory VII) to review the money payments sent by his predecessors to Rome, assuring the pope that the sum already collected was on its way and that the balance would follow in due course.[259] In another context, we find that Giso made accusations of an unspecified kind against the abbots of Athelney and Muchelney, and it seems to have been in the council at Gloucester, in 1080, that Archbishop Lanfranc raised the matter for a formal hearing.[260] The abbots were defiant, in their different ways; and in their support Thurstan, abbot of Glastonbury, is said to have recited from memory various charters of former kings, to the effect that only the abbot of Glastonbury had any jurisdiction over the abbots of Athelney and Muchelney. When the king urged that Bishop Giso should settle the matter in the chapter at Glastonbury, Thurstan made another moving speech, insisting that his charters were genuine and that Giso could only come to the chapter at his own invitation. *Quid plura?*, as they say. The bishop came to Glastonbury, on Thurstan's terms; whereupon the abbots of Athelney and Muchelney successfully defended themselves against the accusations, and the bishop was forced to retreat ignominiously back to Wells. Giso himself was good at charters, but he was evidently no match for an Anglo-Saxon monk.

It is some consolation that Bishop Giso could still be effective on his own ground. In a writ addressed to William de Mohun, sheriff of Somerset, and probably issued, therefore, in the early 1080s, Queen Mathilda let it be known that at her request Osbert (Osbern fitzOsbern), bishop of Exeter (1072–1103), had given the church of **Wedmore**, with all its appurtenances, to Bishop Giso.[261] She remarks that Giso had often laid claim to the church; and if we may imagine that Osbern had gained his interest there as a royal priest, in the 1060s,[262] and had retained it in spite of the fact that Edward the Confessor had given the estate itself to Bishop Giso for the church of Wells, we can well imagine why Giso should have been so concerned to have his way. Mathilda may have been acting on her husband's behalf; but it seems more likely, in a matter of this kind, that she was simply acting in the way that Queen Edith had acted before her.

---

256 *Councils & Synods*, no. 92, at 612 and 615; *Lanfranc's Letters*, 72–9.
257 *Councils & Synods*, no. 97, at 631.
258 Appendix I, no. 18.
259 *Councils & Synods*, no. 96; *Lanfranc's Letters*, no. 39.
260 William of Malmesbury, *De antiquitate Glastonie ecclesie*, ch. 76 (ed. Scott, 154–6).
261 Appendix I, no. 19.
262 Barlow, *English Church 1000–1066*, 157; Keynes, 'Regenbald the Chancellor', 208.

Bishop Giso and the 'Terra Gisonis'

At the time of the Domesday survey, Bishop Giso presided over a substantial estate, the greater part of which was reckoned, for purposes of taxation, as a separate hundred, and the whole of which was known (perhaps significantly) as the 'Terra Gisonis'.[263] In 1066 the 'Terra Gisonis' comprised about 220 hides; by 1086 it comprised 282 hides, accounted at an annual value of about £330. An estate of this size in lay hands would have put its owner in a very prominent position (though some way below the level of the principal earls); and it otherwise set the bishopric of Wells in the same league as Peterborough and Ramsey abbeys, not on a par with Glastonbury and Ely but a long way above Bath and the other Somerset houses.[264] The detailed breakdown of the separate manors in the 'Terra Gisonis' reveals that Giso retained a high proportion of his land under his own control,[265] and that only a small proportion of the whole had been assigned to the canons, comprising 14 of the 50 hides at Wells, the 4 hides at Wanstrow, and the 8½ hides at Litton. What (if anything) this may signify is not immediately apparent, and the question arises whether it becomes more meaningful when put in another context.

An obvious effect of the presence of Lotharingian (or Lotharingian-trained) priests in the eleventh-century English church was the promotion of the *uita communis* in secular chapters, and an enthusiasm for the organisation of the communal life in accordance with a canonical rule.[266] The standards were set by the 'Enlarged Rule of Chrodegang', compiled in the second quarter of the ninth century, and itself based in part on the *Institutio canonicorum* (also known as the Rule of Aachen), promulgated in 816–17, and in part on the earlier 'Rule of Chrodegang', compiled by Chrodegang, bishop of Metz (742–66). Leofric, bishop of Exeter, and Ealdred, archbishop of York, are among those known to have introduced these practices in the churches under their control; and Giso, of course, was another. According to the text which purports to be his autobiography, Giso increased the size of the newly-enriched community at Wells, and trained the brethren in canonical obedience; he also built 'a cloister, a refectory, and a dormitory', and instituted other necessary reforms, 'according to the custom of my country'.[267] The text recounts further how the brethren chose one of their own number, called Isaac, as the person best suited to take charge of their internal and external affairs; and since Isaac, 'prepositus canonicorum sancti andree', is

---

[263] Exon DB 156r–160r ('Terra Gisonis Episcopi in Sumerseta'); and GDB 89rv ('Terra Episcopi Wellensis') (*DB Som.* 6.1–19). The geld accounts (1086) for the hundreds of Somerset, preserved in Exon DB 75r–82v (*VCH Somerset* i, 527–37), assess a part of the 'Terra Gisonis', amounting to 218 hides, as a separate hundred (Exon DB 78v: *VCH Somerset* i, 531), and the rest (Banwell, Yatton, Wedmore, Wanstrow), amounting to a further 64 hides, in other hundreds. See also Eyton, *Domesday Studies: Somerset* i, 142–6, and ii, 23–4; *DB Som.*, 354–5; and F.R. Thorn, 'Hundreds and Wapentakes', *Somerset Domesday*, ed. Williams and Erskine, 32–41.

[264] For a table showing the comparative value of monastic estates, see Knowles, *Monastic Order*, 702–3. For a table showing the most valuable lay estates, see Clarke, *English Nobility*, 14.

[265] Loud, 'Somerset Domesday', 16 and 20. See also Appendix V.

[266] See Barrow, 'Cathedrals, Provosts and Prebends', 553–5; Barrow, 'English Cathedral Communities', 30–4; Barlow, *English Church 1000–1066*, 239–42; and B. Langefeld, '*Regula canonicorum* or *Regula monasterialis uitae*? The Rule of Chrodegang and Archbishop Wulfred's Reforms at Canterbury', *Anglo-Saxon England* xxv, 1996, 21–36.

[267] Giso's autobiography (Appendix IV, §11).

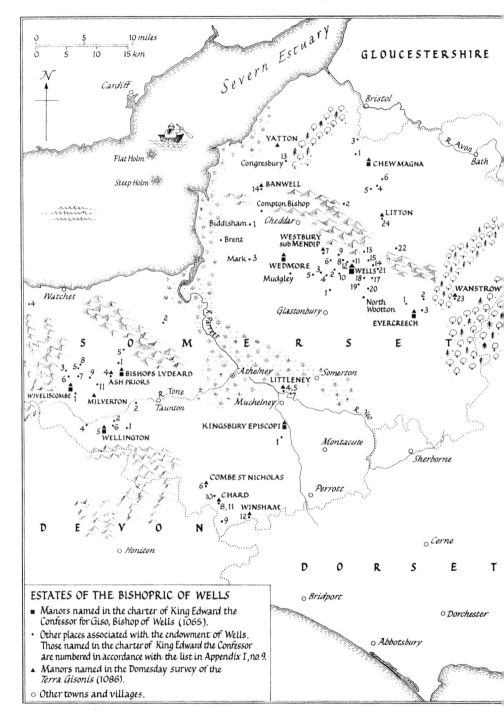

Fig. 2. Estates of the bishopric of Wells (drawn by Reginald Piggott)

mentioned in the 'Geld Inquest' of 1086,[268] we may at least be sure that the information in the autobiography has a secure foundation. For any deeper understanding of the nature or effectiveness of Giso's reforms at Wells, we are dependent in part on the evidence of the charters, discussed above, and in part on our interpretation of the organisation of the 'Terra Gisonis' at the time of the Domesday survey in 1086; though of course it is also instructive to compare the evidence from Wells with the evidence from other churches. Dr Julia Barrow has drawn attention, most interestingly, to some of the basic distinctions which existed between the various cathedral churches in the eleventh century: at London (for example), there seems from an early stage to have been a clear sense of separation between episcopal and chapter lands, and the chapter lands were themselves divided up into separate prebends; at Wells and at Exeter (for example), the episcopal and chapter lands were separate, and a sense was retained of the ownership of the latter by the *community* of canons; and at Hereford (for example), the cathedral canons did not have much of their own, and it was the bishop's lands which were divided up among them into separate prebends.[269] Earl Harold's community of canons at Waltham Holy Cross was, of course, a different kind of matter; but although a well-developed system of separate prebends is described in the late-twelfth-century Waltham Chronicle,[270] it is possible that the situation in the 1060s and 1070s was more in accord with the spirit of communal life.[271] There can be no doubt that Giso himself augmented and consolidated the endowment of his church, and that he did so in general terms for the greater good of the community of canons. Yet one feels, whatever was believed to the contrary in the twelfth century, that Giso did rather less for the canons than he did for himself; and perhaps one can better understand, on this basis, why his successor, Bishop John de Villula, was able to afford to remove the see from the church of St Andrew at Wells to the church of St Peter at Bath.[272]

The 'Sacramentary of Bishop Giso'

We may turn, finally, to the so-called 'Sacramentary of Bishop Giso' (BL Cotton Vitellius A. xviii), lest it should prove to throw any light on the liturgical interests of an expatriate Lotharingian priest in eleventh-century England. It has to be said at once that the sacramentary does not contain any direct evidence of an original association with the bishop of Wells; and it is simply by virtue of a set of observations, which in combination might seem to point in Giso's direction, that it has come to be known by his name. In the first place, the calendar (fos 3r–8v) is said to contain a number of distinctively 'personal' elements, pertaining to one who would appear to have been singularly well-disposed towards saints of the Low

---

[268] Exon DB 78v; *VCH Somerset* i, 531.

[269] Barrow, 'Cathedrals, Provosts, and Prebends', esp. 555–60; Barrow, 'A Lotharingian at Hereford', 30 and 34–42; and above, n. 113. For Exeter, see also Blake, 'The Development of the Chapter of the Diocese of Exeter', cited above, n. 36.

[270] For the organisation of the estates at Waltham, see *The Waltham Chronicle*, ed. Watkiss and Chibnall, 28–30, with discussion, xxiv–xxv and xl.

[271] Cf. S 1036 (above, n. 229) and LDB 15v–16v (*DB Ess.* 7.1 and 8.1–11).

[272] Cf. Crosby, *Bishop and Chapter in Twelfth-Century England*, 53–4.

Countries.[273] Secondly, the sacramentary contains a 'Missa pro congregatione' which begins with a prayer invoking divine aid, through the intercession of St Andrew, for 'the community of this holy monastery [*coenobium*]' (fo. 162rv), and (rather less significantly) a blessing for St Andrew's day (fo. 216v) – observations taken to suggest that the sacramentary was intended for use in a church dedicated to St Andrew.[274] And thirdly, the calendar contains an entry for St Congar (27 November), a Welsh saint whose body was believed to repose at Congresbury, in Somerset,[275] on land which had been given by Duduc to the church of Wells, and whose cult would appear to have been local to that part of the country.[276] Bishop Giso, who was indeed from Lorraine, established himself in the church of St Andrew, at Wells, in Somerset; accordingly, the calendar has entered into liturgical scholarship as that of Giso, bishop of Wells, and has been treated as an expression of his personal interests.[277] It must suffice for present purposes to emphasise that the evidence, such as it is, may be capable of other interpretations. Professor David Dumville is inclined to assign the manuscript to Canterbury;[278] and Dr Alicia Corrêa, developing the argument on liturgical grounds, has observed that the grading of the feasts points in the same direction, with certain elements reflecting Winchester and Glastonbury interests.[279] Nor is it clear that the inclusion of St Congar in the calendar is necessarily symptomatic of Somerset; for it could be

---

[273] Abbot Gasquet and E. Bishop, *The Bosworth Psalter: an Account of a Manuscript Formerly Belonging to O. Turville-Petre Esq. of Bosworth Hall, Now Addit. MS 37517 at the British Museum*, London 1908, 61, n. 1 (describing the calendar in Vitellius A. xviii as a specimen of a new type, displaying admixture of foreign elements, originating with Herman, bishop of Sherborne, or 'more probably' with his neighbour Giso), 162 (with reference to the earlier suggestion that it may be 'a calendar of the church of Wells under bishop Giso the "Lorrainer" '), and 163–4 (with more specific reference to the 'personal elements' in the 'abnormal' calendar). See also Barlow, *English Church 1000–1066*, 82, n. 7. J.A. Robinson, 'Mediæval Calendars of Somerset', *Muchelney Memoranda*, ed. B. Schofield, Somerset Record Society 42, 1927, 143–79, at 166–9, emphasises the importance of making a distinction between 'foreign' entries which are original and 'foreign' entries which are contemporary additions.

[274] The suggestion was made on the sheet pasted at the front of the manuscript, in a hand identified as that of J.A. Herbert. Another hand, identified as that of Francis Wormald, points out that the blessing for St Andrew occurs in other manuscripts, and that the suggestion 'must be received with caution'. I am grateful to Dr Nigel Ramsay for identifying the hands on my behalf. For a variant form of the prayer for the community, see J.W. Legg, *Missale ad Usum Ecclesie Westmonasteriensis* II, Henry Bradshaw Society 5, London 1893, col. 1145.

[275] D.W. Rollason, 'Lists of Saints' Resting-Places in Anglo-Saxon England', *Anglo-Saxon England* vii, 1978, 61–93, at 64 and 92; see also *Liber Vitae*, ed. Keynes, 99–101.

[276] Robinson, 'Calendars of Somerset', 147 and 164–72.

[277] *English Kalendars before AD 1100*, ed. F. Wormald, Henry Bradshaw Society 72, London 1934, vi and 99–111 (no. 8), 'Wells, co. Somerset, under bishop Giso'. See also, e.g., *The Missal of the New Minster, Winchester*, ed. D.H. Turner, Henry Bradshaw Society 93, London 1962, vii (though cf. xxiv–vi); Barlow, *English Church 1000–1066*, 82, n. 7; *Wulfstan of Winchester: the Life of St Æthelwold*, ed. M. Lapidge and M. Winterbottom, Oxford 1991, cxxiii–iv; Ortenberg, *English Church and the Continent*, esp. 74–6, 247; and R.W. Pfaff, 'Massbooks', *Liturgical Books of Anglo-Saxon England*, ed. Pfaff, 7–34, at 19–21.

[278] D.N. Dumville, *Liturgy and the Ecclesiastical History of Late Anglo-Saxon England*, Woodbridge 1992, 25, 53–4, 61 (with reference to St Congar), and 90–1 ('assigned, though on very inadequate evidence, to Giso, bishop of Wells').

[279] A. Corrêa, 'A Mass for St Patrick in an Anglo-Saxon Sacramentary', in D.N. Dumville *et al.*, *Saint Patrick, AD 493–1993*, Woodbridge 1993, 245–52.

explained as a reflection of a 'Winchester' component in the book as a whole.[280] Yet while the scribe of the sacramentary had material in front of him which makes his calendar reek of nothing more distinctive than the inter-connected world of the eleventh-century English church, that does not help much to explain the inclusion (and addition) of several unusual feasts likely to be of particular interest to a man from Lorraine. No doubt we should bear in mind that there were many men from Lorraine in eleventh-century England, and perhaps we should therefore allow the 'Sacramentary of Bishop Giso' to speak for them all. Or perhaps we should pursue a different train of thought. As we have seen, one of the Lorrainers in England was Herman, bishop of Ramsbury (1045–55), a monk at Saint-Bertin's (1055–8), bishop of Ramsbury again (1058–62+), and ultimately bishop 'of Berkshire, Wiltshire, and Dorset', at Sherborne and then at Old Sarum.[281] Herman died in 1078; and one of the very few obits added in the calendar in the 'Sacramentary of Bishop Giso' commemorates 'Herimannus episcopus' (21 Mar.),[282] which suggests that the manuscript belonged in the late eleventh century to a church or to a person with special cause to honour his memory. This might well have been a fellow-Lorrainer, like Giso, or it might have been someone with access to the service-books left behind in one of Herman's churches; and while the matter clearly requires further investigation, it should be noted that the calendar in Vitellius A. xviii displays intriguing connections with calendars in manuscripts with 'Sherborne' associations.[283]

Conclusion

As I said at the beginning, I carry no brief for Giso. I was drawn to him in the first instance because he is a manifestation of the Lotharingian Connection, a phenomenon which might well respond to more detailed analysis as one among the many factors which affected the course of affairs in eleventh-century England. I was drawn to him also because of the unusual quality of the source material available, including an instructively varied assortment of charters and writs, and the fascinating text which purports to be his 'autobiography'. It turns out, alas, that the autobiography may not be quite what it seems; but it is some compensation that

---

[280] Congar is included in the litany in the Arundel Psalter (BL MS Arundel 60), written probably at the New Minster, Winchester, in 1073. See *Anglo-Saxon Litanies*, ed. Lapidge, 144, and (for the date of the psalter) *Liber Vitae*, ed. Keynes, 115, n. 47.

[281] Above, 208–9.

[282] ASC, MS E, *s.a.* 1078, gives X Kal. Mar. = 20 February, as opposed to XII Kal. Apr. = 21 March. The obit in the calendar is more likely to be correct. The calendar also contains obits for 'Freesendis & Albereda' (25 Mar.), presumably representing two women of continental origin (Frithesuind and Alberada), and for a monk called William (6 Nov.). See also J. Gerchow, *Die Gedenküberlieferung der Angelsachsen*, Berlin 1988, 231–2 (no. 16).

[283] Robinson, 'Calendars of Somerset', 169–71, citing the 'Red Book of Darley' (Cambridge, Corpus Christi College, MS 422). C.H. Hohler, 'Some Service Books of the Later Saxon Church', *Tenth-Century Studies: Essays in Commemoration of the Millennium of the Council of Winchester and 'Regularis Concordia'*, ed. D. Parsons, Chichester 1975, 60–83 and 217–27, at 70–1 and 76–7, citing the much later 'Sherborne Missal', on which see J. Wickham Legg, *Liturgical Notes on the Sherborne Missal, a Manuscript in the Possession of the Duke of Northumberland at Alnwick Castle*, London 1896, [reptd from *Transactions of the St Paul's Ecclesiological Society*, vol. IV], 2, and *The Sherborne Missal*, Oxford 1920.

Giso himself should emerge as the draftsman of at least three royal diplomas, issued in 1061, 1065, and 1068, and that other records should show him as he went about his business in Somerset, and, on a particular occasion in 1072, conducting his affairs in the presence of the Lady Edith in her stone church at Wilton. Yet Giso was not, as I said, a figure of any outstanding importance in the politics of his age. True, there is something appealing about the way he pestered the high and the mighty in the interests of his church: first Pope Nicholas, then King Edward and Queen Edith, then King Harold, and finally King William and Queen Mathilda; for this is a man who was nothing if not a determined and effective operator. There is also something instructive about his readiness, as a bishop, to come to terms with the new regime, especially when contrasted with the apparent reluctance of the majority of abbots, with their communities, to do the same. In some senses Giso's good work was undone, c.1090 when the conventual buildings were demolished and when the see was removed to Bath, and c.1180 when the pre-Conquest and Anglo-Norman cathedral was itself demolished in order to make way for its Gothic successor. One should emphasise, however, that Giso's enduring legacy to his church lay in the consolidation and management of the 'Terra Gisonis' itself; and it is not least for this reason that he earns his place among those whose work for the glory of God finds its ultimate expression in the magnificent architecture and statuary of the medieval cathedral of Wells.

APPENDIX I

The Giso File

All of the writs, charters, and other documents associated in one way or another with Giso, bishop of Wells, are listed below in their apparent or approximate chronological order. The list is intended to convey an impression of the variety of material available, and to bring together into a single series documents produced before and after the Norman Conquest. Two of the less accessible texts (nos 9 and 16) are printed below, as Appendix II and Appendix III. The information on the Wells estates should be compared with statements in the 'autobiography' of Bishop Giso (Appendix IV) and in the Domesday survey of the 'Terra Gisonis' (Appendix V). For the abbreviations (S, Pelteret, KCD, *PUE*), see above, n. 1; *ECW* = H. P. R. Finberg, *The Early Charters of Wessex*, Leicester 1964. The numbering of places in no. 9, below, relates to the numbering of places on the map of estates of the bishopric of Wells, Fig. 2, above.

Duduc, bishop of Wells, was consecrated bishop on 11 June 1033, and died on 18 January 1061. Giso (Gisa) was appointed to succeed Duduc, presumably in late January or February 1061. He travelled to Rome with Bishop Ealdred, Walter (bishop-elect of Hereford), Earl Tostig, and others, and was consecrated bishop by Pope Nicholas on Easter Day (15 April) 1061. He received a papal privilege for the church of Wells on 25 April 1061, and returned to Wells during the week 17–23 June 1061.

Reign of King Edward the Confessor (1042–66)

1   Writ of King Edward, addressed to Earl Harold, Abbot Æthelnoth [of Glaston-bury], Godwine the sheriff, and all the king's thegns in Somerset: announcing that he has granted the bishopric [of Wells] to Giso, his priest, 'as fully and as completely as ever Bishop Duduc or any bishop had it before him, in all things; and if any land here has been taken away from the bishopric, it is my will that it be restored or that it be held on such conditions as may be agreeable to him, according to such arrangements with him as can be devised'. ? 1061, after 18 January. *English.*

MS: Wells, D. & C., Liber Albus I, fo. 14r (English) and 14v (Latin)
Ptd: Harmer, *Anglo-Saxon Writs*, no. 64 (with translation); *Councils & Synods*, no. 76 (with translation).
Listed: *ECW*, no. 534; S 1111.
Comment. Above, pp. 227–8. Cast in much the same terms as S 1102 (Harmer, *Anglo-Saxon Writs*, no. 50), a writ of King Edward granting the bishopric of Hereford to Bishop Walter.

2   Letter of Pope Nicholas II to Giso, bishop of Wells, confirming him in the rights of his see. 25 April 1061. *Latin.*

MS: Wells, D. & C., Cathedral Charters, no. 2 (original)
Ptd: *PUE* ii, 131–2 (no. 1); *Councils & Synods*, no. 77.
Listed: *Regesta Pontificum Romanorum*, ed. P. Jaffé, 2nd edn, 2 vols, Leipzig 1885–8, no. 4457.
Translated: *EHD* ii, no. 76.
Comment. Above, p. 228. Pope Nicholas's privilege for Wulfwig, bishop of Dorchester, issued on 3 May 1061, is cast in similar terms (*Councils & Synods*, no. 78; *EHD* ii, no. 75).

3   Writ of King Edward, addressed to Earl Harold, Abbot Æthelnoth [of Glaston-bury], Godwine, and all the king's thegns in Somerset: announcing that Bishop Giso shall legally possess the bishopric [of Wells]. 1061 x May 1065 (? 1061, late April/June). *English.*

MS: Wells, D. & C., Liber Albus I, fo. 14r (English) and 14rv (Latin)
Ptd: Harmer, *Anglo-Saxon Writs*, no. 65 (with translation); *Councils & Synods*, no. 79 (with translation).
Listed: *ECW*, no. 535; S 1112.
Comment. Above, pp. 228–9.

4   Writ of King Edward, addressed to Earl Harold, Abbot Æthelnoth [of Glaston-bury], Godwine the sheriff, and all the king's thegns in Somerset: announcing that Bishop Giso shall discharge the obligations on his land at Chew, Somerset, 'now at the same rate as his predecessor did before him'. April 1061 x May 1065 (? 1061). *English.*

MS: Wells, D. & C., Liber Albus I, fos 17v–18r (English and Latin)
Ptd: Harmer, *Anglo-Saxon Writs*, no. 66 (with translation).
Listed: *ECW*, no. 537; S 1113.
Comment. Above, p. 229. S 1114 (Harmer, *Anglo-Saxon Writs*, no. 67) is a spurious variation of this writ, entered in the Liber Fuscus, fo. 14.

5 Diploma of King Edward for Wulfwold, abbot of Bath: grant of land at Ash-wick, Somerset; witness-list headed by Bishop Giso ('Ego Giso dei gratia epis-copus hanc cartam dictaui'), followed by King Edward and others. 1061. *Latin, with English bounds.*

MSS: 1 Cambridge, Corpus Christi College, MS 111, pp. 90–2 (s. xii)
2 Cambridge, Corpus Christi College, MS 111, p. 127 (s. xiii)

Ptd: KCD 811, and vol. vi, p. 244 (bounds); Hunt, *Bath Chartularies*, vol. i, pp. 33–5 (ex MS 1) and 65–6 (ex MS 2)

Listed: *ECW*, no. 533; S 1034.

Comment. Above, pp. 231–2. Cf. no. 6 (S 1427). Harmer, *Anglo-Saxon Writs*, 39, n. 3, and 430; Keynes, 'Regenbald the Chancellor', 203 and 213, n. 170, drawn up by Bishop Giso.

6 Writ of Wulfwold, abbot of Bath, addressed to Bishop Giso, Abbot Æthelnoth [of Glastonbury], Tofig the sheriff, and all the thegns in Somerset: announcing that King Edward gave him the land at Evesty ('which my father owned'), and the four homesteads at Ashwick; and announcing that he has given the land to St Peter's monastery at Bath, 'for the provision of clothing and food for the monks'. 1061 x 1066. *English.*

MS: Cambridge, Corpus Christi College, MS 111, p. 92

Ptd: Hunt, *Bath Chartularies*, vol. i, p. 35; Harmer, *Anglo-Saxon Writs*, no. 6 (with translation).

Listed: *ECW*, no. 536; S 1427.

Comment. Above, p. 232. For King Edward's grant of Ashwick to Abbot Wulfwold, drawn up by Bishop Giso, see no. 5; the final clauses in the writ may have been suggested by the combined blessing and sanction in the charter.

7 Writ of King Edward, addressed to Earl Harold, Tofig the sheriff, and all the king's thegns in Somerset: announcing that Alfred has sold his land at Litton, Somerset, to Bishop Giso, in the presence of the king and others (including Edith and Earl Harold) at Perrott, Somerset; and that the bishop is legally to possess the land for the bishopric. April 1061 x May 1065. *English.*

MS: Wells, D. & C., Liber Albus I, fo. 14r (English) and 14v (Latin)

Ptd: Harmer, *Anglo-Saxon Writs*, no. 69 (with translation).

Listed: *ECW*, no. 540; S 1116.

Comment. Above, p. 239.

8 Writ of King Edward, addressed to Earl Harold, Abbot Æthelnoth [of Glaston-bury], Tofig the sheriff, and all the king's thegns in Somerset: announcing that he has given the land at Wedmore, Somerset, to Bishop Giso, 'for the maintenance of his clerks (*inne to his clerken bileua*; Lat. *ad sustentationem cleri*) at St Andrew's at Wells'; 'and my will is that the bishop draw up a *priuilegium* concerning this, with my full permission'. April 1061 x May 1065. *English.*

MS: Wells, D. & C., Liber Albus I, fo. 17v (English and Latin)

Ptd: Harmer, *Anglo-Saxon Writs*, no. 68 (with translation).

Listed: *ECW*, no. 539; S 1115.

Comment. Above, pp. 229–30.

9 Diploma of King Edward for the bishopric of Wells, at the request of Bishop Giso (with reference to his earlier visit to Rome) and of Queen Edith. General confirmation of lands (totalling 207 hides, all in Somerset), comprising: (**i**) 50 hides at WELLS (formerly *Tidingtun*), with appurtenances at ¹Polsham, ²Wookey, ³Henton, ⁴Yarley, ⁵Bleadney and ⁶Easton, ⁷Westbury, ⁸Wookey Hole and ⁹Ebbor, ¹⁰Burcott, (Upper) ¹¹Milton and the other (Lower) ¹²Milton, ¹³Pen (Hill), (East) ¹⁴Horrington and the other (West) ¹⁵Horrington, ¹⁶Whitchurch, ¹⁷Dinder, ¹⁸Dulcote, ¹⁹Wellesley, ²⁰Worminster, ²¹Chilcote, ²²Binegar, ²³Wanstrow, and ²⁴Litton; (**ii**) 50 hides at CHEW, with appurtenances at ¹Littleton, ²Hazel (Farm) [in Compton Martin], ³Dundry, (Bishops) ⁴Sutton, ⁵Sutton (Wick) and ⁶Sutton (Court); (**iii**) 20 hides at EVERCREECH, with ¹Prestleigh, ²Chesterblade and (Stony) ³Stratton; (**iv**) 38 hides at KINGSBURY, with appurtenances at ¹Lambrook, ²*Readewelle*, ³*æt tham Beorge*, ⁴Littleney [lost, in Huish], ⁵Huish (Episcopi), ⁶Combe (St Nicholas), ⁷Pibsbury, ⁸Chard, and⁹*other frusa Cerdren* [? S. Chard], ¹⁰Crimchard, ¹¹Langham [in Chard], ¹²Winsham, and ¹³Congresbury and ¹⁴Banwell with all their appurtenances; (**v**) 15 hides at WELLINGTON, comprising (West) ¹Buckland, ²Ham, ³*Huntanapoth*, ⁴Harpford, ⁵Pinksmoor [in Wellington Without], and ⁶Chelston; (**vi**) 15 hides at WIVELISCOMBE, comprising ¹Nunnington, ²Upcott, ³Whitefield, ⁴Withycombe, ⁵Oakhampton, ⁶Langley, ⁷Ford, ⁸Pitsford, ⁹Fitzhead, the ¹⁰other *Fifhyda*, ¹¹Dean, ¹²*Slæp*, and ¹³*Hwrentimor*; (**vii**) 15 hides at (Bishops) LYDEARD, with appurtenances at (East) ¹Combe, ²Padnoller [in Charlynch], ³*Wuduland*, ⁴Ash (Priors), ⁵Bagborough, ⁶*Anacota*, and ⁷*Hylle* [? Lydeard Hill]; and (**viii**) 4 hides at WEDMORE, with appurtenances at Tarnock in ¹Biddisham, ²*Heawycan* and ³Mark. Drawn up at Windsor, 20 May 1065 (MS 2) or 24 May 1065 (MS 1). *Latin.*

MSS: 1 Wells, D. & C., Liber Albus II, fos 241r–242r (s. xv/xvi), dated 24 May 1065

2 BL MS Cotton Tib. E viii, pt i, fo. 218rv (s. xvi/xvii), from a lost single sheet (without witness-list), dated 20 May 1065

3 London, College of Arms, MS WE, fos 121r–123r (s. xvii), from MS 2 (before it was damaged by fire)

Ptd: *Monasticon* i, 187, *ex* MS 2; *Monasticon* (rev. edn) ii, 285–6 (no. 2); KCD 816, *ex* MS 2 and *Monasticon*; below, Appendix II, *ex* MS 1.

Listed: *ECW*, no. 542; S 1042.

Comment. Above, pp. 232–8. Keynes, 'Regenbald the Chancellor', 203–4, drawn up by Bishop Giso.

10 Writ of Queen Edith, addressed to Earl Harold, Tofig, and all their thegns in Somerset: announcing that Bishop Giso is to be entitled to the land at Milverton, Somerset, 'as fully and completely as I myself possessed it, on the terms that we have agreed on'. April 1061 (? 24 May 1065) x 5 January 1066. *English.*

MS: Wells, D. & C., Liber Albus I, fo. 18r (English and Latin)

Ptd: Harmer, *Anglo-Saxon Writs*, no. 70 (with translation).

Listed: *ECW*, no. 541; S 1240.

Comment. Above, pp. 238–9.

Reign of King Harold (1066)

11 Writ of King Harold, addressed to Abbot Æthelnoth [of Glastonbury], Tofig, and all his thegns in Somerset: announcing that Bishop Giso is to be entitled to his sake and his soke over his lands and over his men, 'as fully and as completely as ever he was in King Edward's time in all things'. 6 January 1066 x 14 October 1066. *English.*

> MS: Wells, D. & C., Liber Albus I, fo. 14r (English) and 14v (Latin)
> Ptd: Harmer, *Anglo-Saxon Writs*, no. 71 (with translation).
> Listed: *ECW*, no. 543; S 1163.
> Comment. Above, pp. 239–40.

Reign of King William I (1066–87)

12 Writ of King William I and Earl William [fitz Osbern], addressed to Bishop Giso, Eadnoth the staller, Tofig the sheriff, and all the thegns in Somerset: announcing that he has given Abbot Wulfwold the land at Charlcombe, Somerset, for the church of St Peter, Bath. 1067. *English.*

> MS: Cambridge, Corpus Christi College, MS 111, p. 94
> Ptd: Hunt, *Bath Chartularies*, vol. i, p. 36; *Acta of William I*, ed. Bates, no. 11.
> Listed: *Regesta* i, no. 7; Pelteret, no. 1.
> Translated: *EHD* ii, no. 33.
> Comment. Above, p. 241.

13 Writ of King William I, addressed to Abbot Æthelnoth [of Glastonbury], Tofig the sheriff, and all the thegns in Somerset: announcing that, at the request of Bishop Giso, he has granted Winsham, Somerset, to the church of Wells, for the maintenance of the canons (*ad sustentationem canonicorum*). 1066 x 1082. *Latin.*

> MS: Wells, D. & C., Liber Albus I, fo. 49r
> Ptd: *Acta of William I*, ed. Bates, no. 287.
> Listed: *Regesta* i, no. 160.
> Comment. Above, p. 241.

14 Diploma of King William I for Giso, bishop of Wells: restoration to the church of St Andrew of 30 hides at Banwell, Somerset, given by Bishop Duduc but taken away by King Harold, 'for the proper increase of the dignity of the church, for the demesne of the episcopal see and for the maintenance of the brethren of the church of Wells'. '1067', *recte* 1068 (? Whitsuntide (11 May), at Westminster). *Latin, with bounds, in English, of Banwell and Compton Bishop, and with a note, in English, concerning 5 hides and some meadow at Hewish [in Brentmarsh] and 9 flocks at Cheddar Minster and some common land.*

> MS: Wells, D. & C., Liber Albus II, fos 246v–248v
> Ptd: *Acta of William I*, ed. Bates, no. 286.
> Listed: *Regesta* i, no. 23; Pelteret, no. 11.
> Translated: *EHD* ii, no. 77.
> Comment. Above, pp. 242–3. Dated '1067', in the sixth indiction [=1068].

Keynes, 'Regenbald the Chancellor', 219–20, probably drawn up by Bishop Giso.

15 Writ of the Lady Edith, widow of King Edward, addressed to all the hundred at Wedmore: announcing that she has given Bishop Giso the land at Mark, Somerset, 'for his canons at St Andrew's at Wells'; 'and I pray you that you will pronounce for me a just judgement concerning Wudumann to whom I entrusted my horses and who has for six years withheld my rent—both honey and money also'. 6 January 1066 x 18 December 1075. *English.*

MS: Wells, D. & C., Liber Albus I, fo. 17v (English and Latin)

Ptd: Harmer, *Anglo-Saxon Writs*, no. 72 (with translation).

Listed: *ECW*, no. 545; S 1241; Pelteret, no. 57.

Comment. Above, p. 239.

16 Record of Bishop Giso's purchase of land at Combe (St Nicholas), Somerset, from Azur, son of Thored. Conducted on the upper floor of the stone church at Wilton, Wiltshire, in the presence of the Lady Edith, widow of King Edward, with the permission of King William. 29 February 1072. *English.*

MS: Wells, D. & C., Liber Albus II, fo. 254v

Ptd: F. H. Dickinson, 'The Sale of Combe', *Proc. of the Somerset Archæol. and Nat. Hist. Society* xxii, 1876, 106–13; below, Appendix III.

Listed: Pelteret, no. 56.

Comment. Above, pp. 243–7. [E.A. Freeman], 'A Sale in 1072', *The Saturday Review* xlii, 1876, 688–9; *Life of Edward*, ed. Barlow, 139; Williams, *The English and the Norman Conquest*, 22, n. 110. For the expression 'ær dæg(e) and æfter (dæge)', see Harmer, *Anglo-Saxon Writs*, 431, n. to line 8.

17 Record of dues which pertained to the bishop of Winchester's manor of Taunton, Somerset, on the day of King Edward's death (5 January 1066). Attested by Bishop Giso, Abbot Ælfsige, Abbot Wulfgeat, Ælfnoth prior, Wulfweard White, and others, including Harding, son of Eadnoth. 1066 x 1086. *English.*

MS: BL, MS Add. 15350, fo. 27rv

Ptd: *Anglo-Saxon Charters*, ed. Robertson, App. I, no. 4.

Listed: *ECW*, no. 544; Pelteret, no. 144.

Comment. Above, p. 243. The text in the 'Codex Wintoniensis' was copied from a chirograph.

18 Writ of King William I, addressed to William de Courseulles (? in his capacity as sheriff of Somerset): ordering him to see to it that *Rom feoh* (Peter's Pence) be paid by the coming Michaelmas, by the king's men and by all the thegns and their men; and he is to make this known at Montacute and at Bristol, so that those who have not done it may do it; and the bishop and William are to make enquiry about those who do not pay; and neither William nor any of his men is to take any pledge in the land of Bishop Giso, in the bishop's absence. c.1068 x 1083 (before no. 19), ? c.1080. *English.*

MS: Wells, D. & C., Liber Albus I, fo. 18r (English and Latin)

Ptd: *Acta of William I*, ed. Bates, no. 288.

Listed: *Regesta* I, no. 187; Pelteret, no. 29.

Comment. Above, p. 248.

19 Writ of Queen Mathilda, addressed to William de Mohun, sheriff, and all the men in Somerset: announcing that Osbern, bishop of Exeter, has, at her request, given Bishop Giso the church at Wedmore, Somerset, to which Giso had frequently laid claim; William de Mohun is to give the bishop seisin. c.1068 (after no. 18) x 1083. *Latin.*

MS: Wells, D. & C., Liber Albus I, fo. 58r
Ptd: *Acta of William I*, ed. Bates, no. 289.
Listed: *EEA* xi: *Exeter 1046–1184*, ed. Barlow, no. *9.
Comment. Above, p. 248.

APPENDIX II

Charter of King Edward the Confessor
for the Bishopric of Wells
24 May 1065

King Edward the Confessor's charter for the bishopric of Wells (Appendix I, no. 9) has generally been regarded as a forgery; but it is argued above, pp. 232–8, that its irregular or suspicious features can be explained on the presumption that the charter was drawn up by Bishop Giso himself, and reflects his own understanding of the estates which constituted the endowment of his church. The text is printed below from Wells, D. & C., 'Liber Albus II', fos 241r–242r. Previous editions of the charter have been derived from the transcript in BL MS Cotton Tiberius E viii, pt i, fo. 218rv, which lacks the witness-list. The transcript is headed 'A true copy of the charter of Edw. the Confessor into the Bishop & Church of Welles', and was clearly taken from a version of the charter copied on a single sheet (dated 20 May 1065, indiction 3); the copy of the charter in London, College of Arms, MS WE, fos 121r–123r, was taken from this transcript some time before Tiberius was damaged in the Cotton fire of 1731. It is interesting to note in this connection that Francis Godwin, canon of Wells and latterly bishop of Llandaff (1601–17) and Hereford (1617–33), remarks in a letter to William Camden, dated 27 May 1608, that he had made a transcript of what was evidently this charter 'out of the *Autographum* remaining in the Archives of the Church of Wells', and enclosed a copy; see *Gulielmi Camdeni et Illustrium Virorum ad G. Camdenum Epistolæ*, ed. T. Smith, London 1691, p. 109, from BL MS Cotton Julius C v, fo. 94. Godwin's particular interest in the bishops of Bath and Wells is shown by the catalogue of them which he compiled and wrote out for himself in 1594 (Cambridge, Trinity College, MS R. 7. 12); his well known catalogue of the bishops of England, in general, was first published in 1601.

Rubric (representing the endorsement on the original single sheet): Þis is eallra þæra landa landboc þe mid rihte hyrað into þam biscoprice þe Eadweard cyngc gebocode Sancto Andrea apostolo // into þam biscopstole to Wyllan on ece yrfe.

✠ ℞ Regnante in perpetuum domino nostro Iesu Christo omnium regum principe. Ego Eadweardus secundum uoluntatem eius monarcha totius Britanniae, sciens gloriosis regibus nihil esse felicius et preclaro populo salubrius quam ius aecclesiastice rectitudinis in omnibus seruare, et in diuinis atque secularibus negociis iusta iudicia agere, proposui iuste et clementer regendo mihi subditis prodesse et *sic* singulorum utilitatibus prouidere, ut confirmatis nostra auctoritate que quibusque contingunt haereditario iure per posteritates sibi succedentes inuiolata queant esse. Unde rogatus a Gisone Wellensi episcopo, quem ante hoc triennium Rome cum commendaticiis litteris direxi, et apostolica ordinatione Nicolai pape functum recepi, et maxime ab Eadgida regina mihi matrimonio sociata, et sibi gratuite miserationis dignatione propitia, ut ea que antecessorum meorum largitate donata sunt, uel sagacitate confirmata, apicibus nostre auctoritatis, ecclesie sedis sue literato confirmarem, et que in multis cyrographis regum priorum essent aliquibus iam uetustate pene consumptis in armariolo unius cartule congregari permitterem. Eorum iustis petitionibus libens annuo, et non solum ea que ipse a me uel antecessores eius a meis impetrauerunt uel etiam pretio acquisiuerunt ex his que regibus debentur, habere eum, et omnes successores eius inuiolabiliter permitto; sed etiam quicquid possidere uidetur ecclesia quam regit, constituo in perpetua libertate, exceptis tribus, expeditione, pontis arcisue restauratione. Quod ut per succedentia sibi seculorum tempora apud filios iusticie perduret fixum, in hac cartula coram subnotatis testibus manu propria dominice crucis depingo signum, et mee ymaginis adnecto sigillum. Si quisque a me canonice decreta sunt infregerit, anathemate irremediabili multatus sententie damnationis eterne subiaceat, nisi resipuerit.

✠ Ego Edwardus rex crucis titulo hanc confirmo libertatem. ✠ Ego Eadgyda regina eodem sigillo adhibeo confirmationem. ✠ Ego Stigandus archiepiscopus subscribo. ✠ Ego Aldredus archiepiscopus assentio. ✠ Ego Heremannus episcopus laudo. ✠ Ego Leofricus episcopus consolido. ✠ Ego Willhelmus episcopus. ✠ Ego Egelricus episcopus. ✠ Ego Eilmer episcopus. ✠ Ego Leofwinus episcopus. ✠ Ego Wulfwinus episcopus. ✠ Ego Waldere episcopus. ✠ Ego Wulfstanus episcopus. ✠ Ego Egelnodus abbas. ✠ Ego Leofweardus abbas. ✠ Ego Sewold abbas. ✠ Ego Haroldus dux. ✠ Ego Tostig dux. ✠ Ego Gyrd dux. ✠ Ego Leofwine dux. ✠ Ego Eadwine dux. ✠ Ego Walþeof dux. ✠ Ego Rotbertus procurator. ✠ Ego Esgar procurator. ✠ Ego Raulf procurator. ✠ Ego Bundi procurator. ✠ Ego Wigod pincerna. ✠ Ego Heardyng pincerna. ✠ Ego Winsi cubicularius. ✠ Ego Brihtric p[rinceps] ✠ Ego Elfstan p[rinceps] ✠ Ego Elfgar p[rinceps] ✠ Ego Tov[i]g ✠ Ego Agelwi ✠ Ego Evorwacer ✠ Ego Eilwi ✠ Ego Egelmer m[inister] ✠ Ego Egilfrid m[inister] ✠ Ego Wikyng m[inister] ✠ Ego Siweard m[inister] ✠ Ego Nordman m[inister] ✠ Ego Elfgeat m[inister] ✠ Ego Osmund m[inister]

Quamuis autem in singulis cyrographis possessiones eiusdem ecclesie pleniter annotate habeantur, tamen non infructuosum ratus sum, si in hoc quoque recapitulentur. <i> Inprimis in territorio Wellensi, quod antiquo uocabulo dicitur Tidington, et in singulis uiculis ad se pertinentibus sunt .line mansus, hoc est, Paulesham, Woky, Hentun, Gyrdleg, Bleddenhyð et Eastun, Westbyrig, Wokyhole et Æbbe wyrð, Burcotan, Middeltun et oðer Middeltun, et æt þam Pænne, Hornningdun et oðer Horningdun, et Hwitecirce, Denrenn, Dulticotan, Welsleg, Wuormestorr, Celicotan, Begenhangra, Wandestreow, Hlittun. <ii> Item in alio quod Circ dicitur .line et hii sunt uiculi sibi adiacentes, Litletun, Hæsele, Dundreg et .iii. Suðtunes. <iii> In alio autem quod dicitur Euorcric .xx. mansus, Preostle, Cesterbled, Strettun. <iv> Et in illo quod uocatur Cyncgesbyrig .xxxviii. mansus et hii sunt eius uiculi, Landbroc, Readewelle, et æt þam Beorge, et Lytlenige, Hwisc, Cuma, Pibbesbyrig, Cerdren et oðer frusa Cerdren, Cynemerestun, Langanham, Winesham atque Cungaresbyrig, necnon et Banawell cum omnibus ad se pertinentibus. <v> In eo quoque quod Welingtun nuncupatur est possessio .xv. cassatorum, et hæ sunt uillule eorum, Bocland, Hamme, Huntanapoð, Herpoðford, Pitnocesmor, Ceolfestun. **<vi>** Sunt .xv. in altero Wyfelescombe nominato, in his uillis distributi, Nunnetun, Upcotan, Hwitefeld, Hwiðigcum, Acumetun, Langele, Forda, Peddesford, Fifhida et oðer Fifhyda, Dene, Slep, Hwrentimor. **<vii>** Habentur etiam in eo quod Lidegeard dicitur .xv. cassati, et hee curticule adiacentes sibi, Cuma, Peddenallras, et þ wudu land, Æsce, Baggabeorc, Anacota, Hylle. **<viii>** In eo loco quod Weddmor dicitur .iiii. mansuum est possessio, et he sunt uillule huc pertinentes, Biddesham quod Tarnuc proprie appellatur, et alia que dicitur Heawycan, et Mercern.

Hec igitur cum omnibus ad se pertinentibus, id est siluis, campis, pratis, paschuis, piscuariis, molendinis, ecclesiae prefate uel episcopo, ut predixi, confirmo, et libertatem eius secundum antecessorum meorum statuta amplifico. Scripta est haec karta ab eodem Gisone episcopo iussu meo anno dominice incarnationis mill'io .lxv. indictione .iiii. vicesima .iiii. die mensis Mai in regali uilla Wendlesore nuncupata. <> Signum manus Gisonis episcopi. ✠

APPENDIX III

Record of Bishop Giso's Purchase of Land
at Combe (St Nicholas), Somerset
29 February 1072

The text of the charter recording Bishop Giso's purchase of land at Combe (St Nicholas) from Azor, son of Thored (Appendix I, no. 16), is printed below from Wells, D. & C., 'Liber Albus II', fo. 254v. In the Old English text, the letter wynn is here represented by w.

Rubric (representing the endorsement on the original single sheet): Bæc be Cume

✠ Her cyð embe þ land æt Cume. Þa biscop Giso of Sumorsetescyre wæs on Wiltune inn þære stænena cyrcean on þære upfleringe to foren Eadgyþe þere hlefdian Edweardes cyncges lafe mid Willelmes cyncges geleafan þ Adzor Þuredes sunu moste hyt sellan 7 gyfan þ land æt Cume Gisan b. 7 hi wurþan sæhte þ se b. gef him .vi. marc. goldes and sceolde þ land gan inn to þam b'rice. æt Welle eall swa hit stode mid mete and mid mannum 7 mid eallum æhtan swa swa hyt hym on handa stod on æcce yrfe ær dæg 7 æfter 7 his gebedredene sceolde beon bynnan þam mynstre 7 his fæder 7 his meder 7 his geswustra 7 his sunu. a tha hwile þe crystendom. wunede on Engle lande on gewittnæste þære manna þe þær mid wæron.

✠ Sæxi preost. ✠ Kyppincg pr*eost.* ✠ Brihtmær pr*eost.* ✠ Godric diac'. ✠ Waldere diac'. ✠ Sumorlæte subdiac'. ✠ Herdincg. ✠ Wulfweard hwite. ✠ Ægelsig stiweard. ✠ Alfwold burþen. ✠ Vitela. ✠ Alfwold. ✠ Brihtric Doddasunu. ✠ Brixi Ceolsig sunu. ✠ Godwine hos. Leofwine Godwinessunu. ✠ Leofwine Edwines sunu. ✠ Siweard Godmannes sunu. ✠ Agamund. ✠ Ælfric lange. ✠ Ælfric Ælfheges sunu.

✠ Þiederic goldsmið. ✠ Ægelsig goldsmið. ✠ Norðmann Ioh*anne*s sunu. ✠ Ægelric coc. ✠ Rabel coc ✠.

7 þis wes gedon on þone Wednesday binnan hlenctene þa man sang Reminiscere miseracionum tuarum Domine. on þam vi geare þæs þe Willelm cyng rixode 7 Mathyld. his gebedde, 7 Rotb. æþeling hyre sunu 7 Landfranc arceb. 7 þa ylce geare gewiten þa twegen biscopes Stigand arceb' 7 Leofric b. of Exacestre. 7 þa wæs agan fram Xpes gebyrdtide þusen geare 7 lxxii geare on þæt xi geare. þæs he Giso b. feng to rice.

Translation

Charter concerning Combe

Here it is made known concerning the land at Combe: when Bishop Giso of Somersetshire was at Wilton, on the up-floor of the stone church, before the Lady Edith, King Edward's widow, with the permission of King William, in order that Adzor, son of Thored, might sell it and give the land at Combe to Bishop Giso. And they came to an agreement that the bishop should give him 6 marks of gold, and the land should go to the bishopric at Wells just as it stood, with provisions and with men and with all goods, as it stood in his hands, in perpetual inheritance, at any time whatever; and there should be a service for him in the minster, and for his father, and his mother, and his sisters, and his son, for as long as Christendom should continue in England. In the witness of the men who were there:
+ Sæxi, priest. + Kyppincg, priest. + Brihtmær, priest. + Godric, deacon. + Waldere, deacon. + Sumorlæte, subdeacon. + Hearding. + Wulfweard White. + Æthelsige, steward. + Ælfwold, chamberlain. + Vitela. + Ælfwold. + Brihtric, son of Dodda. + Brixi, son of Ceolsige. + Godwine *hos.* Leofwine, son of Godwine. + Leofwine, son of Eadwine. + Siweard, son of Godman. + Agamund. + Ælfric the Long. + Ælfric, son of Ælfheah. + Thiederic, goldsmith. + Æthelsige, goldsmith. + Northmann, son of John. + Æthelric, cook. + Rabel, cook. +.

And this was done on the Wednesday in Lent when they sing 'Reminiscere miserationum tuarum Domine', in the sixth year that King William reigned, and Mathilda, his consort, and Robert ætheling, their son, and Lanfranc, archbishop. And the same year died the two bishops, Archbishop Stigand and Leofric, bishop of Exeter. And then was gone from the time of Christ's birth one thousand and seventy-two years, in the eleventh year since Bishop Giso succeeded to power.

APPENDIX IV

The 'Autobiography' of Bishop Giso

The text which purports to be the 'autobiography' of Bishop Giso is embedded in an anonymous tract on the bishopric of Wells (known to modern scholarship as the *Historiola de Primordiis Episcopatus Somersetensis*), compiled probably by a canon of Wells in the late twelfth or the early thirteenth century; for discussion, see above, pp. 213–26. The *Historiola* is preserved only in a fourteenth-century register of the cathedral priory of Bath (London, Lincoln's Inn, MS 185, fos 96r–99r), and was printed in *Ecclesiastical Documents*, ed. Joseph Hunter, Camden Society 8, London 1840, 9–28. Hunter's edition is accompanied by an English translation, and is furnished with an introduction (3–7) and notes (29–41). A new edition of the *Historiola* is needed, in which the work as a whole could be studied in relation to other manifestations of historical writing at Wells, notably the *Historia Minor* and the *Historia Major* (printed in T.F. Palmer, *Collectanea i: a Collection of Documents from Various Sources*, Somerset Record Society 39 (1924), 48–71). It is to be hoped that someone will be moved to undertake this task. For present purposes, it must suffice to provide a provisional text of the 'autobiography' on its own, divided editorially into sections numbered from §1 to §13, and accompanied by a revised translation.

Text

Ecce iam audistis ob quam causam, quo casu, qua ratione, quando et quis transtulit cathedram ad Wellam. Daniel uero, cum annis quadraginta tres sedisset in pontificatu, relicta terra morientium transiuit ad terram uiuentium. Cui successerunt plurimi successores in Wella, pontifices subscripti Sigarus, Alwynus, qui subplantauit Sigarum ab episcopatu, post cuius obitum cum .xiii. diebus uixisset episcopus exspirauit; Brithelmus; Burthwoldus, Liowyngus, Brithtumus, Elwynus, quibus successerunt Brithwynus, et Duduco uir iustus et timoratus; de quibus scripsit successor eorum, uenerabilis et preclare memorie Gyso episcopus, cuius scriptum en profertur in medium:

§1 Anno dominice incarnationis .m.xxx. Cnuth rege Danorum et Norweynensium optinente etiam <97r> principatum totius Brittannie, Brythcri episcopus Wellie ecclesie Merechyyt cognominatus .ii. Idus Aprilis obiit, et in Glasstingensi cenobio, in quo ante episcopatum abbas fuit, est sepultus. Huic successit Duduco, natione Saxo, .iii. Idus Iunii ordinatus, qui possessiones quas hereditario iure a rege ante episcopatum promeruerat, monasterium uidelicet Sancti Petri in ciuitate Gloucestrensi situm cum omnibus ad se pertinentibus, et uillam que Kunigresbiria dicitur, atque aliam Banewelle nuncupatam, roboratas cyrographis regie autoritatis ac donationis Deo Sanctoque Andree tempore Edwardi piissimi regis obtulit; uestimenta quoque sacerdotalia, reliquias sanctorum, uasa altarea concupiscibilia, libros plurimos, et omnia que habere poterat, iam, imminente die uocationis sue, adhibuit; et .xx.uii. ordinationis sue agens annum menses quoque .uii. et dies .uii. obdormiuit in Domino .xu. kalendas Februarii, et sepultus est in ecclesia sedis sue.

§2 Haroldus uero, tunc temporis dux occidentalium Saxonum, non solum terras inuadere, uerum etiam episcopalem sedem omnibus hiis spoliare non timuit; set et Stigandus archiepiscopus Cantuariorum, postea, tempore Willielmi regis, in conciliis episcoporum, a legatis Alexandri pape in ciuitate Wyncestrie degradatus, prefatum monasterium iniusta ambitione a rege sibi dari petiit et impetratum ad horam optinuit.

§3 Huic predicto Duduco episcopo successi ego, G. Hasbaniensis incola ex uico Sancti Trudonis anno Dominice Incarnationis .m.lx. quem Rex Edwardus, licet uite meritis indignum, Rome direxit et a Nicholao papa ordinatum, die Paschali, id est .xvii. kalendas Maii; post peractam ibi sinodum, ebdomada secunda post albas, priuilegium Apostolice autoritatis mecum deferentem, honorifice recepit.

§4 Tunc ecclesiam sedis mee perspiciens esse mediocrem, clericos quoque .iiii.^{or} uel .u.^{que} absque claustro et rra [refectorio] esse ibidem, uoluntarium me ad eorum astruxi adinstaurationem. Igitur, pietate nulli secundo cum huiusmodi indigentiam intimarem, possessionem que Wedmor dicitur, pro remuneratione eterne recompensationis, in augmentum et sustentationem fratrum ibidem Deo seruientium, ab eo inpetraui. Regina quoque Eadgid, cuius adminuculo et suggestione hoc ad effectum uenit, partem eiusdem terre que sui iuris erat, Merken et Moddesleh ab incolis nuncupatam, fideli beniuolentia ad idem adauxit.

§5 Uillam deinde que Wynesham appellatur, a quodam antecessorum meorum prestitam, set per multorum annorum curricula absque obauditione a successoribus retentam, a quodam Alsie nomine tunc temporis eam in dominio habente, cepi repetere; quem crebro canonice ammonitum, et post iudicium prouincialium, quo ille excludi et ego debebam introduci, armis repugnantem, non timui anathematizare.

§6 Haroldum etiam ducem, qui ecclesiam michi commissam <spoliauerat>, nunc secreto nunc palam correctum, pari sententia cogitabam ferire; sed, defuncto rege Edwardo, anno ab Incarnatione Domini m.lxv, cum ille regni gubernacula suscepisset, non solum ea que tulerat se redditurum, uerum etiam ampliora spopondit daturum. Preoccupante autem illum iudicio diuine ultionis, post uictoriam qua potitus est de equiuoco suo rege Norweyniensium .xxi. die reparato exercitu, contra Willielmum ducem Normannorum qui iam meridianam terre eius plagam inuaserat, arma corripuit, et mense .x. regni sui, cum duobus fratribus suis, et maxima populi sui strage, occubuit.

§7 Dux uero uictoria potitus, cum regni gubernacula post <97v> eum suscepisset, et a me de iniuria michi illata querimoniam audisset, Wynesham ecclesie resignauit, priuilegio confirmauit, ea conditione, ut fratres in eadem Deo sacrificium laudis offerentes, pro sua suorumque antecessorum et successorum perpetua salute, eam iure hereditario inuiolabiliter possiderent;

§8 et monasterium Oswaldi se additurum, cum citius posset, spopondit.

§9 Ego deinde ut amplificarem ecclesie mee adhuc beneficia, predium quod Cumbe nuncupatur, a quodam meo parochiano Atsere dicto, cum consensu regis Willielmi, emptum, cum quibusdam aliis, Wurmeston et Littone nuncupatis, ad augmentum cleri et sustentationem eius, uelud prenominata, assignaui.

§10 Aliud quoque, Kulmetone uocatum, quod sibi, defuncta matre, iure hereditario prouenerat, Elnedou Glastingensi abbate, ecclesie mee donari, impetraui; sed illud, diabolica cuiusdam potentis inuasione, diu non tenui.

§11 Hiis itaque mansionibus ad sustentationem fratrum, regum liberalitate, cum summa libertate ecclesie, delegatis, eorum numerum adauxi; et quos, publice uiuere et inhoneste mendicare, necessariorum inopia antea coegerat, canonicali, ditatos, instruxi obedientia. Claustrum uero et refectorium et dormitorium illis preparaui, et omnia que ad hec necessaria et competentia fore cognoui, ad modum patrie mee, laudabiliter aduocaui. Unum uero ex ipsis, Ysaac nomine, uelud pre ceteris etate et sensu ministerio ydoneum, unanimes elegerunt, qui bonis eorum exterioribus curam impenderet, et interius fratribus. Sententiam anathematis inflixi in omnes illos, qui uel institutionem meam canonice factam in aliquo lederent, uel de possessionibus, uel per me uel antecessores meos appositis, aliquid tollerent.

§12 Huius rei prelibationem ideo premisi, ut, cum in sequentibus de istis et omnibus que ad episcopalem pertinent dignitatem terris confuse tractauero, que ad usum canonicorum, que ad episcopi dominium uel dispensationem, proprie, innotescat, et posteritas, ab ambiguitate libera, terminos suos infra habitantes, aliena non inuadat.

§13 Successores uero meos fraterne dilectionis affectu moneo, et deprecor, ut supra ecclesie huius per me et antecessores meos positam beneficii sui sarcinam, unusquisque rem augeat, ut fructum recompensationis post huius uite transitum a Christo gloriosus possideat. Si quis cuiuslibet ordinis decreti huius uiolator exstiterit, qui uel ordinationis mee statum inuertere, uel de possessionibus canonicorum usui deputatis quamlibet parum ad aliud transferre presumpserit, illum episcopus paterna ammonitione et consilio regat et reuocet, uel induratum diuine ultionis seueritate compescat, ne, dum male agentem negligenter tollerauerit, non a se sed aliunde ad modum Hely, dampnationi incurrat.

Ecce rei ueritas de conuenientia Wellensis ecclesie quam uenerande memorie Gyso scriptam reliquit. Qui, cum annos circiter .xxviii. in cathedra pontificali sedisset, decurso dierum suorum circulo, obdormiuit in Domino, et sepultus est in ecclesia quam rexerat, in emiciclo facto in pariete a parte aquilonali prope altare, sicut Duduco predecessor eius sepultus est a meridie iuxta altare.

Translation

So, now you have heard for what reason, by what chance, in what manner, when, and by whom the episcopal see was transferred to Wells. Daniel, indeed, having held the bishopric for 43 years, left the land of the dying and passed to the land of living. Many successors followed him at Wells, (including) the bishops written hereafter: Sigar; Ælfwine, who displaced Sigar from the episcopal office, who survived as bishop for 13 days after his death, and died; Brihthelm; Buruhwold; Lyfing; *Brithtum* [=Brihtwine]; *Elwyn* [=Æthelwine]. To whom succeeded Brihtwine [*recte* Brihtwig] and Duduc, a man who was just and devout; concerning whom their successor Bishop Giso, of venerable and famous memory, has written – whose account may be introduced at this point:

§1 In the year of the Lord's Incarnation 1030 [*recte* 1033], when Cnut, king of the Danes and Norwegians, was holding control of the whole of Britain, *Brythcri* [=Brihtwig] bishop of the church of Wells, whose surname was *Merechyyt* [=Merehwit], died, on II Id. Apr. [12 Apr.], and was buried in the monastery of Glastonbury, in which he was abbot before he became bishop. He was succeeded by Duduc, a Saxon by birth, who was consecrated on III Id. Jun. [11 Jun.], and who, in the time of Edward, the most pious king, gave to God and to St Andrew the possessions which he had obtained from the king in hereditary right, before he became bishop, namely, the monastery of St Peter [*probably an error for St Oswald*] in the city of Gloucester, with all things pertaining to it, as well as the estate called CONGRESBURY and another called BANWELL, strengthened by charters [*lit.* chirographs] of royal authority and donation. He also gave sacerdotal vestments, relics of saints, beautiful vessels for the altar, many books, and, as the day of his death drew near, everything which he possessed; and in the twenty-seventh year of his ordination [*11 Jun. 1059–10 Jun. 1060, if calculated from 1033*], plus 7 months and 7 days, he fell asleep in the Lord, on XV Kal. Feb. [18 Jan.], and was buried in the church of his see.

§2 But Harold, at that time Earl of the West Saxons, did not hesitate not only to invade the lands but also to despoil the episcopal see of all these things. Moreover,

Stigand, archbishop of Canterbury – afterwards, in the time of King William, degraded in councils of bishops by the legates of Pope Alexander, in the city of Winchester – sought with unjust desire to be given the aforesaid monastery by the king, and obtained his request.

§3 I, Giso, a Hasbanian from the town of Saint Trond, succeeded the aforesaid Bishop Duduc in the year of the Lord's Incarnation 1060; whom, although unworthy of any such merit, King Edward sent to Rome, and, when the synod there was over, received back with honour, in the second week after Albs [*i.e. after Whitsunday, i.e. 17–23 June*], duly consecrated by Pope Nicholas on Easter Day, XVII Kal. Maii [15 Apr. (1061)], and bringing with me a privilege of Apostolic authority.

§4 Then, perceiving my episcopal church to be small, and the four or five clerks there to be without cloister, or refectory, I undertook of my own volition the establishment of these things. Accordingly, I mentioned this poverty to the one who in piety was second to none, and I obtained from him the possession which is called WEDMORE, for the remuneration of an eternal recompense, for the increase and maintenance of the brethren there serving God. And Queen Edith, through whose assistance and suggestion this was brought into effect, added to it, with faithful benevolence, a part of the same land which was in her own possession, called MARK and MUDGLEY by the inhabitants.

§5 Then the estate called WINSHAM, which had been granted out by one of my predecessors but kept from successors for a period of many years, without any service, I began to reclaim from a certain Ælfsige, who at that time held it in lordship. He was frequently admonished canonically; and when, after a judgement of the provincials that he was to be deprived and I ought to be put in possession, he resisted by force, I did not hesitate to anathematize him.

§6 I even considered striking Earl Harold, who <had despoliated> the church committed to me, and whom I rebuked sometimes in private and sometimes openly, with a sentence of the same kind; but, after King Edward's death in the year of the Lord's Incarnation 1065 [*correct for 5 January 1066, if the year was reckoned from the Annunciation*], and on taking up the government of the kingdom, he promised not only to restore what he had taken away, but also to give fresh donations. However, the judgement of divine vengeance overtook him on the twenty-first day after the victory which he obtained over his namesake, the king of the Norwegians, when, having recruited his army, he engaged in battle with William, duke of the Normans, who had invaded the southern shore of his land, and was slain, in the tenth month of his reign, with his two brothers, and a great slaughter of his people.

§7 The duke, having obtained the victory, and when he had taken up the government of the kingdom after him, and had heard from me a complaint about the injury which had been done to me, surrendered WINSHAM to the church, and confirmed it by a charter (*priuilegium*) which specified that the brethren, offering the sacrifice of praise to God in that church, for the eternal welfare of himself and of his predecessors and successors, should possess it inviolably, by hereditary right.

§8 And he promised that he would add the monastery of Oswald [*i.e. St Oswald's, Gloucester*], as soon as he could.

§9 In order that I might still further enlarge the property of my church, I bought the estate called COMBE from one of my parishoners, called Atsere, with the consent of King William, and assigned it, with certain other estates, called

WORMINSTER and LITTON, for the increase of the clerks and for their maintenance, in the same way as above.

§10 Another estate, called KILMINGTON, I prevailed with Æthelnoth, abbot of Glastonbury, to give to my church, to whom it had descended by hereditary right on the death of his mother; but this, owing to the diabolical interference of a certain powerful person, I did not hold for any length of time.

§11 Once these estates had been handed over by the generosity of kings, with full liberty of the church, for the maintenance of the brethren, I increased their number; and those whom the want of the necessities of life had previously compelled to live among the people and to beg in a mean manner, and who were now enriched, I trained in canonical obedience. Indeed, I prepared for them a cloister, a refectory, and a dormitory; and I brought together, in praiseworthy manner, all those things which I knew to be necessary and appropriate for the purpose, according to the custom of my country. They unanimously chose one of their own number, called Isaac, as fitter for the office than the rest by age and understanding, who was to take care of their temporal concerns without, and of the brethren within. I pronounced the sentence of anathema against all who should in any thing violate the arrangement thus canonically made, or should take away any part of the possessions thus assigned by me or my predecessors.

§12 I have thus given a foretaste of this subject, that when hereafter I shall have treated of these and all the lands which pertain generally to this episcopal see, it may be known what belongs peculiarly to the use of the canons and what to the demesne and disposal of the bishop; and so, posterity being freed from all uncertainty on this subject, one party may not encroach upon the rights of another.

§13 But now I warn my successors in the spirit of fraternal affection, and I entreat them out of regard to the benefits conferred on this church by me and my predecessors, that each of them would endeavour to add to its property, that they may possess in glory the fruit of a recompense from Christ when they have passed out of this present life. If any one, of whatever rank, shall violate this decree, either as overturning this my ordinance, or presuming to transfer to some other purpose any part, however small, of the possessions set apart to the use of the canons, him let the bishop, by paternal admonition and counsel, rule and advise, or, if he is hardened, restrain by the severity of divine vengeance, lest while he negligently suffer the evil-doer to proceed, he may, after the manner of Eli, incur a sentence of condemnation not from himself but from another quarter.

Behold, now you have the truth concerning the settlement of the possessions of the church of Wells which Giso of venerable memory left in writing. When he had occupied the episcopal see for about 28 years – the circle of his days being completed – he fell asleep in the Lord, and was buried in the church which he had ruled, in a little niche in the wall, on the north side near the altar, just as Duduc his predecessor was buried on the south side of the altar.

APPENDIX V

The *Terra Gisonis* in 1086

The account of the estates belonging to the bishopric of Wells, drawn up in 1086 for the purposes of the Domesday survey, is here reduced to its essentials, so that the information can be compared more easily with the charters and writs which bear on the activities of Bishop Giso between 1061 and 1088 (Appendix I), and with the details given in Giso's 'autobiography' (Appendix IV). The information is derived from the survey of the 'Terra Gisonis episcopi in Sumerseta', in Exon DB 156r–160r, and from the abbreviated version in GDB 89rv (*DB Som.* 6.1–19). Some further details emerge from the geld accounts for the hundreds of Somerset, in Exon DB 75r–82v.

1. WELLS (50 hides), held TRE by the bishop
   8 hides held by the bishop in lordship
   6 hides held by villeins, etc.
   14 hides held by the canons (6 hides in lordship)
   6 hides held by Fastrad (4 hides in lordship)
   5 hides held by Richard (3 hides in lordship)
   5 hides held by Erneis (4 hides in lordship)
   2 hides held by Fastrad
   2 hides held by Ralph (1 hide in lordship)
   2 hides held by Manasseh's wife, not from the bishop
   2 hides over and above the 50, which never paid geld, held by Ælfward crocco and Eadric from the bishop

2. COMBE (St Nicholas) (20 hides), held TRE by Azor, son of Thorold
   8 hides in lordship
   12 hides held by villeins, etc.

3. KINGSBURY (Episcopi) (20 hides), held TRE by the bishop
   6 hides in lordship
   6 hides held by villeins, etc.
   8 hides held by 3 *milites* and 1 *clericus*

4. CHARD (8 hides), held TRE by the bishop
   2 hides in lordship
   6 hides held by villeins, etc.
   2 hides held by 1 *tainus*

5. LITTLENEY [in Huish] (2 hides), held TRE by the bishop
   1 hide in lordship
   1 hide held by villeins, etc.

6. WIVELISCOMBE (15 hides), held TRE by the bishop
   3 hides in lordship
   3 hides held by villeins, etc.
   9 hides held by 3 *milites*

7. WELLINGTON (14 hides), held TRE by the bishop
       3 hides in lordship
       9 hides held by villeins, etc.
       2 hides of the villeins' land held by John *hostiarius*
       1 hide added, held TRE by Ælfgifu

8. (Bishops) LYDEARD (10 hides, less 1 virgate), held TRE by the bishop
       3 hides in lordship
       4 hides held by villeins, etc.
       3 hides of the villeins' land held by 2 *milites*

9. BANWELL (30 hides), held TRE by Earl Harold
       6 hides in lordship
       7 hides held by villeins, etc.
       3 hides held by Serlo de Borci
       5½ hides held by Ralph tortesmanus
       5½ hides held by Rohard (2 hides in lordship)
       1 hide held by Fastrad
       1 hide held by Bovo
       1 hide held by Ælfwig Haussonna

10. EVERCREECH (20 hides), held TRE by the bishop
       3 hides in lordship
       2 hides held by villeins, etc.
       7 hides held by Erneis (4 hides in lordship)
       1½ hides held by Maghere
       1 hide held by Hildebert
       5 hides and 1 virgate held by 3 Englishmen (2 laymen and a priest)

11. WESTBURY (sub Mendip) (6 hides), held TRE by the bishop
       3 hides in lordship
       3 hides held by villeins, etc.

12. WINSHAM (10 hides), held TRE by Ælfsige, and TRW by Osmund from the bishop
       4 hides in lordship
       6 hides held by villeins, etc.

13. CHEW (Magna) (30 hides), held TRE by the bishop
       4 hides in lordship
       6 hides held by villeins, etc.
       5 hides held by Richard (4 hides in lordship)
       6 hides held by Roghard (3 hides in lordship)
       5 hides held by Stephen (4 hides and 3 virgates in lordship)
       7 virgates held by Ælfric of Stowey (1½ hides in lordship)
       2 hides held by Wulfric (1 hide and 3 virgates in lordship)

14. YATTON (20 hides), held TRE by John Danus
       6 hides in lordship

2 hides held by villeins, etc.

5 hides held by Fastrad (2 hides in lordship)

4 hides held by Hildebert (2 hides in lordship), of which 1 hide was held
TRE by Ailrun, to which belongs the pasture called Wemberham (which
belonged TRE to the manor of Congresbury)

1 hide held by Benzelin the Archdeacon

15. WEDMORE (10 hides; 11 hides are there), held TRE by the bishop

4 hides and 3 virgates in lordship

5 hides and 1 virgate held by villeins, etc.

The bishop's holding at Wedmore is also registered under the 'Terra Regis', as a
member of the manor of Cheddar (*DB Som.* 1.2).

16. WANSTROW (4 hides), held TRE by the Canons (Exon DB: by the bishop
himself), and held TRW by the Canons from the bishop

2 hides in lordship

2 hides held by villeins, etc.

17. LITTON (8½ hides), held TRE by the Canons (Exon DB: by the bishop himself), and TRW by the Canons (from the bishop)

6½ hides in lordship

2 hides held by villeins, etc.

18. MILVERTON (1 virgate), held TRE by the bishop, and held TRW by the king

A holding at Milverton, assessed at half a virgate, is registered under the lands
which were held 'in Queen Edith's time' (i.e. in 1075) by Queen Edith (*DB Som.*
1.26)

19. ASH (Priors) (3 hides and 1 virgate), held TRE by the bishop (in the bishop's
manor of Lydeard), and held TRW by Roger Arundel from the king, wrongfully

This holding is also registered under the land of Roger Arundel, in two parts: 2
hides held TRE by Ailric, and 1 hide and 1 virgate held TRE by Sæwine from the
bishop of Wells (*DB Som.* 22.20)

A LOMBARD ABBEY IN A NORMAN WORLD:
ST SOPHIA, BENEVENTO, 1050–1200

G.A. Loud

The monastery of St Sophia, Benevento, was one of a number of wealthy and influential Benedictine monasteries which collectively dominated the Church in southern Italy during the eleventh and early twelfth centuries. Benedictine influence was even more marked in the south of Italy than in the rest of Christendom at this period, and it endured for a considerable period after the Black Monks' predominance had elsewhere been overtaken by newer currents of monasticism. The great south Italian abbeys such as Montecassino, the Holy Trinity at Cava and St Clement at Casauria in the Abruzzi profited both from the major changes in the power structure and landholding brought about by the Norman conquest of the southern third of the peninsula, and also from the influence of the Gregorian reform movement which led to them receiving the donation of numerous churches formerly in lay hands. In southern Italy, as elsewhere in Christendom, laymen surrendered *Eigenkirchen* to the Church on a large scale, and most of these were given into monastic hands rather than back to the bishops who had abandoned or been deprived of their rights over them.

That in southern Italy the monastic element enjoyed a role even more prominent than elsewhere in the Christian west was primarily a product of the way in which the secular Church was structured. The period immediately before the Norman Conquest and that of the Conquest itself saw a proliferation of new bishoprics, until virtually every hill town in the south had its cathedral. Thus in Apulia, where in 900 there had been only eight bishoprics, by the later twelfth century there were forty-six.[1] Indeed the twelfth-century kingdom of Sicily had in all some 144 dioceses. Not surprisingly most of these sees were restricted in size, often (as in the Terra di Bari) cheek by jowl with each other, and they were even more restricted in income. The provision of an adequately educated and effective episcopate in dioceses which were too poor either to have proper schools to train local clergy or to attract qualified outsiders to seek bishoprics and canonries remained problematic, at least until the thirteenth-century development of the mendicant orders, whose members' vows of poverty made them ideally suited for staffing many south

The research for this essay was facilitated by my tenure of a Balsdon Senior Research Fellowship at the British School of Rome in spring 1990, and grants from the Wolfson Foundation, the British Academy and the University of Leeds. It would have been impossible without the help of Professore Elio Galasso, Direttore of the Museo del Sannio at Benevento, Mgr. Leonard Boyle, Prefect of the Vatican Library, and their staffs. To all of these I am very grateful. This essay is dedicated to the memory of my mother, who died on 28 July 1996, a few days after it was completed.

[1] J.-M. Martin, *La Pouille du VIe au XIIe siècle*, Rome 1993, 563.

Map 1. The property of St Sophia, Benevento, late twelfth century

Italian bishoprics.[2] If the influence of monasteries was always strongly regional, it was by no means confined to the exiguous territory of a single diocese. The larger monasteries possessed the schools and libraries which many cathedrals lacked, through which they could instruct their recruits and maintain reputations for piety and learning. They were therefore more likely to attract the religious instincts and generosity of the predominantly (though not exclusively) Norman/French upper class which the conquest had created. And until the end of the twelfth century south Italian monasticism remained overwhelmingly Benedictine. The new currents of eremitic monasticism had some effect from the 1120s onwards, but such foundations were few and their impact limited until relatively late in the twelfth century, while until the very last years of that century the Cistercians and the canonical orders were largely conspicuous by their absence.[3]

Within this context, however, St Sophia, Benevento, is a case study of particular interest. This is in part because it is well-documented. Its chartulary, written in 1119, is the oldest such manuscript to have survived from southern Italy, even though it was not the first actually to have been written. (It has been shown that the late twelfth-century Casauria chartulary was based on an archetype produced as early as the 1030s.)[4] In addition a substantial number of original charters from St Sophia still exist, even though the scale of their survival has inevitably been considerably less than that for those monasteries which have retained a continuous existence up to the present day, as Montecassino, Cava and Montevergine. By contrast, St Sophia was converted to a canonical house in the late fifteenth century and eventually suppressed in 1806, though the dispersal of its manuscripts seems to have occurred primarily in the late sixteenth century.[5] But more significantly there was its location. The city of Benevento, situated in the centre of southern Italy on a strongly defensible site at the junction of the Rivers Calore and Sabato, and on the old Roman *Via Appia*, still in the Middle Ages the principal route across the mountainous spine of this part of the peninsula, was the one place in southern Italy which the Norman invaders never succeeded in incorporating into their dominions. (Naples admittedly retained its independence in the eleventh century but

---

2   See especially N. Kamp, 'Soziale Herkunft und geistlicher Bildungsweg der unteritalienischen Bischöfe im normannischen-staufischen Zeit', *Le Istituzioni ecclesiastiche della 'Societas Christiana' dei secoli XI e XII*, Miscellanea del centro di studi medievali 8, Milan 1977, 87–116. Also G.A. Loud, 'Churches and Churchmen in an Age of Conquest: Southern Italy 1030–1130', *The Haskins Society Journal* iv, 1992, 37–53, Martin, *Pouille*, 563–627 (for the Terra di Bari, *ibid.*, 582).
3   The best general survey is now H. Houben, *Die Abtei Venosa und das Mönchtum im normanisch-staufischen Süditalien*, Tübingen 1995, especially 13–77.
4   Cod. Vat. Lat. 4939, fos 25–217. J.-M. Martin, 'Quelques reflexions en vue de 'edition du *Chronicon Sanctae Sophiae*', *Bullettino dell'istituto storico italiano per il medio evo* xcix, 1993, 301–17, at 302–3. Cf. L. Feller, 'Le Cartulaire-chronique de San Clemente a Casauria', *Les Cartulaires*, ed. O. Guyotjeannin *et al.*, Memoires et documents de l'école des chartes 39, Paris 1993, 261–77, at 274–5. There is an execrable, and for scholarly purposes almost useless, edition of the chartulary in F. Ughelli, *Italia Sacra*, 2nd edn by N. Colletti, vol. x, Venice 1721. Citations here are from the manuscript, to the contents of which there is a helpful guide in O. Bertolini, 'I Documenti trascritti nel "Liber Preceptorum Beneventani monasterii S. Sophiae" ', *Studi di storia napoletana in onore di Michelangelo Schipa*, Naples 1926, 11–47. A new edition by J.-M. Martin is now in preparation.
5   O. Bertolini, 'Gli Annales Beneventani', *Bullettino dell'istituto storico italiano per il medio evo* xlii, 1923, 25–7. G.A. Loud, 'The Medieval Records of the Monastery of St Sophia, Benevento', *Archives* xix, 1991, 364–73.

eventually submitted to Roger II in 1137.) The principality of Benevento, which in the early eleventh century comprised most of the inland mountain region of the south, stretching up to the Adriatic coast north of the River Fortore, fell prey to the invaders, but the town of Benevento and its immediate *contado* did not.

The survival of Benevento itself as an independent enclave within what became the kingdom of Sicily was certainly not for want of trying on the part of the Normans. They were already encroaching significantly on its surrounding territories in the 1040s. A Beneventan count called Madelfridus was killed fighting against them in the Caudine Valley to the south-west of the city in June 1045. He was buried in St Sophia which acquired part of his property, for he was unmarried and childless.[6] It cannot have been very much later that the father of Desiderius, the future abbot of Montecassino and pope, who was born into a Beneventan noble family, was killed by the Normans.[7] By 1050 Pope Leo IX was trying to persuade Drogo de Hauteville, the leader of the Apulian Normans, to restrain his followers from their attacks on the town and its lands, albeit with negligible success.[8] When the Normans gathered their forces to resist Pope Leo's army at the battle of Civitate in 1053 there was a distinct, and clearly sizeable, contingent from the Benevento region and from Telese (20 km to the north-west of Benevento), commanded by Count Gerard, whose descendants, the counts of Ariano, were to become important patrons of St Sophia.[9] The first recorded donation by a Norman to St Sophia came in 1062 from a certain Count Guimund, one of the sons of Guimund des Moulins, whose family were to give their name to the later county of Molise. His charter proclaimed that 'since we have with our relations invaded the lands of the Beneventans', he had acquired the village of Cerreto (6 km to the north of Telese), and he gave the monastery various properties formerly belonging to certain Lombards there.[10]

By 1073 the situation of Benevento had become so serious that its prince, Landulf VI, surrendered the town into the hands of Pope Gregory VII, hoping that this papal overlordship would protect it against his rapacious neighbours. A year later his only son was killed fighting the invaders, and when Landulf himself died in November 1077 the Norman duke of Apulia, Robert Guiscard, laid siege to the city. He was however unable to capture it, and thereafter Benevento remained as a papal dominion within Norman southern Italy. Ironically when the town did

---

[6] Benevento, Museo del Sannio, Fondo S. Sofia, vol. 12 no. 16: 'declaro q(uam) ante (h)os menses quidam madelfridus comes qui fuit nepotem meum filium quondam madelferium comitem qui fuit consobrino fratre meo de hoc seculo decessit pro quo cecidit in bello in finibus caude . . . non reliquit nec filium nec filiam de sua uxore quia non habuit uxorem in coniugio sociata'. Cf. Pergamene Aldobrandini [formerly, to autumn 1990, in the Biblioteca Apostolica Vaticana, now at Frascati], Cartolario I no. 36: 'quondam Madelfrid(us) comes nepote meo in predicta mense et ind(ictione) cecidit in bello a nefandissimis normannis in finibus caudense unde de hoc sec(u)lo decessit et sepultus est in sepulchro ubi predictus suus genitor sepultus fuit in monaster(io) beate sofie'.

[7] *Chronica Monasterii Casinensis*, lib. III c. 2, ed. H. Hoffmann, MGH SS XXXIV, Hanover 1980, 364. [Henceforth *Chron. Cas.*]

[8] *Storia de' normanni di Amato di Montecassino*, lib. III cc. 17–19, ed. V. de Bartholomeis, Fonti per la storia d'Italia 76, Rome 1935, 131–3.

[9] *Guillaume de Pouille. La Geste de Robert Guiscard*, lib. II lines 133–4. ed. M. Mathieu, Palermo 1961, 138.

[10] W. Jahn, *Untersuchungen zur normannischer Herrschaft in Süditalien (1040–1100)*, Frankfurt 1989, 363–6 no. 2.

surrender to a Norman army, led by Guiscard's son Roger Borsa, in 1101, this was at the behest of the then pope, Paschal II, who was reacting to the growing consolidation of power within the city by its governors, a local noble called Dacomirius and his son Anso, who were nominally the papacy's representatives but were becoming increasingly independent. Paschal therefore sought to use the Normans as allies through whom he could enforce his own authority over Benevento. But though in the short term he was successful, in practice even after 1101 Benevento enjoyed a considerable degree of self-government, and this tendency was undoubtedly growing during the second half of the twelfth century.[11]

Benevento was thus never ruled by the Normans, and indeed remained something of a bastion of native Lombard sentiment in the new Norman-dominated world of southern Italy. At times in the early twelfth century its relations with its Norman neighbours were extremely tense. The city's chronicler Falco recorded that in 1113 the prince of Capua and the two leading Norman nobles of the region, Counts Robert of Caiazzo and Jordan of Ariano, with whom the town was in dispute, 'were convulsed with envy and hatred of the Lombards', a statement which may well tell us more about his feelings than theirs.[12] But while Falco is certainly a tendentious witness, and was a fierce partisan in the bitter factional disputes which convulsed the city at this time, not least concerning what policy to adopt towards its Norman neighbours, his opinion cannot be entirely discounted. Nor can feelings towards the Normans have been improved by the presence in the city of those whose families had been dispossessed by the invaders, such as the grandson of a former Lombard prince of Capua who in 1109 gave his share in the collective ownership of two churches, one inside the city and one just outside the walls, to St Sophia.[13] *[Appendix I, document no. 1]*

But Benevento did not exist in a vacuum. The territory which was left to it was very limited, some of the lands owned by the citizens were subject to local Norman nobles and owed dues to them (an obligation from which they were anxious to escape and eventually did so), and in particular a number of the churches and monasteries therein had property at a considerable distance from the city. This inevitably brought them into contact with the Normans, and none more so than St Sophia, which became the most important and by far the most wealthy of the several monastic houses, both for men and women, located within Benevento.[14] For St Sophia enjoyed an extraordinary growth in its property at this period, both in terms of landed possessions and dependent churches. This occurred primarily in the fifty years from 1080 until the creation of the unified kingdom of Sicily in 1130, and very largely because of the pious generosity of the new Norman ruling class. Not only did the monastery expand its existing property in and around Benevento itself, but it acquired important possessions both in Molise to the north and in the Capitanata in northern Apulia to the east. In both these regions the bulk

---

[11] For a detailed discussion, O. Vehse, 'Benevent als Territorium des Kirchenstaates bis zum Beginn der Avignonesischen Epoche, I Bis zum Ausgang der normannischen Dynastie', *Quellen und Forschungen aus italienischen Archiven und Bibliotheken* xxii, 1930/1, 87–160, at 99–115.

[12] *Falconis Beneventani Chronicon*, ed. G. Del Re, *Cronisti e scrittori sincroni napoletani* I, Naples 1845, 164. [Henceforth *Falco*].

[13] Pergamene Aldobrandini, Cart. I no. 40.

[14] See G.A. Loud, 'Politics, Piety and Ecclesiastical Patronage in Twelfth-Century Benevento', to appear in *Studi in memoria di Leon-Robert Ménager*, ed. E. Cuozzo and J.-M. Martin, Rome 1997. Dues owed by the citizens: *Falco*, 187, 234, 237–8.

of what was acquired by the abbey was given to it by Normans. Benevento remained a Lombard town, and, apart from a very few who took monastic vows, there is no evidence that those of Norman descent lived there, although some clearly visited it temporarily.[15] But its premier religious house attracted generous benefactions from the Normans over an extended period. The consequences of this for St Sophia were striking. By the early fourteenth century, when papal taxation lists enable us to compare the wealth of different churches, St Sophia, while it was nowhere near as rich as the great abbey of Montecassino, nor indeed Cava, enjoyed an income four times that of the archbishop of Benevento and eight times that of the next wealthiest monastic house in the city, the monastery of St Modestus.[16]

However, by the time of its first endowment by a Norman in 1062, the church of St Sophia had already been in existence for some three centuries. Before we examine the development of the abbey's possessions and its links with the aristocracy of southern Italy during the later eleventh and early twelfth centuries, a brief sketch of its complicated earlier history is needed, not least because this had important repercussions for its status during the period after 1050.

The church of St Sophia was founded between 758 and 768 by Duke Arichis of Benevento as his private chapel, situated next door to his palace, and modelled, albeit on a much smaller scale, on the great church of the Byzantine emperors at Constantinople after which it took its name, and from which it copied its circular shape. He may also have been influenced by the construction of a chapel in the royal palace at Pavia by King Luitprand a generation earlier.[17] This church was therefore an expression of the regal pretensions which led Arichis later on in his reign to adopt the princely title which was thereafter borne by his successors. However this was not the only church dedicated to the Holy Wisdom in Benevento, for at about the same time and certainly pre-774 a nunnery with that name was founded which was made subject to the monastery of St Benedict of Montecassino, already much favoured by the Lombard dukes. There was indeed also a third church with that dedication, a monastery for men founded outside the walls c.721, but that may not have lasted very long.[18] The nunnery however was still in existence in 923 when Abbess Rodelgarda received a privilege from Prince Landulf I, and perhaps until 938, for one recension of the *Annales Beneventani* has a cryptic reference to her in that year (perhaps when she died?).[19] But by 945 it had been converted into a monastery for men, using the princely chapel as its church; and in a legal case of that year, held before Prince Landulf II in his palace at Benevento,

---

[15] Normans as monks/nuns in Benevento: Mihera, the son of Hugh Falloc, c.1088, *De Rebus Gestis Rogerii Calabriae et Siciliae Comitis auctore Gaufredo Malaterra*, ed. E. Pontieri, Rerum Italicarum Scriptores, Bologna 1927/8, lib. IV c.11, pp. 91–2. Bethlem, daughter of Dauferius of Greci, who became Abbess of S. Maria di Porta Somma in the city in 1121, *Falco*, 183. 'Altruda normanna et monacha' recorded on 10th July in the copy of the St Sophia necrology in Cod. Vat. Borgiani 296, fo. 75r.

[16] *Rationes Decimarum Italiae – Campania*, ed. P. Sella, M. Inguanez L. Matteo-Cerasoli, Studi e testi 69, Vatican City 1936, 317–20, cf. 41 (Montecassino), 339 (Montevergine), 390 (Cava). St Sophia was worth 400 ounces, compared with Montevirgine 580 ounces, Cava 700 and Montecassino 2000 in 1308/10.

[17] H. Belting, 'Studien zum Beneventanischen Hof im 8. Jahrhundert', *Dumbarton Oaks Papers* xvi, 1962, 180, 182–6, and for a description of the building 175–80.

[18] *Ibid.*, 180–2.

[19] Cod. Vat. Lat. 4939, fos 61v–62v (= Ughelli x.440–1). Bertolini, 'Gli Annales Beneventani' [as note 5], 121.

Abbot Ursus vindicated the freedom of his monastery from the claims of the abbot of Montecassino, claiming that it had from its foundation been under the jurisdiction of the princes of Benevento.[20] With regard to the princely chapel this was of course true, but it looks as though Ursus was skilfully exploiting the ambiguity as to which of the two churches which had been combined he was representing, for the new monastery certainly took over the property and rights pertaining to the former nunnery.

Until the Lombard princely line died out, St Sophia remained their *Eigenkloster*. It was apparently where their inauguration ceremonies took place, and probably where they were buried, at least after the definitive split of the principality of Benevento from that of Capua in 981. We have express evidence of such a burial only in the case of Pandulf II (died August 1014), but this must also have been true for Pandulf III who became a monk there in 1060.[21] The surviving privileges do not suggest any very extensive gifts of land by the princes (probably because with the haemorrhage of princely authority in the later tenth century there was very little of their fisc left to give) but they confirmed and extended the abbey's rights: for example to allow freemen to settle on its lands free from dues and service to them, and to possess any free woman who married one of the abbey's serfs and the offspring of such unions.[22] While the abbey enjoyed this relationship with the princes who lived next door to it, any claims of ownership by Montecassino were clearly a dead letter, although it appears that an attempt was made to raise the issue by the abbot of Montecassino in the early years of the eleventh century, and the independent status of St Sophia was expressly confirmed by both Pope Benedict VIII and the Emperor Henry II in 1022.[23]

However after 1077 the situation was very different. The papacy was now the lord of Benevento, and Montecassino was one of the principal allies of the Gregorian reform papacy. Its own abbot, Desiderius, was himself chosen as pope in 1086, and Cassinese monks played important roles at the Curia, notably John of Gaeta (the later Gelasius II) as papal chancellor from 1089 onwards. Furthermore, one of the most important concerns of the Cassinese abbots Desiderius and Oderisius who rebuilt and developed that monastery after 1058 was the recovery of alienated properties and churches which they felt should rightly belong to their house. It was therefore hardly surprising that Montecassino's historic claims to St Sophia were raised only a few months after the death of Landulf VI by that abbey's librarian and historian, Leo Marsicanus, at the Lenten synod of 1078. However the parlous position of the papacy in Gregory VII's later years, and in particular the troubled relationship between him and Montecassino after 1079, ensured that these claims failed.[24] But the Cassinese were nothing if not persistent. Leo tried again at the synod of Melfi in 1089. Then, after Urban II had issued a bull confirming St

---

[20] Museo del Sannio, Fondo S. Sofia, vol. 8 no. 8. Surprisingly this document is not in the chartulary.
[21] Museo del Sannio, Fondo S. Sofia, vol. 12 no. 8. Bertolini, 'Gli Annales Beneventani', 141. For inauguration ceremonies, Belting, 'Studien', 184–5.
[22] Cod. Vat. Lat. 4939, fos 60r–61v (= Ughelli x.440), July 961.
[23] *Italia Pontificia*, ed. P.F. Kehr, 10 vols, Berlin 1905–74, ix *Samnium-Apulia-Lucania*, ed. W. Holtzmann, 1963, 82 no. 2, *MGH Diplomatum* iii. 600 no. 471 (from Cod. Vat. Lat. 4939 fos 137r–v, 139r–40v).
[24] *Chron. Cas.*, III. 42, p. 420. For Montecassino: G.A. Loud, 'Abbot Desiderius of Montecassino and the Gregorian Papacy', *Journal of Ecclesiastical History* xxx (1979), 305–26; H.E.J. Cowdrey,

Sophia's direct and sole dependence on the Roman church in 1092, Abbot Oderisius of Montecassino raised the case once more at the synod of Troia in 1093. Here, according to the Montecassino Chronicle, 'because of outbreaks of warfare he was then unable to secure justice'.[25] A much more determined effort was made a few years later, first at Urban II's Lenten synod in Rome in 1097, then at the Council of Bari in October 1098 and at a council held immediately afterwards in Benevento. The only account which we have of what transpired there is the by no means unbiased one of Leo Marsicanus, who was once again Montecassino's spokesman. He claimed that Urban admitted the justice of his abbey's case. What rings true in this account is the corollary, that though sympathetic the pope was powerless to put these claims into effect because of local opposition within Benevento (over which his control at this period was anyway extremely fragile).[26] Given the hints that we have in other sources of the extraordinarily close relationship between Abbot Madelmus of St Sophia and the civic leaders, it is very clear why Urban's orders to the rector Anso to render justice to Montecassino had no effect.[27] Further efforts made by Abbot Gerard of Montecassino at papal synods in Benevento in 1113 and Rome in 1116 proved equally fruitless, although this renewal of Cassinese claims was probably one of the reasons for the collection and copying of St Sophia's privileges in the chartulary of 1119.[28] Anyway, after this date Montecassino had its own troubles, and its claims over the Beneventan monastery appear to have been abandoned.

The period during which St Sophia successfully defended its independence against Montecassino was precisely that during which its own material fortunes were spectacularly enhanced by the benefactions of a number of Norman aristocrats, and it is to these gifts and what they tell us of the relations between the Normans and Benevento that we must now turn. Furthermore, their effect was to create for St Sophia an entirely new landed endowment, above all in Molise, the mountainous region stretching away to the north of Benevento up towards the Abruzzi.

Though the original nunnery of St Sophia had been generously endowed, it is highly unlikely that by the early eleventh century the new monastery retained much of that property outside the immediate vicinity of Benevento itself. Certainly the confirmations of the abbey's property granted by the Ottonian emperors on their sporadic visits to Benevento after 972 contain impressively long lists of churches and other possessions allegedly owned by St Sophia over a wide area of southern Italy, but it is probable that there was a strong element of wishful thinking

---

The Age of Abbot Desiderius. Montecassino, the Papacy and the Normans in the Eleventh and Early Twelfth Centuries, Oxford 1983, especially 131–76.

25 *Chron. Cas.* IV. 7, p. 471. Cod. Vat. Lat. 4939, fos 145v–147v. *Italia Pontificia* ix. 85–6 nos 13–14.

26 E. Gattula, *Historia Abbatiae Casinensis*, Venice 1733, 54–6. I was able to check this passage thanks to the kindness of Jane Martindale who sent me a microfilm of the relevant pages.

27 Thus in 1082 the rector Stephen, Dacomirius and a large crowd of Beneventan nobles gathered to celebrate the feast of St Mercurius in the cloister of the abbey (which possessed the saint's relics). There they heard a sermon from Madelmus 'urging them to turn away from worldly pleasures and to love the Lord with all their power', Cod. Vat. Lat. 4939 fo. 195v. Cf. Gattula, *Historia* 55–6 for the order to Anso.

28 *Chron. Cas.*, IV. 48, 60, pp. 514–15, 523. Martin, 'Quelques reflexions' [as n. 4], 308–10.

here.[29] In particular it seems very unlikely that the abbey still actually possessed properties along the Apulian coast such as the fisheries at Siponto and Lesina listed here, given the extension of Byzantine rule northwards into the Capitanata at this period. A number of monasteries from the Lombard principalities had once had extensive property in this area, notably Montecassino and St Vincent on Volturno, but nearly all of what they had once possessed there had been alienated by the late tenth century and it seems highly unlikely that St Sophia was any better off.[30] Similarly control over properties in the principality of Capua would have been difficult after the split between the two principalities of Capua and Benevento in 981. Certainly there is little correspondence between the possessions named in these tenth-century confirmations and the similar lists contained in a series of papal bulls between 1084 and 1131. The disruption caused by the Norman takeover obviously might explain this discontinuity, though one ought not to assume that the Normans would necessarily be the ones responsible for such losses, even in the mid-eleventh century. When Abbot Amicus I complained to the archbishop of Benevento's synod in 1061 it was about the (probably Lombard) bishop of Dragonara, who had deprived the abbey of two churches within his diocese. To judge by a identical complaint made in another synod by Abbot Madelmus four-teen years later, St Sophia did not get them back.[31] It is however probable that the more widespread losses had occurred a century or more earlier, and it may well be that only the new properties not present in Otto I's 972 diploma which were added to the lists in the later Ottonian confirmations actually correspond to the reality of the abbey's property at the turn of the millennium. Certainly churches such as St Angelo in Altissimo near the River Biferno, first mentioned in Otto III's diploma of March 999, and the monastery of St Angelo in Ariano (25 km to the east of Benevento), confirmed for the first time in Henry II's diploma of 1022, continued to be important parts of the abbey's endowment into the twelfth and thirteenth centuries. The monastery at Ariano is elsewhere described as being subject to St Sophia in a charter of 1006.[32] The 1022 confirmation also contained the first reference to the church of St Donatus at Leocubante (to the south of Benevento), round which a village and complex of lands was to develop which remained the abbey's economically most important possession in the immediate vicinity of Benevento right through the Middle Ages.[33]

The scale of St Sophia's endowment at the height of its prosperity can be seen from a charter confirming its property issued in the name of King William II of Sicily in 1170 (which is probably genuine despite doubts which some scholars have expressed). This mentions by name four churches within Benevento and some

[29] *MGH Diplomatum* i. 554–6 no. 408 (972), ii(1). 306–7 no. 264 (981), ii (2). 736–7 no. 310 (999), iii. 596–7 no. 468 (1022) [from Cod. Vat. Lat. 4939, fos 126r–134v].

[30] Martin, *Pouille* [as n. 1], 295–9, 677–9.

[31] Cod. Vat. Lat. 4939, fos 166r–170r, Pergamene Aldobrandini, Cart. I no. 23 (the original of the 1075 document). Ughelli x.507–10 gives a very careless edition. (The version of the 1061 document in Ughelli x.550 is forged.) One of these churches, St Maria in Oliano, was recorded as deserted in 1143, when it was given by the then bishop of Dragonara to the canons of St Leonard of Siponto, *Regesto di S. Leonardo di Siponto*, ed. F. Camobreco, Rome 1913, 13 no. 19.

[32] Cod. Vat. Lat. 13490, document no. 2. This 'manuscript' is, like the Pergamene Aldobrandini, actually a folder of original charters, nos 1–31 of which are from S. Angelo.

[33] A. Zazo, 'Chiese, feudi e possessi della badia benedettina di Santa Sofia di Benevento nel secolo XIV', *Samnium* xxxvii, 1964, 36–40.

forty elsewhere, as well as nine *castella* (that is fortified villages) and nine (unfortified) *casales*.[34] The great majority of what was listed here had been acquired during the century before 1170. The list of churches cannot be complete: Paschal II's confirmation of the abbey's property named over a hundred subordinate churches as early as 1101, even though some of these entries may have represented unenforceable claims (and the 1170 list seems to omit chapels themselves subject to the abbey's dependent churches).[35] This growth of the abbey's ecclesiastical empire was (as with the other major south Italian monasteries) the product of the widespread inculcation among the laity of Gregorian views as to the sinfulness of the proprietary church, hitherto ubiquitous in the region. Already in 1117 the donors to St Sophia of a church in the south-western Capitanata could record that their donation was of 'the patronage and right that therein pertains to the lay power', one of the earliest south Italian examples of such 'Gregorian' phrase-ology.[36] [*See Appendix I, document no. 2*] But unfortunately the surviving sources do not permit us to follow the chronology of church donations in any detailed way, as can be done for Montecassino at the same period.[37]

However the chronology of donation is clear with regard to the *castella*: each of which comprised a fortified village, dependent tenants, a defined territory and judicial and fiscal rights within it, and forming therefore the most significant elements within the monastery's territorial lordship of the later twelfth century. The first of these, Ripalonga (near Troia in the Capitanata) was apparently given to the abbey by Robert Guiscard in March 1065, though he may in fact have simply been confirming a donation by one of his vassals, a certain Niel or Nigel who had been the actual builder of the *castellum*.[38] This was to remain the monastery's only *castellum* in this region. Of the others two, Fragneto and Botticella, were very close together some 15 km north of Benevento; the other six were all in Molise [*See map*]. Six of the eight were donated to St Sophia in the period between the death of Guiscard in 1085 and the coronation of King Roger in 1130, and a seventh probably just after 1130. All five of those where details of the donation have survived were given to the abbey by Norman nobles.

In chronological order these gifts of *castella* occurred as follows. Assuming that we can trust the charter text in the chartulary, *Toro* was given by Robert *de Principatu* son of Tristain, in December 1092. (There are two other versions of this document, dated 1090 and 1124; the first is undoubtedly a forgery, the second

---

[34] A. Pratesi, 'I Documenti originali dei re normanni di Sicilia', *Archivio paleografico italiano* xiv, 1956, plates 31–2, transcription in *Bullettino dell'archivio paleografico italiano*, ns i, 1955, 176–8. At least one of the grounds on which Pratesi suggests that this was a forgery, that Abbot John IV was not (as described in the charter) a cardinal, is demonstrably wrong [below n. 113]. The forthcoming edition of William II's charters by H. Enzensberger will provide a definitive verdict.

[35] Cod. Vat. Lat. 4939, fos 147v–150v (Ughelli x.495–7).

[36] Pergamene Aldobrandini, Cart. I no. 47. For similar phraseology, cf. Museo del Sannio, Fondo S. Sofia, vol. 12 no. 42 (May 1124), where the owner of a church said that belonged to him 'legibus et iure patronatu'. The earliest reference to the *ius patronatus* that I can find in the Cava archive is in an 1142 charter of Bishop John of Paestum, Badia di S. Trinità, Arm. Mag. G. 36. For a helpful discussion, H. Dormeier, *Montecassino und die Laien im 11. und 12. Jahrhundert*, Stuttgart 1979, 81–7.

[37] Cf. Dormeier, *Montecassino und die Laien*, 28–58, especially the table at 56.

[38] *Recueil des actes des ducs normands d'Italie [1046–1127]* i *Les Premiers Ducs (1046–1087)*, ed. L-R. Ménager, Bari 1981), 62–5 no. 14. [N.B. vol. ii of this edition has never appeared].

occurs only in a late thirteenth-century copy.)[39] *Castelvecchio* was given by Count Rodulf of Boiano before January 1094, when his donation was confirmed by his sons Hugh and Roger.[40] *Fragneto* was donated by Count Herbert of Ariano, whose family was closely linked with the abbey over several generations, in February 1100.[41] *Cantalupo* was given by Richard *de lu Guastu* before July 1121 when his overlord Robert fitz Richard confirmed the gift at the request of Abbot John III of St Sophia.[42] *Archipresbitero* was given by a certain Raleri son of Aimeric in August 1127, though in this case the donor and his father reserved for themselves a life interest in half the income from the *castellum*.[43] In two further cases details how the abbey acquired the lordship do not survive, but *Botticella* must have been given between 1119 when the chartulary was written and February 1131 when it was listed among St Sophia's possessions in a bull of Anacletus II which was added into a blank section of the chartulary.[44] *S. Giovanni in Gualdo* was confirmed to the abbey, along with the neighbouring *castella* of Castelvecchio and Toro by Count Hugh II of Molise in March 1149. One might suggest that St Sophia acquired it during the 1130s, but from whom cannot be ascertained. It seems unlikely to have been from the Count of Boiano himself, or from one of his predecessors, for in this charter he expressly distinguished Castelvecchio, which had been given by his grandfather, from the other two *castella*.[45]

There remain two problematic cases. One is the *castellum* of Ubiano, mentioned in the papal confirmations of abbatial property in 1120 and 1131 but not in the 1170 royal document, and concerning which nothing else is known, not even its location. Was this perhaps a property lost during the civil war of the 1130s? The other is the last of the nine *castella* listed in 1170, S. Angelo in Altissimo, the most northerly of St Sophia's *castella* in Molise. The church of S. Angelo had, as we have seen, belonged to the abbey since the late tenth century, and indeed seems to have been virtually its only possession in Molise before the arrival of the Normans. In 1147, when in the court of Count Hugh of Molise Abbot John IV successfully obtained the return of its 'tribute and income' from a local nobleman called Hugh Markese who had illegally alienated this, what was in dispute was the income from the church of S. Angelo and its men, not a *castellum*, though the charter does have an incidental reference to the *villa* of S. Angelo.[46] Nor was there any mention of a *castellum* in September 1168 when Abbot John leased the church to a priest, Mazzarus, for the latter's lifetime, or in a donation to the church by Malfridus

---

[39] Cod. Vat. Lat. 4939, fos 161r–162v (Ughelli x.504–5, very inaccurate). The forged version is Museo del Sannio, Fondo S. Sofia, vol. 12 no. 26. The 1124 version is in a copy of April 1270, along with two (genuine) charters of the counts of Molise, *ibid.*, vol. 12 no. 41.

[40] Cod. Vat. Lat. 4939, fos 188v–189v (Ughelli x.523–4, where the witness list is fiction).

[41] Cod. Vat. Lat. 4939, fos 183v–184v (Ughelli x.519–20, again very inaccurate, especially the witness list).

[42] Museo del Sannio, Fondo S. Sofia, vol. 2 no. 5.

[43] Pergamene Aldobrandini, Cart. I no. 57, ed. G.A. Loud, 'The Genesis and Context of the Chronicle of Falco of Benevento', *ANS* xv, 1992, 197–8.

[44] Cod. Vat. Lat. 4939, fo. 157v.

[45] E.M. Jamison, 'I Conti di Molise e di Marsia nei secoli xii e xiii', *Convegno storico abruzzese-molisano. 25–29 marzo 1931, Atti e memorie*, Casalbordino 1933, i, 155–6 no. 2.

[46] E.M. Jamison, 'The Administration of the County of Molise in the Twelfth and Thirteenth Centuries, I', *EHR* xliv, 1929, 554–6 no. 1.

Markese, son of Hugh, in October 1179.[47] It must therefore be possible that S. Angelo was included in the list of *castella* rather than that of *casales* in 1170 through scribal error. But if this was not the case, then it would represent the only example of a village provided with defences by the abbey, rather than as with all its other *castella* an existing fortified settlement given to the monastery. Given both the tight royal control exercised over fortifications after 1140, which makes abbatial initiative unlikely, and the lack of any other evidence for its castral status, the case of S. Angelo in Altissimo must remain very doubtful, though there was certainly some sort of settlement there.

In contrast to its *castella* which, insofar as we can analyse them, were already in existence when they were donated to St Sophia, most of its *casales* attested by the later twelfth century were the product of either organic growth, or in some cases perhaps of deliberate development, around existing churches belonging to the abbey. The earliest example of this, and the clearest one of abbatial initiative, was Leocubante, where in the early 1060s the abbots were seeking to develop the land around the church of St Donatus by leasing plots to cultivators who were obliged to plant vines there, usually on favourable terms for the first seven years of cultivation (in other words before the vines were fully productive), and in two cases with the obligation of building a house there.[48] This initiative was obviously successful, for Gregory VII's confirmation of the abbey's property of 1084 mentioned the *villa* of Leocubante, which the royal charter of 1170 classified as a *casale*.[49]

A number of the other villages listed in the 1170 charter of William II developed around churches which St Sophia had been given during the half-century of growth from 1080 to 1130. Thus two churches in the Capitanata were given to the abbey by vassals of Count Henry of Monte Sant'Angelo, and confirmed by him in September 1091: St Salvator outside Fiorentino by William of Nonant and St Nicholas of Sfilizzo on the Gargano peninsula by Godfrey of Vieste.[50] In October 1114 Count Robert II of Loritello, who had extended his lordship southwards into the central Capitanata after the Counts of Monte Sant'Angelo had died out, granted Abbot Bernard of St Sophia the right to settle colonists at a number of churches in his dominions, including that of St Salvator.[51] The casale of St Salvator *Abbatis Aldi* (named after the original founder of the church) is duly attested not just by the 1170 charter, but by the grant to its men of rights of pasture and gathering wood in her lands by Adelicia, the daughter and heiress of Count Robert IV of Loritello in April 1187.[52] A *casale* was established at Sfilizzo by May 1152 when Abbot John

---

47 Museo del Sannio, Fondo S. Sofia, vol. 13 no. 17.

48 Museo del Sannio, Fondo S. Sofia, vol. 28 no. 4 (May 1063), Pergamene Aldobrandini, Cart. I no. 14 (containing two separate leases of September 1063) and I no. 10 (January 1064). For the dating, G.A. Loud, 'The Abbots of St Sophia, Benevento, in the Eleventh Century', *Quellen und Forschungen aus Italienischen Archiven und Bibliotheken* lxxi, 1991, 8–9. Cf. Museo del Sannio, Fondo S. Sofia, vol. 28 no. 5 (1069), which is less specific than the other documents.

49 L. Santifaller, *Quellen und Forschungen zum Urkunden und Kanzleiwesen Papst Gregor VII* i, Vatican City 1957, 261–5 no. 217 (from Cod. Vat. Lat. 4939, fos 142v–145r).

50 A. Petrucci, 'Note di diplomatica normanna II Enrico conte di Montesangelo ed i suoi documenti, *Bullettino del istituto storico italiano per il medio evo* lxxii, 1960, 175–6 no. 3 (from Cod. Vat. Lat. 4939, fos 193v–195r). William de Nonant's charter: Jahn, *Untersuchungen zur normannischer Herrschaft* [above n. 10], 379–83.

51 Jahn, *Untersuchungen zur normannischer Herrschaft*, 400–1 no. 16 (from Cod. Vat. Lat. 4939, fos 192v–193v). For the background, Jahn, 329–41, Martin, *Pouille*, 721–7.

52 Museo del Sannio, Fondo S. Sofia, vol. 2 no. 10. For the possession of Fiorentino by the Counts

IV leased this village, one of the monastery's more outlying properties, to a local knight and his family.[53] [*See Appendix I, document no. 4*]. Similarly in March 1126 St Sophia was given the church of St Peter *ad Lauretum*, not far from its *castellum* of Fragneto, by a Norman vassal of the Count of Ariano called Gerard de Marcia. He died soon afterwards, but in the next year his son Robert formally confirmed his father's oral promise of a further adjoining section of land.[54] S. Pietro was described as a *casale* both in the 1170 list and in a charter of Gerard's grandson Richard in May 1180.[55] [*See Appendix I, document no. 71*]

Two other churches which were already in the monastery's possession by 1084 were later to become the foci of *casales*, though we do not know through whom or exactly when it acquired them. St Peter in Cucciano (10 km to the north of the abbey's *castellum* of Fragneto) was described as a chapel in Gregory's bull of 1084. It should surely be identified with the *casale* of St Peter 'in Gaudetano' of the 1170 royal charter: it was anyway certainly a *casale* by October 1193 when Abbot Bartholomew came to an agreement with thirty of its inhabitants (presumably the total of the adult male population) who renounced in favour of the monastery various legal disputes about the olive groves of the *casale*.[56] St Ephraim in Deliceto, near Bovino, was also the focus of a *casale* before the death of King William II of Sicily in 1189.[57] Similarly *casales* developed around several of the abbey's churches in Molise during the twelfth century: notably St Sophia in Jelsi by 1148, and the two churches of St Lucy and St Mark near Campolieto by 1185. None of these villages were listed as such in the 1170 charter, but we know nothing about the previous history of these three churches, nor when they were acquired, except that St Lucy, Campolieto, was in its possession before 1101.[58]

There were only two exceptions to this pattern: where already existing open settlements were given to the monastery. The papal bull of 1092 recorded the recent acquisition of the *villa* of St Stephen de Francisca in the Capitanata (subsequently described as a *casale* in a charter of 1120), and in March 1122 Gerard de Marcia gave St Sophia the church of St Mary *de Sipagno* and its *casale* within the territory of his *castellum* of Reino (5 km north east of Fragneto, and about 20 km north of Benevento itself). Neither settlement was recorded as such in the 1170 list, although the *church* of St Maria de Sipagno was. The *casale* was certainly still in existence at this time for in 1175 another of Gerard's grandsons, Robert, the head of the senior branch of the kin group, came to an agreement with the abbey concerning what dues the inhabitants still owed to his family at harvest time.[59] This

of Loritello at this later period, cf. *Regesto di S. Leonardo di Siponto*, 53–4 no. 85 (1179). For Abbot Aldo, see a 1079/80 charter of William of Nonant, Jahn, *Untersuchungen zur normannischer Herrschaft*, 369–71 no. 4.

[53] Pergamene Aldobrandini, Cart. II no. 8.

[54] Pergamene Aldobrandini, Cart. II nos 56, 59.

[55] Museo del Sannio, Fondo S. Sofia, vol. 13 no. 18.

[56] Museo del Sannio, Fondo S. Sofia, vol. 13 no. 26.

[57] Museo del Sannio, Fondo S. Sofia, vol. 12 no. 2 (the dating clause of which is damaged; what is legible is 'September, Indiction VII, *regnante* King William of Sicily'. The possible dates are thus 1158, 1173, 1188.).

[58] E.M. Jamison, 'Notes on S. Maria della Strada at Matrice: its History and Sculpture', *Papers of the British School at Rome* xiv, 1938, 76–9 no. 1, at 78. Jamison, 'Administration of Molise I', 557–9 no. 3.

[59] Cod. Vat. Lat. 4939, fos 146r–v, Museo del Sannio, Fondo S. Sofia, vol. 10 no. 26 (1120), vol. 2

once again suggests that the list of abbatial property in the 1170 royal charter can only be an approximate guide to the abbey's estates at that period: nonetheless it is still helpful, nor should the inconsistencies in that list be taken to impugn the veracity of the document.

The overall picture of the abbey and its dependent settlements may thus be summarised as follows. St Sophia's possessions in the *regno* lay for the most part in three regions. In Molise the monastery was given several already existing *castella*, though there is also evidence for the development of *casales* around a number of its churches. However in the Capitanata, with the exception of the very early grant of Ripalonga, St Sophia did not have *castella* – rather open villages were developed around the churches which the abbey acquired in the period after 1085. In Irpinia, the area to the immediate north and east of Benevento, we find both two abbatial *castella* and several open villages. But nowhere did the abbey itself fortify existing settlements (that this occurred in the case of S. Angelo in Altissimo seems improbable). The development of villages around its churches was part of the general expansion of settlement, fuelled by demographic growth, in southern Italy during the Norman period. This phenomenon was particularly marked in the Capitanata, an area which had up to the late eleventh century been only very thinly populated, but which was opened up for settlement and cultivation on a large scale in the century after 1080.[60] St Sophia acquired a number of churches in this area (in which there were few other monasteries to be competitors in attracting such donations), and these subordinate churches played an important part in the development of southern part of the region.[61]

The abbey's benefactors came from two contrasting groups. It was always a focus for religious aspirations within Benevento itself, and the consolidation and exploitation of its urban and immediately suburban property remained an important concern throughout this period (though space does not permit its discussion here). But St Sophia's acquisition of a more extended nexus of churches and properties came very largely from benefactions from the new Normanno-French nobility. The three most powerful families with whom the abbey was linked over an extended period were those of the dukes of Apulia, the counts of Boiano and the counts of Ariano.

Admittedly ducal benefactions were limited. Apart from Guiscard's gift of Ripalonga in 1065 (and as we have seen this may have been no more than a confirmation of another's donation), there was only his grant of a church in the territory of Frigento in 1077, a minor donation of land in the vicinity of Troia by his son Roger Borsa in 1094, and the latter's grant of exemption from *herbaticum* and *plateaticum* dues in 1110.[62] The dukes were only very intermittently concerned with the affairs of the Benevento region, and ducal ecclesiastical patronage was directed far more at Montecassino and Cava than towards St Sophia. But where

no. 6 (1122), Pergamene Aldobrandini, Cart. I no. 51 is another copy of the same charter. Pergamene Aldobrandini, Cart. II no. 28b (1175).

[60] Martin, *Pouille*, 286–9, 354–8.

[61] Martin, *Pouille*, 672.

[62] Ménager, *Recueil des actes des ducs* i. 91–4 no. 26, Museo del Sannio, Fondo S. Sofia, vol. 12 no. 29 (*ibid.*, no. 30 is a forged version of c.1280), Cod. Vat. Lat. 4939, fos 181r–182r (Ughelli x.517–18 with the usual fictional witness list). Three months later, in November 1110, Duke Roger similarly exempted the animals of Montecassino from such dues, *Le Colonie Cassinesi in Capitanata* ii *Gargano*, ed. T. Leccisotti, Miscellanea Cassinese 15, 1938, 49–50 no. 9.

relations with the duke were important, especially in the early twelfth century – and similarly relations with the king after 1130 – was in the protection of the property and dependencies that St Sophia already possessed.

To some extent this was true too of the counts of Boiano, after Count Rodulf's donation of Castelvecchio pre-1094; though it is difficult to know if it was one of the counts or one of their vassals who gave St Sophia the monastery of St Mary of Saepino before 1101. But certainly it was comital protection and confirmations of its rights which allowed St Sophia's property to expand and flourish in Molise; and the monastery was at pains to secure such confirmation from each succeeding count from the family of Moulins.[63] In the very different world after 1140, when royal authority had been consolidated over southern Italy, the counts of Molise (as they now became known) continued to favour St Sophia, whether preventing their barons from alienating monastic property, restraining their own bailiffs from infringing on the judicial immunity of the abbey's *castella*, or remitting the customary food renders (*prandia*) which up to 1170 they had still received from Castelvecchio. The charter embodying this last concession was granted by Richard of Mandra, the royal *familiaris* who played such an important part in the disputes at the royal court during the minority of William II and who was appointed count of Molise in succession to the childless Hugh II in 1166. It was made while he was at the baths of Pozzuoli in November 1170. [*Appendix I, document no. 5*]. His presence there may suggest ill-health, and perhaps significantly this is the last known evidence for him being alive.[64]

However the abbey's relationship with the counts of Ariano was more complex, and reveals something of the difficulties and ambiguities of monastic relations with powerful patrons, especially in the confused state of Apulia after the death of Robert Guiscard. A major factor in the relationship was the presence of St Sophia's cell of St Angelo immediately outside the walls of their principal town. Indeed the first mark of comital favour to St Sophia was Count Gerard's confirmation of a gift by an inhabitant of Ariano to this cell in October 1070.[65] This was followed by his donation of the monastery of St Benedict at Morcone and a number of other churches to the mother house in January 1079, an undated remission of various customary payments from the abbey's land at a place called Pantano, and his son Count Herbert's gift of Fragneto in 1100.[66] But in the years 1113–14 Herbert's son Jordan was at war with Benevento, and it was only with the conclusion of a peace agreement with the city in the summer of 1114 that he issued two charters in favour of St Sophia. The first, in July 1114, was simply the confirmation of the cession to St Sophia of the hitherto-independent monastery of St Onuphrius *de gualdo mazzoca* by its prior Adam, and would not be very significant were it not for the interesting phrase that he confirmed this 'in everything insofar as it belongs to me

---

[63] Cod. Vat. Lat. 4939, fos 188v–191r (1094, 1113), 208v–209v (1119), Jamison, 'I Conti', 155–6 no. 2 (1149).

[64] Pergamene Aldobrandini, Cart. II no. 21. Richard had saved King William I's life during the attempted coup of 1161. His career was discussed at length by *La Historia o Liber de Regno Sicilie di Ugo Falcando*, ed. G.B. Siragusa, Rome, Fonti per la storia d'Italia 22, 1897, 56 (the coup), 69 (appointed royal constable), 98 (made count of Molise), 101, 104–5, 124–6, 139–42 (trial and imprisonment in 1168), 153–4 (release), 161–2 (one of the minority council). See also C.M. Kauffman, *The Baths of Pozzuoli*, Oxford 1959, especially 4–5.

[65] Cod. Vat. Lat. 13490, no. 16.

[66] Cod. Vat. Lat. 4939, fos 182r–184v, 202r–v.

from the lay power' (another sign that Gregorian ideas were beginning to have some effect among the south Italian laity).[67] Two months later however, he formally restored to the Beneventan monastery its long-time dependency of St Angelo, which his father (the abbey's erstwhile benefactor) had 'unjustly and unsuitably' converted to a house of secular canons, an arrangement which he had continued.[68] Subsequently in 1119 Jordan became embroiled in a bitter conflict, fought out in and around Benevento, with a rival Count, Rainulf of Caiazzo (who held a major territorial lordship to the west of the city), and his own uncle and disobedient vassal, Robert of Montefusco. In May 1121 the latter was murdered in Benevento. His mutilated and headless body was brought in from the street where it lay and buried in St Sophia, on the personal initiative of Abbot John III. Not long afterwards Jordan was driven from Ariano and deprived of almost all his other lands by Duke William of Apulia, helped by six hundred knights and a substantial subsidy obtained from his cousin Roger of Sicily.[69]

We do not know in what light Jordan regarded the monks' burial of his uncle. But it may be significant that in July 1122 a court at Ariano, held in the presence of a ducal constable (and thus clearly after Jordan's expulsion), once again vindicated St Sophia's possession of its cell of S. Angelo against the claims of one Alferius, cleric and doctor, who fled before formal judgement could be given against him.[70] Had a renewed threat to this cell been the count's response to the burial of his treacherous uncle? Certainly relations had been restored by May 1125 when Jordan gave the abbey a mill at Morcone (where he had lived since his expulsion from Ariano) for the soul of one of his men, Iollemus.[71] [*Appendix I, document no. 3*]. But it is clear that, for all their benefactions to St Sophia, the abbey's relationship to its powerful neighbours was an uneasy and fluctuating one.

These difficulties, and a subsequent legal case in 1125 when the monk provost of St Angelo complained of a violent attack on his monastery by a number of local men, were symptomatic of a more general problem for St Sophia and for other churches in the 1120s.[72] Duke William's troubles with the over-mighty count of Ariano were only part of a break-down in authority and order within the duchy at this period. At the papal council of Troia in November 1120, when Calixtus II proclaimed the Truce of God, the abbot of St Sophia came to an agreement with a local noble, William de Hauteville (the younger brother of the count of Loritello), to whom he had entrusted its *casale* of Francisca since 'that *casale* had been captured and plundered by its neighbours, and raised to the ground'. William had been unable to defend it, and returned it to the abbot, albeit in return for a money

---

[67] Cod. Vat. Lat. 4939, fos 187v–188v: 'in omnibus quantum ab laycam potestatem michi pertinet' (the use of the wrong case is all too typical of south Italian Latin at this period). Cf. *Falco*, 164–8 for the background.

[68] Cod. Vat. Lat. 4939, fos 185r–186v. This may have been one of the 'many sins' which made Count Jordan reluctant to attend the papal council of Ceprano in October 1114, *Falco*, 169.

[69] *Falco*, 176–8, 180, 183–4 (Robert's assassination), 186–7. Count Robert of Caiazzo (Rainulf's father) had made a minor benefaction to St Sophia in 1099, Cod. Vat. Lat. 4939, fos 191v–192r, but his major religious ties were with Montecassino.

[70] Cod. Vat. Lat. 13491, no. 16. This 'manuscript' is another folder of original charters.

[71] Museo del Sannio, Fondo S. Sofia, vol. 12 no. 43.

[72] Museo del Sannio, Fondo S. Sofia, vol. 12 no. 44.

payment.[73] Not long afterwards Abbot John III travelled to Salerno to see Duke William to beg his help about a problem concerning the abbey's lands at Corleto near Ascoli Satriano, threatened by 'wars and the oppression of enemies'. It is noteworthy that, despite the difficulties the duke faced in Apulia at this period (and the comments of later chroniclers about his character deficiencies), he was still seen as the source of redress by churchmen, and in this case his local representative in Ascoli appears to have been successful in helping the monastery.[74]

Furthermore, while the claims of Montecassino were one reason for the compilation of St Sophia's chartulary in 1119, one might suggest that the more general need to defend the abbey's rights at a time when public authority and order was weak was also a factor. The introduction to the chartulary stated explicitly that should questions arise about the monastery's property it would enable ' the written title (*preceptum*) to be sought without trouble or ambiguity'.[75] That a copyist should expend the considerable effort of writing nearly 200 folios and transcribing 170 documents, the older of which were clearly very difficult to read, suggests that an evident need was felt for such proof.

After 1140, with the creation of the unified kingdom of Sicily and an effective royal administration functioning throughout the southern mainland, the situation was obviously very different from that which prevailed twenty years earlier. Nonetheless, any ecclesiastical institution with an extensive network of churches and lands still faced potential problems, both in maintaining its hold on its possessions – especially those at a distance from the mother church – and in defending and defining its rights and privileges. Although Benevento remained an independent papal enclave within, but not part of, the kingdom of Sicily, its numerous properties in the regno inevitably involved St Sophia in frequent dealings with the crown and its officials.

These contacts may be categorized as being of three main types. First, the abbey still had to defend its property from illegal alienations by local nobles, and in this the creation of a rule of law in the new kingdom that was much more effective than hitherto was all in its favour. Thus in October 1158 a representative of the abbey went to the court of the royal justiciars Florius of Camerota and Aimeric of Monte Morcone in the citadel in Capua and charged a certain Geoffrey de Petrabaldi with the illegal seizure of its church of St Peter *in Balneo*. Though the defendant claimed that he had done this lawfully and with the sanction of the late Count Hugh [of Molise], both the church and various animals and renders belonging to it which Geoffrey had also seized, were returned to the abbey.[76] In November 1164 a court

---

[73] Museo del Sannio, Fondo S. Sofia, vol. 10 no. 26: 'casale(m) ipsum a vicinis captum et depredatum et usque ad solum destructum est'.

[74] Museo del Sannio, Fondo S. Sofia, vol. 8 no. 34. Cf. *Les Chartes de Troia (1064–1266)*, ed. J.-M. Martin, Codice diplomatico pugliese 21, Bari 1976, 168–71 no. 43, both for the Truce of God and for a restitution by William to another monastery. Loud, 'Churches and Churchmen in an Age of Conquest' [above n. 1], 52–3.

[75] Cod. Vat. Lat. 4939, fo. 26v: 'Quatenus si quid rerum tam possessarum quam concessarum eidem ecclesie. sive instanti sive in p(re)terito. sive in future tempore pr(ae) supra dictarum personarum precepta questionis oriatur. facile in primis ad hunc libellum quasi generaliter recurratur. de inde per singulum quod queritur preceptum sine labore atque ambiguitate titulo ei(us) inspecto et libelli divisione considerate; specialiter perveniatur'.

[76] Pergamene Aldobrandini, Cart. II no. 13. For Geoffrey, *Catalogus Baronum*, ed. E.M. Jamison, Fonti per la storia d'Italia 101, Rome 1972, art. 795, [henceforth *Cat. Bar.*]. For Florius of Camerota's long career as a royal official, E.M. Jamison, 'The Norman Administration of Apulia

at Lesina (on the Adriatic coast north of the Gargano peninsula) vindicated St Sophia's ownership of the casale of Sfilizzo against a family to whom this village had been leased some twelve years earlier, and then through the mediation of (among others) the royal justiciar Count Geoffrey of Lesina and the royal chamberlain Roger son of Giroie, arranged a new lease on terms agreeable to the abbey and protecting its rights.[77] And in March 1173 a case concerning the theft of foodstuffs from St Sophia's *castrum* of Toro was heard in front of the Master Justiciar of Apulia and Terra di Lavoro, Count Robert of Caserta, first at Alife and then once again at Capua.[78] There were other similar problems which did not reach a royal court, such as the October 1147 case heard by Count Hugh II of Molise concerning his baron Hugh Markese's seizure of St Angelo in Altissimo, which he appears to have judged as part of his private jurisdiction (though Hugh also acted as a royal justiciar on occasion).[79] And in 1148 another Molise baron, Gerald de Fay, returned a church which he had taken from St Sophia through the mediation of the archbishop of Benevento, who was at the time visiting that part of the area which lay within his diocese – and if we are to believe the arenga of his charter, also as a result of the offender's pangs of conscience.[80]

Perhaps more common than outright seizure of abbatial property was a second type of case: disputes concerning abbatial rights, the exemption of the monastery's dependents from local baronial jurisdiction, boundary disputes, and certain residual claims on abbatial property by descendants of the original donors. Gerald de Fay was once again in dispute with St Sophia in May 1151 concerning the boundaries between his *castellum* of Jelsi and the monastery's neighbouring one of Cantalupo. The case was eventually settled in the court of the royal Justiciar Robert fitz Robert at Montecorvino.[81] In May 1172 Abbot John IV went in person to the royal court, then at Barletta on the Apulian coast where King William was waiting (in vain) for the Byzantine bride promised him by Manuel Comnenus, to complain about the exactions of a Molise baron, Robert of Mignanello, on the lands and men of one of its churches, St Agnellus of Pietrafinda. Robert promised not only to cease such exactions, but to allow the monastery's men rights to pasture and gathering wood in his lands (this last quite a common but clearly important privilege).[82] The problems which might occur with the descendants of donors can be illustrated from the de Marchia family, which survived the dispossession of its

---

and Capua more especially under Roger II and William I, 1127–1166', *Papers of the British School at Rome* vi, 1913 [reprint as a separate volume Aalen 1987), 365–6, 478–80. Aimeric has not hitherto been noted as a justiciar.

[77] Pergamene Aldobrandini, Cart. II no. 15. This is the earliest explicit evidence for Count Geoffrey as justiciar, though he may have acted as such since 1156: Jamison, 'Norman Administration', 315–16, 353, 363. Roger son of Girole has been unknown to previous students of the royal administration.

[78] Pergamene Aldobrandini, Cart. II no. 27.

[79] Jamison, 'Administration of Molise, I', 554–6 no. 1 [cf. n. 46 above].

[80] Jamison, 'Notes on S. Maria della Strada' [above n. 58], 76–80 no. 1.

[81] Pergamene Aldobrandini, Cart. II no. 6. The justiciar is otherwise unattested, but his presence judging a case in Molise has important implications for the interaction of the royal administration and comital authority in King Roger's last years. Montecorvino is now deserted; it was 25km E. of Jelsi, and 18km W. of Lucera

[82] Pergamene Aldobrandini, Cart. II no. 25. For the king's wait, Romuald of Salerno, *Chronicon sive Annales*, ed. C.A. Garufi, Rerum Italicarum Scriptores, Città di Castello 1935, 261.

erstwhile overlord the count of Ariano by King Roger in the late 1130s.[83] In 1175 Robert de Marchia remitted the labour services which his uncle Malgerius had formerly and unjustly exacted from every household in St Sophia's *casale* of Sipagno (which had, as we have seen, developed round a church given to the abbey by his grandfather). Robert promised that in future each *feudum* would owe only four 'works' a year, two at sowing and two at harvest. (Notice by the way the characteristic south Italian use of 'fief' to describe a peasant's agricultural tenement, not a military holding.)[84] However in May 1180 his first cousin Richard, Malgerius's son, was the subject of a complaint by Abbot William to the Master Justiciar Count Tancred of Lecce about infringement of the abbey's rights in its *casale* of S. Pietro in Laureto (the church of which their grandfather had given to St Sophia fifty-four years earlier). Richard had formally to renounce his claims over the mountain of Torre di Ermula near the *casale* and acknowledge his fault in infringing its rights by arresting one of its men.[85] [*Appendix I, document no. 7*]. A year later Richard completed his reconciliation with the monastery by granting its men rights of gathering wood and pasture on his lands.[86]

In all these cases the abbey benefited from the rule of law enforced by royal officials. However the development of the royal administration also gave rise to a potential problem: the fiscal exactions of royal (as well as baronial) officers on abbatial property. The third type of external contact was therefore the vindication of the abbey's privileges and immunities. Sometimes such cases might be very minor, as when in April 1168 the royal bailiffs of Montefusco (10 km south-east of Benevento) exacted more than the due rate of *herbaticum* from the sheep and cattle of the abbey's men from its *casale* of Leocubante.[87] But such cases as the infringement of its judicial immunities by the bailiffs of the count of Molise in 1153 (seemingly acting on behalf of the crown), and the attempt by a Molise baron to levy an aid on two of its *casales* in 1185 (almost certainly connected with the royal expedition against Byzantium in that year) were potentially much more serious.[88] The abbey was certainly prepared to enlist the royal court at Palermo on its side, as when at some point late in William II's reign the royal bailiffs of Ascoli had illegally taken over some of land at Ascoli. The abbot secured a mandate from the court to the Master of the *Duana Baronum* (the king's chief financial officer on the mainland) to secure restitution.[89] St Sophia continued successfully to maintain its privileged status after the German conquest, as was shown in 1197 when Henry VI ordered those collecting the tax for his forthcoming Crusade to respect the immunity of the abbey's lands, villages and obediences, although it was not to be so fortunate in this respect in the thirteenth century.[90]

---

[83] *Falco*, 245, 249, who describes how Count Roger was sent as a prisoner to Sicily in 1139. Subsequently he was in exile at the German court, along with Prince Robert II of Capua, *MGH Diplomatum* ix. 176–7 no. 99 (1144).

[84] Pergamene Aldobrandini, Cart. II no. 28b.

[85] Museo del Sannio, Fondo S. Sofia, vol. 13 no. 18.

[86] Museo del Sannio, Fondo S. Sofia, vol. 13 no. 20.

[87] Museo del Sannio, Fondo S. Sofia, vol. 10 no. 5.

[88] Jamison, 'Administration of Molise, I', 556–9 nos. 2–3.

[89] E.M. Jamison, *Admiral Eugenius of Sicily*, 1957, 319–21 no. 2. For the *Duana Baronum*, H. Takayama, *The Administration of the Norman Kingdom of Sicily*, Leiden 1993, 145–57.

[90] F. Bartoloni, 'Due documenti per la storia della terra santa', *Bullettino dell'archivio paleografico italiano*, ns i, 1955 137–8.

The organisation and exploitation during the twelfth century of St Sophia's extensive property is less easy to explore than its defence. It seems probable that the *castella* and its lands at Leocubante provided the lion's share of its economic underpinning. Each of them was in the charge of an abbey provost, almost always a monk.[91] As one might expect those in such responsible posts might go on to higher office. The former provost of Toro, Bartholomew, was dean of St Sophia between March 1173 and April 1179, and may well be the same Bartholomew who was abbot 1192–1207.[92] In addition a monk called Seguala appears to have been the provost in general charge of the abbey's properties in the Capitanata in the 1160s and early 1170s.[93] By 1218 St Sophia had an official called the *Maior Prepositus*, to whom was entrusted the overall supervision of its property. But one cannot be sure whether the provosts who were occasionally mentioned in twelfth-century documents without being linked to a specific property, as for example the 'John, priest, monk and provost of the monastery' who was with Abbot Franco when he made arrangements for the staffing of one of the monastery's dependent churches in Benevento in 1131, fulfilled the same role.[94] The monastery was usually represented by its own monks in property transactions, but not invariably so. In 1174–76 a knight called Bartholomew acted as its *procurator* in and around Benevento, and it was also represented by a knight (albeit accompanied by two monks) when in 1197 Count John of Alife restored a mill to it which he had taken.[95]

Some at least of the inhabitants of the abbey's *castella* owed the *dazio*, a money payment, *angaria* (labour services, probably mostly commuted) and various customary payments and obligations, lumped together as *servitia*. These payments and obligations seem to have derived from their holdings rather than their personal status.[96] Here of course St Sophia held the lordship over the village. Even men of superior social status resident in the *castella* might owe obligations to the monastery, as when in a legal case of February 1177 a knight at Toro agreed that he and his men were liable for the repair of the sluice gate of the abbey's mill.[97] The lands of the abbey and its dependent churches outside the *castella* were generally leased, with rents either in money or kind, or indeed a combination of the two. Thus in September 1179 Abbot William personally leased some land of the abbey's cell of St Mercurius at Alife for twenty-five years in return for a annual rent of a tenth of

91 Provosts of Leocubante: Alcerius, Museo del Sannio, Fondo S. Sofia, vol. 13 no. 5 (February 1140), a monk Mercurius, *ibid.*, vol. 10 no. 6 (March 1155), a monk Maynardus, *ibid.*, vol. 10 no. 35 (April 1168), two monks John and Rosatus, *ibid.*, vol. 36 no. 15 (January 1182). Cf. Tancred, monk and provost of Botticella in August 1218, *ibid.*, vol. 28 no. 14.

92 Pergamene Aldobrandini, Cart. II no. 27 (in which he gave evidence in a court case because he was the former provost of Toro), Museo del Sannio, Fondo S. Sofia, vol. 28 no. 9.

93 Pergamene Aldobrandini, Cart. II no. 15, Museo del Sannio, Fondo S. Sofia, vol. 36 no. 12 (March 1167), *Chartes de Troia*, pp. 265–70 no. 88 (July 1172). He was also one of those with the abbot at Barletta in May 1172 [above n. 82].

94 Museo del Sannio, Fondo S. Sofia, vol. 4 no. 1, vol. 28 no. 14.

95 Museo del Sannio, Fondo S. Sofia, vol. 36 no. 13, vol. 10 no. 30, vol. 13 no. 52. Bartholomew's two sons, both knights too, accompanied the abbot on a visit to Alife in August 1183, by which time their father was dead, *ibid.*, vol. 28 no. 12.

96 Museo del Sannio, Fondo S. Sofia, vol. 10 no. 21 (December 1164), in which Abbot John IV remits to one of his *fideles* the obligations owed from his *feudum* in S. Giovanni in Gualdo.

97 Jamison, 'Notes on St Maria della Strada', 80–1 no. 2. The document is dated 1176, but the calendar year at Benevento began on 1st March, and the indiction number and pontifical year indicate 1177.

the fruits and four pounds of wax a year, with the prospect of renewal thereafter for the same terms and an entry fine of 20 tari. However four years later he leased this same land for twenty-nine years to someone else for a money rent of 12 tari a year.[98] The abbey also had considerable urban property within Benevento, almost always leased out in return for money rents, as well as land and profitable riverine rights and mills in the immediate environs of the town. One of the abbots' chief local concerns in the twelfth century was to secure an adequate water supply for its property at Benevento itself, including by irrigation, as for example in March 1150 when the archbishop personally oversaw an agreement to this end between St Sophia and the church of St Paul, allowing the former to make a water course through the latter's land.[99] It seems probable therefore that some of this local property was directly cultivated by the abbey.

However, some of the abbey's more distant properties were not directly administered but leased out on a long term basis as complete units. Most of what property it still possessed (or claimed) in the Terra di Lavoro, including the churches of St Faith at Juniano and St Martin at Maddaloni, was leased to the monastery of St Lawrence at Aversa by Abbot Madelmus at the papal synod of Troia in 1093. After some dispute, for the monks were not at first keen to continue this arrangement, the lease was renewed for a further twenty-nine years in 1123 in another agreement brokered by the papal *curia*. This was in turn renewed for a further term of twenty-nine years in 1152 (and the 1123 agreement had expressly envisaged such a renewal so this was clearly intended as a semi-permanent arrangement).[100] What happened thereafter we do not know, although the *casale* of St Faith (clearly another which had sprung up during the twelfth century around one of the monastery's churches) appears to have been back in the direct possession of St Sophia for at least a short time in the early thirteenth century, before being leased once again, to a layman, in 1235.[101] Similarly the church and *casale* of Sfilizzo on the Gargano peninsula was leased in 1152 to a local knight (apparently in perpetuity) [*Appendix I, document no. 4*], and twelve years later after a court case this was renewed in favour of his niece and her heirs.[102] The documents relating to these leases make clear that St Sophia was alive to the danger of permanent alienation inherent in such long-term arrangements, for there was provision for the abbey's immediate recovery of the property if the rent was unpaid. But such leases clearly made sense for possessions at a distance from Benevento, direct management of which would be administratively inconvenient. They could also be profitable – in 1123 St Lawrence, Aversa, agreed to a payment of 3000 tari for renewal of the lease and an annual rent of 160 tari, with double rent being payable in the year of renewal. The Sfilizzo lease was for an annual rent of 50 pounds of wax and one *romanatum* (i.e. 30 pence).

St Sophia also increasingly resorted to the lease of its subordinate churches,

---

98 Museo del Sannio, Fondo S. Sofia, vol. 28 nos 10, 12.
99 Museo del Sannio, Fondo S. Sofia, vol. 10 no. 4.
100 F. Bartoloni, 'Additiones Kehrianae', *Quellen und Forschungen aus italienischen Archiven und Bibliotheken*, xxxiv, 1954, 43–5 no. 4. D. Girgensohn, 'Documenti beneventani inediti del secolo xii', *Samnium* xl, 1967, 290–6 no. 5, 300–2 no. 8. The *curtis* of Juniano had been confirmed to St Sophia by Otto II in 982, MGH *Diplomatum* ii (1). 333–4 no. 286.
101 Pergamene Aldobrandini, Cart. IV nos 18 (1230), 23 (the 1235 lease). Cf. *Les Registres de Gregoire IX*, ed. L. Auvray, 3 vols, Paris 1890–1955, i. 656 no. 1154 (1233).
102 Pergamene Aldobrandini, Cart. II nos 8, 15. The legal case may have been the product of a squabble within the family rather than a dispute with the monastery.

though here the motive may have been less an economic one than the provision of adequate spiritual provision for the parishioners of such churches. Certainly these leases were always to clerics and contained the obligation that the office should be said on a regular basis (a provision also included in the Sfilizzo lease of 1152). In one example, in 1131, it was expressly laid down that the holder should be unmarried. The rents specified may have been as much reminders of the abbey's ultimate ownership as for its real economic benefit, for the sums involved were not usually very large, although in 1180 the *infirmarius* of St Sophia leased a church apparently pertaining to his office for an annual rent of eight *romanati*, payable in three instalments.[103] (By contrast in 1147 the abbey came to an agreement with the bishop of Lucera to pay him two *romanati* a year as recognition of his episcopal rights over its churches in his diocese.)[104] Such payments might be in kind as well as cash: thus in 1187 a church at Saepino was leased for 12 tari and 12 measures of corn.[105] Even if often small individually, collectively such payments were no doubt a useful addition to the monastery's income. The lease rather than the appropriation of dependent churches may also have been a product of some decline in the number of monks, though here our evidence can only be inferential. At the time of the disputed abbatial election of 1120 there were almost fifty monks at St Sophia.[106] How big the community was later is unknown, but it is probably significant that while at least one of its dependent cells, St Mercurius of Alife, seems to have remained as a monastery until well into the thirteenth century, some others which once had monastic communities appear no longer to have had them by c.1200.[107] This may be one reason why many of its churches came to be entrusted to secular clerics, though there was always a strong argument for not scattering monks away from the mother house. One should note that in his 1147 agreement with St Sophia the bishop of Lucera assumed that its churches in his diocese would be staffed by secular priests, albeit ones appointed by the monastery.[108]

The twelfth century also saw, as one might expect, an increasing role played in the internal organisation of the monastery by its obedientiaries. At the beginning of

---

103 Museo del Sannio, Fondo S. Sofia, vol. 4 nos 1, 4. In 1192 a church near Ariano was leased for 11 tari a year, Cod. Vat. Lat. 13491, no. 22.

104 A. Pratesi, 'Note di diplomatica vescovile beneventana II', *Bullettino dell'archivio paleografico italiano*, ns i, 1955, 70–2 no. 9.

105 Museo del Sannio, Fondo S. Sofia, vol. 4 no. 5.

106 *Falco*, 182.

107 St Mercurius was described as a monastery in 1223, Cod. Vat. Lat. 13491 no. 73, and 1237, Museo del Sannio, Fondo S. Sofia, vol. 28 no. 19. An undated, but by its script late twelfth-century, charter shows St Agnellus, Trivento, as a monastery, Pergamene Aldobrandini, Cart. II no. 70, and it was so described in the royal charter of 1170 [above n. 34], as was St Onuphrius *de gualdo mazocca*, which was undoubtedly so in July 1143, when its monks were granted the right of freely electing their own abbot, Museo del Sannio, Fondo S. Sofia, vol. 2 no. 7. But S. Angelo, Ariano, which was still a monastery in 1135, was by 1178 described as a church, and had a provost who was a priest but not a monk, Museo del Sannio, Fondo S. Sofia, vol. 13 no. 3, Pergamene Aldobrandini, Cart. II no. 31. St Salvatore *abbatis aldi* which had been a monastic establishment in the eleventh century, may already have ceased to be by 1114 [above n. 51]. For St Arontius of Vaccarizza, see below n. 115.

108 However, the lease of the church of S. Angelo in Altissimo in September 1168 stated that no annual census was required but that the priest lessee should hold it on the same terms as would one of the monks, Girgensohn, 'Documenti beneventani inediti', 306–7 no. 11. This clearly implies that some churches were staffed by monks. That of S. Arcangelo, Ascoli, had a monastic prior in 1200 but was described as a 'church', not a monastery, Museo del Sannio, Fondo S. Sofia, vol. 13 no. 29.

this period Abbot Madelmus had allowed them to receive deathbed bequests. In December 1130 the 'provost of the infirmary' bought a vineyard and land outside Benevento on its behalf, and after 1140 a few donors directed their gifts to specific obedientaries rather than to the monastery as a whole: we may in particular note two donations by Trasemundus the notary, almost certainly the son of the chronicler Falco, to the infirmary in 1161.[109] At the end of our period, the role of the obedientaries was defined and rules for hospitality, clothing and discipline laid down in a privilege of Abbot Albert in August 1211.[110] Yet not surprisingly the internal life of the monastery remains largely elusive. There is however one interesting vignette. The earliest recorded act of Abbot William was when in April 1179 he assigned some houses in Benevento and a piece of land just outside the town to the *vestiarium*, which would in turn provide from the rents of these properties the extra dish for the brothers on the feast of St Thomas Becket, hitherto paid for by the abbot. [*Appendix I, document no. 6*]. Here the domestic concerns of the Beneventan monastery intersected with the wider affairs of Christendom, no doubt through the influence of Archbishop Lombard (1171–79), who had once been a member of Becket's *familia*.[111]

The years between the end of King Roger's campaigns to unite southern Italy in 1139 and the death of his grandson William II in 1189 saw St Sophia at the peak of its prosperity and reputation. This was especially the case during the long rule of Abbot John IV (attested between August 1142 and February 1177), who was responsible for the building of the still surviving abbey cloister, with its exquisitely sculptured capitals suggesting both the wealth and the taste of its patron.[112] Furthermore at some stage before September 1168, while Pope Alexander III was living in Benevento to escape the forces of Frederick Barbarossa, he appointed Abbot John as a cardinal.[113] St Sophia was thus clearly an institution of consequence within the Church as a whole.

Yet the period of prosperity was relatively brief. The years after 1189 were to be for St Sophia, as for so many south Italian Benedictine houses, ones of difficulty and ultimately of decline. The disputes over the crown and the problems of royal authority before 1220 played their part in this, as did Frederick II's later quarrels with the papacy. Benevento itself may not have been in the *regno*, but the extent of its property within the *regno* meant that the destiny of its premier religious institution was inextricably linked with that kingdom. Signs of difficulty were already present by the late twelfth century. In October 1193 we have the first reference to debt, a problem which was over the next forty years to become crippling.[114] And in

[109] Museo del Sannio, Fondo S. Sofia, vol. 36 no. 7, vol. 13 nos 12–13 (this last edited by Loud, 'Genesis and Context' [above n. 43], 197–8 no. 2. Cf. Museo del Sannio, Fondo S. Sofia, vol. 36 no. 9 (August 1143), a sale to the sacristy, and *ibid.*, vol. 13 no. 6 (September 1143), a donation of which half was to go to the monastery as a whole and half to the refectory.

[110] Museo del Sannio, Fondo S Sofia, vol. 4 no. 7, which refers to the regulations of Abbot Madelmus.

[111] Museo del Sannio, Fondo S. Sofia, vol. 28 no. 9. *The Letters of John of Salisbury* ii, *The Later Letters (1163–1180)*, ed. W.J. Millor and C.N.L. Brooke, Oxford 1979, 400–1 no. 228, 416–17 no. 231.

[112] An inscription on one of them reads: 'Perpetuis annis stat quarti fame Iohannis / Per quem pastorem domus hunc habet ista decorem'.

[113] Girgensohn, 'Documenti beneventani inediti', 306–7 no. 11 is the first record of this dignity. There are a number of other instances, e.g. Pergamene Aldobrandini, Cart. II no. 23 (April 1171).

[114] Museo del Sannio, Fondo S. Sofia, vol. 15 no. 3: Abbot Bartholomew received 8 ounces of gold

September 1200 the abbot's representatives leased a church near Troia to two citizens of that town, laymen not clerics. That church, St Arontius of Vaccarizza, had once itself been a monastery (given to St Sophia in 1099), and clearly was one no longer. The rent was to be in kind: large quantities of wheat, barley, oil and loaves, an unusual feature, and symptom of a time of instability. This was made clear by clauses in the lease which, both with regard to the rent and to the saying of the office in the church, referred to possible interruptions caused by war.[115] In 1050, despite the Norman conquest, the future for St Sophia was bright. But in 1200 it was already looking distinctly ominous.

I   **The Counts of Ariano**

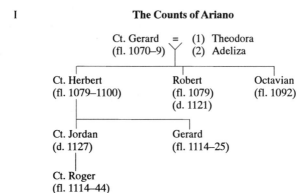

II   **The De Marcia Family**

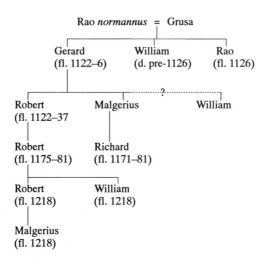

in return for the concession of a tenement at Leocubante, and immediately gave this sum to the widow of an inhabitant of Benevento in payment of a debt. For the thirteenth century, G.A. Loud, 'Monarchy and Monastery in the Mezzogiorno: the Abbey of St Sophia, Benevento and the Staufen', *Papers of the British School at Rome* lix, 1991, 283–318, especially 293–4.
115 Pergamene Aldobrandini, Cart. III no. 14. It was renewed three years later, *ibid.*, Cart. III no. 10. For the original donation, Cod. Vat. Lat. 4939, fos 203r–204v.

APPENDIX I

Documents

(1) (August 1109) Donation to the monastery of St Sophia, Benevento, by Guidelmus, grandson of Prince Pandulf [V?] of Capua[116] of his share of the churches of St Benedict and St Paul of Benevento. Beneventan script, some damp marks. Pergamene Aldobrandini, Cartolario I no. 40.

In nomine domini. Anno millesimo centesimo nono ab incarnatione domini nostri iehsu christi. Et undecimo anno pontificatus domini paschalis secundi. summi pontificis / et universalis pap(a)e. Mense augusti. secunda indic(tione). Ego guidelmus filius atenolfi qui fuit filius domini pandolfi principis capuanensis civitatis. Declaro me / ad convenientiam habere cum monasterio sancte sophie quod est edificatum intus benev(entanam?) veterem civitatem.[117] non longe a porta summa. et cum aliis nostris consortibus ecclesiam mo/nast(erialem?) vocatam sancti benedicti que est constructa foras non longe ab hac beneventana civitate prope fluvium caloris. atque prope ecclesiam vocatam sancti marci. Quam et decla/ro me ad comune habere cum eodem monasterio sancte sophie aliam ecclesiam monast(erialem?) sancti pauli que est subdita et pertinens eidem monasterio sancti benedicti edificata quod (?) / intus eadem beneventana civitate iuxta trasenda publica que vocatur de leone iudice. De quibus ecclesiis et de omnibus earum pertinentiis et ornatu et regimine pertinet / mihi legibus portio. Nunc autem pro remedio et salute anime mee et genitoris mei et parentum meorum congruum mihi est integram ipsam portionem meam ipsarum ecclesiarum / et de omnibus suis pertinentiis et ornatu et regimine offere deo in iamdicto monasterio sancte sophie ubi nunc deo auxiliante dominus bernardus abbes pre esse / cognoscitur. Qua propter ego qui supra guidelmus dum mihi congruum est bona mea voluntate ante iohannem gastaldum et iudicem aliosque subscriptos testes. per hanc / videlicet cartam pro anima mea et genitoris mei meorumque parentum optuli deo in prephato monasterio sancte sophie integram portionem meam predictarum ecclesiarum videlicet / sancti benedicti et sancti pauli et de omnibus earum pertinentiis et ornatu et regimine. Ea exinde nec mihi nec cuique alicui inde reservavi habendum. sed integra(m?) / ipsam portionem meam ipsarum ecclesiarum et omnium earum pertinentiarum (?) et ornatu et regimine. cum inferius et superius cum viis et anditis suis simulque cum muniminibus / propriis cum portione omnium muniminum inde pertinentium et continen(tium?). atque cum omnibus aliis inde pertinentiis omnino pro anima mea et genitoris mei et parentum meorum in prephato / monasterio optuli. Ea itaque ratione ut amodo et semper tam ipse dominus bernardus abbas quam eius successores et pars eiusdem monasterii et illi quibus a parte predicti / monasterii datum paruerit et eorum heredes integram eandem meam oblationem habere et possidere valeant securiter inde faciendo omnia quecumque voluerint sine contradictione / mea et meorum heredum et sine cuiusque requisitione. Unde obligo me ego qui supra Guidelmus et meos obligo heredes antistare et

---

[116] Probably the last Lombard prince of that name, Pandulf V (1049–57).
[117] The original Lombard town, the upper part of the twelfth-century town around the princely palace.

defendere eidem abbati eiusque successoribus et quibus / ab eis datum paruerit et eorum heredes et parti prephati monasterii integram ipsam meam oblationem ab omnibus hominibus ab omnibusque partibus. Quod si taliter ut dictum est / integram ipsam meam oblationem nos qui supra non defenderimus. aut si aliquo tempore ego et mei heredes cum eodem abbate suisque successoribus et quibus ab eis datum paruerit et / heredibus aut cum parte predicti monasterii ex eodem mea oblatione per quamlibet inventam rationem causare aut contendere presumpserimus querendo illud vel exinde eis tollere / aut contrare seu minuere aut si hoc removere quesierimus inde ante omnia mille solidos constantinos penam me et meos heredes eidem abbati suisque successoribus et parte / predicti monasterii et quibus ab eis datum paruerit et eorum heredibus componere obligavi. Et in antea omni tempori inde ad usque eos inviti taciti et contempti maneamus atque / inviti illam eis defendamus sicut supra obligati sumus per eandem obligationem pendere. Et quando ipse dominus Bernardus abbas et successores et pars eiusdem / monasterii seu illi quibus ab eis datum paruerit vel eorum heredes ex inde voluerint fieri auctores et defensores per se ipsos potestatem habeant munimit(a?) inde / pertinentia et continentia ad legem ostendere et cum suis causatoribus inde causare et contendere omnemque definitionem cum eis inde facere debuissimus. / et per se ipsos illam sibi defendant et securiter possideant. Quam te Falconem notarium[118] taliter scribere rogavi. Actum Beneventi feliciter.

+ Ego qui supra Iohannes castaldus et iudex
+ Ego Lupus clericus
+ Ego Poto

(2) (May 1117) Donation to St Sophia of lands and the *ius patronatus* of two churches in the castello of Panni[119] by Ptolomerius and his wife Magalda, and their son Ptolomerius. Beneventan script, torn and badly faded in the middle, with two lines almost entirely obscured. Pergamene Aldobrandini, Cartolario I no. 47.

Nos sumus Ptolomerius filius quondam bonae memoriae guarini. et Magalda uxor eius filia quondam aitardi. et ptolomerius filius eorum amb(orum). / pro salute animarum nostrarum et dionisii filii nostri qui anno preterito obiit. et guidelmi de parisio cognati meique ptolomerii, et om(nium) / aliorum parentum nostrorum; quatinus in future vita d(o)m(ini) habeamus propitium et veniam mereamur peccatorum. In presentia iohannis cast(aldi) et iudicis/ et aliorum plurimorum nobiscum habendo prefatum guidelmum de parisio. et Riccardum de fonta(na?) rosa nepotem nostrum. et martinum presbiterum cap/pellanum nostrum. et malorinum. et ursileum abbatem sancti petri. Per hoc scriptum offerimus deo et in monasterio sanctae Sophiae de benevento. videlicet / in manus domini Bernardi venerabilis abbatis eiusdem monasterii. videlicet terras et silvas. coniunctas cum terris et silvis quas preterito tempore / in eodem monasterio ego ipse cum predicto dionisio filio nostro concessimus. et (obtu?)limus in eodem monasterio coniunctis cum aliis terris beati Bartholo/mei de loco castelli nostri Pandi. de qua ecclesia beati Bartholomei. et Sanctae Mariae ibique. cum omnibus eorum [*sic*] pertinentiis et

---

[118] The chronicler Falco, see Loud, 'Genesis and Context', 194.
[119] Panni, 6km SW. of Bovino, *Cat. Bar.*, arts 277, 343, where it was held by Leo of Foggia, a royal chamberlain. Errico Cuozzo kindly identified this placename for me.

possessionibus / patronatum et ius quod inde layce potestati pertine(tur?). in eodem monasterio similiter tunc optulimus et concessimus. Verumptamen terrae ipsae et / silvae quas modo ibi add . . . . . . concessimus. his finibus includuntur. De una parte incipiente a vado vecclo de rivo cupo / et per rivum ipsum ascend(it) [usque?] ad fontanam que dicitur rivi supi. Et ab ipsa fontana revolven(do) et vadit recte inter hoc et terram quam . . . em . . . / . . . . . . descendit in vallonem . . . . . . [va]llone[m] . . . / . . . et r . . . revolvit . . . . . . que / dicitur strata. Ab inde vad(it) aliquantum vadit per eandem viam usque in alteram viam. iterum revolven(do) per eandem viam et descend(it) usque in vallone / et per hunc vallonem descend(it) usque in rivum que dicitur labella. De alia parte vadit per ipsam labellam. De aliis partibus qualiter vadit revolvendo / per loca. et coniungendo cum predictis terris et silvis quae preterito tempore in eodem monasterio concessimus. et coniungitur in pri-orem finem. / Infra hos omnes fines nec nobis neque nostris heredibus vel succes-soribus aut vicariis aliquid reservavimus. sed ea omnia qualiter predictis finibus / includuntur. cum inferioribus et superioribus. cum viis et aquis et anditis. montibus et planis. cultum et incultum. atque cum omnibus eorum pertinentiis. pro remedio et salute animarum nostrarum et predicti filii nostri dionisii et omnium parentum nostrorum. libere et absolute et transac/tive [?] in eodem monasterio optulimus et concessimus. Ea ratione; ut amodo et semper tu ipse dominus Bernardus venerabi-lis abbas et tui successores et / pars eiusdem monasterii integram eandem nostram oblationem firmiter et securiter habere et possidere valeatis sine aliqua contradic-tio(ne) nostra vel / nostrorum heredum vel successorum aut vicariorum; et sine cuiuscumque personae contrarieta(te). Et per nostram defensionem amodo et sem-per ab omnibus / hominibus ab omnibusque partibus. Quod si aliqua hominis persona contra hanc nostram oblationem temerario ausu inimico generis humani / instigante agere aut causari temptaverit. cum iuda miserrimo magistri et domini sui proditore sortiatur portionem. Nec non / cum dathan et abyran quos vivos terra absorbuit perpetualiter dampneritur. et in futuro ex anime cum impiis et dampnatis / iudicentur. anathematis vinculo dampnandi in perpetuum. Omnis vero illud con-servantes et manutenentes ad honorem et proficuum eiusdem / monasterii gratia divina protegat et tueatur. Quod tibi Transoni clerico et notario atque advocato taliter scribere iussimus in anno / dominice incar(natione). millesimo centesimo septimo decimo. Pontificatus vero domini nostri secundi Paschal(is) papae anno octavodecimo. mense madio. Ind(ictione) . . . / In camera monasterii Sanctae So-phiae. Feliciter.

+ Signum crucis propriae manus ptolomerii.
+ Signum crucis propriae manus predicti ptolomerii filii.
+ Signum crucis propriae manus prefati Guidelmi de parisio.[120]
+ Signum crucis propriae manus predicti riccardi de font(ana?) rosa.[121]
+ Signum crucis propriae manus marini presbiteri cappellani.
+ Signum crucis propriae manus malorini.

---

[120] An ancestor of Roger de Parisio, lord of Castelnuovo della Daunia, who was one of the knights present at the court judging the dispute between St Sophia and Gerald de Fay in 1151, Pergamene Aldobrandini, Cart. II no. 6, *Cat. Bar.*, art. 391.

[121] In the *Cat. Bar.*, art. 428, William of Fontanarosa held fiefs at Paduli and S. Arcangelo Trimonte, east of Benevento.

+ Signum crucis proprie manus guidelmi filii roffridi.
+ Ego qui supra Iohannis castald(us) et iudex.

(3) (1125, May) Count Jordan of Ariano gives the abbey of St Sophia, Benevento, a mill near its subject monastery of St Benedict, Morcone, and a piece of land, for the soul of Iollemus son of Raino Equalis. Beneventan script, generally good condition but with some damp marking on the right-hand side and a piece missing from the right margin, Benevento, Museo del Sannio, Fondo S. Sofia, vol. 12 no. 43.

In nomine domini. Anno millesimo centesimo vicesimo quinto ab incarnatione domini nostri yehsu christi. mense madio et tertia indictione. / Ego IORDANUS Comes filius ERBERTI comitis. presentibus militibus aliisque bonis hominibus. Bona mea voluntate. Concedo et dono / pro redemptione anime Iollemi filii Rainonis equalis monasterio sancte sophie totum et integrum quoddam molendinum quod situm est in alvio saxinore / prope monasterium sancti benedicti in pertinentiis morconis subditi eiusdem monasterii sancte sophie. cum viis et aquis et anditis suis. et cum omnibus propriis inde / pertinentiis et continentiis ut in tempore vetusto fuit. Similiter concedo et dono quandam petiam terre in loco acristoliete cum viis et anditiis suis (et) / cum omnibus propriis inde pertinentiis et continentiis quamquam Iollemus filius Rainonis equalis ante tempus sue mortis trasactivo nomine ten . . . / infra supradicta pertinentia eiusdem molendini et iamdicte terre; nec michi nec cuilibet alteri exinde reservavi. sed integrum illud sicut perlegitur trasac . . . / donavi eiusdem monasterio sancte sophie. Ea videlicet ratione ut amodo et semper faciat inde quodcumque facere voluerit sine meam meorumque heredum ali(quam) / contradictionem. et sine cuiuscumque requisitione. Unde obligo me et meos heredes nos illud antistare et defendere ab omnibus hominibus omnibusque partibus. / Quam si taliter ut dictum est illud non defensaverimus aut si aliquo portione illud tornare aut removere quesiverimus querendo exinde tol(lere) / vel contrare seu minuiere aut si subtraere presumserimus (no)s et quicumque hoc fecerint sub anathemate mane . . . is. Quam te / PETRO notario taliter scribere iussi.

+ Ego comes Iordanus.
+ Ego comes Rocgerius filius comitis Iordani propria manu me subscripsi
+ Ego Robbertus de cossiano consensi et me subscripsi.
+ Ego Girardus avunculus comitis testis sum.
+ Ego Girardus frater comitis testis sum.[122]
+ Ego Rainone testis sum.
+ Ego guilelmus aldone testis sum.
+ Ego aribertus de amandra testis sum.[123]
+ Ego Robbertus Iaconus testis sum.
+ Ego Landofus de padule testis sum.
+ Ego audialdus testis sum.
+ Ego Iohannes testis sum.
+ Ego Iohannes I(udex?) testis sum.

[122] Witnessed Jordan's July 1114 charter for St Sophia, Cod. Vat. Lat. 4939, fo. 188v.
[123] Richard de Amandra witnessed Jordan's September 1114 charter to St Sophia, Cod. Vat. Lat. 4939, fo. 186v.

(4) (1152, May) Abbot John (IV) of the monastery of St Sophia leases the *casale* of Sfilizzo in the territory of Vieste, and its church of St Nicholas, to the knight Richard son of William and his heirs.[124] Probably a copy rather than an original since it is written in minuscule; some bad staining over the left part of the parchment renders a number of words illegible. Pergamene Aldobrandini, Cartolario II no. 8.

In nomine domini. Anno dominice incarnationis millesimo centesimo quinquaginta secundo. Et octavo anno pontificatus domini Eugenii tertii summi pontificis et universalis pape. mense madio xv indictione. Memoratorium factum a me Iohanne / dei gratia monasterii sancte sophie abbate de hoc quod ante idoneos homines coniunxi me in bonam convenientiam cum Riccardo milite filio quondam guidelmi. et statim mecum habendo alcerium decanum / dominum albertum dominum Romualdum. dominum maynardum dominum gregorium dominum iohannem. dominum Placidum. dominum Nycolaum; dedi et tradidi ei unum casalem Sfilizzum nomine. cum hominibus et omnibus / possessionibus et pertinentiis suis et unam ecclesiam vocatam s(anctem) nycolay in eodem casale. ipsi eidem nostro monasterio pertinentem in territorio de civitate nomine vestana. Ea ratione. ut amodo et / cunctis diebus vite sue et vita suorum heredum potestatem habeunt ipse et sui heredes et missi eorum ipsam ecclesiam et ipsum casalem tenere dominari. et predictam ecclesiam die noctuque facere officiare / si . . . ssos ipsius ecclesie refic(ere) (?) ecclesiam sicut decet. et vineas et terras suas tempore suo laborare et cultare sicut mereant. et dare ad laborandum cui voluerit. Quicquid / vero (?) . . . d . . . possessionibus (i)dem casalis exierit sue sit prop(r)ietam. Et cum ego vel aliquis confratrum nostrorum ibi applicuerimus. debeant nos ibidem suscipere et honeste / ser . . . . . . id semper debeant dirigere ad ipsum nostrum monasterium sancte sophie censum inde unum romanatum de bono monete et quinquaginta / libros de (cera) . . . u . . . nobis dirigere usque ad sequen(tes) kalendas mense novemb(ris). tunc debeant nobis duplicatum ipsum censum dirigere. Ita quod si ad sequentem domini / nati(vitatem) . . . diem . . . duplicatum censum et de super decem romanatos. ab inde in antea potestatem habeamus accipere nostre proprietati ipsum casalem et / iam dictam ecclesiam . . . omnibus per(tin)e(ntiis) . . . o tempore nostre potestati illud tenere et frui. usque dum ipsum censum duplicatum cum ipsos romanatos decem nobis soluerint. / ad obitum . . . heredum s(uorum) . . . eiusdem nostri monasterii duplicare censum ipsum. et sic ab inde in antea debeant ipsi heredes sui per singulos annos / parti predicti nostri monasterii solvere censum inde videlicet unum romanatum et quinquaginta libras de cera in omni predicto tenore et condicione. Et si ipsum / censum sui heredes ut dictum est ab eorum . . . i parti iam dicti monasterii solvere et dirigere noluerint. tunc pars iam dicti nostri monasterii / habeant potestatem ipsis heredibus suis ipsum casalem eandem ecclesiam auferre et dare cui voluerimus sine sue contradictione. Hanc vero / traditionem sed ei. salva omni ratione filiarum quondam iordani germani sui. quam habentem in predicto casale et eadem ecclesia et pertinentiis suis a parte / predicti nostri monasterii. de . . . omnibus ad impleundum (?) guadiam mihi dedit et mediatorem mihi posuit Robbertum cognomento de ullia filius . . . ad pignorandum / illos

---

[124] *Cat. Bar.*, art. 374 records him holding one knight's fee, which E. Cuozzo, *Catalogus Baronum. Commentario*, Fonti per la storia d' Italia 101b, Rome 1984, 93 suggests was near Chieuti, west of the Gargano massif.

et illorum heredum in omnibus rebus ipsis . . . sis. Ego trasemundus notarius
interfui.

+ Signum crucis proprie manus (Ric)cardi.
+ Signum crucis proprie manus Robberti de ullia.[125]
+ Signum crucis proprie manus saruli filii raoni (?)
+ Ego landulfus index rogatus . . . d . . . ndi subscripsi.

(5)   (November 1170) Count Richard of Molise, while at the baths of Pozzuoli,
gives to St Sophia and Abbot John [IV] the food renders *[prandia]* which he and
his predecessors have received from Castelvecchio, to be paid instead (the most
probable interpretation, although here the document is defective) to the abbey's
dependency of St Maria of Saepino. Minuscule, some damp marks on the right
hand side and a large hole in the middle of the parchment. Pergamene Aldobrandini, Cartolario II no. 21.

In nomine sancte et individue trinitatis. Anno ab incarna/tione domini Millesimo
Centesimo Septuagesimo. Mense novembris / Indictione quarta. Nos Riccardus.
dei et Regia gratia de molis(io) / comes et domini Regis familiaris. Quia morum et
legum iura commendat / ut contractum inter mortales habitorum series. m(em)bra-
nis ad posteros / memoriam describantur. cum ab humane sepissime nisi scriptis /
detente solea(n)t dilabi memoria fatemur quam nostra bona voluntate. In presentia
baronum nostrorum aliorum que subscriptorum pro remissione delictorum nostrorum ac pro anime nostre nostrorum que [parentum?] . . . / redemptione deo et
monasterio Beate Sophie in man[ibus?] domini Iohanni(s) / venerabilis abbatis
eiusdem monasterii. prandia que habere debem(u)s / de castello vetulo sicut antecessores nostri soliti sunt habere in perpetuum dimitt . . . ve scilicet apud sanctam
mariam / de sepino . . . obligantes nos nostrosque / heredes hanc . . . (fir)mam
atque stabilam tenere. nec de / cetero predict(um) castellum a nobis seu a nostris
heredibus pro prandiis / ipsius molestiam vel infestationem sustinere. Et ut hoc
donum et relaxatio perpetuum. firmitatis robur obtineat presens scriptum / in quo
signum sancte et vivice crucis manibus nostris designavimus. per / manus Goffridi
nostri notarii scribi precepimus. actum apud balnea puteolana. feliciteR.

+ Nos Ricc(ardus) dei et Regia gratia de molis(io) Comes. et domini Regis familia-
ris / signum hoc vivifice crucis fecimus.
+ Signum crucis proprie manus taliacoti.
+ Signum crucis proprie manus Robberti Sancti Agapeti.[126]
+ Signum crucis proprie manus Gualter(ii) de molinis.[127]
+ Signum crucis proprie manus Robberti de molinis.[128]

[125] Otherwise unattested, but clearly a relative of the royal justiciar Henry de Ollia (d. c.1155) and
his son Geoffrey, count of Lesina 1155–c.1180), Jamison 'Norman Administration of Apulia and
Capua', 309, 315, Cuozzo, *Catalogus Baronum. Commentario*, 93–8. The family derived from
Oully-le-Tesson (Calvados).
[126] In the *Cat. Bar.*, art. 311, he held Gildone as a rear vassal of the count of Civitate. He later
witnessed the 1185 charter of Count Roger of Molise to St Sophia [n. 88 above] where he was
described as a 'royal baron' (i.e. a tenant-in-chief).
[127] Witnessed the 1185 charter of Count Roger.
[128] Probably the same man as in *Cat. Bar.*, art. 962. In 1180 he was a royal justiciar [*document no. 7*

+ Signum crucis proprie manus Simonis de molinis.[129]
+ Signum crucis proprie manus Berardi de rivo negro.[130]
+ Signum crucis proprie manus Raonis de molinis.[131]

(6) (April 1179) Abbot William of St Sophia assigns to the *vestiarium* of the abbey a piece of land near the church of St Mark, a house next to the main square of Benevento, and some other houses just outside the Porta Somma, all of which have been recently acquired. He specifies that in future the *vestiarium* shall pay for the extra dish for the brothers which the abbot has provided on the feast of St Thomas Becket. Neat, clear Beneventan script; the parchment is torn on the right hand side but otherwise in good condition. Benevento, Museo del Sannio, Fondo S. Sofia, vol. 28 no. 9.

In nomine domini. Anno dominice incarnationis millesimo centesimo septuagesimo nono. Et vicesimo anno pontificatus domini nostri / allexandri tertii summi pontificis et universalis papae. Mense Aprilis. duodecimo indictione. Nos Guilielmus dei gratia humilis / Abbatis monasterii Sancte Sophie. Cum ipsius nostri monasterii congregatio dei faciente clementia a quo / bona cuncta procedunt innumero nostris temporibus et religione augmentata esse dinoscitur. cum equ(alis?) / sit et rationi conveniens ut fratribus nostris regulariter inventibus nichil deese valeat unde scr(ibetur iudi?)/cium dei cui plurimum intenti sunt obleat in unde aliquo minorari. sed magis more solito in ecclesia mona(sterii) / divina valeant celebrari officia; divino moti spiramine. providemus de rebus m(ona)/sterii nostris diebus et per nos acquisitas. vestiario fratrum concedere. Ut omni ab eis exclusa na..st (?)../ sublato quoque murmure secundum regulam beati Benedicti quam diligere noscuntur malis o . . . / et conservare. Incessant(er) valeant oracioni vacare. Congregatio igitur in claustro fratribus / et voluntate nostra et proposito eis expositis. cum gratiam illud admodum acceptumque tenerent / a deo quo postmodum omnibus fere flexis genibus nobis gratias agerent. coram Iohanne iudice ipsis ecclesiam presentibus fratribus. et falcone notario et scriba per infulem eiusdem notarii. obdimus tradimus atque concessimus vobis domino / Bartholomeo prescripti nostri cenobii decano. et domino Madelmo monacho et vestiario. et domino Nycola / monacho ad partem ipsius vestiarii. totam terram que dicitur yscla quam nuper a malanoctibus emi(mus?) / foris et prope ecclesiam Sancti Marci. et totam unam casam quam similiter acquisivimus secus plateam publicam maiorem / et prope ecclesiam sancti Iohannis a porta summa. que videlicet fuit quondam Iohannis carammanni. et alias casas que / fuerunt heredum magistri Roggerii flasconarii. que scilicet sunt extra porta summa secus murum civitatis a sinistre / parte descenditibus ad Iudicetum. Ea quod ratione ait amodo et imperpetuum. pars ipsius vestiarii integras ipsas possessiones habeas et possideat. et earum censum et

---

below]. He also witnessed the 1185 charter of Count Roger, where he was described as the count's constable.

[129] Cf. *Le Cartulaire de S. Matteo di Sculgola en Capitanate (1177–1239)*, ed. J.-M. Martin (Codice diplomatico pugliese xxx, Bari 1987), 42–3, no. 23 (December 1183).

[130] Probably a relative of the Oderisius de Rivo Negro of *Cat. Bar.*, arts 731, 750, whose various lordships totalled nine knights' fees.

[131] Cf. *Cat. Bar.*, arts 733–4. He witnessed the 1153 charter of Count Hugh II of Molise, Jamison, 'Administration of Molise, I', 556–7 no. 2.

frudium pro fratrum sustentatione percipiat. (sine) / nostra et nostrorum successorum contradictione et requisitione. et per nostram et nostrorum successorum defensionem ab omnibus / hominibus omnibusque partibus. dando pars ipsius vestiarii omni anno octo tar(enos) pro ferculo fratribus ipsius (nostri?) cenobii / quod nos in festo beati Thome Cantuariensis archiepiscopi et martiris dare consuevimus. Illud quoque a nobis et / a cunctis fratribus statutum est. Ut si quis hanc nostram concessionem infringere temptaverit. vel ab ipso vestiario removere. excommunicationis vinculo teneatur astrictus. et cum Dathan et Abiron. et Iuda domini et magistri sui traditore. eternis flammis debeat cruciari. Quod si prefatum falconem notarium et / scribam sacri beneventani palatii taliter scribere rogavimus. quia interfuisti.

+ Ego qui supra Iohannes iudex.

(7) (May 1180) Richard de Marchia, son of Malgerius,[132] expresses his remorse about his seizure of a man belonging to the monastery of St Sophia's *casale* of S. Pietro in Laurito, and then, in the bishop's palace at Aversa, in the presence of Count Tancred of Lecce, Master Constable and Justiciar of Apulia and Terra di Lavoro,[133] and other noblemen, pledges himself to abandon his claims against the monastery concerning the mountain called Torre di Ermula.[134] Minuscule, small, neat, notarial hand, good condition. Benevento, Museo del Sannio, Fondo S. Sofia, vol. 13 no. 18.

In nomine domini nostri Iehsu Christi dei eterni. Anno ab incarnatione eius millesimo centesimo octagesimo. mense ma/dii. Indic(tione) tertiadecima. Et quintodecimo anno domini nostri Willelmi dei gratia Sicilie. ducatus Apulie. et principatus / Capue Gloriosissimi Regis. Scriptum memorie de hoc quod Ego Riccardus cognomento de marchia filius quondam Malgerii eiusdem cogno/minis. Cognoscens me contra monasterium sancte Sophie de benevento deliq(u)isse. de quodam videlicet homine quem Ego / iniuste ceperam. in quodam casale predicti monasterii. quod sanctus Petrus de Laurito vocatur. Et quia vidi me graviter / offendisse. cum amicis et consanguineis meis. scilicet cum Robberto de marchia. et Romaildo de troia. dominem Gui/lielmum venerabilem abbatem supradicti monasterii Sancte Sophie adivi. preces multimodis apud eum deponens. pro dei amore. et / sue sancte religionis optentu. suppliciter rogavi. ut delictum illud mihi remitteret; Qui habito fratrum suorum consilio. solita / pietate peccatum illud mihi indulxit. Taliter ut quia ipse dominus abbas querulam inde apud dominum Egregium Comitem Tancredum / licie. et magistrum Comestabulum. et magistrum Iusticiarium tocius apulii et terre laboris deposuerat. In presentiam suam venirem. et coram eo / omne conditione. quam Ego qui supra Riccardus habebam in quodam monte qui vocatur torus de ermula. qui mons est iuris predicti mona/sterii Sancte Sophie. Ipsi monasterio remitterem in perpetuum. Unde Ego qui supra Riccardus de Marchia aput aversam. ubi iamdictus egregius dominus / Comes et magister comestabulus et magister iusticiarius tocius apulie et terre laboris Regiam curiam tenebat;

---

132 Lord of Pesco Sannita, 12 km NE of Benevento, *Cat. Bar.*, art. 346.
133 The future king 1190–4, Master Justiciar 1176–85.
134 Mentioned in the boundary clause of his uncle Robert's charter to St Sophia in 1127 as being not far from the church of St Peter, Pergamene Aldobrandini, Cart. I no. 59.

adivi et coram eo in camera palacii episcopii me presentavi. et bona mea voluntate in presentia predicti egregii domini Comitis. presentibus ibi Robberto de / molini Regio iusticiario. Silvestro de Cavello. Magistro Maczulino iudice Sancti iermani. Aczone iudice bulani. Si/mone de grecia et Robberto malescal(co) predicti domini Comitis. remisi per pannum mantelli mei in manus domini Amici venerabilis / prepositi iamdicti Sancte Sophie pro parte et vice ipsius monasterii et Rectorum eius presentium et futurorum. quicquid iuris et conditio/nis habebam vel habere poteram in supradicto monte qui vocatur torus de ermula. et omnino illud qui nunc clamavi; Obli/gavi etiam me Ego Riccardus et meos heredes supradicto domino Amico venerabili preposito iamdicti monasterii. propter et vice ipsius mo/nasterii et Rectorum eius presentium et futurorum. Coram videlicet predicto egregio dom-ino Comite. mag(istro) Comest(abulo) et mag(istro) Iustic(iario) tocius apulie et / terre labor(is). sedentibus ibi et audientibus supradictis viris. quod numquam de decetero contra monasterium querulam intromovere presum(ps)imus. et / si aliquin quod absit ego vel mei heredes hanc remissionem irritam facere temptaverimus; vel calumpniam aliquam predicto monasterio / in(tro)movere presumpserimus; quod triginta unciarum auri penam iamdicto monasterio componamus. et fiat (?) inviti causa firma manente / taciti maneamus. hoc breve scripsi ego Alex(ander) notarius averse[135] rogatu supradicti Riccardi de marchia.

+ Signum crucis manus supradicti Robberti de molini Regii iusticiarii[136]
+ Signum crucis manus predicti Silvestri de Cavello
+ Ego Aczo iudex
+ Signum manus supradicti Ricc(ardi) de marchia
+ Signum manus prefati Simonis de grecia[137]
+ Signum manus predicti Robberti malescalci[138]
+ Signum proprie manus mac(zolini?)

---

[135] Some 22 other charters written by him at Aversa between 1156 and 1183 have survived, *Codice diplomatico normanno di Aversa*, ed. A. Gallo, Naples 1927, no. 68 *et seq.*
[136] See above n. 128.
[137] Otherwise unattested, but he must have been a relative of the lords of Greci, Brien (d. pre-1163) and his son Gerard, a royal justiciar (fl. 1155–77), for whom E.M. Jamison, 'The Abbess Bethlem of S. Maria di Porta Somma and the barons of the Terra Beneventana', *Oxford Essays in Medieval History Presented to Herbert Edward Salter*, Oxford 1934, 33–67.
[138] Cf. *Le Pergamene di San Giovanni Evangelista di Lecce*, ed. M. Pastore, Lecce 1970, 24 (1181).

APPENDIX II

The Abbots of St Sophia, Benevento[139]

Ursus	945
Azzo	July 961 – August 986
Gregory I	February 998 – April 1022
Bisantius	July 1033 – May 1038
Gregory II	December 1041 – March 1052 (deposed)
Sikenulfus	May 1052 – March 1056
Amicus I	September 1058 – April 1062 (died early 1063)
Peter	March 1063 – January 1064
Amicus II	March 1065 – October 1068
John [II?]	August 1069 – March 1072
Madelmus	March 1074/5 – died 27/28 September 1107[140]
Bernard	29 September 1107 – died 30 July 1120[141]
John [III] 'the Grammarian'	14 August 1120 – died 23 November 1128[142]
Franco	November 1128 – February 1140
John IV	August 1142 – February 1177
William	April 1179 – June 1191
Bartholomew	October 1192 – August 1207
Albert	August 1211 – April 1216
Matthew	April 1219 – July 1239
	[long vacancy]
Peter of Capua	November 1254 – January 1255

[139] The dates given are those firmly attested for each abbot. The list is clearly incomplete insofar as the early abbots are concerned. Since John IV is several times identified by this number there must have been three earlier abbots of this name, but only two can be identified.
[140] Bertolini, 'Annales Beneventani' 153, Cod. Vat. Borgiani 296, fo. 78v.
[141] *Falco*, 162, 181.
[142] *Falco*, 182, 200.

'QUOT HOMINES?' THE POPULATION OF DOMESDAY ENGLAND[1]

John S. Moore

To adapt an aphorism of Jane Austen in *Pride and Prejudice,*

> It is a truth universally acknowledged, that an economic historian in possession of a good topic must be in want of statistics.

This immediately calls to mind another aphorism by Jane Austen's contemporary, the Duke of Wellington: 'lies, more lies, damned lies, and statistics'. Why, then, is a knowledge of the number of people in Domesday England desirable? The short answer is that King William, his officials and his barons, after the 'much thought and deep discussion . . . about this country, how it was occupied and with what sort of people' at the Gloucester Council in January 1086,[2] clearly thought that 'numbering the people' was an important aspect of the Domesday survey, and this is evident from the first edition of the survey's questionnaire, the only version to survive, included in the *Inquisitio Eliensis* (*IE*):

> How many men? How many villagers? How many cottars? How many slaves? How many freemen? How many sokemen?[3]

King William and his councillors were in fact 'quantifiers'! Unless we think that they were simply silly (in which case the survey was indeed the 'vast administrative mistake' of Richardson and Sayles),[4] clearly they did regard

[1] My thanks are due to Professor Christopher Harper-Bill, current Director of the Battle Conference, for his invitation to present this paper; to all my friends at the Conference for their help; to my fellow medievalists at the University of Bristol, Marcus Bull, Brendan Smith and Ian Wei, for their continued friendship and support; to past and present undergraduate members of my 'Domesday England' seminar and to past and present postgraduates in the M.A. in Medieval Studies course at Bristol, whose ability to ask stimulating if sometimes unanswerable questions is a prophylactic against premature senile decay. I am particularly grateful to my very good friend Ann Williams for discussion of, and advice on, the Shaftesbury Abbey estate-surveys, and providing me with a preliminary analysis of them. I am most grateful to Mrs Vivien Brown for giving me a retyped copy of the chapter in R.A. Brown's Ph.D. thesis dealing with garrisons, and to Professor Joan Greatrex for information on monastic population. I also thank Caroline Thorn for providing me with copies of some of the Evesham 'satellites' at short notice. I am grateful for help from Professor Joan Greatrex before the Conference and for constructive criticism from Dr Charles Coulson and Dr Jennifer Ward after this paper was delivered. Finally, my wife and children know well how much I owe them for their support and forbearance.

[2] For the more precise redating of the Council meeting to January 1086, see J.S. Moore, 'Post-Mortem of an Invasion', in R. Smith and H.R. Loyn, eds, *Domesday: 900 Years of England's Norman Heritage*, London 1986, 69.

[3] Translated from N.E.S.A. Hamilton, ed., *Inquisitio Comitatus Cantabrigiensis*, London 1876, 97.

[4] H.G. Richardson and G.O. Sayles, *The Governance of Medieval England from the Conquest to Magna Carta*, Edinburgh 1963, 28.

such numbering as an important aspect of their inquiry. Indeed, as I have pointed out elsewhere, 'numbering the people' *was* important to both kings and magnates both in 1086 and far later: kings and their officials needed to know the numbers of taxpayers and of potential military recruits, as did lords, who also needed to know the numbers of tenants and how much rent and labour would be forthcoming from them.[5] Since the *Anglo-Saxon Chronicle*'s account of the Domesday survey immediately followed on from its description of the Danish 'invasion scare' in 1085 which had caused King William to bring over 'a larger force of mounted men and infantry . . . than had ever come to this country', the problems resulting from billeting this army are now seen as a major factor leading the king to consider the advisability of a nationwide survey.[6] In part, therefore, the Domesday survey was also a reaction to urgent military necessity, and the crisis did not recede until the assassination of Cnut IV of Denmark in July 1086. Although the Domesday survey was many things – geld book, register of title, feodary, etc. – it was in part a census, as William of Malmesbury noted in describing the achievements of King William in England:

> He so subdued the inhabitants to his will that without opposition he conducted the first census of all heads, compiled for his information a written record of the rents of all landed estates, and bound all free men, whosoever's they were, to his fealty by an oath.[7]

William thus clearly distinguished between the demographic aspects (*censum omnium capitum*) and the economic aspects (*omnium praediorum redditus*) of *DB*, which I believe he is the first writer to discern.

After a somewhat extended 'short answer' to the question of why a knowledge of Domesday population is desirable, a short 'long answer': Anglo-Norman England was an example of what economic historians classify as a 'pre-industrial' (or, better, 'pre-industrialised') economy, in which land was the source of most wealth, and control of land was the source of status and power. Before the 'Industrial Revolution', all economies in the world were of this type, and 'Third World' economies to this day are basically of the same character.[8] In such an economy, the balance between population and land is clearly crucial, and the evidence of the Domesday survey arguably enables historians to examine this type of economy in Anglo-Norman England perhaps better than in any other large medieval European region. But it does not necessarily follow that what figures now exist are of adequate quality for their intended use. The existence of large numbers of figures must not prevent their critical evaluation. Even though statistical manipulation does require some special mathematical techniques, other kinds of historical evidence also require their own specialist techniques, such as palaeography and diplomatic in the case of charters: what should be common to the use of all historical evidence, whether quantitative or non-quantitative, is accurate evaluation of both its accuracy and its utility for its proposed purpose by historians.

5 J.S. Moore, 'Introduction', in J.S. Moore and R. Smith, eds, *The House of Lords: a Thousand Years of British Tradition*, London 1994, 13.
6 N.J. Higham, 'The Domesday Survey: Context and Purpose', *History* lxxviii, 1993, 7–21.
7 *De Gestis Regum* ii, 317.
8 P. Crone, *Pre-Industrial Societies*, London 1989, repr. 1994.

Historians' opinions on the accuracy of Domesday Book have varied widely. One Victorian scholar pompously pronounced that

> I believe the text of . . . Domesday to be almost faultless . . . As Domesday Book was a work of man, there are also no doubt . . . mistakes and omissions, but to acknowledge this is not to acknowledge that the man is living who can point them out and correct them . . .[9]

As I commented when I first unearthed this gem, 'an attitude, one would think, more appropriate in the cathedral canon towards his bishop or dean than in a critical historian towards his major source'.[10] Nowadays, given the strife at Lincoln Cathedral, my comment has lost some of its force. It might be thought that such uncritical adulation would long ago have been abandoned, but it is still alive in Australia in the 1990s. G.D. Snooks refers to 'the comprehensive and reliable data-set presented . . . in Domesday Book' and goes on to state

> The underlying data . . . basically estimates of numbers of families . . . are far more robust and reliable than those used by Gregory King six hundred years later.[11]

Given that Gregory King's basic demographic source, the Hearth Tax returns, comprised nominal lists of heads of household at parish level compiled by local officials, supplemented by detailed household 'listings' made under the Marriage Duty Act of 1695, I find Snooks' comparison totally incomprehensible: perhaps living on the other side of the globe induces an upside-down view of reality! Moreover, apart from boroughs, the earlier work of McDonald and Snooks devoted little attention to problems of population.[12] Confronted with such nonsense, it is understandable that others besides Chris Lewis are 'already skeptical (*sic*) enough about Domesday numerology',[13] or that A.R. Bridbury should argue

> The numbers game is played out. Counting tenants in Domesday Book and adding something to compensate for Domesday's omissions cannot possibly tell us how many people occupied the land as sub-tenants or as tenants of sub-tenants or even as squatters.[14]

But this comment goes too far. Dr Bridbury simply assumes that there were 'sub-tenants or . . . tenants of sub-tenants' in 1086 because such people undoubtedly existed in what most other historians would regard as the very different, more densely populated, England of c.1300, in which the pressure of people on land had greatly intensified and in which, as a result, a considerable section of that population was indeed landless.[15] To be fair, Dr Bridbury has also argued that

[9] C.S. Taylor, *An Analysis of the Gloucestershire Domesday*, Bristol 1889, 16, 19.

[10] J.S. Moore, 'The Gloucestershire Section of Domesday Book: Geographical Problems of the Text, part 1', *Trans. Bristol and Glos. Arch. Soc.* cv, 1987, 110.

[11] R.H. Britnell and B.M.S. Campbell, eds, *A Commercialising Economy: England, 1085 to c.1300*, Manchester 1995, 28, 31.

[12] J. McDonald and G.D. Snooks, *Domesday Economy: a New Approach to Anglo-Norman History*, Oxford 1986, 17–19.

[13] C.P. Lewis, 'The Domesday Jurors', *Haskins Soc. Journ.* v, 1993, 33.

[14] A.R. Bridbury, *The English Economy from Bede to the Reformation*, Woodbridge 1992, 124.

[15] For example, at Halesowen (Worcs.), the number of manorial tenants tripled between 1086 and

We can no longer countenance the assumption that there was a population explosion in the century or so after Domesday . . . It may well be that we should postulate a Domesday population which was very much bigger than everyone has yet thought possible. But there is no point in attempting to assign numbers to our guesses.[16]

Although recent estimates of the total population in 1086 have risen, and whilst there is still disagreement about the extent of population-growth in the twelfth and even more in the thirteenth centuries, no-one apart from Bridbury has seriously argued for 'zero-growth' after 1086. If he wishes to establish his 'guesses', then he must produce the evidence and he must 'assign numbers'.

So far as the Domesday statistics are concerned, I would argue for a middle position. Clearly they are not, and cannot be, totally 'comprehensive and reliable', as Snooks suggested. The implications of modern views about 'the making of Domesday Book' for the problematic accuracy of its figures are considerable. It is, as any medievalist knows, extremely easy to miscopy roman numerals, and if, as is now thought, there was a succession of stages of summarisation and recopying of data, at county, circuit and national levels, the probability of copying errors occurring is even greater, the more so if we allow for the probability that work on the Domesday survey was being done under pressure to meet a final deadline.[17] Even without such pressure of time, even if there had been no copying errors, the information originally collected was itself incomplete. For one of the manors of Woodchester (Glos.), we are told

Nobody has rendered account of this manor to the king's commissioners, nor has any of them come to this survey

an omission for which an obvious reason was stated:

Edward [of Salisbury, sheriff of Wiltshire] holds this land in the *feorm* of Wiltshire, wrongfully as the county [of Gloucestershire] states.[18]

1315, from 71 to 215, but the total population probably quadrupled (Z. Razi, *Life, Marriage and Death in a Medieval Parish. Economy, Society and Demography in Halesowen, 1270–1400*, Cambridge 1980, 28–32). Numerous 'undersettlers' are also recorded, exceptionally, on the surveys of the archbishop of Canterbury's estates c.1285: B.C. Redwood and A.E. Wilson, eds, 'Custumals of the Archbishop's Manors in Sussex', *Sussex Rec. Soc.* lvii, 1958, xxxvi–ii and *passim*; F.R.H. Du Boulay, *The Lordship of Canterbury. An Essay on Medieval Society*, London 1966, 137.

[16] Bridbury, *The English Economy*, 124.

[17] H. Jenkinson, ed., *Domesday Book Re-bound*, London 1954, 30–7; V.H. Galbraith, *The Making of Domesday Book*, Oxford 1961, 180–2, 185–8, 202–4; R.W. Finn, *The Domesday Inquest and the Making of Domesday Book*, London 1961, 189–91; S.P.J. Harvey, 'Domesday Book and Anglo-Norman Governance', *TRHS* 5th ser., xxv, 1975, 190; S.P.J. Harvey, 'Recent Domesday Studies', *EHR* xcv, 1980, 126–7; Moore, 'Post-Mortem of an Invasion', 69–70; J.C. Holt, '1086', in J.C. Holt, ed., *Domesday Studies*, Woodbridge 1987, 43–7. The deadline for completing *DB* cannot have been 1 August 1086 as Sir James Holt thought: we now know work was still in progress 'well into 1088' and possibly later (C.P. Lewis, 'The Earldom of Surrey and the Date of Domesday Book', *Historical Research* lxiii, 1990, 329–36; D. Bates, 'Two Ramsey Abbey Writs and the Domesday Survey', *Historical Research* lxiii, 1990, 337–9).

[18] *DB, Glos.*, fo. 164b, *1*, 63. References to Domesday Book (*DB*) are to the Phillimore series, edited by John Morris, because this is the only readily available edition permitting precise reference to individual entries. A county abbreviation is followed by the folio number and column letter, using Vinogradoff's system, a chapter number (italicised) and the entry number. Some of John Morris'

For whatever reason, there was 'no return' from Hankham (Sussex),[19] and numerous similar examples could be cited; the omissions include major honorial centres such as Tonbridge (Kent), whilst at Battle (Sussex), as the late and much missed Cecily Clark showed, a thriving town had grown up outside the abbey gate by the early 1100s: it is difficult to believe that there were no townsmen twenty years earlier.[20]

Even where manorial entries were submitted, the relevant information was not always to hand and blank spaces had to be left which never were filled-in, for example for the number of villagers to be added, as at Billingborough (Lincs.) and at Leckhampsted (Bucks.).[21] Groups of men or their possessions are often mentioned *en passant* but not enumerated, such as the 'sokemen's land' at Wye (Kent), where the sokemen themselves do not occur, or the unnumbered 'foresters' mentioned under Wallop but nowhere else in mainland Hampshire. At Newport Pagnell (Bucks.) demographic uncertainty reigns supreme: 'the burgesses', number not given, 'have 6½ ploughs of the other men', also unnumbered, 'who work outside the 5 hides' of the manor, who may, or may not, be identical with 'the men who live in the woodland', again unnumbered.[22] In most counties there were manors, not described as 'waste', usually with ploughs or other resources mentioned, usually also with a value stated, but nevertheless apparently unpopulated.[23] In those counties affected by the 'harrying of the north', 'waste' vills are plentiful and the resulting dislocation sufficiently explains why some other entries lack details of population.[24] As we shall see, there are also some problems in the recording of urban populations, but what is less easy to explain is the absence of any recorded people in the three great Cheshire salt-making centres of Nantwich, Northwich and

more otiose translations, notably 'man-at-arms' for *miles*, instead of 'knight', lordship' for *dominium*, instead of 'demesne', and 'freeman' for *sochemannus*, instead of 'sokeman', have been changed. All references are to the 'Exchequer' or 'Great' Domesday (vol. I) unless *DB* is followed by *II*.

[19] *DB, Sussex*, fo. 22b, *10*, 82.

[20] H.C. Darby, E.M.J. Campbell, *Domesday Geography of South-East England*, Cambridge 1962 [hereafter *DGSEE*], 417–18, 435, 492, 514. For Battle, see C. Clark, 'Battle c.1110: An Anthroponymist looks at an Anglo-Norman New Town', *ANS* ii, 1980, 21–41, 168–72, repr. in P. Jackson, ed., *Words, Names and History*, Cambridge 1995, 221–40, and E. Searle, ' "Inter Amicos": The Abbey, Town and Early Charters of Battle', *ANS* xiii, 1991, 1–14.

[21] *DB, Lincs.*, fo. 348a, *12*, 55; *DB, Bucks.*, fo. 149d, *21*, 7.

[22] *DB, Kent*, fo. 11d, *6*, 1; *DB, Hants*, fo. 38d, *1*, 23; *DB, Bucks.*, fo. 148d, *17*, 17. For other examples of such omissions, see *DB, Middx*, fo. 127c, *3*, 12, fo. 128b, *4*, 1; *DB, Herts.*, fo. 138c, *26*, 1; *DB, Bucks.*, fo. 152b, *45*, 1; *DB, Oxon.*, fo. 155d, 7, 16, fo. 156b, *7*, 41; *DB, Glos.*, fo. 163a, *1*, 15, fo. 164d, *3*, 4, fo. 165a, *4*, 1, fo. 166d, *31*, 7, fo. 168c, *52*, 3; *DB, Worcs.*, fo. 174c, *8*, 8; *DB, Herefs.*, fo. 180d–1a, *1*, 48–9, fo. 182a, *2*, 27, fo. 184c, *10*, 44; *DB, Cambs.*, fo. 199c, *29*, 1; *DB, Hunts.*, fo. 203c, *1*, 3; *DB, Beds.*, fo. 209d, *2*, 9, fo. 210b, *4*, 1; *DB, Nhants.*, fo. 228a, *55*, 5; *DB, Leics.*, fo. 234b, *17*, 7–8; *DB, II, Norfolk*, fo. 139a, *1*, 221; *DB, II, Suffolk*, fo. 359b, *14*, 26, fo. 365b, *14*, 79.

[23] *DGSEE*, 21–2, 66, 116, 156, 206, 243, 307, 310, 377–8, 435, 492, 516; H.C. Darby, R.W. Finn, *Domesday Geography of South-West England*, Cambridge 1967 [hereafter *DGSWE*], 9, 23, 89–91, 161–2, 246, 317; H.C. Darby, I.B. Terrett, *Domesday Geography of Midland England*, Cambridge 1954 [hereafter *DGME*], 8, 17, 62, 74, 115–16, 125, 162, 169, 185, 224, 234, 286, 332, 393; H.C. Darby, *Domesday Geography of Eastern England*, Cambridge 1952 [hereafter *DGEE*], 28, 50, 291, 328; H.C. Darby, I.S. Maxwell, *Domesday Geography of Northern England*, Cambridge 1962 [hereafter *DGNE*], 251.

[24] *DGNE*, 9–11, 33, 36, 59–71, 93–6, 114–16, 118, 139–50, 192–4, 212–21, 265–7, 296–9, 313–19, 343, 346, 365–76, 405–7, 412–13.

Middlewich: these had been derelict early in the 1070s, but they were all producing income in 1086.[25]

It is therefore clear that the recorded population in *DB* is a minimum count even of heads of households, and that any claims for its complete statistical accuracy are utterly unjustified. But, 'then and now', to use *DB*'s own terminology, the fault lies in our own expectations of statistical precision. Even modern British censuses, regularly collected and tabulated by an experienced and highly professional civil service after much previous preparation, have been demonstrated to be inaccurate by up to 2 – 3 per cent after being rechecked by sample surveys.[26] We should be grateful that the royal and baronial officials of 1086 achieved so much in such a short time without any previous experience to guide them: instead of carping about their deficiencies, we should devote ourselves to remedying them. For it is inherently unlikely that any of the groups of men recorded without numbers were of large size: at most one or two dozen heads of household each in the majority of cases, one would guess, given the small size of most rural settlements in Anglo-Norman England. With regard to those settlements which were apparently economically active but had no recorded population, in most instances (if they were not worked by men from adjacent vills) they were probably of small size, to judge from the recorded resources and values, and probably allowing no more than ten heads of household for each place would suffice. An additional few hundred heads of household per county would probably compensate for these textual deficiencies. In short, although our source material is not flawless – what historical source is flawless? – this does not mean that we should abandon all attempts to use it with due care and caution.

What specific questions do we wish to answer and what specific problems need to be considered in trying to answer these questions? Obviously we want to know the total size of the population of England in 1086, its geographical distribution between counties and between town and countryside, and its social distribution between different groups. We would also want to know if the population was rising or falling before and after 1086. (This last question, however, I shall not attempt to answer now: it seems to me to be quite premature to consider the population-level *before* and *after* 1086 until we have first established with reasonable certitude the level of population *in* 1086.) To answer any of these questions, we need first to resolve some preliminary crucial issues. The first, obviously, is the basic accuracy of the population figures, indeed all the figures, presented to us in *DB* and its 'satellites'. This crucial question has been ignored by previous scholars, as can be seen from David Bates' *Bibliography*.[27] Although *DB* has long been used as a source of statistics, notably by Maitland, Baring and Darby, the validity of its statistics has not been seriously considered, and even McDonald and Snooks have given little thought to its demographic figures.[28] The second question is what

[25] *DGNE*, 346–7; *DB, Ches.*, fos 268a–b, *S*, 1–3.

[26] T.H. Hollingsworth, *Historical Demography*, London 1969, 32.

[27] D. Bates, *A Bibliography of Domesday Book*, Woodbridge 1985, esp. 1–34. Professor Bates has confirmed in conversation that he knows of no more recent work dealing with either copying error or the accuracy of *DB* statistics.

[28] F.W. Maitland, *Domesday Book and Beyond*, Cambridge 1897; F.H. Baring, *Domesday Tables for the Counties of Surrey, Berkshire, Middlesex, Hertford, Buckingham and Bedford and the New Forest*, London 1909; *DGEE*; *DGME*; *DGNE*; *DGSWE*; H.C. Darby, *Domesday England*, Cambridge 1977, repr. 1979, 1986. Galbraith remarked that 'sooner or later the Domesday geographers

sections of the 1086 population were partly omitted or totally excluded from *DB*, but which we need to add to our calculations based on the recorded figures. Third, there is the 'multiplier problem', that is, the factor or factors needed to convert figures of heads of household (which it is generally agreed most of the *DB* figures were) into estimates of total population. Let us first look at these problems.

It is generally accepted that none of the figures in *DB* can be taken for granted, given the high probability of copying errors involved in using roman numerals, the use of which even Round admitted was 'almost fatal to accuracy'.[29] But given the uniqueness of *DB*, the possibility of checking the bulk of these figures is slim. Three approaches, two major and one minor, can be envisaged. The first is to compare numerical data in *DB* with their proximate source in the preceding stage of returns, *Exon DB* for circuit II, the *Inquisitio Comitatus Cantabrigiensis* (*ICC*) for Cambridgeshire, *IE* for the Ely Abbey estates in Cambridgeshire, Essex, Hertfordshire, Huntingdonshire, Norfolk and Suffolk. Whilst such a comparison would not facilitate any decision about the degree of accuracy of the original data in *DB*, it would enable us to calculate the rate of error in copying between different stages in the compilation of *DB*. The second method is to compare the numerical data in *DB* with those given in the monastic estate-surveys of the first half of the twelfth century, since the latter can be assumed to be accurate (apart from copying errors). Some historians may want to argue that the landholders and their officials who supplied most of the detailed information, and in particular most of the numerical data, for the Domesday survey perhaps 'massaged' the data in order to mislead the king and his officials about their true wealth and resources. But there would be no point at all in the compilers of the ecclesiastical estate-surveys including data that was not as accurate as possible, since inaccuracy would invalidate the very purpose for which the surveys were being made, namely the efficient running of the estates. The third approach to checking the accuracy of the data in *DB* would involve the reconstruction of hundreds and wapentakes and their constituent vills to ascertain if the tax assessments conformed to the 'five-hide' or 'six carucate' rules respectively. Although Round believed he had established these rules, and his work has been supported more recently,[30] doubt has also been cast on their reality;[31] it thus seems unsafe to assume that these rules were so well established that we can use them to check for scribal errors in the tax assessments themselves. We are, therefore, thrown back on the first two approaches.

Although Round himself made much comparative use of *ICC* and *IE*, this was mainly to establish the meaning of *DB*'s formulae and the method of compilation of *DB* rather than to test the accuracy of the copying of data, and his use of both

---

will have to face the question of the validity of their statistics.' (Galbraith, *The Making of Domesday Book*, 222.) For McDonald and Snooks, see above, n. 12.

[29] J.H. Round, *Feudal England*, London 1895, 20.

[30] Round, *Feudal England*, 44–98; R.A. Leaver, 'Five Hides in Ten Counties', *Econ. Hist. Rev.* 2nd ser., 41, 1988, 525–42. The valuable works of Cyril Hart assume the existence of units of five hides or six carucates as much as proving their existence. (C.R. Hart, 'The Hidation of Huntingdonshire', *Proc. Cambridge Antiq. Soc.* lxi, 1968, 55–66; *The Hidation of Northamptonshire*, Leicester 1970; *The Hidation of Cambridgeshire*, Leicester 1974; *The Danelaw*, London 1992, chs. 11–12).

[31] Maitland. *Domesday Book and Beyond*, 463–6, argued that the hide was related to value; this point is also supported by McDonald and Snooks, *Domesday Economy: a New Approach to Anglo-Norman History*, ch. 4.

Table 1. Comparison of population figures in *DB* and *IE*

Number of manors	Total number of tenants in *DB*	Total number of tenants in *IE*	Change in number of tenants
DB, I			
Cambridgeshire			
86	1266	1266	0 (0%)
Hertfordshire			
26	256	244	−12 (−4.9%)
Huntingdonshire			
5	140	155	15 (+9.7%)
(excluding slaves in *IE*)			
5	140	140	140 (0%)
DB, II			
Essex			
16	416	394	−22 (−5.6%)
Norfolk			
55	972	992	20 (+2.0%)
Suffolk			
218	1740	1705	−35 (−2.1%)
All counties in *IE*			
406	4790	4756	−34 (−0.7%)

these 'satellites' was unsystematic.[32] Notoriously also, he ignored *Exon DB*, dismissing it in an infamous one-line footnote, 'It will be observed that I do not touch the *Liber Exoniensis*.'[33] To be blunt, this was dishonest: *Exon DB* was utterly fatal to most of his hypotheses. No systematic and thorough comparison of the statistical data of *DB* with the figures in any of the 'satellite' texts has ever been made, doubtless because of the labour involved, but some partial comparisons have been made in the introductions to the *Victoria County History* volumes dealing with *DB*, in the notes in the Phillimore editions for the relevant counties, and in the *Domesday Geography* volumes for eastern and south-eastern England.[34] The general,

[32] Round, *Feudal England*, 3–146.
[33] Round, *Feudal England*, 146, n. 265.
[34] *ICC* and *IE*: *DGEE*, 99–100, 114, 153–4, 164, 171, 209, 264–6, 278–9, 291, 315, 319, 329–31; *DGSWE*, 48, 55, 66; *VCH Cambridgeshire* i, 335, 337–8; *VCH Hertfordshire* i, 263–5; *VCH Norfolk* ii, 4; *VCH Suffolk* i, 357, 394; A. Rumble, ed., *Domesday Book: Cambridgeshire*, Chichester 1981, 'The Cambridgeshire Inquiry', 'The Ely Inquiry', Notes; J. Morris, ed., *Domesday Book: Hertfordshire*, Chichester 1976, Appendix and Notes; J. Morris, ed., *Domesday Book: Huntingdonshire*, Chichester 1975, Appendix. *Exon DB*: *DGSWE*, esp. Appendix 1; *VCH Cornwall* ii, pt.8, 45–6; *VCH Devon* i, 375–80; *VCH Dorset* iii, 1–5; *VCH Somerset* i, 383–5; C. Thorn, F. Thorn, eds, *Domesday Book: Cornwall*, Chichester 1979, 'The Exeter Domesday', Notes; C. Thorn, F. Thorn, eds, *Domesday Book: Devon*, Chichester, 2 vols, 1985, 'The Exeter Domesday', Notes; C. Thorn, F. Thorn, eds, *Domesday Book: Dorset*, Chichester 1983, 'The Exeter Domesday', Notes; C. Thorn, F. Thorn, eds, *Domesday Book: Wiltshire*, Chichester 1979, 'The Exeter Domesday', Notes.

subjective, impression given by previous writers is that the discrepancies were minor, but this belief has not been verified objectively or quantified. My present analysis is confined to a comparison of the *DB* population-figures for 1086 with those in *IE* for the six counties where Ely Abbey had estates, and in *The Feudal Book of Abbot Baldwin* for the estates of the abbey of Bury St Edmunds mainly in Norfolk and Suffolk. Ideally, we should also compare the population-figures in *DB* with those in *ICC* (for Cambridgeshire) and *Exon DB* for the south-western counties, but the time necessary for such a laborious comparison has so far precluded its accomplishment.

The results of my detailed analysis of the population-figures in *DB* and *IE* are summarised on a county basis in Table 1. (In all the Tables, 'half-freemen' and 'half-villagers' have been counted as single individuals, since the 'half' refers simply to the shared jurisdiction over them: one recalls Maitland's words on the unreality of a *semi-bos*: 'not in any monstrous birth do we find the explanation ...').[35] It is perhaps also worth stating that the figures relate not just to those estates still held by Ely Abbey in 1086 but also to the large number of estates which had been held by the abbey in 1066 but were subsequently stolen by Norman lords. Recognition of this fact throws some additional light on the 'making of Domesday Book'. How did the Ely officials obtain the detailed information for 1086 for those estates which were no longer held by the abbey? Hardly either from the stewards of the current lords or from their own inspection of the lost estates (which these new lords would certainly have resisted as prejudicial to their own tenure). Since the Ely officials clearly did have access to detailed information on the lost estates, it seems to follow that this information had been made publicly available, 'laid on the table' to use a modern Parliamentary phrase, presumably at county courts, as part of the process of checking the data by the jurors who are so carefully listed in *ICC* and *IE*.[36] Galbraith, in reacting justifiably against Round's excessive reliance on the *ICC* and *IE*, against his belief in the 'original returns' as purely a series of hundred rolls, and against his rejection of *Exon DB*, as a consequence underplayed the importance of the oral testimony of the hundredal jurors in validating or modifying the written information submitted by the lords and their officials.

Let us now return to studying the results summarised in Table 1. Obviously, in considering aggregative totals, there is the possibility of small errors in both sets of data cancelling each other: in Cambridgeshire, for instance, the overall total number of tenants in *DB* and *IE* are the same, but there are a few discrepancies within individual manors. Still, these results demonstrate the care taken by the scribes during the Domesday inquest to copy figures accurately, in spite of the undoubted pressure of time under which they were working. The highest degree of copying-error (+9.8 per cent in Huntingdonshire) is exceptional because of the omission of slaves from the main section of *IE* and from the relevant *DB* folios (the data on slaves on the Huntingdonshire manors appear only in the 'Breviate' of *IE*). If we ignore these slaves, Huntingdonshire, like its neighbour Cambridgeshire, appears almost free from scribal error. Another way of assessing the data-set is to consider the number of manors where there are no discrepancies between *DB* and *IE*. Of the 406 manors in Table 1, 383 appear in both *DB* and *IE*: of those 383, 304

[35] Maitland, *Domesday Book and Beyond*, 142.
[36] Lewis, 'The Domesday Jurors', 35–44.

(79 per cent) have identical figures in the two sources, and in a further 29 manors (8 per cent) the difference is no greater than plus or minus 2. At county level, the range of error runs from plus or minus 2.1 per cent to minus 5.6 per cent, and the overall level of error is 0.7 per cent. Moreover, these levels of error must be considered as maxima, not minima, since the surviving texts of the *ICC* and *IE* are themselves copies of the originals made in the second half of the twelfth century, and it is entirely possible that some errors may have crept in during this stage of copying. Even if we allow for three or four intermediate stages of recopying and summarisation during the Domesday inquest – and, as Sally Harvey remarked, the speed at which the inquest was conducted rules out further stages in the time available[37] – this results in a degree of copying-error of between 2.1 and 2.8 per cent, error of the same order of magnitude as that found in modern British censuses!

A second estimation of copying-error can be made from the *Feudal Book of Abbot Baldwin* which covers some of the area covered by *IE*. The *Feudal Book* was apparently made between King William's death in September 1087 and Abbot Baldwin's death in January 1098, though Reginald Lennard considered that it was probably made after Abbot Baldwin's death and before that of Abbot Ailbold in 1119.[38] The survey, which was admirably edited by the late David Douglas, covers the manors of the abbey of Bury St Edmunds, chiefly in Norfolk and Suffolk, and the chief text is again a late twelfth-century copy: the prologue to the first section explicitly dates it to the period 1086–87,

> at the time when, by King William's order, the survey of all England was made . . . The saint and his men also held these [lands] on the day when the same king who ordered [the survey] was alive and dead.

The second section of the *Feudal Book* is similarly headed by a clear indication of date: 'These are the lands of the enfeoffed men of St Edmund and of Abbot Baldwin.'[39] Whilst Lennard fully accepted that the first two sections of the 'Feudal Book' were based on Domesday material, he nevertheless asserted that 'there is really no evidence that even the first two sections were compiled by or for Abbot Baldwin',[40] but the statements I have just quoted from the MS seem to me decisive. (It is worthwhile mentioning that the second part of the *Feudal Book* is not simply a re-arrangement of the first part, but is an independent compilation from the 'original returns', since it contains data not in the first part nor in *DB, II*. Thus for Preston and Wattisfield (Suffolk), where *DB, II* simply states the existence of 'others', the second part supplies full details of these people.[41]) The third part of the *Feudal Book* has no internal dating, but Douglas, after comparing its detailed figures, argued strongly that 'in this section . . . we are dealing with the names, estates, and rents of the Domesday freemen and sokemen.'[42] This I doubt, since, like Lennard, I can see no close correlation between the population-figures in *DB*,

---

[37] S. Harvey, 'Recent Domesday Studies', *EHR* xcv, 1980, 127.

[38] R. Lennard, *Rural England, 1086–1135*, Oxford 1959, 359.

[39] D.C. Douglas, ed., *Feudal Documents from the Abbey of Bury St Edmunds*, Oxford 1932, xx, xlvi (date of MS), xlvii, 3 (prologue to section 1), l, 15 (prologue to section 2), 3–44.

[40] Lennard, *Rural England, 1086–1135*, 359 and n. 1.

[41] *DB, Suffolk*, fo. 359b, *14*, 26 (Preston); fo. 365b, *14*, 79 (Wattisfield); Douglas, ed., *Feudal Documents*, 19–20.

[42] Douglas, ed., *Feudal Documents*, lix–x, lxxv.

II and the third section of the *Feudal Book*, which is up to a generation later than 1086.[43] Opinions about the reliability of the *Feudal Book* vary: Douglas was much impressed both by its similar terminology to that of *DB* and by the correspondence between its figures and those of *DB, II*, but Alex Rumble has observed 'frequent discrepancies between the statistics given in [the] F[eudal] B[ook] and in L[ittle] D[omesday] B[ook]'.[44] Nevertheless, it seems clear that the first two sections of the *Feudal Book* were composed in William Rufus's reign, and they are a genuine Domesday 'satellite'. These two sections cannot be later copies from *DB, II* since they are not in the same hundredal order as *DB, II* and, crucially, include details not in *DB, II*, in two cases rectifying the latter's admitted deficiencies. My own analysis of the discrepancies between *DB, II* and the *Feudal Book*, limited to the demographic statistics, is summarised in Table 2.

Table 2. Comparison of population figures in *DB* and the *Feudal Book of Abbot Baldwin*, Part I

Number of manors	Total number of tenants in *DB, II*	Total number of tenants in *Feudal Book*	Change in number of tenants
All manors with data in both *DB, II* and *Feudal Book*			
194	3824	3595	−229 (−6.0%)
Manors excluding those with slaves omitted			
143	2622	2517	−105 (−4.0%)

In 1086 the abbey of Bury St Edmunds held 220 manors in Essex, Norfolk and Suffolk, but 26 of these manors do not have any corresponding entries in the *Feudal Book*. For the remaining 194 manors there is a difference of 6 per cent between the total numbers of tenants in the two sources. But this comparison is invalid, since the first part of the *Feudal Book* omits the slaves recorded in *DB, II*, for reasons now unknown. Perhaps it was unclear to Abbot Baldwin whether slaves should be included: after all, his brother abbot of Ely, like all other landholders in the nearby county of Huntingdonshire, did not return their slaves for manors in that county. More probably, since the first two parts of the *Feudal Book* could have been updated at any time between 1087 and late 1097, Abbot Baldwin may have abolished slavery on the abbey estates as other lords were doing at the time.[45] If we omit the 47 manors where the different totals resulted from slaves being left out, and a further four manors where the differences were caused by the omission of undertenants of freemen or sokemen in the *Feudal Book*, the overall discrepancy falls to 4 per cent. Of these 143 manors, 99 (69 per cent) had the same number of tenants in the two sources, and the discrepancies in the remaining manors are not

[43] Lennard, *Rural England, 1086–1135*, 359.
[44] Douglas, ed., *Feudal Documents*, lix–x, lxv–xx; A. Rumble, ed., *Domesday Book: Suffolk*, Chichester 1986, Appendix II.
[45] J.S. Moore, 'Anglo-Norman Slavery', *ANS* xi, 1989, 219–20; D.A.E. Pelteret, *Slavery in Early Medieval England from the reign of Alfred until the Twelfth Century*, Woodbridge 1995, 185–240, 251–9.

Table 3. Comparison of *DB* Evesham surveys

Evesham J: A. Hidage and demesne ploughs

DB Folio	Chapter number	Entry number	Manor	Hides	Demesne ploughs	Evesham survey	Hides	Demesne ploughs
Worcestershire								
175d	10	6	Wickhamford	3	4	J 1	8	4
			Bretforton	6	0	J 1	0	0
175d	10	7	Badsey	6.5	2	J 2	5.5	3
175d	10	5	Aldington	1	2	J 3	1.5	3
175d	10	12	Bengeworth	4	2	J 4	4	2
175d	10	11	Hampton	5	3	J 5	5	4
175d	10	5	Offenham	7	3	J 6	16	4
175d	10	8	Littleton	7	2	J 7	6	3
175d	10	9	Church Honeybourne	2.5	4	J 8	3	3
175d	10	14	Atch Lench	4.5	1	J 9	3.5	1
175d	10	16	Church Lench	4	2	J 10	4	N/A
175c	10	3	Lenchwick, Norton	8	5	J 11	10	5
Northamptonshire								
222c	11	6	Badby	4	4	J 12	4	5
Totals				62.5	34		66.5	32+?

Evesham J: B. Population

Manor	DB: Free-men	Vill-agers	Small-holders	Slaves	Total	EvJ: Free-men	Vill-agers/ rustics	Small-holders	Slaves/ oxmen	Total
Worcestershire (*DB*, fos 175c–d, *10*, 5–9, 11–12, 14; *EvJ*, 1–9)										
Wickhamford	0	0	7	0	7	0	0	0	0 }	35
Bretforton	0	16	0	0	16	0	20	15	0 }	
Badsey	0	12	0	4	16	0	9	5	6	20
Aldington	0	0	5	4	9	0	0	2	6	8
Bengeworth	0	5	2	6	13	0	0	6	4	10
Hampton	1	15	4	8	28	2	13	6	8	29
Offenham	4	25	20	0	49	7	7	14	8	43
Littleton	1	15	2	3	21	0	12	5	6	23
Church Honeybourne	0	11	4	4	19	0	10	2	6	18
Atch Lench	0	3	4	2	9	0	5	0	2	7

Manor	DB: Free-men	Vill-agers	Small-holders	Slaves	Total	EvJ: Free-men	Vill-agers/ rustics	Small-holders	Slaves/ oxmen	Total
Northamptonshire (*DB*, fo. 222c, *11*; *EvJ* 12)										
Badby	0	12	8	8	28	0	21	11	10	42
Totals	6	114	56	39	215	9	104	66	56	235
Worcestershire (not comparable)										
Church Lench	0	2	4	2	10	N/A	N/A	N/A	N/A	N/A
Lenchwick, Norton	1	13	11	10	35	N/A	N/A	N/A	10	10

Evesham L: A. Hidage and demesne ploughs

Chapter Folio number	DB Entry number	Manor	Hides	Demesne ploughs	Evesham survey	Hides	Demesne ploughs
Gloucestershire							
164a-b 1	59	Beckford	11	3	L ⎱	16	10
164b 1	60	Ashton under Hill	8	4	L ⎰		

Evesham L: B. Population

Manor	DB: Free-men	Vill-agers	Small-holders	Slaves	Total	EvL: Free-men	Vill-agers/ rustics	Small-holders	Slaves/ oxmen	Total
Beckford	0	34	17	12	63	7	46	15	5	73
Ashton under Hill	0	10	4	8	22	N/A	N/A	N/A	N/A	N/A

large, indeed there are only three manors where the difference exceeds plus or minus 10. The overall copying error in the *Feudal Book* thus falls within the range indicated by the previous analysis of *IE*, again suggesting a remarkable degree of care on the part of the scribes responsible.

With regard to the second question posed earlier, even if there were very few scribal errors in the copying of numbers of people in the compilation of *DB*, as we have just seen, it does not follow that the original figures were accurate. Whether they were accurate can only be determined by a comparison of *DB* with the ecclesiastical estate-surveys made after 1086 and before the 1130s. Because these form a very small sample for comparison, I have studied all the available data in the surveys, not just the population-figures. Given that there will inevitably be changes in village and manorial populations in any period of time, it is unrealistic to expect exact equivalence between the population-figures in *DB* and later surveys, indeed, exact equivalence would arouse the suspicion that the later source

Table 4. Comparison of *DB* and the Caen Survey A

A. Demesne ploughs

DB:					*Caen A*:	
Folio number	Chapter number	Entry	Manor	Demesne ploughs	Demesne ploughs	Charters and Custumals, page
DB, II						
Essex						
21b	15	1	Felsted	3	7	33–4
Norfolk						
140a	1	231	Horstead	2	2	36
DB, I						
Dorset						
79a	21	1	Tarrant Launceston	2	0	35
Hertfordshire						
132d	1	9	Temple Dinsley	3	3	37
Gloucestershire						
166c	23	1	Pinbury	3	3	34–5
166c	23	2	Minchin-hampton	5	5	35–6
163d	1	49	Avening	8	8	37–8
Totals				26	28	

B. Population

	DB:					*Caen A:*				
Manor	Free-men/soke-men	Vill-agers	Small-holders	Slaves	Total	Free-men/soke-men	Vill-agers	Small-holders	Slaves	Total
Essex										
Felsted	4	20	35	11	70	5	26	39	11	81
Norfolk										
Horstead	0	16	9	4	29	4	23	8	1	36
Dorset										
Tarrant Launceston	0	9	1	14	24	0	9	15	0	24

Manor	DB: Free-men/ soke-men	Vill-agers	Small-holders	Slaves	Total	Caen A: Free-men/ soke-men	Vill-agers	Small-holders	Slaves	Total
Hertfordshire										
Temple										
Dinsley	1	19	14	6	40	0	14	11	5	30
Gloucestershire										
Pinbury	0	8	1	9	18	0	8	4	6	18
Minchin-										
hampton	0	33	10	10	53	6	28	11	9	54
Avening	0	24	5	30	59	3	25	9	[16]	53
Totals	5	129	75	84	293	18	133	97	48	296

may be copying *DB* or a local 'satellite'. We cannot, therefore, directly assess the accuracy of the demographic data of *DB*, but if the order of magnitude of the later figures is similar to that of the earlier, we may then reasonably accept that the *DB* figures were as accurate as can be expected, allowing for copying errors.

We can start with two Evesham documents recently brought to light by Dr Howard Clarke, whose edition in the *Worcestershire Historical Society* series is eagerly awaited. In chronological order these are Evesham J, a survey of 13 manors of Evesham Abbey in Northamptonshire and Worcestershire dateable to c.1104, and Evesham L, a survey of two Gloucestershire manors of Evesham abbey c.1126.[46] Both these Evesham documents provide details of hidage [demesne] ploughs and population which are compared with *DB* in Table 3. Of the 13 manors in Evesham J, two (Church Lench and Lenchwick with Norton) have no details of population c.1104; the remaining data show a rough equivalence of hides and demesne ploughs, and a small overall increase in total population of 9.3 per cent; the two manors in Evesham L, by contrast, appear to reveal a drop in population of 19 per cent. But it is clear that the population has increased since an earlier, unspecified, 'said time', when there were 32 villagers and 9 smallholders, figures much more comparable with Beckford alone in *DB*. If we compare the Evesham L figures with the *DB* figures just for Beckford, the change in population becomes a rise of 15.9 per cent. A rise of 9.3 per cent between 1086 and c.1104 (Evesham J) and the probable rise of 15.9 per cent by c.1126 (Evesham L) both suggest that the *DB* figures for all these manors are indeed plausible. The same conclusion can be drawn from the records for the English estates of Holy Trinity, Caen (Table 4), on which there is virtually no overall change between the manorial populations in 1086 and in Survey A of c.1113, and where also the distribution between the major groups of peasantry appears to be roughly the same. My comparison for the Caen estates has excluded the hidage: some assessments have been reduced, whilst others are missing. Nevertheless, apart from Avening (Glos.)

---

[46] BL Cotton MS Vespasian B XXIV, fos 49v, 53r (Evesham J), 57v (Evesham L). Evesham Q, a survey of Droitwich (Worcs.) also c.1126 (BL Harleian MS 3763, fo. 82r), is a hidage schedule with no other relevant details for this analysis and has not been further considered.

where Survey A appears to be incomplete, hence the addition of 16 oxmen to the figures stated in the MS, the manors seem to be identical units and therefore afford a fair basis for comparison.[47]

Finally, the evidence of the *Black Book of Peterborough*, dating from the royal seizure of the abbey lands following the death of Abbot John de Séez in 1125, shows an overall increase of 33 per cent in manorial population in the forty years since the Domesday inquest (see Table 5).[48]

Although the numbers of the groups of rural society in 1125 are still roughly in proportion to those of 1086, the pressure of growing numbers of men on the available land was leading to an extension of the cultivated area both by assarting of woodland and drainage of fens where feasible but also to the subdivision of standard villagers' tenements and the creation of a new group of 'half-villagers'.[49] By the 1130s, therefore, comparison with monastic surveys becomes less useful as a means of determining the accuracy of *DB* statistics, because continued population-growth is rendering a comparison with conditions in 1086 increasingly problematic. Nevertheless, on the basis of all the estate-surveys so far considered, the numbers of manorial tenants given in *DB* do fit well with those of the later surveys, and in general they seem as accurate as we can now reasonably expect. But there are at least two known exceptions to this conclusion.

The first, which I owe entirely to Ann Williams, comprises the Shaftesbury Abbey estate-surveys of c.1130 in BL Harley MS 61: whilst the figures in these surveys for the villagers and lesser groups of dependent peasants are comparable with those in *DB*, it is abundantly clear that *DB* has omitted some knights and free peasants who are recorded in the abbey's survey. But the proportion of omissions to the total tenantry of c.1130 is not high: 8 per cent in Wiltshire, 3 per cent in Dorset, 5 per cent in both counties combined. The second, even more problematic case, is the Burton Abbey surveys which have long been known to record rent-payers not seemingly represented in *DB*.[50] This opinion, however, has not gone uncriticised. Dr Bridbury has argued that the *DB* valuations of the Burton Abbey manors 'correlated very closely to the aggregate of cash payments made by the tenants of each of these manors' in Survey B of c.1115. If that were so, then the *censarii* must have been present in 1086, even though not recorded in *DB*.[51] But Bridbury's belief is hardly borne out by any high correlation in his own figures. Some *DB* valuations are close to the total rent-receipts of c.1115 (e.g. Abbot's Bromley, Darlaston, Leigh and Wetmore), some are higher than the later rentals (e.g. Branston, Mickleover) and some are lower (e.g. Stretton). The total of *DB* values is £34 7s, the total

[47] M. Chibnall, ed., *Charters and Custumals of the Abbey of Holy Trinity, Caen*, Oxford 1982, 33–8.

[48] T. Stapleton, ed., 'Chronicon Petroburgense', *Camden Soc.*, os xlvii, 1849, 157–66.

[49] The 'half-villagers' appear in Stapleton, ed., *Chronicon Petroburgense*, 158–9, 160–6. For drainage of the Fens and assarting in the E. Midlands region, see H.C. Darby, *The Medieval Fenland*, Cambridge 1940, 43–8, 79–80, 141–2; E. Miller, *The Abbey and Bishopric of Ely*, Cambridge 1951, 95–9, 120–1, 147; J.A. Raftis, *The Estates of Ramsey Abbey*, Toronto 1957, 40, 71–5, 87–9, 105; H.E. Hallam, ed., *Agrarian History of England and Wales, ii: 1042–1350*, Cambridge 1988, 139–74, 189–202, 497–507.

[50] F.H. Baring, 'Domesday Book and the Burton Cartulary', *EHR* xi, 1896, 98–102; J.H. Round, 'The Burton Abbey Surveys', *EHR* xx, 1905, 275–89; J.F.R. Walmsley, 'The *Censarii* of Burton Abbey and the Domesday Population', *N. Staffs. Journ. of Field Studies* viii, 1968, 73–80.

[51] Bridbury, *The English Economy*, 115.

rents of *censarii* is £27 1s, a difference of nearly 23 per cent.[52] My own reservations relate rather to the nature of Staffordshire and Derbyshire, counties with low population-densities (especially Derbyshire and the north of Staffordshire where most of the Burton Abbey estates lay) in which much 'waste' was recorded in 1086.[53] I regard the Burton Abbey *censarii* as representing recolonization after 1086, as in Yorkshire and other parts of northern England: Maitland, Vinogradoff and Bridgman (the local editor of the Burton Abbey surveys) all shared my opinion about this.[54] A different and much more likely omission, to judge from the evidence of the Cheshire and Shropshire folios of *DB*, are under-tenants and demesne lessees, the 'missing third level', as they have been christened. Accepting that such people were omitted, what allowance can be made for them? There can hardly have been more than one or two such people on each manor, if that, and since there were about 13,000 manors recorded in *DB*, at most an additional 25,000 heads, or about 120,000 people in all, need to be included in our final summary.

Allowance also needs to be made for the population of some towns. Although the first edition of the Domesday questionnaire made no mention of burgesses, this omission was clearly rectified in a subsequent version at a late stage in the Domesday inquest, since most county towns and major boroughs were added at the beginning of each county section, and blank folios (*DB*, fos 37r, 125v, 126r) were left at the beginning of the Hampshire and Middlesex gatherings for the addition of entries for Winchester and London respectively which were never provided. The existence of the *Winton Domesday*, containing surveys of the royal land in Winchester c.1057 and c.1110, and a full survey of the city c.1148, enables us to estimate its Domesday population as about 5,500.[55] London's population is more controversial: the figure of 52,000 in 1196 given by one chronicler is clearly exaggerated, but another contemporary figure of 40,000 in 1199 may not be far off the mark.[56] For modern estimates of the medieval population of London have been rising, and it probably had 20,000 inhabitants in 1086.[57] Though there was only a

---

[52] Bridbury, *The English Economy*, 127.

[53] *DGNE*, 283–4, 297–301, 313–19; *DGNE*, 169, 184–9, 198–202.

[54] T.A.M. Bishop, 'The Norman Settlement of Yorkshire', in R.W. Hunt, W.A. Pantin, R.W. Southern, eds, *Studies in Medieval History presented to Frederick Maurice Powicke*, Oxford 1948, 6–14; W.E. Kapelle, *The Norman Conquest of the North*, London 1979, chs 6–8. Maitland, *Domesday Book and Beyond*, 363, n. 7, and P. Vinogradoff, *English Society in the Eleventh Century*, Oxford 1908, 462–3, as well as the local editor of the surveys (C.G.O. Bridgman, 'The Burton Abbey Twelfth-Century Surveys', *Staffordshire Historical Collections* ns, 1916, 268) have also argued for new settlement after 1086.

[55] F. Barlow, M. Biddle, O. Von Feilitzen, D.J. Keene, eds, *Winchester in the Early Middle Ages*, London 1976, 360, 467–9.

[56] *Chronicles of the Reigns of Stephen, Henry II and Richard I*, ed. R. Howlett, RS lxxxii, 1885, ii, 468; G.A. Williams, *From Commune to Capital*, London 1963, 317, gives Peter of Blois's estimate of 120 parish churches and 40,000 people in 1199; the number of churches is near that of William FitzStephen (126) and 'could be precisely correct' (C.N.L. Brooke, G. Keir, *London, 800–1216*, London 1975, 120–1). Peter as archdeacon of London was in a good position to estimate the number of inhabitants.

[57] J.C. Russell, *British Medieval Population*, Albuquerque 1947, 285–7, estimated London's population as 17,850 (1086), 30,000 (c.1200) and 60,000 (c.1340), but the basis for the 1086 estimate is certainly faulty. J. Clark, *Saxon and Norman London*, London, 1989, 30, put the 1086 population at 10 – 15,000; Williams, *From Commune to Capital*, 19–20, 315–17, accepting a figure of 35 – 40,000 based on the 1377 Poll Tax, argued for 20,000 c.1200 and 40,000+ c.1320; Brooke and Keir, *London, 800–1216*, 70, noted estimates for the peak population c.1300 between 20,000 and 50,000;

Table 5. Comparison of *DB* and Peterborough *Black Book*

A. Hidage and demesne ploughs

	DB:					Black Book:		
Folio	Chapter number	Entry number	Manor	Hides	Demesne ploughs	Hides	Demesne ploughs	Black Bk page
Bedfordshire/Northamptonshire								
218c	Beds., 7	1	Stanwick	2.5	1	2.5		
221c	Nhants, 6	16	Stanwick	1.25	2	0.5	2	166
Huntingdonshire								
205b	8	1	Fletton	5	2	5	2	165
205b	8	2	Alwalton	5	2	5	2	160–1
Leicestershire								
231b	5	2	Great Easton	12 C	2			
231b	5	3	Great Easton	2 C	0	3	0	159–60
Lincolnshire								
345c	8	1	Fiskerton	3 C	0			
345c	8	2	Scothern	5.5 C	0	11.75 C	3	164
345c	8	3	Reepham	4.75 C	0			
345d	8	17–18	Scotter	11 C	4	11.75 C	4	164–5
344c	7	36	Gosberton	1.75C	1	3 C	0	165
Northamptonshire								
221b	6	1	Peterborough	8	5	5.75	4	?
221b	6	2	Cottingham	7	2	5.25	2	?
221b	6	3	Thorpe	2	2	2.25	2	158–9
221b	6	4	Castor	3	2	4.5	4	163–4
221b	6	6	Pilsgate	6	1	3	1	158
221b	6	7	Glinton	3	3	3	3	162–3
221b	6	8	Werrington	8.25	5	3	2	161
221b	6	10a	Oundle	6	3	4	3	158
221c	6	11	Warmington	7.5	4	7	4	160
221c	6	12	Ashton	4.5	2	3.75	2	162
221c	6	13	Tinwell	5.25	2	4.5	2	158
221c	6	15	Irthling-borough	5.25	2	[5.25]	2	166
221c	6	17	Kettering	10	1	10	4	157–8
222a	6a	25	Pytchley	5.25	2	5.5	4	161–2
222a	6a	27	Aldwincle	3	1	3	2	166
Nottinghamshire								
284b	8	1	Collingham	4 C	2	4 C	2	?
Totals				N/A	53	N/A	56	
Boroughs								
219a	B	4	Northampton	N/A	N/A	N/A	N/A	166
221b	6	1	Peterborough	N/A	N/A	5.75	N/A	161

Population

Manor	DB: Free-men/soke-men	Vill-agers	Small-holders	Slaves	Total	Black Book: Free-men/soke-men	Vill-agers/rustics	Half vill-agers	Small-holders	Oxmen	Total
Bedfordshire/Northamptonshire											
anwick	0	2	2	0	4 }	1	9	13	2	3	28
anwick	0	8	4	1	13 }						
Huntingdonshire											
etton	0	14	3	0	17	0	6	10	6	0	22
walton	0	20	0	0	20	0	8	22	6	0	36
Leicestershire											
reat Easton	12	10	5	0	27 }	12	21	0	0	0	33
reat Easton	0	10	0	0	10 }						
Lincolnshire											
skerton	1	18	3	0	22]						
cothern etc.	32	0	0	0	32 }	20	26	12	4	0	62
eepham	0	12	2	0	14]						
cotter etc.	23	36	13	0	72	29	24	11	10	2	76
osberton	1	12	9	0	22	0	12	8	0	0	20
Northamptonshire											
eterborough	0	37	8	0	7	0	32	12	15	0	59
ottingham	0	29	10	4	43	3	17	0	7	0	27
horpe	3	12	2	2	19	0	12	6	6	0	24
astor	0	13	2	1	16	4	25	4	6	10	49
ilsgate	26	9	2	1	38	44	8	0	1	3	56
linton	8	10	6	0	24	15	14	8	10	7	54
Werrington	19	30	4	4	57	17	11	8	1	0	37
undle	0	23	10	3	36	15	25	0	10	6	56
farmington	0	32	0	3	35	9	20	29	0	0	58
shton	0	11	2	1	14	4	14	2	0	5	25
inwell	0	24	11	0	35	0	20	13	6	4	43
thlingborough	4	9	8	2	23	3	4	10	2	4	23
ettering	0	31	0	0	31	1	40	0	8	2	51
ytchley	4	5	5	2	16	5	11	9	5	8	38
ldwincle	2	9	2	0	13	1	14	0	2	4	21
Nottinghamshire											
ollingham	37	9	20	0	66	50	20	0	0	0	70
otals	172	435	133	24	726	233	393	177	107	58	968

oroughs

orthampton	15 houses; 2 waste houses.	14 'men'; 2 waste houses.	
eterborough		18 burgesses, ? 18 knights, 16 sergeants, 3 fishermen	110 110

passing reference to its burgesses in *DB*, Bristol also was a rapidly growing new town, with four to five moneyers at work in the late eleventh century, a prosperous port whose slave-trading was denounced by Bishop Wulfstan of Worcester: Bristol probably had at least 3 – 4,000 inhabitants in 1086.[58] It is obviously very unfortunate that three out of the probable six major towns in Anglo-Norman England are partially or wholly omitted in *DB*. The population-record of some other towns is either non-existent or deficient: such towns include Dover, Rochester, Arundel, Hastings, Southwark, Marlborough, Salisbury, Frome, Milverton, Okehampton, Worcester, Hereford, Newport Pagnell and Bedford; the population of the sixth ward of Stamford, in Northamptonshire, is not given, and the populations of both Derby and Nottingham are given only for 1066.[59] Although the accounts of both Gloucester and Winchcombe in *DB* are also defective, these can be rectified from the Evesham K 'satellite' text.[60]

Apart from the towns, which were obviously an afterthought, we can accept that on the whole *DB* preserved a good record within its terms of reference, with remarkably few copying errors. But by no means all the existing population came within the stated terms of reference either because the people concerned did not generate revenue, or because they were of no possible military significance, or both. In short, we need to move on to the second major problem on the agenda I outlined earlier, that of omissions and exclusions. In addition to incompletely recorded data on groups of people who were intended to be fully included in *DB*, it is clear that, whether by accident or design, other groups of people were not enumerated at all even though they undoubtedly existed in Anglo-Norman England and, indeed, their presence is often implied by *DB*. The Domesday survey mentions many castles, at the latest count 51,[61] although modern scholars have shown that the record of castles in *DB* is very deficient, the total fairly certainly being about 500. Earlier estimates of 5–600 castles by Painter and Beeler may appear excessively high, by comparison with the 327 recorded castles, including castles

---

E. Miller, J. Hatcher, *Medieval England: Towns, Commerce and Trade*, London 1995, 264, 274, accept an estimate of 80,000 c.1300 which had doubled since 1200. If the population doubled during the thirteenth century, as is generally accepted, c.1200 it would have been about the 40,000 level estimated by Peter of Blois c.1200, hence the 1086 figure must have been at least 20,000 if not more.

[58] Bristol's four moneyers in William I's reign were matched in number by Chester, Colchester, Dover, Exeter, Gloucester, Hereford, Ipswich, Oxford, Southwark, Worcester and York; the five moneyers under William Rufus were equalled only by Norwich (R.H.M. Dolley, *The Norman Conquest and the English Coinage*, London 1966, 14). Later work suggests there were six moneyers at work at Bristol in William I's reign, but two only worked on one coin-issue each (E.J. Harris, 'The Moneyers of the Norman Kings and the Types they are Known to have Struck, Part 2', *Seaby's Coin and Medal Bulletin*, 774, 1983, 34–5). The population of the towns listed above can be estimated as follows: Chester, 1,500 (*DGNE*, 378); Colchester, 2,250 (*DGEE*, 253–4); Exeter, 2,000 (*DGSWE*, 280–1); Gloucester, 1,800 (Evesham K 1); Ipswich, 1,400 (*DGEE*, 193); Norwich, ?5,000 (*DGEE*, 140); Oxford, 2,300, earlier ?4,700 (*DGSEE*, 227–8); York, 4,000 (*DGNE*, 155–6) (The evidence for Hereford and Southwark is fragmentary, and for Worcester is incomplete). These figures suggest that Bristol's population was probably over 3,000 and perhaps over 4,000 in 1086.

[59] *DGSEE*, 179, 274–8, 398–400, 463–72, 546–54; *DGSWE*, 55, 57, 204–5, 284–5; *DGME*, 101–3, 260–1; *DGEE*, 80; *DGNE*, 272, 322

[60] J.S. Moore, ed., *Domesday Book: Gloucestershire*, Chichester 1982, Appendix EvK 1, 116; C. Thorn, ed., *Domesday Book: Worcestershire*, Chichester 1982, Appendix II.

[61] C.G. Harfield, 'A Hand-List of Castles Recorded in the Domesday Book', *EHR* cvi, 1991, 371–92.

built after 1086, in Angevin England *and Wales*, of which no more than 275 existed at any one time.[62] But a recent re-examination of this question has concluded that there was an accelerating fall in the number of castles between 1100 and 1154, so that there were indeed probably 500 castles in being in 1086.[63] To be effective, these Anglo-Norman castles must have had garrisons, but *DB*, with one exception, provides no details of them. (The exception is Richard's Castle (Herefs.) where the presence of '23 men' were recorded because, unusually, they paid rent to their lord, Osbern Fitz Richard (*DB, Herefs.*, fo. 186d, *24*, 1).) We know that most castles also functioned as the chief residence of their holders, who of course were listed in *DB* but whose households were, yet again, excluded. Moreover, *DB* also mentions cathedrals, many monasteries and a few nunneries, both English and Norman, *as landholders*, but once more says virtually nothing of episcopal or abbatial households, the chapters of secular cathedrals, monks and nuns and their lay servants in England. Although more is said about secular canons in *DB*, it is a very incomplete record of secular minsters and collegiate churches, as John Blair has shown.[64] There are two entries which include monks or their servants, both in *DB, II*, both in Suffolk. At Wissett, it was stated that 'In this church are 12 monks' (*DB, Suffolk*, fo. 293a, *3*, 14), which was in fact the priory of Rumburgh mentioned by name in another entry (*DB, Suffolk*, fo. 298a, *3*, 105); at Bury St Edmunds are noted the

75 bakers, brewers, tailors, washers, shoemakers, robemakers, cooks, porters and stewards [who] daily serve the Saint, the abbot and the brethren

(*DB, Suffolk*, fo. 372a, *14*, 167). For information on castles, lordly households, great and small, and monasteries, we must look to other sources. At this point I should state that this paper, like the Domesday inquest itself, has generated a number of 'satellite texts', and that my treatment of the topics I have mentioned will summarise conclusions to be discussed in detail in a series of forthcoming publications.[65]

Though historians have long studied castles, their interest has concentrated on castles as buildings, as military strongpoints, as centres of political control and of administration. By contrast, much less work has been done on castles as residences: if, as Ann Williams has recently reminded us, 'an Englishman's home is his castle', it is equally true that his lord's castle (or at any rate his lord's main castle) is also his lord's home.[66] Even less work has been focussed on castle-garrisons by military historians, even though they recognise that the Anglo-Norman period was an age of sieges rather than battles.[67] In the 'crisis conditions' of 1085 'care and

---

[62] S. Painter, 'English Castles in the Early Middle Ages', *Speculum* x, 1935, 321–32; J. Beeler, *Warfare in England, 1066–1189*, Ithaca 1966; R.A. Brown, 'A List of Castles, 1154–1216', *EHR* lxxiv, 1959, 249–80.

[63] R. Eales, 'Royal Power and Castles in Norman England', in C. Harper-Bill, R. Harvey, eds, *The Ideals and Practice of Medieval Knighthood* iii, 1990, 54–63.

[64] J. Blair, 'Secular Minsters in Domesday Book', in P.H. Sawyer, ed., *Domesday Book: A Reassessment*, London 1985, 104–42; J. Blair, ed., *Minsters and Parish Churches: the Local Church in Transition, 950–1200*, Oxford 1988.

[65] J. S. Moore, 'Anglo-Norman Garrisons', forthcoming. Other articles are in preparation.

[66] A. Williams, 'A Bell-house and a Burh-geat: Lordly Residences in England before the Norman Conquest', in C. Harper-Bill, R. Harvey, eds, *Medieval Knighthood* iv, 1992, 240.

[67] Useful but not comprehensive coverage of data on garrisons, and references to original sources, neither of which are always accurately reported, occur in P. Warner, *Sieges of the Middle Ages*,

maintenance' garrisons of part-timers provided by castle-guard service would certainly have been supplemented in many instances by detachments from the mercenary army brought to England by the king, a force which was soberly estimated by Florence of Worcester at 'many thousands'.[68] In the twelfth and later centuries, analysis of the detailed archives then available shows that wartime garrisons consisted of knights and serjeants serving for pay, who, from the available evidence in the Anglo-Norman world – which is, apart from the Pipe Roll for 31 Henry I, mainly literary – numbered on average about 200, thus being much larger than the peacetime garrisons, if indeed there was a peacetime garrison apart from the permanent castle staff and contingents fulfilling castle-guard duties. The average estimated size of a normal full-time peace-time garrison, where these existed, was no more than 12 to 15 in number. In the light of Richard Eales' recent work on Norman castles, I have put the number of castles existing in 1086 as 500. Since Charles Coulson has persuaded me that such wartime garrisons would have been drawn mainly from the mercenary army imported in 1085, the normal garrison-element in Anglo-Norman England comprised peace-time garrisons totalling no more than 6–7,000 and, allowing for the defence of lesser castles by castle-guard contingents, more probably numbering about 4,000.

Besides castle-garrisons, *DB* also excluded any details of the households of both the secular landholders, whether magnates or small manorial lords, and bishops and abbots. Again, because of the lack of contemporary evidence on the size of such households in the eleventh century, it is necessary to utilise what comparative evidence is available later in the medieval period. The third Lateran Council of 1179, for example, limited the size of retinues during visitations to 40 or 50 for archbishops and 20 or 30 for bishops:[69] we may reasonably presume that retinues had previously exceeded these levels, particularly in England, whose dioceses were among the richest in western Europe. Moreover, the whole archepiscopal or episcopal household would not have gone on visitation, so that the total numbers, including domestic servants, would have been higher, probably of the order of 60–75 for archbishops and 40–50 for bishops. Eadmer tells how Archbishop Anselm was unable to live with his monks in Canterbury 'partly by the large retinue which his episcopal dignity and the custom of the country did not allow him to be without'.[70] Abbots also had sizeable retinues: thus the newly-appointed Abbot Turold of Peterborough 'came to the monastery with one hundred and sixty Normans well armed' in 1069.[71] This was undoubtedly exceptional, but Gilbert

London 1968; R.A. Brown, *English Castles*, London 3rd edn, 1976, 173, 185–9, 191–4, 198–9; N.J.G. Pounds, *The Medieval Castle in England and Wales: a Social and Political History*, Cambridge 1990, 90, 122–3; J. Bradbury, *The Medieval Siege*, Woodbridge 1992. For examples of military historians who have ignored garrisons, see C. Oman, *A History of the Art of War in the Middle Ages*, London 2nd edn, 2 vols, 1924, i, 381, 400; ii, 43; P. Contamine, *War in the Middle Ages*, Oxford 1984, 101.

68 *ASC*, 161 ('E' text, *s.a.* 1085); Worcester ii, 18.

69 *Chronicles of the Reigns of Stephen, Henry II and Richard I*, ed. R. Howlett, RS lxxxii, 1885–90, i, 216; *Gesta Regis Henrici Secundi Benedicti Abbatis*, ed. W. Stubbs, RS xlix, 1867, i, 224; *Chronica Magistri Rogeri de Houedene*, ed. W. Stubbs, RS li, 1868–71, ii, 173–4; *Gervasii Cantuariensis Opera Historica*, ed. W. Stubbs, RS lxiii, 1879–80, i, 291–2.

70 R.W. Southern, ed., *The Life of St Anselm by Eadmer*, Oxford 1962, 71.

71 *ASC*, 152 ('E', text, *s.a.* 1069); W.T. Mellows, ed., *The Peterborough Chronicle of Hugh Candidus*, Peterborough 1941, 40: another text puts the number at 140.

Table 6. Population-estimates: monks, nuns, canons in 1086

native Benedictine monasteries		1,930
alien cells		50
all monks	not exceeding	2,000
nuns		400
secular canons/collegiate priests	at least	700

Crispin as abbot of Westminster had a dozen or more knights housed around the abbey.[72] I have therefore allowed 60 men to each of the archbishops, and 40 to each of the 13 bishops, 30 to each of 63 abbots or priors, and 10 to each of 15 abbesses. In the light of discussion after this paper was read, I now accept that episcopal and abbatial servants were usually unmarried individuals (the reason for the separate housing of knights outside monasteries being their well-known disruptive influence on monastic life), and that the abbesses' servants were usually unmarried women or widows, but a few senior servants may have been married heads of household. In all, servants of the prelates may have totalled about 4,000 persons.

Despite the work of earlier scholars, the number of inmates in English monasteries and nunneries is a difficult problem.[73] Knowles and Hadcock calculated a total number of Benedictine monks (including those of affiliated orders) as lying between 835 and 2,135 in the period 1066–1100, and the number of Benedictine nuns in the same period as lying between 340 and 440,[74] but they do not provide any reasoned basis for these figures (or, indeed, any of their estimated totals) apart from the comment that 'in a great number of cases they have had to be estimated from valuations and by comparison'.[75] Whilst I fully accept that interpolation based on valuations and comparison with other houses are often the only possible basis for estimates, or in default the use of backwards extrapolation from known figures for later dates, rather more argued justification is surely needed. For a full study of this matter, it is necessary to list the existing monastic communities in Domesday England, together with the known figures for inmates. This is, again, work still in progress: it is not helped by the fact that Knowles and Hadcock's *Medieval Religious Houses*, a pioneer work in its time, has not been revised for 25 years and has some significant errors, especially in relation to monastic populations: it is not a complete list of religious houses, especially in the case of collegiate churches, as John Blair's work has shown, but even omits some monastic houses, such as the nunnery at Hereford recorded in *DB, Herefs.*, fo. 181d, 2, 17 (which is also therefore not mentioned in Sally Thomson's *Women Religious*). Neither Hadcock nor Knowles worked through *DB* or the 'satellites' systematically, and their system of references has many errors and frequently refers back to

---

[72] *DB, Middx*, fo. 128b, *4*, 1.

[73] D. Knowles, *The Monastic Order in England, 940–1216*, Cambridge 1940, 713–14; J.C. Russell, 'The Clerical Population of Medieval England', *Traditio* ii, 1944, 177–212; D. Knowles, R. Hadcock, *Medieval Religious Houses: England and Wales*, London 2nd edn, 1971, 489–90.

[74] Russell, 'The Clerical Population of Medieval England', 179, 182, 185, 188.

[75] Knowles and Hadcock, *Medieval Religious Houses*, 489, 493.

J.C. Russell who, when checked, normally cites Knowles's *Monastic Order in England* for houses in Anglo-Norman England. My own preliminary totals are summarised in Table 6. I should say that the last line of Table 6 is the most fragile: Blair has traced over 300 secular minsters in 1086, and I suspect my own popula- tion- estimate is too low, perhaps 50 per cent too low. Otherwise, my figures are at the top end of the ranges postulated by Knowles and Hadcock for the period 1066–1100, which are self-evidently too low, since further houses were established in the 1090s. But, of course, monks and nuns were not the only inhabitants of their establishments.

For the Benedictine monasteries certainly had large numbers of lay servants, and we may suspect that this would have been even more true of Benedictine nunner- ies, which also needed the services of a secular priest. Dom David Knowles commented that 'the number of servants and dependants who lived about the abbey . . . always equalled and often exceeded the number of monks'.[76] As a rough approximation, therefore, I have assumed that there were as many lay servants as monks and nuns in 1086. To judge from the *DB* evidence for the servants of Bury St Edmunds and Westminster, the monks' lay servants were probably married people living outside the monastic precincts, hence an additional 2,000 heads of household has been included for them in the final estimated population of Domes- day England, but the nuns' servants have been assumed to be mostly widows and unmarried women, and thus 400 has been allowed for them.

The third problem on my agenda was that of the 'multiplier', that is, the factor necessary to convert heads of household into estimates of total population. For the manorial tenants in the countryside, my previous work on Domesday slavery concluded that the Domesday slaves were usually married heads of household, like the other members of the village community, and my later work on the Anglo- Norman family concluded that the figure of 4.75 for the average size of household used by the historical demographers of the early modern period was perfectly acceptable for the Anglo-Norman period and was justified by contemporary evi- dence.[77] However, evidence from later periods suggests that an appropriate multi- plier for urban populations would be at least the five favoured by Darby in his *Domesday Geography* series: townsmen were much more likely to have servants, apprentices and lodgers.[78] For higher social levels, nevertheless, I believe that Darby is quite wrong to use a multiplier of five (or anything of the same order). As Peter Laslett many years ago pointed out, the great distinguishing feature of the upper and middle groups of early modern society, as opposed to the lower orders, was that the former employed servants in large numbers.[79] This was also clearly true of the medieval period, in which the classic division between the *pugnantes, orantes et laborantes* implied, *inter alia*, that neither the knights nor the clergy were supposed to work with their hands. The king's household, as we know from the '*Constitutio Domus Regis*', was probably over 150, and this figure probably

---

[76] Knowles, *Monastic Order in England*, 440. For a full discussion of lay servants, see *ibid.*, 439–41.
[77] J.S. Moore, 'The Anglo-Norman Family: Size and Structure', *ANS* xiv, 1992, 193.
[78] E.g. Williams, *From Commune to Capital*, 317.
[79] P. Laslett, *The World We Have Lost Further Explored*, London 3rd edn, 1983, esp. 46, 64, 69, 91.

does not include every menial;[80] to it should be added the several hundred royal household knights who were the core of the royal army.[81] Evidence from later in the medieval period confirms that baronial and knightly households were large and continued to be large until well into the sixteenth century, partly because there was a strong military element, corresponding to the royal household knights, in most aristocratic households. Even the ordinary 'rustic' knight with a single manor house would still have had his household servants.[82] The evidence of the surviving later medieval household accounts, many of which are now in print, is not easy to interpret: diet accounts usually total quantities of food consumed and rarely give the number of people at meals; just occasionally the number of horses fed provides a hint of household size, as with the mid-thirteenth-century De Veres travelling with between 42 and 46 horses, and the wages paid by Henry, earl of Lincoln in 1299 show he was served by about 50 'young men and pages'; it was not until the fifteenth century that the bishop of Salisbury's diet account of 1406–7 regularly gives the number of people fed at each meal and distinguishes between regular members of the household, usually numbering between 50 and 90, and visitors.[83] It is only fairly infrequently that surviving accounts list the entire household as in the case of Thomas, duke of Clarence, who travelled to France c.1418–21 with over 150 attendants.[84] But the better quality evidence from the later medieval period has to be offset to some extent by changing conditions: the higher nobility of fifteenth-century England was both smaller and richer than its equivalent three centuries earlier, its members had more sophisticated standards and were less peripatetic.[85] With some hesitation I suggest that earls and greater barons in Anglo-Norman England (roughly 200) had households in excess of 100 and in some cases probably over 200; that lesser barons and greater knights (roughly 900) would have households of over 50, and that lesser knights (about 6,000) had between 10 and 20 in their households.[86] I also conclude from the use of words such as 'yeomen', 'boys', 'pages' and 'valets' in the surviving household accounts that the servants in such households generally consisted of young unmarried men and women, since we also know that households containing more than one married couple have been

---

[80] C. Johnson, ed., *Dialogus de Scaccario*, Oxford 2nd edn, 1983, 129–43, enumerated at least 143 men, but in several cases recorded only an unnumbered plural; G.H. White, 'The Household of the Norman Kings', *TRHS* 4th ser., xxx, 1948, 127–55; J.A. Green, *The Government of England under Henry I*, Cambridge 1986, 27–37.

[81] C.W. Hollister, *The Military Organization of Anglo-Norman England*, Oxford 1965, 167–8, 174–5, 177–81; M. Chibnall, 'Mercenaries and the *Familia Regis* under Henry I', *History* lxii, 1977, 15–23; J.O. Prestwich, 'The Military Household of the Norman Kings', *EHR* xcvi, 1981, 5–35; Green, *The Government of England under Henry I*, 24–6.

[82] K. Mertes, *The English Noble Household, 1250–1600*, Oxford 1988; M. Girouard, *Life in the English Country House*, New Haven (USA) 1978, 12–15, 82–5; F. Heal, *Hospitality in Early Modern England*, Oxford 1990, 44–8.

[83] C.M. Woolgar, ed., *Household Accounts from Medieval England*, Oxford, 2 vols, 1992–3, i, 151–9, 164–70, 265–430.

[84] Woolgar, ed., *Household Accounts from Medieval England* ii, 651–5.

[85] Moore, 'Introduction', 2–4, and references cited, 179, nn. 3–7; C.C. Dyer, *Standards of Living in the Later Middle Ages*, Cambridge 1989, chs 1–4; Mertes, *The English Noble Household, 1250–1600*; T.B. James, *The Palaces of Medieval England, c.1050–1550*, London 1990.

[86] D. Crouch, *The Image of Aristocracy in Britain, 1000–1300*, London 1992, 293–4, guessed that a typical magnate household c.1130 would contain about 40 people; no justification is offered, and the figure seems far too low.

rare throughout English history.[87] As with the prelates' households, allowance has been made for the possibility that a few senior servants in the baronial households may have been married.

At long last we are in a position to calculate the total population of Domesday England. For this purpose I have accepted Darby's counts of recorded heads because no better basic figures yet exist: Robin Fleming tells me that her data-base never will cover the East Anglian counties in *DB, II*. Darby counted 268,984 heads of rural households, but he made no numerical allowance for the omission or undercounting of slaves in various counties: I have therefore adopted my own revised estimate of 272,700 heads.[88] For these rural heads of household, I again adopt my own multiplier of 4.75, making a total estimated rural population of, in rounded terms, 1,300,000. To this I have already suggested we need to add a few hundreds per county to allow for the omission of numbers of groups of tenants which were of fairly small size, and this would imply an addition of about the 5 per cent level proposed by Darby, which is also the level of omission suggested by the Shaftesbury survey of c.1130, as we have seen earlier.[89] On my figures this amounts to a further 65,000 people, to which we should also add 'about 120,000 people in all' for the 'missing level three'. Darby allowed 120,000 for *DB* burgesses but gave no reasoned justification for this figure; my feeling is that it should perhaps be raised to 150,000.[90] We need also to include the figures for peacetime garrisons, noble and prelatical households, monks and nuns and their servants as discussed in the text.

Finally, there are the lower clergy. The secular canons and collegiate priests probably numbered over, perhaps well over, 700, some but not all of whom were included in *DB*; most were married men, and they thus represent at least 3,300 individuals and perhaps as many as 6,500. Parish priests are a much greater problem: *DB*, it is well known, did not enumerate the parish priests completely or even consistently between circuits, and on Darby's calculations 'churches' and 'priests' together totalled 2,287 on the 13,418 recorded manors, so that only 17 per cent of manors had a priest.[91] This calculation is obviously an under-estimation since in parts of England there were two or more manors in a later parish, but against that there is the strong possibility that, just as churches were often 'appraised with the manors' (as was stated several times in *DB, II*), so priests were often included with the villagers with whom, when they are separately mentioned, they are usually linked. A comparison of entries in *ICC* and *IE* with the corresponding entries in *DB* sometimes reveals that the formula 'X villagers and 1 priest' in the former has become 'X+1' villagers in the latter.[92] Perhaps, therefore, the 'missing' priests were all subsumed within the villagers. But perhaps not, at any rate in every circuit: Lennard argued that only in Huntingdonshire, with 53

87 Moore, 'The Anglo-Norman Family: Size and Structure', 153–4, 167, 174, 188, 193; R.A. Houlbrooke, *The English Family, 1450–1700*, London 1984, 10, 18–26; P. Laslett, R. Wall, *Household and Family in Past Time*, Cambridge 1974, esp. chs 1, 4–7; Laslett, *The World We Have Lost Further Explored*, 97–102.

88 Moore, 'Domesday Slavery', 210–11.

89 H.C. Darby, *Domesday England*, Cambridge 1977, repr 1979, 1986, 88–9; see above, 322.

90 Darby, *Domesday England*, 89.

91 Darby, *Domesday England*, 346.

92 E.g. '6 villagers and 1 priest' (Hamilton, ed., *Inquisitio Comitatus Cantabrigiensis*, 1) becomes '7 villagers' (*DB, Cambs.*, fo. 196c, *18*, 8: Kennett).

Table 7. Total estimated population of Domesday England

Category of people	Recorded heads	Estimated total population
Rural manorial tenants	272,700	1,300,000
Omissions (5%)	13,600	65,000
'Level 3'	25,000	120,000
Burgesses	?25,000	120,000
Normal garrisons	4,000	4,000
Royal household	500	500
Bishops' and abbots' households	2,700	4,000
Greater baronial households	30,000	34,000
Lesser baronial households	45,000	63,000
Knightly households	90,000	90,000
Monks and nuns	2,400	2,400
Monastic servants	2,500	10,000
Canons/collegiate priests	700	3,300
Parish priests omitted	6,000	28,500
Lancashire	?1,800	8,500
Four northern counties	N/A	25,000
Totals	527,200	1,878,200
(Omissions at 10%)	540,800	1,943,200
(Omissions at 15%)	554,400	2,008,200

churches in 83 places (64 per cent), and in Suffolk, with 345 churches in 639 places (54 per cent), was the *DB* record of churches and priests reasonably complete.[93] If we assume that roughly 60 per cent of all the 13,400 places recorded in *DB* 'ought' to have had a priest, then there were about 8,000 parish priests in Anglo-Norman England (a figure that seems quite plausible in view of the 9 – 10,000 English parishes around 1300).[94] Of these 8,000, *DB* records less than a quarter (1,800 in round numbers). I have therefore added 6,000 priests and their families to Table 7, together with Darby's estimates for Lancashire and the four northern counties. Even if we remove the wartime garrisons, as King William doubtless removed them in the autumn of 1086, when the threat of a Danish invasion receded, and substitute the much smaller peacetime garrisons, the 'normal' peacetime population of Anglo-Norman England can hardly have been less than 1.88 millions, as Table 7 shows. It could well have been somewhat higher, but

[93] Lennard, *Rural England, 1086–1135*, 288–9, 292.
[94] J.R.H. Moorman, *Church Life in England in the Thirteenth Century*, Cambridge 1945, 4–5; J.C. Dickinson, *An Ecclesiastical History of England: the Later Middle Ages*, London 1979, 27, 46.

unless the omission rate, which is probably the most dubious of all my calculations, was not 5 per cent but 15 per cent, it is difficult to justify even Sally Harvey's estimate of 2 millions in 1086, whilst Hallam's estimate of 2.5 millions remains a wild and quite unsubstantiated guess.[95] Even with a 15 per cent omission-rate, and raising the numbers of burgesses to 150,000 and of secular canons to 6,500, the 1086 population barely exceeds 2.04 millions.

So far as the social and geographical distribution of the population is concerned, I can offer little advance on Darby's calculations, apart from modifications necessary to take into account my revised estimates of slaves. Where advances can be made in the future are in two areas: the estimation of urban populations using archaeological and numismatic evidence and later as well as contemporary historical sources, and the determination of trends in English population before and after 1086.

To adapt an aphorism of Jane Austen in *Pride and Prejudice*,
It is a truth universally acknowledged, that an economic historian in possession of a good topic must be in want of statistics.

I trust I have demonstrated that this want is neither silly nor impossible of attainment, even if my own answers fail to convince you. I have tried to provide the basis for all my calculations, and the assumptions I have made, so that future attention can be focussed precisely on those areas where others disagree with me. What I would assert is that any estimate of total population in 1086 must be compatible with estimates for population at the peak of the demographic boom of the high middle ages c.1300, after growth in the twelfth and thirteenth centuries. Any estimate which is much greater than 2 million in 1086, allowing for subsequent increases, runs up against the ceiling of population in 1300 which can hardly be greater than 6 million and is probably rather less.[96] Thus, to end, as I always like to end, with the wisdom of Maitland:

The most efficient method of protecting ourselves against such errors is that of reading our history backwards as well as forwards, of making sure of our middle ages before we talk about the 'archaic', of accustoming our eyes to the twilight before we go out into the night.[97]

I hope that this study has thrown some light on the subject!

[95] See my own review of Hallam, ed., *Agrarian History of England and Wales ii: 1042–1350*, in *History* lxxv, 1990, 293–5.
[96] Hallam, ed., *Agrarian History of England and Wales ii: 1042–1350*, 510–13, 536–7.
[97] Maitland, *Domesday Book and Beyond*, 356.

THE EMERGENCE OF ANGLO-NORMAN ARCHITECTURE: DURHAM CATHEDRAL*

Lisa Reilly

By any standards, the changes wrought by the Norman Conquest on the built environment of eleventh-century England are enormous. The sheer scale and energy of Norman architectural patronage guaranteed a noticeable change as very nearly every major Anglo-Saxon abbey church and cathedral was replaced or in the process of being replaced by 1100. At least fifteen cathedrals and major abbey churches were built or under construction by this date and several others were undertaken in the early twelfth century. This transformation was not restricted to the ecclesiastical world. The secular realm was also altered by the construction of motte and bailey defences throughout the country in large numbers, the most impressive ones capped by stone towers. Anyone surveying the English landscape even within twenty years of the Conquest would have noticed a difference, as magnificent new churches were under construction in Lincoln (1072), St Albans (1077), Winchester (1079), Ely (1081) and Worcester (1084). Castles had sprung up at Castle Acre and London soon after 1066 and at Durham c.1072 among other places.

Unlike later additions to medieval architecture in which two styles such as Anglo-Norman and Early English stand side by side as at St Albans, none of the major Anglo-Norman churches built over earlier structures preserve any trace of their Anglo-Saxon predecessors above ground. The situation is different, however, for contemporary parish churches where pre-Conquest fabric is often found. This may indicate a deliberate decision by Norman patrons initially to eradicate the past as well as reflecting the tremendous differences between the two traditions. This Norman erasure of Anglo-Saxon architecture has left us with a very sketchy understanding of the earlier tradition. Relatively few buildings survive and these are scattered throughout the country so it has not been possible to establish whether this architecture has a strongly regional quality.[1] Most of the sites of particular importance to Anglo-Saxon society were either rapidly rebuilt, such as Winchester, or abandoned when the episcopal see was moved elsewhere, as was the case when Norwich replaced North Elmham as the see and Lincoln took over from Dorchester in 1072. This history of destruction at major sites leaves us with buildings which

* I would like to thank the Thomas Jefferson Fellowship Program at Downing College, Cambridge and the University of Virginia Summer Research Grant Program for support of the research for this article. I would also like to thank the R. Allen Brown Memorial Fund and the Department of Architectural History, University of Virginia, for assisting with the expenses of attending the conference.

[1] See E. Fernie, *The Architecture of the Anglo-Saxons*, London 1983, for an overview of this period.

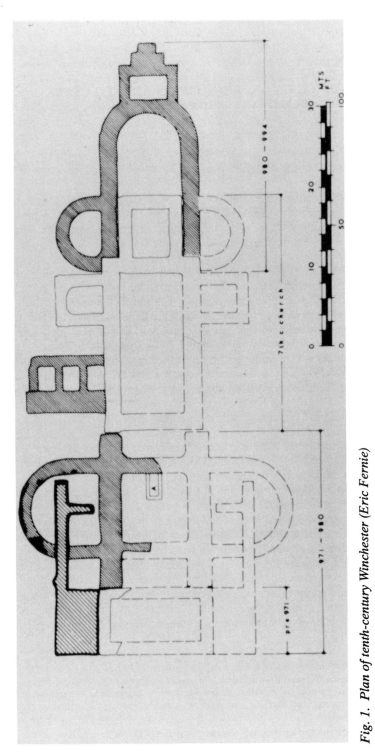

Fig. 1. Plan of tenth-century Winchester (Eric Fernie)

may not represent the most sophisticated or well patronised examples of Anglo-Saxon architecture.

Still, it has been possible for architectural historians to develop certain generalisations about pre-Conquest architecture from these very limited survivals. Anglo-Saxon churches were typically small. Recent excavations at Canterbury and Winchester, however, have challenged this view in terms of the overall length of some buildings, but most evidence suggests that Anglo-Saxon structures were typically small scale in height and often composed of a series of small spaces often added to the original fabric over a prolonged period of time.[2] The distinctive arrangement of these discrete chambers is sometimes regarded as possibly reflecting liturgical or cult practices.[3] These are not sufficiently understood, however, as evidence is sketchy. In any case, the spatial arrangements as identified through excavation examples, such as Winchester (tenth century) (Fig. 1), or surviving monuments, such as Bradford on Avon (eleventh century) (Fig. 2), suggest that neither symmetry nor axiality was particularly valued in Anglo-Saxon architecture. Decoration was apparently important and, as was the case in manuscripts of the period, was often linear in pattern, as suggested by the pilaster strip work at Earls Barton (eleventh century) or the spiral piers of Repton crypt (after 970) (Fig. 3). An interest in decorative effects is also suggested by the frequent ornamentation of arch mouldings as seen at Wittering (mid eleventh century). Further experimentation with such effects can be seen in the wide variety of pier forms often varying within the same building as at Great Paxton (mid eleventh century) (Fig. 4).

Such manipulation of effects, although small scale, suggests that while Anglo-Saxon architecture may not conform to later notions of grandeur in terms of scale, symmetry or unified effects, it was sophisticated in certain aspects of its design. The loss of possible painted decoration and furnishings for these, as for other medieval buildings, further reduces our understanding of their interiors in particular.

It was once common to regard Anglo-Saxon architecture as the insular product of an isolated region. Eric Fernie's study of Anglo-Saxon architecture established that in fact, although English architecture is distinctive during this period, it does display a wide variety of continental influences, as at Great Paxton (mid eleventh century) which he connects to Lotharingian architecture.[4]

Some discussion of the period has focused on Edward the Confessor's introduction of Norman culture to the Anglo-Saxon court, particularly his construction of Westminster Abbey in 1050–65 based on Norman models. Norman artistic ideas were infiltrating Anglo-Saxon society before the Conquest and would have continued to do so had Harold won at Hastings, thus effecting a change in the native tradition, albeit more slowly. The appearance of Norman influences or forms traceable to Norman models is not necessarily, at least to my mind, the most interesting issue. The pattern of absorption of those ideas as well as the end result would have been markedly different had Anglo-Saxon architecture remained intact, with native patrons and masons selecting from the cross channel repertoire. Additionally, their experience of Norman architecture is quite different from that of the natives. The Conquest ruptures artistic traditions and brings a new group of

[2] K. Blockley, 'Canterbury Cathedral', *Current Archaeology* xii, no. 4, Oct./Dec. 1993, 124–36.
[3] Fernie, *Anglo-Saxons*, 42.
[4] Fernie, *Anglo-Saxons*, 132.

Fig. 2. Bradford on Avon exterior (National Buildings Record)

architectural patrons to England from Normandy. The result of their patronage is different from what would have occurred had the patrons remained Anglo-Saxon. The more interesting issues, to my mind, have to do with how and why Norman architecture was transformed by its contact with indigenous traditions following the Conquest.

But first I should identify what that Norman tradition was. Most obvious of all is the fact that Norman churches and, even more to the point, Anglo-Norman churches were big by anyone's standards in Romanesque Europe. The three largest churches on the continent were St Peter's (133 metres in overall length), Speyer (128 metres) and Cluny III (from 1088) (172 metres), a group into which post-Conquest Winchester (from 1079) at 157 metres fits comfortably. Two different elevational compositions predominated in Norman architecture, both of which are found in post-Conquest architecture in England. The first, as seen at Jumièges Abbey, has a double bay system of alternating supports. The abbey church of St Étienne (1064/6–77), built by the Conqueror in his second capital city of Caen, shows the other system, one of uniform supports and three large nearly equal openings. The buildings tended to have timber ceilings over the nave flanked by groin vaulted aisles. The use of such lightweight roofing material over the central space made large openings possible at all three levels of the elevation, as seen at St Étienne, Caen. The Norman preference for rational articulation of forms can be seen in the one to one correspondence between each element of the arch, for example, and its support. Both buildings display the Norman emphasis on the west end in their twin towered facades with an austere impenetrable quality. This represents a continuing development of the Carolingian west work tradition as seen at ninth-century Corvey, which the Normans encountered upon their arrival in Normandy in the tenth century. St Étienne's facade continues to display the concern for logical articulation in its expression of the inner three story elevation and aisle nave aisle division in the composition of its exterior. Norman ground plans also fall into two types as seen at Jumièges and Bernay (1017–c.1055). The former has the ambulatory east end associated with pilgrimage sites while the latter has three parallel apses usually in echelon; one at the end of the nave and flanked by two others, at the end of each aisle. These two patterns are both transported to England. The symmetry, axiality and clarity apparent in the plans suggest the monumental and unified appearance of these buildings.

Comparison of the plans of some Anglo-Saxon buildings with Norman examples highlights the contrast which should now be evident between these two architectural traditions. The plan of Jumièges compared with Winchester shows the additive piecemeal quality of Anglo-Saxon plans in which a series of disparate, quite distinct spaces are created over time. It has been speculated that Anglo-Saxons had a particular reverence for the sanctity of specific sites and were reluctant to tear down their older structures, preferring to add to rather than replace them.[5]

As mentioned above, these two architectural traditions had encountered one another in a limited way under Edward the Confessor. The arrival of a new ruling class following the Conquest meant Anglo-Saxon architecture was subject to the scrutiny and control of outsiders who may not have fully understood its traditions or subtleties. The widespread replacement of Anglo-Saxon buildings initially suggested to architectural historians, as to scholars of other aspects of Anglo-Norman culture, that Norman patrons were contemptuous of Anglo-Saxon architecture, hence they replaced it with buildings of their own as soon as possible. As Peter Kidson put it, in a view widely representative of the field: 'The contempt which the Normans felt for English church buildings was only a part of their wider contempt for almost everything connected with the religious life of the country.'[6] A.W. Clapham wrote: 'Hardly ever before or since has a national culture been so easily, so rapidly or so completely submerged as was the Anglo-Saxon in the last thirty

---

[5] D. Whitelock, 'The Anglo-Saxon Achievement', in D. Whitelock *et al.*, *The Norman Conquest*, New York 1966, 42. See also R. Gem, 'England and the Resistance to Romanesque Architecture', *Studies in Medieval History Presented to R. Allen Brown*, Woodbridge 1989, 129–39.

[6] P. Kidson, P. Murray and P. Thompson, *A History of English Architecture*, Harmondsworth 1978, 34.

Fig. 3. Repton crypt (National Buildings Record)

years of the eleventh century.'[7] This view has been revised for other aspects of post-Conquest Britain as the work of Susan Ridyard, for example, demonstrates with regard to the Norman view of Anglo-Saxon saints and cults.[8] It is clearly simplistic to say that Normans dismissed Anglo-Saxon culture out of hand, for as Kidson goes on to say '. . . Norman architecture in England was always Norman architecture with a difference.'[9] While first generation buildings such as Winchester (1079) (Fig. 5) or Ely's transepts (1080s) show close affinities with Norman examples, influence from elsewhere is also apparent in buildings of this period, such as the use of cushion capitals, basically unknown in Normandy but common in the Rhineland.[10] The 'difference' becomes apparent with one building in particular, Durham Cathedral, begun in 1093. The choir was finished by 1104 and the nave by 1133 (Fig. 6). While its plan and wall composition display close similarities to Norman models, its overall effect is dramatically different. The arrangement of double bays with alternating supports is reminiscent of Jumièges. The proportions have been altered, however, to give emphasis to the ground storey and its tremendously plastic piers. These piers begin 37½ inches above the current floor level, resting on massive plinths which enhance the monumental scale of the arcade. The walls are nearly ten feet thick, a considerable difference from the 4 feet 9 inches found at St Étienne with an overall length of approximately 123 metres.[11] The impression created by this building through its site, piers, length and wall thickness is obviously one of tremendous power and wealth. The bold plastic decorations of the piers, with grooves up to four inches deep along with the ornate arch mouldings and ribs, give a distinctly sculptural quality to the interior. The patterns used to create this sculptural effect are linear in their basis. They, like many other distinctive features, are Anglo-Saxon in origin. The elaboration of the arch mouldings can be seen in pre-Conquest buildings such as Stow (mid eleventh century). The interlacing dado arcade along the aisle walls also has not been seen in Norman architecture before, although this pattern, like those found on the columns, is commonly found in Anglo-Saxon manuscript illuminations, such as BL Royal MS IE VI (known as the Canterbury Bible, later eighth century).

Thus Durham can be regarded as having the scale, plan and elevation of a Norman church combined with the decorative sensibility of Anglo-Saxon culture. Historically, Durham has been emphasised in surveys of medieval architecture for its rib vaults, which are particularly significant for understanding the development of French Gothic architecture.[12] Beginning with John Bilson's analysis of the vaults at the turn of the century, which established their early date, scholarly interest has tended to focus on the technical aspects of the building, as seen more recently in the late Stephen Gardner's article on the galleries of Durham.[13] Indeed

---

7   A.W. Clapham, *Anglo-Saxon Architecture after the Conquest*, Oxford 1934, 1.

8   S.J. Ridyard, '*Condigna veneratio*: Post-Conquest Attitudes to the Saints of the Anglo-Saxons', *ANS* ix, 1987, 179–206.

9   Kidson, *English Architecture*, 36.

10   Kidson, *English Architecture*, 48.

11   The measurements of the wall thickness are discussed in Kidson, *English Architecture*, 41.

12   For example, see Geoffrey Webb, *Architecture in Britain The Middle Ages*, Baltimore 1965, 35 and Marilyn Stokstad, *Medieval Art*, New York 1986, 254.

13   John Bilson, 'Durham Cathedral: The Chronology of its Vaults', *Arch. Journ.*, 2nd series, lxxix (1922), 101–60 and Stephen Gardner, 'The Nave Galleries of Durham Cathedral', *Art Bulletin* lxiv, Dec. 1982, 564–79.

Fig. 4. Great Paxton interior

the vaults do seem to be the most significant feature for the development of medieval architecture outside England. From the developmental point of view, it is Durham's decorative sensibility and motifs such as the interlaced dado arcading which are significant for the immediate development of English medieval architecture. For instance, with regard to the increased elaboration of the arcade arches Peter Kidson notes: 'In this respect the Durham arches stand at the head of a long and extremely rich tradition in English medieval architecture and mark a definite bifurcation between English and Continental ideas on this subject.'[14] Explanations for the dazzling elaborateness of Durham's decoration have generally and quite logically ascribed it to the building's function as a container for the shrine of St Cuthbert.[15] The scale and magnificence of the church surely were designed with this in mind, as well perhaps as the desire for a prominent symbol of the Norman presence in a region troubled by rebellion. This does not, however, explain the strongly indigenous quality of the decorative elements which resurface at Durham.

Studies of Durham which have tried to account for its decorative appearance and the Anglo-Saxon quality of these features have tended to approach the problem from the archaeological angle which has dominated the field of medieval architectural history.[16] Specific sources for the Anglo-Saxon features have been sought, but given the poor survival rate of pre-Conquest buildings in general and those related to Durham in particular, the evidence available is limited. It should be noted here that the rebuilding of Durham was undertaken by monks who had come to the north, initially to Jarrow and Wearmouth, from the west of England, Winchcombe Abbey in particular.[17] Unfortunately, nothing is known of the appearance of Winchcombe Abbey. Thus, this line of inquiry has not been highly successful. A second type of archaeological approach has been followed, chiefly by Jean Bony, in which he uses these Anglo-Saxon features to discuss the nationality of the master mason through careful examination of the construction and stone cutting methods employed at Durham.[18] While Bony's study has yielded much valuable information about the construction of Durham, it has not satisfactorily resolved the nationality issue. Such an issue may well be beside the point in any case. Would the existence of such a person mean that Anglo-Saxon masons had been working in a Norman mode until 1093, when at Durham one was given the opportunity to express a native style? Or were Norman master masons in charge elsewhere in England until this time when a Saxon master, who had absorbed Norman concepts of scale, plan, elevation etc., created a synthesis of the two traditions? Such conjectural scenarios fail to discuss the role of the patron, implying at times that,

---

[14] Kidson, *English Architecture*, 53.

[15] See for example Malcolm Thurlby, 'Patron and Master Mason of Durham Cathedral', *Anglo-Norman Durham*, ed. D. Rollason, M. Harvey and M. Prestwich, Woodbridge 1994, 161–84.

[16] Obvious exceptions include work by Arnold Klukas such as 'The Architectural Implications of the *Decreti Lanfranci*', *ANS* vi, 1983, 136–71, and Eric Fernie's article 'Archaeology and Iconography', *Architectural History* xxxii, 1989, 18–29. On pp. 25–8 Fernie discusses Durham and also suggests, in more general terms, that iconography may be at the root of the Anglo-Saxon features at Durham.

[17] D. Rollason, *Saints and Relics in Anglo-Saxon England*, Oxford 1989, 235.

[18] J. Bony, 'The Stonework Planning of the First Durham Master', *Medieval Architecture and its Intellectual Context*, ed. P. Crossley and E. Fernie, London 1990, 19–34, and 'Durham et la Tradition Saxonne', *Études d'Art Médiéval Offertes à Louis Grodecki*, ed. A. Prache, A. Chastel and A. Chatelet, Paris 1981, 79–85.

Fig. 5. Winchester north transept interior (Conway Library, Courtauld Institute of Art)

contrary to Norman wishes, a master mason was able to sneak this radically new conception past an unwitting sponsor.

These types of investigations seem to me to have been overly specific in their search for a particular Anglo-Saxon source or master mason. The questions asked do not fully acknowledge the nature of Durham's synthesis of these two traditions. In fact, it seems to me that Durham may not call to mind a particular Saxon building in any specific way we understand. The Saxon features employed seem very conceptual, i.e. reminiscent of the Saxon artistic tradition in a very general way, which may be why specific precedents have not been found. The Anglo-Saxon past is being celebrated here, albeit in a very post-Conquest way, just as post-Modern architecture offers a re-interpretation of the past giving us classical architecture with a difference.

The Normans seem to have been masters of adaptive re-use of the native cultures of the areas under their control. As we have already seen, the Carolingian westwork was integrated into the Norman architectural tradition of clarity and monumentality at St Étienne, for example. In Sicily, the previous Roman, Byzantine and Islamic traditions are clearly evident in twelfth-century Norman buildings such as Cefalu, Monreale and the Cappella Palatina at Palermo. They have synthesised these three traditions together with their own facade type and sense of scale. In their use of Islamic institutions, the Normans in Sicily also integrated themselves into the island's history and traditions.[19]

Durham is exceptional in many ways. Its prince-bishop enjoyed unique powers as a secular and religious overlord.[20] The shrine of St Cuthbert is also a significant factor in its architectural development. Finally, the recent reorganisation of Durham from a community of lay clerks to a Benedictine monastery in 1083 would also seem to be a significant factor in the architectural development of the church. While apparently representing a rupture with the immediate pre-Conquest past, the introduction of monasticism is carefully presented by Symeon as a restoration of the original community as led by the saintly Cuthbert and best suited to guard his shrine and relics.[21] As A.J. Piper wrote:

> The sweeping away of the old community in 1083 removed from the scene those whose historic identity involved the preservation of traditions from the more immediate past, for whom conservatism was a matter of living memory. The new community was in a position to seek its own historic identity far further back in the seventh century community of Lindisfarne . . . Bede's writings were the primary source.[22]

The invocation of the Anglo-Saxon past at Durham may be read as a Norman manipulation of the historical past to make their presence part of an ongoing tradition and to gloss over the rupture their conquest represents. The new community, whether installed to restore a more sanctified atmosphere to Cuthbert's shrine

[19] D. Douglas, *The Norman Achievement*, Berkeley 1969, 183.
[20] See G.T. Lapsley, *The County Palatinate of Durham*, Cambridge 1924 , chapter 2 in particular.
[21] D. Rollason, 'Symeon of Durham and the Community of Durham in the Eleventh Century', *England in the Eleventh Century*, Proceedings of the 1990 Harlaxton Symposium, ed. Carola Hicks, Stamford 1992, 183–98.
[22] A.J. Piper, 'The First Generations of Durham Monks and the Cult of St Cuthbert', *St Cuthbert, His Cult and Community*, ed. G. Bonner, D. Rollason and C. Stancliffe, Woodbridge 1989, 445.

Fig. 6. Durham nave interior

or, as others have more cynically suggested, to establish a more pro-Norman atmosphere at Durham, was careful to legitimise itself historically, to invoke a purer Anglo-Saxon past closely associated with the revered saint.[23] Affiliation with Cuthbert may have been part of a wider Norman strategy in the years after the Conquest as they struggled to consolidate their power in this critical region. William the Conqueror's visit to the shrine suggests that he, like earlier outsiders such as Alfred, may have regarded approval by Cuthbert as a way of gaining acceptability as a ruler of Northumbria. Cuthbert is regarded as integral to constructing legitimate political power in the region, as well as the historical justification of the new monastic community. Symeon used historical writing to integrate the monks into the history of Cuthbert's community. Visually the arts were similarly employed to establish links with the past. Barbara Abou-el-Haj has suggested that the Anglo-Saxon style of the 'Life of St Cuthbert' (University College Oxford MS 165) from early twelfth-century Durham may be deliberately archaising to underscore the Anglo-Norman community's connection with the past, its appropriation of the cult's earlier tradition (Fig. 7).[24] Malcolm Baker observed that this manuscript emphasises Cuthbert's duties as an abbot as a way of linking the new Benedictine community with Anglo-Saxon Lindisfarne where Cuthbert had been abbot and introduced Benedictine practice.[25] Janet Backhouse described this manuscript as being in a recognisably Romanesque style but very much in the pre-Conquest mould as particularly evidenced by the use of coloured outline.[26]

Equally, the architectural forms of the church are delivering the same type of message. The church is richly decorated and conceived on a massive scale, as has often been pointed out, to provide a suitable setting for the shrine of Cuthbert. Indeed the nature of the decoration, the spiral piers in particular, is specifically appropriate for a saintly reliquary, as the form apparently originated at the shrine of St Peter's in Rome and was widely used in northern Europe.[27] Anglo-Saxon structures such as Repton were among those using the form. But Durham's features can be read more specifically than simply as statements of saintly magnificence; they can be seen as a new Durham's connection to its Anglo-Saxon past and the age of Cuthbert. The nearly contemporary construction of Lindisfarne using similar motifs can and has been interpreted as an effort to create a past for Durham visually by linking it with Cuthbert's monastery, just as Symeon stressed the historical connection in his writings.[28] At Lindisfarne, too, can be seen rib vaults, alternating compound and cylindrical piers, incised decoration, chevron, and moulding profiles similar to Durham. David Rollason has seen the need to justify the introduction of monks to Durham in 1083 as Symeon's chief purpose in writing the *Libellus*.[29] He

[23] Rollason, 'Symeon of Durham', 194–5.

[24] B. Abou-el-Haj, *The Medieval Cult of Saints: Formations and Transformations*, Cambridge 1994, 41.

[25] M. Baker, 'Medieval Illustrations of Bede's Life of St Cuthbert', *Journal of the Warburg and Courtauld Institutes* xli, 1978, 10.

[26] J. Backhouse, D. Turner and L. Webster, eds, *Golden Age of Anglo-Saxon Art*, London 1984, 202.

[27] E. Fernie, 'The Spiral Piers of Durham Cathedral', *Medieval Art and Architecture at Durham Cathedral*, ed. N. Coldstream and P. Draper, Proceedings of the BAA Annual Conference for 1997, 49–58.

[28] E. Cambridge, 'The Medieval Priory', *Lindisfarne*, ed. D. O'Sullivan and R. Young, London 1995, 68–9.

[29] Rollason, 'Symeon of Durham', 183.

Fig. 7. University College Oxford MS 165, fo. 130 (University College, Oxford)

goes on to say that Symeon's 'aim seems to be to present the introduction of monks to Durham in 1083 as a natural consequence of that history.'[30] The new community was composed largely of Anglo-Saxons, but they were from the south-west and thus without close ties to the local community. Rollason refers to Anne Dawtry's work which established that the monastery's learning and culture owed little to English traditions apart perhaps from a self-conscious desire to establish a spurious continuity with the community of Lindisfarne. Instead, she suggests, they looked to the learning of the continent: 'The replacement of the secular community of Durham by a monastery may have been as much a part of the advancement of Norman control in the north as of a process of ecclesiastical reform.'[31]

The architecture of Durham has several distinctive decorative features in addition to the famous rib vaults and incised pier patterns which seem to have struck a chord in those responsible for English church design. The rib vaults were apparently more widely taken up by continental designers in the succeeding generation. The addition of a roll moulding to the arcade arches, for which, as mentioned above, there are Anglo-Saxon precedents, represents a divide between Norman and Anglo-Norman aesthetics which continues throughout English medieval architectural history. While chevron ornament appears earlier elsewhere, its widespread use at Durham is new and seems to promote similar highly decorative interiors elsewhere as at Peterborough. Finally, interlacing arcading also becomes widely used after Durham, without perhaps appropriating its meaning. The pier decorations, arch forms, and dado arcading all have connections to earlier Anglo-Saxon

---

[30] Rollason, 'Symeon of Durham', 185.
[31] A. Dawtry, 'The Benedictine Revival in the North: The Last Bulwark of Anglo-Saxon Monasticism?', *Studies in Church History* xviii, 1982, 87–98.

forms. Whether these refer to forms which are specifically Durhamesque cannot be determined, as Cuthbert's Lindisfarne and Bishop Aldhuin's *alba ecclesia* (consecrated in 998) were both destroyed, the latter by St Calais in 1093. Literary accounts record that the White Church had two stone towers with bronze pinnacles, one at the west end and one over the choir. The west tower was completed between 1021 and 1042.[32] St John Hope in 1909 believed excavations placed this church in the south west corner of the present cloister. Nothing else is known of its appearance.[33]

Information from a range of sites throughout the medieval period, however, suggests that a consciousness of past buildings was very much a part of the medieval mentality. For example, after describing how distraught the Canterbury monks were following the destruction of their famous choir by fire, Gervase notes that the new piers are of the same distinctive shape as their predecessors on the site.[34] Suger's use of columnar piers and double aisled ambulatory as well as his west front apparently refers to the previous east and west ends of the earlier St Denis.[35] The location of St Oswald's shrine in the south transept of Peterborough Cathedral may have to do with the association of that part of the church with the earlier Anglo-Saxon church whose remains now lie below that part of the present building. The distinctive polygonal pier shapes found throughout Romanesque Peterborough (Fig. 8) together with those found at a number of other sites such as Norwich, Thetford and Castle Acre have been described by Bridget Cherry as forming an eastern England group sharing similar attitudes towards design.[36] The varied forms found at nearby Great Paxton suggest that experimentation with pier forms may reflect a local Anglo-Saxon tradition and those at buildings such as Peterborough may refer to this earlier tradition.

Long ago, Richard Krautheimer brilliantly demonstrated that the medieval notion of a copy is very conceptual, that buildings were considered to be copies based simply on a similar shape for example (e.g. polygonal and round).[37] Often it is hard for us to see the shared characteristics that were apparent to medieval eyes. As with medieval art generally, the value of such imitation was not aesthetic, not due to a preference for one form's appearance over another's but rather derived from the association with a specific building or shrine and its meaning. Krautheimer states: 'Foremost among these elements is the principle that any medieval structure was

---

[32] Reginald of Durham, cited by W. St John Hope, 'Notes on Recent Excavations in the Cloister of Durham', *Proceedings of the Society of Antiquaries*, 2nd series xxii, 1909, 418.

[33] St John Hope, 'Recent Excavations', 416–23. See also H.D. Briggs, E. Cambridge and R.N. Bailey, 'A New Approach to Church Archaeology: Dowsing, Excavation and Documentary Work at Woodhorn, Ponteland and the pre-Norman Cathedral at Durham', *Archaeologia Aeliana*, 5th ser. xi, 1983, 91–7.

[34] Gervase, translated by R. Willis in *The Architectural History of Canterbury Cathedral*, London 1845, 58–9. This aspect of Canterbury is also discussed in my forthcoming book *An Architectural History of Peterborough Cathedral* scheduled for publication by Clarendon Press during spring of 1997.

[35] For a discussion of this and other ways in which the present church at St Denis reflects its predecessor see: E. Fernie, 'Suger's "Completion" of St Denis', and W. Clark , 'The Recollection of the Past is the Promise of the Future', in *Artistic Integration in Gothic Buildings*, ed. V. Raguin, P. Draper and K. Brush, Toronto 1995, 84–91 and 82–113.

[36] B. Cherry, 'Romanesque Architecture in Eastern England', *Journ. BAA* cxxxi, 1978, 1–29.

[37] R. Krautheimer, 'Introduction to an "Iconography of Medieval Architecture" ', *JWCI* v, 1942, 1–33.

Fig. 8. Peterborough choir and north transept interior

meant to convey a meaning which transcends the visual pattern of the structure.'[38] His analysis of copies of the Holy Sepulchre finds examples from throughout Europe including Cambridge (first quarter of twelfth century) and Northampton (c.1120). Plans and descriptions of the model stress the very points which prevail in actual architectural copies such as the number of altars, columns and doors, as well as its shape. He cites William of Malmesbury's description of Bishop Robert of Lorraine's chapel at Hereford as an imitation of the Palatine Chapel at Aachen.[39] The disparities between these apparent to modern eyes leads to the conclusion that the medieval conception of what made one edifice comparable to another was utterly different from our own. Durham may also be reflecting earlier buildings in ways we do not yet understand.

The forms at Durham may in some way reflect local pre-Conquest traditions but this is not determinable given the poor survival rate of related buildings. What is clear is that the community responsible for the construction of Durham, including its leader Bishop William of St Calais, was keenly concerned to present itself as part of a long-standing cultural tradition specifically associated with St Cuthbert. R.B. Dobson describes the transfer from a clerical to a monastic community as taking place 'amidst a wave of conscious and indeed almost antiquarian revivalism'.[40] This association with the Anglo-Saxon past was promoted in texts such as Symeon's *Libellus* as well as manuscript illustrations such as those found in University College Manuscript 165 and in the church's architectural forms. It was used to promote the legitimacy of the newly arrived Benedictine monks as Cuthbert's heirs and possibly Cuthbert's connection with and approval of the Norman political regime, apparently reflecting a long tradition of outsiders seeking his endorsement in their efforts to rule Northumbria.

The incorporation of particularly English forms in the second generation of Anglo-Norman architecture as led by Durham should be viewed against the backdrop of an increased reverence for Anglo-Saxon saints generally and a particular agenda for the new community of Durham monks to link itself with the Anglo-Saxon past. This seems more rewarding than using archaeological techniques which have answered so many questions about Durham to establish a particular mason as responsible for the appearance of these traits. Architectural design, then as now, was essentially a collaborative process, with the distinction between patron's and mason's input difficult if not impossible to determine.

Admittedly there is much speculation in the above scenario, but it does suggest a response to the questions of why Durham should provide a new direction for the development of post-Conquest architecture and why it has such an aspect combined with its Norman monumentality, plan, and elevation, but one which cannot be specifically connected with any known Anglo-Saxon building.

This approach of considering the institutional history of the building together with the physical evidence may prove fruitful at other sites in understanding how and why architectural forms developed as they did for this period. The meaning of the forms, so critical to the medieval viewer, may become more apparent when the context which generated them is more clearly understood.

---

[38] Krautheimer, 'Iconography', 20.
[39] Krautheimer, 'Iconography', 2.
[40] R.B. Dobson, *Durham Priory 1400–1450*, Cambridge 1973, 26.

MILITARY TECHNOLOGY AND CONQUEST:
THE ANOMALY OF ANGLO-SAXON-ENGLAND*

Matthew Strickland

Shortly after Harold Godwineson was crowned king of England on Christmas Day, 1066, Duke William of Normandy took counsel with his magnates to discuss the feasability of an invasion. According to the duke's encomiast, William of Poitiers, many of the nobles voiced grave doubts:

> In the ensuing discussion, despair made them exaggerate Harold's strength and diminish their own. He abounded in riches whereby powerful kings and princes were brought into his alliance; he had a numberless fleet with expert crews long experienced in maritime dangers and battles; the wealth and therefore military resources of his country far exceeded those of our land . . .[1]

It was Poitiers's *own* purpose, of course, to magnify the duke's eventual triumph by inflating the puissance of the enemy, but his assessment of the primary elements of danger to a Norman 'enterprise of England' are revealing; 'a numberless fleet with expert crews' and the great material resources available to Harold. In my ensuing discussion, despair will not, I hope, make me exaggerate the strength of Anglo-Saxon England. Rather, what I propose is to offer some reflections on its military potential in the light of the cogent and provocative thesis propounded by Robert Bartlett in his important and wide-ranging book, *The Making of Europe*.[2]

Taking the period c.950–1350, Bartlett's central contention is that in conjunction with an aristocratic diaspora an advanced military technology was disseminated to the Celtic and Slav peripheries of Europe from a 'central area' comprising the Frankish and German heartlands, together with England *after* 1066.[3] Such technology had three main components: missile weapons (notably the crossbow), heavy cavalry, and castles together with related siege techniques. The assimilation of such

---

* My thanks are due to John Hudson, who kindly read this paper in draft and offered valuable criticism, and for the helpful comments of friends and colleagues at the 1996 Battle Conference.

[1] *Gesta Guillelmi*, 156; R.A. Brown, *The Norman Conquest*, London 1984, 27–8. William of Malmesbury sites this council at Lillebonne (*De gestis regum* ii, 299). For the treatment of these deliberations by subsequent Anglo-Norman chroniclers and by Wace in particular see E.C.M. van Houts, 'The Ship List of William the Conqueror', *ANS* x, 1987, 159–83 at 161–2.

[2] R. Bartlett, *The Making of Europe: Conquest, Colonization and Cultural Change, 950–1350*, London 1993, repr. 1994, chapter 3, 'Military Technology and Political Power', 60–84, which follows his earlier article, 'Technique militaire et pouvoir politique, 900–1300', *Annales; économies – sociétés – civilisations* xli, 1986, 1135–59. Cf *idem, War and Lordship: The Military Component of Political Power, 900–1300* (Fourth Annual Phi Alpha Theta Lecture on History, State University of New York at Albany, 1984).

[3] Bartlett, *The Making of Europe*, 24ff.

superior equipment, fortifications and fighting techniques by peripheral cultures occurred not simply through the direct conquests which they facilitated, but through defensive imitation and cultural emulation.[4]

Few, I suggest, would take issue with the fundamentals of Bartlett's thesis in relation to the Celtic lands or those beyond the German Ostmark, though qualifications have been suggested by more specific case studies such as Frederick Suppe's *Military Institutions on the Welsh Marches*.[5] Suppe not only follows Gerald of Wales in pointing to the power of the native elm bows of the men of Gwent and the inadequacies of heavy cavalry in rough and mountainous terrain – factors readily acknowledged by Bartlett[6] – but has stressed the effectiveness of Welsh guerilla tactics and the inability of castles either to prevent raiding or to resist sustained assault. The Anglo-Norman experience in Wales, he would argue, represented not the inexorable triumph of a superior Frankish technology, but the clash of two highly divergent forms of warfare neither of which could achieve effective dominance over the other, and which resulted in an amalgam and cross-fertilization of military techniques.[7]

But what of England *before* 1066? How far does Bartlett's model hold true of a kingdom which, unlike Scotland, Ireland and the Welsh principalities, had by the early eleventh century achieved a degree of political unification, governmental sophistication, and economic development that rivalled if not far outmatched any of the political units existing within the 'central area' of Europe.[8] By first considering the three main categories of military technology proposed by Bartlett – missile weapons, cavalry and fortifications – then by exploring the additional but crucial dimension of naval power, I would like to argue that in terms of its military potential and methods of fighting, Anglo-Saxon England was anything but a periphery before 1066; it was distinct, to be sure, but no less sophisticated or effective than its Norman assailant. By the nature of its broad remit, what follows can only be an outline sketch, but it may, I hope, not only question the extent to which the Conquest can be viewed as a 'military revolution' – a theme which has long been inherent in discussions of the Norman Conquest – but also contribute to the wider debate concerning 'military revolutions', which, from the initial sixteenth- and seventeenth-century battleground of Roberts and Parker, is now firmly encamped in the later middle ages and marching, it seems, steadily earlier.[9]

---

[4] Bartlett, *The Making of Europe*, 60–84.

[5] F.C. Suppe, *Military Institutions on the Welsh Marches. Shropshire, 1066–1300*, Woodbridge 1994.

[6] Bartlett, *The Making of Europe*, 63, 77.

[7] Suppe, *Military Institutions*, 1–33, 143–9. It could be added that much the same theme of assimilation and amalgamation of systems of recruitment and even methods of fighting characterize elements of military development in post-Conquest England (C.W. Hollister, *The Military Organization of Norman England*, Oxford 1965, 216–67; *idem, Anglo-Saxon Military Institutions on the Eve of the Norman Conquest*, Oxford 1962, 131–2; and below, 369).

[8] J. Campbell, 'Observations on English Government from the Tenth to the Twelfth Century', *TRHS*, 5th series, xxv, 1975, 39–54; *idem*, 'Some Agents and Agencies of the Late Anglo-Saxon State', in *Domesday Studies*, ed J.C. Holt, Woodbridge 1986, 201–18; *idem*, 'Was it Infancy in England? Some Questions of Comparison', in *England and her Neighbours, 1066–1453. Essays in Honour of Pierre Chaplais*, ed. M. Jones and M. Vale, 1989, 1–17; 'England c.991', in *The Battle of Maldon. Fact and Fiction*, ed. J. Cooper, London 1993, 1–17.

[9] *The Military Revolution Debate*, ed. C.J. Rogers, Boulder 1995; *idem*, 'The Military Revolutions of the Hundred Years' War', *The Journal of Military History* lvii, 1993, 241–78; *The Medieval*

Turning first to missile weapons, not only does the testimony of Gerald of Wales indicate the independent existence of powerful bows in Wales before any Anglo-Norman penetration,[10] but increasingly the distinction between the 'shortbow' and the 'longbow' as separate categories of weapon linked teleologically is coming to be seen as more a semantic distortion than a reality.[11] Certainly there is no evidence to suggest that the self-bow deployed by Norman archers at Hastings was any different from that used by their Saxon opponents, who had a long tradition of archery even though its military application remains obscure.[12] If there was a crucial distinction at Hastings, it was in numbers of archers deployed. Whether the absence of an adequate Anglo-Saxon missile arm was due to the speed of Harold's march south from Stamford Bridge, which left the archers – poor and therefore unhorsed – behind,[13] or to other circumstances now lost to us, the deficiency was a crucial one, arguably far more so than any absence of cavalry. For a closely-formed defensive formation of well-equipped men-at-arms supported by adequate missile-fire could defeat cavalry, as the battle of Bourgthéroulde (1124) was to show in microcosm,[14] anticipating the successful English tactics of the Hundred Years War.[15] At Hastings, however, Harold lacked the ability to neutralise the Norman archery by keeping it at a distance,[16] while his densely packed ranks must have offered an easy target to the bowmen and crossbowmen who clearly comprised a significant element in William's army of invasion.[17]

Military Revolution: State, Society and Military Change in Medieval and Early Modern Europe, ed. A. Ayton and J.L. Price, London 1995; M. Prestwich, 'Was there a Military Revolution in Medieval England?', in *Recognitions: Essays Presented to Edmund Fryde*, ed. C. Richmond and I. Harvey, Aberystwyth 1996, 19–38.

[10] *Itinerarium Kambriae* in *Giraldi Cambrensis Opera*, ed. J.F. Dimock, 8 vols, RS XXI, 1861–91, vi, 123, 177, 179.

[11] J. Bradbury, *The Medieval Archer*, Woodbridge 1985, 12–16, 65, 71–75; and R. Hardy and M.J. Strickland, *The Great War Bow* (forthcoming). The most succinct comment, however, remains that of J.C. Holt, *Robin Hood*, London 1982, 79:

> Some historians have been misled by a semantic confusion. Almost inevitably, the longbow has been contrasted with the 'short bow' which is alleged to have preceed it as the conventional weapon of the twelfth and thirteenth centuries. But the longbow was so described to distinguish it not from a short, but from a crossbow. There were short bows. There were short men . . . But the short bow as a category of weapon was invented by the military historian, Sir Charles Oman, in the nineteenth century.

[12] R. Glover, 'The English Army in 1066', *EHR* lxvii, 1952, 1–18, at 117; Bradbury, *The Medieval Archer*, 17–22; J. Manley, 'The Archer and the Army in the Late Saxon Period', *Anglo-Saxon Studies in Archaeology and History* iv, 1985, 223–35.

[13] As argued by Glover, 'English Warfare in 1066', 181–2.

[14] Orderic vi, 348–52; *Jumièges* ii, 234–5. It is possible that archers were employed with similar effect at Brémule in 1119 (Orderic vi, xxi, 238).

[15] For a valuable summary of these tactics see M. Bennett, 'The Development of Battle Tactics in the Hundred Years War', in *Arms, Armies and Fortifications in the Hundred Years War*, ed. A. Curry and M. Hughes, Woodbridge 1994, 1–20.

[16] It was the same fatal weakness that led to Wallace's defeat at Falkirk in 1298. See G.W.S. Barrow, *Robert Bruce and the Community of the Realm of Scotland*, Edinburgh 3rd edn. 1988, 102–3. The analogies between these two battles are instructive.

[17] Bradbury, *The Medieval Archer*, 22–32. One wonders whether this substantial provision of a missile arm was a reflection of William's knowledge of Anglo-Saxon tactics, though his ability to assemble such a corps reflects the relative importance of bows and crossbows in contemporary Frankish warfare.

Fig. 1. The Pictish stone at Aberlemno, which probably represents the defeat of the Northumbrian king Ecgfrith at Nechtansmere in 685. The Northumbrians, on the right, are depicted as heavily armed horsemen with helmets and mail-coats. The rider in the central panel is either about to throw his spear, or is jabbing overarm with it. To the left, Pictish horsemen flank a body of infantry, one of whom holds a long spear in both hands, his shield suspended by a baldric. (Historic Scotland)

Fig. 2. The Coppergate helmet, found at York, and dating to c.750–775. It is strikingly similar in form to those depicted on the Aberlemno stone, and indicates the sophisticated defensive equipment available to the Northumbrian aristocracy. (The York Archaeological Trust)

Deployed by William at Hastings,[18] the crossbow indeed appears to have been a continental import hitherto unknown in England,[19] though it had been in use in France since at least the tenth century.[20] Evidence for the earlier use of crossbows among the Picts is at best ambiguous; the Drosten symbol stone seems to depict not a cross-bow, but rather a 'spring-bow' or mechanical trap used for hunting,[21] while crannog finds of antler and bone cross-bow nuts suggest a late medieval date.[22] This aside, there is little evidence for Anglo-Saxon use of the weapon.[23] Yet if the crossbow played a significant role in achieving Norman victory at Hastings, and both the *Carmen* and Baudri of Bourgeuil believed it did, this was precisely because its great penetrative power was needed against the close-packed ranks of an Anglo-Saxon warrior aristocracy who were as heavily armed and equipped as their Franco-Norman opponents.[24] Thereafter, however, the contribution of the crossbow in the subsequent process of conquest and Anglo-Norman expansion within Britain is hard to trace.[25] And against a fast, mobile enemy employing guerilla tactics in difficult terrain, as in Wales and Ireland, the need was less for the massive power of the crossbow – for defensive armour was far less widespread among Celtic warriors – than for nimble archers capable of rapid fire, as Gerald of Wales pointed out to would-be conquerors of these lands.[26]

Nor should the impact of the crossbow in subsequent Anglo-Norman warfare be over-stated. It was *par excellence* a weapon for siege (the context in which it claimed many of its most notable victims),[27] for its slow rate of fire limited its

---

[18] *Gesta Guillelmi*, 184, notes how at Hastings William '*pedites in fronte locavit, sagittis armatos et balistis*'.

[19] This ignorance is explicitly stated by Baudri of Bourgueil, *Carmen cxcvi*, ed. P. Abrahams, Paris 1926, lines 409–12, and is implied by the use of the loan word *arbalete* by the ASC 'D', 1079. If the the artists of the Bayeux Tapestry were indeed Anglo-Saxons, such unfamiliarity might account for the absence of crossbowmen in this work.

[20] The evidence for the use of the crossbow in ninth- and tenth-century France is helpfully collected and discussed in *Carmen*, Appendix C, 'The Use of the Crossbow at Hastings', 112–15.

[21] J.M. Gilbert, 'Crossbows on Pictish Stones', *Proceedings of the Society of Antiquaries of Scotland* cvii, 1975–6, 316–17, argues for crossbows, but while the bow depicted on the Drosten stone clearly has a form of tiller, the archer's grip on it is not that employed on a crossbow, and he draws back the string with one hand.

[22] A. MacGregor, 'Two Antler Crossbow Nuts and some Notes on the Early Development of the Crossbow', *Proceedings of the Society of Antiquaries of Scotland* cvii, 1975–6, 317–21.

[23] Riddle 17 from the Exeter Book refers to a form of mechanical bow, but it is unclear whether this is a crossbow or a larger siege balista (*Exeter Book*, ed. I. Gollancz, 2 vols, London 1895–1934, ii, 106). In either case, the reference stands in virtual isolation before 1066.

[24] Below, 367. The weapon's power is noted by the *Carmen*, lines 411–12, 'the crossbow-men destroyed the shields as if by a hail-storm, shattered them by countless blows'; and line 382, 'against crossbow-bolts shields are of no avail'.

[25] In 1075, following the suppression of the 'revolt of the earls', Lanfranc informed King William that Norwich Castle had been taken and garrisoned with many crossbowmen and siege engineers (*cum balistariis et artificibus*) as well as 300 knights, but similar details of the deployment of archers and crossbowmen in William's campaigns are scanty (*Lanfranc's Letters*, no. 35, 126–7, where *balistarii* is mysteriously translated as 'slingers').

[26] Gerald of Wales, *Expugnatio Hibernica*, ed. A.B. Scott and F.X. Martin, Dublin 1978, 246–9. These comments are repeated almost verbatim in his *Descriptio Kambriae*, *Giraldi Cambrensis Opera* vi, 220–1.

[27] Amongst those fatally wounded by crossbow bolts at sieges were Geoffrey Martel, count of Anjou, shot at Candé in 1106; Matthew, count of Boulogne at Drincourt, 1173; Richard Coeur de Lion at Chaluz Chabrol, 1199; and Eustace de Vesci at Barnard Castle in 1216 (Orderic vi, 76; *The*

effectiveness in open battle. Of the series of battles between 1066 and 1144, the crossbow is only mentioned as being in use at Hastings and at Alençon in 1118 – not at Tinchebrai (1106), Brémule (1119), Bourgthéroulde (1124) or the first battle of Lincoln (1141), which may perhaps reflect a reluctance, particularly in situations of civil war, to deploy the crossbow *en masse* against knightly opponents.[28]

There is little need here to rehearse the well-known arguments concerning the absence, or otherwise, of cavalry in Anglo-Saxon England,[29] though it is perhaps symptomatic of the paucity of evidence that the most recent debate has focused on the late seventh- or early eighth-century Pictish stone at Aberlemno (see Fig. 1), which shows Pictish warriors defeating heavily armed opponents fighting from the saddle, one of whom jabs overarm with his spear in a manner similiar to some of the Norman cavalry on the Bayeux Tapestry.[30] If the Aberlemno stone does indeed represent the defeat of the Northumbrian king Ecgfrith at Nechtansmere in 685 – and the striking correlation between the equipment of the enemy horsemen it portrays and the Coppergate helmet strongly suggests that it does (see Fig. 2)[31] – then we must guard against the assumption that all Anglo-Saxon armies fought in the same manner, or that tactics and strategy remained unaltered from the days of the heptarchy to Hastings.[32] It is perhaps significant that of the three Pictish

Historical Works of Gervase of Canterbury, ed. W. Stubbs, 2 vols, RS LXXIII, 1879–80, i, 246); *Radulphi de Coggeshall Chronicon Anglicanum*, ed. J. Stevenson, RS LXVI, 1875, 94–6; *Matthei Parisiensis monarchi Sancti Albani chronica majora*, ed. H.R. Luard, 7 vols, RS LVII, 1872–3, ii, 666. By contrast, Toki, son of the prominent Anglo-Saxon lord Wigod of Wallingford, was killed in battle by a crossbow bolt at Gerberoi, 1079 (*ASC* (D), *s.a.* 1079).

[28] For Alençon, see L. Halphen and R. Poupardin, *Chroniques des Comtes d'Anjou et des Seigneurs d'Amboise*, Paris 1913, 155–61, crossbows being mentioned at 159. At the second battle of Lincoln in 1217, Fawkes de Bréauté explicitly ordered his crossbowmen to shoot the horses of the Franco-baronial forces, not the riders (Matthew Paris, *Chronica majora* iii, 21).

[29] For the essence of the debate see Glover, 'English Warfare in 1066', 174–88; Hollister, *Anglo-Saxon Military Institutions*, 134–40; R.A. Brown, *Origins of English Feudalism*, London 1973, 34–43; and cf. R.H.C. Davis, in *The Medieval Warhorse*, London 1989, 75–8; *idem*, 'Did the Anglo-Saxons have Warhorses?', *Weapons and Warfare in Anglo-Saxon England*, ed. S.C. Hawkes, Oxford University Committee for Archaeology Monograph no. 21, Oxford 1989, 141–4.

[30] N.J. Higham, 'Cavalry in Early Bernicia?', *Northern History* xxvii, 1991, 236–41; C. Cessford, 'Cavalry in Early Bernicia: A Reply', *Northern History* xxix, 1993, 185–7; N. Hooper, 'The Aberlemno Stone and Cavalry in Anglo-Saxon England', *Northern History* xxix, 1993, 189–96. For the stone itself see C. Thomas, 'The Pictish Class 1 Symbol Stones', in *Pictish Studies: Settlement, Burial and Art in Dark Age Northern Britain*, ed. J.G.P. Friell and W.G. Watson, Oxford 1984, 169–87; and R. Ritchie, *Picts*, Edinburgh 1989, 22–5. Cf. L. Alcock, 'The Rhind Lectures 1988–89: a Synopsis. An Heroic Age: War and Society in Northern Britain, AD 450–850', *Proceedings of the Society of Antiquaries of Scotland* cxviii, 1988, 327–34, at 331.

[31] D. Tweddle, *The Coppergate Helmet*, York 1984. Hooper, 'The Aberlemno Stone', 191 and n. 16, draws a further parallel, 'close rather than complete', with the helmets depicted on the Franks casket.

[32] Such a caveat is reinforced by the diversity of fighting practices among the German tribes recorded by Tacitus in his *Germania*. Though he notes that 'generally speaking, their strength lies in infantry rather than cavalry', Tacitus speaks of mixed formations of cavalry and infantry, and tribes such as the Tencteri are singled out for their skill in horsemanship (Tacitus, *The Agricola and the Germania*, trans. H. Mattingley, revised S.A. Handford, Harmondsworth 1970, 106, 128–9). Cf. Hooper, 'The Aberlemno Stone', 192, and for a good chronological overview of Anglo-Saxon warfare see *idem*, 'The Anglo-Saxons at War', in *Weapons and Warfare in Anglo-Saxon England*, ed. S.C. Hawkes, Oxford University Committee for Archaeology Monograph no. 21, Oxford 1989, 191–202.

infantrymen, seemingly in close formation and confronting an attacking horseman, one is shown with a shield slung by a baldric round his neck, holding in both hands a long spear (in a manner reminiscent of the Macedonian phalanx), the length of which protrudes past his sword-armed companion who preceeds him.[33] It can be no more than conjecture, but may this not be an early representation of the infantry formation of spearmen later known as the schiltrom,[34] used to such effect against the heavy cavalry of the Edwardian armies during the Wars of Independence?

The Aberlemno stone notwithstanding, however, the evidence from the later Anglo-Saxon period, fragmentary and inadequate though it is, gives the overwhelming impression that by the tenth century if not well before, warriors did not as a rule fight from the saddle as drilled cavalry but rode to battle and dismounted to fight. Bryhtnoth's orders for his men to dismount to fight in *The Battle of Maldon*; the *Chronicle* entry for 1055 telling how Earl Ralph ordered the Anglo-Saxons to fight on horseback against the Welsh contrary to their custom with disastrous results; the complete untrustworthiness of Snorri Sturlasson's *Harald Hardrada's Saga* for the use of cavalry at Stamford Bridge; and the fact that Harold's army fought on foot at Hastings despite the potential of a devastating downhill charge – all these point to the same inescapable conclusion that the Anglo-Saxons fought predominantly, if not exclusively, as infantry.[35]

But here we are concerned with two important points. First, there has been growing recognition that the effectiveness of heavy cavalry as the all powerful military arm of medieval Europe has been considerably exaggerated.[36] In a recent paper, Matthew Bennett has suggested a more realistic picture of the medieval warhorse as a form of cob rather than the towering eighteen hands beast of popular but unfounded assumption.[37] Equally, the ability of disciplined and closely formed infantry successfully to resist and even defeat cavalry equally serves seriously to qualify the supposed supremacy of the heavy horsemen's 'shock tactics'.[38] At Hastings, the Norman cavalry only became effective once they were able to isolate

---

[33] Such long spears were later described by Ailred of Rievaux and Gerald of Wales as the chief weapon of the Galwegians and the men of North Wales respectively (*Relatio venerabilis Aelredi, abbatis Rievallensis, de Standardo*, in *Chronicles and Memorials of the Reigns of Stephen, Henry II and Richard I*, ed. R. Howlett, 4 vols, RS XXXVIII, 1884–90, iii, 186; Gerald, *Descriptio Kambriae*, 177, 181).

[34] If so, this would be the earliest – if not the only – known medieval representation of the schiltrom. On this formation see W.M. Mackenzie, *The Battle of Bannockburn: A Study in Medieval Warfare*, Glasgow 1913, 47–8; and Barrow, *Robert Bruce*, 220–1, 226–9. Compare such schematic representation with the Tapestry's vivid attempt to display the massed formation of Norman knights at Hastings (D. Wilson, *The Bayeux Tapestry*, London 1985, pls 52–3).

[35] Brown, *Origins of Feudalism*, 34–43, and 100, 102, 108–13 where these sources are discussed and given in extract.

[36] J. Gillingham, 'Conquering the Barbarians: War and Chivalry in Twelfth-Century Britain', *Haskins Society Journal* iv, 1992, 67–84, at 75–6; J. France, *Victory in the East. A Military History of the First Crusade*, Cambridge 1994, 30–1, 71–4.

[37] M. Bennett, 'The Medieval Warhorse Reconsidered', *Medieval Knighthood V. Papers from the Sixth Strawberry Hill Conference, 1994*, ed. S. Church and R. Harvey, Woodbridge 1995, 19–40, at 21–6; and cf. *idem*, 'The Myth of the Military Supremacy of Knightly Cavalry', in *Armies, Chivalry and Warfare. Proceedings of the 1995 Harlaxton Symposium*, ed. M.J. Strickland (forthcoming, Stamford 1997). For an important new study see A. Hyland, *The Medieval Warhorse From Byzantium to the Crusades*, Stroud 1994.

[38] Bennett, 'The Medieval Warhorse Reconsidered', 33–4.

groups of Anglo-Saxons in the open as a result of the feigned flight tactics, and then exploit the resulting gaps in the enemy's main formation.[39]

Space here precludes a detailed re-examination of the vexed question of the couched lance.[40] But for the present I would only add that evidence for a tactical revolution as a result of the adoption of couched lance is tellingly elusive, whether we search for it in the period of Charles Martel or around the year 1100, when the supposedly 'embryonic' cavalry techniques of the Bayeux Tapestry are alleged to have achieved maturity.[41] Just as it is now recognized that the stirrup spread only gradually after its appearance in Western Europe, so I would argue that the 'invention' of the couched lance – itself an inherently implausible idea – is a chimera. Horsemen, whether heavily or lightly equipped, used a variety of lance blows throughout the whole period. If the *Psalterium Aureum* of c.880 shows a Carolingian horseman with a couched lance just as 'developed' as those in the Bayeux Tapestry (see Figs 3, 4 and 5),[42] then equally a variety of later medieval manuscripts from the thirteenth to fifteenth centuries show knights jabbing overarm in the supposed 'old fashioned' method as well as other techniques (see Figs 6 and 7).[43]

The teleological view of a development from spear-wielding Carolingian horsemen to the 'true' knight with couched lance of c.1100 confuses the availability of more detailed and expansive literary and visual sources (particularly *The Song of Roland* and the *Bayeux Tapestry*), with the emergence of a new technique of cavalry combat. But the novelty lies only in the survival of the sources; no comparable vernacular *chansons* or secular embroidery are extant from the earlier Frankish period,[44] while what little depiction of battle there is in earlier manuscript

---

[39] Bennett, 'The Medieval Warhorse Reconsidered', 36. On the feigned flight manouevre, which demanded considerable skill and discipline from the knights, see B. Bachrach, 'The Feigned Retreat at Hastings', *Mediaeval Studies* xxxiii, 1971, 344–7.

[40] D.J.A. Ross, 'L'originalité de Turoldus: le maniement de la lance', *Cahiers de Civilisation Médiévale* vi, 1963, 127–38; V. Cirlot, 'Techniques guerrières en Catalogne féodale; le maniement de la lance', *Cahiers de Civilisation Médiévale* xxviii, 1985, 36–43; J. Flori, 'Encore l'usage de la lance: la technique du combat vers l'an 1100', *Cahiers de Civilisation Médiévale* xxxi, 1988, 213–40; J. France, *Victory in the East: A Military History of the Third Crusade*, Cambridge 1994, 30–1, 70–1, 73. Cf. B. Bachrach, '*Caballus et Caballarius* in Medieval Warfare', in *The Study of Chivalry: Resources and Approaches*, ed. H. Chickering and T.H. Seiler, Kalamazoo 1988, 173–212; idem, 'Animals and Warfare in Early Medieval Europe', in *L'uomo di fronte del mondo animale nell'alto medioevo*, Settimane di studio del centro italiano di studi sull'alto medioevo, xxxi, 1985, i, 706–64.

[41] The essential revisionist work on the debate concerning the stirrup and the introduction of feudalism into early Frankia is B. Bachrach, 'Charles Martel, Mounted Shock Combat, the Stirrup and Feudalism', *Studies in Medieval and Renaissance History* vii, 1970, 49–75.

[42] F. Mütherich and J.E. Gaehde, *Carolingian Painting*, London 1977, pls 46–7; cf. BT, pls 60–72. Just as in the Tapestry, warriors are here shown using the overarm thrust as well, though perhaps significantly, when they are attacking a town, not other horsemen.

[43] See, for example, Matthew Paris's *Life of St Alban*, Trinity College, Dublin, MS 177, fo. 41v; the Maciejowski Bible (Pierpont Morgan MS 638), reproduced in S.C. Cockerell, *Old Testament Minatures*, London, fos 10r, 12r, 42r, 45v; and for a later illustration of mixed lance techniques see Marsal de Sas's altar-piece, c.1400, showing James I of Aragon's victory at Puig de Cebolla (R. Rudorff, *The Knights and their World*, London 1974, 161). Examples could be multiplied from sculpture, such as the early twelfth-century north door of S. Nicola at Bari, which shows knights striking overarm with their lances (R.H.C. Davis, *The Medieval Warhorse*, London 1989, 60).

[44] For surviving epic literature, such as the Old High German *Ludwigslied* and *Waltharius*, see J.K. Bostock, *A Handbook on Old High German Literature*, revised by K.C. King and D.R. McLintock,

Fig. 3. Late Carolingian horsemen from the Psalterium Aureum, produced at St Gall before 883. While on the opposite folio cavalrymen attack a city using lances overarm, the central rider here employs the couched lance, in a manner indistinguishable from the Norman knights on the Bayeux Tapestry. (Stiftsbibliothek, St Gallen, Cod. 22, 140v)

Figs 4 and 5. Norman knights from the Bayeux Tapestry. The horsemen here employ a variety of methods to wield their lances, not because the technique of the 'couched lance' was as yet nascent, but because at Hastings, they were forced to adapt to fighting against closely-formed infantry in a strong defensive position. Until the Anglo-Saxon 'shield-wall' had begun to fragment, throwing lances or jabbing overarm must have been as effective, if not more so, than the couched lance, designed primarily for fighting against other cavalry. (Victoria and Albert Museum)

Fig. 6. *In this scene of the massacre of the converts from his Life of St Alban (c.1245–52), Matthew Paris depicts knights thrusting overarm with their lances. (The Board of Trinity College, Dublin; Trinity College Library, MS 177 fo. 41v)*

Fig. 7. *Knights adopt an unusual two-handed method of attack with their lances, from the Maciejowski Bible, French c.1250. While this book of Old Testament scenes far more frequently depicts the attack with the couched lance, illustrations such as this should warn us against assuming both a rigid teleology or a complete uniformity in methods of cavalry combat even by the mid-thirteenth century. (The Pierpont Morgan Library, MS 638, fo. 12r)*

illumination is often derivative and fraught with problems of interpretation.[45] These factors, coupled with the silence or ambiguity of written texts as to horse-men's actual methods of combat, mean that we are almost wholly ignorant of *how* earlier Frankish cavalry fought,[46] and caution against the simple assumption that such mounted warfare was somehow more 'primitive' and ineffectual.[47] Certainly, the equipment demanded of a heavy cavalryman by the capitularies differs little from that required of knights by Henry II's Assize of Arms of 1181.[48] The fact that as early as 531, the Thuringians were sufficiently conscious of the efficacy of a Frankish charge to dig concealed pits before their ranks to break the impact of Theudebert's cavalry,[49] should remind us that irrespective of how warriors wielded their lances, a charge of heavy cavalry must have been a terrifying experience in any era, and that this psychological impact was as, if not more, important than any 'shock tactics'.

To be sure, there were developments from the twelfth century: leather or mail barding afforded increased protection to costly mounts, while the high-backed, wrap-around saddle and possibly double girthing served to make the rider more secure.[50] Perhaps too, there was an improvement in breeds of war horse. But, I would suggest, these marked gradual improvements (themselves offset by other developments such as the mass deployment of pole-armed infantry), not some military 'big bang' attained through the couched lance which has been located with a precision more apparent than real at various stages from the late eleventh to the mid-twelfth century, but which is hard to trace on the battlefield itself. This is not to dismiss the charge with the couched lance, which was undoubtedly very effec-tive,[51] but rather to challenge its use as a *deus ex machina* of technical determinism to explain social or military change.[52] As Bennett notes, the couched lance was a method best employed against other horsemen; the knights on the Tapestry are throwing or jabbing with their lances not because some of them had not yet learned the 'new way' in war, but because they were attacking infantry in close formation and on rising ground[53] – just as at Bannockburn the English knights, unable to

Oxford 1976, and C. Edwards, 'German Vernacular Literature: A Survey', in *Carolingian Culture: Emulation and Innovation*, ed. R. McKitterick, Cambridge 1994, 141–201. Such works, however, are scarcely comparable to the detailed (and often formulaic) descriptions of combat in *chansons* such as *Roland*.

[45] Cf. S. Coupland, 'Carolingian Arms and Armour in the Ninth Century', *Viator* xx, 1989, 29–50.

[46] For the ambiguity of an important (and isolated) passage on mounted combat with the lance in Gregory of Tours' *History of the Franks*, see Davis, *The Medieval Warhorse*, 15, where Davis's own interpretation is perhaps open to question. The laconic and equally opaque evidence of later writers such as Flodoard and Richer on cavalry techniques is carefully studied by J. France, 'La guerre dans la France féodale à la fin du IX et au X siècles', *Revue Belge d'Histoire Militaire* xxiii, 1979, 177–98.

[47] M.J. Strickland, *War and Chivalry. The Conduct and Perception of War in England and Nor-mandy, 1066–1217*, Cambridge 1996, 144–6.

[48] F.L. Ganshof, *Frankish Institutions under Charlemagne*, New York 1968, 65–6 and ns. 47–53; *Gesta regis Henrici secundi Benedicti abbatis*, ed. W. Stubbs, 2 vols, RS XLIX, i, 278, cc. 1–2.

[49] Gregory of Tours, *The History of the Franks*, trans. L. Thorpe, Harmondsworth 1974, 168.

[50] Bachrach, '*Caballus et Caballarius*', 193–7.

[51] Armour could not withstand a lance blow thus delivered, while non-European contemporaries felt moved to comment on the power of the Frankish charge (Strickland, *War and Chivalry*, 174; Bennett, 'The Medieval Warhorse Reconsidered', 34–6).

[52] Strickland, *War and Chivalry*, 23, 146.

[53] For a very different view, that the Tapestry shows only the nascent charge, and that it was the

penetrate the tightly packed and bristling Scottish schiltroms, threw their lances – and even swords and maces – at the enemy in their frustrated impotence.[54]

The second main point is that if the Anglo-Saxons did not deploy cavalry then it was out of choice, not because of a lack of the necessary technology. As Brooks has demonstrated, the tenth and eleventh centuries saw an increasing dissemination of helmets, armour and swords which formerly had been restricted to a much smaller elite, a process undoubtedly accelerated first by the expansion of West Saxon power then by the pressing needs of defence against the renewed Scandinavian threat.[55] If the heriots of II Cnut still are concerned with the highest echelons of society, the notice in the *ASC* for 1008 that a helmet and mail shirt were required from every eight hides suggests that a goodly number of warriors in the hosts of Aethelred must have been respectably armed.[56] By the later eleventh century, the equipment of Normans and Saxons on the Bayeux Tapestry, save for the shape of some shields, is virtually identical.[57]

Hence Bartlett's striking comment that 'the heavy horsemen of the Middle Ages lived in the wheat age but looked like men from the steel age' applies just as much to the gesiths and thegns of Anglo-Saxon England.[58] As John Gillingham has argued, it was not the techniques of fighting which mattered so much when 'conquering the barbarians' but the superiority in defensive armour reflecting a more wealthy and developed economy.[59] Nor did such superiority of arms and equipment over the Celts need to await the coming of the Normans; it was equally enjoyed by the Anglo-Saxons, and may well find its earliest visual representation on the Aberlemno stone, whose sculptors were clearly attempting to stress the technological superiority of the enemy, and hence magnify the achievement of their own victory.

As with defensive armour, so too with equestrian equipment. The evidence of both manuscript illumination and archaeology reveals the use of stirrups at least by the early eleventh century,[60] while Anglo-Scandinavian sculpture, such as the tenth-century tomb from Sockburn, depicts saddles with high cantles and pommels virtually identical to those depicted on the Bayeux Tapestry in use by Saxon and Norman alike.[61] And, as the late R.H.C. Davis pointed out, there is considerable

---

First Crusade that acted as an important catalyst for its subsequent development, see France, *Victory in the East*, 31, 71, 73 and the important comments at 372 n. 5.

[54] Barrow, *Robert the Bruce*, 220.

[55] N.P. Brooks, 'Arms, Status and Warfare in Late Anglo-Saxon England', in *Ethelred the Unready*, ed. D. Hill, British Archaeological Reports, British Series lix, 1978, 81–103; and cf. *idem*, 'Weapons and Armour', in *The Battle of Maldon AD 991*, ed. D.G. Scragg, Manchester 1991, 208–19. For an important contextual discussion see J. Gillingham, 'Thegns and Knights in Eleventh-Century England: Who was then the Gentleman?', *TRHS*, 6th ser. v, 1995, 129–53, especially 135–7.

[56] II Cnut, c.71 (*EHD* i, 465); *ASC* (C) *s.a* 1008.

[57] *BT*, pls 61–72; and cf. N.P. Brooks and H.E. Walker, 'The Authority and Interpretation of the Bayeux Tapestry', *ANS* i, 1978, 1–34, at 19–20.

[58] Bartlett, *The Making of Europe*, 61.

[59] Gillingham, 'Conquering the Barbarians', 75–6.

[60] J. Kiff, 'Images of War: Illustrations of Warfare in Early Eleventh-Century England', *ANS* vii, 1984, 177–94 at 192 and pl. 6; W.A. Seaby and P. Woodfield, 'Viking Stirrups from England and their Background', *Medieval Archaeology* xxiv, 1980, 87–122; J. Graham-Campbell, 'Anglo-Scandinavian Equestrian Equipment in Eleventh-Century England', *ANS* xiv, 1991, 77–90.

[61] For the Sockburn sculpture see R. Cramp, *Corpus of Anglo-Saxon Stone Sculpture, Vol. i: County Durham and Northumberland*, 2 vols, Oxford 1984, ii, pl. 745; N.J. Higham, *The Kingdom*

evidence for selective breeding of high quality horses in stud farms in tenth- and eleventh-century England if not earlier.[62] Horses were not only symbols of rank and status, as Gale Owen-Crocker and James Graham-Campbell have shown, but the automatic association of horses and arms in heriots, notably those listed in II Cnut, indicate them to have been regarded as an integral aspect of military equipment.[63]

But if, as is well attested, the use of horses was a key factor in the mobility of Anglo-Saxon forces from the 'mounted force' of Ecgfrith in 683 mentioned by Eddius Stephanus[64] to Harold's campaigns of 1066, why then did the Anglo-Saxons generally choose not to fight from the saddle? Essentially, I would suggest, because unlike the Viking settlers in Normandy from 911, who came to assimilate Frankish military techniques including castles and cavalry, there was no cultural or military catalyst before 1066 for changing their highly effective and seemingly time-honoured methods of infantry combat. Neither their Celtic or Viking enemies fought as drilled heavy cavalry. While Celtic chiefs may have possessed good equipment and expensive horses – one instantly thinks here of the Gododdin[65] – the majority of Welsh, Scottish and Pictish horsemen seem to have fought as light skirmishers, to exploit the advantages of their fast mounts in rough terrain.[66] The Vikings were as well, if not better, armed than the Anglo-Saxons, but the evidence suggests that in Britain at least, they too rode to battle but dismounted to fight on foot.[67]

Nor is it hard to see why. Hastings itself is a key example of the effectiveness of closely formed infantry, and the battle was so hard fought that contemporaries on both sides believed that only divine intervention could account for the Normans' victory.[68] William was victorious through a combination of superior generalship and sheer good fortune, not because of the innate superiority of Frankish cavalry over Anglo-Saxon infantry. Had he rather than Harold been killed or had he failed

---

of Northumbria, AD 350–1100, Stroud 1993, 198. Cf. Graham-Campbell, 'Anglo-Scandinavian Equestrian Equipment', 80.

[62] R.H.C. Davis, 'The Warhorses of the Normans', *ANS* x, 1987, 67–82, at 80–82; *idem, The Medieval Warhorse*, 70–8; Davis, 'Did the Anglo-Saxons Have Warhorses?', 141–4.

[63] G.R. Owen-Crocker, 'Hawks and Horse Trappings: the Insignia of Rank', in *The Battle of Maldon AD 911*, 220–37; Graham-Campbell, 'Anglo-Scandinavian Equestrian Equipment', 77–90; Davis, 'Did the Anglo-Saxons Have Warhorses?', 142.

[64] *The Life of Bishop Wilfrid by Eddius Stephanus*, ed. and trans. B. Colgrave (Cambridge, 1927, repr. 1985), 40–1.

[65] *The Gododdin: The Oldest Scottish Poem*, ed. K.H. Jackson, 1969.

[66] Higham, 'Cavalry in Early Bernicia?', 239–40, is surely mistaken in dismissing the ability of horsemen to throw javelins, a method of fighting explicitly stated in the *Gododdin*, for this was a time honoured role of light cavalry in the ancient world and well beyond, as pointed out by Cessford, 'Cavalry in Bernicia: A Reply', 185–6 and Hooper, 'The Aberlemno Stone', 189–90. Here it should be noted, however, that the heavy cavalryman in the central scene is not necessarily throwing his spear as Cessford assumes, but could just as well be stabbing overarm with it.

[67] A useful survey of Viking arms, armour and tactics is given by P. Griffiths, *The Viking Art of War*, London 1995, 162–208; see also L. Musset, 'Problèmes militaires du monde scandinave', *Ordinamenti militari in occidente nell'alto medioevo*, 2 vols, Spoleto 1968, i, 245–53. For the Viking use of horses in England see J.H. Clapham, 'The Horsing of the Danes', *EHR* xxv, 1910, 287–93.

[68] *ASC* (D) *s.a.* 1066: 'even as God granted it to them because of the sins of the people'; and for a Norman view, reported by Eadmer, see *Eadmeri historia novorum in Anglia*, ed. M. Rule, RS LXXXI, 1884, 9.

to rally his men when the Breton left collapsed at a crucial stage, the outcome could have been a bloody slaughter of the invader, as had occurred at Stamford Bridge.[69] The memory of this cataclysmic battle permeated the consciousness of the Anglo-Normans well into the twelfth century,[70] and it is hard to believe that the deployment of dismounted knights, supported by cavalry, as a key tactical element in a consecutive series of battles occuring after Hastings – Tinchebrai, Brémule, Bourgthéroulde, the Standard, and Lincoln – did not reflect to some degree the valuable lessons drawn from the desperately fought battle on Senlac ridge.[71] In their blend of cavalry with dismounted knights as heavy infantry, sometimes supported by missilemen, Anglo-Norman tactics represented a highly effective fusion of two divergent military traditions.[72]

The question of castles, the third of Bartlett's technological trinity, is perhaps the most complex and one which requires far more extensive treatment than is possible here. As Bartlett himself notes 'there will always be areas of ambiguity and overlap' between earlier fortifications and the forms of castle developing in Europe from the tenth century.[73] And while burghs were clearly the key military installations of Anglo-Saxon England, the excavations at Goltho and Sulgrave, together with the work of Ann Williams and Derek Renn on the nature of aristocratic fortified residences, have increasingly emphasized the far more diverse and multi-faceted role of defensive works in pre-Conquest England than a simply polarity of 'burghs pre-1066, castles post-1066' would allow.[74]

Conversely, few would wish to deny the crucial role played by the castle both in the subjugation of England after 1066 and in the further expansion, settlement and consolidation of Anglo-Norman royal and seigneurial power.[75] Nor, despite the recognition of the diversity of forms of Norman castles employed post-Conquest and important analogies between 'ringworks' of the early duchy such as Le Plessis Grimoult and fortified Anglo-Saxon sites such as Goltho and Sulgrave, can it be seriously contested that the predominant motte and bailey types and still less stone

[69] Hooper, 'The Anglo-Saxons at War', 200.

[70] Cf. the remark of Richard de Lucy at Battle Abbey, *The Chronicle of Battle Abbey*, ed. E. Searle, Oxford 1980, 178–9.

[71] Jim Bradbury, 'Battles in England', 192–3, admits the possibility of English influence but argues for such dismounting tactics as equally a reflection of existing Frankish tradition. Frankish warriors could dismount to fight, though several examples occur either in the context of siege (such as at the Dyle, 891) or *in extremis*, rather than in a consistent series of engagements as occured between 1106 and 1144. The chief point, however, is that knights were flexible in their methods of combat, and appreciated the value of strong defensive formations on foot.

[72] Hollister, *Anglo-Saxon Military Institutions*, 129–34.

[73] Bartlett, *The Making of Europe*, 65.

[74] G. Beresford, 'Goltho Manor, Lincolnshire: the Buildings and their Surrounding Defences, c.850–1150', *ANS* iv, 1981, 13–36; *idem, Goltho: The Development of an Early Medieval Manor c.850–1150*, London 1987; S. Basset, 'Beyond the Edge of Excavation: The Topographical Context of Goltho', in *Studies in Medieval History Presented to R.H.C. Davis*, ed. H. Mayr-Harting and R.I. Moore, London 1985, 21–39; B.K. Davidson, 'Excavations at Sulgrave, Northamptonshire', *Archaeological Journal* cxxxiv, 1977, 105–14; A. Williams, 'A Bell-house and a Burgh-geat: Lordly Residences in England before the Norman Conquest', *Medieval Knighthood IV. Papers From the Fifth Strawberry Hill Conference*, 1990, ed. C. Harper-Bill and R. Harvey, Woodbridge 1992, 221–40; D. Renn, 'Burhgeat and Gonfanon: Two Side-lights from the Bayeux Tapestry', *ANS* xvi, 1993, 177–98.

[75] N.J.G. Pounds, *The Medieval Castle in England and Wales*, Cambridge 1990, 3–71, provides an admirable survey with extensive bibliography.

keeps were a Frankish import into England.[76] And as Ann Williams has pointed out, although we are probably justified in regarding fortified thegnly residences as being widespread in pre-Conquest England, nevertheless their use as bases for noble rebellion or civil war was limited[77] – the fortifications of Wimborne and Christchurch by the aetheling Aethelwold against Edward the Elder in 900 is an example standing in relative isolation.[78] Rather it was fleets which furnished the crucial mechanism for expressing political discontent, as witness the sea-borne raids, for example, by Osgod Clapa in 1049 and those by Harold and Godwine in 1052 and Tostig in 1066, to which we might add the incursions from Ireland by the sons of Harold in 1067 and 1069.[79] It would seem too that the majority of such sites were not as heavily fortified as many post-Conquest castles – Goltho at least was considerably strengthened by its subsequent Norman occupants;[80] the relative political stability of late Anglo-Saxon England, the power of the king, and the predominant military role of the burghs made powerful private fortifications either unnecessary or undesirable.[81]

Burghs differed from castles in many important respects: in ground area they were usually far larger; they were communal not seigneurial; their construction and defence was part of a national military obligation, with this nowhere more strikingly revealed than in the Burghal Hidage; and many were designed to combine military needs with those of urban development as vital tools of increasing royal wealth and authority. They were essentially a response to large-scale external invasion, not, as with many of the castles of the duchy, to small-scale private war.[82]

Yet if we think less in terms of physical structures or social and economic roles and more in terms of military function and effectiveness, we must ask how significant a difference there really was between the castle and earlier Anglo-Scandinavian fortifications. Just as castles served to protect a relatively small number of horsemen in hostile territory and act as bases for offensive operations, so this phenomenon is equally apparent in the Vikings' use both of pre-existing indigenous fortification in England and Frankia and the construction of their own defended bases.[83] The Alfredian burghs show a carefully planned system of defence in depth which succeeded in effectively neutralizing the renewed Viking threat to Wessex

---

[76] R.A. Brown, 'The Norman Conquest and the Genesis of English Castles', *Château-Gaillard* iii, 1966, 1–14; *idem*, 'An Historian's Approach to the Origins of the Castle in England', *Archaeological Journal* cxxvi, 1970, 131–48; Pounds, *The Medieval Castle*, 9–25.

[77] Williams, 'A Bell-house and Burgh-geat', 239.

[78] *ASC* (C) *s.a.* 900.

[79] Williams, 'A Bell-house and Burgh-geat', 239; *ASC* (C, D) *s.a.* 1049; *ASC* (C, D, E) *s.a.* 1052; *ASC* (C, D, E) *s.a.* 1066; *ASC* (D) *s.a.* 1067; *ASC* (D) *s.a.* 1069.

[80] Beresford, 'Goltho Manor', 27–36.

[81] Brown, 'Origins of the Castle', 139; Williams, 'A Bell-house and Burgh-geat', 238–40.

[82] C.A.R. Radford, 'The Pre-Conquest Boroughs of England, 9–11th Centuries', *Proceedings of the British Academy* lxiv, 1980, 131–53; *idem*, 'The Later Pre-Conquest Boroughs and their Defences', *Medieval Archaeology* xiv, 1970, 83–103; M. Biddle and D. Hill, 'Late Saxon Planned Towns', *Antiquaries Journal* li, 1971, 70–85; A.P. Smyth, *King Alfred the Great*, Oxford 1995, 135–46. I have been unable as yet to consult *The Defence of Wessex: The Burghal Hidage and Anglo-Saxon Fortifications*, ed. D. Hill and A. Rumble, New York and Manchester 1996.

[83] N.P. Brooks, 'England in the Ninth Century: The Crucible of Defeat', *TRHS*, 5th ser., xxix, 1979, 1–20, at 9–11; Smyth, *King Alfred*, 139–40.

after 885, and, just as castles might, served to contain raiding, to defend the local population, and supply garrison forces for field armies when needed.[84]

But still more striking is the offensive use of burghs under Edward the Elder, Ealdorman Aethelred and Aethelflaed, in what Stenton described as 'one of the best sustained and most decisive campaigns in the whole of the Dark Ages',[85] and which closely parallels the castle-building of the Conqueror in the years between 1066 and 1070. Here we see the aggressive use of burghs as marching camps, as bases to drive deep into Danish held territory, then to consolidate conquest, as fortified bridge heads, as siege fortifications to contain key Danish boroughs and to block access along vital river networks.[86]

Given the suggestive parallels between the burghs and the Frankish fortresses and fortified bridges initiated by Charles the Bald's Edict of Pitres in 864,[87] it might be argued that here is an earlier instance of the export of military developments from a Frankish 'central area' to a more peripheral part of Europe. Doubtless Alfred and his heirs were well aware of Frankish practice,[88] but given earlier indigenous fortification[89] and the extent of pre-existing Roman defences, it is probably better to think in terms of a fusion of insular development and continental influences. And while links between the courts of Wessex and Frankia may well have been close, the flow of military, as well as cultural ideas may not necessarily have been all one way. If the suggestion is correct that Henry the Fowler's fortifications against the Magyars, manned by *agrarii milites*, may have drawn on the successful use of burghs by Alfred and Edward the Elder,[90] then here we have an example of an Anglo-Saxon England already firmly within the 'central area' of military technology, influencing developments in Saxony, which in the first part of the tenth century may itself, as Leyser has argued, be seen as militarily less sophisticated and more on the periphery than its Frankish neighbours to the west.[91]

Evidence for the nature of siege techniques in Anglo-Saxon England is extremely

---

[84] See especially Abels, *Lordship and Military Obligation*, 69–78; and for a detailed discussion of the successful containment of Hastein and the campaigns of 892–9, see Smyth, *King Alfred*, 117–46.

[85] F.M. Stenton, *Anglo-Saxon England*, Oxford 3rd edn 1971, 335. B.S. Bachrach and R. Aris, 'Military Technology and Garrison Organization: Some Observations on Anglo-Saxon Military Thinking in the Light of the Burghal Hidage', *Technology and Culture* xxxi, 1990, 1–17.

[86] See the *Anglo-Saxon Chronicle*, including the Mercian Register, from 900–924, *passim*.

[87] For Frankish fortification see C. Gillmor, 'The Logistics of Fortified Bridge Building on the Seine under Charles the Bald', *ANS* xi, 1988, 87–106 and bibliography there cited; cf. Smyth, *King Alfred*, 140–2, for a summary of Charles's fortress building.

[88] J.M. Hassal and D. Hill, 'Pont de l'Arche: Frankish Influence on the West Saxon Burgh?', *Archaeological Journal* cxxvii, 1970, 188–95; Smyth, *King Alfred*, 140–2.

[89] Brooks, 'The Development of Military Obligations in Eighth- and Ninth-Century England', in *England before the Conquest: Studies presented to D. Whitelock*, ed. P. Clemoes and K. Hughes, Cambridge 1971, 69–84; *idem*, 'England in the Ninth Century', 9–10;

[90] P. Wormald, 'The Burghs', in *The Anglo-Saxons*, ed. J. Campbell, E. John and P. Wormald, Oxford 1982, 152–3; M.W. Thompson, *The Rise of the Castle*, Cambridge 1991, 13–27; and cf. K.-U. Jäschke, *Burgenbau und Landesverteidigung um 900. Uberlegungen zu Beispielen aus Deutschland, Frankreich und England*, Sigmaringen 1975, 118–33, 115–21. This view, however, has been recently questioned by E.J. Schoenfeld, 'Anglo-Saxon *Burhs* and Continental *Burgen*: Early Medieval Fortifications in Constitutional Perspective', *Haskins Society Journal* vi, 1994, 49–66, particularly valuable for its review of the substantial German literature.

[91] K. Leyser, 'Henry I and the Beginnings of the Saxon Empire', *EHR* lxxxiii, 1968, 1–32.

limited, but the Viking siege of Paris as reported by Abbo of St Germain reveals that they had access to an impressive range of siege equipment.[92] Their knowledge of such technology may have been absorbed from the Franks, just as Bartlett shows how the Estonians and Russians quickly adopted skills in making siege engines learned from the Danes and Germans.[93] But as Bradbury has pointed out, the post Roman legacy of siege methods was widespread,[94] and given that Gotfried of Denmark, who was capable of constructing part of the Danevirke, was viewed as a severe threat by Charlemagne, we should not perhaps underestimate the Danes' indigenous technological capabilities.[95] Indeed, in this context of the flow of military ideas, it becomes of even greater interest to ask – though answers appear elusive – whence came the influences behind Harald Bluetooth's great Danish fortresses of Trelleborg, Aggersborg, Nonnebakken and Fyrkat.[96] For if the inspiration for these highly sophisticated geometric fortresses came not from German but from earlier Baltic or Slav types of fortification, we must add further qualification to Bartlett's centre-periphery model, or at least consider that within the period under discussion, the axis of such polarities could change.[97]

The military reputation of the burghs has suffered by their failure under Aethelred, though the valiant and sustained defence of London, which finally yielded not by storm but by negotiation, hints at what was possible by the combination of powerful defences and more inspired resistance.[98] It is difficult to assess the condition in which the burghs were maintained under Edward the Confessor and Harold, but it would be surprising had the ever-present invasion scares from Norway and Denmark, coupled with memories of the bitter experience of Aethelred's reign, not led to a significant degree of readiness. The key point, however, is that because of the decisive nature of Hastings and the rapid and widespread political capitulation in its immediate aftermath, William never had to fight a war of sieges which could have slowly worn down his forces by attrition and disease. The defensive potential of the burghs is suggested by the ability of the men of Bristol to drive off the sons of Harold in 1067 – here both fortifications and garrison were operating for the new king, not against him – and more revealingly, the difficulty William had in 1068 in besieging Exeter, which only surrendered because of internal divisions.[99] It

---

[92] Abbo, *La siège de Paris par les Normands*, ed. H. Waquet, Paris 1942, 22ff; J. Bradbury, *The Medieval Siege*, Woodbridge 1992, 42–7.

[93] Bartlett, *The Making of Europe*, 74–5.

[94] Bradbury, *Medieval Siege*, 12–25.

[95] On Gotfried and the Danevirke see D. Wilson, *Civil and Military Engineering in Viking Age Scandinavia*, First Paul Johnstone Memorial Lecture, London 1978, 3–5; E. Roesdahl, *Viking Age Denmark*, London 1982, 141–6; and cf. K.L. Maund, ' "A Turmoil of Warring Princes": Political Leadership in Ninth-century Denmark', *Haskins Society Journal* vi, 1994, 29–47.

[96] E. Roesdahl, 'The Danish Geometrical Viking Fortresses and their Context', *ANS* ix, 1986, 209–226; *idem*, *Viking Age Denmark*, 147–55.

[97] Significantly, however, these fortresses seemingly had a only a brief working life, and 'after them we know of no others (nor or private fortresses or castles) for more than a hundred years. These were episodes' (Roesdahl, 'The Danish Geometrical Viking Fortresses', 217); *idem*, 'The End of Viking-age Fortifications in Denmark and What Followed', *Château Gaillard* xii, 1985, 39–47.

[98] *ASC* (C, D, E) *s.a.* 994, 1009, 1013, 1016. Probably written within the city or by a native, these annals are naturally highly partisan, but there seems little reason to doubt the effectiveness of the city's defences which they reflect.

[99] *ASC* (D) *s.a.* 1067; J.O. Prestwich, 'Military Intelligence under the Norman and Angevin Kings',

was his recognition in 1066 that London could not be taken by direct assault that led William to launch his great harrying march of encirclement, while Kapelle has argued that the burning of York by the retiring Norman garrison in late 1069 crucially deprived the Danish expeditionary force of suitable winter quarters.[100] Had they been able to hold and occupy York till the arrival of Svein Estrithson the following spring, William might have been in severe trouble.

Let me turn now to the military arm which, I would suggest, is of crucial importance in appreciating the full military potential of late Anglo-Saxon England – naval power. And here it is important to bear in mind when discussing the Anglo-Saxon 'navy' or 'fleet' that we are hardly dealing with a discrete arm or separate military institutions, but rather with forces that had a ship-borne capability aboard vessels often designed more for the rapid transportation of troops than for battle at sea. Men who served, whether the mercenary lithsmen or those raised by territorial obligation which comprised part of the *trimoda necessitas*, did so in the double capacity as warriors and seamen.[101] Yet despite important discussions on the nature of the late Saxon navy by Hollister and Hooper, the concentration by historians on land warfare – on the composition of armies, the use of cavalry and infantry tactics, and on the role of castles in conquest and settlement – still serves to overshadow the offensive capabilities of Anglo-Saxon fleets.[102] Equally, in regard to naval activity in 1066, scholarly attention has focused primarily on the raising of the Norman fleet and the logistics of invasion.[103] Yet as we have seen, William of Poitiers reflects a healthy respect for the power of Harold's fleet, and it is he who informs us of the king's intention to bar any Norman withdrawal by intercepting them at sea.[104] The C and D versions of the *Chronicle* record that Harold commanded 'a naval force and a land force larger than any king had assembled before in this country'.[105] As it transpired, William's delayed sailing – whether by accident or design – compelled Harold's fleet stationed off the Isle of

---

in *Law and Government in Medieval England and Normandy. Essays in Honour of Sir James Holt*, Cambridge 1994, 1–30, at 4–8; and cf. I. Burrow, 'The Town Defences of Exeter', *Transactions of the Devonshire Archaeological Association* cix, 1977, 13–40.

[100] Douglas, *William the Conqueror*, 205–6; W. Kapelle, *The Norman Conquest of the North. The Region and its Transformation, 1000–1135*, London 1979, 115–16.

[101] Hollister, *Anglo-Saxon Military Institutions*, 104–7; N. Hooper, 'Some Observations on the Navy in Late Anglo-Saxon England', in *Studies in Medieval History Presented to R.A. Brown*, ed. C. Harper-Bill, C.J. Holdsworth and J.L. Nelson, Woodbridge 1989, 203–13, at 206.

[102] Hollister, *Anglo-Saxon Military Institutions*, 103–26; Hooper, 'Some Observations on the Navy', 203–13. Cf. Abels, *Lordship and Military Obligation*, 109–10, 158–9.

[103] J. Laporte, 'Les opérations navales en Manche et Mer du Nord pendant l'année 1066', *Annales de Normandie* xvii, 1967, 3–42; M. Graindor, 'Le débarquement du Guillaume en 1066: un coup de maitre de la marine normande', *Archaeologia* xxx, 1969; B. Bachrach, 'On the Origins of William the Conqueror's Horse Transports', *Technology and Culture* xxvi, 1983, 505–31; *idem*, 'The Military Administration of the Norman Conquest', *ANS* viii, 1986, 1–25; C.M. Gillmor, 'Naval Logistics of the Cross-Channel Operation, 1066', *ANS* vii, 1984, 105–31; J. Neumann, 'Hydrographic and Ship-Hydrodynamic Aspects of the Norman Invasion, AD 1066', *ANS* xi, 1988, 221–44. The offensive use of Norman fleets in the Mediterranean, however, is discussed by D.P. Waley, 'Combined Operations in Sicily, AD 1060–78', *Papers of the British School at Rome* xxii, 1954, 118–25; and M. Bennett, 'Norman Naval Activity in the Mediterranean, c.1060–c.1108', *ANS* xv, 1992, 41–58.

[104] *Gesta Guillelmi*, 180; 'And so that they should find no refuge in withdrawal he had sent a fleet of 700 warships to cut them off at sea.' The number, of course, is a hopeless exaggeration.

[105] *ASC* (D, E) *s.a.* 1066.

Wight to disband, though not after having held station for an impressive four months, while part of it was wrecked by storms while returning to the Thames.[106] But this should not blind us to the possibility that the Norman fleet could have easily suffered the same fate as befell later French invasion forces at Damme in 1213, where an English fleet destroyed Philip's invasion force at its anchorage in the Zwynn estuary (an event largely repeated at the later battle at Sluys, 1340), or at Sandwich in 1217, where the French invasion fleet was caught at sea and routed.[107] Had Harold's ships intercepted William's heavily laden transports or blockaded his beach-head at Pevensey,[108] historians might have been writing not of a Norman military revolution but of the wooden walls of Anglo-Saxon England. Harold may indeed have attempted some offensive action with his fleet. The 'E' version of the *Chronicle* alone notes that Harold 'went out with a naval force against William', placing this concurrently with Tostig's arrival in the Humber, and the occurrence of some form of naval engagement is confirmed by references in Domesday Book to Englishmen losing their lands because they fought against William in a naval battle.[109]

Ships and seafaring ability had, as John Haywood's excellent study *Dark Age Naval Power* shows, been integral to the process of raiding, conquest and settlement by Angles, Jutes and Saxons, in ways which closely parallel later Viking attacks and invasion.[110] With Bede's fleeting reference to Ecgfrith's raid on Ireland in 684, we have a tantalizing hint of the extent to which the power of seventh-century Northumbria, whose power centres were predominantly coastal, was based on supremacy at sea as well as on land.[111] It has always been seen as an irony that the island seclusion of many Anglo-Saxon monastic sites left them vulnerable to Viking raiders from 793, but may it be that these coastal sites were established in the knowledge of a powerful home fleet, and that their vulnerability only occured with the decline of Northumbrian power, just as happened in the decades following the death of Edgar?

It would seem more than likely that other kingdoms of the heptarchy kept naval units, and evidence for trade suggests flourishing seafaring activity. As in Frankia, the onset of Viking raiding may well have acted as an incentive to strengthen such forces, and the *Anglo-Saxon Chronicle* records that in 851, considerably prior to Alfred's famous reforms, Aethelstan, son of Aethelwulf, 'fought in ships and slew a great army at Sandwich in Kent, and captured nine ships and put the others to

---

[106] *ASC* (C) s.a. 1066.
[107] For the battle of Damme, W.L. Warren, *King John*, London repr. 1964, 204–5; for Sandwich, D. Carpenter, *The Minority of Henry III*, London 1990, 43–4; and for Sluys, 'a naval catastrophe on a scale unequalled until modern times', J. Sumption, *The Hundred Years War. Trial by Battle*, London 1990, 325–9.
[108] Hollister, *Anglo-Saxon Military Institutions*, 125, 'Had the term of shipfyrd service not expired in the early autumn of 1066, the Conqueror might never have managed a landing on the English coast.' The successful blockade of Pevensey by English ships in 1088, which forced the rebel garrison to sue for peace with Rufus, affords an instructive parallel (*ASC* (E) s.a. 1088).
[109] *ASC* (E) s.a. 1066; A. Williams, *The English and the Norman Conquest*, Woodbridge 1995, 19.
[110] J. Haywood, *Dark Age Naval Power*, London and New York 1991, 51–76.
[111] *Bede's Ecclesiastical History of the English People*, ed. B. Colgrave and R.A.B. Mynors, Oxford 1969, 426. On this raid see H. Moisl, 'The Bernician Royal Dynasty and the Irish in the Seventh Century', *Peritia* ii, 1983, 120–4.

flight'.[112] Subsequently, fleets may have played an important role in the conquest of the Danelaw by the West Saxon kings. In the initial stages of containment, they were used to raid into Danish-held territory. In 885, an Anglo-Saxon naval force from Kent raided East Anglia, and seized a Viking force of sixteen ships at the mouth of the Stour before being defeated by a much larger Viking fleet.[113] Similarly in 910, Edward the Elder assembled a force of 100 ships, again in Kent, and it was because the Danes believed 'that the greater part of his forces were on the ships' that Edward was able to catch and heavily defeat the Viking army at Tettenhall.[114] Subsequently, the navy served to support campaigns further north, as in 934, when Aethelstan invaded Scotland in conjunction with a fleet which ravaged as far as Caithness.[115]

The size, composition and methods of raising these early fleets are largely obscure, though it seems likely that as more of the Danelaw came within the sway of the West Saxon kings, their naval forces became augmented by the ships, crews and naval expertise of client rulers, in a fusion of Anglo-Danish military capabilities analogous to that occurring after the accession of Cnut. This was certainly the case at the apogee of the dynasty's power under Edgar, for the *Chronicle* records that the sub-kings who submitted to him at Chester in 973 'gave him pledges that they would be his allies on sea and on land'.[116] The fact that on this occasion these eight rulers rowed Edgar on the Dee, while the king himself skilfully steered the ship,[117] was itself symbolic – doubtless consciously so – of his hegemony over a maritime empire and of sub-kings whose main puissance was sea- rather than land-based.[118]

---

[112] *ASC* (A, B, D), *s.a.* 851.

[113] *ASC* (A, B, D), *s.a.* 885.

[114] *ASC* (A, B, C, D) *s.a.* 910.

[115] *Symeonis monachi opera omnia*, ed. T. Arnold, 2 vols, RS LXXV, 1885, ii, 124. Operations this far north suggest that the fleet was also targeting Norwegian settlers in northeast Scotland (A.P. Smyth, *Scandinavian York and Dublin*, 2 vols, New Jersey and Dublin 1975–9, ii, 65).

[116] *ASC* (D, E) *s.a.* 973; John of Worcester ii, 422–5, 'eight sub-kings . . . swore that they would be loyal to, and co-operate with, him by land and sea'. The latter chronicle subsequently notes how in 1064, the Welsh promised to serve Edward 'by sea and by land' (*ibid.* ii, 596–7; Hollister, *Anglo-Saxon Military Institutions*, 106).

[117] John of Worcester ii, 424–5. The *ASC* (D) *s.a* 973 saw this secular ceremony as the immediate sequel to Edgar's consecration at Bath in May, on which see A. Jones, 'The Significance of the Regal Consecration of Edgar in 973', *Journal of Ecclesiastical History* xxxiii, 1982, 375–90. The extent to which Anglo-Saxon kings were seen as 'sea-kings' is further suggested by the prominence of ships as the ultimate in high status diplomatic gifts. Harald Finehair of Norway sent Aethelstan a fine warship with a purple sail and gilded prow and stern, while Godwine attempted to appease Harthacnut with a magnificent ship with a gilded prow, complete with eighty splendidly accoutred warriors (*De gestis regum* i, 149; John of Worcester ii, 530–1). Similarly leading ecclesiastics might bequeath the king fine ships (Hollister, *Anglo-Saxon Military Institutions*, 108). Conversely, when Gruffyd ap Llewelyn was slain in 1063, his head and the ornamented prow of his ship were presented to Earl Harold, who sent them in turn to King Edward (*ASC* (D) *s.a.* 1063).

[118] The point is well illustrated by the *Senchus fer nAlban*, a tenth-century text of a probable seventh-century tract from the kingdom of Dalriada, which is concerned with territorial assessment for tribute and for the provision of ship service, with two seven-bench boats owed from every twenty 'houses' (M.O. Anderson, *Kings and Kingship in Early Scotland*, Edinburgh 1973, 158–65; A.A.M. Duncan, *Scotland. The Making of the Kingdom*, Edinburgh 1975, 74–5; J. Bannerman, *Studies in the History of Dalriada*, Edinburgh 1974, 27–156).

The great coalition that confronted Aethelstan at Brunanburgh was sea-borne. According to Symeon of Durham, the army numbered (an improbable) 615 ships, while the Brunanburgh poem

In this context, the choice of Chester for this grand ceremony was itself signifi-cant. With the growing power of the Hiberno-Norse kingdom of Dublin and substantial settlement on the north-west coast, the Irish Sea became an area of crucial strategic importance, and still more so after the annexation of York.[119] Chester was therefore a vital link in the defences of northern Mercia.[120] By the time of Edgar, it was not only an important regional administrative centre with 'an exceptionally active mint',[121] but was probably also a key naval base guarding the western approaches. According to the *Chronicle* for 973, Edgar himself arrived there following his coronation at Bath with 'his whole naval force', and it is possible that Chester was the base for the 'northern fleet' mentioned in the striking elaboration of this annal in John of Worcester. The passage is worth quoting *in extenso*:

> Now he had assembled during his lifetime 3,600 strong ships for his own use, from which, when the Easter feast was over, he used to assemble 1,200 on the east coasts of the island, 1,200 on the west and 1,200 on the north coasts, and sail to the western fleet with the eastern, and, when he had sent that back, to the northern fleet with the western, and that sent back, with the northern fleet to the eastern, and in that way he used to circumnavigate the whole island every summer, acting thus vigorously for the defence of the kingdom against foreigners and to train himself and his men in military exercises.[122]

This remarkable annal clearly is not contemporary,[123] nor can one place any confi-dence in its estimate of the size of Edgar's fleet. Nevertheless, it is remarkable testimony to the perception of Edgar's reign as a golden age in which an Anglo-Saxon 'empire' was bound together and defended by a powerful navy, a perception which began as early as the reign of Aethelred II.[124] That such was more than mere creative nostalgia, however, is suggested by the kingdom's impressive military

stresses the escape of the shattered remnants of Olaf's forces by sea (Symeon of Durham i, 76; *ASC* (C) *s.a.* 937).

[119] Smyth, *Scandinavian York and Dublin* i, 75ff. Cf. N.J. Higham, 'The Cheshire *Burhs* and the Mercian Frontier to 924', *Transactions of the Antiquarian Society of Lancashire and Cheshire* lxxxv, 1988, 193–221; *idem*, 'The Scandinavians in North Cumbria: Raids and Settlement in the Later Ninth to Mid-Tenth Centuries', in *The Scandinavians in Cumbria*, ed. J.R. Baldwin and I.D. White, Edinburgh 1985, 37–51; *idem*, 'Northumbria, Mercia and the Irish Sea Norse, 893–926', in *Viking Treasure from the North West: The Cuerdale Hoard in its Context*, ed. J. Graham-Campbell, Liverpool 1992, 21–30.

[120] N.J. Higham, *The Origins of Cheshire*, Manchester 1993, 115–17. The city's Roman walls were still standing by the tenth century, though the later Saxon defences may not have employed all of its extensive circuit, *ibid.*, 116.

[121] Higham, *Origins of Cheshire*, 184–7.

[122] John of Worcester ii, 424–7.

[123] R.R. Darlington and P. McGurk, 'The "Chronicon ex Chronicis" of "Florence" of Worcester and its Use of Sources for English History Before 1066', *ANS* v, 1982, 185–96 at 185, 191–2, where the influence of Byrthferth's *Life of Oswald* on this passage is also noted.

[124] The annal should in this regard be compared with the obituary to Edgar in *ASC* (D) *s.a.* 975, clearly written with hindsight and experience of renewed Viking attack: 'Nor was there fleet so proud nor host so strong that it got itself prey in England as long as the noble king held the throne'. So too Aelfric, in his *Life of St Swithun*, noted of Edgar's reign that 'his kingdom continued ever at peace, so that no fleet was ever heard of except of our own people who held this land. And all the kings who were in this island, Cumbrians and Scots, came to Edgar, once eight kings in one day,

capacity which comes more clearly into view under Aethelred, ironically precisely because of the manifold threats which beset him. The famous *Chronicle* entry for 1008, for example, records how 'the king ordered that ships should be built unremittingly over all England, namely a warship from 310 hides', and it may well be that the ship sokes and the organizational basis which allowed such rapid and widespread mobilization of ships pre-date Aethelred's reign.[125]

If the extreme paucity of information for secular affairs in Edgar's reign prevents a realistic assessment of the navy's role in the achievement of West Saxon hegemony in Britain, the power and confidence of the fleet may be glimpsed earlier in Aethelstan's willingness to commit naval forces to continental ventures. It was the fear that Louis d'Outremer would make a revanche backed by an Anglo-Saxon fleet that led both to the overtures of Hugh duke of the Franks to Aethelstan in 926, and to Henry the Fowler marrying his son Otto to Edith, Aethelstan's sister. Henry's fears were realized when Aethelstan's ships aided Louis in his attempt to regain Lotharingia, annexed by Henry in 925, though with little success.[126]

Similarly, despite the ultimate failure of Aethelred's navy, it too was capable of offensive action; his fleet may well have harried the Cotentin in reprisal for the Normans harbouring Viking fleets, while in 1000, he attempted to co-ordinate a land and sea attack on Cumberland.[127] Significantly, the fleet 'went out round by Chester', and although they failed to rendezvous with the king, they ravaged the Isle of Man. This was not a sporadic and unfocused act of aggression, but an attempt to reassert Anglo-Saxon command of the western approaches enjoyed under Edgar by striking at Viking bases around the Irish Sea.[128]

With the accession of Cnut, this naval potential was united with powerful fleets at the disposal of the Danish kings, which have been studied in depth by Nicholas Hooper and Niels Lund, and which made possible Cnut's pretensions to dominance in the Baltic and the North Sea.[129] And if the navy under Edward the Confessor appears as essentially a coastal defence force, stationed off the Isle of Wight or Sandwich on an almost annual basis, we should remember that this was because of policy, not because it lacked an offensive potential. If Godwine had had his way in 1047–48, the Anglo-Saxon navy would have been embroiled in a large scale martime war in support of Svein Estrithson against the Norwegians, and in 1049,

and they all submitted to Edgar's direction' (*Aelfric's Lives of the Saints*, ed. W.W. Skeat, *EETS* 1881–1900, i, 468; *EHD* i, 927).

[125] E. John, *Land Tenure in Early England*, Leicester 1960, 115–23; Hollister, *Anglo-Saxon Military Institutions*, 108–17; Hooper, 'Some Observations on the Navy', 208–10; Abels, *Lordship and Military Obligation*, 93 and n. 78. Cf. D. Hill, *An Atlas of Anglo-Saxon England*, Oxford revised edn 1984, 92–3.

[126] Stenton, *Anglo-Saxon England*, 345–7.

[127] *Jumièges* ii, 10–15; *ASC* (C) s.a. 1000.

[128] Hill, *An Atlas of Anglo-Saxon England*, 63–4.

[129] N. Hooper, 'Some Observations on the Navy', 204–8; *idem*, 'Military Developments in the Reign of Cnut', in *The Reign of Cnut: King of England, Demark and Norway*, ed. A.R. Rumble, Leicester 1994, 89–101; N. Lund, 'The Armies of Svein Forkbeard and Cnut: *leding* or *lith*', *Anglo-Saxon England* xv, 1986, 105–18; *idem*, 'Danish Military Organization', in *The Battle of Maldon. Fiction and Fact*, ed. J. Cooper, London 1993, 109–26. For Cnut's ambitions in northern Europe see M.K. Lawson, *Cnut: The Danes in England in the Early Eleventh Century*, London 1993, 81–116, and cf. 177–84.

Edward assisted Henry III, the German emperor, by a naval blockade against Baldwin V of Flanders.[130]

Two main points emerge from this discussion of the fleet. The first is that to discuss Anglo-Saxon military potential without fully acknowledging the offensive role of fleets is to minimize the arm to which the Anglo-Saxons themselves attached great, if not supreme, significance. Second, the whole question of maritime warfare suggests an important additional dimension to Bartlett's model of the diffusion and direction of military technology.

Although it is important, as Haywood has argued, to set Viking activity firmly within the context of a long familiarity with seafaring by Anglo-Saxons, Franks and Frisians,[131] the successes achieved by Viking forces in the ninth century and still more in the decades either side of 1000 reinforce the impression that at least at sea the Scandinavian raiders and invaders retained their edge in maritime expertise. The role of ship technology and seamanship in Viking expansion, conquest and settlement from the later eighth century has long been axiomatic.[132] The shallow draught of fast, manoeuvrable longships allowed both rapid coastal raids and the penetration of river networks deep inland while the more capacious *knarr* could be used in a supportive role as transports. In war, mobility was the hallmark of Viking strategy,[133] and it was the effectiveness of Viking ships, used in conjunction with defensive fortification and highly mobile horsed units, which forced the Franks and Anglo-Saxons to develop and expand existing defensive systems with fortified bridges, burghs and fleets.[134] Here surely is a striking case where in terms of a diaspora of military technology, a crucial dimension of it emanated not from a Frankish core to a Scandinavian periphery, but vice versa, compelling 'defensive imitation' in exactly the opposite direction. And if the Normans introduced the warhorse and crossbow into England in 1066, they did so it seems from transport ships which may have drawn as much on Scandinavian as on Mediterranean influences.[135]

How far in other respects the naval forces of the early Norman duchy were influenced by Viking technology, seamanship and naval tactics can only be a matter of speculation. The Scandinavian maritime legacy must have remained strong through much of the tenth century, and even as Rollo's successors and their men began in turn to assimilate the castles and cavalry warfare of the Franks, such

---

[130] F. Barlow, *Edward the Confessor*, London 1970, 91–3, 98–9. In 1048, Svein Estrithson had requested 'naval assistance, which was to be fifty ships at least', but was refused (*ASC* (D) *s.a.* 1048).

[131] Haywood, *Dark Age Naval Power*, 75–6.

[132] The literature on Viking ships and seafaring is extensive, but see *inter alia* A.W. Brogger and H. Shetelig, *The Viking Ships*, London repr. 1971; O. Olsen and O. Crumlin-Pedersen, *Five Viking Ships from Roskilde Fjord*, Roskilde 1978; and for general surveys, P.G. Foote and D.M. Wilson, *The Viking Achievement*, London 1970, 232–54; and S. McGrail, 'Ships, Shipwrights and Seamen', in J. Graham-Campbell, *The Viking World*, London 1980, 37–63.

[133] For an unorthodox but thought-provoking analysis see Griffiths, *The Viking Art of War*, especially ch. 3, 'Strategic Mobility' and ch. 4, 'The Viking Notion of Strategy'.

[134] Cf. C. Gillmor, 'War on the Rivers: Viking Numbers and Mobility on the Seine and Loire, 841–886', *Viator* xix, 1988, 79–109.

[135] Gillmor, 'Naval Logistics', 110–14, who favours predominantly Scandinavian influence, and for an opposing view, stressing William's debt to Byzantine and Norman-Sicilian practice, B. Bachrach, 'On the Origin of William the Conqueror's Horse Transports', *Technology and Culture* xxvi, 1983, 505–31.

influences cannot but have been re-inforced by the use of Norman ports by Viking fleets and the vibrant commerce which greatly contributed to the flourish of Rouen and other towns.[136] Duke Richard II (996–1026) made an agreement with Svein Forkbeard whereby in return for shelter and care of any wounded, the Danes agreed to sell their booty in Normandy,[137] while in 1013/14 he sought the aid of Olaf Haraldson to raid Brittany and in his war against Odo of Chartres.[138]

Olaf's activities are of particular interest. In Brittany, his forces not only captured the castle of Dol (where in 1076 the Conqueror would suffer one of his worst military reverses),[139] but successfully defeated the attack of Breton cavalry by digging concealed trenches which broke the charge of the horsemen.[140] Olaf, moreover, successfully repeated this tactic against William V of Aquitaine; the Aquitainian knights were thrown as their horses stumbled and broke their legs in trenches dug secretly and concealed with sods.[141] The form of warfare practised by Viking warriors was, in favourable circumstances, clearly capable of overcoming both castles and cavalry.

The employment of such Viking freebooters by Frankish territorial rulers, as much as by Aethelred the Unready,[142] must have resulted in an amalgam of diverse forms of warfare and military traditions, and one in which the role of fleets remained important. If William of Jumièges is to be believed, the Norman fleet was capable of offensive action as late as 1034, the year in which Duke Robert assembled a naval force to assist an attempted invasion by Edward, but which after being hindered by storms was diverted to aid an attack on Brittany.[143] The unsuccessful landings by Edward and his brother Alfred two years later were presumably supported by Norman ships,[144] while despite the misgivings which William of Poitiers has the Norman magnates voice, the speed with which Duke William could raise a

---

[136] L. Musset, 'Rouen et l'Angleterre vers l'an mil', *Annales de Normandie* xxiv, 1974, 287–90; L.W. Breese, 'The Persistence of Scandinavian Connections in Normandy in the Tenth and Early Eleventh Centuries', *Viator* viii, 1977, 47–61; J. Campbell, 'England, France, Flanders and Germany, Some Comparisons and Connections', in *Ethelred the Unready*, 255–70; D. Bates, *Normandy before 1066*, London 1982, 37–8.

[137] *Jumièges* ii, 16–19, and *ibid.*, p. 17 n. 4 for the date of this treaty (either 1003 or 1013); cf. M. Fauroux, *Recueil des actes des ducs de Normandie (911–1066)*, Caen 1961, 22. Such booty included slaves, and Rouen possessed a flourishing slave market (E.M.C. van Houts, 'Scandinavian Influence in Norman Literature of the Eleventh Century', *ANS* vi, 1983, 106–21 at 107–8). See also L. Musset, 'L'image de la Scandinavie dans les ouevres Normandes de la période ducale (911–1204)', in *Les relations littéraires Franco-Scandinaves au Moyen Age* (Bibliothèque de la Faculté de Philosophie et Lettres de l'Université de Liège, 208, Paris 1975), 193–215.

[138] *Jumièges* ii, 24–7, and 24 n. 3.

[139] Douglas, *William the Conqueror*, 233–4.

[140] *Jumièges* ii, 24–7.

[141] *Adémar of Chabannes, Chronique*, ed. J. Chavanon, Paris 1897, 176. Ademar does not mention Olaf by name, but his presence is confirmed by the *Víkingavísur* of his skald Sigvatr (*Jumièges* ii, 24–5, ns.3–4). On this campaign and its background see J. Martindale, 'Peace and War in Early Eleventh Century Aquitaine', *Medieval Knighthood* iv, 147–76, at 171–4.

[142] *ASC* (A), *s.a.* 1000; *ASC* (C), *s.a.* 1012, 1013.

[143] *Jumièges* ii, 76–8; S.D. Keynes, 'The Aethelings in England and Normandy', *ANS* xiii, 1990, 193–4 and n. 100; Bates, *Normandy before 1066*, 67–8; E.M.C. van Houts, 'The Political Relations between Normandy and England before 1066 according to the *Gesta Normannorum Ducum*', in *Les mutations socio-culturelles au tournant des XIe–XIIe siècles*, ed. R. Foreville *et al.*, Actes du IVe colloque internationale Anselmien (1984), 85–97.

[144] *Jumièges* ii, 104–7; Keynes, 'The Aethelings in Normandy', 195–6.

fleet suggests ready and plentiful access to shipwrights and materials.[145] As we have seen, there may well have been a naval engagement with Anglo-Saxon ships before William's main landing, suggesting a continued offensive role, and J.O. Prestwich has suggested that the Norman knights seized on landing at Exeter in 1068 were part of a reconnaissance force sent by William to assess the threat in the South West from Gytha, widow of Godwine, and the sons of Harold.[146]

One final consideration reinforces the contention that any discussion of military conquest and technology must address the question of maritime power. In the twenty years following Hastings, the gravest military threat to the consolidation of Norman power in England came not from the defeated Anglo-Saxons or insular neighbours, but from Danish fleets. In 1069–70, despite tenacious and widespread local resistance, it was only the arrival of Danish ships which transformed the potential strategic danger by furnishing armies powerful enough to have fought William in open battle, while as the letter of Lanfranc to Walcher of Durham reveals, the imminent arrival of the Danes was expected in 1075 in support of the rebellion of Roger of Hereford, Ralph de Gael and Waltheof.[147] The planned invasion in 1085 by Cnut IV of Denmark, which brought together the overwhelmingly powerful naval forces of Cnut, Olaf of Norway and Count Robert of Flanders, was arguably the most dangerous military threat ever faced by the Conqueror.[148] Certainly William's own actions reveal the gravity of the supposed danger; he layed waste a broad coastal strip on the east coast to deny supplies to any invader, and brought over a huge mercenary army which he billeted on his vassals.[149] And it was in all probability the need to assess his available resources after this invasion scare which led to deep speech at Gloucester and the creation of Domesday Book.[150]

William's measures for coastal defence, such as the rapes of Sussex, Odo's earldom of Kent, and castles such as Norwich, Dover and the great stone keep at Colchester, were designed primarily to counter invasion from Scandinavia rather than France – compared to the Danish or Norwegian fleets, Eustace of Boulogne's botched coup of 1067 must have seemed very small beer.[151] It was not, however, any technological superiority which saved the Normans' precarious hold on England but a combination of the Conqueror's fine generalship and great good fortune. His ability as a commander, supported by excellent military intelligence, is shown by his pre-emptive strike against Exeter in 1068. Held by Gytha, who was not only Harold's mother but Svein Estrithson's aunt, the city offered a perfect base for the sons of Harold and their fleet operating from Ireland. William besieged it, however,

---

[145] Shipwrights may, however, have been hired from all over Europe. On this, and the raising of the Norman fleet, see Gillmor, 'Naval Logistics', 105–31.

[146] Prestwich, 'Norman and Angevin Military Intelligence', 7–8.

[147] Douglas, *William the Conqueror*, 232–3; *Lanfranc's Letters*, 126–7.

[148] Stenton, *Anglo-Saxon England*, 617.

[149] *ASC* (E) *s.a* 1085; F.M. Stenton, *The First Century of English Feudalism*, Oxford 2nd edn. 1961, 149–51; Douglas, *William the Conqueror*, 346–7. For the possible devastation of Thanet by William with the same intention see Barlow, *Edward the Confessor*, 91 n. 5.

[150] S. Harvey, 'Domesday Book and Anglo-Norman Governance', *TRHS*, 5th ser., xxv, 1975, 175–93 at 181–2; cf. J.C. Holt, '1086', in *Domesday Studies*, 41–64 at 62.

[151] Orderic ii, 204–7.

before they could co-ordinate an attack with a Danish invasion in the east, thereby imitating the strategy of the successful Godwinist revanche of 1052.[152]

In 1069, William was able to exploit both the burning of York, which denied the Danish army suitable winter quarters, and the enemy's strategic indecision, which allowed him to press home a relentless advance, driving them back from the south bank of the Humber before they could complete the fortification of the Isle of Axholme, then outflanking them in their efforts to hold the line of the Aire.[153] Possibly the absence of King Svein was crucial here, but the Danish expeditionary force allowed itself to be bought off, as did Svein himself following his own arrival in 1070, thereby dooming the Anglo-Saxon opposition to failure.[154] With Danish naval support, Ely had been a formidable base for resistance; their departure, however, allowed William to impose a blockade by sea with a fleet which, as a crowning irony, was comprised at least in part of Anglo-Saxon *butsecarls*.[155]

It would be intriguing to know what the military outcome would have been had a Norman army fought a pitched battle with a major Norwegian or Danish force, but the hard fought battle of Stamford Bridge, if not distant memories of Cnut's triumph at Ashingdon in 1016, doubtless made William consider himself fortunate that it was Harold Godwineson and not himself who had had to face Harald Hardraada in the field. He was fortunate too that the Danes eschewed battle in 1069 and a major landing in 1070, and that they failed to properly co-ordinate their efforts with the 'rising of the earls' in 1075. Orderic believed that William's 'victory luck' deserted him after 1076 as divine punishment for the unjust execution of Waltheof, but he was surely overlooking the Danes' internal quarrels that led first to the postponment of Cnut IV's invasion in 1085, then to his murder the following year.[156] Thus apart from the campaign of late 1069, William's hold on his newly won kingdom was never really tested in the field by his most powerful opponents. The history of the Anglo-Norman state might have been very different had William's England been subjected to the kind of sustained seaborne attacks and king-led invasions that had brought Ethelred's powerful kingdom to its knees.

In conclusion, in terms of conduct in war, with the widespread killing of non-combatants, the enslavement of prisoners and the general absence of ransom, Anglo-Saxon England can indeed be seen as more closely analogous to the Celtic lands than to France and its developing notions of chivalric behaviour.[157] But though the Normans may have viewed the Anglo-Saxons as barbarians – and doubtless the Danes still more so – few of them would have dismissed the military potential of these enemies in the same way that Anglo-Norman writers could

---

[152] Prestwich, 'Norman and Angevin Military Intelligence', 4–8. Exeter's potential had been fully appreciated by the Vikings in 876–7 (*ASC*, *s.a.* 876, 877; cf. *ASC* (C) *s.a.* 1003).

[153] Kapelle, *The Norman Conquest of the North*, 114–16.

[154] Kapelle, *The Norman Conquest of the North*, 117; Stenton, *Anglo-Saxon England*, 605–6.

[155] *ASC* (D, E) *s.a.* 1071. For the siege of Ely, see the references cited in J. Beeler, *Warfare in England, 1066–89*, 43–6.

[156] Orderic ii, 350–1, and iv, 52–5; Douglas, *William the Conqueror*, 356.

[157] M.J. Strickland, 'Slaughter, Slavery or Ransom? The Impact of the Conquest on Conduct in Warfare', in *England in the Eleventh Century*, ed. C. Hicks, Stamford 1992, 41–60; Gillingham, 'Conquering the Barbarians', 67–83; *idem*, 'The Beginnings of English Imperialism', *Journal of Historical Sociology* v, 1992, 392–409.

deride the skipping kerns and the 'worthless Scot with half-bare buttocks' of the Celtic world.[158]

Rather, in terms of resources, structure and military capacity, late Anglo-Saxon England was not, as William of Poitiers well recognized, a society on the periphery of a 'non-Mediterranean Europe', but one which was very much a 'central area' long before 1066. It could boast a warrior aristocracy as well armed and equipped as any in Frankia, and if they did not fight from the saddle, then it was because of the effectiveness of their infantry tactics, not their unfamiliarity with horsemanship. An extensive series of fortifications, some stone-built and many of formidable dimensions, was complimented by a powerful fleet, which as recently as 1063 had shown its capacity to conduct successful combined operations against the Welsh.[159]

Robert Bartlett has drawn an important contrast between the successes enjoyed by the Franks against the Celts and Slavs, and their far more limited achievements against the Greek and Muslim societies of the Mediterranean and Levant.[160] For these latter, despite markedly different fighting techniques, enjoyed an equal if not superior military technology and were capable of containing – and in the case of the Muslims, finally defeating – their Frankish opponents. Here, I would suggest, is a far better analogy for late Anglo-Saxon England than the Celtic or Slav lands. Not, of course, that Anglo-Saxon England had Greek fire, or sophisticated fortifications like Nicaea or Antioch encountered by the First Crusade – but then neither did the great majority of the Frankish principalities. Both Byzantine and Muslim armies could be defeated in the field by the Franks, but a Durazzo or a Dorylaeum was never so cataclysmic as to deny effective recovery and ultimate survival or even eventual triumph. Anglo-Saxon England, by contrast, suffered ultimate defeat not because of any technological inferiority or the absence of crossbows, cavalry or castles, but because of an unusually decisive victory which annihilated effective dynastic members, paralyzed the remaining leadership and resulted in a rapid and widespread political submission. This capitulation served not only to neutralise key elements of defence – the burghs and the fleet – but even allowed them to be deployed by William himself as powerful tools in his own consolidation of power and conquest.

---

[158] Ailred, *Relatio*, 186; J. Gillingham, 'The Context and Purposes of the *History of the Kings of Britain*', *ANS* xiii (1990), at 106–9.

[159] *ASC* (D) *s.a.* 1063; *Vita Aedwardi*, 57–8. Cf. Barlow, *Edward the Confessor*, 210–11; 'Not since Agricola, and never again for many a year, was Wales so insolently invaded.' John of Salisbury later cited the campaign as a model of military planning in his *Policraticus* (*The Statesman's Book of John of Salisbury*, trans. J. Dickinson, New York 1927, 195).

[160] Bartlett, *The Making of Europe*, 71.

THE SPOLIATION OF WORCESTER

Ann Williams

Shortly before his death in 1095, Bishop Wulfstan of Worcester commanded his monk Hemming to begin work on the cartulary which goes by his name. It is concerned with the lands set aside for the use of the monks, as opposed to the episcopal *familia*, and its first section, the *Codicellus possessionum*, describes the losses suffered in the period from the Danish wars of Æthelred II's reign up to the time when Hemming began to write.[1] The later losses chronicled by Hemming can be compared with the account of Worcester's land in Domesday Book, but for the earlier period, he is often the sole authority. Some at least of his information came from St Wulfstan himself, who was born about 1006.[2] But memory is fallible; and Hemming's treatment of the documents available to him suggests that his unsupported word must be treated with due caution.[3] Despite these reservations, what he has to say is of great value for the history of his church and its lands and raises questions of general import for the history of eleventh-century England. For the purposes of this essay, I have re-arranged Hemming's material from a geographical order, which, I think, obscures much of its interest, into a chronological account of Worcester's vicissitudes from the Danish conquest to Domesday Book.[4] The accompanying tables summarize Hemming's information for each stage of the process.

The lands lost to the church of Worcester in the period of the Danish conquest and settlement are detailed in Table I. A monk of Worcester might have access to traditions about this *magna turbatio patriae*, for some of its most damaging campaigns were fought in Mercia.[5] In the Christmas season of 1015–16, Cnut and his ally Eadric Streona, ealdorman of Mercia, crossed into Warwickshire and there

---

[1] BL MS Cotton Tib. A xiii (Hemming's Cartulary), fos 119–34; printed in *Hemingi Chartularium*, ed. Thomas Hearne, Oxford 1723 (hereafter cited as *HC*), 248–81. See N.P. Ker, 'Hemming's Cartulary: a Description of the Two Worcester Cartularies in Cotton Tiberius A xiii', in *Studies in Medieval History presented to F.M. Powicke*, ed. R.W. Hunt, W.A. Pantin and R.W. Southern, Oxford 1948, 49–75; reprinted in *Books, Collectors and Libraries*, ed. Andrew G. Watson, London 1988, 31–49. I should like to thank the members of the Battle Conference, especially Professor Robin Fleming and Professor Hugh Thomas, for an illuminating discussion of this paper; all remaining errors and misconceptions are of course my own.
[2] He gives St Wulfstan as his authority for the seizure of Clent and Tardebigge (*HC*, 276–7).
[3] He says, for example, that Cnut's daughter Gunnhildr married the Emperor Conrad (*Cono*), when in fact her husband was Conrad's son, the future Henry III (*HC*, 267).
[4] Hemming, of course, was interested not in the history of the estates *in toto* but the specific histories of each one of them. His purpose is shown by the fact that the descriptions of each individual estate could have been used in judicial pleas for their recovery, providing details for the Church's *ontalu* (formal claim) in court; I owe this point to Professor Robin Fleming.
[5] *HC*, 277.

'ravaged and burned, and killed all they came across'.[6] Hemming claims that Worcestershire too was ravaged by the Danes, who seized the estates of nobles and commoners, rich and poor alike, so that they held almost the entire province by force.[7] Another cause of disruption was the establishment of three Danish earls and their followers in Herefordshire, Gloucestershire and Worcestershire in the early years of Cnut's reign.[8] As well as the passage of armies, the west midlands suffered frequent demands for geld, which Hemming claims were heavy enough to require the melting-down and sale of church plate and treasure.[9] Similar complaints are heard after the Norman Conquest.[10]

Geld appears as a frequent cause of the losses of the church. Hemming records an 'unbearable levy' (*vectigal importabile*) in the time of Cnut (perhaps the geld of 1018) which caused the loss of five estates in Warwickshire; for if the tax was not paid by the appointed time, whoever produced the money could claim the land, and thus Danes who coveted the church's estates paid over the outstanding sums to the sheriff and took possession.[11] Hemming says that these lands were lost *vi et fraude*, by force and fraud, and uses similar language of two estates in Oxfordshire, seized

---

[6] *ASC*, 1016. At least some of the Mercians still supported Cnut at the battle of Sherston in 1016, not just those Shropshire thegns who might be regarded as adherents of Eadric Streona, but also men from Gloucestershire; to the Chronicle's list of Eadric Streona and Ælfmær *deorling*, John of Worcester adds Ælfgar son of [Æthelweard] *mæw*, whose son Beorhtric held extensive lands, including Tewkesbury, Glos., on the eve of the Norman Conquest (*The Chronicle of John of Worcester*, ed. R.R. Darlington and P. McGurk, 2 vols, Oxford 1995 (hereafter cited as *JnW*), ii, 487–8; *Great Domesday: Facsimile*, ed. R.W.H. Erskine, London 1986 (hereafter cited as *GDB*), fos 163–163v: John Moore, ed., *Domesday Book: Gloucestershire*, Chichester 1983, nos 1, 24–52).

[7] *HC*, 251. Hemming's account is borne out by an Evesham lease of c.1016x1023, confirming to a certain Æthelmær land at Norton, which he had bought 'when it lay waste' in the witness of the whole shire (P.H. Sawyer, *Anglo-Saxon Charters: an Annotated List and Bibliography*, London 1968 (hereafter cited as S.) 1423; A.J. Robertson, *Anglo-Saxon Charters*, Cambridge 1956, no. 81). Norton was part of the manor of Lenchwick, held by Evesham Abbey in 1086 (*GDB* fo. 175v).

[8] Ranig of Herefordshire, Hakon of Worcestershire and Eilifr (Eilaf) of Gloucestershire, see Ann Williams, 'Cockles amongst the Wheat: Danes and English in the West Midlands in the First Half of the Eleventh Century', *Midland History* xi, 1986, 2–22; Simon Keynes, 'Cnut's Earls', *The Reign of Cnut*, ed. Alexander Rumble, Leicester 1994, 59–62. Hemming seems to imply that Earl Ranig was established in Herefordshire as early as 1016, the year when 'King Edmund Ironside fought three battles in one year against Cnut, and the kingdom was divided between them'. This is not intrinsically unlikely; Eirikr of Hladir was appointed earl in the north even before the death of Æthelred II (*ASC*, 1016).

[9] *HC*, 248–9. Eadric, abbot of St Peter's, Gloucester from 1022, had to loan two of the church's manors in return for a payment of £15, to redeem the rest of its lands from 'the great heregeld levied throughout England' (S.1424; the estates, at Hatherley and Badgeworth, did not belong to Gloucester in 1086). These gelds may also be reflected in the reduced assessment on Much Wenlock obtained from Cnut by the community of St Milburg's (*GDB* fo. 252v; Frank and Caroline Thorne, ed., *Domesday Book: Shropshire*, Chichester 1986, no. 3c,2; *VCH Shropshire*, i, 312).

[10] See the list of payments made by Worcester to King William 'apart from the geld on every hide, which no man but God alone can reckon' (Robertson, *Anglo-Saxon Charters*, 242–3).

[11] *HC*, 277–8, and see II Cnut 79: 'And he who has performed the obligations on an estate with the witness of the shire (and he who owned it before would not or could not) is to have it uncontested for his lifetime and give it to whom he pleases after his lifetime.' See also Cnut's charter for his housecarl Bovi (S.989, dated 1033), whose endorsement included the statement that 'Bovi defended the land successfully at law with his money in payment of tax due on it, the whole shire being witness' (Mary-Ann O'Donovan, *Charters of Sherborne*, Oxford (British Academy) 1988, 72). It is possible that Worcester sold or leased some land to raise cash to pay the geld (see also n. 9 above).

by the Danes 'through force and fraud and secular power'.[12] It was not only the Danes, however, who employed such methods; Wychbold, Worcs., and Bickmarsh, Glos., were obtained in exactly the same way by the Englishman Edwin, son of Leofwine, ealdorman of the Hwicce.[13]

All the men specifically accused by Hemming of spoliation are high-ranking officials in command of the shires, whether Danish or English. In Herefordshire the culprits are Earl Ranig and his *milites*, who seized the lands and vills (*terras et villas*) of *Pencovan*, Cowarne, Upleadon, Ocle Pychard and Rochford, with everything that belonged to them, partly because of the incompetence (*debilitatem*) of those in charge of them, and partly because of burdensome taxation and 'other misfortunes'.[14] In Worcestershire likewise, Earl Hakon and his *milites* seized Clifton-on-Teme, Tenbury Wells, Kyre, Hamcastle and Eastham with 'Bastwood'; after Hakon's death, his widow Gunnhildr made various gifts to Worcester, including a golden image of the Virgin, but kept the estates.[15] Beside these Danish predators appear the English spoilers. Edwin, who has already been mentioned, seized lands in Shropshire as well as Bickmarsh and Wychbold. He was perhaps Earl Hakon's deputy in Herefordshire; he may even have been sheriff, for he was killed in 1039, leading the western levies against the Welsh.[16] Æfic, sheriff of Staffordshire, appropriated the revenues of Clent and Tardebigge, both in Worcestershire, to the royal manor of Kingswinford, Staffs., at a time, as Hemming says, when there was no-one to do justice to the church of Worcester, since the kingdom was in turmoil and not yet stabilized under the rule of a single king.[17] The date must be 1016 or 1017, and it was presumably at the same time that Eadric Streona seized three of the church's estates in Gloucestershire, for his spoliation is dated to the time of Leofsige, who became bishop in 1016, and Eadric himself was murdered by Cnut at Christmas 1017.[18]

The secular authorities continue to figure among the enemies of Worcester in Hemming's account of the years between the Danish settlement and the Norman Conquest (see Table II). Swein Godwineson, who in 1043 was created earl of an extensive command based on Hereford, comes in for some swingeing criticism. Hemming cites first the earl's unfilial doubts concerning his parentage: 'he gave himself out to be of the kin of Cnut, that most energetic king, and bore lying testimony that Cnut and no other was his father'. Earl Godwine's reaction is not recorded, but Swein's mother Gytha, 'appalled by his arrogance and vanity,

[12] *Dolis et fraudibus et seculari potentia* (*HC*, 280; the lands were at Heythrop and Upper Kiddington, see Table I).

[13] *HC*, 278–9. Edwin's father Leofwine may have succeeded to the earldom of Mercia after Eadric Streona's murder in 1017, but see Keynes, 'Cnut's Earls', 74–5.

[14] *HC*, 274.

[15] *HC*, 251–2.

[16] *HC*, 278; *ASC*, 1039, 1052 (Hemming, of course, regards his death as a judgement). Hemming refers to the Edwin's Shropshire depredations as 'the aforementioned lands', implying that these are the estates at Tetstill, Hopton Wafers and Cleobury North later seized by Swein Godwineson, as he has already described (see n. 19 below).

[17] *HC*, 277. See also nn. 48 and 51 below.

[18] *HC*, 280–1. The estates were Batsford, Glos., Eisey, Wilts, and the unidentified *Keingeham*. Hemming says of Eadric that 'as he had been the destroyer of many monasteries and the oppressor of almost all', he was refused burial and his body was thrown over the walls of London; this story is also in John of Worcester (*JnW* ii, 504–5).

gathered together many noble West Saxon ladies, and proved by their testimony and many great oaths that she was his mother and Godwine his father'; Swein, however, continued to maintain that 'he did not spring from that kindred'. Hemming proceeds from this to Swein's addiction to 'the lusts of the flesh' and records his abduction of the abbess of Leominster, whom he kept as his wife for a whole year, until threatened with excommunication by Eadsige, archbishop of Canterbury and Lyfing, bishop of Worcester. In revenge he seized three of the church of Worcester's estates in Shropshire, namely Tetstill, Hopton Wafers and Cleobury North.[19]

There are problems with Hemming's account of this episode, quite apart from the fact that Worcester had no charters relating to the disputed estates, and no land in Shropshire at the time of the Domesday survey (see below). Swein's abduction of the abbess of Leominster is recorded by the *Anglo-Saxon Chronicle*, which places the event after the completion of Swein's expedition into Wales in 1046.[20] But her return is unlikely to have been prompted by threats from Bishop Lyfing and Archbishop Eadsige. Lyfing died on 23 March 1046, so that unless Swein's Welsh campaign was completed before then, the bishop was dead even before the abbess' abduction, let alone her year-long residence as the earl's wife. Moreover Eadsige was at this time in retirement from his office, which he resigned on grounds of ill-health in 1044 and resumed only in 1048, by which time Swein had fled first to Denmark and thence to Flanders.[21] As for Swein's denial of his parentage and Gytha's oath, all one can say is that it is not recorded elsewhere. Swein is the only member of his kindred to be accused by Hemming, which might explain the peculiar animus displayed. This is a point to which I shall return.

Most of the church's losses in this period are due to the family and followers of Leofric, earl of Mercia from the 1020s until 1057.[22] Leofric is more usually portrayed as a benefactor than a spoiler of the church; indeed John of Worcester, in recording his many acts of benevolence calls him a 'praiseworthy man of excellent memory'.[23] Hemming paints a different picture, not only of Leofric himself, but also of his brothers Edwin and Godwine, his nephew Æthelwine and his grandsons, Edwin and Morcar; of the whole family, only Leofric's wife Godgifu appears in Worcester's obituary list.[24]

Leofric himself held six of the church's estates in Worcestershire, which may also have been in his father's possession.[25] Towards the end of his life he restored two, at Wolverley and Blackwell; his charter, datable to 1052 x 1057, claims that

[19] *HC*, 275–6. For the identification of Hemming's *Mærebroc* as Tetstill with Marlbrook, see *DB Shropshire*, no. 5,2 and note and see also nos 7,1;3 and notes. Hemming implies that these are the estates seized earlier by Edwin son of Leofwine (see n. 16 above).

[20] *ASC* 'C', 1046.

[21] *ASC* 'E', 1047; 'D', 1049.

[22] See Keynes, 'Cnut's Earls', 74–5, 77–8 for the uncertainties surrounding Leofric's appointment.

[23] *JnW* ii, 582–3.

[24] Sir Ivor Atkins, 'The church of Worcester from the Eighth to the Twelfth Centuries', *Antiqs Journ.* xx, 1940, 31. The Æthelwine in the obituary list might be Earl Leofric's mutilated nephew (see n. 30 below). Only Ealdorman Leofwine's eldest son, Northmann, killed along with Eadric Streona at Christmas 1017, and Leofric's son Earl Ælfgar do not appear in Hemming's rogues' gallery; for Ælfgar, see also n. 106 below.

[25] *HC*, 261. Hemming says merely that Leofric held the estates 'after the death of his father Leofwine' (*defuncto patre suo Leofwino*); but see also Leofric's charter of restitution (next note).

they had previously been held by 'Danes and other enemies of God'.[26] He promised that the remaining estates should revert to the church on his death, but when
he died, on 31 August 1057, they were re-granted to his widow Godgifu for life in
return for an annual cash rent.[27] Subsequently her grandsons Edwin and Morcar,
'inspired by the devil', seized the estates, and as a result one perished miserably,
'abandoned by his friends' (*a suis peremptus*), and the other died in captivity.[28]

We are not told how Leofric's brother Godwine obtained the land he held at
Salwarpe, Worcestershire, merely that Godwine made a deathbed restoration of the
estate at some time between c.1055 and 1058. His son Æthelwine repudiated his
father's bequest, and retained the land with the aid of his uncle the earl. Eventually,
'by the just judgement of God', Æthelwine lost all that he had and perished
miserably in the hut of an oxherd (*bovarius*), being buried by two of his servants.[29]
Æthelwine *cild* is recorded as the pre-Conquest holder of Salwarpe in Domesday
but was not necessarily living in 1066; and Hemming's unreliability in matters of
detail forbids us to use this anecdote as evidence for conditions in Worcestershire
after the Norman Conquest.[30]

Worcester's lands were appropriated by Leofric's men as well as by members of
his kindred. It was Earl Leofric's support which prevented Wulfstan (as prior) from
recovering Hampton Lovett from Earngeat son of Grimr; he secured a legal judgement in his church's favour, but Earngeat, supported by the earl, retained the land
by force. When Earngeat's son wished to become a monk of Worcester, Wulfstan
demanded the return of the estate, or at least the portion known as '*Thiccanapeltreo*'; Earngeat promised that his sons (*filii*) should hold after his death, with
reversion to the monks, but soon 'not one of that whole kin remained to inherit'
and all Earngeat's lands passed into the hands of strangers.[31] A little earlier, while
Æthelwine was prior (before c.1055), one Sigmundr, *genere Danus*, held one of the
estates in the vill of Crowle, Worcestershire, but not content with his own holding,
also coveted that of the monks of Worcester, 'as the men of that race were wont to

---

[26] S.1232, *HC*, 408–9.

[27] *HC*, 261–2. Godgifu also presented various gifts to the Church of Worcester, consisting of three
pallia, two hangings, two bench-covers, two candlesticks *bene et honorifice parata*, and a *bib-
liotheca* in two parts.

[28] *HC*, 262. Presumably Edwin and Morcar's seizure took place after the death of their father,
Ælfgar, whom Hemming does not mention; this probably occurred in 1062. Edwin was killed in
1071, in flight from the Conqueror's men, and Morcar was captured and imprisoned after the siege
of Ely in the same year. Taken literally, Hemming's words would imply that Morcar was dead by the
time of writing in the late 1090s; he is last heard of attesting a charter of his gaoler, Roger de
Beaumont (d. after 1095) in 1086 (C.P. Lewis, 'The Early Earls of Norman England', *ANS* xiii,
1991, 215). Hemming's savage attitude to the young earls should be contrasted with the sympathetic
treatment they receive from the Shropshire-born Ordericus Vitalis (Orderic ii, 214–17, 256–9).
William of Malmesbury is also unsympathetic to the Mercian earls and John of Worcester, like his
source (the *Anglo-Saxon Chronicle*), virtually ignores them.

[29] *HC*, 259–60. Godwine's restoration was made when Wulfstan was prior, that is after c.1055, but
before the election of Wilstan as abbot of Gloucester in 1058.

[30] *GDB* fo. 176. Æthelwine, who 'had his hands cut off by the Danes', may have been one of the
hostages mutilated by Cnut when he was expelled in 1014 (*ASC*, 1014).

[31] *HC*, 260–1. In this passage Hemming gives Wulfstan his episcopal title, though he did not
become bishop until 1062, five years after the death of Leofric in 1057; it is probable, however, that
Hemming has used Wulfstan's title retrospectively. After 1066, Hampton Lovett passed to Urse
d'Abetot and *Thiccanapeltreo* [the 'thick [? sturdy] appletree'] to Hugh l'Asne (see n. 56 below).

do' (*ut illius generis homines erant soliti*).[32] Sigmundr was a *miles* of Earl Leofric, and 'by force and the power of himself and his lord' so burdened the monks' estate with pleas and lawsuits that it became untenable; and thus Prior Æthelwine was forced to loan it to him for life. Hemming gives the terms of the agreement: military service by land and sea, and an 'acceptable' sum of money or a horse (*caballus*) to be rendered annually to the prior.[33]

Sigmundr's appropriation of Crowle was a forced loan rather than an outright seizure.[34] *Lænland*, granted for a specific term with reversion to the grantor at the end of it, was not always easily recovered. Hemming reports that a *cassatus* at Oddingley, Worcs., was leased to the *clericus* Cynethegn, but his heirs withdrew the land from the church.[35] Leopard, also in Worcestershire, was leased by Bishop Brihtheah (1033–38) to Herluin the priest, who had accompanied him to Saxony when he conducted Cnut's daughter Gunnhildr to her marriage with the future king Henry III. Hemming implies that the church lost the service as a result, but Domesday Book includes Leopard as part of the monks' manor of Hallow; in 1086 it was held of them by Hugh de Grandmesnil and of Hugh by Baldwin, who can be identified as Herluin's son. It might be concluded that Baldwin, and indeed Hugh de Grandmesnil, were rendering the due service to the monks.[36]

Lænland was especially endangered if the holder was exiled or forfeited for some offence. In such a case, only the offender's bookland ought to be confiscated by the king, whereas any *lænland* should revert to the lord who loaned it; but this distinction was not always observed.[37] Hemming says that Cotheridge was loaned by its reeve Earnwig to his brother Spirites the priest, but when Spirites was exiled by King Edward (in 1065), Richard fitzScrob seized the land.[38] Richard fitzScrob was one of the king's foreign favourites and a royal staller, and it was probably the king who gave him Cotheridge, as he gave Spirites' forfeited prebend at St Mary's Bromfield, in Shropshire, to another of his stallers, Robert fitzWymarc. Though Hemming presents this as a loss to Worcester, Richard was rendering Cotheridge's dues on the eve of the Conquest and in 1086 his son Osbern fitzRichard still held

---

[32] *HC*, 264–5. It should be noticed that Hemming himself has a Danish name.

[33] Hemming says that military expeditions were very frequent at that time (*tunc crebo agebatur*), which suggests the period of the late 1040s and early 1050s.

[34] Even in the case of seizure, a compromise might be reached whereby the land was held by the alleged spoliator for life with reversion to the church.

[35] *HC*, 264. Bishop Oswald's lease (S.1297, dated 963) of 2½ hides at Oddingley and Laugherne to Cynethegn *clericus* (who ceases to attest episcopal charters in 996) appears in the earlier Worcester cartulary (the *Liber Wigornensis*); the term was for three lives, with reversion to the bishopric (*HC*, 160–1 and see Vanessa J. King, 'St Oswald's Tenants', *St Oswald of Worcester: Life and Influence*, ed. Nicholas Brooks and Catherine Cubitt, Leicester 1996, 112–13). Cynethegn's name is uncommon and the first element suggests a connection with the family of Cyneweard, sheriff of Worcester temp. Bishop Wulfstan, who also held land at Laugherne (see nn. 77 and 79 below).

[36] *GDB* fo. 174; Frank and Caroline Thorne, *Domesday Book: Worcestershire*, Chichester 1982, no. 2,71. For Baldwin son of Herluin, Hugh de Grandmesnil's normal *antecessor*, see Ann Williams, 'An Introduction to the Worcestershire Domesday', *The Worcestershire Domesday*, ed. Ann Williams and R.W.H. Erskine, London 1988, 31 and n. 44 below.

[37] II Cnut, 77, 77i.

[38] *HC*, 254; the date of Spirites' exile is provided by Domesday Book (*GDB* fo. 252v; *DB Shropshire*, no. 3d,7). Spirites was a royal chaplain, richly endowed, with 77 hides of land spread over Kent, Hampshire, Wiltshire, Somerset, Herefordshire and Shropshire (Frank Barlow, *The English Church 1000–1066*, London 1963, 135–6).

of the bishop.[39] But Richard had also seized Lower Sapey and given it to his son Osbern, who held it in chief in 1086, without reference to the rights of the church.[40]

Before proceeding to what Hemming says about the effects of the Norman Conquest on the church's land, let us look at some aspects of his account of the earlier losses. The first question to ask is whether any evidence exists (apart from Hemming) that the lands concerned ever belonged to Worcester, and the answer, in some cases, is precious little. On Tables I and II, I have included all charters which purport to grant these lands to the church; those which are regarded with suspicion are marked with asterisks.[41] Hemming is the only authority for a grant by Offa of Heythrop and Over Kiddington, Oxon. (Table I), a shire where Worcester held no land at the time of Domesday. The same king's grant of the unidentified *Pencovan* (also Table I) is known only from a list of benefactions bound up with John of Worcester's Chronicle.[42] Some of the charters which do survive seem to have been fabricated or at least 'improved' in the eleventh century, perhaps during the very process of overhauling the archives on which Hemming and his colleagues were engaged. This is the case with S.179, an alleged grant of Hallow and its appurtenances by Coenwulf of Mercia in 816, which is the only authority for the church's possession of Lapworth, Warks. (Table I). S.179 is based on a genuine charter of Coenwulf (S.180) but the place-names have been 'up-dated', and the various outliers belonging to Hallow in the eleventh century added.[43] S.181, the authority for Worcester's possession of Belbroughton, Bell Hall, Fairfield and Salwarpe (Table II), is also based on S.180, and was probably fabricated at the same time as S.179.

Such updating of the charters does not necessarily mean that Worcester had not possessed the lands concerned. In the case of Lapworth, Domesday Book reveals that it was held before the Norman Conquest by Baldwin, identifiable as Baldwin son of Herluin, whose father had been given *lænland* at Leopard, Worcs., by Bishop Brihtheah.[44] As Baldwin and his lord Hugh de Grandmesnil still held

[39] *GDB* fo. 172; *DB Worcestershire*, no. 2,14.

[40] *HC*, 255; *GDB* fo.176v: *DB Worcestershire*, no. 19,9.

[41] S.731, of course, is the celebrated *Altitonantis*, fabricated in the mid-twelfth century (Julia Barrow, 'How the Twelfth-century Monks of Worcester Perceived their Past', *The Perception of the Past in Twelfth-Century Europe*, ed. Paul Magdalino, London 1992, 53–74).

[42] Patrick McGurk, personal communication; for Offa's alleged grant, see *Monasticon* i, 608; H.P.R. Finberg, *The Early Charters of the West Midlands*, Leicester 1961, 140.

[43] Finberg, *Early Charters of the West Midlands*, 184–8. Hemming himself records elsewhere that one of the appurtenant estates, at Oddingley, had been given to the church by Bishop Coenwald (d. 957), 150 years after the alleged grant of Coenwulf (*HC*, 573; Finberg, *Early Charters of the West Midlands*, 111, 187).

[44] *GDB* fo. 242: Judy Plaistner, *Domesday Book: Warwickshire*, Chichester 1976, no. 18,7. Lapworth was held in 1086 by Baldwin's usual successor, Hugh de Grandmesnil. Finberg indeed identified Lapworth as the land at *Lippard* given by Bishop Brihtheah to Baldwin's father Herluin (see above, n. 36), but this is Leopard (or Lyppard), Worcs., held in 1086 by Baldwin of Hugh de Grandmesnil, and by Hugh of the bishop of Worcester (*GDB* fo. 174: *DB Worcestershire*, no. 2,71). Baldwin had been Archbishop Ealdred's steward and in the early 1050s Ealdred granted him *lænland* at Weston-on-Avon, Warks. (S.1407: the text describes Baldwin simply as Ealdred's man (*homo*) but he is identified as the bishop's steward in the endorsement). Baldwin received a life-lease with reversion to the monks of Worcester, but in 1086 Weston-on-Avon was held by Hugh de Grandmesnil (*GDB* fo. 169: *DB Gloucestershire*, no. 62,5 and note).

Leopard of the bishop of Worcester in 1086, it is possible, though Domesday does not say so, that Baldwin held Lapworth too as a tenant of Worcester.

Other fabrications are rather less convincing. S.75, an alleged charter of Æthel-red of Mercia for Wychbold (Table I) is an eleventh-century forgery with little to recommend it. S.751, King Edgar's charter for Bickmarsh (also Table I), seems to be 'a reworked charter . . . for the thegn Brihtnoth', with the addition of an assignment by the recipient to the church of Worcester.[45] Something similar seems to have occurred with S.190, which constitutes the monks' title to Crowle (Table II) but here the tampering took place in the tenth century, so it can be presumed that Crowle belonged to the church at that date.[46] Though outright forgery is compara-tively rare, there are some cases where the church's title is dubious in the extreme. S.1421, an undated lease of Luddington (Table I) to one *Fulder* in return for a loan of £3, may have been written by Hemming himself; and S.406 an alleged grant of Clifton-on-Teme (also Table I) by King Athelstan in 930, was constructed at Worcester in the 1090s, the moment at which the church was laying claim to the estate.[47]

There is a particular suspicion in the case of Clifton-on-Teme, for it was a member of the royal manor of Westbury-on-Severn, Glos., as were Kyre and Hamcastle.[48] All three were among the estates allegedly seized from Worcester by Hakon, earl of Worcestershire in the 1020s (Table I). Other royal and comital manors claimed as Worcester's property are Clent and Tardebigge, in Worcester-shire, and Cowarne, Herefords (all in Table I). Domesday shows that Clent and Tardebigge were royal estates in 1066 and Cowarne, to which the third penny (the earl's share) of three hundreds was attached, was held on the eve of the Conquest by Harold Godwineson as earl of Herefordshire. Upleadon, Herefords (Table I), may also have been a comital estate; it was allegedly seized by Earl Ranig of Herefordshire (d. c.1041) and was later held by Eadgyth, sister of Odda of Deerhurst, earl of Worcestershire in the 1050s.[49] As for the three manors in Shrop-shire allegedly taken by Earl Swein (Table II), Hemming clearly implies that they are the estates in Shropshire previously appropriated by Edwin (Table I), who, as we have seen, was perhaps sheriff of Herefordshire. Swein's manors later appear in the hands of Siward son of Æthelgar, King Edward's great-nephew, and grandson

[45] S.75, 751, and see Susan Kelly, *Anglo-Saxon Charters*, revised edition, Cambridge forthcoming.
[46] S.190 is a genuine charter of Wiglaf of Mercia for the minster of Hanbury, with counter-grants to the king, and to Ealdorman Mucel; 'a later scribe (? 10th-century) has tampered with the text to suggest that the grant of land to the king and to Ealdorman Mucel was in fact a life-lease on the estates, with reversion to Worcester' (Kelly, *Anglo-Saxon Charters*, forthcoming).
[47] S.1421, and see Kelly, *Anglo-Saxon Charters*, forthcoming; the term is three years, a very unusual feature, and the lease may have been fabricated to support the claim in the *Codicellus possessionum*. For S.406, see David Dumville, *Wessex and England from Alfred to Edgar*, Wood-bridge 1995, 167, 168 n. 182. Other dubious charters perhaps compiled in the 1090s include S.118 (see n. 76 below); S.1475 (*HC*, p. 335), an alleged grant to the community of Condicote, Glos., which according to Domesday Book (fo. 146v) belonged to St Peter's of Gloucester; and S.1486, a spurious memorandum recording Ealdred's gift of land at Hampnett, Glos., to the monks of Worces-ter, presumably intended to bolster their claim to this disputed estate (see also below, n. 58).
[48] On the eve of the Conquest Clifton and Kyre were in the king's hands and Hamcastle was held by Osbern son of Richard fitzScrob, a royal staller; by 1086 all three estates were held by Osbern (*GDB* fo. 176v; *DB Worcestershire*, nos 18,3;4;8).
[49] *GDB* fo. 186; *DB Herefordshire*, no. 18,1 (see also n. 104 below).

of Eadric Streona, ealdorman of Mercia, so it may be that they too were once comital lands, held by Edwin and Swein as Eadric Streona's successors.[50]

In the case of Clent and Tardebigge, Hemming presents a plausible account of the church's acquisition of the land. He says that they were purchased by Æthelsige, *decanus* of Worcester, from Æthelred II for £200 of silver *in ius perpetuum monasterii*; but after the king's death (in 1016) they were appropriated by Æfic, sheriff of Staffordshire and still lie in that shrievalty. Domesday could have provided Hemming with the last piece of information, for Clent and Tardebigge, though in Worcestershire, are indeed valued with Kingswinford, Staffs., and held by the sheriff of that shire.[51] For the rest, however, he gives Bishop Wulfstan as his informant.[52] There is nothing inherently improbable in the account, and one can envisage circumstances in which Æthelred II might temporarily alienate parts of the royal manors for cash to pay the various gelds occasioned by the Danish wars.[53] Some royal and comital estates might well have passed in this way to Worcester in the latter years of Æthelred's reign, but it is unlikely that they were permanently alienated, and once the kingdom was restored, they presumably reverted to the king, or to his earls.

As for the church's *lænland*, it is important to remember that we have only Worcester's side of the case; the laymen concerned might have had more right than Hemming allows. As Professor Barlow has remarked: 'it is axiomatic in the chronicles and other memorials produced by the clergy that no church held an estate illegally or was deprived of it with justice'.[54] As we have seen, Domesday represents Richard fitzScrob as performing the service from Cotheridge, and Sigmundr *danus* too as paying his dues on Crowle.[55] Only Hampton Lovett and *Thiccanapeltreo* had been withdrawn from the church's control; in 1066 the lands were held by Alweald, perhaps the heir of Earngeat son of Grimr, without reference to the rights of Worcester.[56]

The estates lost in the aftermath of the Norman Conquest are set out in Tables IV and V. It is rarely possible to provide accurate dates for the seizures, but those which were effected by Earl William, or on his authority (Table IV), must belong to the period between 1067, when he became earl, and February 1071, when he was killed at the Battle of Cassel. Likewise, Ralph de Bernay's activities must be dated before 1076, when he was dispossessed and imprisoned for his part in the rebellion of the three earls. This rebellion, and the forfeiture of Earl William's son, Roger de Breteuil, disrupted the earliest post-Conquest patterns of lordship and tenure in the west, a factor which must be borne in mind when comparing Hemming's account of the church's losses with the description of the same lands in Domesday Book.

There are very few indications of what we might call smash and grab. Hemming says that Roger d'Ivri, a royal *pincerna*, 'invaded' Hampnett, Glos. (see Table IV),

[50] *GDB* fo. 260; *DB Shropshire*, nos 5,2:7,1–2 (for Siward son of Æthelgar, see Ann Williams, *The English and the Norman Conquest*, Woodbridge 1995, 94–5). See also nn. 16 and 19 above.

[51] *GDB* fo. 172v; *DB Worcestershire*, nos 1,4–6.

[52] *HC*, 276–7.

[53] There was a dean of Worcester called Æthelsige, who died c.1016 (*Heads of Religious Houses, England and Wales, 940–1216*, ed. David Knowles, C.N.L. Brooke and Vera C.M. London, Cambridge 1972, 83).

[54] Barlow, *The English Church, 1000–1066*, 175.

[55] *GDB* fos 174, 176v; *DB Worcestershire*, nos 2,78;19,6.

[56] *HC*, 260–1; *GDB* fo. 177v; *DB Worcestershire*, nos 26,10;27,1.

while Bishop Wulfstan was at Chester 'on the king's business' (*in legatione regis*). Since Wulfstan was unable to recover Hampnett because of the disagreement between himself and Archbishop Thomas, the date must be 1071–2, when Wulfstan was administering the see of Lichfield after the resignation of Bishop Leofwine.[57] The suit with Thomas concerned the twelve episcopal manors retained by Ealdred after his elevation to the see of York, and claimed by Thomas as his successor. Domesday Book reveals that Hampnett had actually belonged to Archbishop Ealdred, and we might suspect that it was one of the disputed manors, and that Roger d'Ivri might have been acting in some official capacity.[58]

What Domesday shows is that all the lands lost were *lænland*; it is not so much the church of Worcester as its tenants who have been dispossessed. As we have seen, *lænland* was prone (even before 1066) to be confiscated along with the personal holdings of the lessee. Witley, Worcs., seized by Ralph de Bernay and therefore before 1076, had been loaned to Earnwig the priest, at the request of Eadric the Wild.[59] Eadric the Wild, who may be identical with Eadric of Hindlip, the bishop's military commander, was involved in the English rebellion of 1069, and though he was subsequently pardoned, he lost most of his land; Earnwig the priest's holding may have been seized along with his lord's estates.[60]

Some of the Normans and Frenchmen endowed after 1066 received the lands of named Englishmen – their *antecessores* – from whom their title derived. Hemming himself refers to this process, complaining of 'Frenchmen (*francigeni*) who usurped the inheritances of Englishmen'.[61] *Lænland* held by men whose estates were thus transferred *en bloc* to a Norman or French incomer was subject to the same insecurity as any other forfeited land. Thus the Worcester *lænland* held by Baldwin son of Herluin went to Baldwin's successor Hugh de Grandmesnil, though Baldwin continued to hold at least some of it as Hugh's subtenant in 1086, and in one case Hugh seems to have acknowledged the bishop of Worcester's rights in the land.[62]

Problems could also arise when a man who was personally commended to one lord held land owing service to another. In such cases the land ought to go to the

[57] *HC*, 281. Bishop Leofwine of Lichfield formally resigned his see at Easter 1071 (*Lanfranc's Letters*, 37).

[58] *GDB* fo. 168; *DB Gloucestershire*, no. 41,1; for S.1486, a spurious charter of Ealdred, forged (presumably) to bolster the monks' claim, see n. 47 above. Roger d'Ivri seems to have had some ministerial office in Gloucestershire; he had been farming the royal manor of King's Barton, with which Archbishop Ealdred too had been associated (*GDB* fo. 162v; *DB Gloucestershire*, no. 1,2).

[59] *HC*, 256–7; *GDB* fo. 172v; *DB Worcestershire*, no. 2,8 (the TRE tenant is named as Earnwine, a common error for Earnwig). The lease was granted by Bishop Ealdred while Wulfstan was prior, that is, between c.1055 and 1062. For Ealdred's other grants to laymen, all with reversion to the bishopric, see S.1405–7, 1409.

[60] Eadric the steersman held Hindlip of the bishop on the eve of the Conquest (*GDB* fo. 173v; *DB Worcestershire*, no. 2,52) but by 1086 it had passed to Urse d'Abetot. Hemming says elsewhere that after 1066 Eadric held nothing of the bishopric but was the man of Robert, bishop of Hereford, but he attests the agreement of Wulfstan of Worcester and Walter of Evesham, concluded before the Domesday commissioners, as Eadric of Hindlip (*HC*, 75–6, 81–82, 297; *DB Worcestershire*, Appendix H; R.C. van Caeneghem, *English Lawsuits from William I to Richard I*, Selden Society, London 1990–91, i, 38). For the possible identity of Eadric of Hindlip and Eadric the Wild, see Williams, *The English and the Norman Conquest*, 92–3.

[61] *HC*, 269.

[62] See above, nn. 36, 44.

Frenchman who succeeded to the lord to whom service was due (the landlord, or in OE *landrica*); but it was often appropriated by the successor of the personal lord (*hlaford*).[63] For instance, whereas Hemming claims that Sigmundr the Dane held Shelsey Walsh (Table IV) of the monks of Worcester (*ex concessione fratrum*) for the usual service, Domesday not only describes Sigmundr as 'Earl Edwin's *teinus*' but adds that 'he could not withdraw from [the land] without his permission', which implies that Sigmundr held Shelsey of Edwin and not of the monks.[64] Osbern may have appropriated Sigmundr's land at Shelsey when he received some of the lands forfeited by Sigmundr's *hlaford*, Earl Edwin, after 1071, even though, as *lænland*, it should have reverted to Worcester as *landrica*.[65]

The tensions between personal commendation on the one hand and tenurial obligation on the other may have intensified after 1066.[66] The death of Archbishop Ealdred in 1069 and the downfall of Earl Edwin in 1071 must have caused their commended men to seek new protectors, either among the incoming Normans, or the surviving English lords. Hemming describes how, after the downfall of 'all the leading magnates (*baronibus*) of this province', numerous rich men sought the protection of Æthelwig, abbot of Evesham, because 'he surpassed everyone by his intelligence, his shrewdness and his knowledge of secular laws (the only ones he studied)'. Having acquired the personal homage of many thegns, some of them holding *lænland* of Worcester, Æthelwig then 'circumvented them by his slyness and defrauded them of their lands'. Hemming specifies the Worcester estates lost in this way: Acton, Eastbury, Milcote, Westmancote and one of the two holdings at Bengeworth, all belonging to the monks, and Daylesford and Evenlode, which belonged to the bishop.[67] On Æthelwig's death, all were seized by Odo, bishop of Bayeux (for their subsequent fate, see Tables V and VI).[68] Naturally the Evesham

---

[63] The distinction between personal lordship and lordship over land has been clarified by David Roffe, 'Brought to Book: Lordship and Land in Pre-Conquest England', forthcoming; for a summary of Dr Roffe's conclusions, see Williams, *The English and the Norman Conquest*, 71–6.

[64] *HC*, 251; *GDB* fo. 176v; *DB Worcestershire*, no. 19,6. There is a similar dispute over Alvestone, Warks. (*GDB* fo. 238v; *DB Warwickshire*, no. 3,4; see Williams, *The English and the Norman Conquest*, 75, 143–4).

[65] Osbern also held that part of Crowle which had originally belonged to Sigmundr himself (see above, p. 387); it was held on the eve of the Conquest by Ketelbert, presumably either a tenant of Sigmundr or possibly his son (see Williams, ' "Cockles amongst the Wheat" ', 14; 'An Introduction to the Worcestershire Domesday', 22).

[66] It was suggested in the discussion following this paper that the incomers were not especially concerned with the niceties of English tenure, having customs of their own in this matter. Undoubtedly they did, though the differences between English and Norman custom can be exaggerated (see Williams, *The English and the Norman Conquest*, 190–3). I agree that disputes such as those described, and the various compromises which arose from them, became more common after 1066 (though observable before the Conquest and not at Worcester alone); I agree moreover that the effect of such disputes was ultimately to change perceptions about tenure; but I still believe that such changed perceptions were the result of disputes like those recorded by Hemming (and in Domesday Book generally), and not the cause of them.

[67] *HC*, 270–3; van Caeneghem, *English Lawsuits from William I to Richard I*, i, 31.

[68] For Eastbury, seized by Urse d'Abetot, see also *HC*, 257–8; Urse also held Westmancote, which Hemming does not mention again, but of the bishop, not the monks (*GDB* fo. 173, *DB Worcestershire*, no. 2,28). Acton Beauchamp (Table V) was allegedly given to Worcester by Ordwig, Abbot Æthelwig's father (*HC*, 251–2; *VCH Warks.*, i, 274; *GDB* fo. 176; *DB Worcestershire*, no. 11,1). There were two estates at Milcote, Warks., one claimed by Worcester and the other by Evesham; in 1086 both were held by Stephen the steersman, one of Bishop Odo's men, who also held

Chronicle puts a different gloss upon Æthelwig's actions, but it was easy for personal protection to slide into tenurial lordship, especially in the kind of confusion which attended the re-distribution of lands after the Norman Conquest.[69] There was a long dispute between Worcester and Evesham over Bengeworth (and Hampton, which Hemming does not mention). After much litigation, the case was finally settled before the Domesday commissioners; Evesham retained the land, but acknowledged that it lay in the bishop's triple-hundred of Oswaldslow and ought to pay the dues common to all land therein.[70]

Much of Worcester's lost *lænland* had belonged to the kinsmen of Bishop Brihtheah (see Table III and the associated family tree). Hemming says that Brihtheah, as 'a West Saxon from Berkshire', had no kin in the west, and thus lavished the endowment of the church on his relatives and followers.[71] Hemming does not make such complaints against Lyfing and Ealdred, though both were generous donors, perhaps because most of the recipients were in fact still Brihtheah's kinsmen.[72] They include Brihtheah's half-brother Æthelric, who received lands at Himbleton, Spetchley, Wolverton and Whittington, all members of the monks' manor of Hallow; his unnamed brother-in-law, who was given land at Alton-in-Rock and Lower Sapey; his kinsman Brihtwine, who got land at Ravenshill; and his kinsman and chamberlain, Azur, who received land at Bengeworth.[73]

Dorsington, Warks., which had belonged to Ordwig, presumably Æthelwig's father (*GDB* fo. 243v; *DB Warwickshire*, nos 36,1–2; *VCH Warks.*, i, 274). In Worcestershire, Stephen appears as the bishop of Worcester's tenant at Daylesford, presumably by the gift of his lord, Bishop Odo; Evenlode too had passed through Odo's hands (*GDB* fo. 173; *DB Worcestershire*, nos 2,42–3). As for Bengeworth, Hemming describes how when Urse d'Abetot seized the land of Azur, Bishop Brihtheah's kinsman, the thegn Earngrimr, who held the other tenement in the vill, became alarmed, and sought the protection of Æthelwig, who thereupon appropriated his land (*HC*, 269–70). In 1086, both parts of Bengeworth were held of Worcester, Earngrimr's portion by Evesham, and Azur's by Urse (*GDB* fos 174, 175v; *DB Worcestershire*, nos 2,75;10,12).

69 *Chronicon Abbatiae de Evesham*, ed. William Dunn Macray, RS XXIX, 1863, 96–7; van Caeneghem, *English Lawsuits from William I to Richard I*, i, 29–32, and see R.R. Darlington, 'Æthelwig, abbot of Evesham', *EHR* xliv, 1933, *passim*.

70 *HC*, 75–9; 80–3; 296–7; the various documents are printed, with translation, in *DB Worcestershire*, Appendix H and van Caeneghem, *English Lawsuits from William I to Richard I*, i, 37–41. Both parties possessed charters relating to the disputed lands, most of them forged; in the case of Bengeworth, Evesham had S.80 and 1250, both spurious, and S.991, a writ of Cnut granting 5 hides at Bengeworth to Brihtwine, with reversion to Evesham, which may be genuine (see also S.1664). Worcester had the spurious S.118 (for which see n. 76 below) and S.1282 and the possibly genuine S.1341, a lease of Bishop Oswald dated 980.

71 Since they were episcopal and not monastic lands, Hemming does not mention Brihtheah's lease of 2 hides at Aston, Glos., to his *cniht* Wulfmær, to hold as he had held under Bishop Leofsige (S.1399, Robertson, *Anglo-Saxon Charters*, 172–3), nor his lease of 2 hides at Cutsdean, Worcs., to Dodda (*GDB* fo. 173). Aston was part of the episcopal manor of Withington, Glos. and Cutsdean of Bredon, Worcs. (*GDB*, fos 164v–165, 173, *DB Gloucestershire*, no. 3,5, *DB Worcestershire*, no. 2,24).

72 Vanessa J. King, 'Ealdred, Archbishop of York: the Worcester Years', *ANS* xviii, 1996, 135–7. For Lyfing's leases, see S.1058, 1392–8, 1849–56; for Ealdred, see S.1405–9, 1857, and *GDB*, fos 173, 173v; *DB Worcestershire*, nos 2,24;63.

73 *HC*, 255 (Alton), 266 (Himbleton, etc.), 267 (Ravenshill), 269 (Bengeworth). Brihtwine is perhaps identical with Brihtwine *predives*, who gave Hadzor to the church when his grandson Edwin became a monk of Worcester; the gift was fulfilled by Brihtwine's son Brihtmær, but later seized by William fitzOsbern and given to Gilbert fitzTurold (*HC*, 262–4; *GDB* fo. 177; *DB Worcestershire*, no. 20,6). He in turn is probably the Brihtmær whose tenancy at Clopton passed to

Brihtheah's loan of Leopard to his priest Herluin has already been mentioned.[74] He also loaned Elmley Castle to an unnamed thegn (*minister*), from whom it was recovered by his successor Bishop Lyfing, who in turn loaned it to Æthelric *Kiu*, probably Brihtheah's brother.[75] It may have been Brihtheah who loaned Charlton to 'a certain wealthy man', for it passed first to the original lessee's son and then to Godric *finc*, who is probably the son of Brihtheah's brother Æthelric.[76] For similar reasons, it was probably from Brihtheah that the parents of Cyneweard, sheriff of Worcestershire, received Laugherne, since Cyneweard too seems to have been a kinsman, perhaps a son of Æthelric.[77]

Hemming presents Brihtheah as a West Saxon interloper, but the bishop, far from being a newcomer, had before his elevation been abbot of Pershore, and before that a monk at Worcester itself. Moreover, his mother was the sister of Archbishop Wulfstan, bishop of Worcester from 1002 to 1016. Between 1016 and 1023, Brihtheah's mother married the Gloucestershire thegn Wulfric.[78] It may be

---

Urse d'Abetot; this land had formerly been leased to one Ælfweard and his wife Matilda, *cameraria* of Queen Edith (*HC*, 253–4; *GDB* fo. 172; *DB Worcestershire*, no. 2,10). Hemming says that Urse appropriated the lands of Brihtmær's son Alwine on his death, specifically Waresley (HC, 261), leased to Alwine during the priorate of Alstan (1062–after 1077, see *Heads of Religious Houses*, 83). Ælfwine son of Brihtmær attests the Worcester/Evesham agreement of 1086 (*DB Worcestershire*, Appendix V, Worcester H; van Caeneghem, *English Lawsuits from William I to Richard I*, i, 40) and also witnesses a charter of Bishop Wulfstan in 1089 (R.R. Darlington, *The Cartulary of Worcester Cathedral Priory*, PRS, ns xxxviii, London 1968, no. 4, pp. 9–10).

[74] See n. 36 above.

[75] *HC*, 267–8; Hemming gives the terms as one life with reversion to the church, but the surviving charter (S.1396) specifies three lives with reversion to the bishopric. See also Williams, 'An Introduction to the Worcestershire Domesday', 25, where the author's inability to proof-read her own material has resulted in the substitution of 'Bentley[-in-Holt]' for the correct 'Elmley' (see also n. 80 below). For Lyfing's other loans (three of which are also in favour of Æthelric), see S.1392–5, 1396–8.

[76] *HC*, 268–9; for Æthelric's son Godric, see *HC*, 255. In 1086, Charlton and Elmley (11 hides) were held by Robert *dispensator* in succession to Cyneweard and Godric, as members of the Church's manor of Cropthorne; the other members of the manor were 5 hides at Hampton (held by Evesham), and 10 hides at Bengeworth, divided between two manors, one held by Evesham, the other by Urse d'Abetot in succession to Azur, Bishop Brihtheah's kinsman. In all, these tenancies accounted for 26 hides out of the 50 hides at which Cropthorne was assessed (*GDB* fo. 174; *DB Worcestershire*, nos 2,72–5). Though the details of the hidage vary, it is worth noting the spurious charter of Offa, granting 50 hides at Cropthorne to Bishop Tilhere (S.118), with permission to grant 25 of the 50 hides to his kinsmen, 'who shall render to the bishop all the service which they owe to the king', the land to revert to Worcester in the case of forfeiture. The charter might have been worded with the post-Conquest fate of the estates in mind; and probably was.

[77] *HC*, 252–3. In 1066, Cyneweard was holding Elmley (*GDB* fo. 174; *DB Worcestershire*, no. 2,73 and notes), an estate formerly leased to Æthelric (see n. 75 above), and the connections between Cyneweard and Æthelric's undoubted son, Godric, seem unusually close (see n. 92 below).

[78] S.1459, Robertson, *Anglo-Saxon Charters*, 148–9. Wulfric promised his wife (presumably the Wulfgifu to whom Wulfstan gave land at Perry, see n. 81 below) a life-interest in lands at Orletone and Ribbesford, both Worcs., and undertook to obtain for her a three-life lease of land at Knightwick from the abbey of Winchcombe. Orleton, which Hemming does not mention, was held in 1086 by Gilbert fitzTurold in succession to Eadwig and Edwin (*GDB* fo. 177; *DB Worcestershire*, no. 20,5). Ribbesford, according to Hemming, was seized first by 'Danes', and (after the Conquest) by Turstin the Fleming, who later forfeited his lands. Like Gilbert fitzTurold, Turstin was an adherent of Earl William fitzOsbern and forfeited in 1076, for his part in the rebellion of the earl's son, Roger de Breteuil; Ribbesford was in the king's hands in 1086 (*HC*, 256; *GDB* fo. 172; *DB Worcestershire*, no. 1,2). For Knightwick, see n. 94 below.

assumed that Æthelric was the son of Wulfric, but since Brihtheah himself attests the marriage agreement, he was presumably the child of a previous husband.[79]

The descent of their estates helps to clarify the family's relationships (see family tree). Bentley-in-Holt was loaned by Archbishop Wulfstan to his brother Ælfwig and subsequently by Bishop Lyfing to Æthelric, half-brother of Wulfstan's nephew, Brihtheah.[80] Alton-in-Rock was settled on Bishop Brihtheah's mother by her second husband, and subsequently leased by Brihtheah to his brother-in-law, from whom it passed first to his half-brother Æthelric, and thence to Æthelric's son Godric. Godric in turn may be identified with the Godric *finc* who held Charlton of the church of Worcester, and also with Godric of Perry, an estate originally loaned by Archbishop Wulfstan to Wulfgifu, presumably his sister and the mother of Brihtheah and Æthelric.[81] Cyneweard, sheriff of Worcestershire, holder of Laugherne, also held Æthelric's former *lænland* at Elmley, and was perhaps another of his sons. Domesday Book reveals that Æthelric, brother of Bishop Brihtheah, held land at Queenhill, part of the episcopal manor of Ripple, and he is almost certainly the Æthelric to whom Bishop Lyfing leased lands at Hill Croome and Baughton, Worcs., and Armscott in Tredington, Warks.[82] As Æthelric 'the bishop's brother' he attested two leases of Bishop Ealdred around 1055; one is also attested by Godric *finc*.[83]

Brihtheah's kinsmen were a powerful and prosperous local family, but the Norman Conquest brought a change in their fortunes.[84] Earl William himself took Æthelric's lands at Himbleton, Spetchley, Wolverton and Whittington, but offered to do the service on Himbleton and Spetchley, which in 1086 were still part of the manor of Hallow, though held by Roger de Lacy (see Table IV).[85] Earl William's sheriff, Ralph de Bernay, had appropriated Alton-in-Rock, held in turn by Æthelric and his son Godric, but after his forfeiture (in 1076) the king did not return the land to Worcester, giving it instead to Ralph de Tosny.[86] Æthelric's land at Queenhill,

---

[79] It is profitless to speculate, but her first husband may have been a kinsman of Cynethegn *clericus* to whom Bishop Oswald loaned 2½ hides at Oddingley and Laugherne in 963 (S.1297 and see n. 35 above). Laugherne is later found in the hands of Cyneweard (see n. 92 below), perhaps a grandson of Wulfgifu and Wulfric (see n. 77 above); it may be that the land passed to Wulfgifu and thence to her descendants by her second husband. Oddingley, which Hemming complains was withdrawn by Cynethegn's heirs, belonged to the bishopric in 1086, and before the Conquest (*GDB* fo. 173v; *DB Worcestershire*, no. 2,56).

[80] S.1384, 1395 and see Williams, 'An Introduction to the Worcestershire Domesday', 25 (where 'Elmley' has been substituted for 'Bentley', see n. 75 above).

[81] *HC*, 255; S.1385. Godric of Perry attested the final agreement between Bishop Wulfstan and Walter of Evesham in 1086 (see n. 96 below).

[82] *GDB* fo. 180v; Frank and Caroline Thorne, *Domesday Book: Herefordshire*, Chichester 1983, no. 1,45 (reading 'Brihtheah' for *Brictrec*); S.1392, 1394.

[83] S.1406, 1409, dated 1046x53 and 1051x55 respectively.

[84] As well as Laugherne and Elmley, Cyneweard held at Wyre Puddle and Hanley, Worcs. (*GDB* fos 173, 177; *DB Worcestershire*, nos 2,19:20,4) and is probably the Cyneweard with estates in Gloucestershire and Warwickshire (Williams, 'An Introduction to the Worcestershire Domesday', 24). Godric held a hide at Wadborough of the abbey of Pershore, of which his uncle Brihtheah had been abbot (*GDB* fo. 175; *DB Worcestershire*, no. 9,1e).

[85] *HC*, 266; *GDB* fo. 173v; *DB Worcestershire*, no. 2,70. In 1086, Wolverton was attached to the episcopal manor of Kempsey and Whittington to Northwick (*GDB* fos 172v, 173v; *DB Worcestershire*, nos 2,4;58)

[86] *HC*, 255. The same fate befell Worcester's land at Astley, which Ralph de Bernay seized from *Ocea danus* (*HC*, 255–6); Earnsige, whom Domesday names as the pre-Conquest tenant, is

which does not concern Hemming because it belonged to the bishop, not the monks, had also passed through the hands of Earl William and Ralph de Bernay, and was in the king's possession in 1086.[87]

Domesday Book describes Godric as a thegn of Earl Ælfgar, and we might suppose that he had been involved either in the English rebellion of 1069, or the fall of Edwin and his brother Morcar in 1071, were it not that, as will appear, Godric may not have been dispossessed entirely.[88] This fate seems to have befallen only one member of the family, Brihtheah's kinsman and chamberlain Azur, who was outlawed.[89] It was probably because of this that his land at Bengeworth was confiscated by Urse d'Abetot, sheriff of Worcestershire, at some time between 1069 and 1077.[90] Urse had also come into possession of Azur's land at Comberton, held of the abbey of Pershore, of which Brihtheah had been abbot.[91]

Urse d'Abetot and his brother Robert *dispensator* held other lands belonging to Æthelric's family (see Table V). Robert held Elmley Castle, leased to Æthelric but held on the eve of the Conquest by Cyneweard; he also had Cyneweard's estate at Laugherne, and Godric *finc*'s land at Charlton.[92] Robert also held Cyneweard's land at Wyre Puddle, while Herlebald, who appears elsewhere as a tenant of Urse d'Abetot, held Godric's land at Perry; both estates were episcopal tenures and therefore not recorded by Hemming (see Table VI).[93] The interest of Urse and Robert in the lands of Cyneweard and Godric, who were probably brothers, might stem from the fact that Cyneweard was Urse's predecessor as sheriff of Worcestershire.[94]

---

identified as Earnsige son of *Ocea* in the Evesham Chronicle (*Chron. Evesham*, 94; S.1026; Williams, 'Cockles amongst the Wheat' 14). Ribbesford, taken by another of Earl William's men, Turstin the Fleming (or Turstin of Wigmore) was retained by the king when Turstin lost his lands and was exiled, again in 1076 (*HC*, 256; *GDB* fo. 172; *DB Worcestershire*, no. 1,2).

[87] *GDB* fos 173, 180v; *DB Worcestershire*, no. 2,36; *DB Herefordshire*, no. 1,45.

[88] See below, n. 97.

[89] *GDB* 175; *DB Worcestershire*, no. 9,1b. Azur held land at Comberton (see n. 91 below) on a two-life lease from Pershore Abbey, and the agreement was that the land should revert to the church after his wife's death. Azur was living at the time of King Edward's death 'but later, his wife having died, he was made an outlaw'.

[90] *HC*, 269; *GDB* fo. 174; *DB Worcestershire*, no. 2,75. The date of the seizure is after Urse's appointment to the shrievalty in 1069 and before the death of Abbot Æthelwig of Evesham in 1077.

[91] *GDB* fo. 173; *DB Worcestershire*, nos 8,27;9,1b; Appendix IV (Evesham A, 154). Part of Azur's holding at Comberton had passed to Westminster Abbey, which received two-thirds of Pershore's land in Worcs. by gift of King Edward; the remnant, retained by Pershore, is unnamed in Domesday Book but identified in the satellite text, Evesham A.

[92] Elmley Castle: *HC*, 267–8; S.1396; *GDB* fo. 174; *DB Worcestershire*, no. 2,73 and note; Laugherne: *HC*, 252–3; *GDB* fo. 172v; *DB Worcestershire*, no. 2,13; Charlton: *HC*, 268–9; *GDB*, fo. 174; *DB Worcestershire*, no. 2,73 and note. It is in his account of Charlton that Hemming complains of the *francigenae* who usurped the inheritances of Englishmen, perhaps implying that Godric was one of Robert's *antecessores* (see above, n. 61).

[93] *GDB*, fos 173, 173v; *DB Worcestershire*, nos 2,19 (Wyre Piddle, part of Fladbury), 2,61 (Perry, part of Northwick). Herlebald also held, of Urse, Godric's land at Cookhill (*GDB* fo. 177v; *DB Worcestershire*, no. 26, 1). Godric's land at Wadborough, which he held of Pershore Abbey for three lives, had passed to Urse, as the third life (*GDB*, fo. 175; *DB Worcestershire*, no. 9,1e).

[94] Eadgyth *monialis*, whose land at Knightwick passed to Robert *dispensator*, may be a sister of Godric and Cyneweard, for Knightwick (which Hemming does not mention) was settled on Archbishop Wulfstan's sister by her husband (S.1459; *GDB* fo. 173v; *DB Worcestershire*, no. 2,67). Eadgyth was living in 1086, but had restored Knightwick to the church when the numbers of the community increased in King William's time. She may be identical with the Eadgyth who held

Hemming specifically says that Laugherne was seized after the death of Cyneweard, but gives no indication of date. Cyneweard attested a charter of Robert of Stafford in 1072 as Cyneweard of Laugherne, and testified in the dispute between Worcester and Evesham after the death of Æthelwig in 1077.[95] Thereafter he disappears from view. As for Charlton, Hemming says both that Robert *dispensator* seized it after the death of Godric, and that Robert acted *per potentiam reginae*, which implies that the seizure took place before Queen Matilda's death in 1083. Godric, however, was living in 1086, when, as Godric of Perry, he attested the final agreement between Bishop Wulfstan and Walter, abbot of Evesham, concerning the bishop's rights in Oswaldslow.[96] Perry was in Herlebald's hands in 1086 (see Table VI), but it may be that Godric was still holding as an under-tenant, and thus of no concern to the Domesday commissioners.[97]

As we saw with the earlier losses, Worcester's version of events is not the only one; and not all the thefts chronicled by Hemming resulted in permanent loss to the church. At least some of the villains were in fact rendering the services due from their estates (see Tables IV and V). Some, however, were clearly forced loans, of the kind we have already seen in the case of Earl Leofric and Sigmundr of Crowle. Hemming says that when Urse seized their lands at Greenhill and Eastbury, the monks loaned them to him for fear of his power, but though he began by rendering the service, he soon ceased to do so; nor did he perform the services from Clopton or Redmarley.[98] Charlton, held by his brother Robert, had been the subject of a lawsuit; by giving the king a valuable gold chalice, Bishop Wulfstan obtained his writ in respect of the estate, which was nevertheless seized by Robert *dispensator*.[99] The subsequent history of these and other lands held of the church and bishopric by the brothers d'Abetot and their heirs tends to suggest that any service would be hard to obtain.[100]

Urse's motives are not far to seek. In their account of the king's rights in Worcestershire, the Domesday commissioners recorded that 'in the shire there are twelve hundreds, seven of which are quit, as the shire-court testifies, so that the sheriff has nothing in them, and therefore, as he says, he loses much on his farm'. Urse paid £17 by weight and £16 at face-value for the pleas of the shire and hundred, and, as the commissioners reported, 'if he does not receive it from them, he pays out of his own [money]'.[101] The seven hundreds whose holders were entitled to their profits must have been a bitter pill to swallow. All belonged to the Church: Evesham's hundred of *Fisseberge*; the triple hundred of Pershore, now

---

Greenhill, part of the episcopal manor of Wick Episcopi; by 1086, this land had passed to Urse d'Abetot (*GDB* fo. 172v; *DB Worcestershire*, no. 2,12).

[95] R.W. Eyton, 'The Staffordshire Cartulary', *Collections for a History of Staffordshire* ii, 1881, 178; *HC*, 82; *DB Worcestershire*, Appendix V, Worcester H; van Caeneghem, *English Lawsuits from William I to Richard I*, i, 38.

[96] *HC*, 76, 297; *DB Worcestershire*, Appendix V, Worcester H; van Caeneghem, *English Lawsuits from William I to Richard I*, i, 40.

[97] For the levels of holders below the mesne-tenants, rarely recorded in Domesday Book, see Williams, *The English and the Norman Conquest*, 83, 86–7, 89–97.

[98] *HC*, 254, 257–8.

[99] *HC*, 268–9.

[100] See Emma Mason, *The Beauchamp Cartulary Charters, 1100–1268*, PRS ns xliii, London 1988.

[101] *GDB* fo. 172; *DB Worcestershire*, nos C,2–3.

unequally split between Pershore and Westminster; and Worcester's triple hundred of Oswaldslow. Bishop Wulfstan's successful presentation of Oswaldslow as a continental-style immunity from which the sheriff and his agents were excluded exacerbated Urse's problem, but did not cause it; it was the bishop's control of the court of Oswaldslow and its profits that was the root of the trouble. The same applies to the other ecclesiastical hundreds, and it is significant that Urse had seized lands and forced loans from Evesham, Pershore and Westminster, as well as Worcester.

The political and tenurial dominance of the bishop of Worcester was based upon his possession of Oswaldslow, whose privileges reflected his position as a royal agent, responsible for Oswaldslow's military service by land and sea. Urse d'Abetot's rivalry with Bishop Wulfstan was not a new phenomenon; a similar strife had informed the relations between Ælfhere, ealdorman of Mercia and Bishop Oswald of Worcester in the tenth century. I must stress again that this has nothing to do with Oswaldslow's alleged immunity, now shown up beyond reasonable doubt as a post-Conquest fabrication.[102] The tension was political, not institutional, as the most powerful authorities in the west strove for dominance. This tension, I suggest, is reflected in Hemming's *Codicellus possessionum*. A glance at Tables IV and V will show that, as with the earlier losses, most of the post-Conquest spoilers are royal or comital officers: William fitzOsbern, who received Harold II's earldom in Herefordshire as well as western Wessex; Ralph de Bernay, Earl William's sheriff in Herefordshire, and other men in his following; Æthelwig of Evesham, who from about 1069 was what amounts to a local justiciar in the west; and of course Urse himself as sheriff of Worcestershire, and his brother Robert *dispensator*. Moreover the same people whom Hemming names as despoilers of the monks turn up in Domesday among those in dispute with the bishop (the details, derived from Domesday Book, are summarized in Table VI).

It seems that throughout the eleventh century, the church of Worcester had been under constant attack from the secular authorities, intent on its spoliation. Urse d'Abetot's complaint, however, recorded by the Domesday commissioners, suggests that if we had the accounts of the other earls and sheriffs, the boot might well be upon the other foot, with the bishops of Worcester as the villains of the piece.[103] Indeed it is the faces absent from Hemming's rogues' gallery which give the game away. I cannot account for the non-appearance of King Edward's nephew Ralph, earl of Herefordshire from 1051 to 1057, but some of the other absences are more understandable. Odda of Deerhurst, earl of Worcestershire from 1052 to 1056, does not figure as a despoiler of Worcester, despite the fact that one of its disputed manors, Upleadon in Herefordshire, passed through the hands of his sister Eadgyth (see Table I). Could this be because he was a friend of Archbishop Ealdred, and patron of Pershore, of which Bishop Brihtheah had been abbot?[104]

The remaining 'missing persons' are even more interesting. In his account of the Danish settlement, Hemming accuses Earl Hakon of Worcestershire and Earl Ranig of Herefordshire as despoilers of the church, but he omits their colleague, Earl

---

[102] Patrick Wormald, 'Oswaldslow: an "Immunity"?', in *St Oswald of Worcester: Life and Influence*, ed. Brooks and Cubitt, 117–28.

[103] The Bengeworth/Hampton affair, for which we have both sides of the case, is very instructive (see n. 70 above).

[104] For Odda, see Ann Williams, 'Odda of Deerhurst', The Deerhurst lecture, 1996, Deerhurst 1997.

Eilifr Thorgilson of Gloucestershire. Eilifr's sister Gytha married Godwine, earl of Wessex, and her second son is another absentee: Harold, earl of Wessex, earl of Herefordshire, and eventually (though briefly) king. Harold and his father Godwine were the friends and allies of successive bishops of Worcester; Godwine and Lyfing, Godwine and Ealdred, Harold and Wulfstan. Naturally they do not figure among the predators on the church's lands, even though one of the disputed estates, Cowarne in Herefordshire, was actually held by Harold on the eve of the Conquest (Table I). In this case there was a political alliance, not a political rivalry, between the bishops and the earls.[105] Perhaps this is why Hemming is so hard on Harold's elder brother, Earl Swein, whose moral character has to be shown to be totally depraved; only thus can Hemming explain why someone who should have supported Worcester could in fact despoil it.[106]

---

[105] For Godwine's relations with Lyfing and Ealdred, see King, 'Ealdred, Archbishop of York: the Worcester Years', 125–6, 127, 134; for Harold and Wulfstan, see *Vita Wulfstani*, ed. R.R. Darlington, Camden Society 3rd series xl, London 1928, 13, 22–4.

[106] Earl Ælfgar's absence might be explained in a similar way; whereas most of the Mercian earls figure among Worcester's rivals – and thus despoilers – he was a benefactor, who gave Church Icomb, Glos., to the monks of Worcester (*HC*, 406; see *GDB* fo. 173; *DB Worcestershire* no. 2,41).

Table I. The Danish conquest

Estate	Despoiler	Charters	*GDB* (TRE)
Heythrop	'Danes'	[Offa]	Godric
Kiddington	'Danes'	[Offa]	Godric
Luddington	'Danes'	S.*1421	4 *taini*
Drayton	'Danes'	S.198,1257[1]	Bp Worcester
Loxley	'Danes'		Bp Worcester
Lapworth	'Danes'	S.*179	Baldwin
Milcote	'Danes'	S.1289,1311	Bp Worcester
Pencovan	Earl Ranig	[Offa]	unidentified
Cowarne	Earl Ranig		Earl Harold
Upleadon	Earl Ranig		Eadgyth, Earl Odda's sister
Ocle Pychard	Earl Ranig		6 free men
Rochford	Earl Ranig		Leofnoth
Ribbesford	'Danes'	S.1459	King Edward
Clifton-on-Teme	Earl Hakon	S.*406	King Edward
Kyre	Earl Hakon		King Edward
Hamcastle	Earl Hakon		Osbern fitzRichard
Tenbury	Earl Hakon		Richard fitzScrob
Eastham	Earl Hakon		Eadric
'Bastwood'	Earl Hakon		Eadric
Clent	Æfic, sheriff of Staffs		King Edward
Tardebigge	as above		King Edward
Wychbold	Edwin	S.*75	Earl Godwine[2]
Bickmarsh	Edwin	S.*751	Eadgyth
'lands in Shrops'	Edwin		see Table II[3]
Batsford	Eadric Streona	S.1859 (incomplete)	Brihtmær
Eisey	Eadric Streona	S.*145,206	[Earl Harold][4]
Keingeham	as above		unidentified

---

[1] The charters, and the TRE tenancy, relate to Stratford-upon-Avon, of which Drayton was part.

[2] Perhaps an error for Earl Edwin.

[3] These are the lands at Tetstill, Hopton Wafers and Cleobury North later seized by Swein Godwineson.

[4] See *Regesta* i, no. 9, King William's grant of Latton and Eisey, Wilts, to Regenbald the chancellor, as they were held by King (*sic*) Harold.

Table II. Losses c.1030–1066

Estate	Charters	Despoiler	*GDB* (TRE)
Tetstill, Salop		Earl Swein	Siward [son of Æthelgar]
Hopton Wafers, Salop		Earl Swein	Siward [son of Æthelgar]
Cleobury North, Salop		Earl Swein	Siward [son of Æthelgar]
Wolverley	S.*211, 1232	Earl Leofric	Mo Worcester
Blackwell	S.*731, 1232, 1337	Earl Leofric	Mo Worcester
Belbroughton	S.*181	Earl Leofric	Godgifu
Bell Hall	S.*181	Earl Leofric	Leofnoth
Chaddesley Corbett	S.*179, 180	Earl Leofric	Ea[l]dgifu
Fairfield	S.*181	Earl Leofric	Not in *DB*
Salwarpe	S.*181	Æthelwine, nephew of Earl Leofric	Æthelwine *cild*
Crowle	S.*190, *205	Sigmundr *danus*	Bp Worcester: Sigmundr
Hampton Lovett	S.83, *181	Earngeat Grim's son	Alweald
Thiccanapel-treo		Earngeat Grim's son	Alweald
Oddingley	S.*179,1297	Cynethegn's heirs	Bp Worcester: Thorkel
Leopard		Herluin	Mo Worcester: [Baldwin][1]
Cotheridge	S.1303	Richard Scrob	Osbern fitzRichard
Lower Sapey		Richard Scrob	Osbern fitzRichard

[1] Baldwin held (of Hugh de Grandmesnil) in 1086.

op **Brihtheah's kinsmen**

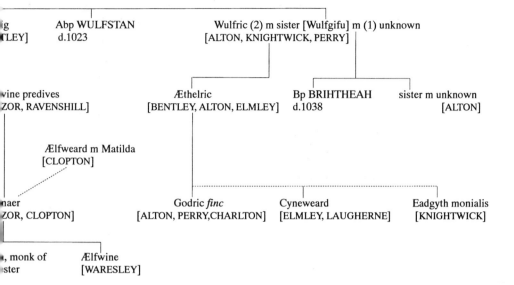

ig [LEY]	Abp WULFSTAN d.1023	Wulfric (2) m sister [Wulfgifu] m (1) unknown [ALTON, KNIGHTWICK, PERRY]

vine predives
ZOR, RAVENSHILL]

Æthelric
[BENTLEY, ALTON, ELMLEY]

Bp BRIHTHEAH
d.1038

sister m unknown
[ALTON]

Ælfweard m Matilda
[CLOPTON]

naer
ZOR, CLOPTON]

Godric *finc*
[ALTON, PERRY,CHARLTON]

Cyneweard
[ELMLEY, LAUGHERNE]

Eadgyth monialis
[KNIGHTWICK]

, monk of
ster

Ælfwine
[WARESLEY]

Broken line = hypothetical relationship

Table III. Bishop Brihtheah's leases

Estate	Lessee	Holder TRE	Seized
Himbleton	Æthelric (brother)	Mo Worcester: Æthelric	see Table IV
Spetchley	Æthelric	Mo Worcester: Æthelric	see Table IV
Wolverton	Æthelric	Bp Worcester: Æthelric	see Table IV
Whittington	Æthelric	Bp Worcester: Æthelric	see Table IV
Lower Sapey	brother-in-law	Osbern fitzRichard Scrob	see Table II
Alton-in-Rock[1]	(1) brother-in-law, (2) Æthelric and his son Godric	Godric, *tainus* of Earl Ælfgar	see Table IV
[Charlton][2]	[Godric *finc*]	Bp Worcester: Godric	see Table V
Elmley Castle	a *minister* [Æthelric][3]	Bp Worcester: Cyneweard	see Table V
[Laugherne][4]	[Cyneweard]	Bp Worcester: Cyneweard	see Table V
Ravenshill	Brihtwine, kinsman	Not in *DB*	see Table V
Bengeworth I	Azur, kinsman & chamberlain	Bp Worcester: Azur	see Table V
Leopard	Herluin	Bp Worcester: [Baldwin][5]	see Table II

1 Given by Wulfric to his wife (Wulfgifu), Archbishop Wulfstan's sister.
2 Loaned for three lives to 'a certain wealthy man', then held by his son and finally Godric *finc*.
3 Leased to Æthelric *Kiu*, miles, by Bishop Lyfing (S.1396).
4 Held from the monastery by Cyneweard and his parents; lessor not named.
5 Baldwin held (of Hugh de Grandmesnil) in 1086.

Table IV. Losses post-Conquest: Earl William and his men

Estate	Tenant	Taken by	1086
Himbleton	Æthelric	Earl William	Mo Worcester: Roger de Lacy
Spetchley	Æthelric	Earl William	as above
Wolverton	Æthelric	Earl William	Bp Worcester: Roger de Lacy
Whittington	Æthelric	Earl William	Bp Worcester: Walter Ponther
Bredicote	Brihtweald	'Normans'	as above
Hadzor	Brihtmær, son of Brihtwine[1]	Earl William	Gilbert fitzTurold[2]
Alton-in-Rock	Godric, Earl Ælfgar's *tainus*	Ralph de Bernay	Ralph de Tosny
Astley	Earnsige son of *Ocea danus*	Ralph de Bernay	Ralph de Tosny
Witley	Earnwig the priest	Ralph de Bernay	Bp Worcester: Urse d'Abetot
Pendock	Godwine	Ralph de Bernay	Bp Worcester: Urse d'Abetot
Ribbesford[3]	no TRE tenant named	Turstin of Flanders	King William
Hampnett (Glos.)	Archbishop Ealdred[4]	Roger d'Ivry	Roger d'Ivry
Shelsey	Sigmundr, Earl Edwin's *tainus*	'Normans'	Osbern fitzRichard Scrob

[1] See also Table V.
[2] Given by Earl William.
[3] See also Table I.
[4] Hemming says this was monastic land; see S.1480, a spurious grant of Ealdred to St Mary's, Worcester.

Table V. Post-conquest losses: Æthelwig, Urse and Robert

Estate	TRE holder	Taken by	1086
Redmarley	Wulfmær and Ulfkell	Urse d'Abetot	Ralph de Tosny
Elmley Castle	Cyneweard	Robert *dispensator*	Mo Worcester: Robert
Laugherne	Cyneweard	Robert *dispensator*	Bp Worcester: Robert
Charlton	Godric [*finc*]	Robert *dispensator*	Mo Worcester: Robert
Knightwick	Eadgyth *monialis*	Not in Hemming	Mo Worcester: Robert
Greenhill	Eadgyth	Urse d'Abetot	Bp Worcester: Urse d'Abetot
Clopton	Brihtmær	Urse d'Abetot	Bp Worcester: Urse d'Abetot
Waresley[1]	Ælfwine son of Brihtmær[2]	Urse d'Abetot	Not in *DB*
Ravenshill	Brihtwine	Urse d'Abetot	Not in *DB*
Westmancote	Brihtwine	(1) Æthelwig, (2) Odo of Bayeux	Bp Worcester: Urse d'Abetot
Bengeworth I	Azur, kin of Brihtheah	Urse d'Abetot	Mo Worcester: Urse d'Abetot
Bengeworth II	Earngrim	Æthelwig	Mo Worcester: Evesham Abbey
Acton Beauchamp	Evesham Abbey	(1) Æthelwig, (2) Urse	Odo of Bayeux: Urse
Eastbury	Alric	(1) Æthelwig, (2) Urse	Mo Worcester: Walter
Milcote	Bishop Wulfstan	(1) Æthelwig, (2) Odo of Bayeux	Stephen [the steersman]
Hampton	Evesham Abbey	Not in Hemming	Odo of Bayeux: Urse

[1] Hemming says that Wulfstan leased it to Ælfwine, Brihtmær's son, apparently after 1077 (it belonged to the monks in the days of Prior Ælfstan and Witheric the reeve, i.e., c.1062–77), but that on Ælfwine's death Urse seized it with the rest of his land.

[2] See also Table IV.

Table VI. Episcopal land in dispute after 1066

Land	Service TRE	Service TRW	Holder 1086
OSWALDSLOW (WORCS.)			
Mucknell	*ad victum*		Urse
Holt	*consuetudines*		Urse
Kenswick	*consuetudines*		Urse
Laugherne	demesne		Urse
Ab Lench	service		Urse
Rous Lench	service		Urse
Holdfast	*de episcopo*		Urse
Hindlip and Overton	*servicium regis et episcopi*		Urse
Warndon/White Ladies Aston	*terra villanorum*		Urse
Cudley	service		Urse
Redmarley	service		Urse
Washbourne			Urse
Perry	*ad voluntatem episopi*		Herlebald [? of Urse]
Wyre Piddle	service		Robert *dispensator*
Bushley[1]	*servicium regis/firma*	no service	[Earl William]
Barley[2]	service		the king
Churchill	service		Walter Ponther
Queenhill[3]	service		[Ralph de Bernay]
Longdon	service		Gilbert fitzTurold
Daylesford[4]	*de victu monachorum*		Stephen [Bishop of Bayeux]
Evenlode	*de victu monachorum*		[Bishop of Bayeux]
Bishampton	[sake and soke]	service as TRE	Roger de Lacy
Hill Croome	[lease, S.1392]		Roger de Lacy

---

[1] In the king's hands 1086 (*GDB* fo. 180v; *DB Herefordshire*, no. 1,44).
[2] Barley and Bushley (above) were held TRE by Beorhtric son of Ælfgar, who also held Stoke Orchard (see n. 6 below).
[3] In the king's hands, 1086 (*GDB* fo. 180v; *DB Herefordshire*, no. 1,45).

Land	Service TRE	Service TRW	Holder 1086
Bredon's Norton	Leofwine, *radman*		Durand [of Gloucester]
Ditchford	service		Richard
GLOUCESTERSHIRE			
Compton Greenfield			Gilbert fitzTurold
Itchington			Constantine
Stoke Gifford		no service	Osbern Giffard
Colesbourne			Walter fitzRoger[5]
Barnsley			Durand [of Gloucester] and Eudo
Southam			Durand [of Gloucester]
Sapperton			Ralph
Gotherington			Turstin fitzRolf
Aust			Turstin fitzRolf
Stoke Orchard[6]		service refused	Bernard and Reginald

4   Daylesford and Evenlode were among the lands taken by Æthelwig of Evesham when the holders commended themselves to him; later they were seized by Odo of Bayeux.
5   Roger de Pitres, sheriff of Gloucestershire, brother of Durand of Gloucester.
6   Stoke Orchard had been appropriated by one of the lords of Tewkesbury, successively Beorhtric son of Ælfgar, William fitzOsbern, Queen Matilda and King William (*GDB* fo. 163v; *DB Gloucestershire*, no. 1,47).